Career Counseling

Career Counseling 7e
A Holistic Approach

Vernon G. Zunker

Texas State University

BROOKS/COLE
CENGAGE Learning™

Australia • Brazil • Japan • Korea • Mexico • Singapore • Spain • United Kingdom • United States

BROOKS/COLE
CENGAGE Learning™

Career Counseling: A Holistic Approach, 7e
Vernon G. Zunker

Executive Editor: Lisa Gebo

Counseling Editor: Marquita Flemming

Assistant Editor: Monica Sarmiento Arvin

Editorial Assistant: Christine Northup

Technology Project Manager: Barry Connolly

Marketing Manager: Rebecca Weisman

Marketing Assistant: Caroline Concilla

Marketing Communications Manager:
Tami Strang

Project Manager, Editorial Production:
Rita Jaramillo

Art Director: Vernon Boes

Print Buyer: Rebecca Cross

Permissions Editor: Stephanie Lee

Production Service:
Stratford Publishing Services

Text Designer: Jeanne Calabrese

Copy Editor: Hilary Farquhar

Cover Designer: Irene Morris

Cover Images: Getty Images, Inc.

Compositor: Stratford Publishing Services

Library of Congress Control Number: 2004117329

ISBN-13: 978-0-534-64017-0
ISBN-10: 0-534-64017-6

Brooks/Cole
10 Davis Drive
Belmont, CA 94002-3098
USA

Cengage Learning is a leading provider of customized learning solutions with office locations around the globe, including Singapore, the United Kingdom, Australia, Mexico, Brazil, and Japan. Locate your local office at: **international.cengage.com/region**

Cengage Learning products are represented in Canada by Nelson Education, Ltd.

For your course and learning solutions, visit **academic.cengage.com**

Purchase any of our products at your local college store or at our preferred online store **www.ichapters.com**

Printed in the United States of America
5 6 7 8 9 11 10 09

Brief Contents

Contents

Preface

It seems as though it was just a few years ago that the following scenario took place. At the end of a long day I was resting comfortably in my office chair when the phone rang. The ringing interrupted some very pleasant thoughts! The spring semester was just over and I was looking forward to the freedom that accompanies a hot, lazy summer. My wife and I also had plans to visit friends in Mexico City. But it didn't happen!

The dean who called explained that the instructor who was assigned to teach the summer course in career counseling was taken to the hospital for emergency treatment and, of course, he needed a replacement. It was a Friday afternoon and classes were to begin the following Monday. The point of this discussion is that the ill instructor had opted to not use a textbook for the class. It was during that weekend that I wrote the first words of what eventually was to become a textbook. In the semesters that followed I compiled information about career counseling that I shared with my students. In 1981, the first edition of this book was published.

We now come to the 7th edition and more than likely the last edition I will write as the sole author. It has been a journey that was unexpected but one that gave my work role greater meaning. My own career path was both linear and cyclical, but more important, most interesting and challenging. My work influenced and was influenced by my lifestyle and other life roles that fortunately were well balanced. As I reflect on the past, I am overwhelmed by the opportunities I was given and the work satisfaction I experienced. Hence the driving force to write about career counseling eventually became a personal goal to help counselors help others find a meaningful work role. As you read the following pages, I hope you will develop a fuller understanding of my personal quest.

In each edition I have endorsed the scientist-practitioner counseling role. The rationale for this approach is that, in my opinion, counselors are most effective when they are aware of the underlying reasons for methods, procedures, and interventions they select. This rationale is underscored by the current increasing emphasis on research-based interventions in counseling. The major emphasis in all editions, however, has been directed toward the *practice of career development,* that is, how counselors can apply the findings of research in the practitioner role.

This 7th revision is truly a revised edition! The subtitle is now *A Holistic Approach* to reflect the new emphasis in this edition. I have written five new chapters. The first is the introduction to career counseling in Chapter 1, which contains a chronological historical development of career counseling and some basic issues to be addressed in the 21st century. Chapter 4, completely new, introduces a holistic approach to career counseling as it focuses on how to manage sets of client concerns. Counselors are to recognize that client concerns may be interrelated. In other words, counselors are to fuse career and personal concerns. Chapter 9 is also new to this text and introduces ethical procedures in career counseling. Boundaries of ethical concerns are discussed along with examples of violations. Chapter 11, on gender issues in career counseling, replaces two chapters that were devoted to issues of men and women. This new chapter contents that more emphasis should be placed on shared work roles in the new millennium. Finally, Chapter 15, on elementary school counseling, highlighteds national career development competencies and offers suggestions for developing career-related programs with community support.

Special attention was given to Chapter 2 on career development theories. In this new edition, theories have been grouped together into four categories. The purpose here was to take the opportunity to discuss how each group of theories has provided the foundation for the practice of career development. More emphasis has been placed on the practical application of theories, with a case example at the end of the chapter. All career development theories discussed in this text are summarized in Appendix A.

All chapters have been updated. Chapter 8, for example, addresses technology in the new millennium. In addition to a discussion of computer-based career guidance programs, a variety of technologically driven learning platforms is presented. Chapter 18 takes an inclusive view of the work role, underscoring the argument that work in our lives is a very pervasive issue. The restructuring of how and for whom one works will touch the families of many citizens in the next society. In sum, counselors are to build an understanding of how work will change in the new millennium. Specifically, more attention needs to be directed toward effective career counseling programs for adults in transition.

Career Counseling is divided into four parts. Part One, "Foundations and Resources," covers historical developments, basic issues, career development theories, career counseling models, managing sets of client concerns, intake interviews, use of assessment results, computer-based programs, technologically driven training programs, and ethical standards. The first chapter provides a perspective of career counseling's historical development and some basic issues of the 21st century. Chapter 2 is devoted to career development theories and their practical application. The third chapter covers five career counseling models using case illustrations. Managing sets of client concerns in a holistic counseling approach is discussed in Chapter 4. Chapter 5 covers the intake interview with case examples. Chapter 6 covers the use of standardized tests. Nonstandardized methods of using assessment results are reviewed in Chapter 7, which also includes a model for using assessment results. Chapter 8 focuses on interactive and information-oriented computer programs designed to enhance the career counseling process, including the appropriate use of Internet resources, and technological platforms for training. The final chapter in this part introduces ethical boundaries and examples of violations.

Part Two, "Career Counseling for Special Populations," includes a discussion of innovative counseling models and career counseling programs for special populations. Chapter 10, focusing on multicultural groups, has been completely revised to

emphasize how counselors can apply culturally appropriate techniques and procedures. Gender issues are discussed in Chapter 11. Chapter 12 covers the family's influence on career development and the issues facing dual-career marriages. Special
counseling components for meeting the unique needs of persons with disabilities are
discussed in Chapter 13. In Chapter 14, issues and needs of gays, lesbians, and bisexuals are discussed, followed by suggested intervention strategies.

Part Three, "Career Counseling in Educational Settings," provides innovative
counseling models and programs for elementary through senior high school and for
postsecondary institutions of higher learning. Chapter 15 presents implications of
human development and relevant research for career guidance programs in elementary schools and some practical suggestions. Chapter 16 explores a variety of approaches to career counseling for middle/junior schools and senior high schools. The
development of career-related and counseling programs to help meet their varied
needs of college students are offered in Chapter 17.

Part Four, "Career Counseling in Work Settings and Career Transitions Throughout Life," is intended to build an understanding of adults' career development in new
and developing organizations, changes in work requirements and in workplace environments, stages and transitions in adult development, and career counseling programs designed to meet their needs. Chapter 18 discusses several work-related issues
and the pervasive nature of the work role. Chapter 19 identifies adult concerns and
covers counseling components for adults in career transition.

A companion text, *Using Assessment Results in Career Development,* 7th Edition
(Osborn & Zunker, 2006), has been developed as a supplement to this book. This
ancillary text illustrates how assessment results can be used to increase self-awareness
and rational choices. Readers will find that *Using Assessment Results* provides detailed
information about applying knowledge of tests and measurements in counseling
encounters and using assessment results in a wide variety of counseling situations.

I am most appreciative of the reviewers of this edition: Laurie Williamson,
Appalachian State University; Jodi Caldwell, Georgia Southern University; Paul For-
nell, CSU Long Beach; William Kolodinsky, Northern Arizona University, Yuma; Joyce
Hickson, Columbus State University; Dale Septeowski, Concordia University; Ann
Carter-Obayuwana, Howard University; Louis Downs, CSU San Bernardino; William
Salazar, Morehead State University; William E. Stillwell, University of Kentucky; Joan
Hartzke McIlroy, Lewis and Clark College; Marla Peterson, University of Tennessee;
and Debra Osborn, University of South Florida.

Marquita Flemming and her staff at Wadsworth provided superb assistance for
this edition. So did David Wilder who gave me step-by-step instructions for making
the most effective use of a new software program. Thanks to Ken Macinga for
unearthing some very signifcant and key references. A special accolade goes to my
constant canine companion Toddi, who faithfully stayed by my side throughout this
project.

1 Historical Development and Some Basic Issues

Chapter Highlights

- Chronology of career counseling and guidance movement

- Beginnings of the counseling profession

- Early contributors

- Early governmental programs

- Development of professional organizations

- Career counseling from past and future perspectives

- Some basic issues that reflect current and future needs of career counseling

  The case for the individual

  Career life perspective

  Career choice

  Working in the 21st century

  Lifelong learning

  Counseling in a culturally diverse society

  Effective use of career information

  Focusing on a multiple spectrum of domains

THIS BOOK is about career counseling in an ever changing world. Professional counselors assist individuals with career and personal concerns. This specialized content includes initial career choice, the connection between career and personal problems, adaptations to changes in the work place, multiple career dilemmas, and maintenance of a balanced lifestyle. The career counseling process does not separate career and personal concerns but integrates them to better evaluate how all life roles are interrelated. Understanding the whole person as a member of complex social systems is the cornerstone of effective career counseling. Counselors are to recognize the relationship between career issues and all other life roles, and assist people and systems to discover healthier ways of living.

We begin with a chronology of the birth and growth of "career guidance." The term "career guidance" is used in a historical context to represent all components of services and activities in educational institutions, agencies, and other career-related educational programs. This book, however, includes both the career counseling role and components of career services, but is primarily devoted to developing counseling skills for integrating career and personal concerns. One of the major purposes of the historical perspective in this opening chapter is to illustrate how the birth and growth of career counseling was influenced by a number of factors, including sociocultural changes, the Industrial Revolution, world wars, federal programs, advanced technology, and advances in the study of human development. The second section of this chapter is devoted to some basic issues in career counseling that provide a means of discovering some significant challenges that currently face the counseling profession. Using the historical development section as a backdrop, basic issues introduce some current and future challenges of a growing and ever expanding career counseling movement. You will discover that counselors are very flexible and continually modify programs, methods, and procedures for solution-focused strength-based counseling approaches.

Historical Development and Some Basic Issues

The career counseling movement is a product of our development as a nation. It is the story of human progress in a nation founded on the principle of human rights. Career counseling touches all aspects of human life, for it has involved political, economic, educational, philosophical, and social progress and change. To think of the career counseling movement as merely another educational event is a gross misinterpretation of its broader significance for social progress. In fact, this movement has had and will have a tremendous impact on the working lives of many individuals. Understanding the historical perspectives of this movement will provide a greater insight into the development of the career counselor's role in the 21st century.

Six Stages of Development from 1890

Pope (2000) has suggested that the development of career counseling in the United States has evolved in six stages starting in 1890 to the present time. These stages have been paraphrased as follows:

- Stage one (1890–1919) began the growth of placement services in urban areas to meet the needs of growing industrial organizations.

- Stage two (1920–1939) marked the growth of educational guidance in elementary and secondary schools.
- Stage three (1940–1959) was a time of significant growth of guidance needs in colleges and universities and in the training of counselors.
- Stage four (1960–1979) was highlighted by organizational career development. The nature of work became more appropriately viewed as a very pervasive life role.
- Stage five (1980–1989) was a period of significant transitions brought on by information technology and the beginning of career counseling private practice and outplacement services.
- Stage six (1990–present) is viewed as a time of changing demographics, the beginning of multicultural counseling, continued development of technology, and a focus on school-to-work transitions.

The next stage in our development as a nation will certainly be impacted by the September 11, 2001, terrorists' attack on the United States and the subsequent war on terrorism. The uncertainties, threatening conditions, and concerns for the safety of family members, combined with changing economic conditions, makes a strong case for solution-based, self-directed counseling goals.

These stages representing the growth of career counseling and service programs include vast changes in our society and especially in the work role of many Americans. Career counseling was created to meet the needs of a society during the shift from rural to urban living in the industrial age and has expanded its focus during other transitional periods of changes in how and where we work and live. Intertwined in this movement are significant databases of information that have enlightened our knowledge of human behavior and development, social issues, political events, and studies of career development and life roles. The growth of career counseling therefore has been influenced by a number of variables, factors, and events in a changing society. The following chronology of the career counseling movement provides an overview that can be supplemented by reviewing the major sources of this chronology: Herr (2001), Pichioni and Bonk (1983), Pope (2000), and Zunker (2002).

A Chronology of Historical Events from Mid-1800s

1850–1920

- The rise of industrialism in the late 1800s significantly changed the way people worked and lived. Urban areas grew quickly, attracting many immigrants and people from rural areas. Work and living environments were significantly changed for both men and women. Men worked in factories and women worked at home.
- There was a significant loss of jobs in the agricultural sector.
- Early in the 20th century, George Merrill developed a plan for students to explore industrial arts courses in San Francisco.
- Between 1898 and 1907, Jeff Davis was designated as an educational and vocational counselor at Central High in Detroit. Later, as a school principal in Grand Rapids, Michigan, he provided class time to offer career-related information to students.
- Frank Parson, often referred to as the father of the vocational guidance movement, founded the Vocations Bureau of Boston in 1908. He published *Choosing a*

Vocation in 1909, establishing a three-step procedure for career decision making that remains as a significant benchmark. He also lobbied to eliminate child labor.

- By 1910 about 35 cities had some form of vocational guidance in their schools. The first National Conference on Vocational Guidance took place in Boston in 1910. Other conferences followed and in 1913 the National Vocational Guidance Association (NVGA) was incorporated.
- The first vocational guidance course was taught at Harvard by Meyer Bloomfield in 1911. Hugo Munsterberg of Harvard established industrial psychology as a relevant field of applied psychology.
- His book *Psychological and Industrial Efficiency,* published in 1913, included studies of occupational choice and worker performance. This movement focused attention on work organizations and their employees.
- In 1915 the NVGA began publishing the *Vocational Guidance Bulletin.*
- In 1917 the Smith-Hughes Act was passed to provide funds for vocational guidance services. As a direct result, nationwide vocational guidance programs were launched.
- During the late 1800s the mental measurement movement also grew and flourished. In 1890, James M. Cattell introduced the concept of mental tests to determine mental abilities as an important factor of human traits. In 1909 the first intelligence test was developed by Binet and Simon in France. In 1916, L. M. Terman of Stanford published the *Stanford-Binet Intelligence Test.*
- During World War I (1914–1918), large numbers of recruits were administered ability tests, known as Army Alpha and Beta tests for classification and placement in the armed services. These tests also served as an example for the development of assessment measures used in career counseling.
- E. K. Strong of Stanford introduced the *Strong Vocational Interest Blank* in 1927. This measure of interest, constructed from the responses of individuals in certain occupations, provided an important tool for linking assessment of interests with certain occupations.
- In 1928, Clark L. Hull published *Aptitude Testing,* suggesting that human traits could be matched with job requirements.
- Achievement testing in schools made rapid progress during the 1920s. Personality testing was used during World War I but was much slower in development.

1930–1950

- The significant events that took place during this time were the Great Depression and World War II (1939–1945) and its aftermath. Unemployment was a major social issue in this country and in many others.
- During the Great Depression in the 1930s, the federal government passed several legislative acts designed to help individuals find work. Two federal agencies that helped create jobs were the Works Progress Administration and the Civilian Conservation Corps.
- In addition, the U.S. Employment Service was established in 1933 by the Wagner-Peyser Act.
- The Occupational Information and Guidance service was established in 1938 under the George-Dean Act.

- The first edition of the *Dictionary of Occupational Titles* was published in 1939 by the U.S. Department of Labor.
- In the private sector, the B'nai B'rith Vocational Service Bureau was established in 1938 and offered vocational guidance programs in metropolitan areas.
- During World War II, the armed services once again needed testing procedures to classify recruits. As a result, the *Army General Classification Test* (AGCT) was developed in 1940.
- In 1944 the Veterans Administration established centers throughout the country for career-related services that were offered to returning veterans.
- The George-Barden Act was passed in 1946, making funds available to establish counselor-training programs in all states.
- *How to Counsel Students* by E. G. Williamson was published in 1939; this work was characterized by some as supporting a directive counseling approach of matching abilities and interests with job requirements.
- Carl Rogers's famous book *Counseling and Psychotherapy* was published in 1942. He and his colleagues joined together to attack directive counseling by suggesting that more attention should be given to clients' needs of gaining an understanding of self and taking steps to control their own destiny. More emphasis was directed to the client and his or her ability to solve personal concerns.
- The *Occupational Outlook* was first published in 1948 by the U.S. Department of Labor.
- The measurement movement continued its growth with the establishment of the Educational Testing Service in 1948. They published the *Scholastic Aptitude Tests*, which were designed to measure one's potential of success in college.

1950–1980

- Two events that stand out at the beginning of this period were the Korean War (1950–1953) and the expansion of the "cold war."
- In 1951, an important merger of professional organizations took place. The following organizations merged to form the American Personnel and Guidance Association (APGA): American College Personnel Association, National Association of Guidance Supervisors and College Trainers, National Vocational Guidance Association, and Student Personnel Association for Teacher Education.
- In the early 1950s, Ginzberg, Ginsburg, Axelrad, and Herma (1951); Roe (1956); and Super (1957) developed and published career development and occupational choice theories. These were followed by theories from Blau, Gustad, Jessor, Parnes, and Wilcox (1956) and Tiedeman and O'Hara (1963). Career development theories became landmarks in the career counseling movement. More theories followed, including one by Holland (1966), and others continue to be developed.
- The American College Testing Program (ACT) was founded in 1959. Other commercial test publishers merged into larger companies and corporations.
- Working conditions generally improved after the World War II years. By 1960, the career counseling movement increasingly was supported by federal and local governmental bodies, including schools and universities.
- Manpower legislation designed to create new jobs through occupational training was passed by Congress.

- Civil rights legislation was enacted in 1964. The 1960s were known for major value upheavals in response to the Vietnam War.
- Amendments to the Vocational Educational Act of 1963 provided guidance services for elementary and secondary schools, public community colleges, and technical institutes. Counselor training programs expanded and flourished.
- The career education movement in the 1970s was created to specifically address career development, attitudes, and values infused within traditional learning. Career education focused on career awareness, career exploration, value clarification, decision-making skills, career orientation, and career preparation.
- In 1976 the National Occupational Information Coordinating Committee was established by Congress. Its purpose was to sponsor projects to establish national career counseling and development guidelines at state and local levels.

1980–Present

- During this period of time, the career counseling movement continued to flourish and expanded its services with a greater concentration on the needs of minorities and women. The global economy became a driving force behind changes in how and where people work.
- The Joint Training Partnership Act (JTPA) was enacted in 1982. It provided career services for retraining workers and for disadvantaged youth. The Carl Perkins Vocational Education Act of 1984 expanded career services to address the needs of vocational education students. Other expansions of this act in the 1990s have continued to support career services.
- In 1984, the National Certified Career Counselors organization was founded in order to offer national certification to counselors.
- The NVGA changed its name to the National Career Development Association (NCDA) in 1985. In 1986, its publication *Vocational Guidance Quarterly* became the *Career Development Quarterly*.
- The Americans with Disabilities Act (ADA) was passed in 1992, which provided that employers are to have reasonable work accommodations for persons with disabilities.
- In the 1990s the Internet offered career counseling Web sites that are increasingly being used by job seekers and adults in career transition. Ethical standards continue to be developed concerning the use of Web sites for job search, assessment, and career counseling.
- The School-to-Work Opportunities Act was passed in 1994. This act provided funds to enhance school-to-school and school-to-work transitions.
- In 1998 the Workforce Investment Act offered career services to disadvantaged youth, adults, and dislocated workers.
- In 1999 the NCDA board of directors endorsed a new Council on Workforce and Career Development Associations reflecting a broad scope of interests and collaborations with private practice, business, and agency counselors both domestically and internationally (Pope, 2000).
- On September 11, 2001, terrorists attacked the United States and the war on terrorism was launched. Career counseling will continue to focus on the relationship between career issues and other life issues that evolve from these events.

A Glance into the Past and a Look into the Future

In the beginning of this discussion, we referred to events and social conditions that determined the course of the career counseling movement. The chronology of the career counseling movement reflects the continuous influence of social, political, economic, and other changes in our nation. In the political arena, the career counseling movement has found support in federal legislation that has provided funds for career-related service programs and counselor training programs.

This field has been influenced by foresight, dedication, and pioneering efforts of many individuals. Those who came forth with conceptualizations of career counseling that have endured for many decades provided the guidelines for contemporary practices. Other individuals concentrating on basic research in human development also contributed immeasurably to the career counseling movement. The leaders in related branches of applied psychology and contributors to technological advancements all played a part in developing what has become the mainstream of this movement.

The basic issues that follow are examples of career counseling perspectives that reflect current services in career counseling and project future needs that are ingrained in our development as a nation. As in the past, events, conditions, and situations will greatly determine the needs of our society. In our early development the focus on career services was driven primarily by conditions within our geographical boundaries. The immediate future, however, is inextricably intertwined with a global economy and as mentioned earlier, the impact of significant events such as the September 11, 2001, attacks and the war on terrorism. Market forces and workplace changes driven by a global economy have created vast changes in how work is structured and how it will be accomplished. The psychological environment created by the war on terrorism, however, has many implications for the counseling profession. Threatening conditions, risks associated with a family member on the war front, and the interruption of family life and work role suggest that client concerns are interrelated and must be approached from a whole-person perspective. We attempt to address some personal and career issues in the pages that follow.

Some Basic Issues

We now turn to identifying some basic issues in career counseling that provide a means of discovering some of the significant challenges that currently face the counseling profession. These issues are discussed in a straightforward manner in an attempt to transcend the clutter usually associated with controversy. We have attempted to go after the jugular instead of the capillaries and briefly make direct and simple statements about each issue. The reader is encouraged to learn more about basic issues from references and the chapters that follow.

Be aware that we do not suggest that our list of basic issues is complete. We have, however, included those issues that are thought to introduce some of the challenges associated with learning to become an effective career counselor. The basic issues selected, not necessarily in order of importance, are as follows: The Case for the Individual, Career Life Perspective, Career Choice, Working in the 21st Century, Lifelong

Learning, Counseling in a Culturally Diverse Society, Effective Use of Career Information, and Focusing on a Multiple Spectrum of Domains. Some terms used in career counseling are identified in Box 1-1.

Box 1.1	Some Terms Defined

Many terms will be introduced and defined throughout this book. Some of the terminology that is briefly described in this chapter to clarify the basic issues discussed will be explained in greater detail in succeeding chapters, within the context of program descriptions and practical illustrations.

The definition of *career* has been developed by the National Career Development Association and cited by Reardon, Lenz, Sampson, and Peterson (2000) as follows: "*Career:* Time extended working out of a purposeful life pattern through work undertaken by the person" (p. 6). Here, career refers to the activities and positions involved in vocations, occupations, and jobs as well as to related activities associated with an individual's lifetime of work.

Hall and Mirvas (1996) suggest an updated definition of *career* that reflects a more current role of flexibility required of contemporary workers. They submit the term "protean career" that "encompasses any kind of flexible, idiosyncratic career course, with peaks and valleys, left turns, moves from one line of work to another, and so forth. Rather than focusing outward on some ideal generalized career path, the protean career is unique to each person—a sort of career fingerprint" (p. 21). Thus, this perception of future work environments realistically points out that some workers in the 21st century, especially those who work for industrial organizations, will make multiple career choices.

As Feldman (2002) points out, many poor and blue-collar workers may view their environments as very constrained, with limited potential for finding work. Therefore, practically any work may be viewed as a necessity to provide for family; *career* is at best a vague term with little or no meaning. Counselors are to provide a more enlightened and encouraging perspective of self-development through learning new skills in trades and basic skills for advancement. Keys

to solutions of current problems and methods to take advantage of opportunities that may occur should be fostered.

Career development as defined by the American Counseling Association "is the total constellation of psychological, sociological, educational, physical, economic, and chance factors that combine to influence the nature and significance of work in the total life span of any given individual" (Engels, 1994, p. 2). Specifically, the term reflects individually developed needs and goals associated with stages of life and with tasks that affect career choices and subsequent fulfillment of purpose.

Career counseling includes all counseling activities associated with career choice over a life span. In the career counseling process, all aspects of individual needs (including family, work, personal concerns, and leisure) are recognized as integral parts of career decision making and planning. Career counseling also includes counseling activities associated with work maladjustment, stress reduction, mental health concerns, and developmental programs that enhance work skills, interpersonal relationships, adaptability, flexibility, and other developmental programs that lead to self-agency.

Career guidance encompasses all components of services and activities in educational institutions, agencies, and other organizations that offer counseling and career-related programs. It is a counselor-coordinated effort designed to facilitate career development through a variety of professional services that fosters each client's ability and desire to manage their own career development.

Practice in career development is used internationally by researchers and counselors in some countries to replace the terms career guidance and counseling (Herr, 2001). It appears

continued

Box 1.1	continued

that this is an effort to remove the confusion of terms that are often used interchangeably, and are not clearly defined. For example, the use of career information can be accomplished through a career guidance curriculum module, but it also can be described verbally in an individual counseling session. Practice in career development therefore suggests a wide range of career services that are to be specifically identified by content and context.

According to Reardon, Lenz, Sampson, and Peterson (2000) *"work* is an activity that produces something of value for oneself or others" (p. 7). This description of work points out that work is a broad term that not only includes work for which one is paid a salary, but unpaid work such as a volunteer who participates in a fund-

raising event for a community project. Thus, work can mean many different things to those who do it. In career counseling, we tend to use this broader perspective of work to communicate to clients that work role is very pervasive in one's life and is interrelated to all life roles.

The term *career intervention* has become more prominent in career-related literature. It is defined by Spokane (1991) as follows: "Any activity (treatment of effort) designed to enhance a person's career development or to enable that person to make more effective career decisions" (p. 22). Thus, a career intervention may include an interpretation of measured interests for career decision making or a group counseling component designed to enhance one's interpersonal skills.

The Case for the Individual

Vocational counseling was founded on the principle of individual differences in assets and strengths. Measures of individual traits were the primary focus of early vocational counseling. The major goal was to match an individual's assets and strengths with job requirements (Picchioni & Bonk, 1983). From these early beginnings, vocational counselors gradually and carefully expanded the scope of human traits used in the vocational choice process. In the meantime, researchers built career development theories and subsequent counseling procedures that are currently being addressed in the career counseling process. The eventual shift from vocational to career counseling reflected a need to include the individual's purposeful life pattern through work.

Current career counseling practices include a concerted effort to build an understanding of an individual's traits, aspirations, motives, preferred lifestyle, and career and personal concerns. With the mindset that accompanies a holistic counseling approach, counselors evaluate how individual problems and subsequent challenges are interrelated. The uniqueness of each individual is used to build tailored individualized intervention strategies. Each strategy may require a variety of techniques and materials, so not everyone takes the same test or uses the same career information resource.

Individual concerns also determine the content and purpose of intervention strategies. Solution-based interventions can take many different paths. Small groups may share family life problems and solutions. A large group may share information about certain training programs. Yet another individual may receive personal counseling and career counseling simultaneously to solve major problems that are interfering with making a career choice. Still another may learn effective communication skills.

The emphasis on individual differences strongly suggests that we address all issues of diversity in the counseling process; for example, counselors focus on gender differences, culture differences, sexual orientation, physical or cognitive disabilities, and differences within groups. Special attention is given to individuals who have experienced discrimination and oppression. Each individual is viewed as a product of their heritage who has been shaped by a variety of experiences and circumstances in a unique environment. Individuals differ, for example, in their values, family structure, and motivation as well as in their worldviews. Career choice, for instance, may be influenced by the lack of family resources rather than what an individual desires. More information about factors that influence career choice can be found in Chapters 10–14 devoted to special populations.

Counselors must ask the question: Who is this person who sits before me? One thing we do know is that this person is human and we both participate in human existence. But, there are many facets about this person that we do not know. What are this person's motives, drives, and aspirations? How much depth of psychological insight does this person have? The client will also seek the answers to such questions as: How do I choose a career? How can I improve? Which job is best for me? These questions and others will to a large extent determine the course of action that will lead to self-discovery, enlightenment, and empowerment in a counseling relationship.

The case for the individual is a simple, straightforward concept that helps counselors to maintain a focus on the uniqueness of each client. An effective counseling approach maintains that each client is indeed a unique individual. This position discourages stereotyping, especially in a society that is culturally diverse. The basic issue here is that clients who come to us with critical unmet concerns must be viewed as unique individuals with unique backgrounds and traits.

Career Life Perspective

The career life perspective is a good example of how career counseling has developed a more inclusive role. The terms *career life* or, as some prefer, *life/career* illuminates the interconnection between all life roles. Donald Super (1984) developed a conceptual model that illustrates the interaction of life roles over the life span that is discussed in Chapter 2. He suggests that because people are involved in several life roles simultaneously, success in one role facilitates success in another and all roles affect one another over the life span. This conceptual model is a prime example of integrating career and life development as well as a need to focus on the interrelationships of all life roles. It also suggests that career life perspective is a basic issue that should be addressed in career counseling.

Following this logic, the career life perspective introduces some key factors that may influence career choice. More specifically, how much does one value time for family and leisure, for instance, and the social status associated with a job, or place of residence, and financial opportunities? These questions are examples of discussion topics that may have been otherwise ignored or overlooked.

One approach to incorporating the career life perspective is to clarify the client's lifestyle orientation. The individual's commitment to work, leisure, volunteer activities, home, and family are relevant topics. In addition, attention could be directed to individual aspirations for social status, a particular work climate, education and training, mobility, and financial security. These factors add depth, direction, and diversity to the counseling process. They provide stimulus for discussion groups and assist individuals in clarifying their individual needs for both career and life roles.

The career life perspective opens the door for counselors to introduce concepts that add meaning and clarity to how work and life are intertwined. From this perspective, the work role is viewed as a major determiner of each individual's life story. On the other hand, the interrelationship of life roles suggests that the joys and frustrations one experiences in life are balanced through an assortment of activities and different roles. Although work occupies a large part of our lives, it is not the only life role in which we can express our individuality. In this context, a balanced lifestyle takes on a more significant meaning.

In the process of clarifying career and life roles an important perspective emerges from which to evaluate potential careers and their interrelationships. The strength of lifestyle orientations for self-improvement through education, leadership roles in work, financial independence, and participation in community activities and services are specific examples of discussion topics. In addition, a comparison of lifestyle factors with skills, interests, and personality, for example, can point out congruence or striking differences. An ever expanding role of career counseling will certainly include the comprehensive nature of career life perspective.

Career Choice

Career counselors traditionally have focused on a number of significant factors that influence career choice. Values, interests, abilities, skills, and work-life experiences are viable factors that are discussed and clarified. There are, however, many other interacting factors and contextual issues that are a significant part of the career choice process. An ever changing workforce and the uncertainties associated with a global economy exacerbate the confusion inherent in future work role projections. Changes in how work is organized may eliminate some jobs and in how and where we will work in the future suggests that individuals may have multiple careers over the life span.

It is no surprise that career choice is considered tentative from the standpoint that practically every choice involves some doubt about the credibility of the chosen career and the possibility that workplace changes may make it obsolete. The individual's uncertainty is compounded by the career possibilities that have disappeared because of economic conditions, and the career uncertainties forecast by imminent technology changes. Moreover, career choice is a process in which one not only chooses but also eliminates—and consequently stifles—some interests and talents. Parts of us are left to lie fallow when a career choice is made. Career choice is also clouded by the search all of us experience for self-identity and meaning in a world society that is drawing closer together.

Career choice is a complex process that cannot be explained in a few paragraphs. In Chapter 2, some theories of career choice are discussed. In Chapter 3, five career counseling models suggest step-by-step procedures that counselors use to assist an individual make an optimal career choice. Finally, you will learn that there are an almost endless number of factors that can influence career choice. The recent growing movement to integrate career and personal counseling will justifiably introduce many more variables into the career choice process. The recognition that career and personal concerns are not inseparable suggests that counselors address the interrelationship of personal and career problems. In essence, career choice is a process that encompasses a concerted effort by both counselor and client. Skills learned by the client in the initial choice process can be used in future decisions.

Working in the 21st Century

Work for most Americans is the focus of their attention for much of their adult life. One's career is a major factor of each individual's life story. To a large extent, work determines the joys and frustrations of daily life. One's work provides the means through which an individual expresses personal identity and accumulates financial resources (Newman & Newman, 2003).

Peter Drucker (2002) has suggested that the next society will be dominated by knowledge workers. Their career development is characterized by finely tuned skills that are built around a solid knowledge base that continually needs updating. Medical doctors, dentists, and psychologists are examples of traditional established knowledge workers. The new breed of knowledge worker, however, has emerged from advances in technology, such as a hi-tech information technologist. Future knowledge workers will replace the current ones as technology continues to change with the introduction of advanced products.

The work environment has also experienced dramatic changes in how work tasks are accomplished. We have witnessed or read about new diagnostic devices currently used in the health care industry. Automobile mechanics are now trained to use computerized diagnostic equipment to determine if our vehicle is operating properly. Large distribution organizations can determine their inventory almost immediately through personalized software programs. Plumbers use advanced technology to locate leaks in underground pipelines. Even the amount of wax in your left ear can be determined by a small camera whose image is enlarged and viewed on a screen. We do not know, however, how future advances in technology will change the way we work and live but they are sure to come. Broadband technology, for example, should offer significant innovations for the future workplace.

We have also witnessed changes from established work patterns of the past. We now have an abundance of independent contractors, self-employed individuals, freelance workers, and consultants. The contingent workforce, for instance, is part of a growing trend of new work arrangements. Originally, contingent workers filled in for an absent employee; however, the emerging contingent worker of today is one who agrees to work for a specified time in an organization. Under these conditions there is no guarantee of future employment.

The rapid growth of temp agencies and professional employment organizations is the result of organizational restructuring and the act of "outsourcing" its employees. More and more organizations have opted to contract with temp agencies or employment organizations for a workforce. They keep a core of employees that devote most of their time to planning and developing strategies for increasing their productivity. The rationale is that organizations are relieved of the increasing amount of "red tape" involved with large groups of employees and are not required to offer certain benefits. They do not make lifetime commitments to employees.

Yet another change for the worker in the 21st century is the practice of contracting for services and/or special personnel. A business group may opt to contract with an organization or with individuals to take over payroll and accounting services. A health care facility may contract with another organization to furnish registered nurses. These two examples suggest that some workers will work at the same site for a considerable time while other workers will shift sites on a regular basis.

Individuals who work for temp agencies, professional organizations, and contract organizations are promoted strictly for their specialized knowledge and their ability to perform. The highest-paid jobs are very competitive and take considerable dedication to updating knowledge and skills. The duties of the knowledge worker can be done equally well by both sexes and by individuals of different cultures and/or race or sexual orientation.

The changes we have discussed in the immediate preceding paragraphs will affect some workers more than others. What has and will change is how we work. Some knowledge workers, for example, will learn to make use of the results of new technological tools. One knowledge worker will gather information for another knowledge worker—thus, it is the new technology that will determine how the work is accomplished. According to Drucker (2002), we will depend heavily on knowledge workers in the next society. See Chapter 18 for more information.

Lifelong Learning

Working in the 21st century and the concept of lifelong learning has much in common. The forecast of a changing workplace underscores the need for developing a lifelong learning plan. Patton and McMahon (1999) suggest the terms "life career development learning" to emphasize the interrelationship of lifelong learning and career development. The basic assumption is that new knowledge bridges changes in work and life in the 21st century.

At first glance, lifelong learning may appear to be a concept we can take for granted. We cannot assume, however, that all our clients have conceptualized the significant relationship between lifelong learning and career development. To some the connection between lifelong learning and living more fully is at best a vague concept. Counselors may be required to offer concrete examples of the interrelationships between education and work in an effort to correct faulty thinking.

In 1994, the School-to-Work Opportunities Act was passed to assist high school students to receive more experiences and coursework that relate directly to the kinds of work they may enter. Follow-up studies of students in these programs suggested that those students who were irregular in school attendance were also irregular in attendance in the workplace (Fouad, 1997). Many of these students continued to need support from counselors, mentors, and supervisors at work. Most important, students need to accumulate positive job experiences before they understand the value of future planning (Gelso & Fretz, 2001).

One of the major counseling goals of lifelong learning is to provide each client with a knowledge base and skills that can be used for current and future concerns and needs. Decision making and communication skills, for instance, are good examples of skills that can be nurtured and used over the life span. Survival skills and networking techniques may be essential during periods of low employment. Information resources that can be accessed for a variety of client interests can be used to locate career projections or leisure and recreational needs. Finally, clients should periodically evaluate their own career development in an effort to determine their individualized learning needs. These suggestions are representative of an almost endless number of potential learning opportunities that can assist clients now and in the future. Counselors will find some challenging situations when promoting lifelong learning that include becoming an advocate for learning programs in a client's community.

Counseling in a Culturally Diverse Society

In the last two decades an abundance of information on the subject of multicultural counseling has been published. Much of it has been directed at developing new and modified counseling procedures to meet the needs of a growing culturally diverse society. Critics have pointed out that the assumptions of Western thought and psychology of human development need to be modified into a broader, more integrated knowledge base. The point to consider in this context is that individuals from different cultures develop their own set of values and work needs that were shaped in their unique environment. Values that differ from those of the dominant white culture are to be recognized and appreciated.

Career choice, for example, may be driven by goals of family as opposed to individual aspirations. In individualistic cultures of Europe and North America, great value is placed on individual accomplishment. In collectivistic cultures of Africa, Asia, and Latin America, the individual focuses on the welfare of the group and their collective survival (Axelson, 1999).

We do not, however, assume that all individuals of a particular culture have maintained the value structure of their parents. Some cultural values do break down as younger generations assimilate the values of the dominant culture. The term *acculturation* refers to the degree a client has assumed beliefs, values, and behaviors of the dominant culture. Differences in worldviews are frequently found in views about family, cooperation versus competition, communication styles, and locus of control (Gelso & Fretz, 2001).

The special needs of multicultural groups are addressed in all chapters of this text. This emphasis signifies the importance of meeting the counseling needs of a culturally diverse society. Counselor training programs for the most part continue to focus on updating competencies for career counselors. Counselors are to be alert to hard copy and online professional association guidelines for effective multicultural counseling.

An introduction to multicultural counseling usually begins with a definition of culture such as the one by Carter and Qureshi (1995) who suggest that "culture is a learned system of meaning and behavior that is passed from one generation to the next" (p. 240). A learned system of meaning and behavior suggests that each individual is indeed shaped by a unique environment of experiences in his or her culture. Two important concepts emerge from this definition. First, individuals develop worldviews shaped in their cultural ethnic groups and second, there are individual differences within ethnic groups. These concepts provide the foundation from which to build multicultural counseling competencies.

The following counseling competencies are introduced here and are followed by a more complete explanation in Chapter 10. Counselor competence begins with counselor self-understanding. Counselors are to increase their awareness of their own culture in order to change their racist behaviors. This process leads to an understanding of biases, stereotypes, and unintentional behaviors. Second, counselors acquire knowledge of each client's culture by focusing on culture-specific behavioral patterns, life experiences, and value systems. Finally, the concept of differences within groups suggests that we view each client as a unique individual. (See Box 1-2.)

In sum, counselors will be challenged to meet the needs of an increasingly culturally diverse society. Counselors modify their procedures, techniques, and tools and learn culturally appropriate ones. Assessment instruments, for example, have to be carefully scrutinized to determine if they are culturally appropriate. The call is for career counselors to not be culture-bound. The role and scope of career counseling should include techniques and tools that are more sensitive to different cultural values and concerns.

Effective Use of Career Information

In the not too distant past, career information consisted of a collection of unappealing, drab files and books containing technical-oriented descriptions of work tasks. In the last three decades there has been an explosion of published career information materials in the form of colorful books, files, audiovisual resources, and computer-based programs. In addition, we now have computer-generated career information and a vast array of Internet resources. It is not unusual to find sections in the local

---

Box 1-2	The Practice of Career Development Is Growing Internationally

The brief examples that follow present some evidence that the career guidance and counseling movement is making great strides of progress internationally. Counselors should be alert to global initiatives that emerge from career counseling programs in other nations.

All secondary students in England are required to maintain records of achievement (ROAs) and individual action plans (IAPs). These records are used by school-leavers to obtain vocational training through a National Record of Achievement action plan sponsored by government policy. Specifically, the information is used to document individual career competencies and work experiences. This is a good example that illustrates the desire to provide career services to students who are about to make the transition from school-to-work or school-to-school. In England, as in many other nations, career development programs are to begin in early childhood and continue over the life span.

Likewise, in Finland an individualized student personal study program (PSP) is developed by government employment offices and is used in individual and group counseling programs before one begins vocational education and training. The PSP contains information about each student's work experiences, previous studies, and leisure activities. It serves as an important component in life planning and in individualizing each student's vocational education.

In Australia, a national Job Network has been created. More than 300 private, community, and government organizations have formed to contract with the national government to provide assistance to job seekers. Services offered are flexible in terms of job matching and individual assistance. At Centrelink centers, similar to one-stop centers in this country, career services are offered across Australia. Services include a national job registry, provisions for overseeing unemployment benefits, assessment of each job seeker's eligibility for work, and instructions on how to use the Job Network. Australia has also developed career education programs for all school levels.

Denmark has also instituted one-stop centers called counseling houses. In these locations, career counselors offer individual counseling and provide a variety of services, including career information, job search skills, educational options, and training opportunities. Denmark is committed to professionalizing career services through its National Council on Educational and Vocational Guidance. They have a strong commitment to developing counselor training programs.

In the Netherlands, career education and guidance are mandatory in secondary schools. Their approach to career development includes a life-

newspaper that are devoted to job openings, a list of online sources of job information, and the usual want ads. The point here is that we now have at our disposal a variety of current career information resources. The significant challenge, however, is how can we most effectively use career information.

Spokane (1991) reviewed the rather meager research on how clients filter and process career information into the career decision process. He focused on information-seeking behavior, the cognitive process involved in assimilating career information, and the social restraints that restrict some individuals in the career search process. All of these elements suggest that more attention and research needs to be directed to the effective use of career information in the career counseling process. To underscore this point we suggest that effective career information processing skills, for example, are key requirements in the decision process.

Rounds and Tracey (1990) and Sampson, Reardon, Peterson, and Lenz (2004) suggest that information processing skills are essential for making optimal career

long learning commitment and the development of a working identity. The government has been very proactive in creating career development services that offer care for sick workers, assistance designed to help the unemployed return to the workforce, aid for persons with disabilities, and welfare intervention.

In Japan, career services are offered through a network of Public Employment Security Offices (PESO). Career information can be obtained through a computer-assisted information system that reports labor supply and demand. Services offered include study courses designed to enhance career decision making, career services especially designed for women, older workers, and dropouts. There appears to be an emphasis to encourage personal responsibility for one's career development.

In the secondary schools in Hong Kong, career teachers provide programs of career services. The focus is on available career guidance resources that contain job opportunities with corresponding requirements. Services include career-related workshops, coaching, career planning, and support networks.

Canada has been an outstanding leader in developing a national career development policy that is very innovative. Career in Canada is viewed as a development of work tasks as op-

posed to a focus on a single field of work. This view is driven by the perception that individuals will make multiple job changes over the life span, placing the focus on improving work tasks rather than specific jobs. Individuals are also to become self-directed, with an emphasis on self-responsibility and self-agency. These recommendations are fostered through computer and Internet career development programs, participation of employers in work experience, cooperative education, career fairs, and numerous youth employment programs.

In sum, we have provided only very brief examples of career guidance and counseling programs in some nations around the globe. In most countries we find a strong commitment to career-related services by national governments. There seems to be agreement that career development should begin at an early age and be enhanced over the life span. Career education in schools stands out as a program that has received universal support. It should not be surprising to find that each nation has tailored its career services to address its economic and cultural traditions and needs. Future cooperative efforts with other nations should offer the potential for exchange of program ideas and research. The information in this box was compiled from Herr, Cramer, and Niles (2004, pp. 57–66).

decisions. They recommended that counselors evaluate client skills in processing information during the career decision process. They also suggest that the timing of intervention strategies is essential to maintaining productive effective information-seeking behaviors. Their methods for assessing levels of information processing skills are summarized and illustrated in Chapter 3.

Sharf (2002) lists a number of specific sources on career information that he recommends. He believes that counselors have the responsibility to know certain types of occupational information and specific sources of information. According to Sharf, counselors are to provide occupational descriptions including salary ranges, outlook, educational requirements, and where more information can be found about an occupation a client selects.

Reardon, Lenz, Sampson, and Peterson (2000) firmly believe that instead of an individual asking for specific information, such as where is the best-paying job, the client should begin career counseling by focusing on self-knowledge. They suggest that clients should focus on past experiences, connect and relate life experiences, and recognize that all life experiences contribute to self-understanding. Self-knowledge is also illuminated through clarification of values, interests, and knowledge of personal skills. Finally, they suggest that career information is more effective in timing and content when a client has gone through a period of readiness that is prompted by an empowerment to evaluate and comprehend self.

Readiness for career information suggests that clients have realistic expectations, are free of faulty beliefs that interfere with rational decision making, have learned how to effectively process career information, and have a fairly accurate perception of self. In other words, clients are capable of projecting self into requirements of work environments found in career exploration and subsequently are able to make appropriate decisions as to their fit. Be aware that the ability of clients to analyze data is of the utmost importance in career decision making. Young adults can be overwhelmed by the number of career possibilities and find themselves with information overload (Feldman, 2002). The lesson here is to prepare clients for effectively evaluating career information. Finally, uncovering underlying constraints that limit client career options is a most worthy objective.

Clients are to begin career exploration by evaluating both negative and positive reactions to all careers. They continue their search by focusing on information obtained from discussions with workers, parents, and other important adults. Productive exploration can come from shadowing workers on the job, and participating in cooperative education programs, internships, and apprenticeships. Finally, the counselor collaborates with the client on each phase of career information processing. (See Appendix H for a description of a high school student's experience in a cooperative education program.)

Focusing on a Multiple Spectrum of Domains

Traditionally, career counseling has been viewed as a counseling process that has focused on career choice and career development over the life span. Historically, career counselors placed clients by matching measured human traits with requirements of jobs. Gradually, a broader approach to career choice and placement included additional variables such as personality, values, lifestyle preferences, and the significance of person-in-environment interactions. This movement was supported by a solid database of research developed during the last century that has provided career counselors with a greater insight into career development theory and effective career-related interventions. The need to integrate career and personal concerns in the practice of career development has emerged as the next challenge in the ever expanding role of career counseling.

Current practice places a strong emphasis on the connection between career development and mental health. A growing database of evidence suggests that faulty cognitions that inhibit systematic, logical thinking, for example, can interfere with the career choice process (Spokane, 1989; Gelso & Fretz, 2001). Severe personality disorders may make it difficult for some clients to function in a work environment. Fear of failure suggests that an individual withholds work efforts for fear of not being successful. Work dysfunctions of poor performance, absence from work, and other maladaptive reactions to the work environment may be the result of complex interactions of personal characteristics and the workplace (Lowman, 1993; Neff, 1985). These examples underscore the rationale of integrating career and personal concerns in the practice of career development.

The implications of interweaving career and personal concerns are very pervasive for both client and counselor. Clients who present concerns that are considered potential mental health problems will best be served by counseling professionals skilled in the integration of services. Counselors will be required to develop skills in diagnosing client personal concerns as well as the competency to provide intervention strategies in the affective, cognitive, and behavioral domains. Obviously, not all clients will present severe personal concerns that require therapy. Clients who can best be served by a holistic counseling approach, can expect to find counselors who are trained in diagnosis, treatment, and managed care, and who favor brief therapies when appropriate.

Counselors focus on sets of client concerns. Some concerns will involve career-related problems and others may represent personal ones that are interrelated to multiple life roles, including the work role. Within this framework, counselors focus on a multiple spectrum of domains of the "whole person" as in a holistic approach to counseling. Career and personal concerns are considered as inseparable and interrelated. We use the example of a depressed client to illustrate the interrelatedness of personal and career concerns.

Case 1-1 The Depressed Worker

Alma, a worker in her late thirties, told her career counselor that she wanted to change jobs. Alma was currently doing secretarial work in a large firm, a job she had held for two years. Her reasons for seeking a change were somewhat vague: She stated, "I just don't like it there any more." And, she added, "I'm very depressed."

Depression can come from a variety of sources, and it can be work-related, nonwork-related, or both. As Lowman (1993) points out, however, depression can both lower work performance and affect nonwork factors. In Alma's case, work seems to be at the center of her problem.

Many aspects of work have been found to influence depression, such as problems with supervision, overly demanding work, ambiguity of authority, lack of social support, and corporate instability (Golding, 1989; Firth & Britton, 1989, cited in Lowman, 1993). The career counselor was able to determine that Alma's depression was related to a poor relationship with her immediate supervisor. Alma also perceived that her work was demanding and that she received little feedback support.

When clients present concerns of depression, there are many questions to be answered. For instance: What are possible sources of stress in the workplace and in the home? Is this client predisposed to depression? How do we decrease depression or anxiety?

Such cases may follow several pathways. If the counselor determines that the client is suffering from work-related depression, the counselor and client focus on concerns the client has about the work environment and other life roles. When job change is the best choice, the client must reevaluate goals, changing values, and developed abilities. Client and counselor seek solutions to the current concerns with work environment and requirements to determine a future work role.

The choice to change the person could involve stress reduction exercises, cognitive-behavioral therapy, addiction treatment, medication, physical activity programs, interpersonal skills training, and logotherapy, among others. Combinations of such programs are often used. More than likely, Alma's counselor would suggest programs of stress reduction to accompany the process of choosing a different occupation.

In this brief review of a case study, several counseling skills were suggested and implied: for example, skills in diagnosing symptoms of depression, skills of interviewing, skills in anxiety-reduction programs, and skills in career decision-making procedures. A more holistic approach in the practice of career development recognizes that an individual's total development includes a broad spectrum of domains; helpers are not just career counselors, helpers counsel individuals. Chapter 4 is devoted to a broader explanation of integrating career and personal concerns.

In sum, basic issues represent both the historical development of career counseling and its exciting future. More information is provided about basic issues in the chapters that follow. At this point you hopefully have gained a greater perspective of the role and scope of career counseling. It is a very inclusive counseling role that is centered around the meaning of work in each person's life. Career counseling is an approach that involves the "whole person." Career counselors focus on balancing all life roles in an ever changing world.

Summary

1. The career counseling movement was embedded in changes in our society, especially in the work role. Career counseling was created to meet the needs of society during transitional periods of change. Its growth was influenced by a number of variables, factors, and events. Some key influences include the rise of industrialism, needs of war veterans and their families, social reform movements, studies of human development, growth of urban areas, the measurement movement, federal acts and initiatives, studies of career development, changing demographics, growth of technology, and global market forces.

2. Some basic issues in career counseling include the case for the individual, career life perspective, working in the 21st century, counseling in a culturally diverse society, effective use of information, and focusing on multiple spectrums of domains.

Supplementary Learning Exercises

1. Should all career counseling focus on individual needs? Elaborate and cite examples.
2. Give at least five reasons the federal government has supported the career counseling and guidance movement.
3. Give at least five examples of how changes in the workplace will influence career choice.
4. What is a knowledge worker? How are they different than other workers?
5. Why is so much importance attributed to the lifelong learning concept? Illustrate your answer with examples.
6. How does one become a culturally competent counselor? Describe changes in counseling approaches, procedures, and assessment instruments.
7. Describe at least four counseling strategies that promote the effective use of career information.
8. How can career counselors integrate multiple life roles in the counseling process? Support your answer with examples.
9. Rank the basic issues discussed in this chapter in order of importance. Support your top three choices in a debate with a classmate.
10. Add at least three additional basic issues that you consider to be essential to effective career counseling in the 21st century.

For More Information

Historical Development

Herr, E. L. (2001). Career development and its practice: A historical approach. *Career Development Quarterly, 49* (3), 196–211.

Picchioni, A. P., & Bonk, E. C. (1981). *A comprehensive history of guidance in the United States.* Austin: Texas Personal and Guidance Association.

Pope, M. (2001). A brief history of career counseling in the United States. *Career Development Quarterly 48,* 194–211.

Zunker, V. G. (2002). *Career counseling: Applied concepts of life planning.* Pacific Grove, CA: Brooks/Cole.

Basic Issues

Drucker, P. F. (2002). *Managing the future.* New York: Truman Talley Books.

Feldman, D. C. (Ed.). (2002). *Work careers: A developmental perspective.* San Francisco, CA: Jossey-Bass.

Gelso, C., & Fretz, B. (2001). *Counseling psychology.* Belmont, CA: Wadsworth.

Herr, E. L., Cramer, S. H., & Niles, S. G. (2004). *Career guidance and counseling through the life span: Systematic approaches.* Boston: Pearson Educational, Inc.

Suggested InfoTrac College Edition Topics

Career choice	Holistic counseling
Career information	Life learning
Counseling history	Multicultural counseling
Human development	Work

Theories
of Career Development

2

Chapter Highlights

- Trait-Oriented Theories

- Social Learning and Cognitive Theories

- Developmental Theories

- Person-in-Environment Perspective

- Implications for Career Guidance

- Case Study

THE CAREER DEVELOPMENT THEORIES discussed in this chapter have been most instrumental in providing the foundation for research in vocational behavior. To comprehend these theories is to understand the priorities in career counseling today. The conceptual shifts in career counseling, test format, work satisfaction studies, and classification systems of occupations have evolved primarily from theories. Understandably, the study of career counseling should begin with some sources of its foundation.

We begin with a brief discussion of how career development theories emerged, what constitutes a theory, and, finally, general information about theories. Next, we review nine theories, grouped according to Gelso and Fretz (2001) as follows: trait-oriented theories, social learning and cognitive theories, developmental theories, and person-in-environment theories.

Vocational counseling's initial focus primarily was on the use of assessment techniques for job placement. Beginning in the early 1950s, vocational counseling started to expand its boundaries by including a broader range of factors in the career choice process, such as self-concept, self-knowledge, and an array of developmental issues. The career development theories that followed in the 1970s and beyond have contributed to an even broader and growing perspective of the career development process. The theories discussed here will include basic assumptions, key terms, outcomes, and practical applications. Be aware that there will be references that are associated with the unfolding of some theories that go back to 1909. Hence, some theories have historical value in the early studies of vocational psychology and as such have significantly influenced current career counseling practices. The overarching objective here, however, is to discover how theories influenced the development of counseling procedures, and the components of theories that are most relevant for building an understanding of and a basic foundation for career counseling. Keep in mind that the purpose of this chapter is to introduce the basic elements of career development theories. More in-depth and extensive information can be found in Brown (2002), Brown and Brooks (1996), Osipow and Fitzgerald (1996), and Sharf (2002).

Career development theories have been criticized by both students and practitioners as being vague about how findings and conclusions can be used and are thought to be "out of touch" with what counselors really want and need—a more direct link between theory and practice. The most compelling and enduring questions have focused on what purpose career development theories serve and, more important, how they contribute to career counseling practice. To answer the first question one must understand the nature of theories. A career development theory is a set of concepts, propositions, and ideas that provides us with insights into what is believed to be true about the process of career development. A theory presents some clues about what is most important to study, how it should be studied, and how results will address counseling concerns (Shaffer, 2002; Sigelman & Rider, 2003). A career development theory is not step-by-step, how-to-do career counseling; however, what is learned from the results of concepts and propositions of theories does provide the guidelines for counseling procedures and interventions discussed in the next chapter's career counseling models. Some theories discussed do offer suggestions for how to do career counseling, and some provide diagnostic measures, workbooks, and other counseling materials. Generally, career development theories present different views of what is most important in the career development process and provide the basis for future research.

One fact we know for certain from career development theories is that the career development process can take many and different pathways. It is often difficult, therefore, to filter out what each theory has contributed to counseling practice and how one theory differs from another. Our major objective in this chapter is to bring theories to life and illustrate how the study of career development has influenced the methods used in counseling all clients who come to us with sets of concerns. Near the end of the chapter a fictitious client will be introduced to briefly illustrate how a client can be helped by a counselor using the outcomes of career development research. A summary of four groups of theories' significant findings and recommendations for counseling offer some practical solutions that can be used to help address client's problems. Be aware that only some of the career development theory positions are discussed in the summaries. The point here is that research efforts on career development have led to a significant number of counseling procedures and interventions that are currently used. Only some have been selected as examples to illustrate helpful links to client concerns.

Trait-Oriented Theories

This first group of theories evolved from the measurement movement in the early part of the 20th century. They are embedded in Parson's (1909) vocational counseling paradigm of matching individual traits with requirements of occupations. From this rather straightforward approach emerged the study of work adjustment and job satisfaction variables. A key finding was potential sets of reinforcers in the work environment that enhance job satisfaction. The position that individuals are attracted to an occupational environment that meets their personal needs and provides them with satisfaction became the driving force behind one of the most popular career counseling approaches. In this section we introduce trait-and-factor theory, person-environment-correspondence counseling, and John Holland's typology. (Holland is recognized worldwide as a most prolific leader in career counseling.)

Trait-and-Factor Theory

Among the earliest theorists on vocational counseling, Parsons (1909) maintained that vocational guidance is accomplished first by *studying the individual,* second by *surveying occupations,* and finally by *matching* the individual with the occupation. This process, called trait-and-factor theory, became the foundation of many vocational counseling programs in the early part of the 20th century, including those used by the Veterans Administration, YMCA, Jewish vocational services, and colleges and universities.

The trait-and-factor approach has been the most durable of all career counseling theories. Simply stated, it means matching the individual's traits with requirements of a specific occupation, subsequently solving the career-search problem. The trait-and-factor theory evolved from early studies of individual differences and developed closely with the psychometric movement. This theory greatly influenced the study of job descriptions and job requirements as theorists attempted to predict future job success by measuring job-related traits. The key characteristic of this theory is the assumption that individuals have unique patterns of ability and/or traits that can be objectively measured and correlated with the requirements of various types of jobs.

The development of assessment instruments and the refinement of occupational information are closely associated with the trait-and-factor theory. The study of aptitudes in relation to job success has been an ongoing process. Occupational interests occupy a major part of the research literature on career development. The importance of individual values in the career decision-making process has also been highlighted by the trait-and-factor theory.

Through the efforts of Parsons (1909) and Williamson (1939, 1965), components of the trait-and-factor theory were developed into step-by-step procedures designed to help clients make wise career decisions. Parsons's three-step procedures—studying the individual, surveying occupations, and using "true reasoning" to match the individual with an occupation—may at first glance be judged to be completely dominated by test results. But, on the contrary, it has been argued that Parsons's first step suggests that evaluating each individual's background is an important part of his counseling paradigm and does not necessarily include psychometric data.

Williamson (1939, 1949) was a prominent advocate of trait-and-factor counseling. Williamson's counseling procedures maintained the early impetus of the trait-and-factor approach that evolved from Parsons's work. This straightforward approach to counseling contained six sequential steps: analysis, synthesis, diagnosis, prognosis, counseling, and follow-up. When integrated into other theories of career counseling, the trait-and-factor approach played a vital role in the development of assessment techniques, whose results are used with other data to reveal congruence between individual and work environment. Thus, a major criticism of this theory has been a dependence on and an overuse of test results.

Brown, Brooks, and associates (1990), however, argued that trait-and-factor theory has never been fully understood. They suggested that advocates of trait-and-factor approaches never approved of excessive use of testing in career counseling. For example, Williamson (1939) suggested that test results are but one means of evaluating individual differences. Other data, such as work experience and general background, are as important as test results in the career counseling process.

Recently, Sharf (2002) summarized the advantages and disadvantages of trait-and-factor theory and suggested that it is a static theory rather than a developmental one. Furthermore, it focuses on identifying individual traits and factors but does not account for how interests, values, aptitudes, achievement, and personalities grow and change. The major point here is that clients can benefit from dialogue that is directed toward continually evolving personal traits and how changes affect career decision making.

The following assumptions of the trait-and-factor approach also raise concerns about this theory: (1) There is a single career goal for everyone, and (2) career decisions are based primarily on measured abilities (Herr, Cramer, & Niles, 2004). These assumptions severely restrict the range of factors that can be considered in the career development process. In essence, it suggests that the trait-and-factor approach is too narrow in scope to be considered a major theory of career development. We should recognize, however, that standardized assessment and occupational analysis procedures stressed in trait-and-factor approaches are useful in career counseling. In fact, assessment instruments designed primarily to assist in career decision making continue to be developed and refined. The same may be said about occupational information, as growing numbers of research projects have focused on optimal use of job descriptions and requirements, work environments, and job satisfaction studies. Finally, bridging the gap between assessment scores and work environments is a huge challenge for career counselors now, as in the past (Prediger, 1995).

Will trait-and-factor theory be revitalized for the 21st century? Prediger (1995) suggests that person-environment fit theory has indeed enhanced the potential for a closer relationship between assessment and career counseling; assessment information can provide the basis for developing career possibilities into realities. For example, assessment results, along with other information, can provide a pathway for growth and propose how that growth can be accomplished. Prediger suggested a *similarity model,* designed not to predict success or to find the "ideal career," but to provide a means of evaluating occupations that "are similar to you in important ways" (Prediger, 1995, p. 2).

Using the similarity model to provide client focus when exploring careers may revitalize the role of trait-and-factor in current career counseling models (Rounds & Tracey, 1990; Zytowski, 1994). The relevant message here is that trait-and-factor theory has an important role in future career development theory and in career counseling practice.

 ## Summary of Practical Applications

1. One of the major career counseling roles of early trait-and-factor approaches was that of diagnosis. In this context, assessment was the process of analyzing data collected through a variety of tests. Individual strengths and weaknesses were evaluated, with the primary purpose of finding a job that matched measured abilities and achievements. Assessment data was used primarily to predict job satisfaction and success.

2. Contemporary career counseling practices are expanding the use of test data. One example is the study of the relationship between human factors and work environment variables. The results of this research are used to find congruence between individual human factors and reinforcers that exist in work environments. In Holland's (1996) typology approach, one major objective is to find work environments that are congruent with a client's personality traits.

3. Instead of predicting the possibility of success in a particular career on the basis of actuarial information, the counselor interprets test data and informs the client of observed similarities to current workers in a career field. For example, a client who has a similar interest pattern to current workers in a particular field of work may find that work to be satisfying. Clients use this information, along with other data, in the career decision process. Finally, assessment data are considered to be one source of information that can be most effectively used in conjunction with other data.

Person-Environment-Correspondence (PEC) Counseling

This theory has a long history, and as late as the early 1990s, it was referred to as the theory of work adjustment (TWA). In 1991, it was revised once again to include descriptions of the differences between personality structure and personality style and between personality style and adjustment style. The theory at that point had become more inclusive, embracing how individuals interact in their everyday lives as well as how they interact in a work environment. The broader label of person-environment-correspondence (PEC) was added in 1991 (Dawis, 2002; Lofquist & Dawis, 1991).

PEC theory has always emphasized that work is more than step-by-step task-oriented procedures. Work includes human interaction and sources of satisfaction, dissatisfaction, rewards, stress, and many other psychological variables. The basic assumption is that individuals seek to achieve and maintain a positive relationship with their work environments. According to Dawis and Lofquist, individuals bring their requirements to a work environment, and the work environment makes its requirements of individuals. To survive, the individual and the work environment must achieve some degree of *congruence* (correspondence).

To achieve this *consonance,* or agreement, the individual must successfully meet the job requirements, and the work environment must fulfill the individual's requirements. Stability on the job, which can lead to tenure, is a function of correspondence between individual and work environment. The process of achieving and maintaining correspondence with a work environment is referred to as *work adjustment.*

Four key points of Dawis's and Lofquist's theory are summarized as follows: (1) work personality and work environment should be amenable, (2) individual needs are most important in determining an individual's fit into the work environment, (3) individual needs and the reinforcer system that characterizes the work setting are important aspects of stability and tenure, and (4) job placement is best accomplished through a match of worker traits with the requirements of a work environment.

Dawis and Lofquist (1984) (Dawis 2002) have identified *occupational reinforcers* found in the work environment that are vital to an individual's work adjustment. They evaluated work settings to derive potential reinforcers of individual behavior. In the career counseling process, individual needs are matched with occupational reinforcers to determine an individual's fit into a work environment. Some examples of occupational reinforcers are achievement, advancement, authority, coworkers, activity, security, social service, social status, and variety.

Lofquist and Dawis (1984) and Dawis (2002) continue to stress the significance between the relationships of job satisfaction and work adjustment. Job satisfaction has been evaluated from outcomes (results or consequences) of work experience, such as tenure, job involvement, productivity, work alienation, and morale. A significant but not surprising conclusion suggests that satisfaction is negatively related to job turnover, withdrawal behavior (such as absenteeism and lateness), and worker alienation. But perhaps more importantly, job satisfaction was found to be positively related to job involvement, morale, and overall life situations or nonwork satisfaction.

This theory assumes that job satisfaction is a significant indicator of work adjustment. For example, job satisfaction is an indicator of the individual's perception of work and the work environment and is highly related to tenure in a work situation. The theory of work adjustment therefore has the following implications for career counselors:

1. Job satisfaction should be evaluated according to several factors, including satisfaction with coworkers and supervisors, type of work, autonomy, responsibility, and opportunities for self-expression of ability and for serving others.
2. Job satisfaction is an important career counseling concern but does not alone measure work adjustment. Work adjustment includes other variables, such as the individual's ability to perform tasks required of work.
3. Job satisfaction is an important predictor of job tenure, and the factors associated with job satisfaction should be recognized in career counseling. An individual's abilities and how they relate to work requirements are not the only career counseling components of work adjustment.
4. Individual needs and values are significant components of job satisfaction. These factors should be delineated in career counseling programs designed to enhance work adjustment.

5. Individuals differ significantly in specific reinforcers of career satisfaction. There-fore, career counseling must be individualized when exploring interests, values, and needs.
6. Career counselors should consider the reinforcers available in work environ-ments and compare them with the individual needs of clients.

What does all this mean for the career counselor? First, it should not be surpris-ing that career counselors should consider clients' job satisfaction needs to help them find amenable work environments. Keep in mind that job satisfaction is a significant variable in determining productivity, job involvement, and career tenure. Second, career counselors should use occupational information to assist clients in matching individual needs, interests, and abilities with patterns and levels of different rein-forcers in the work environment. For example, the reinforcer of "achievement" is re-lated to experiences of accomplishment in the work situation. Social service is related to the opportunities that a work situation offers for performing tasks that will help people. In the following paragraphs some core elements of this theory are briefly reviewed. They include work reinforcers, personality traits, abilities and values, envi-ronmental structure and work adjustment, and future perspectives.

Work Reinforcers. Some significant problems with identifying work reinforcers in the 21st century are constant changes in work requirements, in workplaces, and how and by whom success will be evaluated. Lofquist and Dawis warned that career counselors may have difficulty identifying occupational reinforcers because of the lack of rele-vant research, the vast variety of jobs in the current labor force, and emerging jobs. Meanwhile, the theory of work adjustment has focused more attention on the impor-tance of worker satisfaction. In the future, however, workers may have to adjust to finding satisfaction in a variety of jobs in a work environment that makes use of their individual skills. Workers in the 21st century may work in teams and use sets of skills to meet work requirements.

Personality Traits, Ability, and Values. A core element of PEC is the identification of per-sonality traits, ability, and values. Dawis (1996, 2002) identified personality structure as stable characteristics of personality that consist primarily of abilities and values. *Personality style* is seen as "typical temporal characteristics" of an individual's interac-tion with the environment. In other words, does the worker's behavior and actions fit well in the work environment or are there indications of conflicts. As is usual in other trait-and-factor theories, *ability dimensions* are used to estimate the individual's prob-able levels of work skills or abilities. *Values* are viewed as work needs and are identified primarily through the *Minnesota Importance Questionnaire* (University of Minnesota, 1984), discussed in the next chapter. Work needs resemble a client's "ordinary psycho-logical needs," which develop outside the work environment but also apply to the work setting, such as recognition and need achievement. Most important, this theory emphasizes that both abilities (work skills) and values (work needs) are important components of optimal career selection.

Environmental Structure and Work Adjustment. Two other key elements are *environmental structure and work adjustment.* Environmental structure is identified as the character-istic abilities and values of individuals who inhabit the work environment. The basic assumption here is that clients who have abilities and values similar to individuals already on the job will make it less difficult for an individual to adjust to a work environment. This assumption is an example of "matching" and is one of the core elements of trait-and-factor counseling.

Work adjustment is ideal when person and environment have matching work needs and work skills; however, changes in either can lead to worker dissatisfaction. A worker's attempt to improve his or her fit within the work environment can be viewed as actions designed to achieve work adjustment. Adjustments usually follow one of two modes: active and reactive. In the active mode, the worker attempts to change the work environment, whereas in the reactive mode, the worker attempts to correspond better with the work environment.

Important to the career counselor here is that work adjustment is closely related to personality style, although they are considered to be distinct concepts. Because of changing work conditions, counselors can expect to find more clients with work adjustment problems, thus, work adjustment counseling is one of the areas that should increase in the 21st century. PEC counseling suggests that adjustment behavior includes degrees of flexibility, one's ability to react positively to changes, perseverance, and personality style or style of interaction within the environment. Herein lies a major contribution of this theory—work adjustment counseling. This is a relatively unaddressed issue and should garner more attention in the near future as we witness more violence in the workplace as a result of worker dissatisfaction.

The Future. Some counselors may find that their services may be needed as consultants to organizations. There is a growing awareness among organizations that employees who learn to balance their lifestyle are more satisfied in the workplace, which in turn leads to improved productivity, and less absenteeism. Worker satisfaction among employees has long been the goal of organizations. This goal has taken on a new twist in the 21st century with the violence that has been experienced recently in the workplace. Counselors must recognize that antisocial behavior in the workplace is a complex phenomenon and that it often parallels violence in other life roles (Baron, Hoffman, & Merrill, 2000).

Empirical Support for the Person-Environment-Correspondence Theory

For PEC, see Holland (1992), Spokane (1985), and Gelso and Fretz (2001). For prediction of satisfactoriness, see Hunter and Hunter (1984). For prediction of satisfaction, that is, worker satisfaction from need-reinforcer correspondence, see Dawis (1991). For other studies that offer information about various propositions of the theory, see Rounds (1990), Bretz and Judge (1994), and Dawis (2002).

 ### Summary of Practical Applications

1. The person-environment-correspondence theory depends heavily on client assessment because its major objective is to identify groups of occupations that hold the greatest potential for a client's satisfaction in a work environment and, conversely, those that will be less likely to meet the criteria for satisfaction. Of major concern are a client's abilities (work skills) and values (work needs).

2. The *U.S. Employment Service's General Aptitude Test Battery* (U.S. Department of Labor, 1970a) is recommended for measuring abilities, whereas the *Minnesota Importance Questionnaire* (MIQ) (University of Minnesota, 1984) is used to assess values. Personality style is to be evaluated by the counselor in an interview.

3. The *Minnesota Occupational Classification System III* (Dawis, Dohm, Lofquist, Chartrand, & Due, 1987) provides an index for level and patterns of abilities and reinforcers that different occupations provide. This index is used for matching work skills to requirements of occupations and as a means of determining reinforcers available by occupation. Clearly, reinforcers are becoming more difficult to identify in the current work world.

4. Presentation of assessment information should be tailored to the client's abilities, values, and style. The highly verbal client would probably prefer a verbal presentation with time allowed for discussion. A client high in spatial ability would most likely prefer a graphic presentation. The point here is that the counselor should present the information in the most meaningful way for clients.

5. Career planning should be conceptualized to be most meaningful to the client by determining whether the client is more achievement–oriented (satisfactoriness) or more self-fulfilled–oriented (satisfaction). The rationale here is that the counselor should ascertain client orientation to determine which prediction system to emphasize in the career planning process.

Work adjustment counseling is viewed differently in today's society, where clients are faced with constantly changing work environments. Helping clients learn new skills and develop appropriate work habits that match the needs of changing work environments are relevant counseling strategies for the 21st century (Dawis, 1996). As we have noted already, the nature of work will change along with the workplace in the 21st century. Theories that are based primarily on stable and traditional work environments from which reinforcers for job satisfaction are obtained will be less relevant for career counseling. The general themes of work adjustment, work environment, and job satisfaction derived from this theory, however, should continue to be recognized as viable factors in career counseling.

John Holland's Typology

According to John Holland (1992), individuals are attracted to a given career because of their particular personalities and numerous variables that constitute their backgrounds. First, career choice is an expression of, or an extension of, personality into the world of work, followed by subsequent identification with specific occupational stereotypes. A comparison of self with the perception of an occupation and subsequent acceptance or rejection is a major determinant in career choice. Congruence of one's view of self with occupational preference establishes what Holland refers to as the *modal personal style.*

Modal personal orientation is a developmental process established through heredity and the individual's life history of reacting to environmental demands. Central to Holland's theory is the concept that one chooses a career to satisfy one's preferred modal personal orientation. If the individual has developed a strong dominant orientation, satisfaction is probable in a corresponding occupational environment. If, however, the orientation is one of indecision, the likelihood of satisfaction diminishes. The strength or dominance of the developed modal personal orientation as compared with career environments will be critical to the individual's selection of a preferred lifestyle. Again, the key concept behind Holland's environmental models and environmental influences is that individuals are attracted to a particular role demand of an occupational environment that meets their personal needs and provides them with satisfaction.

For example, a socially oriented individual prefers to work in an environment that provides interaction with others, such as a teaching position. On the other hand, a mechanically inclined individual would seek out an environment where his or her trade could be quietly practiced and where socializing is minimal. Occupational homogeneity therefore provides the best route to self-fulfillment and a consistent career pattern. Individuals out of their elements who have conflicting occupational environmental roles and goals will have inconsistent and divergent career patterns. Holland stressed the *importance of self-knowledge* in the search for vocational satisfaction and stability.

From this frame of reference, Holland proposed six kinds of modal occupational environments and six matching modal personal orientations. These are summarized in Table 2-1, which also offers representative examples of occupations and themes associated with each personal style.

Holland proposed that personality types can be arranged in a coded system following his modal-personal-orientation themes such as R (realistic occupation), I (investigative), A (artistic), S (social), E (enterprising), and C (conventional). In this way, personality types can be arranged according to dominant combinations. For example, a code of CRI would mean that an individual is very much like people in conventional occupations, and somewhat like those in realistic and investigative occupations. Holland's Occupational Classification (HOC) system has corresponding Dictionary of Occupational Titles (DOT) numbers for cross-reference purposes. The four basic assumptions underlying Holland's (1992) theory are as follows:

1. In our culture, most persons can be categorized as one of six types: realistic, investigative, artistic, social, enterprising, or conventional. (p. 2)
2. There are six kinds of environments: realistic, investigative, artistic, social, enterprising, or conventional. (p. 3)
3. People search for environments that will let them exercise their skills and abilities, express their attitudes and values, and take on agreeable problems and roles. (p. 4)
4. A person's behavior is determined by an interaction between his personality and the characteristics of his environment. (p. 4)

The relationships between Holland's personality types are illustrated in Figure 2-1. The hexagonal model provides a visual presentation of the inner relationship of personality styles and occupational environment coefficients of correlation. For example, adjacent categories on the hexagon (e.g., realistic and investigative) are most alike, whereas opposites (e.g., artistic and conventional) are most unlike. Those of intermediate distance (e.g., realistic and enterprising) are somewhat unlike.

Holland's hexagonal model introduces five key concepts. The first, *consistency,* relates to personality as well as to environment. Some types have more in common than others; for instance, artistic and social types have more in common than do

Table 2.1	Holland's Modal Personal Styles and Occupational Environments	
Personal styles	**Themes**	**Occupational environments**
May lack social skills; prefers concrete vs. abstract work tasks; may seem frank, materialistic, and inflexible; usually has mechanical abilities	Realistic	Skilled trades such as plumber, electrician, and machine operator; technician skills such as airplane mechanic, photographer, draftsperson, and some service occupations materialistic, and inflexible; usually has
Very task-oriented; is interested in math and science; may be described as independent, analytical, and intellectual; may be reserved and defers leadership to others	Investigative	Scientific such as chemist, physicist, and mathematician; technician such as laboratory technician, computer programmer, and electronics worker
Prefers self-expression through the arts; may be described as imaginative, introspective, and independent; values aesthetics and creation of art forms	Artistic	Artistic such as sculptor, artist, and designer; musical such as music teacher, orchestra leader, and musician; literary such as editor, writer, and critic
Prefers social interaction and has good communication skills; is concerned with social problems, and is community-service-oriented; has interest in educational activities	Social	Educational such as teacher, educational administrator, and college professor; social welfare such as social worker, sociologist, rehabilitation counselor, and professional nurse
Prefers leadership roles; may be described as domineering, ambitious, and persuasive; makes use of good verbal skills	Enterprising	Managerial such as personnel, production, and sales manager; various sales positions, such as life insurance, real estate, and car salesperson
May be described as practical, well-controlled, sociable, and rather conservative; prefers structured tasks such as systematizing and manipulation of data and word processing	Conventional	Office and clerical worker such as timekeeper, file clerk, teller, accountant, keypunch operator, secretary, bookkeeper, receptionist, and credit manager

Source: Adapted from Holland, 1985a, 1992.

investigative and enterprising types. The closer the types are on the hexagon, the more consistent the individual will be. Therefore, high consistency is seen when an individual expresses a preference for adjoining codes such as ESA or RIC. Less consistency would be indicated by codes RAE or CAS.

The second concept is *differentiation*. Individuals who fit a pure personality type will express little resemblance to other types. Conversely, those individuals who fit

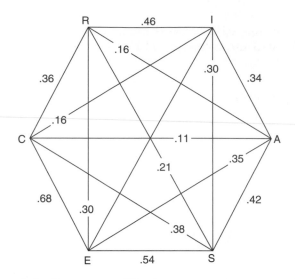

Figure 2.1   Holland's model of personality types and occupational environments

Source: From *An Empirical Occupational Classification Derived from a Theory of Personality and Intended for Practice and Research,* by J. L. Holland, D. R. Whitney, N. S. Cole, and J. M. Richards, Jr., ACT Research Report No. 29, The American College Testing Program, 1969. Copyright 1969 by the American College Testing Program.

several personality types have poorly defined personality styles and are considered undifferentiated or poorly defined.

Identity, the third concept, describes those individuals who have a clear and stable picture of their goals, interests, and talents. In the case of environments, identity refers to the degree to which a workplace has clarity, stability, and integration of goals, tasks, and rewards. For example, individuals who have many occupational goals, as opposed to a few, have low identity.

The fourth concept, *congruence,* occurs when an individual's personality type matches the environment. Social personality types, for example, prefer environments that provide social interaction, concerns with social problems, and interest in educational activities. In reviewing the major studies investigating this concept, Spokane (1985) and Dumenci (1995) concluded that research did support the theory that congruence is highly related to academic performance and persistence, job satisfaction, and stability of choice.

Finally, Holland's model provides a *calculus* (the fifth concept) for his theory. Holland proposed that the theoretical relationships between types of occupational environments lend themselves to empirical research techniques. In essence, further research will provide counselors and clients with a better understanding of Holland's theory as changes in work environments occur.

As important as the individual's self-knowledge is his or her occupational knowledge. Holland believed critical career judgments are drawn partially from an individual's occupational information. The importance of identification with an occupational environment underscores the significance of occupational knowledge in the process of appropriate career choice. Knowledge of both occupational environment and corresponding modal personal orientations is, according to Holland, critical to appropriate career decision making.

In the process of career decision making, Holland postulated that the hierarchy or level of attainment in a career is determined primarily by individual self-evaluations. Intelligence is considered less important than personality and interest. Furthermore, the factor of intelligence is subsumed in the classification of personality types; for example, individuals who resemble the investigative type of modal personal orientation are generally intelligent and naturally have skills such as analytical and abstract reasoning.

According to Holland, the stability of career choice depends primarily on the dominance of personal orientation. Putting it another way, individuals are products of an environment that greatly influences their personal orientations and eventual career choices. Personality development is a primary consideration in Holland's career-typology theory of vocational behavior.

Holland's theory is primarily descriptive, with little emphasis on explaining the causes and the timing of the development of hierarchies of the personal modal styles. He concentrated on the factors that influence career choice rather than on the developmental process that leads to career choice. Holland's early theory was developed from observations made on a population of National Merit Scholarship finalists. He later expanded the database to include a wider sample of the general population. His research has been extensive and longitudinal. Holland (1987a) compared his theories with developmental positions:

> I find experience for a learning theory perspective to be more persuasive [than developmental views]. In my scheme, different types are the outcomes of different learning histories. Stability of type is a common occurrence because careers [types] tend to snowball over the life course. The reciprocal interaction of person and successive jobs usually leads to a series of success and satisfaction cycles. (p. 26)

The RIASEC model has been tested with a wide range of ethnically diverse individuals, including those from different socioeconomic backgrounds, and with international groups. The results are mixed, that is, some studies support Holland's theory and others indicate less support (Rounds & Tracey, 1996; Ryan, Tracey, & Rounds, 1996). There does appear to be enough positive evidence, however, to use instruments that are based on Holland's codes with caution when testing culturally diverse populations (Gelso & Fretz, 2001).

Holland's theory emphasizes the accuracy of self-knowledge and the career information necessary for career decision making. The theory has had a tremendous impact on interest assessment and career counseling procedures; a number of interest inventories present results using the Holland classification format. Its implications for counseling are apparent; a major counseling objective would be to develop strategies to enhance knowledge of self, occupational requirements, and differing occupational environments. According to Hartung and Niles (2000), Holland's "practical experiences have influenced his emphasis of applying abstract concepts to counseling practice" (p. 7).

In sum, Holland's theory has proved to be of more practical usefulness than any of the other theories discussed in this text. In addition, most of his propositions have been clearly defined, and they lend themselves to empirical evaluations. The impact of his scholarly approach to RIASEC theory has had and will continue to exert tremendous influence on career development research and procedures (Spokane, Luchetta, & Richwine, 2002).

Empirical Support for Holland's Theory

Extensive testing of Holland's theory suggests that his constructs are valid, and in fact the body of evidence is extremely large—almost overwhelming. Reviews of research are by Spokane (1996), Osipow and Fitzgerald (1996), Holland, Fritzsche, and Powell (1994), Holland, Powell, and Fritzsche (1994), and Weinrach and Srebalus (1990). Examples of other research topics include the interplay between personality and interests by Gottfredson, Jones, and Holland (1993) and Carson and Mowesian (1993); the studies of the hexagon by Rounds and Tracey (1993); and person-environment congruence and interaction by Spokane (1985) and Meir, Esformes, and Friedland (1994). The best current statements about exploring careers with a typology are by Holland (1996) and, comparing the NEO Five-Factor Model with Holland's typology, by Hogan and Blake (1999). According to Reardon, Lenz, Sampson, and Peterson (2000), there are more than five hundred studies on Holland's typology. The original documents should be read for more details of current research projects. An update and discussion of Holland's theory can be found in Spokane, Luchetta, and Richwine (2002).

 ### Summary of Practical Applications

Applying Holland's theory in career counseling requires a working knowledge of several inventories and diagnostic measures. Some of these instruments will only be introduced here, as more information is given about them in Chapter 6.

1. The *Vocational Preference Inventory* (Holland, 1985b) has undergone several revisions.
2. *My Vocational Situation* (Holland, Daiger, & Power, 1980) and *Vocational Identity Scale* (Holland, Johnston, & Asama, 1993) provide information about goals, interests, and talents.
3. *The Position Classification Inventory* (Gottfredson & Holland, 1991) is a job analysis measure of RIASEC environmental codes.
4. The *Career Attitudes and Strategies Inventory* (Gottfredson & Holland, 1994) measures work environment variables.
5. The *Self-Directed Search* (SDS) (Form R) (Holland, 1994a) is one of the most widely used interest inventories; it has more than 20 foreign language versions, can be administered by a computer that includes computer-based reports, and is available on the Internet. It has gone through several revisions and is continually studied for effectiveness. Accompanying the assessment booklet are several companion materials: *The Occupations Finder* (Rosen, Holmberg, & Holland, 1994b), the *Dictionary of Educational Opportunities* (Rosen, Holmberg, & Holland, 1994a), the *You and Your Career Booklet* (Holland, 1994b), a *Leisure Activities Finder* (Holmberg, Rosen, & Holland, 1990), and a *Dictionary of Holland Occupational Codes* (Gottfredson & Holland, 1989). The *Self-Directed Search and Related Holland Materials: A Practitioner's Guide* by Reardon and Lenz (1998), is a most helpful tool when using the SDS.

Figure 2-2 presents the steps for using the *SDS* assessment booklet and *The Occupations Finder*.

Step 1
Using the assessment booklet,
a person:

– lists occupational aspirations

– indicates preferred activities
  in the six areas

– reports competencies in the
  six areas

– indicates occupational
  preferences in the six areas

– rates abilities in the six areas

– scores the responses he/she
  has given and calculates six
  summary scores

– obtains a three-letter summary
  code from the three highest
  summary scores

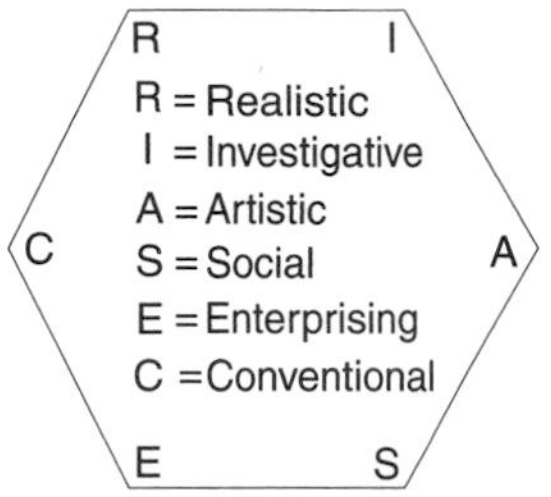

R = Realistic
I = Investigative
A = Artistic
S = Social
E = Enterprising
C = Conventional

Step 2
Using the occupations finder,
a person locates among the
1,335 occupations those with
codes that resemble his/her
summary code.

Step 3
The person compares the
code for his/her current
vocational aspiration with the
summary code to determine
the degree of agreement.

Step 4
The person is encouraged to
take "Some Next Steps" to
enhance the quality of his/her
career decision making.

Figure 2.2   Steps in using the SDS

Source: Adapted and Reproduced by special permission of the Publisher, Psychological Assessment Resources, Inc., Odessa, FL 33556, from the *Self-Directed Search Professional User's Guide,* by J. Holland, A. Powell, and B. Fritzsche. Copyright 1985, 1987, 1994 by PAR, Inc. Further reproduction is prohibited without permission from PAR, Inc.

Summary Comments Concerning Trait-Oriented Theories

Trait-oriented theories emphasize how standardized tests are used and the importance of choosing appropriate testing tools. Human traits such as aptitudes, interests, and personality, for example, can be matched with certain work environments for a means of evaluating potential work sites. An individual's work needs can be compared with components of job satisfaction found in certain occupational environments. Self-knowledge in terms of understanding the level and depth of one's traits and characteristics is an essential element for evaluating career information: Traits of aptitude, interests, and personality type are projected into potential work environments to find congruence and fit.

A significant development in trait-oriented approaches is the position that one observes work environments from several perspectives, including work requirements, personal-environment-fit, and potential reinforcers of one's personal needs. For example, a socially oriented individual prefers to work in an environment that provides interactions with people whereas a mechanically inclined individual would seek out an environment where her trade could be quietly practiced. This very logical approach to career choice suggests that one should consider a number of occupations that matches their personal needs and abilities found in particular work environments rather than just focuses on one specific occupation. Holland's typology approach is a logical and refreshing method to identify certain individual salient characteristics by type such as life goals and values, among other characteristics. Trait-oriented theories have clearly identified and expanded individual characteristics and traits used in the career counseling process.

Finally, more attention needs to be given to work adjustment, job satisfaction, and problems faced by individuals in career transition. It is expected that many individuals in the 21st century will change jobs several times over their life span. The job market will more than likely continue to fluctuate between up and down times. With all the unknowns, workers will be required to adapt quickly to new and different work environments. Workers in the 21st century will be challenged with new procedures, tools, requirements, and culturally diverse coworkers and associates. Keep in mind that many have entered a career with the expectation of a continuous, challenging, intrinsically rewarding work environment only to experience something quite different. For these individuals and others, work adjustment counseling can be very relevant. Although reinforcers may be more difficult to identify in the work world of the 21st century, we have been alerted to address sources of work satisfaction variables in career choice and maintenance. See Chapter 3 for an illustration of a trait-oriented career counseling model.

Social Learning and Cognitive Theories

The theories in this section focus on a wide range of variables that affect career choice and career maintenance over the life span. In general, social conditioning, social position, and life events are thought to significantly influence career choice. More specifically, individuals are thought to be influenced by many factors including genetic endowments and special abilities, contextual experiences, learning experiences, and skills learned in managing tasks. Key elements in the career choice process are problem-solving and decision-making skills. Career choice also involves the interaction of cognitive and affective processes. Individuals must be able to process information effectively and think rationally.

Individuals who resort to personal agency or assume total responsibility for their future model an attitude others should emulate. In addition, individuals are encouraged to develop strategies to overcome barriers that interfere with choice implementation. Learning is a key element in this group of theories; for example, learning experiences can expand and increase the range of occupations one considers exploring. Keep in mind that indecision may be related to a limited educational background. Finally, this group of theories addresses faulty thinking that can obscure rational decision making. Discovering and unlearning faulty beliefs about career choice and multiple life roles is major objective of these theories. We begin with a learning theory, proceed to a cognitive information processing theory, and, finally, explore a social cognitive perspective.

Krumboltz's Learning Theory of Career Counseling

A social-learning theory approach to career decision making was first proposed by Krumboltz, Mitchell, and Gelatt (1975), followed several years later by Mitchell and Krumboltz (1990). More recently, Mitchell and Krumboltz (1996) have extended the earlier social-learning theory approach to include Krumboltz's learning theory of career counseling, and they now suggest that the entire theory be referred to as learning theory of career counseling (LTCC). We review the theory's two parts: Part one explains the origins of career choice, and part two addresses the important question of what career counselors can do to help solve career-related problems.

The theory is an attempt to simplify the process of career selection and is based primarily on life events that are influential in determining career selection. In LTCC, the process of career development involves four factors: (1) genetic endowments and special abilities, (2) environmental conditions and events, (3) learning experiences, and (4) task approach skills.

Genetic endowments and special abilities include inherited qualities that may set limits on the individual's career opportunities. The authors do not attempt to explain the interaction of the genetic characteristics and special abilities but emphasize that these factors should be recognized as influences in the career decision-making process.

Environmental conditions and events are factors of influence that are often beyond the individual's control. What is emphasized here is that certain events and circumstances in the individual's environment influence skills development, activities, and career preferences. For example, government policies regulating certain occupations and the availability of certain natural resources in the individual's environment may largely determine the opportunities and experiences available. Natural disasters, such as droughts and floods that affect economic conditions, are further examples of influences beyond the control of the individuals affected.

The third factor, *learning experiences,* includes instrumental learning experiences and associative learning experiences. Instrumental learning experiences are those the individual learns through reactions to consequences, through direct observable results of actions, and through the reactions of others. The consequences of learning activities and their later influence on career planning and development are primarily determined by the activity's reinforcement or nonreinforcement; by the individual's genetic endowment, special abilities, and skills; and by a task itself.

Associative learning experiences include negative and positive reactions to pairs of previously neutral situations. For example, the statements "all politicians are dishonest" and "all bankers are rich" influence the individual's perceptions of these occupations. These associations can also be learned through observations, written materials, and films.

The fourth factor, *task approach skills,* includes the sets of skills the individual has developed, such as problem-solving skills, work habits, mental sets, emotional responses, and cognitive responses. These sets of developed skills largely determine the outcome of problems and tasks the individual faces.

Task approach skills are often modified as a result of desirable or undesirable experiences. For example, Sue, a high school senior, occasionally takes and studies class notes. Although she was able to make good grades in high school, she may find that this same practice in college results in failure, thus causing her to modify notetaking practices and study habits.

Krumboltz and associates emphatically stress that each individual's unique learning experiences over the life span develop the primary influences that lead to career choice. These influences include (1) generalization of self derived from experiences and performance in relation to learned standards, (2) sets of developed skills used in coping with the environment, and (3) career-entry behavior such as applying for a job or selecting an educational or training institution. This social-learning model therefore emphasizes the importance of learning experiences and their effect on occupational selection. In the scheme of things, genetic endowment is considered primarily as a factor that can limit learning experiences and subsequent career choice. Career decision making is considered to be an important skill that can be used over one's life span.

The factors that influence individual preferences in this social-learning model are composed of numerous cognitive processes, interactions in the environment, and inherited personal characteristics and traits. For example, educational and occupational preferences are a direct, observable result of actions (referred to as self-observation generalizations) and of learning experiences involved with career tasks. If an individual has been positively reinforced while engaging in the activities of a course of study or occupation, the individual is more likely to express a preference for that course of study or field of work. In this way, the consequence of each learning experience, in school or on a job, increases the probability that the individual will have a similar learning experience in the future. As we have learned at the beginning of the 21st century, proficiency in a field of work does not ensure that an individual will remain in that field of work. An economic crisis or even a negative feedback may initiate a change of career direction.

Genetic and environmental factors are also involved in the development of preferences. For example, a basketball coach might reinforce his players for their skills, but the coach will more likely reinforce tall players than those smaller in stature. Other positive factors influencing preferences are valued models who advocate engaging in a field of work or an educational course, or who are observed doing so. Finally, positive words and images, such as a booklet describing an occupation in glamorous terms, will lead to positive reactions to that occupation.

In sum, social-learning theory suggests that learning takes place through observations as well as through direct experiences. The determination of an individual's problematic beliefs and generalizations is very important in this social-learning model (Mitchell & Krumboltz, 1996). For example, identifying content from which certain beliefs and generalizations have evolved is a key ingredient for developing counseling strategies for individuals who have problems making career decisions. The counselor's role is to probe assumptions and presuppositions of expressed beliefs and use this information to explore alternative beliefs and courses of action. Assisting individuals to understand fully the validity of their beliefs is a major component of the social-learning model. Specifically, the counselor should address the following problems (Krumboltz, 1983):

- Persons may fail to recognize that a remediable problem exists (individuals assume that most problems are a normal part of life and cannot be altered).
- Persons may fail to exert the effort needed to make a decision or solve a problem (individuals exert little effort to explore alternatives; they take the familiar way out).
- Persons may eliminate a potentially satisfying alternative for inappropriate reasons (individuals overgeneralize from false assumptions and overlook potentially worthwhile alternatives).
- Persons may choose poor alternatives for inappropriate reasons (individuals are unable to realistically evaluate potential careers because of false beliefs and unrealistic expectations).
- Persons may suffer anguish and anxiety over perceived inability to achieve goals (individual goals may be unrealistic or in conflict with other goals).

LTCC is both descriptive and explanatory: The process of career choice is described and examples of factors that influence choice are given. Although the authors have attempted to simplify the process of career development and career choice, the many variables introduced in this theory make the process of validation extremely complex. Meanwhile, the authors should be commended for specifying counseling objectives based on this theory and for providing strategies designed to accomplish these objectives. They also provided several observations for career counseling (Krumboltz, Mitchell, & Gelatt, 1975, pp. 11–13):

1. Career decision making is a learned skill.
2. Persons who claim to have made a career choice need help, too (career choice may have been made from inaccurate information and faulty alternatives).
3. Success is measured by students' demonstrated skill in decision making (evaluations of decision-making skills are needed).
4. Clients come from a wide array of groups.
5. Clients need not feel guilty if they are not sure of a career to enter.
6. No one occupation is seen as the best for any one individual.

Empirical Support for Krumboltz's Learning Theory

The learning theory of career counseling has yet to be fully tested. The original theory, social-learning theory of career decision making, claimed validity from the development of educational and occupational preferences, the development of task approach skills and factors that cause people to take action, and from an extensive database on general social-learning theory of behavior. Sharf (2002) has suggested that LTCC is an outstanding example of the relationship between social-learning approaches and the human learning process. Gelso and Fretz (2001), however, complain that many of the propositions of this theory have not been researched, especially studies of the use of this theory with culturally diverse groups. More information about the validity of this theory can be obtained from Mitchell and Krumboltz (1996).

Happenstance Approach Theory

In the late 1990s, Mitchell, Levin, and Krumboltz (1999) developed happenstance approach theory for career counseling. The primary premise suggests that chance events over one's life span can have both positive and negative consequences. An individual may learn about an interesting job from an acquaintance, for example, or lose a job as a result of outsourcing only to find a better one. Of course, some life events have negative consequences for career development, for example, the illness or death of a loved one. Unpredictable social factors, environmental conditions, and chance events over the life span are to be recognized as important influences in clients' lives.

In LTCC, the client is viewed as one who is exploring and experimenting and should be empowered to take actions that help to create a satisfying life. Challenges that involve educational opportunities and available work options, for instance, should be approached with a positive attitude that promotes positive outcomes. Happenstance approach therefore suggests that counselors are to assist clients respond to conditions and events in a positive manner. In short, clients are to learn to deal with unplanned events, especially in the give-and-take of life in the 21st-century workforce.

Five critical client skills—curiosity, persistence, flexibility, optimism, and risk taking—are identified by Mitchell, Levin, and Krumboltz (1999) and are paraphrased as follows:

Curiosity suggests that one explore learning opportunities and take advantage of options offered by chance events. *Persistence* is emphasized as a way of dealing with obstacles that may be the result of chance events. *Flexibility* is used in this context to describe how one learns to address a variety of circumstances and events by adapting and adjusting as events unfold. *Optimism* implies a positive attitude when pursuing new opportunities. Thus, positive actions can be productive in a changing workplace when one seeks a new or different career. *Risk taking* in this context may be necessary during unexpected and new events. Clients, for instance, are to learn that risk taking can result in positive outcomes for career development such as finding a more secure job. A client, for example, may decide to enroll full time in a community college for skill development in order to qualify for a future job.

Happenstance approach should be an integral part of the counseling interview. As counselors elaborate person-in-environment experiences, chance events become focus points for conceptualizing counseling interventions. In this respect, happenstance-related questions can reveal how a client has learned to deal with certain situations in the past. From this position the counselor can enable the client to transform these past experiences into opportunities for learning and exploration. As Sharf (2002) points out, "These unexpected events give clients a larger platform from which to make decisions and to deal with new unexpected events" (p. 353).

Counselors can also expect to find that some clients have developed barriers to actions resulting from chance events. In essence, they have difficulty in taking positive actions and are reluctant to address difficult issues. Consequently, attending to a client's belief system is reinforced as a major counseling goal in happenstance theory. The overarching desirable outcome here is to empower and prepare each client for positive actions that take advantage of unexpected events and to help them cope with negative consequences in the future (Mitchell, Levin, & Krumboltz, 1999).

Happenstance theory suggests that clients learn to approach the future with a positive attitude and the curiosity and optimism that produces positive results. Foster an attitude that takes advantage of unplanned events: Clients are to look for solutions to their circumstances and develop strengths based on their past experiences in life and work. The workplace of the 21st century will present unexpected events and consequences for many workers. Some examples are presented in Chapters 5, 18, and 19.

✥ Summary of Practical Applications

According to Mitchell and Krumboltz (1996), when people in modern society make career choices, they must cope with four fundamental trends. Career counselors must recognize these trends and be prepared to help.

1. Clients need to expand their capabilities and interests, not base decisions on existing characteristics only. This first trend centers around the use of interest inventories. Because many individuals have limited experiences with most activities that interest inventories measure, clients may become indifferent to many activities they have not had the chance to experience personally. The point here is that career counselors should assist individuals in exploring new activities, rather than routinely directing them to base career decisions on measured interests that reflect limited past experiences.

2. Clients need to prepare for changing work tasks, not assume that occupations will remain stable. The changing role of job requirements and workplace environ-

ments in our current society suggests that career counselors must be prepared to help individuals learn new skills and attitudes so they can meet the demands of international competition. The radical restructuring of the workforce and the disruptions of expectations can be very stressful. Therefore, career counselors also should be prepared to help individuals cope with stress as they learn to develop new skills on an ongoing basis.

3. Clients need to be empowered to take action, not merely be given a diagnosis. Many issues about career decisions are often overlooked, including a lack of information about working per se, families' reaction to a member's taking a particular job, and how to go about getting a job. These issues and others, such as restructuring of the workplace, could cause fear of the decision-making process itself, referred to as zeteophobia, or cause procrastination about making a decision. Career counselors are directed to help individuals find answers to these questions and others while providing effective support during the exploration process.

4. Career counselors need to play a major role in dealing with all career problems, not just with occupational selection. Krumboltz (1993), Gelso and Fretz (2001), Richardson (1993), and Zunker (1994), among others, have suggested that career and personal counseling should be integrated. Such issues as burnout, career change, peer affiliate relationships, obstacles to career development, and the work role and its effect on other life roles are examples of potential problems that call for interventions by the career counselor.

Other suggestions:

1. The role of career counselors and the goals of career counseling need to be reevaluated. Counselors need to continue to promote client learning, but perhaps in a different way. Counselors may have to become coaches and mentors to help individuals meet the changes in workforce requirements.

2. Learning experiences should be used to increase the range of opportunities that can be considered in career exploration. Counselors should attempt to discover unlimited experiences among clients and offer proper learning solutions.

3. Assessment results can be used to create new learning experiences. For instance, aptitude test results can be used to focus on new learning. Key interests identified through interest inventories need to be developed. Assessment results can be starting points for establishing new learning experiences.

4. Intervention strategies suggested by Mitchell and Krumboltz include the use of job clubs, in which individuals can offer support to each other during the job search process. A wide range of media should be made available to clients, and local employers should offer high school students structured work-based learning experiences.

5. Career counselors should become adept at using cognitive restructuring. For the youngster who is to report to work with fear of doing a poor job, the counselor can suggest another perspective. Cognitive restructuring suggests to such a client that he or she should view the new job as a chance to impress the boss and fellow workers with his or her enthusiasm. "Reframing" the perspective for this client should be helpful in making the first day on a job a satisfactory one.

6. Career counselors should also use behavioral counseling techniques, including role playing or trying new behaviors, desensitization when dealing with phobias,

and paradoxical intention. The latter technique suggests that a client engage in the types of behavior that have created a problem (Mitchell & Krumboltz, 1996).

Career Development from a Cognitive Information Processing Perspective

Our next career development theory is based on cognitive information processing (CIP) theory and was developed by Peterson, Sampson, and Reardon (1991). CIP theory is applied to career development in terms of how individuals make a career decision and use information in career problem solving and decision making. CIP is based on the ten assumptions shown in Table 2-2. Using these assumptions as a focal point, the major strategy of career intervention is to provide learning events that will

Table 2-2	Assumptions Underlying the Cognitive Information Processing (CIP) Perspective of Career Development
Assumption	**Explanation**
1. Career choice results from an interaction of cognitive and affective processes.	CIP emphasizes the cognitive domain in career decision making; but it also acknowledges the presence of an affective source of information in the process (Heppner & Krauskopf, 1987; Zajonc, 1980). Ultimately, commitment to a career goal involves an interaction between affective and cognitive processes.
2. Making career choices is a problem-solving activity.	Individuals can learn to solve career problems (that is, to choose careers) just as they can learn to solve math, physics, or chemistry problems. The major differences between career problems and math or science problems lie in the complexity and ambiguity of the stimulus and the greater uncertainty as to the correctness of the solution.
3. The capabilities of career problem solvers depend on the availability of cognitive operations as well as knowledge.	One's capability as a career problem solver depends on one's self-knowledge and on one's knowledge of occupations. It also depends on the cognitive operations one can draw on to derive relationships between these two domains.
4. Career problem solving is a high-memory-load task.	The realm of self-knowledge is complex; so is the world of work. The drawing of relationships between these two domains entails attending to both domains simultaneously. Such a task may easily overload the working memory store.
5. Motivation.	The motivation to become a better career problem solver stems from the desire to make satisfying career choices through a better understanding of oneself and the occupational world.

develop the individual's processing abilities. In this way, clients develop capabilities as career problem solvers to meet immediate as well as future problems.

The stages of processing information begin with screening, translating, and encoding input in short-term memory; then storing it in long-term memory; and later activating, retrieving, and transforming the input into working memory to arrive at a solution. The counselor's principal function in CIP theory is to identify client's needs and develop interventions to help clients acquire the knowledge and skills to address those needs.

Peterson, Sampson, and Reardon (1991) and Sampson, Reardon, Peterson, and Lenz (2004) stress that career problem solving is primarily a cognitive process that can be improved through a sequential procedure known as CASVE, which includes the following generic processing skills: communication (receiving, encoding, and sending out queries),

Table 2.2	**(continued)**
Assumption	**Explanation**
6. Career development involves continual growth and change in knowledge structures.	Self-knowledge and occupational knowledge consist of sets of organized memory structures called *schemata* that evolve over the person's life span. Both the occupational world and we ourselves are ever-changing. Thus, the need to develop and integrate these domains never ceases.
7. Career identity depends on self-knowledge.	In CIP terms, career identity is defined as the level of development of self-knowledge memory structures. Career identity is a function of the complexity, integration, and stability of the schemata constituting the self-knowledge domain.
8. Career maturity depends on one's ability to solve career problems.	From a CIP perspective, career maturity is defined as the ability to make independent and responsible career decisions based on the thoughtful integration of the best information available about oneself and the occupational world.
9. The ultimate goal of career counseling is achieved by facilitating the growth of information-processing skills.	From a CIP perspective, the goal of career counseling is therefore to provide the conditions of learning that facilitate the growth of memory structures and cognitive skills so as to improve the client's capacity for processing information.
10. The ultimate aim of career counseling is to enhance the client's capabilities as a career problem solver and a decision maker.	From a CIP perspective, the goal of career counseling is to enhance the client's career decision-making capabilities through the development of information-processing skills.

Source: *Career Development and Services: A Cognitive Approach,* by G. Peterson, J. Sampson, and R. Reardon, pp. 7–9. Copyright © 1991. Reprinted with permission of Brooks/Cole, a part of The Thomson Corporation.

analysis (identifying and placing problems in a conceptual framework), synthesis (formulating courses of action), valuing (judging each action as to its likelihood of success and failure and its impact on others), and execution (implementing strategies to carry out plans). Table 2-3 describes the CASVE cycle using career information and media.

This model emphasizes the notion that career information counseling is a learning event. This is consistent with other theories that make this same assumption. One major difference between CIP theory and other theories discussed in this chapter, however, is the role of cognition as a mediating force that leads individuals to greater power and control in determining their own destinies. Take, for example, a client who expresses a need to make a career decision. This client is viewed as one who has a career problem or, as expressed in this theory, a gap exists between the client's current situation and a future career situation. Counselors are to seek out the problems and factors involved in this gap. One problem, for example, could be a family situation that has restricted and limited the client's possible career choices. Another could be the current work environment. Yet another could involve a child care problem. The point here is that career problems can result from a variety of factors that may involve internal domains such as faulty thinking and/or external domains of various personal and social factors. Once the problems are identified the counselor develops problem-solving interventions. Problem solving and decision making are valuable skills that can be used throughout one's life span.

Table 2-3	Career Information and the CASVE Cycle
Phase of the CASVE cycle	**Example of career information and media**
Communication (identifying a need)	A description of the personal and family issues that women typically face in returning to work (information) in a videotaped interview of currently employed women (medium)
Analysis (interrelating problem components)	Explanations of the basic education requirements for degree programs (information) in community college catalogues (medium)
Synthesis (creating likely alternatives)	A presentation of emerging nontraditional career options for women (information) at a seminar on career development for women (medium)
Valuing (prioritizing alternatives)	An exploration of how the roles of parent, spouse, citizen, "leisurite," and homemaker would be affected by the assumption of the worker role (information) in an adult version of a computer-assisted career guidance system (medium)
Execution (forming means-ends strategies)	A description of a functional résumé emphasizing transferable skills, followed by the creation of a résumé (information) presented on a computer-assisted employability skills system (medium)

Source: From *Career Development and Services: A Cognitive Approach,* by G. Peterson, J. Sampson, and R. Reardon, p. 200. Copyright © 1991. Reprinted with permission of Brooks/Cole, a part of The Thomson Corporation.

In this theory, *problem solving* is considered to be a series of thought processes that eventually lead to solutions of problems and remove the gap between a current situation and a preferred one. The accomplishment of this goal involves information-processing domains such as self-knowledge, occupational knowledge, and decision-making skills. In the decision-making process, the individual uses self-talk, concentrates on increasing self-awareness, and develops the ability to monitor and control information processing by recognizing when the next step in the decision process would be beneficial. The strength of this theory is in its practical application to solving career problems. As we learn more about CIP theory, the CASVE approach will be further delineated for the counseling profession.

Empirical Support for the CIP Perspective

For a discussion of metacognitions or executive processing domain, see Helwig (1992). For information about the Career Thoughts Inventory, see Peterson, Sampson, and Reardon (1991), Sampson, Peterson, Lenz, Reardon, and Saunders (1996a), and Sampson, Reardon, Peterson, and Lenz (2004). Major strengths of theory are covered in Krumboltz (1992) and Gelso and Fretz (2001).

 ### Summary of Practical Applications

Peterson, Sampson, Reardon, and Lenz (1996), and Sampson, Reardon, Peterson, and Lenz (2004), the developers of this theory, have also proposed a seven-step sequence for career delivery service, as shown in Figure 2-3. This sequence can be used as a delivery option for both problem solving and decision making, and it can be used for individual, group, self-directed, and curricular programs. Group counseling requires that the counselor do prescreening in steps 1 and 2. In the next chapter, these steps are explained in some detail in a career counseling model referred to as Cognitive Information Processing Approach. We strongly encourage you to read the original source for a more complete understanding of this theory.

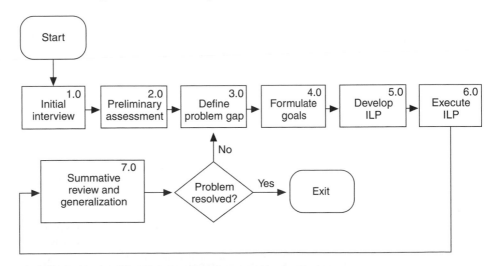

Figure 2.3   A career counseling sequence for individuals

Source: From *Career Development and Services: A Cognitive Approach,* by G. Peterson, J. Sampson, and R. Reardon, p. 231. Copyright © 1991. Reprinted with permission of Brooks/Cole, a part of The Thomson Corporation.

Career Development from a Social Cognitive Perspective

The study of cognitive variables and processes has become a popular topic for researchers, who apply what is often referred to as the "cognitive revolution" to the study of career development. This theory has indeed followed such a script by offering a *Social Cognitive Career Theory* (SCCT) to complement existing theories and to build connecting bridges to other theories of career development.

According to Lent, Brown, and Hackett (1996, 2002), the theory's authors, there are three ways to translate and share knowledge between existing theories and emerging ones. The first is to agree on a common meaning for conceptually related concepts, such as self-concept and self-efficacy. Betz (1992b) defines career self-efficacy as "the possibility that low expectations of efficacy with respect to some aspect of career behavior may serve as a detriment to optimal career choice and the development of the individual" (p. 24). Further delineation of this theory involves Betz's reference to career-choice content (content domains such as math, science, or writing) and career-choice process (behavioral domains that enhance career implementation). From this frame of reference, an individual might avoid areas of course work associated with a career because of low self-efficacy. Likewise, self-efficacy deficits can lead to procrastination in or avoidance of a career decision.

Hackett and Betz (1981) suggest that social beliefs and expectations are the mechanisms through which self-efficacy deficits are developed, particularly for women. Hackett and Betz cite a restricted range of options and underutilization of abilities as important factors hindering women's career development. Using this logic, women's vocational behavior can be at least partially explained.

The second way to translate and share knowledge about existing theories and emerging ones is to fully describe and define common outcomes, such as satisfaction and stability, found in a number of theories. Finally, a third way is to fully explain the relationships among such diverse constructs as interests, self-efficacy, abilities, and needs. Clearly, the challenge is to find a common ground for communicating a conceptual order to the vast number of variables found in career-related literature.

The underlying assumptions and constructs of this theory are embedded in general social cognitive theory (Bandura, 1986), which blends cognitive, self-regulatory, and motivational processes into a lifelong phenomenon. More specifically, SCCT's major goals are to find methods of defining specific mediators from which learning experiences shape and subsequently influence career behavior. Furthermore, the aim is to explain how variables such as interests, abilities, and values interrelate and, most important, how all variables influence individual growth and the contextual factors (environmental influences) that lead to career outcomes. Also emphasized is the term personal agency, which reflects how and why individuals exert power to either achieve a solution, such as a career outcome, or adapt to career changes. To identify and conceptualize the causal influences interacting between individuals and their environment, SCCT subscribes to Bandura's (1986) model of causality known as the triadic reciprocal. Within this bidirectional model, there are three variables: (1) personal and physical attributes, (2) external environmental factors, and (3) overt behavior. All three interact to the point of affecting one another as causal influences of an individual's development. Using this logic, SCCT conceptualizes the interacting influences among individuals, their behavior, and their environments to describe how individuals influence situations that ultimately affect their own thoughts and behavior.

What we have here is a complex, interacting system that is bidirectional and within which behavior, as one factor, and situations in the environment, as another, act as co-determinants in shaping personal thoughts and behaviors and external environmental factors. In essence, this is a person-behavior-situation interaction.

Key Theoretical Constructs

The personal determinants of career development have been conceptualized as *self-efficacy, outcome expectations,* and *personal goals.* The "big three" are considered to be building blocks within the triadic causal system that determine the course of career development and its outcome. Self-efficacy is not viewed as a unitary or fixed trait but, rather, as a set of beliefs about a specific performance domain. Self-efficacy is developed through four types of learning experiences (Lent, Brown, & Hackett, 1996): "(1) personal performance accomplishments, (2) vicarious learning, (3) social persuasion, and (4) physiological states and reactions" (p. 380). Self-efficacy is strengthened when success is experienced within a performance domain, whereas it is weakened when there are repeated failures.

Outcome expectations are also regarded as personal beliefs about expectations or consequences of behavioral activities. Some individuals may be motivated by extrinsic reinforcement, such as receiving an award; others by self-directed activities, such as pride in oneself; and yet others by the actual process of performing an activity. Outcome expectations are shaped by learning activities similar to those of self-efficacy.

One of most important reasons for personal goals in this theory is that they are considered to be guides that sustain behavior. While processing personal goals, individuals generate personal agency that interacts with the three building blocks, which in effect shapes self-directed behavior.

Interest Developmental Model

Individuals develop interests through activities in which they view themselves as competent and generally expect valued outcomes. Interests fail to develop when weak and negative outcomes are expected from an activity. Activities that produce valued outcomes and that have been developed as personal interests are sustained by individuals through goals that ensure their involvement in those activities. Following this logic, activity practice tends to solidify interests and reshape and reinforce self-efficacy.

Attitudes and Values

Within the framework of SCCT, values are subsumed in the concept of outcome expectation. In effect, values are preferences for particular reinforcers, such as money, status, or autonomy. This theory stresses that outcome expectations are influenced by value systems that are positively reinforced when involved with a particular activity.

Gender and Race/Ethnicity

In this theory, we must focus on how career development was influenced from personal reactions to the social and cultural environment. Thus, the individual's socially constructed world, not inherited biological traits, is the focus of gender and race in the SCCT. It therefore is not surprising that this theory focuses on the social, cultural, and economic conditions that shaped learning opportunities to which individuals were exposed, interpersonal reactions experienced for performing certain activities, and the future outcomes that have been generated. In sum, the effects of gender and ethnicity on career interests, choice, and performance are associated primarily with differential learning experiences that influenced and subsequently shaped self-efficacy and outcome expectations.

Choice Model

The choice model is divided into three components: (1) establishing a goal; (2) taking action (by enrolling in a training or school program) to implement a choice; and (3) attaining a level of performance (successes or failures) that determines the direction of future career behavior. One's personal agency is seen as a most important variable in determining the degree of progression in the choice process. The pathways to career choice in SCCT are as follows: (1) self-efficacy and outcome expectations promote career-related interests; (2) interests in turn influence goals; (3) goal-related actions lead to performance experiences; (4) the outcome determines future paths (determined by whether self-efficacy is strengthened or weakened); and (5) finally, one establishes a career decision or redirects goals.

One major hurdle for the individual in the choice model has to do with contextual or environmental influences. The rationale is based on opportunity structure experienced in the environment. For instance, individuals who experience support and other beneficial environmental conditions readily take their goals into actions more so than do those who experience the opposite from their environment.

Performance Model

The SCCT contains a performance model that appears to be a summary description of this theory. Its purpose is twofold: (1) it illustrates concern for the level and quality of an individual's accomplishments and for the personal agency involvement in career-related pursuits; and (2) it points out the interplay of ability, self-efficacy, outcome expectations, and the establishment of goals for judging performance. This model can also serve as a method of determining points of reference for implementing effective intervention strategies.

Empirical Support for Career Self-Efficacy

Selected references on career self-efficacy include Hackett (1995), Hackett and Lent (1992), Betz and Hackett (1986), Zimmerman (1995), and Schunk (1995). For relevant findings to SCCT's major hypotheses, see Coon-Carty (1995), Gelso and Fretz (2001), Multon, Brown, and Lent (1991), Sadri and Robertson (1993), Smith and Fouad (1999), Niles and Hartung (2000), and Sharf (2002).

 ### Summary of Practical Applications

1. Suggestions for expanding interests and facilitating choice in SCCT include educational programs in schools that concentrate on developing interests, values, and talents and also focus on the cognitive basis for linking with these variables.
2. In the SCCT approach, individuals who are experiencing great difficulty with career choice or change should be presented with an array of occupations that correspond with their abilities and values, but not necessarily with their interests. This theory's authors argue that individuals will not consider some occupations because of false impressions of their abilities and, subsequently, will respond

indifferently to such occupations on interest inventories. For example, the individual who does not indicate an interest in nursing may have been told that "you will have to take a lot of science courses." Because he views his ability to pass science courses as poor, he reacts negatively to nursing when in fact his past performance and ability scores indicate he has a better than average chance of being successful in a nursing program.

3. A strategy used in SCCT to combat perceived weaknesses includes using occupational card sorts. The individual is asked to sort occupational titles into categories of "might choose," "in question," and "would not choose." The client is then asked to further sort cards from "in question" and "would not choose" into subcategories by self-efficacy beliefs ("if I had the skills I might choose"), outcome expectations ("might choose if they matched my values"), and definite lack of interest ("not considered a possible choice"), and other. Clearly, the purpose of this procedure is to assist the client in fully understanding the interacting forces that determine self-appraisals in the career decision process. Individuals who have developed false notions about their abilities and values can indeed become indifferent toward certain occupations.

4. Overcoming barriers to choice and success is a significant goal for career counseling in SCCT. The rationale here is that individuals who perceive insurmountable barriers to career entry will be unwilling to pursue occupational interests in the career choice process. A decisional balance sheet is used to assist clients in evaluating perceived barriers. Each client is asked to generate a list of both positive and negative consequences for each career alternative he or she has selected. Each individual is then asked to develop strategies designed to overcome barriers that interfere with choice implementation.

5. School-to-work initiatives suggested by SCCT include designing skill programs that provide for self-efficacy enhancement, realistic outcome expectations, and goal-setting skills (Lent, Brown, & Hackett, 1996).

Summary Comments Concerning Social Learning and Cognitive Theories

The social learning and cognitive theories strongly suggest an emphasis on self-knowledge as the foundation for making a career decision. Information-processing skills, therefore, are considered to be of major importance. These theories also stress the importance of human traits such as ability, personality, and values, but more important, they suggest research be directed to how these variables interrelate to influence growth and development. Other important factors that influence the depth and breadth of self-knowledge are social, cultural, and economic conditions. Hence, counselors are urged to unearth contextual interactions and relationship events and experiences of each client.

Self-efficacy or low expectations of what can be accomplished careerwise are thought to be the result of several factors, including environmental and economic conditions. Hence, career beliefs of a client are considered to be a core element to evaluate in the career counseling process. In all three theories in this group, faulty beliefs are aggressively addressed.

Learning programs are most important for increasing the range of career choices. Learning takes place in many ways, such as observations, reactions to others, situational conditions, and direct experiences. Following this logic, counselors are to have clients observe work activities, and attempt to learn certain work tasks. Standardized tests are used primarily to determine educational and cognitive deficits. Individualized learning program goals and activities designed to debunk faulty thinking are developed from the results of test scores and intake interviews

Finally, learning to process information effectively is a major goal of these theories. The rationale here is that skills learned in an initial career choice process can be used in the future. In this respect, clients also can prepare for future changes in work tasks and working conditions. The learning approach emphasized in these theories suggests that learning to adapt and adjust to multiple life roles in an ever changing society is a lifelong endeavor.

See Chapter 3 for a counseling model developed from LTCC and one from a cognitive information-processing perspective.

Developmental Theories

Career development is viewed as a lifelong process that is very inclusive. One major concept of developmental theories suggests that individuals make changes during developmental stages and adapt to changing life roles. Self-concept is a critical core element in developmental theories. Individuals should project self into work environments during the exploration stage and, ideally, implement a realistic self-concept into the work world. A system of developmental tasks over the life span provides key points for counseling interventions. Counselors are to evaluate the many unique developmental needs of each client when establishing counseling goals.

Adult developmental stages such as establishment and maintenance (Super, 1990) have received greater attention during the last three decades. Some workers have been "outsourced," others opt to change careers, and some become involved in part-time work. Super's life-role approach suggests that work is very pervasive, to the point that one life role may affect others, explaining the current interest in multiple life roles. Super's position points out a weakness of other career development theories: that they have not addressed adult concerns and have focused primarily on initial career choice.

We also learn from developmental theories that individuals circumscribe or narrow career choice through self-awareness that is determined by one's social class, level of interests, and experiences with sex typing. A primary counseling role is to assist clients to understand how their unique development influences perceptions of life roles, including the work role. In this section we introduce a life-span, life-space approach to careers, and circumscription and compromise: a developmental theory of occupational aspirations.

Life-Span, Life-Space Approach to Careers

Donald Super (1972) thought that he had often been mislabeled as a theorist. In fact, Super did not believe that he had developed a theory that could be labeled specifically at that time. On the contrary, he viewed his work as the development of segments of possible future theories. He indicated that if he was to carry a label, it should be broad, such as differential-developmental-social-phenomenological psychologist. His multisided approach to career development was reflected first in his interest in differential psychology, or the trait-and-factor theory, as a medium through which testing instruments and subsequent norms for assessment are developed. He thought that differential psychology is of utmost importance in the continuing attempt to furnish data on occupational differences related to personality, aptitude, and interests. This he viewed as an ongoing process as we learn more about the world of work and the changes that will surely come in work requirements.

As early as the 1940s, Super was promoting the idea that career development is a process that unfolds gradually over the life span. The real impact of this position was a change from the overwhelming emphasis on initial career choice to counseling programs that extended counseling to include work adjustment and multiple life roles. In essence, career development was viewed as a continuous process that involved multiple life roles. Counselors are therefore to be prepared to address client concerns over a lifetime of development, during which individuals encounter situational and personal changes. In the 21st century, for example, it is forecast that a large number of individuals will change jobs several times over their life span (Drucker, 2002). The new buzz words are "multiple jobs" in "multiple places."

Self-Concept

Self-concept theory is the centerpiece of Super's approach to vocational behavior. Research projects generated as early as the 1960s aimed at determining how self-concept is implemented in vocational behavior. The significance of self-concept in the career development process was an ongoing research effort by Super and his colleagues over a span of some fifty years. Their conclusions generally indicated that vocational self-concept develops through physical and mental growth, observations of work, identification with working adults, general environment, and general experiences. Ultimately, differences and similarities between self and others are assimilated. As experiences become broader in relation to awareness of the world of work, the more sophisticated vocational self-concept is formed. Although the vocational self-concept is only part of the total self-concept, it is the driving force that establishes career patterns one will follow throughout life. The major practical application here is that individuals implement their self-concepts into careers as a means of self-expression. Secondly, the self-concept developmental process is multidimensional. Both internal factors (e.g., aptitude, values, and personality) and external situational conditions (e.g., contextual interactions) are major determinants of self-concept development.

In contemporary counseling, self-concept, self-awareness, self-esteem and self-knowledge are considered to be very important concepts to evaluate in the counseling process. These concepts are embedded in Roger's (1942) client-centered therapy. It appears that Super was also influenced by this seminal work as he informed those who counsel that it is imperative to understand that clients have a better chance of making optimal decisions when they are most aware of the work world and themselves. Within this position the principle of "know thyself" becomes a prerequisite for optimal career choice. Herein we find the roots of the career education movement of the 1970s and beyond. Super suggested that students gain career maturity by learning how to plan for the future and understand the benefits of planning. School curriculums that offer opportunities for students to make connections between classroom activities and future work roles were a most important outcome recommendation.

Super also recognized that individuals who are given opportunities to learn more about themselves will learn to expand their career considerations or at least to be more confident of their initial choices. These contributions to career counseling have inspired computer-assisted career guidance programs as well as other resources that provide career information.

Developmental Stages and Tasks

In this section, we quickly review Super's initial developmental stages and tasks. These stages and tasks are core elements of Super's developmental approach to career development.

1. Growth (birth to age 14 or 15), characterized by development of capacity, attitudes, interests, and needs associated with self-concepts.
2. Exploratory (ages 15–24), characterized by a tentative phase in which choices are narrowed but not finalized.
3. Establishment (ages 25–44), characterized by trial and stabilization through work experiences.
4. Maintenance (ages 45–64), characterized by a continual adjustment process to improve working position and situation.
5. Decline (ages 65+), characterized by preretirement considerations, reduced work output, and eventual retirement (Issacson, 1985, pp. 51–53).

These stages of vocational development provide the framework for observing vocational behavior and attitudes, which are evidenced through five activities known as vocational developmental tasks. These five developmental tasks are shown in Table 2-4,

Table 2-4	**Super's Vocational Developmental Tasks**		
Vocational developmental tasks	**Ages**	**General characteristics**	
Crystallization	14–18	A cognitive process period of formulating a general vocational goal through awareness of resources, contingencies, interests, values, and planning for the preferred occupation	
Specification	18–21	A period of moving from tentative vocational preferences toward a specific vocational preference	
Implementation	21–24	A period of completing training for vocational preference and entering employment	
Stabilization	24–35	A period of confirming a preferred career by actual work experience and use of talents to demonstrate career choice as an appropriate one	
Consolidation	35+	A period of establishment in a career by advancement, status, and seniority	

and are delineated by typical age ranges (tasks can occur at other age levels) and by their general characteristics.

The crystallization task begins with the forming of a preferred career plan and the considerations involved in how it might be implemented. Pertinent information is studied with the goal of becoming more aware of preferred choice and if indeed it is a wise one. The specification task follows, in which the individual feels the need to specify the career plan through more specific resources and explicit awareness of cogent variables of preferred choice. The implementation task is accomplished by the completion of training and entry into a career. The stabilization task is reached when the individual is firmly established in a career and develops a feeling of security in the career position. Finally, the consolidation task follows with advancement and seniority in a career (Super, Starishesky, Matlin, & Jordaan, 1963).

Super (1990) modified developmental tasks through the life span, as shown in Table 2-5. He uses the terms cycling and recycling through developmental tasks. This

Table 2-5	The Cycling and Recycling of Developmental Tasks Through the Life Span			
	Age			
Life stage	Adolescence 14–25	Early adulthood 25–45	Middle adulthood 45–65	Late adulthood over 65
Decline	Giving less time to hobbies	Reducing sports participation	Focusing on essential activities	Reducing working hours
Maintenance	Verifying current occupational choice	Making occupational position secure	Holding own against competition	Keeping up what is still enjoyed
Establishment	Getting started in a chosen field	Settling down in a permanent position	Developing new skills	Doing things one has always wanted to do
Exploration	Learning more about more opportunities	Finding opportunity to do desired work	Identifying new problems to work on	Finding a good retirement spot
Growth	Developing a realistic self-concept	Learning to relate to others	Accepting one's limitations	Developing non-occupational roles

Source: From "A Life-Span, Life-Space Approach to Career Development," by D. E. Super. In *Career Choice and Development: Applying Contemporary Theories to Practice,* 2nd ed., by D. Brown, L. Brooks, and Associates, p. 206. Copyright © 1990 by Jossey-Bass, Inc., Publishers. Reprinted by permission.

formulation clarifies Super's position, which might have been misunderstood in the past; in essence, he views ages and transitions as very flexible and as not occurring in a well-ordered sequence. A person can recycle through one or more stages, which Super refers to as a minicycle. For example, an individual who experiences disestablishment in a particular job may undergo new growth and become ready to change occupations. In this instance, the individual has reached the point of maintenance but now recycles through exploration in search of a new and different position.

Career Maturity

One of Super's best-known studies, launched in 1951, followed the vocational development of ninth-grade boys in Middletown, New York (Super & Overstreet, 1960). One emphasis of this study was to identify and validate the vocational developmental tasks relevant to each stage of development. Super thought that the completion of the appropriate tasks at each level was an indication of what he termed vocational maturity, now referred to as career maturity. The findings suggest that the ninth-grade boys in this study had not reached a level of understanding of the world of work or of themselves sufficient enough to make adequate career decisions. Career maturity seemed to be related more to intelligence than to age. Be aware that when Super conducted these studies he primarily studied the career maturity of white males; however, later studies of vocational maturity included ethnic groups and females.

Various traits of career maturity (such as planning, accepting responsibility, and awareness of various aspects of a preferred vocation) proved to be irregular and unstable during a three-year period in high school. However, those individuals who were seen as vocationally mature in the ninth grade (based on their knowledge of an occupation, planning, and interest) were significantly more successful as young adults. This finding suggests that there is a relationship between career maturity and adolescent achievement of a significant degree of self-awareness, knowledge of occupations, and developed planning capability. Thus, ninth-grade vocational behavior does have some predictive validity for the future. In other words, boys who successfully accomplish developmental tasks at periodic stages tend to achieve greater maturity later in life.

The career maturity concepts developed by Super have far-reaching implications for career education and career counseling programs. The critical phases of career maturity development provide points of reference from which the desired attitudes and competencies related to effective career growth can be identified and subsequently assessed. Moreover, the delineation of desired attitudes and competencies within each stage affords the specification of objectives for instructional and counseling projects designed to foster career maturity development. Super (1974, p. 13) identified six dimensions that he thought were relevant and appropriate for adolescents:

1. Orientation to vocational choice, an attitudinal dimension determining whether the individual is concerned with the eventual vocational choice to be made
2. Information and planning, a competence dimension concerning specificity of information individuals had concerning future career decisions and past planning accomplished
3. Consistency of vocational preferences, an individual's consistencies of preferences
4. Crystallization of traits, an individual's progress toward forming a self-concept
5. Vocational independence, such as independence of work experience

6. Wisdom of vocational preferences, a dimension concerned with an individual's ability to make realistic preferences consistent with personal tasks

Super's concept of career maturity should also be considered a major contribution to career developmental theories. An updated version of a standardized measure of career maturity variables by Crites and Savickas (1995) is evidence that this concept remains viable. Conceptually, career maturity is acquired through successfully accomplishing developmental tasks within a continuous series of life stages. Career maturity on this continuum is described in attitudinal and competence dimensions. Points of reference from this continuum provide relevant information for career counseling and career education objectives and strategies.

The concept of career maturity provides some important guidelines for career choice. Some clients simply are not prepared to make an optimal career choice. This may become clear in the intake interview and/or from the results of career maturity and other inventories. Counselors may need to assume the role of teacher or coach and provide learning and exploration activities designed to enhance self-knowledge, improve problem-solving skills, and increase the client's knowledge of work per se.

Life-Stage Model

About four years before Super's death, he developed a life-stage model by using a "life rainbow" as shown in Figure 2-4 (Super, 1990). This two-dimensional graphic schema presents a longitudinal dimension of life span, referred to as a "maxicycle,"

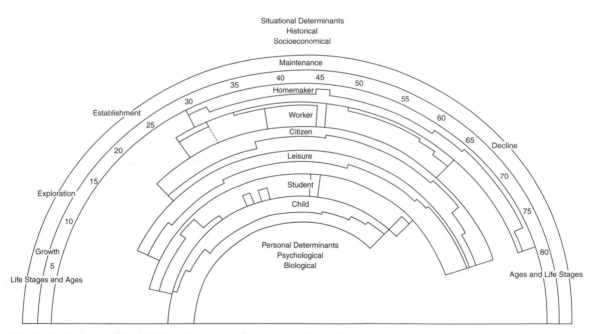

Figure 2.4   **The life-career rainbow: Six life roles in schematic life space**

Source: From "A Life-Span, Life-Space Approach to Career Development," by D. E. Super. In *Career Choice and Development, Applying Contemporary Theories to Practice,* 2nd ed., edited by D. Brown, L. Brooks, and Associates, p. 212. Copyright © 1990 by Jossey-Bass, Inc. This material is used by permission of John Wiley & Sons, Inc.

and corresponding major life stages, labeled "minicycles." A second dimension is "life space," or the roles played by individuals as they progress through developmental stages, such as child, student, "leisurite," citizen, worker, spouse, homemaker, parent, and pensioner. People experience these roles in the following theaters: home, community, school (college and university), and workplace. This conceptual model leads to some interesting observations: (1) Because people are involved in several roles simultaneously within several theaters, success in one role facilitates success in another; and (2) all roles affect one another in the various theaters.

In these early years of the 21st century there appears to be an increased interest in the interrelationships of life roles. How pervasive, for example, is the work role in our lives? Do problems observed in the work role affect the family role or is the source of problems from family role conflicts? Such questions suggest that we use a more holistic approach in solving the concerns that clients bring to counseling. Super's early work on life roles and their interrelationships should provide the impetus for more research on multiple life roles for career and personal counseling.

Archway Model

In the early 1990s, Super also created an "archway model" to delineate the changing diversity of life roles experienced by individuals over the life span. This model is used to clarify how biographical, psychological, and socioeconomic determinants influence career development. Figure 2-5 illustrates the archway model. One base stone in the arch supports the person and his or her psychological characteristics, and the other base stone supports societal aspects such as economic resources, community, school, family, and so on. The point is that societal factors interact with the person's biological and psychological characteristics as he or she functions and grows.

The column that extends from the biological base encompasses the person's needs, intelligence, values, aptitudes, and interests—those factors that constitute personality variables and lead to achievement. The column rising from the geographical base stone includes environmental influences such as family, school, peer group, and labor markets—factors that affect social policy and employment practices.

The arch joining the columns is made up of conceptual components, including developmental stages from childhood to adulthood and developed role self-concepts. The keystone of the archway is the self or person who has experienced the personal and social forces that are major determinants of self-concept formation and active life roles in society.

In essence, interactive learning is the fundamental concept that forms the keystone (self) of the archway as the individual encounters people, ideas, facts, and objects in personal development. The relationship of the model's segments highlights the profound interaction of influences in the career development process. The integration of life activities and developmental stages is a prime example of perceiving career development as a pervasive part of life. Career guidance programs that incorporate developmental concepts must address a broad range of counseling techniques and intervention strategies. This seems to be the message that Super promoted for several decades.

In a publication after Super's death in 1994, his theory was labeled "the life-span, life-space approach to careers" (Super, Savickas, & Super, 1996). Because this theory evolved during 60 years of research, it is no wonder that it stands out as one of the

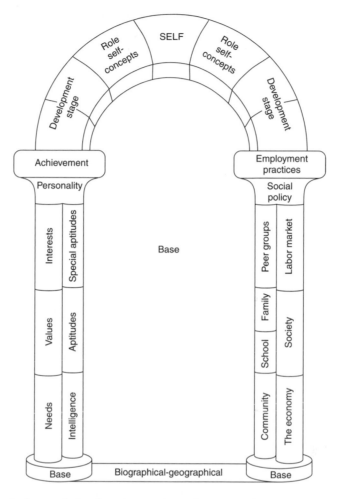

Figure 2.5   A segmental model of career development

Source: From "A Life-Span, Life-Space Approahc to Career Development" by D. E. Super in *Career Choice and Development: Applying Contemporary Theories to Practice,* 2nd ed., by D. Brown, L. Brooks, and Associates, pp. 206–208. Copyright © 1990 by Jossey-Bass, Inc., Publishers. Reprinted by permission.

most comprehensive vocational development models in the career counseling profession. Over this 60-year period, Super's theory was constantly refined and updated, once being labeled "career development theory" and later "developmental self-concept theory." The recent name change reflects contemporary issues related to life-span needs and Super's most recent research of life roles. In this broad-based approach, gender and cultural differences are also addressed; the needs of cultural and ethnic minorities are considered important variables in the career counseling process.

Empirical Evaluations of Super's Theory

Evaluations of Super's theory have been predominantly positive, although empirical research has been difficult to accomplish because of the theory's broad scope (Brown, Brooks, & Associates, 1990). Swanson (1992) has suggested that more segments of the theory be evaluated empirically, especially the life space of adolescents and young adults and the life-span research of adults.

In a very provocative article that traces the development of Super's theory, Salomone (1996) suggested that Super had not offered testable hypotheses for various propositions of his theory. Salomone argued that Super failed to consistently define hypothetical constructs that are operational and that lend themselves to quantitative measures that support his statements. In Salomone's opinion, such constructs as work satisfaction, career maturity, and vocational development are not readily measurable, either because they are rather vague in concept or instruments at a given point in time were not available to measure them. Perhaps Salomone's criticism of Super's concepts can best be explained with the example of Super's definition of career. Salomone contended that Super expanded the concept of career (child, leisurite, and citizen) to be too inclusive for "three ingredients of good definitions—clarity, specificity, and exclusivity"; thus, when concepts are vague and nonspecific, they lose their usefulness. In this respect, Super's theory is very elusive; the relationship between theoretical propositions and empirical findings is not clearly delineated. Despite the limitations of Super's theory as outlined in his article, however, Salomone did recognize that Super has had a monumental impact on career development.

Finally, several outstanding researchers offered support to Super's theory in general, and specifically as one that describes the process of vocational development and one that will provide the mainstream of research for developmental psychology in the future (Hackett, Lent, & Greenhaus, 1991; Osipow & Fitzgerald, 1996).

 ## Summary of Practical Applications

When observing Super's suggestions for practical applications, we must remember that he remained dedicated to the roles of developmental stages within three major segments of his theory—life space, life span, and self-concepts. He and his colleagues developed numerous assessment instruments designed to measure developmental tasks over the life span that are currently used in the career counseling process. Following are summaries of the counseling steps.

1. Assessment: A career development assessment and counseling model (C-DAC) was developed to measure constructs from the basic life-span, life-space theory in four phases: (1) life structure and work-role salience; (2) career development status and resources; (3) vocational identity with its work values, occupational interests, and vocational abilities; and (4) occupational self-concepts and life themes. Sharf (2002) reports that C-DAC assessment programs were expanded recently to include more culturally oriented interventions in the practice of career development. Counselors begin with an intake interview, encouraging the client to express career concerns. Background information is gathered from school records and other sources. After comparing background information with the client's career concerns in the first interview, the counselor begins a four-step procedure to complete the assessment component.

    a. The first step focuses on the client's life structure (social elements that constitute an individual's life) and work-role salience. If the client considers the work role to be important, further assessment will be more meaningful. If not, career orientation programs are recommended. The *Salience Inventory* (Nevill & Super, 1986) is used to determine the client's life space (participation and commitment to five life roles for school, work, family, community, and leisure). Scores for the client's life structure are also obtained from the constellation of 15 scores from the inventory, and they provide clues to the pattern of the client's activity in—and hope for—five major life roles.

b. The second assessment phase measures the client's perception of the work role, referred to as the client's career stage (vocational developmental tasks that concern the client) and career concerns (the amount of concern the client has with exploration, establishment, maintenance, and disengagement). The *Adult Career Concerns Inventory* (ACCI) (Super, Thompson, & Lindeman, 1988) measures career stage and career concerns, or they can be obtained through an interview.

In addition, assessment within this step includes a measure of the client's resources for choosing or coping with tasks when making decisions. The *Career Development Inventory* (Savickas, 1990; Thompson, Lindeman, Super, Jordaan, & Myers, 1984) is used to measure the variables of career planning, career exploration, information about work, and knowledge of occupations. Finally, an assessment is made of the client's resources of adapting through use of the *Career Mastery Inventory* (Crites & Savickas, 1995).

c. The third phase includes measures of abilities, interests, and values. Interest inventories that provide estimates of realistic, investigative, artistic, social, enterprising, and conventional (RIASEC) types as defined in Table 2-6 (Holland, 1992) are recommended. The *Differential Aptitude Test* (Bennett, Seashore, & Wesman, 1974) is recommended to measure aptitudes, and the *Values Inventory* (Nevill & Super, 1986) or the *Work Value Inventory* (Super, 1970) are recommended to measure values.

d. The fourth phase includes assessment of self-concepts and life themes by using adjective checklists, card sorts, or a repertory grid technique to assess the client's self-schema in world space.

2. Data integration and narrative interpretation: After assessment has been accomplished, the counselor interprets the data to the client. The interpretation process is referred to as integrative interpretation, in which the client's life story unfolds.

3. Counseling goals: In the process of setting goals, the counselor attempts to assist the client to develop an accurate picture of his or her self and life roles. Choices are to be based on implementing the self-concept into the work world in a realistic manner.

4. Procedures: Career development counseling procedures pertinent to career development tasks such as exploration, establishment, maintenance, and disengagement are recommended. A variety of techniques may be used that incorporate life stages and developmental tasks.

5. Processes: Counseling to promote career development may use coaching, educating, mentoring, modifying, or restructuring during an interview. Super also recommends cyclical counseling, in which the counseling interviews sometimes are directive but nondirective at other times. For example, directive approaches can be used to provide confrontations with reality, whereas nondirective approaches assist the client with interpreting the meanings associated with confrontations.

Life-span, life-space theory is indeed a comprehensive framework from which career development counseling has emerged. The counseling procedures developed from this theory are designed to foster maximal development (Super, Savickas, & Super, 1996).

Circumscription, Compromise, and Self-Creation: A Developmental Theory of Occupational Aspirations

The development of occupational aspirations is the main theme of Gottfredson's (1981) theory. Incorporating a biosocial developmental approach, her theory describes how people become attracted to certain occupations. Self-concept in vocational development is a key factor to career selection, according to Gottfredson, because people want jobs that are compatible with their self-images. Yet self-concept development in terms of vocational choice theory needs further definition, argued Gottfredson: key determinants of self-concept development are one's social class, level of intelligence, and experiences with sex-typing. According to Gottfredson, individual development progresses through four stages:

1. Orientation to size and power (ages 3–5): Thought process is concrete; children develop some sense through sex roles of what it means to be an adult.
2. Orientation to sex roles (ages 6–8): Self-concept is influenced by gender development.
3. Orientation to social valuation (ages 9–13): Development of concepts of social class contributes to the awareness of self-in-situation. Preferences for level of work develop.
4. Orientation to the internal, unique self (beginning at age 14): Introspective thinking promotes greater self-awareness and perceptions of others. Individual achieves greater perception of vocational aspirations in the context of self, sex role, and social class.

In this model of development, occupational preferences emerge within the complexities that accompany physical and mental growth. A major determinant of occupational preferences is the progressive circumscription of aspirations during self-concept development, that is, from the child's rather simplistic and concrete view of life to the more comprehensive, complex, abstract thinking of the adolescent and adult. For example, in stage 1, the child has a positive view of occupations based on concrete thinking. In stage 2, the child makes more critical assessments of preferences, some of which are based on sex-typing. In stage 3, the child adds more criteria to evaluate preferences. In stage 4, the adolescent develops greater awareness of self, sex-typing, and social class, all of which are used with other criteria in evaluating occupational preferences.

Gottfredson suggested that socioeconomic background and intellectual level greatly influence individuals' self-concept in the dominant society. As people project into the work world, they choose occupations that are appropriate to their "social space," intellectual level, and sex-typing. In the Gottfredson model, social class and intelligence are incorporated in the self-concept theory of vocational choice.

Another unique factor in this theory is the concept of compromise in decision making. According to Gottfredson, compromises are based primarily on generalizations formed about occupations or "cognitive maps" of occupations. Although each person develops a unique map, each uses common methods of evaluating similarities and differences, namely through sex-typing, level of work, and field of work. In this way, individuals create boundaries or tolerable limits of acceptable jobs. Gottfredson suggested that people compromise their occupational choices because of the accessibility of an occupation or even give up vocational interests to take a job that has an appropriate level of prestige and is an appropriate sex-type. In general, individuals are less willing to compromise job level and sex-type because these factors are more closely associated with self-concept and social identity.

In its early stages, this theory had a strong sociological perspective. The external barriers that limit individual goals and opportunities concern Gottfredson, and her theory differed from other theories in four major ways. First, in career development, there is an attempt to implement the social self and, secondarily, the psychological self. Gottfredson places much more emphasis on the idea that individuals establish social identities through work. Second, how cognitions of self and occupations develop from early childhood is a major focus of the theory. Third, the theory's premise is that career choice is a process of eliminating options, thus narrowing one's choices. Fourth, the theory attempts to answer how individuals compromise their goals as they try to implement their aspirations. In Gottfredson's view, career choice proceeds by eliminating the negative rather than by selecting the most positive.

Although these differences make this theory distinctive, the theory also shares some fundamental assumptions with other theories. For example, career choice is a developmental process from early childhood. Second, individuals attempt to implement their self-concepts into career choice selections. Finally, satisfaction of career choice is determined largely by a "good fit" between the choice and the self-concept.

Major Concepts of Gottfredson's Theory

Self-Concept. Following Super, Starichesky, Matlin, and Jordaan (1963), Gottfredson defines self-concept as one's view of self that has many elements, such as one's appearance, abilities, personality, gender, values, and place in society.

Images of Occupations. Images of occupations refer to occupational stereotypes (Holland, 1992) that include personalities of people in different occupations, the work that is done, and the appropriateness of that work for different types of people.

Cognitive Maps of Occupations. These cognitive maps constitute how adolescents and adults distinguish occupations into major dimensions, specifically, masculinity/femininity, occupational prestige level, and field of work. A two-dimensional map of sex-type (Holland's term) and prestige level has been constructed to portray certain occupations by these two dimensions, and Holland's typology is used to indicate field of work. For example, an accountant (field of work), has above-average prestige level, and sex-type is rated as more masculine than female. This map is primarily used to locate "areas" of society that different occupations offer. Individuals use images of themselves to assess their compatibility with different occupations. Some refer to this process as congruence, or person-environment fit. If the core elements of self-concept conflict with an occupation, that occupation is rejected in Gottfredson's scheme.

Social Space. This term refers to the zone of acceptable alternatives in each person's cognitive map of occupations, or each person's view of where he or she fits or would want to fit into society. Gottfredson suggests that career decision making should center around points of reference as "territories," either measured or contemplated, rather than around specific points of reference to a single occupation.

Circumscription. Circumscription reflects the process by which an individual narrows his or her territory when making a decision about social space or acceptable alternatives. The stages of circumscription were outlined earlier.

Compromise. This is a very significant process in Gottfredson's theory. As she puts it, "individuals often discover, when the time comes that they will be unable to implement their most preferred choices" (Gottfredson, 1996, p. 187). Within this process, individuals will settle for a "good" choice but not the best possible one. Compromise is the process of adjusting aspirations to accommodate external reality, such as local availability of educational programs and employment, hiring practices, and family obligations. According to Gottfredson, individuals will not compromise their field of interest by prestige or sex-type when there are small discrepancies. When there are moderate trade-offs within the process of compromise, people avoid abandoning prestige rather than sex-type. In major trade-offs, people will sacrifice interests rather than prestige or sex-type (Gottfredson, 1996).

The scope of this theory has been greatly expanded by Gottfredson (2002), primarily through a biosocial perspective of career counseling. She stresses that career development is to be viewed as a nature-nurture partnership. She was greatly influenced by Eysenck's (1998) findings from genetically sensitive family studies over several decades that suggest both genes and environment drive human experiences, which in turn consolidate individual traits. In other words, genetically distinct individuals create different environments and each individual's genetic uniqueness shapes their experiences. This position differs from socialization theory, which suggests we are passive learners from our environmental experiences and supports the view that we are active participants in creating self-directed experiences. Not only are our experiences self-directed but how we perceive and interpret them is unique for each individual. In this way both genes and environment contribute to one's unique development.

What stands out as a different perspective here is the genetic influence on one's behavior. It seems that genetic propensities drive our evaluations of experiences and as such are precursors of individual uniqueness. The nature-nurture partnership approach therefore adheres to an inner compass from which one may circumscribe and compromise life choices. Gottfredson's theory is distinguished from others by her emphasis on inherited genetic propensities that shape individual traits. Following this logic, individuals "seek and create environments that reinforce their genetic proclivities" (Gottfredson, 2002, p. 115).

The implications for career counseling include a perspective on individual differences that focuses on the influence of genetic individuality. Studies of genetic intelligence support the principle that genetic influence on intelligence is clearly evident (Shaffer, 2002). As early as the late 1920s, Spearman (1927) suggested that a general mental ability exists called the "g" factor that contributes to the ability to perform specific tasks such as numerical reasoning and word memory (Sigelman & Rider, 2003). In addition, there appears to be genetic influences on the development of personality traits in that many personality traits are considered to be moderately heritable (Shaffer, 2002). Most important to recognize here is the interplay of genetic and environmental factors that contribute to behavior. As Gottfredson suggests, individuals and their environments are involved in a continuous state of dynamic interaction that leads to change and modification of both. Thus, counselors are to respect the individuality of all clients and make no assumptions about a client's vocational interests, attitudes, and abilities. More applications of her theory follow.

Empirical Support

Lapan and Jingeleski (1992) found some agreement with the concept of social space in that individuals did assess compatibility with regard to zones of alternatives within the broad scope of the occupational world. Sastre and Mullet (1992) confirmed that gender, social class, and intelligence are related to work field and level of occupational aspirations. Leung, Conoley, and Scheel (1994) studied 149 immigrant and native-born Asian American college students to determine whether the boundaries of social space are set by age 13 (stage 3). They concluded that social space increased in size from age 8 through 17, disconfirming the theory's predictions. Although this one study should not negate Gottfredson's individual development through four stages, there remains the possibility that some students widen their range of career exploration during high school. Also see Armstrong and Crombie (2000), Gottfredson (1997), and McLennan and Arthur (1999).

 ### Summary of Practical Applications

Gottfredson directs career counselors to what she refers to as underappreciated problems and possibilities in career development. Counselors should encourage clients to be as realistic as possible when exploring potential occupational goals. She concludes that reality is either ignored, or the client fails to deal effectively with it. She recommends five developmental criteria to aid the counselee in dealing with reality.

1. The counselee is able to name one or more occupational alternatives. If not, then the counselor is to determine whether indecision reflects the inability to choose among high-quality alternatives or whether there is an unwillingness to attempt to choose. Some questions to be answered are the following: Is there a lack of self-confidence? Are there internal or external conflicts in goals? Is there impaired judgment?
2. The counselee's interests and abilities are adequate for occupations chosen. If not, is this the result of misperceptions about self? Are there external pressures from parents or other important adults?
3. The counselee is satisfied with the alternatives he or she has identified. If dissatisfied, does the counselee consider the selected alternatives as an unacceptable compromise of interests, sex-type, prestige or family concerns, or other concerns? Attempt to determine internal or external constraints.
4. The counselee has not unnecessarily restricted his or her alternatives. Did the counselee consider suitable and accessible alternatives? Has there been a lack of exposure to compatible alternatives? Does the counselee have an adequate knowledge of his or her own abilities?
5. The counselee is aware of opportunities and is not realistic about obstacles for implementing the chosen occupation. What are the reasons the counselee has not been realistic about obstacles? Is there wishful thinking or a lack of information

or planning? Information to seek during the counseling interview includes why certain options seem to be rejected and why some compromises are more acceptable than others. Use the following questions: What is the preferred self, in both sociability and personality type? Are the perceptions of boundaries in social space adequate? Who are the primary reference groups, and what family circumstances influence the counselee?

Finally, Gottfredson suggests that information that provides compatibility and accessibility are essential. One may do this through exploration of social space that includes aptitude requirements of occupations, arrays of occupational clusters, and the counselee's perceptions of sex-type and prestige. Occupational clusters depicted on a map are to be used to focus attention on compatible clusters. As the counselee selects more specific occupations, the characteristics of the occupation and the availability of training should be discussed. Eventually, as the client reaches the realm of constructive realism, a subset of best choices can be selected realistically and, subsequently, one best choice made, with a list of alternatives.

Gottfredson adds a biosocial perspective to the career development of the very young. She strongly suggests that more attention be given to the development of individuals in their young years. Of her key concepts, circumscription and compromise are the most dynamic and need further research to determine how to minimize their limiting effects on career choice. Her theory has been criticized because it is limited to children and leaves much to be said about adult development (Gelso & Fretz, 2001).

Summary Comments Concerning Developmental Theories

Developmental theories give a perspective of career development that is continuous and discontinuous and is indeed multidimensional. The concept of vocational maturity illuminates the proposition that some clients simply are not prepared to make an optimal career decision. Counselors are to assess a client's orientation to work, planning skills, and reality of occupational preferences to determine readiness for career choice. There are developmental tasks and stages in career development that provide windows of opportunity for counseling interventions. Self-concept is the driving force that establishes a career pattern. One of the major goals of developmental theory is to assist each client to develop an accurate picture of self in multiple life roles. The assumption that clients are involved in several life roles simultaneously, and success in one life role facilitates success in another, underscores the important perspective of life-span development. Super has called special attention to adult concerns in the scheme of career development that will be most relevant in the 21st century.

Gottfredson's research underscores a well-known position that career education should begin with the very young. Counselors need to make every effort to empower children to learn more about the work world and promote the proposition that each child should feel free to choose any career. Counselors need to be aware of how parental status influences children and social restraints of circumscription limit their career development.

Finally, each client's unique development should be the focus of the intake interview. Developmental theories point out that each individual's development is unique, multifaceted, and multidimensional. Counselors must recognize that client concerns can emerge from internal and external factors or a combination of both. In the next section we expand the developmental process to include contextual interactions. See Chapter 3 for an illustration of a developmental career counseling model.

Person-in-Environment Perspective

The person-in-environment perspective focuses attention on contextual interaction over the life span. Clients are viewed as products of an environment that is very inclusive but also unique. One's career development is thought to be *influenced and constructed* within several environmental systems such as family, church or synagogue, neighborhood, school, neighbors, friends, workplace, community agencies, culture, and customs of the larger environment. Major tenets of these theories emphatically support the position that concerns of clients do not exist totally within the person.

Counselors are to look not only for internal pathology but also for causes of client concerns that may have developed through a variety of experiences, relationships, and situations. This position is not necessarily a new one in that a number of theorists have stressed the need to unearth background variables of clients. The major differences here, however, are the inclusive nature of influence variables that are viewed as systems, constructs, and the proposition that there is reciprocity affect, that is, individuals influence and are influenced as they interact within their environment. Therefore, effective counseling procedures need to unearth both internal and external variables that contribute to career development.

Person-in-environment and ecological systems are often used interchangeably (Cormier & Nurius, 2003), but an ecological system is *not in itself a career development theory.* An ecological system is one of the most inclusive methods of understanding human development. It is, as the name implies, a study of the relationship between person and environment. An ecological system theory provides a detailed analysis of ongoing environmental influences over the life span. The developing person is viewed as "being at the center of and embedded in several environmental systems that interact with one another" (Shaffer, 2002, p. 59).

Bronfenbrenner (1979) suggested that there are four systems that make up an environment. The first is the microsystem or the person; second is the mesosystem of family, peer group, and schoolmates, among others; third is the exosystem of friends of family, extended family, neighbors, workplaces, media, and others; and, finally, the macrosystem is the sum of broad ideologies expressed and modeled by the sociocultural group. These systems are illustrated in Figure 2-6.

This human development theory posits that people develop in changing historical contexts and in sociocultural interactions and relationships. Such a perspective makes an important point for counselors to contemplate by suggesting that not all client problems are "within" the client, but on the contrary, many concerns are embedded within person-in-environment experiences. Within this view of human development that is both continuous and discontinuous, individuals are also involved in ongoing systems that change. Uniqueness emerges from individualized and shared experiences, and one's unique interpretation of those experiences: Each individual life story unfolds within changing ecological systems.

The ecological systems perspective provides the counselor with the opportunity to view all aspects of a person as a whole. It is a "who" and "where" approach to counseling that offers a balanced view of human development (Cormier & Nuruis, 2003).

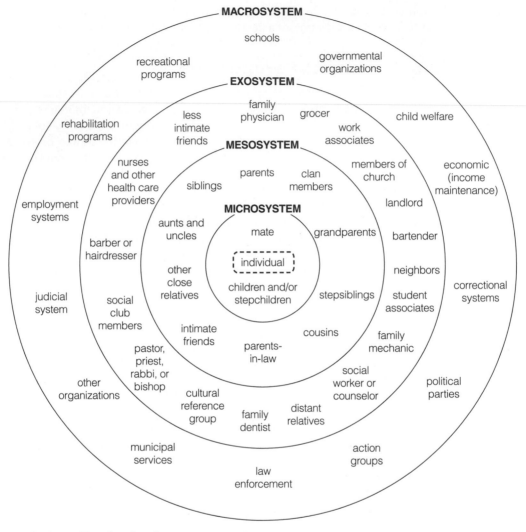

Figure 2.6 **Ecological systems map**

Source: From *Direct Social Work: Theory and Practice*, 5th ed., by D. Hepworth, R. Rooney, and J. Larsen, p. 267. Copyright © 1997. Reprinted by permission of Brooks/Cole, a part of The Thomson Corporation.

The lesson here is that counselors search for causes of client concerns and constructs that have developed from a wide range of interactions in his or her environment. Core assumptions, for instance, may well be embedded in learning experiences within eco- logical systems. For example, are Joy's mood swings the result of faulty perceptions of environmental events or from poor environmental fit? Is Jim's problem in school a learning disability or the result of current marital conflicts between his parents? Is poor self-esteem and lack of assertiveness the reason Jessica has not been promoted or is it because she has a controlling and demanding family? Or both? Dan thinks he is too stupid to get accepted to college. Is this a self-concept problem or the result of underfunded and inadequate schools, or both?

These examples illustrate the significance of unearthing one's life story from environmental factors that may contribute to a client's faulty thinking or inappropriate behavior and the internal conflicts a client brings to counseling. The life story can also be a valuable source of information that can be fostered in the career counseling process. In sum, an ecological system includes a broad perspective of potential influences that can affect learning, thinking, reasoning, decision making, and subsequent behavior. More important, it suggests that human behavior can be understood only in the context in which it occurs. The person-in-environment approach to counseling is touted as a more inclusive and balanced approach to the practice of career development. A greater understanding of person-in-environment perspectives includes an introduction to *constructivism* in the next paragraphs.

Constructivism

Since the early 1980s, the psychological approach of constructivism to career development has emerged from the philosophical position of postmodernism that suggested there is no fixed truth. This position is a reaction to traditional modernist thinking of logical positivism, from which theories with logical proofs were directed to gather empirical data to either approve or disapprove them. The logical positivism approach served the physical sciences well but social scientists turned to alternative paradigms of constructivism to better understand human behavior. The constructivist's viewpoint of career development is quite a departure from other theories that rely on logical proofs supported by empirical data. Constructivists support the belief that individuals define themselves as they participate in events and relationships in their environment. In order to make sense of environmental interactions and events, each individual develops personal constructs in which his or her views of the world differ from others. For example, different worldviews develop from different cultures and within cultures. These sets of personal constructs continue to be modified over the life span. In this context, the client is an active participant in her or his career development and each client is considered as a unique individual who has developed personal constructs from her or his perceptions of unique events and interactions. What is suggested here is that counselors concentrate on assisting individual clients to identify and understand their unique personal constructs as a precursor for intervention strategies. The life history of each client provides them with a means for understanding their own career story and the direction of their vocational behavior (Savickas, 2002).

Gelso and Fretz (2001) suggest that Brown, Brooks, and Associates (1996) have captured the essence of the emergence of constructivism in the following propositions:

- All aspects of the universe are interconnected; it is impossible to separate figure from ground, subject from object, people from environments.
- There are no absolutes; thus, human functioning cannot be reduced to laws or principles, and cause and effect cannot be inferred.
- Human behavior can be understood only in the context in which it occurs.
- The subjective frame of reference of human beings is the only legitimate source of knowledge. Events occur outside human beings. As individuals understand their environments and participate in events, they define themselves and their environments (p. 10).

Following this logic, individual careers are constructed through unique learning experiences in an ecological system. Personal constructs therefore are developed by individuals through the way they interpret and view their lives (Kelly, 1955). Life-role clarity and meaning of life, for example, are expressed in one's career (Sharf, 2002). Thus, counselors emphasize person–work-environment fit from two perspectives— how the person fits into the work role and how the work role fits into the person's lifestyle. Keep in mind that individual sets of constructs are modified continually over a life span, suggesting that individuals are best served by learning to manage their own career development. Clients who learn to understand that the direction of their vocational behavior may change over time are best prepared to make careful and meaningful life and career decisions. The focus of this viewpoint is on individual behavior rather than on the behavior of groups of individuals that may provide a norm from which one judges their own career development. Such norms can be used as guidelines, however, as individuals process and comprehend their own personal agenda. Two career development theories are reviewed: career construction; a developmental theory of vocational behavior; and a contextual explanation of career.

Career Construction: A Developmental Theory of Vocational Behavior

Using our brief introduction to constructivism as a backdrop, we review some of the highlights of a career construction theory by Savickas (2002). Using Super's theory of vocational development, Savickas expands and extends this theory by using the psychological approach of constructivism, which suggests that individuals construct their own reality or truth. Second, he suggests that careers are to be viewed from a developmental contextual viewpoint that focuses on one's adaptation to an environment through the development of inner structures. Savickas carefully states 16 propositions of career construction theory that include (1) developmental contextualism, such as the core roles developed through an individual's life structure, preferences of life roles, and an individual's career pattern; (2) development of vocational self-concepts that include individual differences, vocational characteristics, occupational requirements, work satisfaction, how self-concepts develop and are implemented in work roles, and continuity of self-concepts; and (3) vocational developmental tasks experienced as social expectations, the growth experienced during career transitions, vocational maturity as a psychosocial construct, career adaptability as a psychological construct, and how career construction is fostered. Some of these propositions will be discussed in the following paragraphs but readers are encouraged to read the original text for more complete information.

Developmental contextualism that is used to designate how individual constructs are developed appears to be built around the concepts of Bronfenbrenner's (1979) ecological system discussed earlier. As one develops in a social context, personal constructs evolve from one's perception of events and interactions within a social ecology system. It is the context of reciprocal development in a social ecology that gives meaning to the personal constructs that influence life-role development. For instance, gender differences in work roles may be fostered. Occupational choice could be restrained or embellished as individuals interact within contextual opportunities. The point to remember here is that individuals participate in their own development that leads to perceptions of core roles, so counselors can assist clients to consciously influence the direction of future life roles.

As core roles emerge in the constructivist's view, there is an increasing sense of personal awareness and integration of constructs. As more personal constructs are developed, one becomes increasingly aware of individual differences and dichotomous constructs. Gradually, one integrates constructs into a system that gives clarity to purpose and role. Life in an ever changing society provides for an ongoing process of individual construct development that influences adaptations and modification of life roles. Within this context, Savickas (2002) makes the point that each person's core roles interact to reciprocally shape each other. Therefore, to understand an individual's career choice and commitment, for instance, is to understand and appreciate the inner constructs that give meaning to that individual's life roles.

Following Super's lead, Savickas illuminates the importance of self-concept development. He describes the forming of self-concept in early childhood "as a collection of percepts that is neither integrated nor particularly coherent." In early adolescence a more unified and coherent self-concept permits individuals to form some abstract self-descriptions. Finally, the more organized self-concept becomes a filter through which one forms self-perceptions that guide and control behavior. As one experiences the give-and-take of life, new and different percepts lead to self-concept revision. Thus, in this context, the process of career development is never complete.

There are also dimensions of self-concept that are worthy of mention. The vocational self-concept is viewed as an individual's perception of her or his personal attributes that are considered relevant to certain work roles. Examples of self-concept dimensions of attributes that were suggested by Super include assertiveness and gregariousness, whereas examples of self-concept metadimensions include consistency and stability (Savickas, 2002). This distinction is particularly important in career choice counseling. In Savickas's career construction theory the self-concept dimensions direct the *content* of alternative choices whereas the metadimensions of self-esteem, realism, and clarity, for example, direct the *process* of making a choice. Thus, one individual may project the vocational self-concept into a certain work environment of interest but withdraw from it because of poor self-esteem. This situation illustrates that contradictory self-percepts make it difficult to find occupational fit and provide the counselor with clues for developing tailored interventions.

Career Construction: Developmental Tasks Within Vocational Development Stages

Career construction theory endorses Super's (1990) basic principles of developmental tasks. The basic principles of tasks and stages, for instance, suggest that successful passage from one stage to another is considered as individual progress over the life span. Second, the degree to which one successfully adapts to each task and meshes this progress with career concerns indicates one's level of career maturity. It therefore is important that clients and counselors recognize the relevance of completing the goals of the developmental stages of growth, exploration, establishment, maintenance, and disengagement. In the following paragraphs the developmental tasks within each developmental stage will be briefly discussed, primarily from a constructivist's point of view. A major point here is that each individual's experiences in processing developmental tasks forms the foundation for a greater self-understanding and vocational identity.

Growth, the first developmental stage, is characterized by Super as development of capacity, attitudes, interests, and needs associated with self-concepts. It is a life span developmental process as outlined in Table 2-5 earlier in this chapter. Savickas (2002) emphasizes developmental factors associated with children. He suggests that there are four major tasks that society has imposed upon children as follows:

1. Become *concerned* about one's future as a worker.
2. Increase personal *control* over one's vocational activities.
3. Form *conceptions* about how to make educational and vocational choices.
4. Acquire the *confidence* to make and implement these career choices (p. 168).

In sum, the *concerned* child is influenced by numerous interactive relationships. Among the most significant are interactions between parents and children. Children who have secure attachments to caregivers are more likely to feel positive about themselves and other people. Conversely, those who have insecure attachments develop poor self-perceptions and view others with distrust. (See Roe, 1956, in Chapter 15.) Because children experience and learn from numerous relational activities in early childhood, positive relationships are to be fostered (Tiedeman & O'Hara, 1963). *Career control* refers to self-determination (Blustein & Flum, 1999) and the development of personal agency. The individual gains control of her or his future by fostering her or his own independent actions and intentional behavior that reinforces actions of decisiveness and self-competence. The forming of *career conceptions* involves consideration and reconsideration of possible courses of action. Curiosity about the future prompts some individuals to project into tentative goals and form some tentative results. Thus, distorted career perceptions during this period can hamper future career choices. Sources of one's *career confidence* in this scheme are numerous and most important. Some sources include daily interactions with peers and significant experiences such as learning to solve problems. One outstanding source of career confidence is success in school activities that help build positive attitudes, beliefs, and competencies.

The *exploration stage* is characterized by Super as a tentative phase in which choices are narrowed but not finalized. One learns more about occupational opportunities and self-in-situation. In the process of *constructing* a career, the individual searches for congruent work environments in which to express vocational identity. There is a continued assessment of alternatives; some are discarded but may be reconsidered in other tasks. During this stage, individuals are searching for a clearer definition of self in order to establish a sense of vocational identity (Savickas, 2002).

There are three tasks associated with the exploration stage: crystallization, specification, and actualization. During the *crystallization process,* there is a continued assessment of alternatives. Goals become more definite and formed but are not irreversible. One major goal of the crystallization process is for individuals to stabilize and integrate self-percepts into a stable structure. Those who lag behind and fail to gain clarity of self and role are often classified as being indecisive. Thus, it is not surprising that disharmony significantly interferes with career development. In general, Savickas takes the position that in a structural model of career development, competencies derive from knowledge about one's self and occupations, as in other career theories, and are inextricably intertwined with development of skills needed for problem solving, matching, and life planning.

Specification tasks direct individuals toward specifying an occupational choice. The individual becomes involved in carefully reviewing tentative preferences in an in-depth exploration of reality testing. There is a focus on the particular behaviors that are necessary to meet one's chosen goal. At first glance this task may appear rather simplistic but it is indeed a relevant step in the career choice process. One who makes a declaration of intent suggests that the crystallization process is complete. Thus, in specifying an occupation the individual declares how he views himself in relation to the world and implies a unity and wholeness of purpose that has prompted a significant commitment!

Actualization is a period that is highlighted by one's focus on career identification. It may include trial jobs in the chosen occupational group. During this period, the individual searches for fit in a work environment. One may experiment with a series of related jobs before finding a congruent one. There are internal and external barriers that may delay actualization. Poor attitudes, inappropriate behavior patterns, and beliefs are internal factors that disrupt progress. External barriers can come in many forms, such as outsourcing of jobs, and lack of opportunity to advance. Individuals therefore should be prepared to face a work world where there is little in the way of promises for a lifetime job. In sum, actualization tasks are ongoing, as one may experience multiple jobs over the life span.

The third career stage of *establishment* infers a settling-down process in a permanent job. One begins the implementation of self-concept in an occupational role. Individuals are to refine their occupational role and consolidate their position. This stage is also characterized by greater self-understanding and identification with the total system of a career field. Developing a perspective of positive growth orientation is to be fostered. Individuals must distinguish between real barriers (no growth, slow growth, and organizational decline) and perceived barriers (role confusion, poor career identity, nebulous perceptions of career success and direction) that affect their ability to reach personal goals.

The fourth career stage is *maintenance* or *management.* Here individuals become more aware of life stages in terms of time spans and begin to view career in terms of implementing future opportunities. Savickas suggests that this stage is a time for a renewal of vocational development. It involves re-finding the self and maintaining and preserving one's self-concept. Workers in this stage avoid stagnation by updating their skills and knowledge. They become innovative in developing new and different strategies. They become lifelong learners. In spite of these actions, changes in how and for whom one works makes it apparent to workers who have reached the maintenance stage that they must be resilient and willing to start over in a different career path. Counselors can suggest a recycling through one or more of the career-stage maxicycles.

Finally, career stage five, *disengagement,* is characterized by preretirement considerations. The individual prepares to "let go" of responsibilities and pass them on to others. One major adjustment during late career is learning to accept a reduced work role and changing focus away from a highly involved work identity. It is, as the name implies, a disengagement of vocational self-concept and a recycling to retirement living. One has to organize a new and different lifestyle. One would suspect that the sequence of events for retired workers in the 21st century will be quite different from those of their predecessors in the last century. The new social corporate culture that is being driven by global market forces should drastically change the work history of many citizens.

Empirical Support for Career Construction Theory

Much more research is needed on various aspects of career construction theory; however, empirical research on the theory by Hackett and Lent (1992) and Osipow and Fitzgerald (1996) suggests the following:

1. The data generally support the model.
2. The development segment is well documented.
3. Data relative to the self-concept generally agree with the theory (Savickas, 2002, p. 183).

 ### Summary of Practical Applications

Career construction theory stresses the development and implementation of self-concept into society. Clients are to learn how to construct a career path that fosters individual progress to discovering and experiencing a meaningful life. In order to foster self-concept development and implementation, constructivist career counseling begins with the discovery of career concerns.

Assessment of Career Construction Theory

The intake interview focuses on career concerns that can be identified by the *Adult Career Concerns Inventory* (Super, Thompson, & Lindeman, 1988). This inventory measures concerns with the developmental stages of exploration, establishment, management, and disengagement. Thus, the assessment phase is very inclusive, but does focus on life space, career adaptability, vocational self-concept and career themes, and vocational identity.

The counselor begins by identifying concerns in life space and, more specifically, the work role. Uncovering a client's level of commitment to work role is a major goal of this first phase. Counselors are also to determine the cultural context in which concerns originate. When it is found that a client has a strong commitment to the work role, adaptability, vocational self-concept, and vocational identity become focus points. A major objective is to find out if vocational identity is accurate. If the work role is not a major concern of the client, the counselor shifts to identifying the relative importance of other life roles.

Assessing Career Adaptability.   Inventories that are used include the following: *Career Maturity Inventory* (Crites & Savickas, 1996) for high school students and *Career Development Inventory* (Savickas & Hartung, 1996) for college students.

These inventories generally are used to evaluate competencies for making educational and vocational decisions. They focus on (1) the choice process of crystallizing, specifying, and actualizing, and (2) the implementing process of stabilizing, consolidating, and advancing. The interview may also be used to obtain this information. See Dix and Savickas (1995) and Savickas (2002).

Assessing Vocational Self-Concept and Career Themes.   This step in client assessment attempts to uncover a cross-sectional view of self-concept and a longitudinal view of career themes. Self-concepts may be measured by adjective checklists (Johansson, 1975), card sorts (Hartung, 1999), or a repertory grid technique (Neimeyer, 1989). Career theme assessment usually includes an autobiography, but it can be attained through a career-theme interview (Savickas, 1989).

Assessing Vocational Identity.   To obtain an objective picture of an individual's vocational identity, the counselor is instructed to use measures of interests such as the *Self-Directed Search* (Holland, 1994a) or *Strong Interest Inventory* (Harmon, Hansen, Borgen, & Hammer, 1994). The major purpose of measures of objective interests is to identify how a client resembles workers employed in different occupations. Objective measures of interests that indicate some congruence with certain occupations are compared with vocational self-concepts and career themes to determine their fit.

Finally, Savickas suggests that test results are presented most effectively in an integrated and narrative format. The narrative serves as the client's life story; it includes the importance of life roles and the emerging career experiences. The narrative should include the client's concerns and illuminate the client's character in the context of a client's life space. The client's concerns are to be conceptualized by the counselor as the current predicament and are linked to career themes that encourage speculation about the future. Clients are to connect with alternative choices that make sense out of the work world. One of the key counseling methods used in constructivist career counseling is autobiographical reasoning.

Finally, career narratives consist of career stories that assist clients in relating vocational self-concepts to work roles. Narratives are designed to foster self-concept clarification as a most important connection with self-fulfillment. In sum, constructivist approaches to career development recognize that individuals develop their own constructs and views of what is real for them, thus the career narrative provides an effective tool to connect career themes with one's vocational identity. See Savickas (1993) for more information and Sharf (2002) for a detailed and straightforward account of narrative counseling.

A Contextual Explanation of Career

The contextualism method establishes a contextual action explanation of career research and career counseling. Contextualism is based on the philosophical position known as constructivism (Brown, Brooks, & Associates, 1996). According to Sharf (1996), the constructivist position suggests "that individuals construct their own way of organizing information and that truth or reality is a matter of perception" (p. 405). Understanding how clients construct personal meanings from present actions and subsequent experiences is the core of this theory (Savickas, 2002).

The contextual model for human development is an ever changing, ongoing interplay of forces. The major focus is on the relationship between person and environment because they are considered to be inseparable and are regarded as a unit. As people and the environment interact, development can proceed along many different pathways, depending on how one influences the other (Shaffer, 2002).

Young, Valach, and Collin (1996, 2002) propose that one way to understand a contextualist explanation of career counseling is by action theory. Action, in this sense, focuses on the whole in the context in which action is taken. For example, a career counselor, a client, and a worker in the field the client is currently interested in have a discussion about the work, peer affiliates, and work environment. The total action of all three people is the context in which this particular counseling took place, and their actions form the basis for constructing personal meaning. To break the process into parts would be similar to unraveling an event into meaningless fragments. Thus, the wholeness of an event and the succession of changes that result from interaction with others and their contexts is the contextualist perspective. In essence, contextualists support the idea that events take shape as people engage in them, and only then is an analysis of actions and events practical. Thus, their focus is on "human intention, processes, and change in context rather than on context as a setting (environment) for action" (Young, Valach, & Collin, 2002, p. 207).

The study of actions is the major focus of the contextual viewpoint. Actions are conceptualized as being cognitively and socially directed and as reflecting everyday experiences; actions are social processes and, as such, reflect each individual's social and cultural world. Actions are viewed from three perspectives: they *manifest behavior,* for example, taking notes of a lecture; they are *internal processes,* such as feeling nervous about an examination; and they have *social meaning,* such as being successful in a career.

Action systems are composed of joint and individual actions and two terms, project and career. Joint action simply means that many career-related actions occur among people. According to the contextualist point of view, career values, interests, identity, and behaviors are constructed largely through language in conversation with others. Instead of evaluating the discussions individually between client and counselor, the contextualist conceptualizes joint action as a unit between client and counselor. The major focus here is on the action of the dyad. In other words, each person influences the other and their conclusions may direct some changes in each participant's behavior or cause them to modify their thinking about the subject discussed. Their subsequent actions may result in positive or negative consequences in the future.

Project refers to an agreement of actions between two or more people. For example, a single parent and adolescent child form an agreement of household responsibilities so that both may work. Because of changing work conditions and working hours, parent and child renegotiate responsibilities. In this example, individual and joint actions—including manifest actions—internal processes, and social meaning contribute to the project. The parent's and the child's behavior can be interpreted individually and jointly by this project.

The term career, as used in this theory, is similar to the term project. It can also be used to construct connections among actions and to evaluate plans, goals, emotions, and internal cognitions. The major difference between project and career is that career extends over a longer period of time and subsequently involves more actions. The actions can become complex and include greater social meaning. In this way, career approximates the idea of vocation.

The authors of this theory have developed an aspects-of-action theory to illustrate action systems, perspectives on action, and levels of action organization. Levels of action organization include elements, functional steps, and goals. Elements refer to physical and verbal behavior, such as words, movements, and environmental structures. Functional steps refer to higher-level actions than elements—for example, pleading and reminding can be used to convey a desired action. Goals, the highest level of action, usually represent the general intention of the individual or group.

The major purpose of defining actions in this manner is to organize the interpretation of human actions. Interpretation within this script offers a systematic method of evaluating and interpreting actions and the context in which they happen—what the counselor and client are doing together.

Much more research is needed on how a person affects the environment and how the environment affects that person. As we learn more about the ecology within which significant interactions occur, we may discover some dimensions that are relevant to career development. A good description of how both individuals and the world interact is by Vondracek, Lerner, and Schulenberg (1986), who see "levels of being" as multiple dimensions of interdependent forces that are developing and changing over time. This is a very complex person-context model that will take time to delineate in research.

In the meantime, the effects of salient contextual interactions have some very important implications for career counseling. Our perception of the individual in context can be somewhat conceptualized if we consider individual and environment as a circular interaction, as in Figure 2-6. Within this process an individual brings unique characteristics to an environment, and is influenced by the characteristics of others and situational conditions in the environment. One individual might be greatly influenced to limit career choice according to the mores of his or her environment, while another might not vocally express a lack of agreement, but will adapt his or her behavior to find some fit in the environment.

One very important outcome from our discussion of contextual influences is that development is shaped by the historical and cultural context of one's environment. Perhaps Sigelman and Rider (2003) offer the most clearly stated perspective of person-in-environment as follows:

> (1) humans are inherently neither good or bad; (2) nature and nurture, interacting continually, make us what we are; (3) people are active in their own development; (4) development probably involves some continuity and some discontinuity, some stage-like changes and some gradual ones; and (5) although some aspects of development may be universal, development also varies widely from individual to individual and can change directions depending on experience. (p. 47)

Empirical Support for Action Theory

For more on action theory, see Polkinghorne (1990) and von Cranach and Harre (1982). For discussions on context and environment, see Holland (1992) and Krumboltz and Nichols (1990). For more on this theory in general, see Valach (1990), Young and Valach (1996), Shotter (1993), Richardson (1993), Hermans (1992), Sigelman and Rider (2003), and Shaffer (2002).

 ### Summary of Practical Applications

Narrative counseling represents a practical approach for the practice of career development. Counselors are to ask clients to tell their life story. In this context, the major purpose of a life-story narrative is to discover how clients intentionally interact within segments of their environment. Counselors focus on career as a story to derive meaning from what the client views as important and unimportant. Client and counselor derive meaning from the chronology of events as well as the implied meaning of those events.

Two other goals of narrative counseling are (1) to establish a sense of client identity by how the story is told and constructed, and (2) to gain insight into client's future goals. Counselors are to focus especially on client conceptualizations, concepts, and constructs. Counselors assist clients in developing awareness of self from joint interpretation of narratives that brings meaning to the past and direction for the future (Savickas, 2002; Sharf, 2002).

Summary Comments Concerning Person-in-Environment Perspective

The person-in-environment perspective is indeed an inclusive view of career development. The major focus on initial career choice, for instance, should be expanded to account for interactive influences over the life span. There is to be a greater emphasis on the recognition that initial good fit between person and career may *not* continue to be a good fit over the life span; career development is therefore both continuous and discontinuous. Individuals and work environments change and these changes are bidirectional: In contextual career theory, individuals influence environments and a broad array of factors in the environment influence the individual. From a contextual development viewpoint we are active in our own development. Clients therefore are to assume responsibility for their development in all life roles. A self-directed approach to satisfying changing needs should be fostered. The recognition of reciprocal influence calls for more attention to the interrelationships of continuous changes in work environments and within individuals.

To become effective helpers, counselors also must focus on understanding the dynamics of changes in individual development and the salient messages individuals receive from their environment. Counselors not only address environmental influences in the initial choice but also the relatively fast-moving changes in restructured work environments and the significant demographic changes forecast for the 21st century. What is suggested here is that counselors help clients to explore the meaning and origins of core assumptions to more fully understand self, self-in-situation, and self in multiple life roles. Finally, counselors are to empower clients to challenge the core assumptions that limit career options.

Case Study: Maurice

The following case study illustrates how career development theories have influenced career counseling procedures and development of counseling materials. Counseling methods and procedures suggested by trait-oriented, social learning and cognitive, developmental, and person-in-environment theories have been selected as examples of counseling practice. In addition, client-centered and Gestalt techniques are included to represent a more holistic counseling approach. Maurice's case illustrates initial counseling responses to sets of concerns. As in many counseling encounters, additional problems surface during interventions and require further evaluations to establish counseling goals. The purpose of this case, however, is to provide an example of how some client *career concerns* can be addressed from the results of career development theory research. *Personal client concerns* are addressed by counseling interventions from the affective and cognitive-behavioral theoretical domains.

Maurice, a very shy and soft-spoken 19-year-old male, presented the following concerns: He wanted help to find a job because he had failed in school and had little work experience. The counselor spent considerable time to establish rapport, primarily by offering support and encouragement before interviewing him.

In the intake interview, through probing questions of the presenting concerns, it became clear to the counselor that Maurice was greatly influenced by his family's social status and level of employment of family members. He was convinced that certain kinds of work were "off limits" for him and in fact should not even be considered. His self-concept was judged as poor because of self-deprecating comments he made. He had little knowledge of the work world and, likewise, had little in the way of skills in making appropriate decisions. There were indications of faulty thinking, to the point that he was confused as to what the future held in store for him. He had assumed that his "place in life would be like his family and something would just happen to show the way." After further discussion the counselor *tentatively* conceptualized Maurice's concerns as follows:

1. Lacks self-knowledge concerning skills, interests, personality traits, and aptitudes.
2. Is confused as to how to find a sense of direction.
3. Restrictions of career options are probably the result of limited exposure to work roles and his family's social status.
4. Lacks basic information about the work world.
5. Has a very poor educational background and left high school before graduating.
6. Needs assistance in restructuring faulty perceptions and subsequently in how to rationally solve problems.
7. There appears to be an affective domain problem involving self-identity, self-concept, and feelings of helplessness.

Many concepts and propositions of several career development theories can be used to address Maurice's concerns. Person-in-environment perspectives and developmental theories focus on the relevance of an individual's unique development according to stages and tasks, contextual interactions, and learning experiences. Thus, information about Maurice's background and life story should reveal how he interprets events, situations, and experiences. This information should provide insights into the development of personal constructs and his vocational identity. The goal here is to attempt to gain a perspective of how Maurice constructs meaning from his experiences and relationships and help him to understand the consequences of his unique development. The counselor especially focused on Maurice's development in a social context. The major purpose for this intervention was to help Maurice recognize that his current social expectations may cause him to limit career options.

From a developmental perspective, it appeared that Maurice was not prepared to make a career decision, that is, he lacked career maturity. The problem of self-knowledge, which cuts across several theories, can first be addressed by a similarity model when discussing test results of academic achievement, interests, and personality traits, as suggested in trait-oriented theories. An inventory that measures vocational identity, need for information, and perceived barriers to choice will be administered from Holland's typology approach. All assessment results will be discussed and used as a planning tool for counseling interventions with Maurice's approval. Counseling will be focused on developing a greater sense of self through structured exercises and concrete experiences.

A learning plan stressed in social learning and cognitive theories is designed to improve Maurice's skills and educational development. The development of basic skills will be emphasized. Education is viewed as a key factor to broaden the scope of occupations Maurice will consider. He will learn more about the world of work by using a computerized assisted career guidance system. Maurice will also visit job sites and shadow some workers. What is emphasized here is one of the major principles of social learning theory, which suggests learning takes place through observations as well as through direct experiences.

Maurice will be taught how to use positive self-talk effectively in order to debunk stereotypes and restrictive career aspirations. His ability to sort out and resolve problems will be carefully monitored. He will be given examples of problem-solving exercises for current and future use. Cognitive behavioral interventions will be employed to help him unlearn faulty cognitions gleaned from an inventory that measures one's beliefs about careers (Mitchell & Krumboltz, 1996). Career development learning theory approaches suggest that some individuals overgeneralize from false assumptions and overlook worthwhile alternatives. Thus, in the case of Maurice, he may choose alternatives for inappropriate reasons.

Client-centered therapy and/or Gestalt techniques will focus on building positive self-concepts and help Maurice to understand sources of his feelings of helplessness. Active listening, empathy, and positive regard will be stressed. Coaching designed to reframe his thinking will also be emphasized. Incorporated within interventions are references to self in work role, planning skills, and reality of occupational aspirations.

In Maurice's case, it is clear that counselors should fuse career and personal concerns. A "whole person" holistic approach to Maurice's concerns will place both counselor and client in a better position to judge when an optimal career decision is possible. An integrated counseling approach makes use of strategies that are derived from several career development theories and combines them with client-centered and Gestalt techniques. The counseling suggestions in this case point out both differences and similarities of career development theory approaches, and so, counselors select technical tools from several theoretical frameworks that can best address a client's concerns. Maurice's case suggests that some client concerns may best be addressed from a holistic point of view that fosters the use of the most appropriate interventions that address unique individual needs. Be aware that not all the interventions suggested may be used. Interrelationships found between concerns suggest that some concerns can be addressed simultaneously. More information about holistic counseling is discussed in Chapter 4.

Implications for Career Counseling

Career development theories are conceptual systems designed to delineate apparent relationships between a concomitance of events that lead to causes and effects. Although the theories described in this chapter have a variety of labels, all emphasize the relationships between the unique traits of individuals and the characteristics of society in which development occurs. The major difference among the theories is the nature of the influential factors involved in the career decision process, but all the theories have common implications for career guidance.

1. Career development takes place in stages that are somewhat related to age but are influenced by many factors in the sociocultural milieu. Because career development is a lifelong process, career-related programs must be designed to meet the needs of individuals over their life spans.

2. The tasks associated with stages of career development involve transitions requiring individuals to cope with each stage of life. Helping individuals cope with transitions is a key concept to remember while promoting development.

3. Career maturity is acquired through successfully accomplishing developmental tasks within a continuous series of life stages. Points of reference from this continuum provide relevant information for the practice of career development.

4. Each person should be considered unique. This uniqueness is a product of many sources, including sociocultural background, genetic endowment, personal and educational experiences, family relationships, and community resources. In this context, values, interests, abilities, personal constructs, and behavioral tendencies are important in shaping career development.

5. Self-concept affects career decisions. Self-concept is not a static phenomenon but, rather, is an ongoing process that can gradually or abruptly change as people and situations change. Accurate self-concepts contribute to career maturity.

6. The stability of career choice depends primarily on the strength and dominance of one's personal orientation of personality characteristics, preferences, abilities, and traits. Work environments that match personal orientations provide appropriate outlets for personal and work satisfaction. Finding congruence between personality traits and work environments is a key objective of career development.

7. Individual characteristics and traits can be assessed through standardized assessment instruments. Identified traits are used to predict future outcomes of probable adjustments. Matching job requirements with personal characteristics might not dominate career-counseling strategies but remains a viable part of some programs.

8. Social learning emphasizes the importance of learning experiences and their effect on occupational selection. Learning takes place through observations as well as through direct experiences. Identifying the content of individual beliefs and generalizations is a key ingredient in developing counseling strategies.

9. Introducing occupational information resources and developing skills for their proper use is a relevant goal for all educational institutions. Moreover, this need persists over the life span.

10. Career development involves a lifelong series of choices. Counselors help clients make appropriate choices by teaching decision-making and problem-solving skills. Understanding the individual processes involved in choices enables counselors to better assist during the decision-making process.

11. The concept of human freedom is implied in all career development theories. This concept implies that career counselors should provide avenues of freedom that allow individuals to explore options within the social, political, and economic milieu. The limits of personal freedom are often external (e.g., economic

Box 2.1	Summary of Career Development Theories

The career theories in this chapter and in other chapters are summarized by major assumptions, key terms, and outcomes in Appendix A. Included are the following:

Trait-Oriented Theories
Trait-and-Factor
Person-Environment-Correspondence
John Holland's Typology

Social Learning and Cognitive Theories
Learning Theory of Career Counseling
Cognitive Information Processing
Social Cognitive Perspective

Developmental Theories
Life-Span, Life-Space Approach

Circumscription and Compromise:
A Developmental Theory of Occupational Aspiration

Person-in-Environment
Career Construction: A Developmental Theory of Vocational Behavior
A Contextual Exploration of Career

Other Theories
Ann Roe: A Needs Approach
Ginzberg and Associates
Sociological Perspective of Work and Career Development

conditions, discrimination, and environmental conditions), but freedom also can be constrained by such internal sources as fear, lack of confidence, faulty attitudes, poor self-concept development, and behavioral deficits. Within this context, the career counselor should be concerned not only with career development but with all facets of human development. Counseling strategies must be designed to meet a wide range of needs. (See Box 2-1.)

12. The importance of cognitive development and its relationship to self-concept and subsequent occupational aspirations are receiving greater attention. This focus is concerned primarily with the role of cognitive development in terms of appropriate gender roles, occupational roles, and other generalizations that directly affect career development. This fine-tuning of relationships between human and career development implies that counselors must develop a greater sensitivity to both.

Summary

1. Trait-Oriented Theories include Trait and Factor Approach, Person-Environment-Correspondence Counseling, and John Holland: A Typology Approach.
2. Social Learning and Cognitive Theories include Krumboltz's Learning Theory of Career Counseling, Career Development from a Cognitive Information Processing Perspective, and Career Development in a Social Cognitive Perspective.
3. Developmental Theories include Life-Span, Life-Space Approach to Careers and Circumscription, Compromise, and Creation: A Developmental Theory of Occupational Aspirations.
4. Person-in-Environment Approaches include a Career Construction Theory and Contextual Explanation of Career.

5. A case example is used as an example of how to apply strategies from career development theories.

Supplementary Learning Exercises

1. Explain why the trait-and-factor approach is considered the most durable theory. Give examples of the use of the trait-and-factor theory in current career counseling programs.
2. Defend the statement: Career development is a continuous process. Explain how it is a discontinuous process.
3. Write your own definition of career development and career counseling. Identify theories you agree and disagree with in summary form.
4. What are some of the implications of learning theories? How do these theories affect career development?
5. Compare Holland's approach to career development with person-in-environment theories. Summarize some similarities and differences.
6. Using the following reference, explain the principles behind Holland's theory of vocational choice. Defend or criticize his thesis that vocational interests are not independent of personality. Holland, J. L. (1992). *Making vocational choices* (2nd ed.). Odessa, FL: Psychological Assessment Resources.
7. How is it that some clients limit their career choices? Explain with examples.
8. Outline the factor that you consider most important in the career development of an adult you know or one you interview.
9. Defend and criticize the position of integrating theories in career counseling.
10. Develop your own theory of career development. Identify the components of theories you agree with and why you agree with them.

For More Information

Brown, D., & Associates (Eds). (2002). *Career choice and development.* San Francisco, CA: Jossey-Bass.

Brown, D., Brooks, L., & Associates. (1996). *Career choice and development* (3rd ed.). San Francisco, CA: Jossey-Bass.

Chartrand, J. M. (1991). The evolution of trait-and-factor career counseling: A person-environment fit approach. *Journal of Counseling & Development, 69,* 518–524.

Feldman, D. C. (2002). *Work careers: A developmental perspective.* San Francisco, CA: Jossey-Bass.

Holland, J. L. (1992*). Making vocational choices* (2nd ed.). Odessa, FL: Psychological Assessment Resources.

Patton, W., & McMahon, M. (1999). *Career development and systems theory: A new relationship.* Pacific Grove, CA: Brooks/Cole.

Prediger, D. J. (1995). *Assessment in career counseling.* Greensboro, NC: ERIC Counseling and Student Services Clearinghouse, University of North Carolina.

Sharf, R. S. (2002). *Applying career development theory to counseling.* Pacific Grove, CA: Brooks/Cole.

Suggested InfoTrac College Edition Topics

Career development

Career theories

Cognitive theories

Contextual approaches

Constructivism

Developmental theories

Ecology

Learning theories

Social learning

Career Counseling Models

3

Chapter Highlights

- Relevant issues and concepts emerging from model development

- Suggestions for career guidance from a career life planning model

- Trait-and-factor and person-environment-fit model

- Developmental model

- Learning theory model

- Cognitive information-processing approach model

- Multicultural career counseling model for ethnic women

- Model summary of counseling goals, intake interview techniques, use of assessment, diagnosis, and counseling process

THE CAREER DEVELOPMENT RESEARCH introduced in the preceding chapter has successfully produced guidelines for career counseling practice. However, the working relationship between practicing counselors and those who do career development research has been less than ideal, and researchers continue to search for more effective ways to communicate. An interesting assessment of the status between researchers and practitioners was suggested by Arbona (1996) and Lucas (1996), who point out that career development theories should not be expected to completely guide practice. Arbona and Lucas conclude that research answers theoretical questions but the counselor needs answers to questions that focus on actual practice. Lucas (1996) suggests one solution to this problem: Counselors should build a file of effective minitheories from their own experiences.

In a related publication, Harmon (1996) suggests that the gap between counseling skills and the current needs of a changing, diverse society has increased, making it imperative for counselors to upgrade their training. Clearly, future career counselors should be familiar not only with career development research but also with effective techniques, procedures, and materials used in contemporary models that can be used for building new approaches for the future.

In this chapter we introduce four career counseling models that are embedded in career development theory. A fifth model has been developed for a specific ethnic/racial group. The career counseling models discussed here present suggestions for building a repertoire of practical applications that can serve as a foundation for career counseling models of the future. First, we briefly discuss some basic issues and concepts that have emerged from model development. Next, five career counseling models are outlined and described. The major parameters of the five models are briefly discussed in the final section.

Other career counseling models can be found in Chapters 7, 10, 14 within the context of discussion of special groups. The next six chapters contain techniques used in career counseling models. Chapter 4 is devoted to methods of fusing career and personal concerns. Chapter 5 offers techniques for intake interviewing while Chapters 6 and 7 cover the use of assessment in career counseling. In Chapter 8 we discuss the use of technology in the new millennium. Finally, ethical standards and codes are reviewed in Chapter 9.

Some Issues and Concepts Emerging from Model Development

During the early development of career counseling models, the trait-and-factor approach received the most attention and has survived as a viable part of current trait-oriented models. In fact, Brown and Brooks and Associates (1991, 1996) point out that it may be the most popular theory among contemporary models. The key characteristic of this theory is the assumption that clients have unique traits that can be matched with requirements of occupations. This is often referred to as an actuarial method of predicting success in an occupation from the client's measured trait characteristics and is also associated with what is characterized as objective data (valid standardized test scores), rather than as subjective information (information clients reveal about themselves and perceptions of their environment, usually in an interview). The terms actuarial, objective, and subjective data are often mentioned in current career counseling models.

Diagnosis of client problems, at times referred to as appraisal or simply as problem identification, has involved some interesting criteria. Crites (1981) suggested three types of diagnosis—differential, dynamic, and decisional. Differential diagnosis is based on individual psychology, that is, how individuals differ from norms, and identifies the client's problems in such categories as undecided or indecisive. The focus is on describing the client's problems. A dynamic diagnosis is concerned with the reasons why the client has problems and may identify them as irrational beliefs, anxiety, or lack of information. A decisional diagnosis infers that the client's decision-making style, especially the process, should be addressed.

Three client labels that have been used extensively are decided, undecided, or indecisive. Decided clients are those who have made a career decision. These clients might profit from counseling that is designed to formulate other steps in decision making and to determine if their choice was inappropriately made.

Undecided clients have not made a career decision but might not view their current status as a problem; they prefer to delay making a commitment. The prevalent developmental view of this client is of an uninformed, immature person who generally lacks self-knowledge, information about occupations, or both. Yet, from another perspective, undecided clients could be described as multipotential individuals; they have the competencies to pursue several different types of careers.

The indecisive client is characterized as one who has a high level of anxiety accompanied by dysfunctional thinking. This client type is often labeled as not having cognitive clarity or as having irrational beliefs. For instance, the indecisive client could have problems embedded in a personality disorder that might be accompanied by depression. In general, clients with this label lack self-confidence, tolerance for ambiguity, and a sense of identity. These clients often need psychotherapy or personal counseling before they can benefit from career counseling, although both personal and career needs can be introduced simultaneously (Meara, 1996).

The following diagnostic systems are often used as guidelines for designating client problems: an extensive diagnostic taxonomy by Campbell and Cellini (1981); diagnostic and treatment suggestions by Rounds and Tinsley (1984); categories and suggested treatment by Kinnier and Krumboltz (1984); and a classification of problems suggested by Holland, Daiger, and Power (1980). In sum, contemporary models employ a combination of diagnostic criteria for specifying tailored interventions to meet specific client needs.

Finally, Gysbers and Moore (1987) have envisioned the career counseling process as Life Career Planning in which a strategy is created to help clients embark on a career path that might involve a series of occupations. This plan is very inclusive and incorporates family and leisure roles. In this model the career counseling process has two major phases and several subphases as follows:

I. Client goal or problem identification, clarification, and specification
   A. Establishing a client–counselor relationship, including client–counselor responsibilities
   B. Gathering client self and environmental information to understand the client's goal or problem

     1. Who is the client?
       a. How does the client view himself or herself, others, and his or her world?
       b. What language does the client use to represent these views?
       c. What themes does the client use to organize and direct his or her behavior based on views?
     2. What is the client's current status and environment?
       a. Client's life roles, settings, and events
       b. Relationship to client's goal or problem
  C. Understanding client self- and environmental information by sorting, analyzing, and relating such information to client's goal or problem through
     1. Career development theories
     2. Counseling theories
     3. Classification systems
  D. Drawing conclusions; making diagnosis

II. Client goal or problem resolution
  A. Taking action; interventions selected based on diagnosis. Some examples of interventions include counseling techniques, testing, personal styles analyses, career and labor market information, individual career plans, occupational card sorts, and computerized information and decision systems.
  B. Evaluating the impact of the interventions used; did interventions resolve the client's goal or problem?
     1. If goal or problem was not resolved, recycle.
     2. If goal or problem was resolved, close counseling relationship.

Source: From *Career Counseling: Skills and Techniques for Practitioners,* by N. C. Gysbers and E. J. Moore, p. 172. Copyright 1987 by Prentice-Hall, Inc. Reprinted by permission.

The impact of this conception of career counseling has not been fully appreciated; however, the very inclusive nature of this process suggests that career counseling is not dealing simply with static states of human behavior but, rather, with complex adaptive systems. Also, career counseling is not linear (choose, be trained, and be happy ever after); rather, it is multidimensional, involving interacting contextual variables and sophisticated cognitive domains that process information in an ever changing environment. Finally, career counseling is future oriented. Career development is both a continuous and discontinuous process that requires clients to learn, adapt, make changes, and develop all life roles.

Five Career Counseling Models

Five career counseling models represent a broad spectrum of career counseling strategies that are directed toward a common goal of assisting clients make a career decision. Each of the following models is introduced with some brief comments about its origins: trait-and-factor and person-environment-fit (PEF), developmental, learning theory, cognitive information-processing (CIP) approach, and multicultural career counseling model for ethnic women. Review Chapters 2 and 3 for background information on the career development theory for the first four models. The first model, trait-and-factor and PEF, includes two different career development theories. The developmental model primarily was drawn from Super's (1957, 1980) work, the learning theory model from Mitchell and Krumboltz (1996), and the CIP approach from Peterson, Sampson, and Reardon (1991). The background information for the multicultural career counseling model is contained in Chapter 10. All the models are flexible enough to include occupational classification systems such as Holland's Classification System, assessment instruments discussed in Chapters 6 and 7, and a variety of occupational information resources, including written materials, computer-generated materials, and multimedia aids.

The point here is that the career counseling models described in the following pages can use the very popular Holland typology approach and materials, some of which were described in Chapter 2. All the models discussed endorse an individualized approach to career counseling. Individual needs, therefore, dictate the kind and type of assessment instruments used and the materials and procedures used in the counseling process.

Because occupational information is an important part of intervention strategies in the five counseling models described in this section, some suggestions for its effective use are summarized. The following recommendations for the effective acquisition of occupational information have been compiled by Spokane (1991) and are paraphrased as follows:

1. When exploring occupations, counselors should urge clients to record both negative and positive reactions to each occupation. Both disconfirming and confirming reactions can suggest personal constructs that need further evaluation.
2. Counselors should have clients complete a list of occupations that are most congruent with their interests and abilities and those occupations that are rated as acceptable. Clients should begin with a broad-based exploration and follow it with a more focused, complete study. This process is considered most effective in confirming congruency.
3. Sources of occupational information that are close (proximal), such as parents or friends, should be followed by more distal information (farthest), such as a job site. Counselors should prepare clients to focus their research efforts on more in-depth study of occupations (distal) from which more accurate information can be obtained.
4. Career exploration involves both behavioral and cognitive processes; however, a framework for processing information, such as a form that requires clients to record relevant information, allows clients to derive the most benefits. Counselors can most effectively present sources of information when clients indicate readiness and express an interest in the information.

Trait-and-Factor and Person-Environment-Fit

The brief discussion of the historical development of trait-and-factor theory in Chapter 2 points out its controversial development. Trait-and-factor theory is viewed by some as promoting a very simplistic counseling process that is characterized by "three interviews and a cloud of dust" (Crites, 1981, p. 49), whereas others have argued that the applied concepts of the theory represent a misinterpretation of what Parsons (1909) and later Williamson (1939) intended (Brown, Brooks, & Associates, 1990; Rounds & Tracey, 1990; Spokane, 1991; Swanson, 1996) and Gelso and Fretz (2001).

What appears to have been a theory that met society's needs in the 1930s, within the role and scope of counseling practices at that time, was eventually viewed as a counselor-dominated, very inflexible, simplistic, and extremely test-oriented method.

Current proponents of trait-and-factor approaches strongly suggest that Williamson advocated multiple sources of client information, including subjective domains of cognitive and affective processing. Williamson's (1939) own words about analysis, the first step in his model, supports their observation: "Collecting data from many sources about attitudes, interests, family background, knowledge, educational progress, aptitudes, etc., by means of both subjective and objective techniques" (p. 215). Furthermore, the counseling processes used in trait-and-factor approaches suggest that this is a rational problem-solving approach similar to career counseling models currently in vogue (Rounds & Tracey, 1990; Swanson, 1996). In fact, the basic assumptions of trait-and-factor theory can be easily translated into practice and, with some modifications designed to meet contemporary societal needs, represent a viable philosophical basis for use within current career counseling models. What is needed, according to Rounds and Tracey (1990) and Swanson (1996) is to converge relevant trait-and-factor formulations within currently updated models of career development theory.

Trait-and-Factor and Person-Environment-Fit (PEF) Converge

During the last decade we have seen a gradual convergence of trait-and-factor methods and procedures with person-environment-fit constructs—also referred to as person-environment-correspondence in its early development (Rounds & Tracey, 1990). In general terms, some trait-and-factor methods have been adapted to determine person-environment-fit, but significant changes have also occurred: (1) both cognitive and affective processes are now involved; (2) clinical information and qualitative data are included in the appraisal process; and (3) the counselor's role has shifted from a directive approach to one in which counselor and client negotiate and collaborate (Swanson, 1996).

The following career counseling model has been extrapolated from several sources (Dawis, 1996; Swanson, 1996; Rounds & Tracey, 1990) and should be considered as examples of possible counseling procedures suggested by these authors and explicitly delineated in a career counseling model by Walsh (1990).

The following model includes seven stages, which will be briefly described.

Stage 1. Intake Interview
    a. Establish client–counselor collaboration relationship
    b. Gather background information
    c. Assess emotional status and cognitive clarity
    d. Observe personality style

Stage 2. Identify Developmental Variables
    a. Perception of self and environment
    b. Environmental variables
    c. Contextual interactions
    d. Gender variables
    e. Minority group status

Stage 3. Assessment
    a. Ability patterns

    b. Values
    c. Reinforcer requirements
    d. Interests
    e. Information-processing skills

Stage 4. Identify and Solve Problems
    a. Affective status
    b. Self-knowledge needs
    c. Level of information-processing skills

Stage 5. Generate PEF Analysis
    a. Cognitive schema
    b. Criteria on which to base choice
    c. Optimal prediction system

Stage 6. Confirm, Explore, and Decide
    a. Counselor and client confirm PEF analysis
    b. Client explores potential work environments
    c. Client makes a decision

Stage 7. Follow-Up
    a. Evaluate progress
    b. Recycle if necessary

Dawis (1996) suggests that the major goal of PEF is the enhancement of self-knowledge. Clients who have developed an adequate self-identity are better equipped to self-assess potential satisfaction and congruence with work environments. Thus, self-knowledge promotes optimal career selection.

In Stage 1, the Intake Interview begins with the client and counselor forming a compatible working relationship. Counselors do not assume an authority-expert role; rather, they build a relationship in which they will share responsibility and negotiate options in a collaborative manner.

Background information includes a biographical history that can be obtained from a questionnaire and through discussion. Information about the client's environmental influences are a high priority. During the interview, the counselor evaluates the emotional status of the client and the client's cognitive clarity. Personality style and personality characteristics are also observed. The information obtained in the intake interview is used throughout the counseling process. For example, background variables are used to evaluate personality structure and style. Any problems that surfaced are further evaluated in the stages that follow.

In Stage 2, Identify Developmental Variables, the information obtained in the intake interview is reviewed to account for important elements that are involved in PEF counseling, such as perception. Perception in this context refers to perception of self, such as one's identity, self-concept or self-image and, in addition, perception of environment, that is, its requirements, reinforcers, and demands. Environmental variables and contextual interactions are evaluated to determine a client's opportunities, relevant experiences, and limitations. Restrictions of developmental opportunities from environmental variables for women and minority groups are particularly important.

Assessment, in Stage 3, involves a comprehensive evaluation of the client's cognitive abilities, values, and interests. These measured traits are used with other variables to determine a client's reinforcement needs found in occupational environments. Thus, the major purpose of this information is to match client needs with occupations or groups of occupations that are predicted to result in satisfaction (self-fulfillment) and satisfactoriness (achievement).

Information-processing skills are important for clients to appropriately process information presented to them in PEF counseling. Those clients who need assistance for processing information are assigned intervention strategies designed to improve these skills before PEF counseling continues. More details about information-processing skills can be found in Stage 4.

In Stage 4, Identify and Solve Problems, information gathered in the first three stages is used to identify any affective concerns, self-knowledge needs, and the client's level of information processing. Clients who are identified as having serious emotional problems or dysfunctional thinking are referred for psychotherapy or for a complete psychological evaluation. Clients who have unrealistic or faulty beliefs about self-perceptions or perceptions of work environments or both are provided with tailored intervention strategies designed to assist them.

An important point made here is that counselors are to evaluate each client's ability to process information for optimal career decision making and person-environment-fit. Adhering to this position, differential diagnosis of client problems and subsequent treatment decisions are major objectives of an effective career counseling model. To evaluate specificity of client information-processing problems and to develop appropriate timing of intervention strategies, Rounds and Tracey (1990) have adapted Anderson's (1985) Adaptive Control of Thought theory as a primary focus to determine types of treatment and intervention. Briefly, this theory proclaims that there are three types of knowledge bases: working (active, conscious thought), declarative (knowledge of facts), and procedural (processing the relationship between different pieces of knowledge). Beginners using a trial-and-error procedure tend to use declarative knowledge, whereas experts use procedural knowledge, that is, experts are able to process the relationship of different knowledge and information in decision making. This process in turn involves four steps of information processing: encoding (sorting out the information's meaning), goal setting, plan development and pattern matching, and action. Each step is briefly described in Box 3-1.

In Stage 5, Generate PEF Analysis, the counselor and client develop a cognitive schema or a conceptual framework to direct the search for PEF. In this context each client's ability patterns are used to predict satisfactoriness in different occupations. Values and personality style are used to predict satisfaction with certain occupations and also to describe the client's reinforcer requirements. An occupational classification system is used to locate occupations for abilities required and reinforcers provided. The next step is to list occupations that correspond to the client's satisfaction and satisfactoriness needs. Within this procedure, clients find congruent occupations and choose one that is the optimal fit. The prediction system is more accurate when the client's dominant orientation (satisfactoriness or satisfaction) is known. An illustration of PEF analysis is given in Case 3-1.

Finally, for ethnic groups for which appropriate tests are not available, counselors obtain qualitative information from focused questions, contextual interactions, and nonstandardized exercises as demonstrated in Chapter 7.

Stage 6, Confirm, Explore, and Decide, begins when counselor and client review

Box 3.1	Assessing Level of Information Processing

a. *Encoding* involves the client's perception and interpretation of information. For example, client can recognize relevant advantages and limitations of an occupation.

b. *Goal setting* is best accomplished by concrete, realistic steps in an organized sequential process. For example, recognizing procedural requirements to reach goals.

c. *Effective plan development and pattern matching* involves establishing alternative solutions, several means of reaching goals, and considering the consequences of actions taken.

d. In the *action* step, the client selects an appropriate behavior to solve problems exposed in previous steps.

Rounds and Tracey (1990) also point out that effective information processing includes active and conscious deliberation, which is referred to as central processing, rather than peripheral processing. The counselor's rapport with a client and the counselor's behavior in presenting information can negatively influence the client's motivation to process information and is referred to as peripheral processing. Thus, if clients appear not to be motivated, the counselor should focus on persuasion cues that are related to counselor behavior of projecting warmth, trustworthiness, and competence.

In sum, treatment interventions are a function of the following:

1. Level of client information processing
2. Client motivation
3. "Relative progress in the counseling process." (Rounds & Tracey, 1990, p. 30)

Client levels of information processing are rated as very high, high, medium, and low. Very high levels of information processing indicate clients who have demonstrated competence in the four stages (encoding, goal setting, pattern matching, and action selection) as described earlier. Clients at this level need little treatment and consideration; computer-assisted career guidance programs and self-help procedures are recommended.

Those with high levels of information processing generally lack pattern matching knowledge but have mastered other steps. They should benefit from instructions on career decision-making skills. The focus should be on integrating information for a decision.

Clients rated as having medium-level information-processing skills usually have difficulty with encoding. They exhibit little insightful knowledge about the role and scope of an occupation or an academic major. The treatment should focus on encoding information and depth of insight through individual counseling or by taking a career course. In addition, a thorough analysis of coping and problem-solving skills is recommended.

Clients with low-level skills in information processing are characterized as having significant deficits in problem solving, that is, they are only able to encode and process little information presented to them. These clients may require the counselor to assume a teaching role that directly provides needed skills in a step-by-step fashion. The counselor also assumes a very active role in guiding the client in the decision process.

test data and the prediction analysis to determine if the client is comfortable with the results. If the client does not agree with work environments that are predicted to be congruent, recycling in the model may be recommended. Clients who do agree should be directed to explore potential work environments that are predicted to be congruent. Finally, a decision is reached.

Stage 7, Follow-Up, involves evaluating the client's progress in the counseling process and the procedures used to assist clients in finding a work environment in which they experience satisfactoriness and satisfaction. Counselors also assist clients in their job searches.

In sum, this model emphasizes fit-of-person with an optimal career. Valid and reliable tests are used to determine the client's abilities, values, and interests. This information is used in conjunction with subjective data (cognitive clarity, emotional status, problem-solving processes) in the counseling process. Identifying information-processing skills and improving them are viewed as necessary steps in assisting clients in the career decision-making process. Intervention strategies that are matched to specific identified deficits in information processing are a major focus of the career counseling process. However, the basic assumption of person-environment-fit is that individuals seek to achieve and maintain a positive relationship with their work environments. Thus, counselors assist clients in finding some degree of congruence between themselves and work environments in the career decision process.

Generating a PEF Analysis

Figure 3-1 represents the PEF analysis schematic that is used for optimal career choice.

Following the steps from left to right, the client is administered an abilities test and a values questionnaire. In the second step, ability and value patterns of occupa-

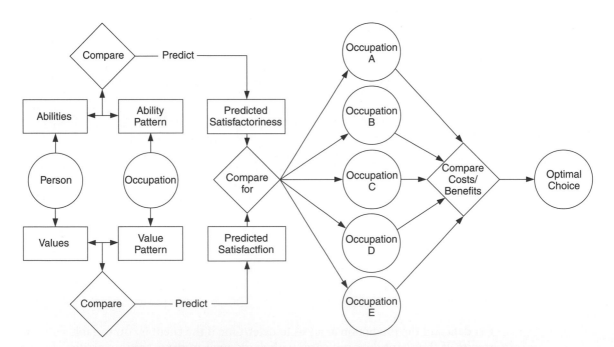

Figure 3.1   Use of the theory of work adjustment in career choice

tions are compared with the client's ability and values. This comparison is used to predict satisfactoriness, or the probability that the worker will satisfy the work requirements in a work environment, and whether the worker will find satisfaction performing the work that is required. These predictions are based on comparing the individual's abilities and values with the work environment requirements and reinforcers available. Finally, the individual selects specific occupations of interest and researches each one until an optimal choice is made.

Case 3-1: Person-Environment-Fit

A counselor's summary of the case of a 19-year-old female who was undecided about a career goal is contained in the paragraphs that follow.

Lee presented a background from a stable home environment, and there were no indications of irrational thinking or faulty beliefs. She appeared to be stable and expressed a positive self-concept. There was no evidence that she felt she must limit her career options because she is female. She felt free to explore any career of interest and was fully aware that some careers are stereotyped as male and female. Lee mentioned that her mother was a Chinese American born in this country and that her father was also American, of Irish and German descent. She identified with the dominant society. She finished high school in the top 20 percent and was in her first semester of college. She was found to have a very high level of skills in information processing. The counselor concluded that Lee was now serious about making a career decision.

During the assessment stage, Lee and the counselor collaborated on the tests that could be helpful.

Counselor: Lee, earlier I explained the idea of career counseling based on PEF. Do you have any questions at this time?

Lee: Not really, but I believe you mentioned that ability and values are used to help people like me find the right kind of job or as you said fit between person and work requirements.

Counselor: Very good!! I'll review the procedure once more. First, we measure your abilities, and values. Second, we will both assess work environments by not only observing work requirements, but also by whether you feel a particular occupation would be satisfying for you. We will do this by matching your traits with work reinforcers found in work environments. When we find a match we refer to this as personal-environment-fit, or simply PEF.

The following tests were chosen after an introduction of the purpose and use of each test: The General Aptitude Test Battery (GATB) (U.S. Department of Labor, 1970b), was chosen to measure nine specific abilities as shown in Lee's score results. The Minnesota Importance Questionnaire (MIQ) (University of Minnesota, 1984) was chosen as a measure of needs; values represent a grouping of needs as shown in Figure 3-2.

Figure 3-2	Values, need scales, and statements from the Minnesota Importance Questionnaire	
Value	**Need Scale**	**Statement**
Achievement	Ability utilization	I could do something that makes use of my abilities.
	Achievement	The job could give me a feeling of accomplishment.
Comfort	Activity	I could be busy all the time.
	Independence	I could work alone on the job.
	Variety	I could do something different every day.
	Compensation	My pay would compare well with that of other workers.
	Security	The job would provide for steady employment.
	Working conditions	The job would have good working conditions.
Status	Advancement	The job would provide an opportunity for advancement.
	Recognition	I could get recognition for the work I do.
	Authority	I could tell people what to do.
	Social status	I could be "somebody" in the community.
Altruism	Co-workers	My co-workers would be easy to make friends with.
	Moral values	I could do the work without feeling it is morally wrong.
	Social service	I could do things for other people.
Safety	Company policies and practices	The company would administer its policies fairly.
	Supervision–human relations	My boss would back up the workers (with top management).
	Supervision-technical	My boss would train the workers well.
Autonomy	Creativity	I could try out some of my ideas.
	Responsibility	I could make decisions on my own.

SOURCE: From *A Psychological Theory of Work Adjustment,* by R. V. Dawis and L. H. Lofquist, p. 29. Copyright 1984 University of Minnesota Press. Reprinted by permission.

Test score results for Lee were grouped by high, moderate, or low for nine abilities and six values as follows:

	High	**Moderate**	**Low**
GATB	Intelligence	Motor coordination	Finger dexterity
	Numerical aptitude	Spatial aptitude	
	Verbal aptitude	Clerical perception	
	Form perception	Manual dexterity	
	Achievement	Status	
MIQ	Comfort	Altruism	
		Safety	
		Autonomy	

The counselor presented assessment results to Lee by carefully explaining the meaning of each ability and value score.

Counselor: Lee, do you recall the meaning of verbal aptitude from our earlier discussion?

Lee: Well, I think it has something to do with my vocabulary.

Counselor: That's right! It was a vocabulary test that required you to identify words that have the same meaning or opposite meaning.

Lee: Yes, that was a tough one!

Counselor: You're right—some people have a difficult time with it. But more important, how does this score link with finding a career?

Lee: I was told by one of my high school teachers that a good vocabulary is important for so many things—like meeting people, making a speech, and even studying. It also is important in work to be able to communicate with other people, like a boss or a customer.

The counselor continued explaining and discussing each of the ability measures. In each case counselor and client linked score results with career choice; the focus was on the decision process. The counselor also emphasized that occupations require a combination of abilities and skills that are listed in references that describe job requirements for a variety of occupations.

After defining each value measured by the MIQ, the counselor turned to the MIQ report form as shown in Figure 3-3. The individual's responses on the MIQ that measure six values and 20 needs are compared with occupational reinforcer patterns (ORPs) for 90 representative occupations. The individual's rating of the importance of a need is represented by a C index. Thus, individual needs are matched with occupational reinforcers to determine an individual's fit into a work environment. Some examples of occupational reinforcers are achievement, advancement, authority, co-workers, activity, security, social service, social status, and variety. ORPs and occupational ability patterns are given for more than 1,700 careers in the Minnesota Occupational Classification System (Rounds, Henly, Dawis, Lofquist, & Weiss, 1981).

Figure 3-3	Correspondence report for SAMPLE REPORT 06/04/93

The MIQ profile is compared with Occupational Reinforcer Patterns (ORPs) for 90 representative occupations. Correspondence is indicated by the C index. A prediction of *Satisfied (S)* results from C values greater than .49, *Likely Satisfied (L)* for C values between .10 and .49, and *Not Satisfied (N)* for C values less than .10. Occupations are clustered by similarity of Occupational Reinforcer Patterns.

	C Index	Pred. Sat.		C Index	Pred. Sat.
CLUSTER A (ACH-AUT-Alt)	.17	L	Locksmith	.45	L
Architect	.11	L	Maintenance Repairer, Factory	.49	L
Dentist	.11	L	Mechanical-Engineering Technician	.28	L
Family Practitioner (M.D.)	.27	L	Office-Machine Servicer	.69	S
Interior Designer/Decorator	.24	L	Photoengraver (Stripper)	.54	S
Lawyer	.27	L	Sales Agent, Real Estate	.18	L
Minister	.11	L	Salesperson, General Hardware	.35	L
Nurse, Occupational Health	.06	N			
Occupational Therapist	.15	L	CLUSTER E (Com)	.47	L
Optometrist	.33	L	Assembler, Production	.35	L
Psychologist, Counseling	.08	N	Baker	.56	S
Recreation Leader	.02	N	Bookbinder	.58	S
Speech Pathologist	.11	L	Bookkeeper I	.55	S
Teacher, Elementary School	.20	L	Bus Driver	.23	L
Teacher, Secondary School	.25	L	Key-Punch Operator	.49	L
Vocational Evaluator	.06	N	Meat Cutter	.49	L
CLUSTER C (ACH-Aut-Com)	.48	L	Post Office Clerk	.43	L
Alteration Tailor	.46	L	Production Helper (Food)	.47	L
Automobile Mechanic	.43	L	Punch-Press Operator	.44	L
Barber	.31	L	Sales, General (Department Store)	.33	L
Beauty Operator	.23	L	Sewing-Machine Operator (Automatic)	.29	L
Caseworker	.31	L	Solderer (Production Line)	.45	L
Claim Adjuster	.47	L	Telephone Operator	.42	L
Commercial Artist, Illustrator	.51	S	Teller (Banking)	.38	L
Electronics Mechanic	.57	S			

Figure 3-3 (continued)

	C Index	Pred. Sat.		C Index	Pred. Sat.
CLUSTER B (ACN-Com)	.36	L	Farm-Equipment Mechanic I	.73	S
Bricklayer	.29	L	Line-Installer-Repairer (Telephone)	.50	S
Carpenter	.44	L			
Cement Mason	−.03	N	Machinist	.67	S
Elevator Repairer	.74	S	Programmer (Business, Engineering Science)	.55	S
Heavy Equipment Operator	.37	L			
Landscape Gardener	.07	N	Sheet Metal Worker	.63	S
Lather	.11	L	Statistical-Machine Servicer	.72	S
Millwright	.29	L	Writer, Technical Publication	.55	S
Painter/Paperhanger	.41	L			
Patternmaker, Metal	.43	L	CLUSTER F (Alt-Com)	.33	L
Pipefitter	.58	S	Airplane Flight Attendant	.09	N
Plasterer	.07	N	Clerk, General Office, Civil Service	.32	L
Plumber	.40	L			
Roofer	.01	N	Dietitian	.21	L
Salesperson, Automobile	.51	S	Fire Fighter	.33	L
			Librarian	.21	L
CLUSTER D (ACH-STA-Com)	.64	S	Medical Technologist	.39	L
Accountant, Certified Public	.51	S	Nurse, Professional	.13	L
Airplane Co-Pilot, Commercial	.60	S	Orderly	−.01	N
Cook (Hotel-Restaurant)	.57	S	Physical Therapist	.24	L
Department Head, Supermarket	.42	L	Police Officer	.23	L
Drafter, Architectural	.48	L	Receptionist, Civil Service	.27	L
Electrician	.66	S	Secretary (General Office)	.30	L
Engineer, Civil	.35	L	Taxi Driver	−.02	N
Engineer, Time Study	.29	L	Telephone Installer	.44	L
			Waiter-Waitress	.26	L

SOURCE: *Minnesota Importance Questionnaire.* Copyright 1984 Vocational Psychology Research, Department of Psychology, University of Minnesota. Reprinted with permission.

Counselor: On this report form a C value indicates the strength or importance of a need. For example, if a C value is greater than .49 then the occupation is considered satisfying or of value to you. If the C value is between .10 and .49 there is likely to be job satisfaction but if the C value is less than .10 it is likely that there would be no job satisfaction.

Lee: That's interesting. Let me see—I have a high value in Cluster A, achievement and autonomy. What does that mean?

Counselor: Good point! Let's look at the definition of each value we discussed earlier.

After reading the description of the two values, Lee was able to summarize how they could be linked to a work environment.

Lee: This means I would like to work on a job that would give me the opportunity to use my skills and be creative. But how will I know if I have the ability to be a lawyer or an architect?

Counselor: Good question, Lee! After you have developed a list of occupations that interest you, we can compare your ability scores with the requirements of each occupation. As you evaluate each occupation, I will be happy to discuss what you have found and refer you to individuals who work in some of the professions.

During the course of the semester, Lee was very diligent in pursuing some specific interests. She visited the university's prelaw advisor and a local attorney. She also had a conference with a representative from the School of Business and an accountant. Shortly before her sophomore year in college, Lee declared an accounting major. Her overall goal was to attend law school eventually and become a tax attorney.

In Lee's case the client's needs and values became the central focus of discussion, which led to a better understanding of how these factors affect job satisfaction and adjustment. In PEC, job satisfaction is considered a significant variable in determining job involvement and career tenure. The PEF analysis stresses the use of occupational information to assist clients in matching needs and abilities with patterns and levels of different reinforcers in the work environment. As work environments change in the future, more research will be needed to maintain the effectiveness of the MIQ.

For more information on PEF counseling and the MIQ, see Zunker and Osborn (2002), Dawis (1996, 2002), and Sharf (2002).

Developmental Model

The developmental model has been built from the premise that career development is a lifelong process and the career counseling needs of individuals must be met at all stages in life (Healy, 1982; Gelso and Fretz, 2001; Sharf, 2002). The development of goals, learning strategies, and the timing of interventions in this model are guided by Super's (1957, 1990) vocational developmental tasks and stages. The overarching goals are problem identification and developing intervention strategies to overcome them. The developmental model also stresses the necessity of discovering each client's uniqueness of development. This individualized career counseling model by Healy (1982) has four stages:

Stage 1. Establishing Client Individuality
   a. Goals
   b. Obstacles
   c. Assets for Securing Goals
   d. Beliefs About Problem Resolution and Counseling
   e. Action Already Taken
   f. Feelings
   g. Learning Style
   h. Goal Impediments

Stage 2. Identifying and Selecting Strategies

Stage 3. Teaching and Aiding Implementation

Stage 4. Verifying Goal Achievement

Source: From *Career Development: Counseling Through the Life Stages,* by C. C. Healy. Copyright 1982 by Allyn & Bacon, Inc.

Stage 1. Establishing Client Individuality

To measure individuality, client and counselor collaborate on and negotiate the traits that are to be measured. Clients are given instructions about how to self-assess, and this information is used to determine further evaluations (Healy, 1990). Generally, unique traits are considered to be abilities and skills, interests, values, and personality variables. Then, the client's social network and support system are obtained through an interview or by a predetermined list of questions.

The seven diagnostic elements and goal impediments of Stage 1, as summarized in the following list, point out the importance of goal identification in this model.

a. Goals. Goals are considered outcomes of counseling or what the client wants to realize, thus, evaluating the client's uniqueness is essential for the counseling process to be effective. The client's traits and background provide information for identifying and understanding obstacles that could block goal attainment. Counselors are to be aware that clients who express vague statements of outcome goals will need more specific guidelines for appropriate future actions.

b. Obstacles. Obstacles that are barriers to goals are classified as internal or external. Examples of internal barriers are cognitive deficiencies, emotional problems, or lack of motivation. External obstacles include unrealistic choices such as financial return of an occupation that will not meet the client's responsibilities.

c. Assets for Securing Goals. Counselors should be alert to make certain that each client has the potential for attaining goals that might not be apparent to the client. Assisting clients in recognizing their assets and linking them to goals is an important counseling responsibility.

d. Beliefs About Problem Resolution and Counseling. Healy (1982) suggests that cultural contextual experiences greatly influence each client's belief system about how to resolve problems. Thus, the counselor explores each client's background from his or her worldview perspective. The counselor's main objective here is to establish a mutually agreed-on relationship with each client. A cooperative and collaborative effort is considered most conducive to resolving problems.

e. Action Already Taken. Knowledge of the client's past actions to resolve problems provides clues of behavior that were ineffective in problem solutions. Correcting actions and guiding clients toward finding effective solutions reinforces a trusting relationship.

f. Feelings. In this context, feelings are related to how the client reacts to processes needed to realize goal attainment. For example, recognizing the rewards of goal attainment engenders motivation to offset frustrations that could distract the client. Counselors need to communicate a recognition and understanding of both positive and negative feelings that are unique to the client's pursuit of goal achievement.

g. Learning Style. At this point in the counseling process, counselor and client identify an individualized learning style that is primarily based on client assets and limitations as applied to problem resolution. For example, clients who are avid readers will welcome library research, but other clients might learn more effectively through observation, such as job shadowing, or through work experience. Still others may opt for computerized career exploratory programs or pursue a combination of learning styles. In sum, counselor and client negotiate the most effective learning situation to overcome goal impediments.

h. Goal Impediments. Healy (1982) has developed a list of impediments to goal establishment that usually emerge during the counseling process.

Before finalizing Stage 1 of this model, he suggests that client and counselor review the following (in Healy's own words, except explanations in parenthesis):

1. The client has unrealistic or unclear goals.
2. The client has insufficient knowledge, ability, interest, training or resources, to reach goals.
3. The client does not try long or hard enough to succeed.
4. The client has misconceptions about how the system operates. (System refers to work systems and what is required in the give-and-take of the workplace.)
5. The client's goals are thwarted by system defects or obstructions. (Clients need information about unfair employment or promotion policies.)
6. The client is unable to decide and commit to one alternative.
7. The client's problem has been formulated incompletely or inaccurately.
8. Interpersonal conflict.
9. The client's affect is inappropriate for his problem (pp. 181–185). (Counselors should assist clients in recognizing frustrating experiences associated with career decisions that often led to distress. Clients need to admit that they are experiencing problems, and some clients will need self-confidence building exercises that lead them to marshalling assets to overcome adversity. Yet other clients may exhibit excessive emotion that calls for the counselor to introduce methods of reducing anxiety to manageable limits.)

At this point in the model, the counselor screens clients who are likely to have problems as suggested by the seven diagnostic elements and nine goal impediments. Some clients may need to be referred for psychotherapy or further evaluation, whereas others may need prevocational training or additional educational instruction.

Stage 2. Identifying and Selecting Strategies

Stage 2 is devoted primarily to a task analysis of actions designed to overcome identified obstacles. The counseling process could include consultation and clarification of goals; for example, some clients may decide to participate in a training program for writing resumés or in interview competence training.

Stage 3. Teaching and Aiding Implementation

The counselor's major task in Stage 3 is to support the client in implementing strategies developed in Stage 2. The counselor may be directly involved with learning projects or secure and oversee assistance from other professionals. Examples of learning strategies include assertiveness training, discussions with employment specialists, job search training, and networking the hidden job market. See Case Example 3-2.

Stage 4. Verifying Goal Achievement

Stage 4 consists of reviewing the effectiveness of learning strategies; revising strategies is an alternative during this stage. The counselor provides support for the client's efforts for goal achievement. One major objective is to increase client confidence for developing learning strategies that can serve as examples for the future.

In sum, this model stresses client individuality, and the client's unique development is used for establishing goals and subsequent strategies to implement goals. Identifying and clarifying problems and potential problems that could hinder the success of the counseling process is very important. A list of specific impediments to goals is a unique feature of this model. Finally, evaluating the most effective learning path to goal attainment is a process that deserves consideration in all career counseling models.

Case 3-2: Multiple Problems

(This case presents problem identification in a developmental model. Only excerpts are used.)

Lou at age 37 needed assistance in finding an appropriate career. She had been employed in several jobs including waitress and bartender, and she is currently working in a nursing home for the elderly as an aide. While serving time in federal penitentiary for transporting illegal aliens, she enjoyed doing landscaping work. No other preferences for a future vocation were stated.

Lou came from a dysfunctional family. Her parents divorced when she was age 3, and she was placed in a foster home. She dropped out of school at age 15 when she became pregnant. She later received a GED. She has been married on two occasions and claimed incompatibility when divorcing her two husbands. She had no children from her marriages but did have a child out of wedlock when she was 16 years of age. That child, now age 21, is serving time for substance abuse. Lou is currently living alone.

Her developmental history also includes substance abuse. She began drinking alcohol at age 13 and started using drugs at age 15. Currently, she is attending a local AA group every evening and claims to have been drug and alcohol free for 26 months.

Lou was appropriately dressed and her speech was spontaneous, goal directed, and of normal rate and rhythm. She was alert, and recent and remote memory were intact. She is obviously streetwise but less academically oriented.

Recent testing results revealed that Lou was functioning in the average range of intelligence. She was weak in academic subjects, including the basics of reading, spelling, and arithmetic.

Lou was disappointed with herself for her past actions and for her current inability to find direction for a career. She described her current condition as constantly being tempted to drink alcohol or to use drugs. As she put it, "It's a daily fight." She feels lonely and has often considered suicide. She expresses despair for not being able to control her thoughts and find a pathway out of this "jungle" she finds herself in. As she stated, "I don't know which way to turn."

The job she now holds and has held for the past year is very stressful. Lou feels that she can do better and is searching for something more stable. When the counselor asked her to specify an interesting job she was only able to mention landscaping. This time Lou wanted to choose a job that has a future but admitted that she has given little thought to what that job may be.

From this data, the counselor was able to build a client profile using a list of impediments to goal establishment (Healy, 1982).

a. Goals. This client has unclear goals and has not developed any planning for finding a satisfying career. She has relatively little knowledge of work requirements and work environments.

b. Obstacles. A support network is needed for remaining substance abuse free. She needs to learn problem-solving and decision-making skills.

c. Assets for Securing Goals. She is of average intelligence but very weak academically. She currently appears to be motivated to find a career direction.

d. Beliefs About Problem Resolution and Counseling. Lou is unrealistic about the counseling process. She expects to be a passive participant and the counselor is magically going to lead her to the optimal career. She has delayed getting help or putting a plan into action.

e. Action Already Taken. There is evidence of insufficient perseverance. She has not been actively involved in helping herself. This may very well be a matter of numerous personal problems, including substance abuse, that have limited her ability to plan time for career counseling.

f. Feelings. Her thinking tends to be very concrete. She oversimplifies solutions to problems. Currently, she is depressed and in immediate need of a support system.

g. Learning Style. Lou would be best equipped to learn by observing. Job shadowing is recommended. Information processing is weak.

h. Goal Impediment. This client has unclear goals. She has insufficient knowledge of resources to reach goals. She has misconceptions about the counseling process per se, that is, that it requires her active participation. There is evidence of emotional instability, suicide ideation, and interpersonal conflict that is going to require psychotherapy.

The counselor decided to refer Lou for further evaluation by a mental health counselor. He approached this referral very carefully.

Counselor: Lou, you have mentioned on several occasions that you have been troubled with your personal life. Could you tell me more?

Lou: I don't know. I believe that I told you most of it. I just didn't get a good start and before I knew it I was in trouble. Then more trouble came along and I just sort of fell into a trap I couldn't get out of. I guess that I should have gotten more help along the way.

Counselor: If you are really serious about wanting help, I believe I can make some recommendations that could help you.

Lou: Sure, I would like some help.

Counselor: I believe you have some personal problems that could be best taken care of by a colleague of mine while I assist you with finding a career. Although you may be counseling with two different counselors, we will have the same goal of helping you establish a more stable future.

Lou appeared satisfied with the recommendation and agreed to the suggestions from the counselor. Personal counseling required Lou to focus on personal problems, which demanded considerable effort and time on her part. Lou was to continue with personal counseling as needed. She eventually continued with career counseling and was successfully placed on a job in a local factory after completing a prevocational training program in which she was given instructions on appropriate interactions with peer affiliates on a job, budget management, and job interview skill training. The career counselor made it clear that he was available for follow-up visits.

Lou's example of problem identification illustrates information that can be attained from the intake interview and supplemented with assessment data. Information from an intake interview should be viewed by the counselor as material from which one can draw tentative conclusions. Such conclusions should be verified by further assessment or with a client referral to a psychologist. In the developmental model, problem identification is considered a most important stage. Armed with relevant information about the source of problems, counselor and client can negotiate intervention strategies that will assist clients in overcoming persistent crises that lead to vague goal statements and subsequent unproductive counseling.

A Learning Theory of Career Counseling (LTCC)

A most comprehensive approach to career decision making has been carefully delineated by Krumboltz, Mitchell, and Gelatt (1975); Krumboltz and Hamel (1977); Krumboltz and Nichols (1990); Mitchell and Krumboltz (1990, 1996); and Krumboltz (1996). These authors emphasize that each individual's unique learning experiences over the life span are most influential in the career choice process. Therefore, learning is a key ingredient in career counseling and career guidance, suggesting that career counselors' major task is to enhance learning opportunities for clients by using a wide array of effective methods that begin in childhood and endure throughout a lifetime.

The scope of the career counselor's role is viewed as very complex and inclusive—suggesting a number of skills, knowledge, and methods to deal with all career and personal problems that act as barriers to goal attainment. Career counselors may take the role of mentor, coach, or educator and should be prepared to solve unique beliefs that hinder personal development. As Krumboltz (1996) sees it, the counselor as educator provides the environment for clients to develop interests, skills, values, work habits, and many other personal qualities. From this learning perspective, clients can be empowered to take actions that promote the creation of satisfying lives now and in the future. For future reference, counselors help clients identify elements of a satisfying life that could change over time and especially how to adapt to changing circumstances and constantly changing work environments.

In this model, the client is viewed as one who is exploring and experimenting with possibilities and tentative decisions. A client should not be condemned for abandoning a goal in the exploratory process of learning about self, workplaces, and careers. In fact, Krumboltz (1996) strongly suggests that clients do not need to make a career decision for the sake of deciding but, rather, should be encouraged to explore, eliminate, and make tentative tryouts in a learning process that makes progress toward accomplishing their personal goals. Within this perspective, indecision is viewed as what is expected from clients who seek assistance; indecision should not be viewed as a negative diagnosis but as an existing condition of a client who is open to learning and exploration.

In sum, the following practical applications for counselors are paraphrased as follows: (1) Assessment instruments are used to stimulate new learning by identifying needed new skills, cultivating new interests, and developing interpersonal competencies; (2) educational interventions should be increased to provide more opportunities of learning about one's abilities to meet career demands, the demands of the workplace, changing work habits, changing beliefs, and values; (3) success criteria should be based on learning outcomes and not solely on whether a client has made a career decision—the focus is on new behaviors, attempts to learn, and revised thoughts; and (4) counselors should integrate career and personal counseling; learning should focus on personal as well as career issues (Krumboltz, 1996).

The following career counseling model relies heavily on a decision-making model developed by Krumboltz and Sorenson (1974) and has been updated by more recent publications as noted in the beginning of this discussion and by Walsh (1990) and Savickas and Walsh (1996).

Stage 1. Interview
- a. Establish client–counselor relationship.
- b. Have client commit to time needed for counseling.
- c. Reinforce insightful and positive client responses.
- d. Focus on all career problems, family life, environmental influences, emotional instability, career beliefs and obstacles, and traditional career domains of skills, interests, values, and personality.
- e. Help clients formulate tentative goals.

Stage 2. Assessment
- a. Objective assessment instruments are used as a means of providing links to learning interventions.
- b. Subjective assessment attempts to attain the accuracy and coherence of the client's information system, identify client's core goals, and faulty or unrealistic strategies to reach goals.
- c. Beliefs and behaviors that typically cause problems are evaluated by using an inventory designed for this purpose.

Stage 3. Generate Activities
- a. Clients are directed to individualized projects such as taking another assessment instrument, reviewing audiovisual materials, computer programs, or studying occupational literature.

b. Some clients may be directed to individualized counseling programs to address personal problems or lack of cognitive clarity.

Stage 4. Collect Information
a. Intervention strategies are reviewed.
b. Individual goals, including newly developed ones, are discussed.
c. A format for previewing an occupation is presented.
d. Clients commit to information gathering by job-site visit or using job-experience kits.

Stage 5. Share Information and Estimate Consequences
a. Client and counselor discuss information gathered about occupations and together estimate the consequences of choosing each occupation.
b. Counselor evaluates client's difficulty in processing information.
c. Counselor evaluates client's faulty strategies in decision processing.
d. Counselor develops remedial interventions.
e. Clients can be directed to collect more information or recycle within the counseling model before moving to next step.

Stage 6. Reevaluate, Decide Tentatively, or Recycle
a. Client and counselor discuss the possibilities of success in specific kinds of occupations.
b. Counselor provides the stimulus for firming up a decision for further exploration of a career, or changing direction and going back to previous steps in making a decision.

Stage 7. Job Search Strategies
a. Client intervention strategies can include using study materials, learning to do an interview or write a resumé, joining a job club, role playing, or doing simulation exercises designed to teach clients the consequences of making life decisions. Client and counselor reintroduce the concepts of career life planning and, specifically, how the procedures of learning to make a career decision can be used with other major decisions in life.

The following paragraphs summarize and highlight additional information to make this model more user-friendly.

In Stage 1, Interview, client–counselor relationships are established and maintained throughout the counseling process. The client must be allotted the status of collaborator and allowed the freedom and given the encouragement to learn, explore, and experiment. A working partnership may best characterize an appropriate relationship.

Some techniques of interviewing, discussed and illustrated in the next two chapters, can be used as examples for at least partially fulfilling the requirements of an intake interview. Counselors obtain more specific information of client learning experiences and environmental conditions that have significantly influenced the development of task approach skills.

In Stage 2, Assessment, results are used in two ways: (1) to suggest to clients how their preferences and skills match requirements found in educational and occupational environments; and (2) to develop new learning experiences for the client (Krumboltz, 1996).

Using test results as a method of identifying what a client may want to learn for the future encourages clients to identify learning intervention strategies that are needed for occupations of interest. In this context, limited skill development is considered as a temporary state that can be improved to enhance a client's potential for career exploration. Following this logic, criterion-referenced tests that evaluate what a client can or cannot do are more desirable than are norm-referenced tests that reveal what percentage of the population the client exceeds.

Assessment designed to measure interests, values, personality, and career beliefs are also used as points of reference for developing learning. In essence, using assessment results for identifying learning needs to improve career decision making suggests that (1) clients should not only base their decisions on existing capabilities and interests but expand them, and (2) occupational requirements are not expected to remain stable—thus, clients need to prepare for changing work tasks and work environments. Tailored and remedial intervention strategies designed to meet each client's unique needs are most effective (Krumboltz, 1996).

Tentative goals formulated during the intake interview are further evaluated during Stage 3, Generate Activities. Client and counselor determine steps necessary to reach goals. Some clients might want to confirm their goals by taking an interest inventory. Another client might want to evaluate abilities. Yet another client might best be served by personal problem counseling before making a goal commitment. Before completing this stage, clients select two or more occupations to explore.

The major objectives of Stage 4, Collect Information, are to introduce clients to career information resources, their purpose, and use. Client and counselor also develop a format for evaluating occupations. Included in the format are opportunities for advancement, pay scales, worker associates, preparation time for certain occupations, and skills that are required. Clients are assigned individual projects involving career exploration and may be required to job shadow or use job-experience kits.

Client and counselor discuss the information gathered for each occupation evaluated in Stage 5, Share Information and Estimate Consequences. Counselors assist clients in estimating their chances of success in a chosen occupation. During this process, the client is directed to state tentative conclusions, reasons for conclusions, and ideas for further exploration. For example, some clients may be directed to collect more information before conclusions can be reached.

In Stage 6, Reevaluate, Decide Tentatively, or Recycle, client and counselor establish a firmer commitment to career direction. Some clients continue to the next step of job search while others recycle for more information or a change in direction. Counselors maintain the position that clients should not be judged harshly for changing their minds during this process of discovery. Some clients require more time and information before deciding tentatively. Counselors should support clients who make reasonable and realistic requests during this stage.

In the final stage, Job Search Strategies, clients become involved in the usual programs of interview training, preparing a resumé, or joining a job club. However, a unique feature of this model is the emphasis on teaching clients the consequences of making a career decision. Client and counselor reintroduce the concepts of career life planning and, specifically, how the procedures of learning to make a career decision can be used with other major decisions in life.

In an attempt to understand how clients arrive at decisions, counselors view core goals as driving forces underlying an individual's motivation toward certain activities and, as such, goals function as a fundamental sense of self. For example, one who has a core goal "to feel superior" might not be motivated to evaluate certain work environments and subsequently lacks motivation to pursue an agreed-on activity. In this case, the counselor assists the client in defining core goals as underlying reasons for a lack of interest in pursuing certain activities. Some clients might be able to identify emotional highs and lows that are influenced by such core goals as an inclination "to feel free and unbound" or in another case "to feel respected." These goals may be considered potent motives for judging career-related activities as worthwhile. Counselors can assist clients in clarifying and resolving core goals, especially those that influence decision making. This step in the career counseling process is considered a key role of the career counselor (Krumboltz & Nichols, 1990).

Two major goals of this model are to build an understanding of what motivates human behavior and how thought processes and actions influence career development and subsequent career decisions. According to "The Living Systems Framework" (LSF) developed by Ford (1987) and Ford and Ford (1987) as discussed in Krumboltz and Nichols (1990, p. 175),

> the primary and most direct influences on decision making are (a) one's accumulated knowledge about the world and about one's self (information processing and storage); (b) one's entire set of desired and undesired outcomes (directive cognitions); (c) evaluative thought processes that determine what one can or should try to accomplish right now (regulatory evaluations); and (d) thought processes that determine strategies for how to accomplish current objectives and coordinate action (control processes).

This explanation underscores the magnitude of extremely complex systems from cognitive science that are used as guidelines to understand what motivates human behavior and how information about self and environment is processed in decision making. See Case 4-3 for a case involving a reluctant decision maker.

In sum, learning is the key to enhancing self-knowledge. A key focus is to develop a greater sensitivity to the advantages and limitations of environmental experiences that influence career decision making. Using learning intervention strategies to develop skills, interests, and abilities to expand a client's outcome potential is a unique feature of this model. Finally, we must recognize that cognitive functions provide clients with a model of the world and their relationship to it. As clients evaluate changing work environments, they also evaluate their skills, abilities, and other personal qualities to meet their perceptions of what is demanded. In this context, appropriate and realistic information processing is essential.

Case 3-3   The Reluctant Decision Maker

Joe was accompanied to a community counseling center by a friend who was also a career counseling client. Joe needed a great deal of support and encouragement before he agreed to make an appointment. He asked for help to find a better job.

Joe dropped out of high school when he was in the 10th grade to work in a fast-food establishment. He recently completed a high school equivalency course and received a diploma. Now 22, he continues to live with his parents. His father is a factory worker, his mother is a homemaker, and he has four siblings.

The counselor immediately recognized that Joe was very uncomfortable asking for help. He seemed very nervous and restless.

Counselor: Joe, I am pleased to know you (shaking hands). Your buddy here has been telling me about what a nice guy you are and what a good friend you have been.

Joe: Well, ah, thank you. He is a good friend too.

Counselor: It's great to have good friends. This reminds me of when a friend of mine helped me get started in college a few years ago.

The counselor continued to make small talk to help Joe feel more at ease. When it appeared that Joe was more relaxed, the counselor outlined his role as counselor and what is expected of a client during the career counseling process. Joe was receptive to suggestions and agreed to keep his appointments and complete work away from the counseling center that might be assigned during the course of counseling.

During the intake interview the counselor discovered that Joe had taken part in career counseling while in a high school equivalency program.

Joe: Yes, I took several tests before I finished training.

Counselor: Do you recall the kind of tests?

Joe: One was for interests and the other was an aptitude test.

Counselor: Good! What did you decide after going over the results?

Joe: Well, I decided to think about two or three different jobs, but I didn't get anywhere.

Counselor: Explain more fully.

Joe: I thought the counselor was supposed to tell me more about what I should do and what I'm qualified for.

As Joe and the counselor continued their discussion, it became apparent that Joe had some faulty beliefs about career decision making. He evidently thought that someone would decide for him or provide a recipe for choosing a job with little effort on his part. In addition, the counselor suspected that there were some underlying reasons Joe was not taking appropriate actions to solve his problems, but this would have to be confirmed by additional data and observation.

Joe: I just was not able to decide, and I really needed some help.

Counselor: Could you tell me about the kind of help you needed?

Joe: I don't exactly know, but I just couldn't see myself in those jobs. I just don't know about all those jobs. My family makes fun of me when I talk about more school.

Counselor: Tell me more about your family.

Joe: They all work hard. They have labor-type jobs and don't make much money. They want me to do the same kinda thing—just live from one paycheck to another and somehow get by. You know sometimes I think they are right! Maybe I'm not cut out to do any other kind of work.

After further discussion, the counselor was greatly concerned that Joe would not progress very far in the career decision-making process with faulty beliefs such as those he had expressed. The counselor jotted the following notes of a thinking pattern that could inhibit Joe's career development:

- Apparent anxiety about career planning
- Lack of flexibility in decision making
- Lack of willingness to consider a variety of occupations
- Faulty beliefs about career decision making and occupational environments
- Lack of family support
- Limited career choices from salient messages in the environment

Counselor: Joe, we can help you make a career decision, but first we both should learn more about your career beliefs. Would you be interested in taking an inventory that would help us understand more about your beliefs and your assumptions about careers?

Joe: Sure, I guess so, but I don't understand how it will help me.

Counselor: Let me explain how we will use the results. We can find out about some of the factors that influence your decisions, what may be necessary to make you feel happy about your future, and changes you are willing to make. Discussing these subjects should help in clarifying your role and my role in the career decision-making process.

The results of the *Career Beliefs Inventory* (CBI) (Krumboltz, 1988) described in Chapter 6, not surprisingly, indicated low scores on several scales, especially on acceptance of uncertainty and on openness. Low scores on these scales indicate that excessive anxiety can lead to viewing career decision making as overwhelming, and Joe's scores also suggested that he had fears about the reactions of others. The counselor felt more certain about his tentative conclusions from the intake interview. In the next session with Joe, and following a review of the purposes of the inventory and its scores, the following exchange took place:

Counselor: Joe, could you tell me the reasons you are uncertain about your career plans?

Joe: Nobody in my family has ever had much schooling. I guess it's not in me to go for more education or training.

Counselor: So you believe that you cannot be successful in higher education because your family has not?

Joe: Yes, I believe that's true.

Counselor: Could you tell me why you feel this way?

Joe: They don't think I can do it.

Counselor: What kind of grades did you make in the high school equivalency courses?

Joe: I made good grades—above C in every course and I got two As.

Counselor: What does this tell you about your ability to do academic work?

Joe: OK, I guess I was successful then, but that does not mean I could do the same in college.

Counselor: You are absolutely right. There are no guarantees, but we have known for a long time that past academic performance is a good indicator of future performance in school.

Joe: But my brother and mom keep telling me that we aren't the kind to go to college.

Counselor: If I provide you with information about your chances of making a C or better in community college, would you be willing to talk with your family about options you are considering for the future?

Joe: Well, I guess so.

Each of the scales with low scores was discussed in a similar manner, that is, faulty beliefs were identified, followed by specific plans of actions. The counselor continued to confront Joe with facts about individuals who were the first in their family to complete a college degree and stressed that he must arrive at a decision based on his own desires and potential.

The counselor and Joe agreed that he should take an achievement test to determine his academic deficiencies. Their plan was to have Joe improve his skills as a means of improving his chances of being a successful college student. In the next four months Joe spent a considerable part of his spare time in studying and being tutored to improve basic academic skills. He also gained a great deal of confidence by being involved in such a project. A follow-up test boosted Joe's confidence when he discovered that he had shown significant academic progress.

The counselor and Joe met on a regular basis to discuss his interests and to change his faulty beliefs. The counselor met with less resistance from Joe as he became more comfortable in the college environment. Finally, Joe convinced his parents to visit with the counselor about his future plans. To everyone's surprise, especially Joe's, they agreed to let Joe "give it a try for a semester."

Joe and the counselor agreed that they would delay making a firm career commitment at this time. They both felt that Joe should be open to look at several options as he progressed in college.

In this case, the CBI provided the stimulus for discussing relevant career problems that inhibited Joe from making choices in his best interests. Faulty beliefs are to be challenged in learning theory counseling. Clients are to be empowered to discover their abilities and improve them as well as to explore various options before making a firm career commitment. Learning to improve his skills gave Joe confidence in his ability to perform at a college level.

Source: Adapted from Zunker and Osborn (2002).

Cognitive Information Processing (CIP) Model

Peterson, Sampson, Reardon, and Lenz (1996) have proposed a seven-step sequence for career delivery service as shown in Chapter 2, Figure 2-3. This sequence can be used as a delivery option for both problem solving and decision making and can be used for individual, group, self-directed, and curricular programs.

This model is an extension of a career development theory, a cognitive information-processing approach to career problem solving and decision making, developed by the same authors and introduced in Chapter 2. This unusual approach of illustrating and carefully describing how a theory can be applied to career counseling should be placed on the practitioner's list of events to celebrate.

A CIP approach to career development and its application to career counseling requires an in-depth understanding of cognitive information process theory. I strongly encourage you to read the original source for more information. This brief introduction to evaluating career information problems within a cognitive processing model should be considered a starting point only for understanding this theory's application to an individual career counseling model.

Information processing for career decision making is conceptualized within this model as a hierarchical system from a base of Knowledge Domains (self-knowledge and occupational knowledge) to a Decision Skills Domain, and finally to an Executive Processing Domain, as shown in Figure 3-4.

In the Knowledge Domain, self-knowledge is related to one's interests, abilities, and values whereas occupational knowledge consists of an individual's view of individual occupations and structural relations between occupations.

The Decision Skills Domain consists of five stages referred to as the CASVE cycle. The acronym CASVE consists of Communication (problem perceived as a gap); Analysis (problem is reduced to components); Synthesis (problem is restructured by creating alternatives); Valuing (problem solutions are evaluated by valuing alternatives); and Execution (problem solutions are accomplished by formulating strategies).

The Executive Processing Domain consists of skills of initiating, coordinating, storing, and retrieving information. These skills are considered to be metacognitions that are used in problem solving and by self-talk, increased self-awareness, and control. Briefly, self-talk ("I think I can be a good engineer") creates expectations and reinforces behavior. Self-awareness influences decision making, in this context, by serving as a balance between individual goals and the goals of important others. Control refers to one's ability to control impulsive actions in the career decision process.

Combining this very brief introduction to cognitive information processing with the material presented in Chapter 2, a career counseling model in a seven-step sequence follows in a paraphrased format (Peterson, Sampson, Reardon, & Lenz, 1996, pp. 450–457):

Step 1: Initial interview. The major purpose of the interview is twofold. The counselor seeks information about the client's career problems and establishes a trusting

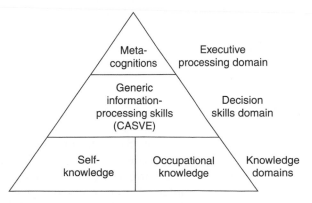

Figure 3.4   Pyramid of information-processing domains

Source: From *Career Development and Services: A Cognitive Approach,* by G. Peterson, J. Sampson, and E. Reardon, p. 28. Copyright © 1991. Reprinted with permission of Brooks/Cole Publishing Company, a part of The Thomson Corporation.

relationship. More specifically, the counselor attends to both the emotional and cognitive components of the client's problems. The counselor recognizes that an effective relationship enhances client self-efficacy and fosters learning.

Step 2: Preliminary assessment. To determine the client's readiness for problem solving and decision making, the Career Thoughts Inventory (Sampson et al., 1996a) is administered. This inventory is used both as a screening assessment and as a needs assessment; as such, it will identify clients who could experience difficulty in the career choice process as a result of dysfunctional thinking.

Step 3: Define problem and analyze causes. In this step, the counselor and the client agree on a preliminary understanding of the client's problem(s). For example, the problem may be defined as a "gap" between the state of the client's indecision and the ideal state of "career decidedness." A word of caution: The client's problem should be explained and stated in neutral, rather than in judgmental, terms.

Step 4: Formulate goals. Formulating goals is a collaborative effort between counselor and client. Goals are put in writing on an individual learning plan (ILP), as shown in Figure 3-5.

Step 5: Develop individual learning plan. Again, the counselor and the client collaborate when developing the ILP, which provides a sequence of resources and activities that will assist the client in meeting goals established earlier. These are very evident on the written ILP. The ILP also serves as a contract between client and counselor.

Step 6: Execute individual learning plan. This step requires that the client take the initiative in proceeding with the agreed-on plan. The counselor encourages and directs the progress and may provide more information, clarification, or reinforcement of the client's progress and may offer planning for future experiences. With dysfunctional clients, a workbook is used as a supplement to learning about the results of the *Career Thoughts Inventory* administered in Step 2. This workbook, entitled *Improving Your Career Thoughts: A Workbook for the* Career Thoughts Inventory (Sampson, Petersen, Lenz, Reardon, & Saunders, 1996b) is used for cognitive restructuring, within which the client uses a four-step procedure (identify, challenge, alter, and take action).

Selected strategies for enhancing career problem solving and decision making are summarized as follows: for discovering self, trace the development of your interests, write an autobiography, and prepare a vocational history; for life experiences, write a description in the third person and analyze emergent themes; for linking measured interests to past experiences, take an interest inventory and relate the results to real-life events.

Step 7: Summative review and generalization. Progress in solving the gap that might have motivated the client to seek counseling is perceived in this last step. A determination is also made about how effective the progress has been in following through with the ILP. The focus through all steps is on the client's career decision-making status. Finally, the lessons learned within the preceding six steps are generalized as skills learned to solve future career and personal problems.

In the initial interview, the counselor's goal is to analyze the characteristics of each client's problem according to a gap, ambiguous cues, interacting courses of action, unpredictability of courses of action, and new problems. Gap is used here to describe a career problem of dissonance between what actually exists and what the client feels should exist. For example, a low-paying job with minimal responsibilities is quite different from the client's mental image of an ideal situation of higher pay,

Individual Learning Plan

Career Resource Center
Central Community College—110 Social Science Building

Goal(s) 1. Understand personal barriers to decision making.

2. Clarify self-knowledge and occupational knowledge.

3. Improve decision-making skills.

4. _____

Goal	Priority	Activity	Purpose/Outcome
1, 2 & 3	1	Individual Counseling	Clarify issues and obtain information
1	2	Modules EP∅ and EP2 and cognitive exercise	Explore Self-Talk
1	3	Monitor thoughts related to a real decision	Monitor Self-Talk
3	4	Module IP∅	Clarify decision-making knowledge
2	5	OCC-U-SORT & Module SK∅	Self knowledge and generate options
2	6	SDS:CV	" "
2	7	Written summary of self-knowledge	" "
2	8	Career key & module OK∅	Identify resources & obtain occ. info.
2	9	CHOICES	Narrow options
2	10	Video tapes, information interviews and shadowing	" "
2	11	Print Materials	" "

Joe Williams   _Marilyn Abley_   _3/12/90_
Client   Career Counselor   Date

Figure 3.5   **Individual learning plan**

Source: From *Career Development and Services: A Cognitive Approach,* by G. Peterson, J. Sampson, and E. Reardon, p. 28. Copyright © 1991. Reprinted with permission of Brooks/Cole, a part of The Thomson Corporation.

higher status, and independence. Recognizing a gap in this manner provides viable information for problem identification and subsequent goal development.

Ambiguous cues are clues the counselor and client can use to understand sources of problems or the underlying reasons for certain behavior patterns. For instance, a client might be experiencing extreme anxiety when faced with a situation in which competing cues are difficult to resolve. A client who might be searching for a stable job that is secure could also be struggling with a desire to be in a position of risk that provides the opportunity of becoming wealthy. In such situations, personal desires and motives or internal drives that are in conflict can be sources of anxiety. Sources of anxiety can also emerge from situational conditions or external factors. Identifying sources of anxiety is a major step toward resolving conflicting ambiguous cues.

Interacting courses of action and uncertainty of outcome also affect decision making and problem solving. For instance, a client might decide to pursue a nursing career and identify requirements, but while doing so might also explore an unrelated career. In this case, this client might lack the confidence to proceed on her own and could need more information about personal traits and career information. Counselors assist clients in identifying actions and elements of actions that provide clues to solving problems. Moreover, the uncertainty of outcome is a major barrier for clients who lack self-confidence to advance on their own. Some issues might be external, such as the lack of financial means for higher education. Another client might be directed toward self-talk or be given support and reinforced by discussing unique assets. Cognitive problems that are identified as dysfunctional are directed toward interventions that replace dualistic thinking with relative thinking, methods of developing self-control strategies, and acquiring effective methods of problem solving.

In addition to uncertainty of outcome, new problems arise during the course of decision making, and they are viewed as sets of subordinate problems. For example, should a decided client seek a low entry position or go through training for a higher-level job? Another client might be searching for which university provides the best program that is affordable. The point here is that subordinate problems can tend to discourage clients who foresee insurmountable barriers to reaching their goals. The uncertainty of outcome and new problems are critical issues at critical stages in a counseling model; the counselor must be prepared to support the client and offer solutions that are discovered in a collaborative relationship between counselor and client.

The next step in the outline, preliminary assessment, is basically a screening and needs assessment procedure. An inventory that can be used for problem identification in the screening process is *My Vocational Situation* (Holland, Daiger, & Power, 1980). This instrument provides scores for vocational identity, need for information, and perceived barriers to occupational choice. Other instruments that measure career maturity, indecision, career beliefs, career decision-making style, and occupational certainty also can be used in the preliminary assessment step.

Defining problems and analyzing causes (Step 3) requires counselor and client to identify probable causes of gaps and subsequent problems. For example, a client who cannot make a decision between two plausible choices might need individual counseling to clarify life roles or other important unique issues. Collaborative interaction between client and counselor is an important relationship that fosters problem identification and, by this process, provides for client agreement and understanding of probable causes.

The formulation of goals (Step 4) follows with continued collaboration for careful detailing of each goal. An active client role reduces the likelihood of misunderstandings and confusion about the sequence of the counseling process.

Client and counselor develop an ILP (Step 5) for each counseling goal, followed by an intervention activity. Learning activities included in the ILP can also be instructional modules (see Zunker, 1998) that contain objectives, self-administered diagnostic tests, alternative learning activities, and a self-administered summary assessment.

In Step 6, execute an ILP, several practical suggestions are given in the outline, including self-talk. Self-talk comments are viewed as self-efficacy beliefs (Bandura, 1989), thus, both negative and positive statements made by clients are discussed with each client. Positive statements are used to reinforce client's actions, and negative statements are considered self-deprecating and should be fully evaluated.

Finally, Step 7, summative review and generalizations, focuses on learned skills that can be used in problem solving and career-making decisions in the future. A review of all steps reinforces client progress and enhances learned experiences.

This model and its theory attempt to answer some important questions about problem solving and the career decision-making process. This career counseling model is basically a learning model built around CIP theory. In applying this theory to a career counseling model, the authors have developed a sound system of steps that are clearly delineated for the practitioner. An ILP is a unique element of this model, which also has a variety of intervention modules. A career counseling case that illustrates some elements of this model is presented in Case 3-4.

Case 3-4　A Lot of Bravado

(This case was recorded by a counselor in the first person. Excerpts from the case are used as an example of one of the important stages in the CIP model.)

When Pat walked in the counseling center he impressed the secretary as someone who has to be very important. Pat had a swagger to his walk that gave the impression of one who is most confident, considers himself attractive, and has got the world by the tail. He didn't ask for a counselor, he wanted to see the director or the "person who is in charge." The secretary did not question Pat's motives but meekly showed him the way to my office.

He quickly made his entry and almost cracked my knuckles while shaking hands. I am sure they could hear him clearly in the adjoining rooms as his first comments went something like this, "Howdy!! My name is Pat. I came to see you today for a little help."

As Pat and I got to know more about each other during our early conversations, he stated that he wanted help in "picking out a good job" and agreed to proceed with career counseling as it was outlined. Pat grew up on a ranch in west Texas that his father managed for a wealthy oil man. In the area where Pat grew up there were extremely large ranches, and many of them contained significant oil and gas deposits. As Pat put it, the people there were "friendly and down home." Pat felt his parents were very supportive of him and it was understood that he would attend college. He had two younger siblings. Pat was now a first-semester freshman. His grades in high school were slightly above average. But he explained that he had to ride the school bus for considerable periods of time because his home was 30 miles from the school. When he got home he had to help his father, which left little time for studying.

After further discussion that was not very productive because of Pat's bravado and guarded comments, we agreed that he should write an autobiography of his life and include his perception of a career goal, his experiences at home, school, and work, and hobbies and interests.

Counselor: I have learned a great deal about your background from our discussion, but I believe it would benefit both of us if you would be willing to write about some events in your life.

Pat: Yes, sir, that might help to get everything down 'cause you see that I like to talk a lot and skip around.

Counselor: I do enjoy hearing about your experiences on such a large ranch. We don't have a lot of students who come in here with a similar background. But we are meeting to help you, and this might be a way to get started.

Pat dropped off his autobiography at the designated time of five days. As I read the autobiography I could not help observing that this was a different Pat than I met only a few days ago. There seemed to be a private Pat who is reflected in his autobiography and a public Pat who you get when you meet face-to-face. Of course I realized we all have our public and private self-concepts, but Pat's behavior appeared to be overcompensating for some reason. The Pat who wrote expressed himself as an individual who is in search of a future that was realistic. He expressed interest in jobs that he evidently observed in his environment, such as geologist, petroleum engineer, and businessman. Yet he admitted he was uncertain about a career choice. Conversely, when he spoke about possible occupations in the counseling center, he mentioned professor so he could drive a Mercedes and stockbroker so he could be rich. Beside being unrealistic about a professor's salary, his statements reflected a naïveté about occupations per se.

The gap between perceived income and actual income had to be resolved before Pat could make appropriate career decisions. In essence, Pat needed to learn more about occupations and options. But what seemed to be the most pressing matter was to discover the sources of anxiety that Pat was currently experiencing.

During the next counseling session when discussing the autobiography, Pat appeared to be very anxious. It appeared that he was experiencing ambiguous cues such as wanting a lot of money regardless of risk but also wanting a secure job that would give him "time to take care of the livestock."

Counselor: I have an inventory that might help us clarify your needs and help you make some decisions. It only takes a few minutes.

Pat: That sounds good to me—let's get started.

Counselor: The inventory is the *Career Thoughts Inventory* (CTI) (Sampson, Peterson, Lenz, Reardon, & Saunders, 1996a). It will give us scores about decision-making problems, anxiety, and conflicts you may have.

Pat scored high on the scale that measures commitment anxiety, and the counselor explained his score as follows:

Counselor: Your high score on this scale may mean that you are having difficulty committing to a career option because you may be afraid of what might happen when you do make a decision.

Pat: I'll have to think about that but it might just be true. To tell the truth I don't really know what I want to do. I suppose that if I decide now it might be wrong and I would be wasting my time and my parents' money.

I informed Pat that many students are undecided about their future and that is understandable, but it is most important to put forth the effort to create some options during the first year in college. This was the first time I met the private Pat face-to-face—he was actually a down-to-earth person struggling to determine an optimal career.

Counselor: Pat, I have met with many students over the years who have struggled to find a career choice. We can help you do that, and I must add that you have made a sincere effort to help yourself and that is most important!

Pat: Thank you. I can really use some help.

Pat and the counselor negotiated an ILP similar to the one displayed in Figure 3-5. Pat was to filter out barriers to decision making and to learn more about himself and about occupations. He was to improve his decision-making skills. This plan involved individual counseling and self-talk to improve his self-esteem and debunk negative thoughts. He was to identify resources for occupational information and use a computer program to narrow his career options. He would be offered training in information interviews that are designed to assist clients in learning about workplaces, and he would be able to do job shadowing to learn more about the give-and-take of specific occupations.

Pat continued to visit with me while reporting his progress with the ILP. We discussed options and the feasibility of choices. Pat's sophistication in career exploration improved significantly as we were able to tease out the sources of his anxiety and point out his assets. Pat's self-talk continued to be monitored to make certain that he concentrated on positive thoughts. It was noticed that he began to walk with that "peacock swagger" again, but this time it was a different Pat—he had a realistic reason for being proud of his progress in college and in the career choice process.

Pat kept in touch after he graduated from college. He married a woman from another state and moved close to the Canadian border where they also have large ranches. He once wrote that he continues to use his business major and information he learned from animal husbandry courses on a ranch that will "all be mine someday where I can take care of the livestock."

In sum, the counselor assisted Pat in closing the gap between reality and what he perceived about some professions that was incorrect. Most important, Pat learned to know more about himself and the anxiety that he had experienced from a lack of confidence that he attempted to mask and deny. A carefully thought-out ILP focused on how to assist Pat make appropriate career decisions and solve personal problems.

The Multicultural Connection

A growing awareness among practitioners of demographics that predicts a more racially and ethnically diverse workforce strongly reinforces the need for modifying career counseling models. Research that addresses the career counseling needs of multicultural groups is in its infancy, although there have been significant increases in numbers of publications that focus on multicultural issues in career counseling (Arbona, 1996). What the practitioner needs is more scientifically rigorous research aimed at providing fully defined career counseling techniques, procedures, and materials for an increasing number of ethnically diverse workers. The research needs of career counseling practice already comprise an extensive list of variables, however, and with the additional dimensions of multicultural domains, we will probably experience a lengthy, time-consuming process. In the meantime, career counselors should carefully evaluate their competencies for multicultural counseling.

A Multicultural Career Counseling Model for Ethnic Women

An introduction to steps or stages in a multicultural model for ethnic women by Bingham and Ward (1996) provides a means of comparing techniques designed to identify specific needs of a special group of clients and the methods and materials used in the counseling process. This model focuses on contextual elements of influence and recognizes that salient racial factors were not a part of theoretical conceptualizations of most of the career development theories discussed in the two preceding chapters. Theories, however, cannot directly guide specific counseling processes at a microlevel that is necessary to meet the special needs of special groups; the development of minitheories may be necessary (Herr, 1996). The potential changes in career counseling models are a clear message to counselors that a lifetime of learning is not only necessary for clients but also for counselors.

This model is presented with the recognition that background issues in multicultural counseling have not been discussed. Chapter 10 is devoted to multicultural counseling and should be considered as an introduction to a vast amount of published material on this subject. However, Bingham's and Ward's model emphasizes contextual factors that limit career choice and stereotypes that hinder career development and introduces counselors to racial identity as a significant variable in client–counselor relationships. These unique features and others are not emphasized in the career counseling models that were developed from career development theories described in the two preceding chapters.

The following are the steps in the multicultural career counseling model for ethnic women developed by Bingham and Ward (1996):

Step 1. Establish Rapport and Culturally Appropriate Relationships

Step 2. Identify Career Issues

Step 3. Assess Impact of Cultural Variables

Step 4. Set Counseling Goals

Step 5. Make Culturally Appropriate Counseling Interventions

Step 6. Make Decision

Step 7. Implement and Follow-Up

Bingham and Ward strongly suggest that counselors are to prepare for clients by using a self-administered *Multicultural Career Counseling Checklist* (MCCC) (Ward & Bingham, 1993) as displayed in Appendix B. The first section of this instrument assesses the counselors' preparation for counseling a culturally different client by identifying both counselor's and client's racial/ethnic backgrounds. The other sections of this instrument concern the counseling process of exploration and assessment and establishing a negotiating and working consensus.

Also in the precounseling phase, the client is administered a *Career Counseling Checklist* (CCC) (Ward & Tate, 1990) displayed in Appendix C. This instrument contains 42 statements that measure such factors as knowledge of the world of work, gender issues, role of family in the decision process, and client's concerns about choosing an occupation.

A Decision Tree (Ward & Bingham, 1993) is a schematic, as displayed in Appendix D, that provides counseling decision points and pathways. One major decision point determines if the client is to be referred for psychological or personal counseling before obtaining career counseling.

A brief explanation of each step in the career counseling model follows:

Step 1: Establish Rapport and Culturally Appropriate Relationships

Client–counselor relationships are considered to be most important in all career counseling models, but especially in this model. When clients feel free to express themselves in a counseling relationship, they can be excellent teachers as cultural informants, provided the counselor makes it clear that discussions of ethnic/racial information is welcome. Trust and collaboration are key factors in a counseling relationship, particularly when client and counselor are from different ethnic group backgrounds.

Counselors must be aware of various specific cultural cues such as nonverbal actions and reactions of the client. For example, some clients may not consider it appropriate to maintain eye contact during counseling; the counselor's reciprocal behavior will enhance the relationship. Counselors should use as much time as necessary to establish a collaborative relationship with a client who has a different worldview than that of the counselor.

Ivey and Ivey (2003) suggest that a counseling relationship should be built on trust that will usually take the entire initial counseling session to develop. Counselors should relay empathy to their clients. Listening to and observing clients is one way to determine how the counselor should respond and to set the context of the working relationship. Counselors should ask clients to clarify some of their comments to demonstrate interest in their thoughts and gain a more adequate understanding of their constructs.

Step 2: Identify Career Issues

Sue and Sue (1990) suggest that a counselor's understanding of the client's worldview issues will facilitate an understanding of barriers that could impede career decision making. Ethnic minority clients who have experienced discrimination, for example, might feel that they cannot overcome the barriers that have conditioned them to limit career choice.

Although ethnic minority clients can experience a sense of responsibility for career identification, they must also be guided to realize that past and present internal and external barriers have in some way influenced their career decisions. Quite possibly, ethnic minority clients have limited experiences with other ethnic social groups and view others as being unreceptive to them. Counselors should realize that cultural groups often share a common set of experiences of oppression that can collectively limit their perspectives of future opportunities.

One major goal of this step is to assist clients in identifying those experiences that limit career choices. A good example is a client who suggests that her gender has limited her future opportunities. She could be reflecting the social mores of her ethnicity in which women are restricted from working outside the home. Yet another client who is looking for a job might be focused on taking care of immediate financial needs rather than searching for a career. This client has been forced to concentrate on short-term goals.

Salient messages received by clients from contextual interaction can cause some ethnic minority clients to circumscribe choices for what is considered an appropriate job. Some clients limit their choices without being fully aware of it. Moreover, ethnic minority groups that have developed worldviews that limit career choices present new and different challenges for career counseling.

Step 3: Assess Impact of Cultural Variables

In this step, counselors identify cultural variables that have the most limiting influence on career choices. This process can be very time-consuming, yet productive, when clients recognize the importance of understanding how their family environment, religion, and cultural history, for example, have shaped their prospects for the future. Counselors need to isolate unique cultural variables that need further delineation in culturally appropriate intervention strategies.

A good example to illustrate the problems associated with this stage is the influence of family on many ethnic minorities. If you ask a Native American how her family is doing, she might respond by telling you how the entire village is attempting to solve their problems. Family for Native Americans is an extended family, which among some tribes means an entire village (Ivey & Ivey, 2003). For other ethnic groups, the extended family can include parents, siblings, grandparents, aunts and uncles, and even godfather. Thus, the influence from family among ethnic minorities, especially first-generation ones, can be very extensive and inclusive. Clients are often in conflict when attempting to decide between what they want to pursue and what their families see as appropriate.

Another related issue is how decisions are made in some ethnic groups. In this country, the rugged individual takes charge of his own destiny and independently determines its course. We as a society have endorsed the individualistic mode of operation within which the individual is empowered to make decisions. In many ethnic minority groups, the opposite is true; collective decision making among family members is considered more appropriate. A friend who grew up in Puerto Rico explained that he consulted his father in all major decisions by telephone from wherever he lived, which included several countries in South America. He had been conditioned that this was the proper way to make a decision. Thus, counselors who include the family in the decision-making process recognize client's needs.

Step 4: Set Counseling Goals

Goal setting is to be a collaborative negotiation between client and counselor. This process encourages clients to be more active in pursuing satisfactory outcomes. A collaborative counseling relationship is especially important for ethnic minority clients. Some ethnic minority clients assume that they are to be passive participants, leaving all decisions to the counselor. In this context, clients are reluctant to share their true feelings and experiences and are uncomfortable being actively involved in the entire career counseling process. Counselors should inform clients that it is proper and acceptable to negotiate activities throughout the counseling process.

Leong (1993) suggests that pragmatic goals are more appropriate for ethnic minority groups than are goals based on self-actualization. The point here seems to be that clients who are more collective oriented, that is, placing family before self, might be more concerned about how a career benefits the family. Also, clients might need immediate placement in a job to support their needs and plan to consider long-term goals in the future. Even though circumstances may determine goal direction, counselors and clients who confer on outcome goals within a relationship that has established trust and respect for each other have the better chance of agreeing on appropriate goals.

Step 5: Make Culturally Appropriate Interventions

Individual needs determine appropriate interventions for members of multicultural groups. For some ethnic minorities, however, family approval and involvement in developing and delivering intervention strategies are recommended. In these cases individuals turn to the family for approval before feeling free to fully involve themselves. Counselors will find that it is very productive to fully investigate which members of the family are empowered to make major decisions.

Group interventions are also considered as very productive for some cultural groups. For example, clients who are struggling to learn English may be served best by group interventions that use the client's native language. In some cases, interpreters may be used to facilitate groups. Groups might be more effective when composed of the same racial group, biracial group, ethnic gender group, and community members.

Bingham and Ward point out counseling interventions may require several sessions because many ethnic minority groups take considerable time to complete an agenda. Finally, if an inventory is used during the course of an intervention strategy, it must be appropriate for the client's racial/ethnic group. (See Chapters 6 and 7.)

Step 6: Make Decision

An important suggestion in this step involves continuing monitoring of the decision process to make certain that the client is free from all barriers to goals. Some barriers can be difficult to remove, and some clients will make a decision mainly to please the counselor. Clients must be invited to recycle in this model without a sense of embarrassment; in fact, a review of the model steps can suggest to the client that it is a legitimate request to continue counseling.

Step 7: Implement and Follow-Up

At this point, clients are usually referred to information resources, individual contacts, or agencies for assistance. Counselors monitor clients' progress and invite them to return for counseling in the future.

The following recommendations for the multicultural career counseling process as suggested by Bingham and Ward (1996) summarize this model:

1. The counselor should be aware of a variety of worldviews.
2. The counselor's preparation for multicultural counseling should be directed by recommendations of Sue, Arredondo, and McDavis (1992).

3. The counselor should fully understand his or her racial identity.
4. The counselor–client relationship should be a collaborative one, that is, a negotiating and working consensus is recommended.
5. The role of the family in the decision-making and counseling process should be emphasized.
6. Worldview, history of client, local sociopolitical issues, and stereotypes should be fully discussed.
7. The influence of racial/ethnic factors that limit career choices should be discussed.
8. Nontraditional interventions such as conversing in groups in the client's native language, using interpreters, and involving community members who can offer insight and direction should be used. Encourage clients to join a biracial network.
9. Client–counselor process should be evaluated continually during counseling and after counseling is terminated.
10. An extensive follow-up should be done and counseling recycled if necessary.

Case 3-5 illustrates the use of the *Career Counseling Checklist* with a Hispanic senior high school student who currently resides in a small town in Texas. Experiencing conflicts between his former culture and the dominant culture, he asks for help from a career counselor. This case illustrates a few examples of the problems faced by individuals from a different culture who want to become working American citizens.

Case 3-5   Questionable Future Status

Carlos wanted to go to college but was unsure of his future status as a citizen. He came from the interior of Mexico at age 8 to join his mother, who had left him for one year with his grandmother while she found a place for them to live in the United States. She married a U.S. citizen and has now established a home. For the first two years of school, Carlos was placed in a bilingual program. Once he learned the English language, he was able to make very good progress in school. He graduated from high school in the top quarter of his class and had made mainly As and Bs on most subjects. His favorite subject was precalculus and his least favorite was economics. He belonged to French and Spanish clubs as well as to a high school spirit club.

Carlos reported that both Spanish and English are spoken in his home. He prefers English and uses it more than his mother does. He and his family belong to the Catholic Church. Carlos does not care to go to Mexico because, as he put it, "of the corruption there." The family celebrates the traditional holidays but relate more to respecting their ancestors on Halloween than is the custom here.

Carlos is now 18 years of age and is working full-time at a mailing service company. He claims to identify more as an American than as a Mexican and plans to make his home permanently in this country. Carlos spoke excellent English and expressed himself very well. It was apparent that he had assimilated many of the dominant culture's social values, but he also had retained many values from his own culture.

Carlos had asked for career counseling because he was not sure about his dream career and needed more information about it and wanted to know which nearby university offered degrees in photography or in how to produce and direct films. He told the counselor that he was interested in photography and the film-making industry because he had worked on some productions at his high school. He would very much like to become a film editor or a producer. The counselor told Carlos that he could be of help but wanted to begin counseling with a *Career Counseling Checklist.*

After Carlos completed the checklist, they discussed their different worldviews and specific items as a way of establishing rapport (Step 1). They agreed to a collaborative working relationship.

Carlos checked several items on the checklist that were thoroughly discussed (Step 2. Identify Career Issues) as follows:

Counselor: I noticed that you checked item 14. "My ethnicity may influence my career choice." Could you tell me more about this item?

Carlos: What I was thinking is that people might not think I can do the kind of work I want to do.

Counselor: Explain more fully.

Carlos: Well, you know how the Mexican man is supposed to work—or not to work hard.

Counselor: You feel others may judge you this way?

Carlos: Yes! But I will work hard at any job if I am given the chance.

Counselor: You are really worried about getting the opportunity to prove yourself. Is that right?

Carlos: Yes, I believe that a lot of Americans will think I can't do it!

Counselor: To an extent, that is a realistic appraisal of what could happen. But on a more positive note, more and more minorities are moving into other than labor-type jobs. I would rather you think of it as a golden opportunity right now to choose the job that you are interested in and pursue it using your best abilities.

Carlos: That is what I want to do and if I am given the chance, I can prove myself.

Counselor: That is a good start, but let us try to remove the negative feelings you still have about getting an equal opportunity in the future.

Counselor and client continued their discussion and during the next session Carlos revealed that part of his worry about the future was that he must try to remain close to his mother. He was afraid that he would be required to move to another location for an education and much farther away from her later to fulfill his dream of being in the film industry.

As they continued their discussion, the counselor identified several career issues, including the following:

- Fear of being stereotyped as an individual who was only capable of doing menial jobs, thus not given consideration for jobs involving creativity and responsibility.
- Fear that family responsibilities would limit his career ambitions.
- Fear that his immigration status would not be taken care of appropriately, or that he might have problems becoming a citizen.

The counselor concluded that Carlos had also evaluated his current situation in a fairly realistic manner. However, it was obvious that he needed more support from his family to fulfill his ambitions. For example, it was clear that his mother did not want him to move far from her, and as a result there was evidence of serious conflicts before he even launched his career journey. Even though Carlos expressed confidence, he was also doubtful about his future that included taking a calculated risk in an environment that has not always been affirmative and friendly to minorities and pursuing a career that was unknown to the family. Carlos stated that he also wanted to remain near his family for consultation on major decisions in the future.

The counselor and Carlos negotiated three goals for the time being: Carlos would (1) gather information about university programs, admission requirements, and financial aid; (2) gather information about related careers in film editing, production, and photography and probable locations of opportunities; and (3) arrange a meeting with his parents and counselor to discuss the information he had gathered.

The counselor made certain that both parents could speak and understand English. The first meeting was a difficult one. It was clear that Carlos's parents were not sure they could trust another "Gringo," but the counselor was prepared to make them as comfortable as possible by introducing a friend who was a highly respected individual in the Mexican-American community. The friend put in a good word for the counselor and made his exit. This ally tremendously helped get the first session going with some sense of trust.

Another ally was used in the second session to explain that her daughter was now attending a university in another state and she was most proud of her. Some of the conversations were in Spanish. As expected, Carlos's parents delayed a decision about his future until they could consider all the information that was discussed. Carlos was to continue working to earn money for college and was encouraged to be tutored by a volunteer from the community who had attended a university.

In this example, the counselor first made certain that he had developed a trusting relationship with Carlos. It was apparent that Carlos felt free to discuss personal and family problems with the counselor. The counselor concluded that Carlos's mother had experienced a great deal of stress in her lifetime and was very protective of her son. Carlos also recognized his mother's reluctance to agree with a plan that might require him to move to another state. There was a genuine concern that Carlos would not be given the opportunity to prove himself because of his race. Goals were set to include parents in the decision process and allies were brought in to encourage trust and an open mind about their son's future. Finally, Carlos and his family compromised by agreeing to let him apply at two universities nearby.

Major Parameters of Five Models

In this section, five career counseling models are summarized by describing each according to its counseling goals, intake interview techniques, use of assessment, diagnosis, and counseling process as shown in the following table. The process of career counseling usually begins with an intake interview, then moves to assessment, on to diagnosis and problem identification, followed by a counseling process that maintains a client-collaborative relationship, then intervention strategies, and ends with an evaluation of outcomes and future plans. Individual needs may dictate different paths for some individuals.

Counseling Goals

Counseling goals provide the reader with goals specific to the model's purpose and procedures that are described in each parameter. For example, the trait-and-factor and PEF model emphasizes optimal fit of clients with an occupation; the developmental model stresses strategies that delineate clients' individual traits to promote career development over the life span; learning theory model suggests interventions to enhance and expand the client's current status; CIP model uses a variety of individual learning plans to improve cognitive processing; and the multicultural model for ethnic women explores avenues of removing salient cultural variables that inhibit and restrict career choice. Within these frameworks, client–counselor relationships are critical. The counselor might simultaneously be a teacher, a mentor, an overseer, and, in most cases, a collaborator who establishes a working consensus relationship.

Intake Interview

The intake interview has many purposes, including building the foundations from which client–counselor relationships are established, and plays a major role by assessing client problems. Ivey and Ivey (1999, p. 12) make a distinction between interviewing and counseling, although they are often used interchangeably: "Interviewing may be considered the most basic process used in information gathering, problem solving, and information and advice giving," whereas "counseling is a more intensive and personal process." In the parameter descriptions that follow, the intake interview is used for information gathering, building client–counselor relationships, assessing problems, determining client's readiness for career counseling, and establishing the process of counseling.

A preliminary assessment of the client's personal and career problems are obtained through background information and observation in the trait-and-factor and PEF model. This information is used with valid test results to form a subjective and objective appraisal of the client. The client's social networks, support system, and unique beliefs are the subject of an intensive interview in the developmental model. This information is used with standardized measures to form a picture of the client's career development. In the learning theory model, the interview identifies both personal and career problems and obstacles such as career beliefs that could block optimal career decisions. The major emphasis is identifying learning opportunities for each client. Both emotional and cognitive problems are emphasized in the CIP model. Furthermore, this model considers a trusting relationship that enhances self-efficacy and fosters learning to be most important. In the multicultural model for ethnic women, culturally appropriate relationships are established. A structural interview is used to determine client needs and to discuss client worldviews.

Use of Assessment

In this parameter, assessment refers to both standardized and nonstandardized methods used in the five models. This broader use of assessment is found in all career models as a part of client problem identification and is used in ongoing career counseling to identify appropriate intervention strategies. Within this framework, counselors not only have to understand the technical aspects of standardized tests that determine their appropriate use but also must sharpen their skills in applying nonstandardized measures. Assessment use is determined through a consensus between client and counselor that generally leads to a client's increased self-knowledge. All models make the point that testing is not the dominant force in making career choices but, rather, is used effectively as a counseling tool.

The trait-and-factor and PEF model uses assessment to provide valid and reliable information of interests, values, and cognitive abilities. Emotional stability, cognitive clarity, and skills in information processing are also evaluated. The developmental model requires assessment of the client's uniqueness in a variety of trait characteristics. This information informs clients of their personal characteristics that are used to determine learning strategies. The learning theory model uses assessment to determine learning experiences and to determine personal beliefs. Two stages of assessment are used in the CIP model. The first stage is used to measure dysfunctional thinking and client's readiness for problem solving. The second stage is used to measure cognitive processing domains and to develop individual learning plans. The major use of assessment in the multicultural model for ethnic women is to assess salient racial factors from interview results and the results of inventories specifically designed for this purpose.

Diagnosis

Identifying client problems is a major focus of the diagnosis parameter—not only for providing a client label but, more important, as a starting point from which goals can be set to resolve client problems. The diagnostic parameter is also used to identify client mental health problems that require further psychological evaluation or treatment. In all five models, diagnosis of irrational or dysfunctional thinking is determined by appraisal systems involving subjective or objective evaluation and, in most cases, both. In sum, diagnosis primarily serves as a means of identifying the client's level of knowledge, information-processing skills, readiness, and motivation to engage in intervention strategies that lead to problem solving and career decision making.

Client deficiencies in information processing are an important function of diagnosis in the trait-and-factor and PEF model. The client's optimal person-environment-fit is determined by valid relationships. Seven diagnostic elements are used in the developmental model to determine intervention strategies. A list of goal impediments also is used to identify client problems. In the learning theory model, faulty beliefs that interfere with goal achievement are identified in the interview and with an inventory designed for this purpose. The status of client skills and their personal qualities are used to determine learning interventions. The effectiveness of cognitive processing is an important element in the CIP model. The causes of gaps between what the client desires in the future and reality provide guidelines for intervention. A decision tree schematic is used as a diagnosis procedure for determining the direction counseling may take in the multicultural model for ethnic women. In this process, clients receive career-style counseling or psychological counseling. Those on the career-style counseling path will be further diagnosed for the impact of cultural variables that influence career choice.

Counseling Process

The career counseling process in all five models involves a multitude of skills; although the following summary is not meant to be an all-inclusive list, it does include the major focus by most models. First, the counselor must be prepared for each counseling encounter that will involve a unique individual whose uniqueness must be accurately delineated. Client and counselors need to form a bond that will endure throughout the entire counseling process. The counselor must be an effective interviewer. The client–counselor relationship is very inclusive, as the counselor may function as a teacher, mentor, coach, advisor, confidante, and overseer, but mainly as a collaborator who involves the client in the ongoing counseling process. Counselors must be knowledgeable of a variety of standardized and nonstandardized assessment instruments. Identifying client problems is a major counseling function. Effectively using intervention strategies including occupational information is an important component of the counseling process within all models. The effective use of decision making is also a major model focus. Finally, clients need to be prepared to recycle in the future.

Counselors introduce clients to the person-environment-fit process and assist them in matching their self-knowledge with congruent work environments in the trait-and-factor and PEF model. This process may follow interventions designed to improve the client's ability to process information. Counselors discuss individual and unique traits with clients in the developmental model. After the client understands specific goal impediments, appropriate goals are established. Learning strategies are developed in collaborative client–counselor relationships. In the learning theory model, counselors assist clients in identifying career beliefs that could interfere with progress in decision making. Counselors try to motivate clients to participate in a learning process that will improve their skills and abilities to function in changing work environments. Clients are to visualize a life span of occupational decisions and learning opportunities. In a CIP model, dysfunctional thinking and cognitive processing problems are a major concern in the opening stages of counseling. Counselors clarify problems and goals and match them with intervention strategies that are developed by consensus between client and counselor. Counselors offer assistance in decision making through cognitive restructuring. The counselor must be prepared to establish and maintain a collaborative, negotiating client–counselor relationship in a multicultural model for ethnic women. An open discussion of worldviews and salient cultural variables that are unique to the client's experience is fundamental in an effective counseling process. Counselors need to respond appropriately to culturally related cues and develop culturally appropriate intervention strategies.

In sum, the parameters of five counseling models discussed in this section provide a wide range of techniques as well as a number of similar procedures. These models were developed during the last two decades of the 20th century and may serve as a foundation for building new models or mini-theories to meet clients' unique needs in the future. There seems to be a consensus among model developers that information gathering is the first step, followed by discovery of unique client needs through subjective and objective data. Standardized assessment does not dominate the counseling process. The locus of control has shifted from counselor dominant to counselor collaborator; client involvement throughout the counseling process is prevalent. The final step in all models is the client learning effective decision-making skills and the counselor extending an open invitation for future counseling.

Summary

1. Career development research has produced a solid database that answers questions about theories. Practitioners need research that focuses on effective counseling procedures and materials. Career development theory research, however, has influenced the development of counseling models.

2. Trait-and-factor is the most popular theory in practical application. Predicting success in occupations from traits measured by objective data is an actuarial method that is widely used.

3. Three types of diagnosis are differential, dynamic, and decisional. Clients can be classified as decided, undecided, or indecisive.

4. A life career planning program points out that career counseling is very inclusive, involves complex adaptive systems, is not linear, and is future oriented.

5. The five career counseling models discussed represent a broad spectrum of techniques. The trait-and-factor theory converged with the person-environment-fit theory and emphasizes optimal fit of client with an occupation. The developmental model stresses promoting career development over the life span. The learning theory model uses learning interventions to improve each client's skills and other personal characteristics. The cognitive approach model stresses individual learning plans and cognitive restructuring. Finally, the multicultural model for ethnic women emphasizes recognizing salient cultural variables that inhibit career choice.

6. The five counseling models use a wide range of techniques but the steps in each model are very similar. A consensus of model procedures includes information gathering, assessment, diagnosis, intervention strategies, and decision making. Standardized assessment does not dominate career counseling, and the locus of control has shifted to give the client equal responsibility in counseling decisions.

Supplementary Learning Exercises

1. Design intervention strategies that you would use for each of the following clients: decided, undecided, and indecisive. Which model would you choose for each?

2. Give an example of the type of intake interview you would use to answer the question of why a client has a particular cultural problem. Explain your choice.

3. Describe the techniques you would use to discover a client's career identity and relevant environmental information about a client to help clarify the client's goal or problem. Identify models you would use.

4. Explain the influence of interacting contextual variables on career choice. What are good references for understanding more about this topic?

5. Give reasons why contemporary career counseling models employ collaborative counselor-client relationships more.

6. Debate the following: trait-and-factor counseling techniques were misinterpreted by users.

7. Which of the five models described in this chapter most often subscribes to and emphasizes the concept of learning over the life span? Give your opinion and reasons.

8. How would you characterize the use of assessment in the five models described in this chapter? Which of the models are most assessment oriented?

9. Explain under what conditions racial identity of the counselor and client are most significant. Explain.
10. Give concrete examples of how salient cultural variables limit career choice of ethnic groups.

For More Information

Axelson, J. A. (1999). *Counseling and development in a multicultural society* (4th ed.). Pacific Grove, CA: Brooks/Cole.

Brown, D., & Associates. (2002). *Career choice and development* (4th ed.). San Francisco: Jossey-Bass.

Brown, D., & Brooks, L. (1991). *Career counseling techniques.* Boston: Allyn & Bacon.

Crites, J. O. (1981). *Career models: Models, methods, and materials.* New York: McGraw-Hill.

Gysbers, N. C., & Moore, E. J. (1987). *Career counseling, skills and techniques for practitioners.* Englewood Cliffs, NJ: Prentice-Hall.

Healy, C. C. (1982). *Career development: Counseling through life stages.* Boston: Allyn & Bacon.

Krumboltz, J. D. (1983). *Private rules in career decision making.* Columbus, OH: National Center for Research in Vocational Education.

Krumboltz, J. D. (1996). A learning theory of career counseling. In M. L. Savickas & W. B. Walsh (Eds.), *Handbook of career counseling and practice* (pp. 55–81).Palo Alto, CA: Davies-Black.

Krumboltz, J. D., & Hamel, D. A. (1977). *Guide to career decision-making skills.* New York: Educational Testing Service.

Krumboltz, J. D., Mitchell, A., & Gelatt, H. G. (1975). Applications of social learning theory of career selection. *Focus on Guidance, 8,* 1–16.

Krumboltz, J. D., & Nichols, C. (1990). Integrating the social learning theory of career decision making. In W. B. Walsh & S. H. Osipow (Eds.), *Career counseling: Contemporary topics in vocational psychology* (pp. 159–192). Hillsdale, NJ: Erlbaum.

Rounds, J. B., & Tracey, T. J. (1990). From trait-and-factor to person-environment-fit counseling: Theory and process. In W. B. Walsh & S. J. Osipow (Eds.), *Career counseling: Contemporary topics in vocational psychology* (pp. 1–44). Hillsdale, NJ: Erlbaum.

Sampson, J. P., Reardon, R. C., Peterson, G. W., & Lenz, J. G. (2004) *Career counseling and services: A cognitive information processing approach.* Belmont, CA: Brooks/Cole-Thomson Learning.

Savickas, M. L., & Walsh, W. B. (Eds.). (1996). *Handbook of career counseling theory and practice.* Palo Alto, CA: Davies-Black.

Sharf, R. S. (1992). *Applying career development theory to counseling.* Pacific Grove, CA: Brooks/Cole.

Spokane, A. R. (1991). *Career intervention.* Englewood Cliffs, NJ: Prentice-Hall.

Suggested InfoTrac College Edition Topics

Career choice   Counseling techniques

Career counseling   Multicultural counseling

Career development

4 Managing Sets of Needs

Chapter Highlights

- Rationale for a holistic approach to career counseling

- Interrelationships of multiple roles

- The call to fuse career and personal counseling

- Domain-sensitive approach as sets of needs

- Using integrative counseling methods and procedures

- A nexus for integrative counseling

- Client concerns by theoretical domains

- Counseling strategies for theoretical domains

- Case study

OUR FOCUS in this chapter is on a counseling approach that addresses both personal and career concerns. The point was made in Chapter 1 that the role and scope of career counseling has been and continues to be influenced by an ever changing society in which the workforce and workplace have also experienced significant changes. How to effectively address career-related concerns in a world that is rapidly changing has been the subject of numerous research projects and debates over several decades. In the meantime, the more sophisticated career development approaches and counseling interventions developed since the latter part of the last century have dramatically expanded the role and scope of career counseling in contemporary society. As pointed out in Chapters 2 and 3, career development theorists currently address a wide range of client concerns, including multiple life roles, learning deficiencies, cognitive difficulties, emotional problems, and social restraints.

Historically, career and personal domains were viewed as separate entities and, as a result, studies of career development were approached as a distinct domain (Spokane, 1991). Following this perspective, counselor training programs also considered career and personal concerns as separate domains. The relationship and interplay of personal and career concerns have focused more attention on strategies that integrate them. Some may complain, however, that the counseling profession has been too cautious in addressing the position of integrating career and personal concerns. In the 1970s, for example, Osipow (1979) put forward the idea of blending vocational development with mental health when working with adults in the workplace. He labeled this effort occupational mental health. Counselors were to address work maladjustment, work-related stress, depression, and other concerns that might involve an interplay between work and personal concerns and all life roles.

The Rationale for a Holistic Approach

In the 1990s, there was considerable dialogue as to whether career counseling should devote more attention to the interrelationships of personal and career problems and how they affect multiple life roles. This debate is not new to the counseling profession. Some researchers have suggested that career and personal concerns should be dealt with separately (Crites, 1981), whereas others, believing that career and personal concerns are intertwined, have promoted a more holistic counseling approach (Krumboltz, 1993; Betz & Corning, 1993). Moreover, Richardson (1996) prudently suggests that the pervasive nature of work in each person's life needs to be researched by several academic disciplines to clarify its position and role in the counseling process. What we have here is a reinforcement of the position that work is a core element of an individual's everyday existence. It gives meaning to many facets of each person's life and as such should be addressed more aggressively in the counseling profession. Conversely, this position also suggests that client personal concerns can significantly affect work roles and career development over the life span. Following this logic, personal concerns that evolve from different life roles and/or interfere with career development should not be ignored in career-related programs and in counseling interventions. Thus, how to effectively integrate an individual's career and personal concerns presents challenges for the practice of career development.

What is being suggested here is a *holistic counseling* approach that is much more inclusive when addressing client concerns. This stance is underscored by the ever expanding role of career counseling, from its early focus on career choice and placement of young adults to today's greater emphasis on the concerns of adults in multiple life roles. The interrelationship of personal and career problems has become more apparent in the lives of adults as they experience changes in work environments and difficulties associated with other life roles. Work maladjustment, career transitions, stress reduction, changing work requirements, concerns of older adults, and changing values and interests are examples of career-related problems that can affect other life roles. In more inclusive counseling models, however, we also address the concerns of some clients who, for example, present depression, behavioral problems, a lack of cognitive clarity, and affective domain concerns of inner conflicts that restrict or interfere with career development.

A review of the five career counseling models in Chapter 3 reveals that a number of similar counseling procedures were used in common. Some personal concerns of clients were addressed in all models. Inherently implied in these counseling models was an interrelationship between personal and career concerns of clients. Later in this chapter we will use five counseling models to explore some interrelationships between concerns clients bring to counseling. Some concerns can be dealt with simultaneously; a more inclusive holistic position requires that all concerns be addressed.

The question here is how to effectively address both personal and career client concerns. Historically, when concerns overlap domains, counselors have turned to integrative or technical eclecticism that combine counseling methods from different theoretical frameworks. An integrative approach to counseling and psychotherapy has a history that spans several decades. A shift toward integrative counseling among mental health helpers was reported as early as the 1970s by Corey (1986). Okun (2002) points out that most helpers at the beginning of the new millennium use an integrated approach, in that they select strategies from a variety of different theoretical frameworks to address personal concerns of clients. The popularity of the integrative movement is underscored by the following journals: *Integrative Psychiatry, Journal of Integrative and Eclectic Psychotherapy,* and the *Journal of Psychotherapy Integration.*

Counselors, therefore, are guided not by a single theoretical orientation but rather choose strategies from theoretical constructs that can best serve the client. One would suspect that some career counselors also use strategies from a variety of career development theoretical constructs. Integrative counseling takes the process a step further: Career and personal concerns, career concerns, mental health issues, and other personal concerns that clients bring to counseling are viewed as being interrelated.

In this chapter we focus on the rationale of a holistic approach to career counseling and the methods and procedures used to integrate career and personal counseling by first reviewing experts' opinions on the subject. We then discuss career counseling models that address personal client problems, and third, we offer methods of overseeing and managing personal and career counseling by theoretical domains, supported by a case study. A word of caution—it is not implied that all client career concerns require intense integrative counseling procedures. Client career concerns can be addressed by a variety of interventions; for instance, one client may be referred to a computer-assisted career guidance program, another to a discussion of how to do a job interview, and yet another to information about connecting a college major with potential work roles. For some clients, however, some integration of career and personal concerns may be necessary.

The Call to Integrate Career and Personal Counseling

The call for the counseling profession to integrate career and personal counseling was heightened in the 1990s, underscored by a profusion of articles in professional journals. In 1993, the *Career Development Quarterly* (Volume 42, pp. 129–173) contained articles that supported the integration of career and personal counseling. Different points of view were expressed, including those predisposed toward a need to integrate career and personal counseling by expanding the role of counseling to address problems of a personal nature that are incurred in multiple life roles over the life span (Gelso & Fretz, 2001).

Super (1993) suggested that "there are two kinds of counseling, situational and personal, and they are not dichotomous but rather a continuum" (p. 132). Counselor and client are to work together to develop the client's self and situational knowledge as shaped in person-in-environment interactions. Clients who are aware of their own needs are empowered to effectively begin an independent exploration that leads to decision making. In this process, career and personal concerns are integrated and not dichotomized.

Krumboltz (1993) strongly advocates integrating career and personal counseling. He suggests that the terms *career counseling* and *personal counseling* convey the impression of a dichotomy that has been reinforced by different training courses and certification. His major point is that personal problems cannot be separated from career problems, as they are inextricably intertwined. He illustrates his point with some case examples, such as, "Linda is depressed because she has lost her job and doesn't think she can ever find another one. Is this a career problem? Or a depression problem?" (p. 144). According to Krumboltz (1993), compartmentalizing client concerns limits our ability as counselors to help them understand, for example, how belief systems and interests are interrelated in the career counseling process.

Davidson and Gilbert (1993) approach career counseling as a highly personal matter that includes the multidimensional self and its relationship to life and work. Counselors, therefore, are to acknowledge and recognize the personal and contextual realities that clients bring to counseling. Career is seen as a personal identity and as such is interrelated with multiple life roles over the life span, including dual-career roles. Finally, these authors conclude that career and personal counseling are the same.

Career issues that engage aspects of the total person are the theme of Haverkamp's and Moore's (1993) research. They suggest that the supposed dichotomy of personal and career counseling was exaggerated by career counseling's narrow focus on career choice with young adults. They argue that more attention should be paid to work adjustment and personal aspects of the whole person. Finally, they conclude that there is little question that career and personal issues are intertwined in adult development.

Betz and Corning (1993) viewed career and personal counseling as inseparable and recommended a "whole person," holistic philosophy of counseling, a belief apparently shared by an increasing number of counselors (Gelso & Fretz, 2001; Schultheiss, 2000). The overwhelming rationale is that career and personal issues are inseparable and intertwined. The most effective mindset when using a holistic approach is one that views each client from a total person perspective. In a collaborative relationship, client and counselor uncover all problems—not just career ones, nor just personal ones, but both—and more important, how they interrelate.

Career and Personal Counseling
in Five Career Counseling Models

In Chapter 3, techniques for five career counseling models were delineated by stages, beginning with client and counselor relationships that enhance and encourage problem identification during the intake interview. Each model contained references to personal-environment-fit problems (e.g., emotional problems) that are to be addressed. In the Trait Factor and Person-Environment-Fit model, for example, counselors are to assess each client's emotional status, cognitive clarity, personality style, and perception of self and environment. Developmental models also call for identifying emotional problems, lack of motivation, and family beliefs. Likewise, the Learning Theory model suggests that counselors focus on faulty career beliefs and obstacles, family life, emotional status, and environmental influences. The Cognitive Information Processing model contains instructions to evaluate emotional and cognitive components of each client's presenting problems. Finally, the counselor's and client's racial/ethnic background issues are highlighted in the Multicultural Model for Ethnic Women. Counselors are to be aware of a variety of client worldviews and the psychological distress that may occur because of clashes between the dominant and non-dominant cultures.

Personal and career-related problems specifically addressed by the five career counseling models appear to support a holistic counseling approach in which personal problems are viewed as an inseparable part of the career counseling process. In all models, person-environment interactions are stressed as a multidimensional developmental process that is unique to each individual. Thus, career development is influenced by many factors in the environment, including a multitude of personal interactions and interrelationships. Consequently, personal and career concerns are to be addressed as interrelated factors that, with some clients, limit or restrict career development and life balance.

Finally, the interrelationship of personal and career concerns is highlighted in the five counseling models by an emphasis on: (1) uncovering faulty beliefs that could interfere with career choice and adapting to work environment requirements, (2) "emotional problems" that are potential deterrents for making optimal career choices and maintaining continuous career development, and (3) existential issues of individual awareness of self, responsibility to self, and finding meaning in life. In addition, career counseling over the life span implies that individuals continually are faced with adjustments and choices in all life roles, the personal as well as career realms. Client Y, for instance, turns down an opportunity to receive higher pay and significantly advance his career. He informs the counselor that he doesn't have the confidence in his ability to assume more responsibilities. Eventually, counselor and client uncover extreme feelings of insecurity that Client Y has managed to hide from his supervisor. This client desperately wanted the advancement but he was afraid to take a chance and risk exposing his feelings of inferiority in a new and different environment. The counselor explored the interactions of Y's beliefs and socialization as well as his role models, or the lack of them. The counselor used interventions to debunk faulty beliefs and patiently had the client explain in a step-by-step fashion his felt inability to perform in a new work role. Insight into this client's concerns was achieved through a careful exploration of how personal and career problems can be intertwined. Recog-

Box 4-1	**A Bipolar Disorder**

I am a divorced mother with three children whose ages are 23, 17, and 16. I am currently employed by a grocery chain that specializes in health foods. Currently I oversee the coffee, tea, and chocolate section in the store. I like my work, but I haven't always been happy in a working situation. In the past I have gone from one job to another including the following jobs: working in a cleaning business, wreath making, waitress, nurse's aide, cook, teacher's aide, truck driver, and health care assistant for disabled individuals. As you can observe I have difficulty sticking to a job and I tend to procrastinate. I seem to be searching for something I can't find or really identify. Sometimes I feel that I could identify what I want to do in the future but I am afraid to try for fear of failure once more. It is hard for me to generate the confidence and energy to get started on a project.

My main problems have been depression, feelings of anger, helplessness, and fear of leaving my home. I have been diagnosed as having a bipolar disorder. There are times when I feel happy and enthusiastic and other times I feel very depressed. It is during the feelings of depression that I cannot focus and function well. Often, I cannot complete even simple tasks. On the other hand, when I feel well, I can relate to other people but I resist becoming involved in close relationships.

I am now 44 years old. My father was in the armed services and we moved quite often. I have lived in Colorado, Virginia, Louisiana, Texas, Germany, and Italy. I have two younger brothers. My parents divorced soon after I graduated from high school. My marriage also failed and my children have become quite discouraged with my mental health problems. One of my major goals is to give them a better home environment.

When I have been able to work it has given me hope for the future. I am currently seeing a therapist and taking antidepressants. I have never had any career counseling even when I was enrolled in college, but work has been very important to me. I feel much better when I can function well on a job, and this feeling of well-being has fostered my lifestyle and other life roles. I still have a secret ambition of owning my own business. I would welcome the opportunity to explore some options. I know from past experience that my personal problems will hinder my progress toward upgrading my vocational skills but I am willing to try to find a pathway to a more fulfilling work role.

SOURCE: The individual who submitted this example of how mental health problems and career issues are intertwined prefers to remain anonymous.

nizing that his internal frame of reference was faulty—to the point that further career development was in jeopardy—this client was now in a better position to make more appropriate decisions. In this case, collaborative effort led to rational decision making that empowers clients to accurately evaluate all situational, interrelated conditions in life and work.

In another example of personal and career concerns, a frustrated client, Z, moved to a job that will allow her more time to be involved with family. She reports, however, that she continues to feel frustrated and unhappy. Client Z felt the source of her problems came from having to work and also manage a family. It was soon discovered, however, that client Z was very impulsive and rather unstable. She had a history of difficulty with establishing long-term goals and was uncertain about future life roles. Her impulsive behavior had interfered with work role functioning and a commitment to work. The counselor suspected that her continued frustration and unhappiness with events at work and at home were driven by her beliefs, traits, and subsequent behavior, which was similar to the profile of a borderline personality disorder. The instability and impulsive nature of borderline clients presents considerable interference with most life roles, including the work role. In this case, interventions were directed toward building an understanding of her beliefs and their connection to how she interprets events in her life. Counseling interventions were directed specifically at her core beliefs, identified during counseling as the primary source of her problems. This case illustrates how faulty beliefs can create unstable interpersonal relations that can distort situational conditions in the workplace, affect work satisfaction, and impact other life roles.

Clients Y and Z are examples of how personal and career concerns are integrated in the counseling process. Even though concerns may be viewed as separate factors in diagnosis, they are often inseparable in the counseling process. The conceptualization of clients' concerns in a holistic counseling approach builds the case for interrelationships. Focusing on the interrelationships of all life roles, the pervasive nature of the work role in each individual's life, and how to effectively relate client problems to life, work, and living more fully in a culturally diverse society is a worthwhile objective. Keep in mind that a balanced lifestyle of work, family, leisure, and health, for example, is a major counseling outcome.

Personal and Career Counseling by Theoretical Domains

It is generally agreed that in an ever changing society, client values, goals, and challenges will change as life roles change over the life span. Counselors, therefore, not only address initial career and personal concerns of young adults but also the multiple choices most people make in a lifetime of work. In addition, counselors also contend with the challenges that emerge from changing work environments and relate these to personal problems in the give-and-take of life in an evolving society. From this perspective one can see the potential of individual challenges that cover a wide range and depth of client problems. In the following paragraphs we will explore some strategies for integrating career and personal concerns.

Blustein and Spengler (1995) have developed a conceptual framework for career counseling that frames client concerns as problem domains. Their "domain-sensitive" approach treats career concerns as one set of needs among others that clients bring to counseling. Their conceptualization of counseling provides a means of developing interventions that address interrelationships of concerns. Take, for example, that client and counselor agree to the following conceptualization of presenting problems as a set of concerns: (1) a lack of positive regard, (2) feelings of anxiety, (3) poor interpersonal relationships, (4) indecision concerning a career change, and (5) a lack of decision-making techniques. The client and counselor also agree that emotional instability has created work-related problems and these problems have been exacerbated by the pressure of work tasks and work environment. In this case the client's poor self-image and lack of personal regard will be addressed through client-centered, Gestalt, or existential counseling techniques. A less stressful work environment will be considered during the process of deciding about a career change. The client will also participate in interventions designed to foster career decision making. One advantage a set-of-needs approach provides is that all client needs are given equal attention, and in some cases are addressed simultaneously.

It should not be surprising to find that with some clients, personal and career problems will overlap. In client Y's case, for example, his poor self-concept and lack of self-regard more than likely contributed to work maladjustment and his inability to be more decisive about a future career or career change. Super (1949) among others emphasized the significance of self-concept in the career choice process. In personal counseling, self-concept pervades intervention strategies and is a very prominent issue in career-related literature as well as personal problems counseling. Self-concept colors how one views the world and interprets situational conditions and, as such, is an interactive influence in the everyday give-and-take of life. Thus, counselors employing a holistic approach deal with the interrelationships of self-concept with all client concerns.

A systematic plan of interventions is needed to address significant career concerns. The overlap of personal and career concerns suggests that interventions are to be designed to find solutions to interrelated domain problems as well as to domain-specific ones. Poor interpersonal skills and faulty thinking, for instance, can significantly affect all life roles. From this perspective, the counselor is sensitive to sets of concerns in terms of how they can most appropriately be addressed and managed in the counseling process. The domain-sensitive approach of sets of concerns fosters the use of research-based interventions that have been developed from theoretical frameworks.

A Nexus for Integrating Counseling

A counseling approach that identifies and addresses personal problems by Doyle (1998) and Okun (2002) also offers counselors some ways to manage and oversee the integration of career and personal counseling. They suggest that counselors who address personal concerns are to identify client problems and subsequent needs according to theoretical domains. Doyle (1998) groups domains as affective- (emotions/feelings), cognitive- (understanding/thinking), and performance- (action/doing) focused strategies. Okun (2002) uses the five domains of affective, cognitive, behavioral, affective-cognitive, and cognitive-behavioral. Her groupings suggest that client problems overlap domains, hence, the affective-cognitive and cognitive-behavioral domains. Gelso and Fretz (2001) group domains as psychoanalytic, behavioral-cognitive, and humanistic-experimental. Finally, Hackney and Cormier (2001) group treatment consideration in five categories as follows: affective, cognitive, behavioral, systematic, and cultural. The choice of domains used for overseeing and managing an integrative approach, however, should be the responsibility of the counselor who is in the best position to judge her or his counseling orientation, training, experiences, competencies, and time limits.

Table 4-1 is modeled after Hackney and Cormier (2001) and contains counseling strategies and corresponding client concerns. The nexus for integrative interventions includes examples of concerns and strategies in four categories or domains—career, affective, cognitive-behavioral, and cultural. Physical health and gender concerns are included in each domain. This perspective provides a means of observing the interrelationships of client concerns within and between four domains. Client concerns that overlap domains call for interventions that cut across categories. A depressed client, for instance, may learn to resolve issues through client-centered therapy while also

Table 4-1	Representative Strategies and Client Concerns in Four Domains

CAREER

Strategies

Trait-Oriented counseling, Developmental counseling, Social Learning and Cognitive counseling, Person-in-Environment counseling

Assessment of traits, clarifying interests, self-concept development, vocational identity development, awareness of developmental stages and tasks, rational decision making, self-directed career maintenance, interpersonal skills development, sources of job satisfaction, work adjustment variables, coping with job loss, and preparing for retirement.

Concerns

Indecisive, deficiencies in basic skills, career maturity issues, poor work identity, work impairment, work maladjustment, deficiencies in basic skills, adjusting to career transitions, balancing life roles, job loss, stress, violence in the workplace, relational problems, failure to adapt to changing work requirements, loss of work identity, and adjustment to retirement.

AFFECTIVE

Strategies

Client-centered therapy, Gestalt experiments, Existential therapy, Psychodynamic therapies

Empathy, active listening, awareness techniques, dignity and worth of individual, ventilation and catharsis, self-regulation, wholeness of individual, insight and awareness, meaning in life, positive regard, and internal frame of reference

Concerns

Emotional instability, sad, anxious, angry, panic attacks, impulsivity, poor self-esteem, feelings of inferiority and helplessness, depressed mood, lethargy, fatigue, and poor personal relationships

focusing on career decision-making interventions. The information in Table 4-1 provides a method of managing client concerns from a "whole person" perspective or holistic approach to counseling that fuses career and personal concerns. Interventions are selected from research-based theoretical frameworks that most appropriately meet client needs. This perspective emphasizes the unique development of each client and her or his concerns that may be addressed most effectively by interventions that incur multiple life roles. It does not eliminate interventions that address specific concerns, such as career exploration or an identified personality disorder, but encourages integrating interventions from a variety of theoretical approaches. Thus, concerns in one domain may be affected by or affect concerns in another domain.

In the context of career concerns, potential presenting problems emerge from career decision making, inadequate basic skills, career immaturity, inadequate problem-solving skills, faulty cognitions, school-to-work transitions, early encounters in the workplace, career identity, work maladjustment, poor interpersonal relationships, career transitions, skill development, loss of job, and work-related stress. The current

Table 4-1	(continued)

COGNITIVE-BEHAVIORAL

Strategies

Behavioral counseling, Cognitive restructuring, Rational-emotive therapy, Reality therapy, Beck's cognitive therapy

Counter-conditioning, bibliotherapy, reframing, A_B_C_D_E analysis, systematic desensitization, modeling, contingency management, homework assignments, assertive training, problem-solving techniques, contracting, and social skills training

Concerns

Faulty thinking, inappropriate behavior, self-destructive behavior, cognitive distortions, maladaptive behavior, faulty beliefs, overgeneralizations of negative experiences, poor information processing skills, and problems in decision making.

CULTURE

Strategies

Culturally based interventions, Multicultural counseling

Focus on level of acculturation and worldview, cultural identity, cultural orientation, work-related values, culturally appropriate assessment techniques and resources, adjustment techniques to new socioeconomic system. Use indigenous helpers, alternative counseling procedures, and expanded repertoire of helping responses

Concerns

Deficiencies in the use of English language and basic skills, poor adjustment to the dominant cultural values, collectivist worldview, cultural shock, lack of job skills, difficulty with assimilating new lifestyle, restrictive emotions, level of cultural identity, effects of discrimination and oppression, and relating to others

conception of a career—that it includes related activities associated with an individual's lifetime of work—suggests that career concerns can be very inclusive. Some clients therefore need to identify and address interrelated concerns in the counseling process.

The affective domain encompasses problems—frequently emotionally driven—that affect mood; self-concept dimensions and metadimensions of self-awareness or self-esteem; and feelings of inferiority, impulsivity, and helplessness, among others. The strategies used are designed to help clients focus inward to achieve self-awareness, self-development, and self-actualization. The cognitive-behavioral domain focuses on the thought process that drives patterns of behavior. The rationale is that faulty thinking can lead to inappropriate behavior. Strategies are designed to unlearn faulty thinking and subsequent actions and to reward appropriate behavior. When deciding about any important life event, one should have a realistic and rational basis on which to reason, think, and act. The ability to conceptualize a problem clearly and then clarify issues it presents provides a much better chance of optimal decision making.

A brief example of the cognitive-behavioral domain is taken from a client who was referred for extreme difficulty in "getting along with work associates." Recurring arguments with fellow workers that almost resulted in violence were reported. During the interview, the counselor discovered that faulty thinking might be the underlying cause of the reported behavioral problem. The following samples of client responses underscore the counselor's conclusion: "You can't trust anyone," "Everybody is out to get you," and "I will slug anyone who messes with me." This client's problem cuts across cognitive (faulty perceptions of fellow workers) and behavioral (inappropriate behavior at work) issues and fits into the cognitive-behavioral domain. The counselor concluded that faulty thinking resulted in inappropriate behavior and poor interpersonal relations with work associates.

Sets of needs to be addressed in the cognitive-behavioral model assumes that there is an interrelationship across domains, within which the problems discovered in one domain are inextricably intertwined with other domains and therefore can be dealt with simultaneously. The choice of strategies in our example can be drawn from Ellis's rational-emotive therapy (1994), Glasser's reality therapy (1989), or Meichenbaum's cognitive-behavioral modification (1977). Anger management interventions also may be used. Career-related interventions may include important interpersonal skills needed for effectively working in teams and an introduction to information for updating work skills. Counselors can select strategies systematically from established theoretical frameworks and are in a much better position to judge if they have the training and skills the strategies require. Be aware that rigorous training to develop skills in counseling techniques drawn from a broad spectrum of theoretical orientations is necessary to meet client concerns of a career counseling approach that fuses career and personal problems.

In the cultural domain, the client's level of acculturation is assessed; worldview is weighed, especially the constructs of individualism versus collectivism. Client cultural identity is attained, and work-related values are uncovered. Culturally based presenting problems provide direction for balancing the focus of interventions. The need to address various dimensions of cultural concerns, discussed in Chapter 10, gives credence to the position of modifying integrative interventions.

At this point we pause to emphasize that counselors follow the ethical code to refer clients when they suspect or identify a problem (or problems) that is beyond the scope of their training. It is just as important to seek assistance or to refer clients when the counselor feels unprepared or confused about a problem at hand (Spokane, 1991). The client's welfare is the first and foremost consideration; this rule should be strictly observed throughout the intake interview and counseling process. Helpers will find that the most appropriate action for some clients is to refer them to another professional who is trained to address their specific needs.

Managing a Holistic Counseling Approach

Overseeing the concerns and progress of several clients is routine for counselors. When one addresses both personal and career concerns, however, effective management skills are essential. Traditionally, career and personal concerns have been viewed as separate entities: The process of fusing career and personal concerns is in its infancy. The "whole person" concept of counseling calls on counselors to handle all client concerns and their interrelationship. Within this framework, counselors search for the most appropriate methods to address a multitude of concerns, including those involving career development and maintenance.

More important, however, are the numerous counseling skills required to meet any number of overlapping client problems in the personal and career domains. Consulting with a colleague about a particular client problem or referring a client for treatment or designated interventions requires that counselors sharpen their communication skills for effective case management. At any point in the counseling process, counselor and client may agree on intervention strategies that require referral to another helper, such as an information technician, a colleague who specializes in certain intervention strategies, a clinical psychologist, or a psychiatrist. Counselors who refer clients to other professionals often continue to oversee the progress of their client toward mutually established goals. Be aware, however, that in some cases counselors may relinquish the responsibilities of overseeing a client's progress to another professional or to an agency. Counselor, colleagues, and client collaborate on content and timing of appropriate intervention strategies. Intervention strategies focus on the interrelationship of presenting problems from theoretical frameworks of both personal and career counseling theories. Thus, counselors may oversee cases that potentially involve an almost endless number of client-interrelated needs and, subsequently, other helpers. Counselors therefore must evaluate each person's training and background to determine which concepts and techniques they can contribute in a holistic counseling approach.

Counselors ideally are to be lifelong learners. Each new client presents the opportunity to learn more about one's effectiveness as a counselor and how to unify techniques when addressing sets of clients' concerns. Counselors also are urged to attend seminars and workshops designed to enhance counseling techniques that effectively integrate career and personal problems. Here are some suggestions to prepare for managing a holistic counseling approach that fuses career and personal concerns:

1. learn more about the pervasive nature of work as a major component of one's existence over the life span,
2. develop an understanding of how one's work role is interrelated to all life roles and how problems in one life role can affect other ones,
3. adopt the position that career and personal concerns are inseparable, hence, a holistic approach to counseling is an effective method of fusing client concerns,
4. support the position that career and personal concerns are to receive equal attention,
5. identify counseling theories that you are most comfortable with as a foundation from which you can expand your counseling skills.

A holistic counseling approach is a framework of guidelines for managing and addressing client concerns, but it is not a rigid set of rules and barriers that discourage innovative counseling approaches. Counselors are on safer grounds ethically, however, when interventions used are from accepted theoretical frameworks. In the following example, some methods of counseling and managing a case are illustrated.

Case 4-1   The Case of Ways of Thinking and Perceiving

Cal's career counseling took place in a community mental health agency. A brief summary of his intake interview provides some significant background information.

Cal reported for his appointment on time. He was very neatly dressed, in freshly pressed clothes that were well coordinated and his shoes looked as though they had just been polished. Cal was very verbal and expressed himself well. He was overly precise with his answers, adding much more information than was asked for. He reported no significant physical health problems. Eye contact was appropriate.

Cal grew up in a small town in which his father had owned a hardware store. He had no siblings. He is now 36 years old. Cal described his father as being very strict and his mother as too judgmental. Cal was divorced after three years of marriage. He had no children and remarked that he felt incapable of being a good parent. He further explained this comment by stating that it was difficult to raise children properly today. Cal's wife asked for a divorce because they had "different beliefs and lifestyle." He explained that his wife stated she could not live up to his expectations and there was always tension between them. Cal lost his job as a bank clerk when the regional office was shut down. He currently lives with his parents.

Cal's stated reason for coming for help was to find a job and to solve some "personal problems." He had worked for his father for several years and then obtained a bank clerk's job, which he held for three years, after his father's store was closed. He was not always pleased with his bank job; as he put it, "I make too many mistakes." Cal viewed his personal problem as a failed marriage. Cal claimed that he tried to be a good husband but his wife complained that he tried to control her every move. Cal reported periodic episodes of depression, for instance, "I felt helpless and slept a lot." He appeared to be fearful of leaving his parents' house for help but they insisted that he find a job. Currently, his demeanor suggests a very poor self-concept. He admits feeling guilty about his failures and is confused about his future.

The counselor made several notations as follows:

Poor self-confidence and self-image

Difficulty in making decisions

Negative expectations of others

Attempts to control important others

Perfectionist attitude

Exhibited dependency needs

Faulty reasoning

Although the counselor realized that there was much more to be learned about Cal, he conceptualized his concerns at this time as follows. In the affective domain there was significant evidence of low self-esteem and negative self-evaluations. In the cognitive-behavioral domain, faulty thinking was driven by a perfectionist attitude from which he evaluates his own behavior and the behavior of others. Understandably, Cal is confused about his future and especially a future work role. His poor self-concept and negative self-evaluations will have to be addressed before Cal is able to make effective rational decisions. The basis for this conclusion is the rationale that successful career decision making requires effective information processing skills and the capability of projecting self into a work role. Hence, the counselor chooses a combination of client-centered and Gestalt therapy to encourage Cal to find some direction for the future. A major objective was to assist Cal in developing his own future agenda.

Cal's thinking process will be addressed by rational emotive behavior therapy and cognitive restructuring from the cognitive-behavioral domain. The counselor suspected that the source of Cal's perfectionist approach to life is internally based constructs that have driven his behavior pattern of attempting to control and harshly judging others. The suspected root of his problem—a distant, critical father and mother—will be the focus of interventions. His attitude is one has to be perfect to please and his fear of failure in the future will make it difficult for Cal to make an optimal career choice.

In addressing career concerns, the counselor uses a combination of interventions from learning theory and cognitive information processing models. Two inventories measuring career beliefs and thoughts will be administered in order to gain more specific information about faulty thinking and how it relates to career choice. Interventions designed to debunk negative self-evaluations will be used, in part to help Cal understand how career choices can be limited from salient messages experienced in his environment. Cal is to be empowered to make decisions on the basis of his own interests and aptitudes.

The counselor made a number of "management" decisions during the process of counseling Cal. Once his needs were identified, the counselor was in the position to determine effective intervention strategies. In this case, the mental health facility had full- and part-time professionals who could assist the counselor. For instance, a counselor who specialized in psychodynamic theories was available to offer suggestions for counseling in the affective domain. At agencies, schools, colleges, and university counseling centers, counselors traditionally share ideas and opinions and participate in learning activities to continually upgrade their counseling skills. Other situations may require the counselor to refer clients to centers staffed with skilled counselors who offer integrated programs.

In sum, Cal's case points out the interrelationship between personal and career concerns. Cal's rigid, strict upbringing led him to believe that he was not capable of pleasing his parents and yet his life seemed to be devoted to attempting to do just that. In his marriage he tried to control his wife as he had been controlled, to the point that she became dissatisfied with the marriage. His perfectionist attitude made it difficult for him to take on a work role for fear of failure. The counselor prudently approached this case as one in which multiple life roles were interrelated to problems in the affective and cognitive-behavioral domains. Cal was encouraged to dig deep into his background to help him understand his current state of mind and to address his faulty thinking when making decisions about his future life and work role.

Career Counselors of the Future

As you read this chapter, you may ask who will do career counseling in the future. One way to answer this question is to identify who is doing career counseling now. According to Liptak (2001), professionals who help people with career problems include licensed counselors, social workers, psychologists, school counselors, mental health counselors, rehabilitation counselors, and addictions counselors. Gelso and Fretz (2001) point out that many psychologists already participate in career-related counseling and, with more training, will become more involved in the future. Most of these professionals have been taught to recognize and treat a broad range of concerns clients bring to counseling and some have specialized training. The point here is that career and personal concerns can be addressed by a number of different mental health professionals. The effective career counselor of the future may well be one who is most skilled at integrating personal and career problems in the counseling process. This shift of emphasis will require changes in professional training programs as well as in how counseling centers are organized. Perhaps in the near future, career and personal counseling will be provided in the same location or at least in an adjacent office. A better working relationship between counselors should provide more effective services to all clients. Be aware that counselors will continue to provide only professional services for which they have been trained.

In sum, a holistic counseling approach suggests that some client concerns are interrelated. All counselors are encouraged to expand their skills to deal with contemporary personal and career concerns of clients in the next society. They, like many of their predecessors, will need our help.

Implications for Career Counseling

Two significant movements in career counseling have been (1) a greater emphasis on fusing personal and career concerns and (2) expanding the research on the pervasive nature of work in people's lives. These two perspectives should create significant future changes in the practice of career development and professional training programs for counselors. Career counseling may become more viable and no longer be viewed by students and faculty as second-rate or lower tier. One suggestion is to offer more opportunities for student internships in career counseling and to present more subject matter in courses that explore the interrelationships between personal and career concerns of clients (Gelso & Fretz, 2001).

Research drawn from more academic disciplines will be a driving force behind any change in counseling focus made by those who design studies to uncover the pervasive nature of work in people's lives. More attention devoted to the interrelationships of multiple life roles should also underscore the need for integrative counseling procedures. In essence, more attention should be directed to the hassles and frustrations faced in the world of work in the 21st century.

The expanding role of career counseling will include a shift of emphasis in research as well as counseling strategies to meet the needs of adults in the workforce who are experiencing interrelated personal and career concerns. We are not implying that we have ignored the needs of adults in the workforce; on the contrary, a solid database of research during the last several decades has established the foundation for career counseling to expand its role to address the pervasive nature of work in our society. Counselors may choose to specialize in work maladjustment; school-to-work programs; consulting with industrial organizations on career management of employees; sensitivity training for work environments; gender issues and work roles, rehabilitation programs; diversity issues and work environments; dual-earner families; mental health issues and career development; curriculum development aimed at exploring the meaning of work in the lives of individuals; and community programs that promote career development to name a few. In essence, there is an exciting and fruitful future for counselors who specialize in career counseling and who address the personal concerns of clients as well.

Finally, it is important to be aware that one can lose sight of career concerns in integrative counseling. As implied earlier, sets of concerns suggest that each concern receives equal attention. The interrelationships of needs suggest that intervention strategies, for example, can be directed toward improving a client's ability to function in multiple life roles. But an initial presenting problem of inappropriate relationships with work associates, however, must remain an overarching counseling goal. In a holistic counseling approach, counselors focus on domain problems that overlap and in the process of identifying and attacking the core element of concerns, career-related needs may be overlooked. Keep in mind that career counseling per se has not been given equal status with mental health counseling among helping professionals.

Summary

1. The pervasive nature of work should be the subject of research by several academic disciplines to clarify its position in counseling programs.
2. Counselors who endorse an integrative counseling approach select strategies from different theoretical frameworks.
3. Experts agree that career and personal problems are inextricably intertwined.
4. A "whole person" holistic approach is recommended for career counseling in the 21st century.
5. Current counseling models support a more holistic approach for career counseling.
6. A domain-sensitive approach treats career concerns as one set of needs among others that clients bring to counseling.
7. Career, affective, cognitive-behavioral, and cultural categories are suggested as the nexus for managing an integrative counseling approach.
8. Affective domain problems include emotionally driven ones that affect mood, self-concept, and feeling of inferiority among others.
9. Cognitive-behavioral problems include faulty thinking and inappropriate behavior.
10. Culturally related concerns are to be addressed through modified intervention strategies.
11. A case example illustrates the interrelationships between personal and career concerns. In this case client problems greatly affected all life roles.
12. Counselor training programs are challenged to provide a broader perspective of career counseling, especially for a holistic counseling approach that addresses both personal and career concerns.

Supplementary Learning Questions

1. Describe major concepts of holistic counseling and its rationale.
2. Describe five examples of Krumboltz's position that career and personal problems are intertwined.
3. Describe integrative career counseling procedures. Support its use.
4. Develop five examples of how career and personal concerns are to be addressed.
5. The career counseling profession has been criticized for devoting most attention to initial choice for young adults. Do you agree? Justify your conclusions.
6. What are the major advantages and disadvantages of using sets of needs in counseling?
7. What do you see as the major obstacles to managing a holistic counseling approach?
8. Defend or criticize the position that career and personal needs are to receive equal attention.
9. Which theoretical domains would you use for managing a holistic counseling approach? Justify your choices.
10. How do you think counselor training programs can be improved to include a broader perspective of counseling needs?

For More Information

Alford, B. A., & Beck, A. T. (1997). *The integrative power of cognitive therapy.* New York: Guilford.

Corey, G. (2001). *The art of integrative counseling.* Belmont, CA: Brooks/Cole-Thomson Learning.

Lazarus, A. (1989). *The practice of multimodal therapy.* Baltimore, MD: Johns Hopkins University Press.

Okun, B. F. (2002). *Effective helping: Interviewing and counseling techniques.* Belmont, CA: Brooks/Cole-Thomson Learning.

Preston, J. (1998). *Integrative brief therapy: Cognitive, psychodynamic, humanistic, and neurobehavioral approaches.* San Luis Obispo, CA: Impact.

Suggested InfoTrac College Edition Topics

Brief therapy	Integrative counseling
Cognitive restructuring	Irrational beliefs
Counseling strategies	Multimodal therapy
Holistic counseling	Social learning

Career Counseling Intake Interview

5

Chapter Highlights

- Rationale for career counseling intake interviews

- Suggested sequence for an interview

- Suggestions for interviewing multicultural groups

- How to assess the significance of life roles and potential conflicts

- How to discover problems that interfere with career development

- Informative tables: personality disorders as related to work impairments; five types of work psychopathology; taxonomy of psychological work-related dysfunctions

- Case examples

THE THEORETICAL PERSPECTIVES and practical solutions addressed in the preceding chapters illuminate some challenges facing career counseling in the 21st century. The call for a more holistic counseling approach also suggests that equal attention should be afforded to personal and career concerns in the intake interview as sets of needs clients bring to counseling. Counselors are encouraged to expand the career counseling intake interview to incorporate a more holistic approach when identifying

149

client problems. To conduct a balanced intake interview, for example, we evaluate both internal (concerns within the client) and external (client's environmental interactions) factors. Internal factors such as emotion, mood, and cognitive functioning are not new to the practice of career development; in a holistic approach, however, every effort is made to uncover all client concerns that could interfere with rational decision making and continuous career development. Counselors also unearth external factors, which include the individual's ecological system and contextual influences in person-in-environment interactions and relationships. From this perspective, counselors focus on gender-role socialization, cultural issues and identity development, and the influence of an individual's sociocultural background of experiences. The alert interviewer recognizes that not all client problems can be attributed to internal conflicts. External situations and conditions such as oppression of minority groups, dysfunctional families, and a lack of community resources are examples of sources of client concerns. Thus, the intake interview can be a most challenging stage of career counseling.

Be aware that we make the assumption that users of this text have been thoroughly trained in interview techniques. That assumption allows us to move quickly to a suggested sequence for an interview; next, to some suggestions for interviewing multicultural groups; third, to the significance of life roles and potential personal conflicts; and fourth, to discovering problems that interfere with career development. In the final part of the chapter some case studies are presented and discussed.

The Intake Interview

The intake interview has different meanings and purposes for mental health professionals. In counseling, the interview assists clients in developing self-understanding, forming conclusions, looking at alternative actions, and so forth; it is viewed as a "helping interview." As a key tool for establishing objectives and goals, the interview is used by social workers to build a social history. Psychiatrists and clinical psychologists use the interview as a diagnostic tool to help form treatment considerations. For career counselors, the proposed purposes of the intake interview borrow from each of these functions. As a diagnostic tool, the interview should help uncover behavioral problems that can lead to work maladjustment and faulty cognitions. In a helping role, the interview assists clients in understanding the integral relationship of all life roles. Finally, all parts of the interview (including historical and demographic data) are used to help develop goals.

A Suggested Sequence for an Interview

The following interview sequence is designed to provide helpers with structured guidelines for observing their clients while in dialogue with them. Most of the topics, such as demographic information and educational history, are typically found in career counseling models; however, the discussion of selected life roles significantly increases the options for obtaining pertinent information. For example, work history and preference for a future career are discussed as part of the work role and in association with other life roles. Individual client needs, however, will directly determine the major focus of the interview and the sequence to be followed. For instance, an interview may be terminated during the discussion of life roles if it is determined that the individual is unable to communicate effectively with a counselor because of major clinical depression. In another case, the interview might focus on only selected life roles, or the counselor might need to focus on a recurring emotional problem. The flexibility suggested for the interview provides a greater opportunity to meet the needs of a wide range of clients. The following outline of the intake interview was adapted from a number of sources including Brown, Brooks, and Associates (1990), Brems (2001), and Cormier and Nurius (2003).

I. Identifying Information

Name, address, age, gender, marital status, occupation, university, school or training facility, work history (Can be taken orally or by written response on preinterview form. Direct questioning has the important advantage of observing client behavior and emotional responses. Therefore, even if a written self-report is used, a discussion of this information should be included in the interview.)

II. Presenting Problems

Reason client has come to counseling

III. Current Status Information

Affect, mood, attitude

IV. Health and Medical Information

Including substance abuse

V. Family Information

Current status and past history

VI. Social/Developmental History

Cultural and religious background
Social interactions
Descriptions of past problems

VII. Life Roles

Current work role
Homemaker
   Spouse
   Parent
Leisure role
Citizen role
Interrelationship of life roles

VIII. Problems That Can Interfere with Career Choice

Ability level, lack of academic achievement and proficiencies
Lack of dominant interest patterns
Affective domain concerns such as poor self-concept and self-awareness
Vocational identity
Information processing skills
Lack of information or training
Career maturity
Barriers (Examples are indecision, faulty thinking, constraints, and contextual influences.)

IX. Problems That Interfere with Career Development
Behaviors that can lead to work maladjustment
Work psychopathology
Work-related dysfunctions
Faulty cognitions
Problems in living

X. Clarifying Problems
Client and counselor collaborate
State problems clearly and concretely

XI. Identify Client Goals
Determine feasibility of goals
Establish subgoals
Assess commitment to goals

As you have heard over and over again, counselors must build rapport with their client. The tone of the interview begins with the initial contact: Conveying a genuine concern to help a client will usually facilitate a working relationship. Expectations on the part of the counselor and counselee should be fully addressed at the first meeting. To facilitate this process, counselors typically use information forms for collecting data in advance of the interview. Information obtained from written forms may differ according to requirements of an agency, school or university, and individual counselor needs. Besides the usual demographic information, other data collected include prior treatment by mental health providers, medical conditions, family history, legal history, drug and alcohol abuse history, presenting problems, current involvement with other helpers or agencies, and expectations of help. This and other information is used to foster productive dialogue and to focus on potential deficits and concerns in career development, multiple life roles, and personal problems. The major purpose of the interview, in this context, is to determine client needs and the subsequent direction that interventions strategies will take. In the next section some suggestions are offered for interviewing multicultural groups.

Suggestions for Interviewing Multicultural Groups

Developing a greater sensitivity to culturally diverse clients has become increasingly important for career counselors; we must foster specific counseling techniques to accommodate the human diversity that exists in our society. The core dimension of interviewing is effective communication between clients and counselors, especially with multicultural groups. Also, during the interview, counselors form opinions and assumptions about clients from both verbal and nonverbal communications. Because of cultural and ethnic differences between counselor and client, the counselor must be alert to a wide spectrum of ethnic and cultural characteristics that influence behavior. Some cultural groups conceptualize their problems differently from those of the dominant culture and seek solutions based on these assumptions. For instance, a client who believes he is being ostracized because of race might be much more interested in finding immediate employment than in pursuing a program for identifying a long-term career goal. Another client might be reluctant to share her personal problems with someone outside the family circle and, in fact, might interpret direct questioning as an infringement of her privacy.

Although it is difficult to generalize techniques suggested for different cultural groups, it seems feasible to first determine the level of acculturation by socioeconomic status, language preference, place of birth, generation level, preferred ethnic identity, and ethnic group social contacts (Ponterotto, 1987). Questions must be carefully selected and presented to avoid offending the client. For example, directness may be judged as demanding, intrusive, or abrupt by some cultural groups. Furthermore, an open person can be seen by some cultures as weak, untrustworthy, and incapable of appropriate restraint (Copeland & Griggs, 1985). Here are some other points to remember when interviewing people from other cultures:

- General appearance can be quite distinctive for some subcultures and should be accepted on that basis.
- Attitude and behavior are considered difficult to ascertain. Major belief themes of certain cultures influence members' attitudes about themselves and others. Their perceptions of the world may be quite different from those of the counselor.
- Affect and mood also are related to cultural beliefs and to what is considered appropriate within a culture. The meaning given to gestures often differs by culture. Work experience may be quite limited because of lack of opportunity. Also, in some cultures, it is considered very immodest to speak highly of yourself and the skills you have mastered.
- Life roles, and particularly relationships, are unique to cultural socialization. In some cultures, females are considered equal to males, whereas in others, females are expected to be subservient.

These examples illustrate the necessity of building an extensive body of resources for interviewing ethnic minorities. Other general recommendations include (1) use straightforward, slang-free language, (2) become familiar with cultural life role models, (3) identify a consultant who can provide helpful information, and (4) become familiar with support networks for different cultural groups.

Most important to remember is that cultural groups are not to be stereotyped as homogeneous. Thus, with our focus on the uniqueness of individuals, we should begin by establishing a collaborative working relationship with each client: A trusting relationship is essential for productive interviewing. The multicultural career counseling model for ethnic women (Bingham & Ward, 1996) discussed in Chapter 3 suggests that a *Multicultural Career Counseling Checklist* that is counselor self-administered (Ward & Bingham, 1993) and a *Career Counseling Checklist* (Ward & Tate, 1990) for clients are to be administered as an aid in establishing rapport. Selected items from the client's checklist can be used as an entry to discussing problems that are related to cultural diversity.

The acculturation level of the client should be assessed in the second step as delineated by Ponterotto (1987) in the previous paragraphs and repeated here:

- Language preference
- Place of birth
- Generation level
- Socioeconomic status
- Preferred ethnic identity
- Ethnic group social contacts

This information may be used to determine the individual's level of assimilation in the transformation process of balancing values, beliefs, and traditions brought from the country of birth with new ideas of lifestyle and traditions of the host country. The stage of identity development should also be evaluated. Additional focus should include the following:

- Neighborhood contextual experiences
- Quality of housing
- Experiences with racism
- Religious beliefs

Interviewing culturally different individuals requires a variety of techniques and skills. Ivey and Ivey (2003) have developed a list of suggestions. Each technique has been listed with an explanation, an illustration, or both. The following suggestions for managing an interview with a culturally diverse individual should be used in conjunction with the previously suggested sequence for an interview.

Eye Contact. In Native American and Latino/a cultural groups, direct eye contact, especially by the young, is considered disrespectful. Okun, Fried, and Okun (1999) note that in many cultures individuals are forbidden to look directly at others who have more power. It is inappropriate in Muslim cultures for women to make direct eye contact with a nonfamily male. Obviously, direct eye contact is interpreted differently among cultures; some cultures consider it to be an invitation to a sexual liaison, whereas others consider it an invitation to conflict.

Touch. Guidelines for touching across gender lines are clearly defined in some cultures. For instance, in many societies, especially in the Middle East and among Asian groups, women do not touch or shake hands with unrelated men. The counselor should let the client initiate the greeting and ending of a counseling session.

Probing Questions. In some cultures, especially among some Asian groups, asking for more in-depth information is considered to be very rude and intrusive. Being aware of this potential problem, counselors restructure their questions to focus on the topic the client has initiated, as shown in the following samples:

COUNSELOR: How do you think you could best help the situation with your brother?

COUNSELOR: What can you tell me about the relationship?

The counselor has a delicate balancing problem with Asian groups that respect individuals who demonstrate proficiency in their profession, but resent those who appear to be too intrusive.

Space and Distance. Be alert to cultural differences in what is considered to be an appropriate distance from another individual when interviewing. Remember that the British prefer more distance than do North Americans (more than an arm's length), Latino/a people like being closer, and those from the Middle East prefer to be "right in your face."

Verbal Style. "I" is not a word in Vietnamese; individuals are defined by their relationships: Son (I) asks Father (you) for permission, Mother speaks to children (them).

Restrictive Emotions. Many cultural groups are taught to mask their emotional feelings. Thus, they might appear to be disinterested and preoccupied. This is particularly true of Native Americans who consider masking of emotional responses as a sign of maturity. In most cases you can expect African Americans and Latino/a people to openly express emotions.

Confrontation Issues. Ivey and Ivey (1999) suggest that "confrontation needs to be used with great sensitivity to individual and cultural differences" (p. 201). They suggest that extreme confrontational statements may not be helpful with certain groups, especially in the opening stages of interviewing. Counselors must remember that personal and family honor are almost sacred among some cultural groups, especially in Asian cultures. Direct confrontation may be perceived as being ill-mannered by some groups. Counselors can learn to be careful and flexible in how they construct questions, such as, "Tell me more about your feelings when that event took place," or "What is your son's typical story of that behavior?" Use the principles of supportive, empathic confrontation to construct questions, and sometimes silence can be helpful to give the client time to struggle with a problem.

Self-Disclosure. This technique is quite paradoxical in that it is most essential when establishing rapport for a trusting client–counselor relationship and can be most damaging to the counseling relationship if the counselor is perceived as being immature. For instance, self-disclosure at the initiation of the interview can be helpful for building trust: "I grew up in the South and I'm white and you are an African American. Do you think we can work together?" However, counselors who focus too much time on their own personal lives and intimacies can lose face with their clients. Again, a delicate balance must be maintained.

Focus on Self-in-Relation and Self-in-Context. The point has been made that in North America we tend to focus on the "I." In many other cultures, the focus is on family or solidarity of groups. In making career decisions the focus can be directed to include the family. The individual perceives himself or herself as a self-in-relationship and makes decisions that meet the needs and approval of the family. Family honor and loyalty may be the driving force that the counselor must recognize.

In sum, what one is expected to remember about the differences between cultures and what are considered to be acceptable and culturally appropriate verbal and nonverbal techniques can be overwhelming. This points out, however, the necessity of preparation for counseling and interviewing encounters, especially with individuals from culturally diverse groups. Counselors must also remember that they are interviewing unique individuals who share some cultural values with others but who have also been shaped by nonshared experiences. The techniques that we have just reviewed are generalized suggestions that might not apply to all members of a particular culture. Nevertheless, the career counseling profession must prepare itself for diversity to be effective in the 21st century.

In the next section we prepare for interviewing by exploring the significance of multiple life roles and their interrelationships. Helpers may use this information in counseling encounters, including initial choice, adults in career transition, and with clients who are experiencing work maladjustment and problems in living.

Discovering the Significance of Life Roles and Potential Conflicts

An abundance of evidence, as suggested in the first four chapters, indicates that career counseling is not concerned just with strategies for selecting a career but is much broader in scope and content. Super (1990), among others, has suggested an integrative approach to career counseling that focuses on the development of life roles over the life span, with emphasis on interrole congruence. A key concept is the effect of the development of one role on others. For instance, has the homemaker role inhibited career development of one spouse? Does the work role leave ample time for other life roles? As Super (1980) pointed out, "Success in one facilitates success in others, and difficulties in one role are likely to lead to difficulties in another" (p. 287).

Hansen's (1996, 2000) Integrative Life Planning (ILP) model incorporates career development, life transitions, gender-role socialization, and social change. This model involves a "lifelong process of identifying our primary needs, roles, and goals and the consequent integration of these within ourselves, our work, and our family" (Hansen, 1990, p. 10). The ILP model evolved from Hansen's (1978) BORN FREE project, which was designed to expand career options for both men and women. Hansen suggested that fragmented approaches to development place limits on decisions clients will make in their lifetimes. A more holistic approach recognizes that an individual's total development includes the broad spectrum of domains: social/emotional, physical, sexual, intellectual, vocational, and spiritual. Finally, in the context of our discussion, this model suggests that life roles are to be integrated in our planning and not isolated from the career decision-making process.

The impact of decisions on lifestyle, including relationships, is a major part of a more comprehensive view of development. The life roles to be evaluated in the interview include worker, homemaker, leisurite, and citizen. Included in the work role is work history, and included in the homemaker role is spouse and parent. Life roles increase and decrease in importance according to the individual's current status. For example, the student role is much more dominant in early life, even though career development is continuous and requires lifetime learning involvement. The potential complexity and variety of life roles over the life span can include a multitude of possible scenarios that warrant exploration. In the following paragraphs, each role is identified and examples of topics to be covered in the interview are presented.

Worker Role

Over time, the term work has generated many definitions and has meant different things to the individuals who do it. Also, the objectives people have for work can be quite different and might change as they pass through stages of career development. For example, some individuals work for the intrinsic enjoyment of it; for others, the primary objective might be as a way of making a living; and yet others work for social status or for self-identity. For many, a combination of objectives and other factors are equally important. Super (1984) suggested an inclusive perspective of the work role that covers most segments of lifestyle. Recently, the approach has shifted from a focus on work alone as a central life concern to an interest in the quality of life, in which work is one central concern in a constellation of roles such as homemaking, citizenship, and leisure that interact to create life satisfaction. The terms *work motivation* and *job satisfaction* are now perhaps displaced by, and certainly are incorporated into, the terms *quality of life* and *life satisfactions* (p. 29).

The different purposes individuals have for the work role should concern us. Herr, Cramer, and Niles (2004) suggested that the purposes of work can be classified as economic, social, and psychological. For example, a major economic purpose is to provide the individual with assets to satisfy current and future basic needs. This is especially the case for some immigrants who seek work that will provide them with subsistence. In the social realm, friendships and social status are established through peer group affiliations through which mutual goals are achieved. A work identity, self-efficacy, and a sense of accomplishment are examples of the psychological purposes of work.

The purposes and meanings of work are uniquely individualized. For example, a family-oriented individual who has a strong need to spend ample time with his or her children could be somewhat unhappy in a work role that limits family activities. A strong orientation for work leadership roles might inhibit an individual's needs associated with the life roles of citizen and leisurite. Although it may be difficult to satisfy the needs of all life roles, a greater balance of roles could enhance some people's quality of life. The following list of topics for discourse and samples of content for work-role interviewing represent only a few of the possibilities that can be discussed. Client needs should dictate the selection of subjects. For a client making an initial choice of work role, the counselor should assess the following:

- Knowledge of life-role concepts
- Acceptance of the idea of different life roles
- Ability to evaluate how work roles affect other life roles
- Ability to project an ideal work role
- Ability to identify purpose of the work role
- Ability to project self into work roles
- Ability to identify future work roles
- Knowledge of personal characteristics
- Level of skill development

Although many variables considered in the initial choice might have to be reevaluated with individuals who wish to change careers, the degree to which the individual is able to do the following should also be explored:

- Adapt to changes (be flexible)
- Learn new and different skills
- Function under different management styles
- Assess reasons for career changes and work commitments
- Assess his or her abilities, limitations, interests, and values to adapt to work environment changes
- Use decision-making procedures
- Identify career resources and how to use them
- Identify sources of stress
- Apply methods of modifying behavior
- Identify educational and training programs

Homemaker Role

The role of homemaker has a wide spectrum of possibilities. For example, a 35-year-old single person might not consider this role a very important one, whereas a married 35-year-old who has children might consider homemaker a major role. A high school student could consider this role as something to be dealt with in the future, whereas a 50-year-old who has reared several children will place less emphasis on this role when planning a career change. The more recent phenomenon of the househusband and a greater emphasis on the male role as homemaker increase the diversity of possible interrole conflicts. The number of working mothers has increased dramatically since the 1970s, as reported by the U.S. Bureau of Census (1997). In another study of working mothers, Shaffer (2002) points out that 60 percent of all mothers work outside the home at least part-time.

A major concern about maternal employment is its effect on children, the family, and the working women themselves. In a comprehensive review of the literature concerning the effects of maternal employment on children, Herr and Cramer (1996) concluded that in general it does no harm to children (infants, preschoolers, and adolescents). Working mothers also seem to fare well, according to Ferree (1984), who conducted a national research study concerning satisfaction variables. She concluded that there were no significant differences in life satisfaction between working mothers and those who did not work outside the home. In a related study, results indicated that stress experienced by working women can be offset by spousal approval, dependable child care, and shared family responsibilities (Scarr, Phillips, & McCartney, 1989; Suchet & Barling, 1985). Research results by Barrett and Hyde (2001) generally support these earlier conclusions.

The issues surrounding the homemaker role in families where both husband and wife work outside the home (dual-earner and dual-career) have major significance. In dual-earner and dual-career families, both husband and wife work outside the home, but dual-career families are characterized as more career-oriented and committed to career development on a continuous basis. Both types of families share some common goals as well as sources of stress, such as role conflict, role overloads, and decreased opportunity for leisure. The following is a list of subjects for general discourse:

- Degree of commitment to the role of homemaker
- Career now and homemaker later
- Woman as a homemaker and the husband as a breadwinner
- Reasons both spouses may have to work
- Homemaker-worker connection
- Family life versus career commitment
- Significance of integrated life roles

Potential conflict issues such as the following should also be assessed:

- Decreased leisure
- Share of homemaker responsibilities
- View of traditional gender-based roles
- Stress from physical and emotional demands
- Multiple role demands
- Commitment to household chores
- Commitment to sharing child care responsibilities

- Commitment to development of spouse's career
- Nonsupport of spouse's career development
- Dissimilar levels of involvement in both work and family needs
- Decision-making procedures for such family matters as when to have children
- Expectations of family roles in dual-career marriages

Leisure Role

A number of clichés about the relationship of work and leisure have endured for generations. The primary message has been that a quality lifestyle is one in which there is a balance between time spent at work and time devoted to leisure activities. This message still prevails and has received renewed recognition as a means of fostering need satisfaction (Cavanaugh & Blanchard-Fields, 2002; Leclair, 1982). Within this frame of reference, quality of life is attained through a more holistic approach to human and career development.

Simply stated, individuals are to recognize that quality of life is associated with all life roles. Central to our concerns as career counselors is a balance of life roles that gives clients the freedom for self-expression to meet their needs. Moreover, when interrole conflicts are discovered, we have at our disposal a menu of suggestions designed to enhance all life roles.

In the early 1970s the complementary role that leisure had to the work role was expressed by Kando and Summers (1971) as two-dimensional, that is, it reinforces positive associations that are also expressed in the work role (supplemental compensation) and provides activities to reduce stress associated with unpleasant work experiences (reactive compensation). Brems (2001) takes a similar position on the relationship between work and leisure in that both can complement each other for a more balanced and healthier lifestyle. In a discussion of dimensions of leisure, Liptak (2001) makes the point that career and work are indeed intertwined. Following this logic, but with a somewhat different twist, Jackson (1988) suggested that individuals can receive psychological benefits from leisure, but only if they learn how to use the time spent in leisure in a purposeful manner. Sources of stress found in work, such as competition, can also become sources of stress in leisure activities.

The availability of time that can be devoted to leisure for any one individual is situational. However, McDaniels (1990) and Liptak (2001) advocated planning for different types of leisure as part of a counseling model. They also suggested that counselors act in an advocacy role to promote leisure activities in schools, workplaces, homes, and communities.

In sum, the leisure role should be assessed as a prolific means of complementing other life roles. The proportion of time a person allocates to leisure should be judged from the perspective of lifestyle. For example, the ambitious accountant might consider leisure activities as a luxury that has little current relevance, whereas the individual who is working full-time as a bus driver and part-time on two other jobs could view leisure as something that other, more fortunate people have. The involvement in leisure might simply be haphazard and left to chance. Although there is not a plethora of research about the benefits of leisure activities, some research indicates that effective participation in leisure can be therapeutic (Guinn, 1999; Ragheb & Griffith, 1982) and can compensate for dissatisfaction found in work (Bloland & Edwards, 1981; Brems, 2001; Kelly, 1996), which suggests that leisure activities are a most important part of lifestyle.

Suggested subjects for discourse are the following:

- Benefits of leisure activities
- Purpose for planning activities
- Types of leisure, including intellectual, creative, social, and physical activities
- Resources for information on leisure activities
- How to become involved in a leisure/work model
- Perspectives of a holistic lifestyle
- Recognition of conflicts with other life roles
- Role of leisure and career development
- Advantages of balancing life roles with leisure
- Identification of needs and values associated with the leisure role
- Psychological needs satisfied through leisure activities
- Work/leisure connection
- Developmental tasks related to leisure development
- Development of a greater level of interest in leisure activities

Citizen Role

Similar to the leisure role's link to quality of life, the citizen role can serve as an additional or compensating source of satisfaction. Also, it provides opportunities for fulfilling individual needs in a variety of activities found in most communities. Local civic organizations offer an abundance of opportunities for individuals to express civic responsibility as a way of responding to community needs. Although involvement in volunteerism was on the increase for community, state, national, and international projects in the late 1980s and the early part of the 1990s, downsizing of the U.S. workforce has created a different atmosphere in many communities. According to Rimer (1996), who reflected on a national poll sponsored by the *New York Times,* many communities had fewer volunteers for community service. Workers who had lost their jobs were desperately searching for ways to maintain their lifestyle and no longer had the time or the inclination to volunteer for civic services. In another study, Newman and Newman (2003) report that volunteerism among older adults is on the increase. Van Willigen (2000) suggests that volunteerism is highly related to general satisfaction with life. Thus, counselors need to observe the citizen role in the context of current conditions within communities.

The concept of balanced life roles implies that there are numerous opportunities to build a quality lifestyle. Individual work situations might not provide outlets to meet client needs associated with, for example, reading to blind students or being a tutor or a hospital aide. Productive opportunities outside the work role, however, are a means of satisfaction that enhance interrole activities. That is, some needs that might otherwise be left unmet or that produce stress can be satisfied through civic activities.

Bolles (2000), among others, has suggested that skills learned and developed through participation in civic organizations and activities can be used in career decision making. These skills can be matched with work requirements in career exploration. Also, volunteer experiences, along with education and other experiences, can be considered in job placement. In the interview, the counselor should assess the client for:

- Perception of the citizen's role
- Knowledge of civic organizations

- Knowledge of benefits from participating in civic activities
- Knowledge of benefits from participating in volunteerism
- Evaluation of skills learned through participation in civic activities
- Knowledge of how skills can be transferred to work roles
- Degree of participation in civic organizations
- Desire to participate in civic organizations
- Reasons for lack of participation in community activities
- Likes and dislikes of civic activities
- Family involvement in civic activities

In the next section we focus on work maladjustment and problems of living in contemporary society. In the 21st century's fluid working and living conditions, more attention should be paid to adult development and the give-and-take of life in an ever changing society. The objective here is to recognize the importance of adult concerns in the world of work, of the interrelationships of multiple life roles, and of career transition over the life span.

Discovering Problems That Interfere with Career Development

This part of the interview focuses on behavioral patterns of maladjustment. Identifying specific behavior domains that could contribute to conflicts in the work environment helps the career counselor identify goals and objectives for counseling intervention. For instance, individuals whose basic behavior style has been identified as overtly hostile and aggressive might respond to programs designed to manage anger and reduce aggression. "Problems in living" and methods of coping with these problems need to be identified. This approach does not rule out psychiatric etiology as a source of work maladjustment but focuses more on the individual's ability to cope with work demands. Perhaps more important, mental disorders do not necessarily affect work behavior. Neff (1985) pointed out that the ability to function on a job is related to the nature of both an individual's mental health and his or her mental illness. More research is needed, however, to establish the relationship between work-related problems and mental disorders.

The fourth edition of the *Diagnostic and Statistical Manual of Mental Disorders* (DSM-IV) (American Psychiatric Association [APA], 1994) has several categories of mental, social, and behavioral disorders. Although all these disorders can appear in the workplace, references to work impairment or dysfunctions are very generalized. The following quote from the DSM-IV (APA, 1994) is a guideline for how we must individualize our interpretation of mental disorders and the subsequent behavior associated with a disorder.

> In DSM-IV, there is no assumption that each category of mental disorder is a completely discrete entity with absolute boundaries dividing it from other mental disorders or from no mental disorder. There is also no assumption that all individuals described as having the same mental disorder are alike in all important ways. The clinician using the DSM-IV should therefore consider that individuals sharing a diagnosis are likely to be heterogeneous even in regard to the defining features of the diagnosis and that boundary cases will be difficult to diagnose in any but a probabilistic fashion. (p. xxii)

Behaviors That Can Lead to Work Maladjustment

One of our objectives in the intake interview is to identify individualized behavior patterns that impair the work role. Table 5-1 presents symptoms of behavior and faulty cognitive functioning that can lead to work impairment. These symptoms were adapted from personality disorders and descriptions of depression found in DSM-IV (APA, 1994). The information can be used as guidelines for identifying similar patterns of behavior in clients being interviewed. The purpose of this table is not to classify clients according to any particular disorder but, more important, to serve as a guide for identifying behavioral contingencies and faulty assumptions that could lead to work impairment. A client identified as having poor social interaction skills, for instance, might also have difficulty relating to work affiliates and, thus, develop negative meanings associated with work.

Table 5-1 identifies disorders by behaviors, beliefs, and traits. The column "Work Impairments" suggests that some clients might have difficulty in the workplace when the behaviors, beliefs, or traits listed in the column are dominant and extreme. On the other hand, behaviors, beliefs, and traits associated with disorders do not necessarily lead to work impairment as suggested in the column "Other Work Role Observations." Using this logic, the interviewer attempts to determine the degree to which an identified behavior or trait affects the work role. For example, work involving interpersonal interactions might be difficult for some clients, but these clients have managed to become productive workers. Perhaps they could improve their potential with interventions designed to help them overcome this problem in all life roles, but their needs are not as obvious as are those of someone who simply cannot function effectively with others. In sum, the severity of the identified needs determines the course and extent of intervention strategies.

In the DSM-IV, personality disorders are grouped into three clusters—A, B, and C—to accommodate the commonalities found among them. For example, career clients who resemble the characteristics, traits, and behaviors found in the Cluster A group might appear strange, peculiar, and bizarre. Likewise, those career clients who resemble the characteristics associated with the Cluster B group could appear highly emotional and dramatic. Those identified with Cluster C might appear anxious and fearful. The commonalities and overlap of symptoms found in personality disorders suggest that clients can demonstrate behaviors, beliefs, and traits of more than one personality disorder.

Patterns of Work Psychopathology

In an attempt to organize qualities of work behavior that lead to failure in work, Neff (1985) identified five types of patterns of work psychopathology using classifications ranging from Type I to Type V, as shown in Table 5-2. Individuals can be "typed" only when the characteristics listed predominate work behavior. Neff warns that not all clients will fit into these categories; some could have characteristics of several.

Taxonomy of Psychological Work-Related Dysfunctions

Lowman (1993) has attempted to devise a clinically useful taxonomy of psychological work-related dysfunctions, as reported in Table 5-3. One of his major premises is to illuminate the distinction between psychopathology and work dysfunctions, but he also reminds mental health workers that the two types of problems can coexist. For example, psychopathology may or may not affect work performance, and the presence of worker dysfunctions may or may not have an impact on psychopathology.

The disturbances in the capacity to work in Table 5-3 are useful categories for delineating worker dysfunctions. These patterns are summarized as follows. Underachievement is an apparent discrepancy between the individual's ability and performance. Possible causes are passive-aggressive behavior, procrastination, or periodic inhibition to work. Fear of success refers to intentional underachievement because of perceived negative consequences associated with being successful. Fear of failure suggests that an individual withholds work efforts for fear of not being successful.

Other disturbances in the capacity to work such as patterns of overcommitment include an obsessive-compulsive personality disorder that is referenced in Table 5-1. The well-known Type A behavior pattern has long been associated with cardiovascular concerns among individuals overcommitted to work. Burnout is used to describe a number of work-related behaviors, such as when an individual plateaus, which suggests that individual has reached her or his highest level in the workplace. Work overload, boredom, lack of advancement opportunities, and time pressure are often associated with burnout. Transient and situational stress (section II F) are associated with job change, loss of job, and with workplace changes. The last category in this section, perceptual inaccuracies (section II G), refers to differences between the individual worker's perception of the workplace and what actually exists. Finally, category III, dysfunctional working conditions, refers to problems associated with the assigned job itself (such as too demanding or too difficult work), the quality or lack of supervision, and the possibility of poor interpersonal relationships. All these issues represent potential conflicts associated with working conditions.

The guidelines for identifying characteristics that could lead to work impairment or work dysfunctions associated with personality disorders, Neff's patterns of work psychopathology, and Lowman's taxonomy of psychological work-related dysfunctions must be used with caution. Identified characteristics must predominate to be significant. Moreover, work behavior is considered to be a semiautonomous area of personality and, as such, might not be affected by personality disorders. On the other hand, work maladaptation might be linked to personality disorders. In essence, work dysfunctions are the result of a complex interaction of personal characteristics and the workplace. In sum, these guidelines present examples of potential work behavior problems and should be used as such.

Faulty Cognitions

Helpers are challenged to give more attention to cognitive processes in career counseling from the social-learning and cognitive theory approaches to career development discussed in Chapter 2. Somewhat similar approaches to cognitive functioning are irrational beliefs (Ellis, 1994) and faulty reasoning (Beck, 1985). More specifically, the individual's perceptions of self and of people, events, experiences, and environment are seen as potential sources of mistaken and troublesome beliefs. Inaccurate information, inadequate alternatives, and negative constructs derived from life experiences are sources of faulty cognitions.

Faulty cognitions inhibit systematic, logical thinking and can be self-defeating. For example, a client's expectations and assumptions can cause distorted perceptions

Table 5-1	Work Role Projections		
Identification	Behaviors, beliefs, traits	Work impairment	Other work role observations
Cluster A[1] Paranoid career client	Suspicious of others, especially authority figures Avoids participation in group activities Reluctant to self-disclose Hostile and defensive Strong need to be self-sufficient	Poor interpersonal relationships with boss and peer group.	May meet demands of work role because of high ambition, especially in work environments that are highly structured and nonthreatening.
Schizoid career client	Very indecisive Vague about goals Does not desire or enjoy close relationships Prefers solitary activities Often aloof	Work involving interpersonal interactions is difficult.	May work well in an environment that provides social isolation.
Cluster B[1] Antisocial career client	Truancy, vandalism, stealing Nonconformity to social norms Very aggressive Inconsistent work behavior Poor emotional control	Difficulty in sustaining productive work.	Clients who are identified as having only several characteristics of this disorder may be able to function successfully in a work role. However, full-blown antisocial career clients have considerable interference with work roles.
Borderline career client	Poor self-concept Difficulty in establishing long-term goals Difficulty with career choice Difficulty with identifying preferred values Impulsive Unstable interpersonal relations Uncertainty about life roles	Impulsive behavior interferes with work role functioning; poor commitment to work.	The instability and impulsive nature of borderline career clients presents considerable interference with most life roles, including the work role.

[1]Not all personality disorders are included in Clusters A, B, and C.

Source: Adapted from *Diagnostic and Statistical Manual of Mental Disorders,* 4th ed. rev., by the American Psychiatric Association, 1994.

Table 5-1	(continued)

Identification	Behaviors, beliefs, traits	Work impairment	Other work role observations
Narcissistic career client	Exploits others Shows little concern for others Expects favorable treatment Excessive feelings of self-importance Constantly seeks attention	Poor interpersonal relationships; may pursue unrealistic goals while exploiting co-workers.	Because of a strong need for success and power, these clients are able to meet requirements and sometimes excel in work role functioning.
Cluster C[1] Obsessive-compulsive career client	Preoccupied with trivial details Seeks perfection in work tasks to the point that task completion is constantly delayed Has strong need for inflexible routines Avoids decision making Unnecessarily devoted to organizing tasks	Poor task completion. Poor productivity. Subject to stress because of indecision.	Because of excessive conscientiousness and extreme attention to detail, these clients are able to function in work roles that require highly organized procedures.
Avoidant career client	Poor interpersonal skills Avoids occupational activities that involve interpersonal contact Is preoccupied with being criticized or being rejected Is reluctant to take personal risks	Work role is affected by poor interpersonal skills.	Work role functioning is limited to environments that are non-threatening and only require minimum social contacts.
Depressed[2] career client	Lacks interest and pleasure in most activities Has difficulty in concentrating on tasks Behavior is typically lethargic and shows loss of energy Has difficulty sleeping or sleeps excessively Expresses negative feelings toward and about self Dejected mood Low self-evaluations	In severe cases, clients are not able to function in work role.	In mild to moderate cases of depression, some interference can be expected, but not all clients are totally inefficient.

[2]The depressed career client is not considered a personality disorder.

Table 5-2	Neff's Patterns of Work Psychopathology

Type	Characteristics
I—Individuals who lack motivation to work	• Have a negative concept of the work role. • Are indifferent to productive work. • Will work if coerced. • Meet minimum standards of work tasks. • Resist work commitment. • Require close supervision. • Lack need or desire to work.
II—Individuals who experience fear and anxiety in response to being productive	• Feel incapable of being productive. • Feel too inept to meet work demands. • Have low self-esteem. • Competition at work is extremely threatening. • Cooperative work efforts are difficult. • Lack self-confidence. • May retreat from work environment if severely threatened.
III—Individuals who are hostile and aggressive	• Underlying hostility is easily aroused. • Peer affiliation is viewed as potentially dangerous. • Are quick to quarrel with others. • Relation with supervisory personnel is precarious and threatening. • Work roles are often viewed as too demanding and restrictive. • Have very poor interpersonal relationships.
IV—Individuals who are very dependent on others	• Early socialization convinces them that the way to self-preservation is to please others. • Believe that the key to work success is pleasing authority figures. • Have a strong need for constant approval, particularly from supervisors.
V—Individuals who display a marked degree of social naivete	• Have very little knowledge of work environment and demands of work role. • Lack simple understanding of work role involvement. • Have no perception of self as a successful worker to meet even minimal standards. • Unable to project self into work role.

SOURCE: Adapted from Neff, 1985.

Table 5-3	Toward a Clinically Useful Taxonomy of Psychological Work-Related Dysfunctions

I. Determining the relation between psychopathology and work dysfunctions
  A. Affecting work performance
  B. Not affecting work performance
  C. Affected by work performance
  D. Not affected by work performance
II. Disturbances in the capacity to work
  A. Patterns of undercommitment
    1. Underachievement
    2. Temporary production impediments
    3. Procrastination
    4. Occupational misfit
    5. Organizational misfit
    6. Fear of success
    7. Fear of failure
  B. Patterns of overcommitment
    1. Obsessive-compulsive addiction to the work role ("workaholism")
    2. Type A behavior pattern
    3. Job and occupational burnout
  C. Work-related anxiety and depression
    1. Anxiety
      a. Performance anxiety
      b. Generalized anxiety
    2. Work-related depression
  D. Personality dysfunctions and work
    1. Problems with authority
    2. Personality disorders and work
  E. Life role conflicts
    1. Work-family conflicts
  F. Transient, situational stress
    1. Reactions to changes in the work role (e.g., new job) whose impact on the work role is time limited.
  G. Other psychologically relevant work difficulties
    1. Perceptual inaccuracies
III. Dysfunctional working conditions
  A. Defective job design (role overload, ambiguity, etc.)
  B. Defective supervision
  C. Dysfunctional interpersonal relationships

and unrealistic thinking such as "There is only one career for me." Doyle (1992) presented the following examples of faulty cognition that he suggested can lead to false conclusions and negative feelings:

1. Self-deprecating statements: These expressions reveal poor self-worth, for example, "I'm not a good student" or "No one really likes me."
2. Absolute or perfectionist terms: When an individual sets up overly stringent guidelines for his or her behavior, the individual sets himself or herself up for self-criticism and a negative self-image. Conclusions that are absolute or perfectionistic often include words such as must, ought, should, unless, or until. For example, "I should have been the one promoted" or "Unless I get an 'A,' I can't go home."
3. Overgeneralization of negative experiences: These are deductions based on too few examples of situations. Frequently, they are based on negative experiences that make clients think there are many obstacles, making the future hopeless and bleak. For example, "Since I failed the first exam, I will fail the course" or "All the children in school hate me."
4. Negative exaggerations: These statements greatly magnify the true meaning of an event or reality. For example, "All professional athletes are greedy" or "You insulted my mother—you hate my family!"
5. Factually inaccurate statements: These remarks are based on inadequate or incorrect information. These erroneous data distort the client's perceptions of reality. For example, "You need an 'A' average to get into college" or "Autistic children are lazy."
6. Ignorance of the effects of time: These assertions ignore growth, maturation, and the effect that the passage of time can have on experience or events. For example, "He was a very poor student last year—he will surely fail this year" or "I have to go back to the lake and relive my vacation there" (p. 85).

Although faulty cognitions can lead to a multitude of personal problems, Mitchell and Krumboltz (1996) argued that the career decision-making process is most affected. Looking at it from a positive viewpoint, individuals with accurate, constructive beliefs will have fewer problems reaching their career goals. Moreover, realistic expectations foster positive emotional reactions to self and others. In sum, this portion of the interview requires an assessment of the client's beliefs, generalities that cause a belief, other bases for a belief, and the actions that are a result of a belief (Mitchell & Krumboltz, 1987).

Examples of faulty cognitions from Doyle (1992) offer a sound basis for assessing a faulty deductive-thinking process. Doyle's (1992) five examples are ways of thinking that reflect negative feelings about oneself. Irrational expectations of career counseling, as suggested by Nevo (1987), are examples of faulty cognitions and irrational thoughts often found in prospective clients:

1. There is only one vocation in the world that is right for me.
2. Until I find my perfect vocational choice, I will not be satisfied.
3. Someone else can discover the vocation suitable for me.
4. Intelligence tests would tell me how much I am worth.
5. I must be an expert or very successful in the field of my work.
6. I can do anything if I try hard, or I can't do anything that doesn't fit my talents.
7. My vocation should satisfy the important people in my life.

8. Entering a vocation will solve all my problems.
9. I must sense intuitively that the vocation is right for me.
10. Choosing a vocation is a one-time act.

The goal for the interviewer is to help clients identify maladaptive thinking. Using "choosing a vocation is a one-time act" as an example, the counselor asked the client to explain this expressed belief in the following case.

The Case of Faulty Cognitions

CLIENT: I want to find my lifetime job now and get it over with so I can go on to other things.

COUNSELOR: What kind of job did you have in mind?

CLIENT: I thought that's what you're supposed to help me with . . . anyway, I want a job that I can start in when I graduate.

The counselor then asked the client to describe the basis for his belief.

COUNSELOR: Do you think you will stay with the job you choose now for the rest of your life?

CLIENT: Well, I guess so. My father has worked as a bookkeeper as long as I can remember.

COUNSELOR: Was he always a bookkeeper?

CLIENT: Umm, come to think of it, he did work somewhere else.

COUNSELOR: Do you think you might also have other job opportunities in the future?

CLIENT: Well . . . I guess I will.

The counselor was now in a position to explain the idea of career development over the life span and the importance of learning career decision-making techniques and adopting a lifelong commitment. In addition, he could help the client analyze faulty reasoning and false assumptions. The path to a more logical approach to career decision making needed to be established.

Doyle (1992) suggested a technique for helping this client work through faulty reasoning. The client writes out beliefs and conclusions and the assumptions on which they are based. For example:

All bankers are rich.

Once you are a banker, you drive a big car.

The only way for me to get rich is to become a banker.

The rationale for this exercise is based on the premise that faulty reasoning and faulty logic usually have underlying faulty assumptions. Having clients write out their assumptions in this manner assists them in recognizing that their beliefs may be inaccurate.

Yet another way of helping clients identify faulty cognitions is through the *Career Beliefs Inventory* (CBI) (Krumboltz, 1991) and *Career Thoughts Inventory* (CTI) (Sampson, Peterson, Lenz, Reardon, & Saunders, 1996a). If a counselor strongly suspects that a client has developed faulty assumptions that are measurable by the CBI or CTI, these instruments could prove to be a valuable counseling tool. Career counselors should be familiar with such inventories particularly those that help clients expose false beliefs that interfere with wise decision making.

Another technique used to help clients recognize that they have some control of their destiny is the concept of locus of control (Rotter, 1966). Counselors arrange learning situations that prove clients can gain control of their lives through appropriate actions.

Clarifying Problems

A most important stage in the career counseling process is client problem identification. You will recall that all five career counseling models in Chapter 3 emphasized methods and procedures that identify problems and concerns clients bring to counseling. Counselors are to clarify client concerns and needs into a format that is straightforward and concrete. This step often requires in-depth probing. A client's presenting problems, for example, may be the client's way of "testing the waters" before a trusting relationship is established. Counselors, therefore, use their interviewing skills to uncover the "real problems." The following questions adapted from Brems (2001) and Cormier and Nurius (2003) are examples that can be used:

In what circumstances does this problem arise?

How intense is this problem and how often does it occur?

When and where does this problem arise?

Could you please describe some of the things that disturb you?

Whiston (2000) suggests that the counselor is to: "(1) Explore the problem from multiple perspectives, (2) Gather specific information on each problem, (3) Assess problem intensity, (4) Assess degree to which client believes the problem is changeable, and (5) Identify methods the client has used to solve the problem previously" (p. 115).

Thus, the importance of clarifying problems is obvious in that it suggests criteria from which one selects counseling goals and effective interventions. In order to be most effective, problems are clarified into concrete statements that clearly state specific examples of the client's environmental influences, emotions, thinking, and behavior. Keep in mind that problems are usually multidimensional. Some examples for clarifying problems follow.

Kent's presenting problem was "difficulty in getting along with the people I work with." Instead of labeling the problem as one of "poor interpersonal relationships," the counselor wisely probed for more specific information. Kent's private beliefs included the feeling that "no one really cares for me." He expressed self-criticism and tended to reject people first so that they would not have the chance to reject him. Kent also revealed that early interactions with his family were very unpleasant and stressful, which resulted in poor self-regard and feeling that he was misunderstood. He seemed convinced that his chances of getting hurt would be less in the future if he ignored others.

Instead of developing interventions from the vague presenting problem, the counselor was now in the position to use specifically stated real problems and subsequent behaviors. The counselor zeroed in on the client's perceptions, feelings, and actions and developed a collaborative relationship in which they agreed jointly on strategies. In this case *underlying reasons* for poor personal interrelationships were addressed as well as strategies in how to effectively relate to others. Client and counselor explored how problems of this type are very pervasive and can affect all life roles. As discussed in Chapter 4, career and personal concerns are inseparable and intertwined.

Carla was referred as an anxious client who was unable to make a career decision. Considerable time was spent with Carla to establish rapport and trust. Eventually, after a number of probing questions, Carla identified her overriding problem as conflicts with her family over career choice. She wanted a career in engineering but the family wanted her to work in a local factory. She was torn between her loyalty to family and what may be best for them and her own individual goals. Carla was raised by a family that expected each member to do what is best for their collective survival as a group. The real problem in this case was a conflict between the influence of an American individualistic view versus another culture's collectivist view. This case points out that some client concerns involve *culturally shaped relationships* that may be different than the dominant society. The major problem for Carla was embedded within cultural contexts of her environment.

In sum, counselors use *all the information* gathered in the intake interview to determine counseling strategies. The rule of thumb is to not overlook the smallest detail that at times may be expressed by the client in a rather cavalier manner. A health problem, for example, may be the clue to an underlying emotional situation. As we discovered in the previous examples, presenting problems do not always tell the whole story. Counselors must have the skills to ask probing questions in a manner that will encourage clients to reveal the real problems that have been held back. Finally, counselor and client are to clarify problems in specific concrete terms and agree on intervention strategies that will meet the client's needs and concerns.

Case Examples

Excerpts of case studies are provided in this final section. The first case of the confused decision maker provides an example of problems associated with initial career choice. The second case of what was left unsaid is an example of incomplete background information about a client. The third case of the anxious computer technician is an example of a troubled adult in the workforce. The case of the fired plumber is an example of interrole conflict involving the interrelationship of family and work roles. The final case of the unfulfilled worker involves a significant search for identifying individual and family needs.

The Case of the Confused Decision Maker

Kris, a 17-year-old high school student, asked for help in choosing a career. She reported to the counselor's office with one of her older brothers. She stated, "I cannot decide what to major in at college."

Kris was neatly dressed and well groomed. Her speech was fluent and of normal rate and rhythm. She tended to speak very softly. She seemed to be somewhat anxious about making a career decision. She did not appear to be depressed. She constantly looked to her brother for approval.

In the top 10% of her class, Kris had a record of being a very capable student. She had good rapport with teachers as well as with her peer group. She strongly identified with several girls her age at the high school.

Kris had five brothers, and her father was a meat inspector in a local plant. He worked hard to maintain the family. Her mother had never worked outside the home.

When the counselor asked Kris to come into his office alone, she seemed very uncomfortable and asked if her brother could attend the session with her. The counselor reassured her that they would have ample time to talk with her brother later. She reluctantly agreed to begin the interview.

From the description Kris gave of her home environment, the counselor assumed it was very traditional. Moreover, the chores assigned to the children typically were based on what the parents considered appropriate work for boys and for girls. There seemed to be strict stereotypical roles embedded in Kris's perception of traditional work roles for women. She appeared to be very passive and gave the impression that she expected someone else to make decisions for her.

When discussing future objectives, Kris seemed quite confused when the counselor suggested she consider all careers, including nontraditional ones. At one time she had expressed an interest in architecture but considered it to be for men only and therefore decided against it as a possible choice.

Kris's behavior pattern reflected little confidence in her abilities and she deferred to others for decision making. She appeared to be quite uneasy when she was asked to leave her brother and constantly referred to him as giving her good advice and reassuring her of what was best for her. The following dialogue demonstrates her dependency needs.

KRIS: My parents will help me choose the right kind of work.

COUNSELOR: Could you tell me more about your parents choosing the right kind of work for you?

KRIS: My mother and father usually help me with most of the things that I decide on, and if they don't, my older brothers do.

From these excerpts, it seemed clear that Kris was quite dependent on others for decision making. Kris's background and behavior patterns closely matched Neff's (1985) Type IV pattern of individuals who are very dependent on others. The counselor feared that Kris might make career decisions on the basis of what her family considered best for her, rather than on her own interests, values, and abilities. Also, the counselor suspected that if Kris's current behavior patterns continued as is, she would suffer the consequences of a Type IV worker and develop work-related dysfunctions as outlined by Lowman (1993).

The counselor's strategy consisted of building greater rapport with Kris and establishing a basic trust, using the following guidelines:

1. Be respectful and genuine.
2. Focus on developing self-awareness by using reflective procedures.
3. Assist her in understanding how environmental circumstances influenced her behavior.
4. Help her establish alternative ways of thinking and behaving.
5. Assist her in recognizing how she can control her own destiny by illustrating the concept of locus of control; that is, how external and internal people think.
6. Help her recognize the relevance of her values and interests in a career decision-making mode.
7. Introduce career decision-making steps as discussed in Chapter 3.

To promote more realistic goals for career decision making, especially toward self-direction, the counselor chose a cognitive behavioral-intervention strategy (Corey, 1991; Ellis, 1994). The first step included techniques to help Kris separate rational beliefs from irrational ones. Second, the counselor assisted Kris in modifying her thinking, especially the thoughts associated with stereotypical gender-role development. Third, the counselor challenged Kris to develop a greater self-awareness and a more realistic philosophy of integrated life role development. To help her reduce stereotyping in career options, Kris visited job sites for the purpose of observing women at work. Kris will need support over a rather lengthy period of time to debunk dependency needs and to develop self-directive behavior in order to make an optimal career choice.

The Case of What Was Left Unsaid

Ida, a 36-year-old woman, was referred by a mental health agency to a state-supported agency that provided career counseling. Information sent with the referral contained demographic data, educational history, a diagnosis of clinical depression, and prescribed medication. The following notes were made by the career counselor as she interviewed Ida.

A. **General appearance**
    Client was appropriately dressed.
    Hair had not been recently washed.
    Wore little or no makeup.
    Wore glasses.
    Gait was normal.
    Movements were without tremor.
    Carried envelope and placed it on desk.

B. **Attitude and behavior**
Introduced herself.
Eye contact was appropriate.
No evidence of unusual behavior.

C. **Affect and mood**
Said she was depressed.
Did appear rather lifeless.
Stated that she was somewhat nervous about being interviewed.
Stated she "felt good" especially when she was alone.
Said she didn't like "being around a lot of people."

D. **Demographic information**
Said she was married four times, but could not remember the birth sequence of four children or which marriage they were from.
High-pitched voice during discussion of marriages.
Currently living with a cousin who helps care for her children.

E. **Work experiences**
Difficulty in recalling work experiences.
Held part-time job in fast-food restaurant during senior year in high school and for several months after graduation.
Waitressed in several local restaurants.
Was a receptionist in accounting firm for about four months.
Disliked restaurant work.
Enjoyed work as a receptionist; claims she left because she was hospitalized.

F. **Medical history**
Stated that she was in good health until age 29 when she was hospitalized for depression. Was placed in a psychiatric hospital for five days. Has been treated as an outpatient with medication for several years but was unable to specify exactly how long.
Felt that failure in marriage was a major cause of depression.
Has difficulty sleeping.
Reported no other significant illnesses.

G. **Educational history**
Finished high school with average grades.
Dropped out of a community college course in computer programming. Said she had a strange feeling "that she should not finish this course."

During the interview the counselor observed vague references to past history. Even with further questioning, she could not get appropriate feedback:

COUNSELOR: Ida, could you tell me more about the feeling you experienced that convinced you not to finish the computer programming course?

IDA: I don't know how to explain it—it was just like something told me not to finish.

COUNSELOR: Something told you not to finish?

IDA: Yeah, I can't explain it.

Another example was expressions about work experiences.

IDA: I quit working with them because my uncle told me to.

COUNSELOR: Does your uncle often give you advice?

IDA: He helps me a lot—he just seems to know what's best.

The counselor decided to end the interview and get more information about Ida's past history. Another appointment was set to continue the interview. In the meantime, a complete report was received from a mental health agency, which contained a signed release, social history, and psychological workup. Ida had been diagnosed as a schizophrenic, undifferentiated type, and had been hospitalized on three occasions in the last five years. When Ida was asked why she didn't mention the hospitalization, she responded with a shrug. The counselor also discovered that the uncle who was currently advising Ida had died ten years earlier.

In the case of severe psychiatric problems, there is usually evidence of marked impairment of life role functioning, particularly in the work role and homemaker role. The client's suggestion of a "sixth sense" telling her to abruptly quit an educational program and the fact that she felt controlled by someone else was enough evidence to request more in-depth information. Because the psychiatric and psychological evaluation was three years old, the counselor requested a complete update.

One of the major learning outcomes of this case is the importance of obtaining all available client information. The documented history of severe psychological problems does not always translate into suspending career counseling but may require an up-to-date evaluation of current psychological status.

The Case of the Anxious Computer Technician

A 28-year-old male computer technician named John sought the services of a career counselor in private practice. His major complaint was a recent upsurge in anxiety when a new group of workers was assigned to his department. He felt threatened by them and, as he saw it, was treated as an outsider and definitely not as part of their group. He feared that he would be fired and considered resigning and finding a different job or asking for reassignment to another department.

John appeared to be anxious; he moved around in his chair and the pitch of his voice changed, particularly when talking about this new group of people. He constantly moved his arms and hands and clenched his fists. He did not appear to be depressed and stated that he felt very anxious.

John had never seriously considered marriage; he saw himself as a "loner." Furthermore, he had few friends and spoke of himself as being shy, with limited social contacts. John evaluated his educational background as average or above in academics. He had received computer training from a local community college. He was currently taking more courses. John characterized his student life in much the same way as his current situation—that is, few social activities and a feeling of isolation.

He interpreted his role as citizen as voting in most elections; he did not participate in any civic activities. He expressed a feeling of rejection by the individuals he had met in organizations. John collected musical records from the Big Band era and enjoyed listening to them when he was alone. He occasionally attended movies, visited his parents, and watched TV.

When expressing work role experiences, his anxiety seemed to peak, as observed by increased motor activity. Earlier trends of isolating himself from contact with others continued in the current work environment; he ate by himself in the cafeteria and did not join bull sessions during breaks. He did not have a "good" friend among the peer group. He characterized his work role as quietly getting the job done.

John's symptoms of anxiety seemed to be related to a long-standing pattern of difficulty with social interactions. Low self-esteem, feelings of rejection, and avoidance of social activities were embedded in most of his statements. These characteristics are found in Neff's (1985) Type II work psychopathology, in Cluster A personality disorders, and in Lowman's (1993) work-related anxiety work dysfunction taxonomy.

However, John does not exhibit all of the Type II characteristics; likewise, he cannot be identified with any one personality disorder but has characteristics of two or more. This example could be quite typical of many career clients and supports the assumption that identified behaviors, actions, beliefs, and thinking can be generically evaluated as contingencies that could lead to work maladjustment. In sum, John had a history of being an acceptable worker. His life roles could be enhanced with better social skills and more positive self-concepts as a worker and social being. John wanted to change jobs for the wrong reasons. The counselor suggested that he could explore other career opportunities and simultaneously participate in a counseling program designed to help him recognize sources of stress. Other intervention strategies selected were anxiety-management training, social skills and assertiveness training, and relaxation training. In addition, thought-stopping techniques (Cautela & Wisock, 1977; Doyle, 1998) and self-talk were used to eliminate inappropriate thinking, negative self-concepts, and worry-oriented thinking.

The counseling intervention strategies proposed for John were based on the following premise: Emotions are often the result of how we think, and a change in John's thinking process could reduce or eliminate emotional disorders and dysfunctional behaviors (Ellis 1994; Lazarus, 1989; Trower, Casey, & Dryden, 1988). This case illustrates that there are many sources of stress in the work environment, including poor communications between management and workers and between peer groups.

The Case of the Fired Plumber

Yuri, a 40-year-old plumber, requested career counseling to change jobs. "I don't like this plumbing work anymore," he said. He was dressed in soiled work clothes and hadn't shaved for several days. Yuri appeared to be anxious; he constantly moved in his chair, raised his arms, and clenched his fists. He was grossly overweight and asked that he be given permission to smoke. His speech was fluent and of normal rate and rhythm.

Yuri completed high school but had no other formal training. He claimed to be an average student and never failed a grade. During on-the-job training, he learned the skills to become a licensed plumber.

Starting at the lowest level in plumbing, he had advanced to master plumber status and had been employed as a plumber for 12 years. He was recently fired for disruptive behavior and fighting with two fellow workers.

Yuri reported no serious medical problems and had no history of psychiatric treatment. He had been a tobacco smoker for 15 years and occasionally drank alcohol.

For leisure, Yuri watched sports on TV and enjoyed renting movies for home viewing. He also enjoyed watching his son play Little League baseball and regularly practiced with him. Short family vacations consisted of visiting relatives and camping.

Yuri was not active in civic affairs, other than annually helping organize the local Little League. He claimed that he had so little time off from his work that it would be difficult for him to actively participate in civic organizations.

Evidently, Yuri felt that household duties were "woman's work," and even though his wife worked full time outside the home, he did not help with tasks such as cooking, shopping, washing, or housecleaning. He did mow the yard and water the grass. Yuri complained that his wife had recently demanded his help with household chores, which resulted in several major arguments that lasted for days. Yuri and his wife were not on very good terms and had seriously considered divorce. Shortly after his wife chose to spend several days with her mother to "sort things out," Yuri was fired for fighting on the job.

The fact that Yuri had worked for the same plumbing company and with most of the same peer affiliates for 15 years is evidence that he had the skills necessary to interact appropriately within a work environment. It was also clear that Yuri's relations with his wife were in turmoil. Although it was difficult for the counselor to determine whether serious marital problems had existed for a long time, it was clear that Yuri's refusal to help with household chores precipitated the most recent problems. Yuri admitted that he enjoyed working as a plumber, but the stress associated with dual-earner problems had probably influenced how he felt about his current work environment.

This case is a good example of how one life role affects another. The major problem was conflict between husband and wife who both worked full time outside the home, not Yuri's desire for a job change. The counselor's plan was to have Yuri and his wife commit to counseling, with an emphasis on sharing responsibilities and household tasks.

The techniques suggested were based on Hansen's (1996, 2000) Integrative Life Planning Model, which encourages couples to move away from dominant-subordinate relationships toward being equal partners. Among other changes suggested in this model is movement from the position of "job to life roles, and from achievement only to achievement and relationships for both women and men" (Hansen, 1991, p. 84). Career decision making for a different job would be deferred for the time being. Yuri agreed to relocate to a different company as a plumber.

Work and family are not separate worlds, and the case of the fired plumber illustrates how conflict in the homemaker role influenced Yuri's behavior in the work role. Other problem areas that can contribute to conflicts include the following:

Shift work

Separation and travel

Relocation

Work spillover (preoccupation with work role)

Relationships with supervisors

The Case of the Unfulfilled Worker

Gui, a 42-year-old married woman, was self-referred to a career counselor in private practice because, as she put it, "I really don't know what's wrong with me. I like my job and I'm happy with my marriage and my family, but something is missing in my life." Gui was very attractive and neatly and appropriately dressed. She had a new hairdo and made an outstanding appearance. She was very fluent and her speech was of normal rate and rhythm. Although Gui had a positive attitude about her work and many other factors of her life, she still felt that she could improve her lifestyle. She expressed dismay at not being able to be more specific about what was troubling her. She seemed to be somewhat depressed but stated that she was feeling well.

Gui had married twice. Her first marriage lasted only a short period, and, as she put it, she married when she was very young and made a mistake. She'd been married the second time for more than 20 years and had one child from this marriage. Her child was now attending college. Her husband was a professional engineer and earned a good income.

Gui had several odd jobs while in high school and college working in fast-food places and dress shops. She was currently managing a local dress shop and had this position for at least six years. She felt very comfortable in this work and enjoyed meeting people and doing the usual tasks that were involved in running and managing the shop. She expressed no particular desire to get another job but would be willing to if she were able to fulfill her needs better.

Gui stated that she was in excellent health and had never had any significant health problems. She was of medium height and weight.

Gui had received an A.A. degree at a local community college and currently was taking courses at a nearby university. She hoped to receive a degree in business management in the near future.

Gui and her husband, a dual-career couple, seemed to have worked out a very satisfactory relationship in their homemaker roles. Her husband participated in household tasks and assumed responsibilities that gave Gui more time to take care of her work and attend classes at college. She expressed no problems with her marital life and stated that her husband also seemed to be very happy.

As stated earlier, Gui felt that her work role was satisfactory. She had dreamed of managing a dress shop while she was an employee several years ago, and now the opportunity had been given to her. The dress shop she currently managed had been very successful, and she had received several awards from the parent company for exceptional sales. She claimed to relate well to both employees and customers. She was taking a business management course to improve her skills in management.

Because of the strong commitment to upgrade their careers, both Gui and her husband devoted little time to leisure activities. They exercised together in the morning by jogging or walking and attended various events in the community such as theater, movies, and art exhibits. Gui stated that they took the usual family vacations, such as trips to national parks and historical places.

When asked about participation in civic activities, Gui seemed somewhat bewildered and stated that she simply wouldn't have time to participate in these activities because of her full schedule. She was not aware of activities in local civic organizations and had not considered volunteerism.

The counselor returned to Gui's statement, "Something's missing in my life." The counselor asked her to express this feeling more fully:

Gui: I don't know how to really explain it, and I feel guilty about even talking to someone about this. For gosh sakes, I have a great husband and a marvelous child and a very good job. I can't put a finger on what's wrong with me, but I seem to have a feeling that I want to do other things that I'm not doing at this time.

Counselor: Tell me more about the feeling that you want to do "other things."

Gui: Well, I have to give that some thought, but I guess what I really mean is I have a lot of interests and I haven't been able to fulfill many of them.

Counselor: Tell me more about your interests.

Gui: The first one that strikes my fancy is that I had dreams of being an artist, but when I took art classes and started painting, I quickly realized that I didn't have the talent to go on. But, I'm still interested in art and miss being around arts-and-crafts people.

Counselor: Have you ever thought of taking an art class in college?

Gui: Yes, I've had several of those, but I don't want to continue taking art classes.

As the conversation continued, the counselor felt that a values inventory might help Gui clarify needs she could not identify. The counselor recalled that values tend to remain fairly stable and endure over the life span. She felt that this might be an area that would help Gui come to some realization of what she would like to do in the future.

The counselor decided to use the Five-Step Process for Using Assessment Results developed by Zunker (1994). The steps are paraphrased as follows:

Step 1: Analyzing Needs

In this step, the counselor ascertains the client's perception of her need for information to foster self-knowledge. In evaluating Gui's lifestyle, the counselor decided that work climate, family responsibilities, and leisure time had been committed, but rewarding activities in the community had been given little attention.

Counselor: Gui, you've expressed a very positive viewpoint of your work, family, and leisure activities. In fact, you had no negative thoughts concerning these life roles. It seems to be that other areas of your lifestyle may be lacking—what do you think?

Gui: You're probably right, but the only thing that you've mentioned so far has been civic activities, and as I told you, I know very little about them.

Counselor: Okay, well, I can give you more information about them, but at the same time I would like to know more about your needs and how you might fulfill them. Since we cannot identify specific needs at this time, let's agree that we do need to identify some unknown needs that triggers the thought that something is "missing in your life."

Step 2: Establishing a Purpose

Following the needs analysis, the counselor and the client decide on the purpose of testing. Both should recognize that testing cannot be expected to meet all identified needs. In Gui's case, however, the counselor was thinking of only one or two tests to foster self-knowledge. The purpose of each test and inventory should be explained in terms that the counselee can understand. In the following dialogue, the counselor attempts to link the purpose of the test to Gui's needs.

COUNSELOR: As you recall, we've been talking about a number of needs that you feel have not been satisfied or, as you put it, fulfilled. Would you agree that an exploration of your values would be helpful?

GUI: Yes, I do, but what kind of test do you have in mind?

COUNSELOR: Well, I was thinking of a values inventory that would help us establish priorities of values and also introduce sets of values for dialogue.

Step 3: Determining the Instrument

The client and the counselor agree on the type of assessment instrument to be administered. The counselor then relates the characteristics of the test and the kinds of information that it will provide.

GUI: Well, I think it would be great to take a values inventory, but I don't quite understand how it's going to help.

COUNSELOR: You expressed a need to fill a gap in your life, and I think a values inventory that provides such measures as ability utilization, aesthetics, altruism, creativity, and lifestyle would be helpful.

GUI: Oh, that sounds great! Maybe they will tell me just what I need to know.

COUNSELOR: A word of caution, Gui. These tests will help us discover some life career values, but they are not designed to tell you what to do in the future. They will provide us with some information to discuss.

Step 4: Using the Results

The counselor interprets the test scores in a manner that the client can understand and relates the results to the established purpose of testing.

COUNSELOR: Gui, here is a profile of your scores. You will notice that you have high scores in aesthetics, creativity, and social interaction. A high score in aesthetics means . . .

As the counselor went through an explanation of scores, she made certain that Gui understood that test scores from a values inventory are not necessarily more valid or accurate than her own perceptions of her problems. However, the results do provide new ideas and opportunities for specificity in the counseling dialogue. In Gui's case, this was important because she had been very vague about what she felt were her unfulfilled needs. As they discussed the results of the test, Gui agreed with the results from the standpoint that she did have a very high value in aesthetics; perhaps this was one area that was lacking in her life. This could be the key that could provide other opportunities and interesting social interactions and creative endeavors.

Step 5: Making a Decision

The final step is to make a decision based on the assessment's results. Gui decided that she would set aside more time to become involved as a volunteer at the local art museum. She also felt that it would be a good idea to eventually become a docent. She would seek agreement for her plans from her husband and son. The counselor was to see Gui after she had established herself at the art museum to continue dialogue and evaluate her progress.

In this case study, the client was searching for a more satisfying and balanced lifestyle. The goal here was to tease out underlying concerns and put them in perspective. The counselor was careful to let this client express herself freely for the purpose of gaining more self-awareness. This client conscientiously pursued answers to her concerns in an effort to balance life roles and the counselor provided the tools and the means for evaluating her current situation. The rationale here is that clients are to consider all life roles in an effort to live life more fully. Putting life in perspective in this manner provides windows of opportunity to diminish the affects of interrole conflicts.

Summary

1. Sequence for an interview includes identifying information, presenting problems, current status, health and medical information, family life, social/development history, life roles, problems that interfere with career choice, problems that interfere with career development, clarifying problems, and identifying goals.

2. Counselors must develop a greater sensitivity to culturally diverse clients when conducting an interview. Technique issues include eye contact, touch, probing questions, space and distance, verbal style, restrictive emotions, confrontation, self-disclosure, and focus on self-in-relation and self-in-context.

3. Life roles selected for interviewing include worker, homemaker, citizen, and leisurite. Life roles are considered an integral part of each individual's development. Success in one role enhances success in another.

4. Symptoms of work-role maladjustment behavior are identified and modified through intervention programs. Attention should be focused on life role development and the interrelationships of these roles. Tables are used to illustrate work behavior include work role projections, work psychopathology, and a taxonomy of work-related dysfunctions. Faulty cognitions inhibit systematic, logical thinking and can be self-defeating. Sources of faulty cognitions are primarily from life experiences.

5. "The Case of Faulty Cognitions" illustrates the rationale that faulty reasoning and faulty logic are based on false assumptions.

6. Counselors are to clarify client problems in specific terms by evaluating all information gathered in the interview. Counselors are to probe in order to uncover client "real" problems.

7. "The Case of the Confused Decision Maker" illustrates how sex role stereotyping can influence behavior and career decision making.

8. "The Case of What Was Left Unsaid" points out the importance of obtaining all client background information available.

9. "The Case of the Anxious Computer Technician" illustrates how fear and anxiety can interfere with work behavior and other life roles. Counseling intervention strategies focused on helping the client recognize the sources of stress.

10. "The Case of the Fired Plumber" illustrates how one life role can influence behavior in another role.

11. "The Case of the Unfulfilled Worker" is an example of how an unidentified need can be clarified through a five-step interpretation procedure using a values inventory.

Supplementary Learning Exercises

1. Using "The Case of What Was Left Unsaid," specify how the interviewer could have probed for more background information. Identify clues to the client's problems.

2. Develop interview objectives for a specific ethnic client. Justify your rationale.

3. Suggest intervention strategies to deal with the following beliefs: "Psychological tests can tell me what to do in the future" and "I am destined to have only one vocation."

4. How can the concept of locus of control be used effectively to assist clients in controlling their futures? Identify symptoms of behavior that would support the use of this procedure.

5. Develop a supportive argument for the idea that life roles have individualized meanings.

6. Present examples of how one life role affects another. Give suggestions for identifying such problems in the interview.

7. Give several examples of behavior that could be identified with client personality disorders in Table 5-1. Explain how these identified behavior patterns would or would not interfere with the work role.

8. Develop a case that illustrates how a narcissistic career client might behave in the workplace.

9. Present suggestions for detecting serious psychological problems in the interview. Illustrate with examples.

10. Discuss how work history can identify work maladjustment. Build two cases to illustrate.

For More Information

Brown, D., & Brooks, L. (1991). *Career counseling techniques.* Boston: Allyn & Bacon.

Cormier, W., & Nurius, P. S. (2003). *Interviewing strategies for helpers: Fundamental skills and cognitive behavioral interventions* (5th ed.). Pacific Grove, CA: Brooks/Cole-Thomson Learning.

Gysbers, N. C., & Moore, E. J. (1987). *Career counseling, skills and techniques for practitioners.* Englewood Cliffs, NJ: Prentice-Hall.

Ivey, A. E., & Ivey, M. B. (2003). *Intentional interviewing and counseling* (5th ed.). Pacific Grove, CA: Brooks/Cole-Thomson Learning..

Lowman, R. L. (1993). *Counseling and psychotherapy of work dysfunctions.* Washington, DC: American Psychological Association.

Neff, W. S. (1985). *Work and human behavior* (2nd ed.). Chicago: Aldine.

Okun, B. F. (2002). *Effective helping: Interviewing and counseling techniques.* Pacific Grove, CA: Brooks/Cole-Thomson Learning.

Othmer, E., & Othmer, S. (1989). *The clinical interview.* Washington, DC: American Psychiatric Press.

Suggested InfoTrac College Edition Topics

Autobiography	Listening techniques
Behavioral assessment	Nonverbal communications
Empathy	Observation skills
Interviewing strategies	Psychological diagnosis

6 Using Standardized Assessment in Career Counseling

Chapter Highlights

- Problems associated with selecting standardized assessment instruments

- Suggestions for evaluating adapted and accommodated versions of standardized tests

- Achieving equity in assessment

- Assessing the acculturation level of multicultural groups

- Identifying career beliefs

- Identifying skills, proficiencies, and abilities

- Identifying academic achievement

- Identifying and confirming interest levels

- Discovering personality variables

- Determining values

- Exploring career maturity variables

- Using computer-assisted career guidance assessment

- Resources for evaluating assessment instruments

THE DEVELOPMENT of standardized tests and assessment inventories has been closely associated with the vocational counseling movement. As early as 1883, the U.S. Civil Service Commission used competitive examinations for job placement (Kavruck, 1956). Multiple aptitude-test batteries developed during the mid-1940s have been widely used in educational and vocational counseling (Anastasi, 1988). Scholastic aptitude tests used as admission criteria for educational institutions were implemented through the Educational Testing Service (ETS) established in 1947 and the American College Testing Program (ACT) established in 1959.

Recently, more emphasis has been placed on skills identification through informal techniques (Bolles, 2000; Healy, 1990; Holland, 1992; Zunker & Osborn, 2002). The growing popularity of informal methods of identifying skills strongly suggests that some assessment of individual aptitudes, skills, and other individual characteristics is vitally important in the career decision process, despite the controversy surrounding standardized aptitude tests and job success predictions. Healy (1990), among others, has also suggested encouraging clients to develop self-assessment skills as a way of focusing more fully on career options. The major issue seems to be how assessment results can be used most effectively in career counseling. A good approach considers assessment results as only one facet of individuality to be evaluated in the career decision process. More specifically, career decision making is seen as a continuous counseling process within which all aspects of individuality receive consideration. Skills, aptitudes, interests, values, achievements, personality characteristics, maturity, contextual interactions, and salient cultural variables are among the more important aspects that can be evaluated by assessment measures. Thus, assessment results constitute counseling information that can provide the individual with an awareness of increased options and alternatives and encourage greater individual exploration in the career decision process.

The career counseling models discussed in Chapter 3 suggest that all relevant information be included in the career decision process to encourage greater individual participation and consideration of a wider range of career options. Furthermore, the more knowledge counselor and client have of individual characteristics, the greater assurance of a balance of considerations in career decision making. Career counseling programs that are designed to incorporate all relevant information should lessen the chances that career decision making could be dominated by any one factor.

Recognizing the increasingly diverse groups in our society for whom tests were not developed, standardized, or validated, the Association for Assessment in Counseling (AAC) issued a document in 1993 entitled *Multicultural Assessment Standards: A Compilation for Counselors* (Prediger, 1994). This document contains vital information for selecting assessment instruments, administration and scoring, and interpreting assessment results. In 1988, a joint committee on testing practices sponsored by the American Psychological Association (APA) published a document entitled *Code of Fair Testing Practices in Education* (see the APA Web site in Appendix I). This document details the responsibilities of test users and test developers. These publications clearly point out the necessity of all counselors to select and use assessment instruments that are appropriate for each client. For instance, extreme caution should be taken when selecting tests for and interpreting test scores to individuals who were not adequately represented in the normative sample.

This chapter will include some suggestions for the appropriate use of standardized assessment results. In Chapter 7, self-assessments and other methods of assessing variables that can be used in career exploration and career decision making are introduced. The first section of this chapter briefly discusses some psychometric procedures used for standardizing tests; validity and reliability are briefly reviewed. These concepts are assumed to be covered in other courses, thus the emphasis here will be assessment use in career counseling. In the next section, we will discuss some issues associated with achieving equity in the use of assessment. Finally, goals of assessment are introduced with example assessment instruments.

Psychometric Concepts for Selecting Assessment Instruments

The career counseling models discussed in Chapter 3 suggest a variety of uses of assessment in career counseling. Although testing does not dominate counseling procedures in all counseling models, assessment usually has an important role in information gathering, accurate client self-assessment, problem identification, interventions, and outcome evaluations. The unique characteristics and identified traits of each client provide the direction for identifying options and guide the structure of intervention strategies that are tailored to meet individual and special needs. There are many other uses of assessment in career counseling, but these examples underscore the importance of selecting appropriate instruments that will result in valid and reliable results for all groups, including diverse groups. Counselors are to be knowledgeable about psychometric concepts that are necessary in selecting and using assessment instruments.

Reliability

The coefficient correlation of reliability is the degree to which a test score is dependable and consistent; repeated trials will yield approximately the same results. Clearly, the consistency and dependability of a test score determines its role in the counseling process. Although measurement errors can reduce reliability, the intended use of assessment results should be the determining factor for a final judgment of test reliability. For instance, when test scores are used in high-stakes decisions, such as placement in a special program, each test should be scrutinized carefully according to its purpose, content, appropriate use, and validity and reliability; valid and reliable test results are critically important. For the individual exploring several occupational options suggested by an interest inventory, a more moderate reliability coefficient may be acceptable. Keep in mind that the test developer is responsible for providing evidence that reliability is sufficient for its intended use (Drummond, 1992).

Finally, reliability coefficients are obtained by test-retest (same test is given twice with certain time intervals), alternate forms (equivalent tests are administered within certain time intervals), and internal consistency (results of one test are divided into parts referred to as split-half). The stability of a test is determined by coefficients of correlation that remain high over long intervals. Factors that affect stability are summarized by Peterson, Sampson, and Reardon (1991, pp. 127–128) as follows:

a. the stability of the human trait itself; for example, daily moods have low stability, whereas verbal aptitude has high stability

b. group differences, such as gender or ethnic background
c. individual differences within groups, such as genetic endowment, age, and learning
d. the nature of performance; for example, whether it is a maximum effort, as in an achievement test, compared with rating what is generally true, as in an interest inventory
e. the internal consistency of the test itself

Validity

According to the Standards for Educational and Psychological Testing (APA, 1999), validity refers to the meaningfulness and usefulness of certain inferences based on a test score derived from a test in question. Counselors need to answer whether a test measures what it purports to measure. For instance, does a nationally administered aptitude test measure success for the freshman year in a particular college when predicting that the chances are "good" a certain client will make a grade of "C" or better? This question and more should be asked about validity—more specifically, content validity, criterion validity, and construct validity.

Content validity involves opinions of experts about whether the items of a test or inventory represent the content domain of characteristics being measured. For instance, do test questions adequately sample measures of skills, abilities, values, interests, or personality? Measures of human traits such as personality, values, and interests require considerable understanding of traits that are to be measured and considerable skill in developing questions that successfully tap the universal content domain of such human traits.

Criterion validity is determined by the degree to which test scores predict success on an outcome criteria. In predicting success in college, as cited earlier, aptitude test scores are related to the behavior (earned grades) during the first semester in college. Criterion-based interest inventories relate an individual's score with a normative group, such as geologists and ministers, that are satisfied and stable in their occupations. The rationale is that individuals who have similar scores will experience satisfaction in those occupations.

Constructs developed from theory and research, such as cognitive ability and anxiety states, are related to test scores that are derived from tests or inventories developed to measure the defined construct. The result, construct validity coefficient of correlation, provides the evidence that the interpretation of scores is associated with the theoretical implications of the construct label (APA, 1999). For example, the construct of intelligence may include one's ability to build colored block designs within time intervals. This part of an intelligence test contributes to an overall score from which the IQ is derived. The point here is that counselors should evaluate carefully the focus of the construct and the items that are used to measure it.

In sum, selecting assessment instruments requires an understanding of psychometric concepts used in the development of standardized tests. As client and counselor collaborate on selecting tests, counselors should be able to explain the purpose of a test, what the test is designed to measure, why a certain test could be useful, how and why a test is considered a valid and reliable instrument, and how the results can be used to assist the client. Finally, the counselor must be certain that the test administration is appropriate for the client and the results fully account for the client's background and diversity.

Issues in Achieving Equity in Assessment

Changing demographic trends during the last quarter of the 20th century have transformed American society into a more diverse culture. More members of our society speak a second language other than English in their homes and, in 1995, more than 5.5 million children entered school without English-language skills (Garcia, 1995; Sandoval, 1998b). Clearly, the clientele of career counselors is changing and will continue to change as the national workforce grows more diverse. Counselors also should be alert to the increasing amount of research conducted in other nations.

Standardized tests must be used with caution or not used at all when assessment techniques, content, and norms are not applicable "because of an individual's gender, age, race ethnicity, national origin, religion, sexual orientation, disability, language, or socioeconomic status" (APA, 1992, p. 1601). It is not clear at this time how test publishers will deal with the issues of diversity, but it should be clear to test users that each test must be chosen carefully for each client. In the meantime, some helpful suggestions for counselors are briefly reviewed in the following paragraphs.

Read the test manual carefully to determine if the client is a member of a group that has been included in the normative sample used for validity and reliability analysis. This information is often included in a separate publication from the test administration manual and is usually referred to as a technical information manual. Specifically, evaluate the test-taking sample and make notes about its composition.

Counselors should also know the relevant background information about their clients: For instance, whether English is their dominant language, and their socioeconomic status, ethnicity, gender, and other variables. If there are language differences, counselors determine if a test version in the client's dominant language is available. You might have to contact test publishers for this information (Geisinger, 1998).

Be aware of information the test publisher should provide about translated, adapted, and accommodated versions of a test. A translated version is usually accomplished by translating the instrument from the original language to the target language, and this is followed by a "back translation": a second translator translates the version of the target language back to the original version. The degree to which they are comparable can best be assessed during this process; significant differences in word meanings can change the nature of a test and make it invalid. Keep in mind that cultural differences among individuals who grew up in different language environments can lead to different interpretations of what test questions are intended to evaluate (Geisinger, 1998).

Adapted and accommodated versions of a test can provide information that is helpful to the counselor, although there are numerous problems that must be solved. Adapting or accommodating a test usually refers to changes made in the test administration, scoring, or norms to accommodate special groups. Counselors should make certain that the nature of the test has not been changed by an adaptation. For example, when a typical paper-and-pencil test is given verbally or by audiotape or the test time has been increased, one must evaluate its effect on the test results. If the scores are derived from norms from the entire population, counselors must determine if a significant proportion of members from the client's ethnic group were represented. It is often helpful if special population norms are given, for instance, a separate test given to a representative group of Hispanics that can be compared with the national norms (Geisinger, 1998). The major purpose here is to make test results as equitable as possible for all groups. One should be cautious, however, when interpreting scores from a sample of Hispanics or any other ethnic-racial group. It must be remembered that ethnic-racial groups such as Hispanics may share some cultural values and environmental influences, but they are not necessarily a homogenous group.

In sum, counselors should be skilled in evaluating assessment instruments and, more important, have resources available for this purpose. Most test-publishing companies now have 800 numbers, e-mail, and Internet access. Published materials can also be helpful, and a list is provided near the end of this chapter. Counselors should also be skilled in evaluating the unique characteristics of each client's environmental background. All clients have been shaped by cultures that are organized according to unique roles, rules, cultural values, behavior patterns, expectations, and interpersonal history (Cormier & Nurius, 2003; Okun, Fried, & Okun, 1999). Understanding how clients construct personal meanings from past experiences provides counselors with vital information for establishing the means of assessment and counseling.

Acculturation

Finally, there is an important central concept, acculturation, that counselors should use in selecting and using assessment. This term refers to the adoption of beliefs, values, and practices of the host culture (Comas-Diaz & Grenier, 1998; Westermeyer, 1993). We will discuss this concept more in Chapter 10—but in this context, acculturation contains contextual developmental issues that should be considered in assessment.

Table 6-1 displays a list of contextual assessment areas that should help assess a client's cultural transition, adaptation, and acculturation. An evaluation process of contextual areas is referred to as an ethnocultural assessment (Comas-Diaz & Grenier, 1998). Information is collected about a client's maternal and paternal cultures of origin, including countries of origin, religions, social class, languages, gender roles, sociopolitical factors, and family roles; and biological factors, such as genetic predisposition to certain health problems. As our society continues to become more diverse, we can expect an increase of intermarriage and blending of cultures. A practical tool such as ethnocultural assessment should prove invaluable for establishing an assessment plan and should guide appropriate interpretation of assessment results.

Assessment Goals in Career Counseling

According to Thorndike (1997), there were more than 3,000 tests in English for sale in 1994. That number appears to be growing, which points out the difficulty of selecting tests, but it is also encouraging that so many choices are available. In this section, assessment goals will be followed by examples of assessment instruments on the current market. These examples should not be considered as endorsements of instruments for use with all clients. With advancing technology, we can expect continuous changes in how we use assessment. No doubt, many of the well-known and highly used instruments will continue to be popular and will be updated for use with all clients. Counselors should remain alert to new tests that have proved to be valid and reliable. More detailed information on the selection and use of career-related inventories can be found in the references listed at the end of this chapter.

Table 6-1	**Contextual Assessment Areas**

1. Ethnocultural heritage
2. Racial and ethnocultural identities
3. Gender and sexual orientation
4. Socioeconomic status
5. Physical appearance, ability or disability
6. Religion when being raised and what now practicing, spiritual beliefs
7. Biological factors (genetic predisposition to certain illness, etc.)
8. Historical era, age cohort
9. Marital status, sexual history
10. History of (im)migration and generations from (im)migrations
11. Acculturation and transculturation levels
12. Family of origin and multigenerational history
13. Family scripts (roles of women and men, prescriptions for success or failure, etc.)
14. Individual and family life cycle development and stages
15. Client's languages and those spoken by family of origin
16. History of individual abuse and trauma (physical; emotional; sexual; political including torture, oppression, and repression)
17. History of collective trauma (slavery, colonization, Holocaust)
18. Gender-specific issues such as battered wife syndrome
19. Recreations and hobbies, avocations, and special social roles
20. Historical and geopolitical reality of ethnic group and relationship with dominant group (including wars and political conflict)

Source: From "Cultural Considerations in Diagnosis," (pp. 159–160) by L. Comas-Diaz, in F. W. Kaslow (Ed.), *Handbook on Relational Diagnosis and Dysfunctional Family Patterns.* Copyright © 1996 by John Wiley & Sons, Inc. This material used by permission of John Wiley & Sons, Inc.

Assessment usually follows the initial interview in which, among other goals, a collaborative client–counselor relationship has been established. The role and implications of assessment should be delineated; counselors should make it clear that clients will be actively involved in the assessment process. Active involvement includes selecting assessment instruments and client self-assessment, as discussed in Chapter 7. In the first stages of career counseling, an inventory that measures career beliefs and dysfunctional thinking can help determine if personal counseling will be integrated into the career counseling provided the client. It should be noted that no inventory is ever a replacement for skilled interviewing in counseling practice.

Goal 1: Identifying Career Beliefs

The inventories and questionnaires used for this purpose reveal some of the client's beliefs about careers, decision-making styles, identity issues, maladaptive behaviors, degrees of anxiety, fear of failure, and reasons why people are undecided. Some of the inventories used are the following:

Career Beliefs Inventory
Consulting Psychologists Press
3803 E. Bayshore Drive
Palo Alto, CA 94303
800-624-1765
Fax 650-969-8608
www.cpp-db.com

This inventory is used as a counseling tool to help clients identify career beliefs that can inhibit their abilities to make career decisions that are in their best interests. The results are computed for 25 scales under the following five headings: My Current Career Situation, What Seems Necessary for My Happiness, Factors That Influence My Decisions, Changes I Am Willing to Make, and Effort I Am Willing to Initiate. Norms are available for junior high school students, and separate norms are available for male and female employed adults. Scores can be interpreted in percentile ranks for each scale.

Career Thoughts Inventory
Psychological Assessment Resources, Inc.
P.O. Box 998
Odessa, FL 33556
800-331-8378
Fax 800-727-9329
www.parinc.com

This inventory is designed to measure the degree of a person's dysfunctional thinking and how that can affect the career decision-making process. The inventory consists of 48 items and 3 scales: Decision-Making Confusion, Commitment Anxiety, and External Conflict. The total score is an indicator of an individual's overall dysfunctional thinking. This inventory can be used for high school, college, and adult clients. The reading level is 6th grade, and the inventory takes about 7 to 15 minutes to complete.

My Vocational Situation
Psychological Assessment Resources, Inc.
P.O. Box 998
Odessa, FL 33556
800-331-8378
Fax 800-727-9329
www.parinc.com

This inventory consists of three scales—Lack of Vocational Identity, Lack of Information or Training, and Emotional or Personal Barriers (that can cause problems). It can be completed in less than 10 minutes.

Identifying problems by assessment plays a major role in establishing rapport and determining intervention strategies during the first phase of counseling. Counselors decide if the client can proceed with career counseling or should be referred for psychological counseling. In some models the career counselor serves a dual purpose and provides the necessary "personal" counseling while beginning career counseling.

Goal 2: Identifying Skills, Proficiencies, and Abilities

Aptitude tests primarily measure specific skills and proficiencies or the ability to acquire a certain proficiency (Cronbach, 1990). More specifically, aptitude test scores provide an index of measured skills that is intended to predict how well an individual may perform on a job or in an educational or training program. In addition, aptitude test scores indicate an individual's cognitive strengths and weaknesses, that is, differential abilities that provide an index to specific skills. For example, a measure of scholastic aptitude tells us the probability of success in educational programs. A clerical aptitude test score provides an index of ability to perform clerical duties. In the former example, we are informed of combinations of aptitudes that predict scholastic success, whereas in the latter we are provided with more specific measures of skills needed to perform well on a specific job.

Aptitude tests may be purchased as batteries measuring a number of aptitudes and skills or as single tests measuring specific aptitudes. Combinations of battery scores provide prediction indexes for certain educational or training criteria, as well as performance criteria on certain occupations that require combinations of skills. An example of an aptitude battery is the *General Aptitude Test Battery* (GATB) published by the U.S. Department of Labor (1970b). This test was originally developed by the U.S. Employment Service for state employment counselors. The GATB measures the following nine aptitudes: intelligence, verbal, numerical, spatial, form perception, clerical perception, motor coordination, finger dexterity, and manual dexterity.

Other aptitude tests published as single-test booklets measure a wide range of specific skills, including dexterity, mechanical comprehension, occupational attitude, clerical aptitude, design judgment, art aptitude, and musical talent.

Although aptitude tests primarily provide a basis for predicting success in an occupation or in training programs, they can also be used as counseling tools for career exploration. In this approach, measured individual traits provide a good frame of reference for evaluating learning needs. The following sample cases illustrate the use of aptitude test batteries:

- Susan is a senior in high school and does not plan to attend college. She is interested in obtaining work after graduation from high school. Her academic record indicates she is an average student with no particular strengths evidenced by academic grades. Her interests have not crystallized to the point at which she would be able to specify a particular occupational interest. Several assessment inventories were administered, including a complete battery of aptitude tests. These scores were used to discover areas of specific strengths and weaknesses for inclusion in Susan's career exploration program. Identification of specific aptitudes was seen as a stimulus for discovering potential career considerations.

- Ron is returning to the workforce after a serious head injury received in a car accident. During several months of recovery, his previous job in construction work was terminated. He is now interested in "looking for other kinds of work." An aptitude battery was administered to determine possible deficits resulting from the head injury. As the counselor suspected, the test scores indicated poor finger and manual dexterity. Jobs requiring fine visual-motor coordination had to be eliminated from consideration in career exploration.

In Susan's case, aptitude scores provided the stimulus for the discussion of measured aptitudes along with other materials used in career counseling. Susan was provided with a specific focus in career exploration. Ron's deficiencies were found and considerable time in career exploration was saved. Following are representative examples of multiple aptitude test batteries available on the market today.

The Differential Aptitude Test (DAT)
The Psychological Corporation
P.O. Box 708912
San Antonio, TX 78270-8912
800-872-1726
Fax 800-232-1223
www.psychcorp.com

This test consists of eight subtests: verbal reasoning, numerical ability, abstract reasoning, spatial relations, mechanical reasoning, clerical speed and accuracy, spelling, and language usage. The entire battery takes more than three hours to administer. This battery was designed primarily for use with high school and college students. When verbal and numerical scores are combined, a scholastic aptitude score is created. Other subtests are used for vocational and educational planning.

The General Aptitude Test Battery (GATB)
U.S. Employment Service
Washington, DC 20210
(Call your regional employment agencies)

This battery is composed of eight paper-and-pencil tests and four apparatus tests. Nine abilities are measured by the 12 tests: intelligence, verbal aptitude, numerical aptitude, spatial aptitude, form perception, clerical perception, motor coordination, finger dexterity, and manual dexterity. This test is administered to senior high school students and adults. Testing time is two and a half hours. Test results may be used for vocational and educational counseling and placement. This test is available to the public through nonprofit agencies, such as Rehabilitation Offices, and in schools.

Flanagan Aptitude Classification Tests (FACT)
J. C. Flanagan
SRA-McGraw-Hill
220 East Daniel Dale
De Soto, TX 75115
800-843-8855
www.sraonline.com/

This test consists of 16 subtests: inspection, coding, memory, precision, assembly, scales, coordination, judgment/comprehension, arithmetic, patterns, components, tables, mechanics, expression, reasoning, and ingenuity. Each test measures behaviors considered critical to job performance. Selected groups of tests may be administered. The entire battery takes several hours. This test is designed primarily for use with high school students and adults.

Armed Services Vocational Aptitude Battery (ASVAB)
ASVAB Career Exploration Program
Defense Manpower Data Center
400 Gigling Road
Seaside, CA 93955
831-583-2400
www.dmdc.osd.mil/asvab/

The ASVAB form 19 consists of 10 short tests: coding speed, word knowledge, paragraph comprehension, arithmetic reasoning, mathematics knowledge, electronic information, mechanical comprehension, auto and shop information, electronics information, and general science. The test yields scores on each subtest and a composite score for academic ability, verbal ability, and mathematical ability. A workbook provides information for interpreting scores. A computer-adapted version will shorten the time necessary for taking the test.

Goal 3: Identifying Academic Achievement

Achievement tests are designed primarily to assess present levels of developed abilities. Current functioning and basic academic skills such as arithmetic, reading, and language usage are relevant to planning for educational intervention strategies. Academic proficiency has long been a key factor in career planning for individuals considering higher education; however, basic academic competencies are also major determinants in qualifying for certain occupations. For example, identified academic competencies and deficiencies are major considerations for placement or training of school dropouts. Achievement test results provide important information to be included in programs for adults who are entering, returning to, or recycling through the workforce. Changing technology and economic conditions will force many workers to enter programs to upgrade their skills or to train for completely different positions. Assessment of present levels of abilities will be needed to determine the possible scope of career exploration for these individuals.

For our use in career counseling programs, we will consider achievement tests in three categories: (1) general survey battery; (2) single-subject tests; and (3) diagnostic batteries. The general survey battery measures knowledge of most subjects taught in school and is standardized on the same population. The single-subject test, as the name implies, measures knowledge of only one subject/content area. Diagnostic batteries measure knowledge of specific proficiencies such as reading, spelling, and arithmetic achievement.

The use of achievement tests in career counseling is illustrated in the two cases that follow. In the first example, achievement test results are used to assist a student in determining a college major. In the second example, a diagnostic battery is used to assist a woman who is returning to the workforce after several years of being a homemaker.

- Juan is a senior in high school who is considering college, but he cannot decide between biology and chemistry as a major. All other factors being equal as far as career opportunities are concerned, the decision is made to determine which is Juan's strongest subject area. The counselor and Juan selected single-subject tests in biology and chemistry, as these tests are relatively more thorough and precise compared with the general survey battery and the diagnostic battery. Thus, single-subject achievement tests provide a more thorough evaluation of specific subject abilities for Juan's consideration.

- Betty quit school when she was in the sixth grade. After several years of marriage, she was deserted by her husband and is seeking employment. Other test data reveal that she is of at least average intelligence. After careful review of alternatives by counselor and client, a diagnostic battery was selected for the specific purpose of determining basic arithmetic skills and reading and spelling levels. Both client and counselor were especially interested in determining academic deficiencies for educational planning; that is, consideration should be given to upgrading basic skills for eventual training for a high school equivalency. This information was seen as essential for both educational and career planning.

Because of the wide range of achievement tests on the market today, individual tests will not be listed here. Instead, the following are representative major publishers of achievement tests.

CTB-Macmillan-McGraw-Hill
20 Ryan Ranch Road
Monterey, CA 93940
800-538-9547
Fax 800-282-0266
www.ctb.com

Educational Testing Service
P.O. Box 6736
Princeton, NJ 08540
609-406-5050
www.ets.org

Houghton Mifflin Company
222 Berkeley Street
Boston, MA 02116
800-225-3362
www.hmco.com

The Psychological Corporation
P.O. Box 708912
San Antonio, TX 78270-8912
800-872-1726
Fax 800-232-1223
www.psychcorp.com

Riverside Publishing Company
425 Spring Lake Drive
Itasca, IL 55440
800-323-9540
Fax 630-647-7192
www.riverpub.com

Goal 4: Identifying and Confirming Interest Levels

A considerable body of literature has been published on the subject of gender bias and unfairness in career interest measurement. The National Institute of Education (NIE) published guidelines in 1975 that identified gender bias as "any factor that might influence a person to limit—or might cause others to limit—his or her consideration of a career solely on the basis of gender" (Diamond, 1975, p. xxiii).

According to Diamond (1975), the guidelines have led to some progress in reducing gender bias in interest inventories by calling for fairness in the construction of item pools ("Items such as statements, questions, and names of occupations used in the inventory should be designed so as not to limit the consideration of a career solely on the basis of gender"), fairness in the presentation of technical information ("Technical information should include evidence that the inventory provides career options for both males and females"), and fairness in interpretive procedures ("Interpretive procedures should provide methods of equal treatment of results for both sexes" [p. xxiii]). Generally, the guidelines are aimed at encouraging both sexes to consider all career and educational opportunities and at eliminating sex-role stereotyping by those using interest inventory results in the career counseling process.

The debate about sex bias in interest inventories has focused on the question of whether men and women have different interests. According to Harmon and Meara (1994) and Hansen, Collins, Swanson, and Fouad (1993), men and women still differ in the way they endorse interest inventory items. Thus, interest inventory results might not reflect actual differences between men and women for occupational groups of specific occupations (Fouad & Spreda, 1995). Counselor and client should evaluate interest inventory items to determine if they appropriately represent interests of both genders (Zunker & Osborn, 2002).

Interest inventories have long been associated with career counseling. Two of the most widely used are the *Strong Interest Inventory (SII),* originally developed by E. K. Strong (1983), and the Kuder interest inventories, developed by G. F. Kuder (1963). Holland's (1992) approach to interest identification (as discussed in Chapter 2) has received considerable attention. For example, a number of interest inventories— including the SII, the *American College Testing Program Interest Inventory,* and the *Self-Directed Search* (Holland, 1987a)—are constructed to correspond with Holland's personality types and corresponding work environments. In most inventories, interests are primarily designated by responses to compiled lists of occupations and lists of activities associated with occupations. The rationale is that individuals having similar interest patterns to those found in an occupational group would probably find satisfaction in that particular group.

Two methods commonly used for reporting results are direct comparison (likes and dislikes) with specific occupations and comparisons with themes or clusters of occupations. Interest inventories that provide direct comparisons with specific occupations usually include a numerical index for comparative purposes. For example, the *Kuder Occupational Interest Survey* (Kuder, 1966) provides a coefficient of correlation as an index for comparing an individual's response with an occupational group—that is, higher correlations indicate similar interest patterns to certain occupational groups (Kuder, 1963). The SII provides a standard score for this purpose. In addition, a number of inventories provide profiles that indicate whether interests are similar or dissimilar to those of occupational criterion groups. For example, an individual might give interest responses very similar to those of accountants and very dissimilar to those of social workers.

Clusters of occupations are presented in a variety of schemes. Some clusters are based on the *Dictionary of Occupational Titles* (DOT) models of people, data, and things. The *Kuder General Interest Survey* (Kuder, 1964) yields ten interest scales as follows: outdoor, mechanical, computational, scientific, persuasive, artistic, literary, musical, social service, and clerical. The SII yields six general occupational theme scales taken from Holland's (1992) six modal personal styles and matching work environments. The cluster systems index a group of occupations rather than a single occupation, although the individual can derive specific occupations from the clusters. For the nonreader, picture interest inventories are used to determine occupational interests. These inventories depict occupational environments, individuals at work, and a variety of job-related activities. Individual response is recorded by circling numbers or pictures or by pointing to pictures. Picture interest inventories also provide a basis for discussion about career exploration. Following are some representative examples of interest inventories.

Kuder Occupational Interest Survey
CTB-Macmillan-McGraw-Hill
20 Ryan Ranch Road
Monterey, CA 93940
800-538-9547
Fax 800-282-0266
www.ctb.com

This survey is computer-scored and consists of 77 occupational scales and 29 college-major scales for men, and 57 occupational scales and 27 college-major scales for women. Recommended uses of the inventory include selection, placement, and career exploration. The survey is untimed, usually taking 30 to 40 minutes. Norms are based on samples of data from college seniors.

Self-Directed Search (SDS)
Psychological Assessment Resources, Inc.
P.O. Box 998
Odessa, FL 33556
800-331-8378
Fax 800-727-9329
www.parinc.com

This interest inventory is based on Holland's (1992) theory of career development. It is self-administered and self-scored, as well as self-interpreted, and takes approximately 30 to 40 minutes to complete. The scores are organized to reveal an occupational code or a summary code of three letters representing the personality types and environmental models from Holland's typology: realistic, investigative, artistic, social, enterprising, and conventional. This inventory is used with high school and college students and with adults.

Strong Interest Inventory
Consulting Psychologists Press
3803 E. Bayshore Dr.

Palo Alto, CA 94303
800-624-1765
Fax 650-969-8608
www.cpp-db.com

This inventory combines the male and female versions of the *Strong Vocational Interest Blank* into one survey. The interpretation of scores is based on Holland's typology. The interpretation format includes six general occupational themes, 23 basic interest scales, and 124 occupational scales. Administrative indexes include an academic-orientation index and an introversion-extroversion index. The time to complete is about 30 to 40 minutes. Both male and female occupational scale scores are available.

Career Assessment Inventory (CAI)
C. B. Johansson
National Computer Systems
P.O. Box 1416
Minneapolis, MN 55440
800-627-7271
www.ncs.com

This computer-scored inventory can be administered in approximately 45 minutes. It is designed for 8th-grade students through adults. General occupational theme scales, basic interest scales, and occupational scales are reported. This inventory is primarily used with noncollege-bound individuals.

Wide Range Interest and Opinion Test
Wide Range
P.O. Box 3410
Wilmington, DE 19804
800-221-9728
Fax 302-652-1644
www.widerange.com

This test consists of 150 sets of three pictures from which the individual is asked to indicate likes and dislikes. The pictures depict activities ranging from unskilled labor to the highest levels of technical, managerial, and professional training. The test evaluates educational and vocational interests of a wide range of individuals, including the educationally disadvantaged and the developmentally disabled.

The Campbell Interest and Skill Survey (CISS)
NCS Assessments
P.O. Box 1416
Minneapolis, MN 55440
800-627-7271
www.ncs.com

This instrument is part of a new integrated battery of psychological surveys that currently includes the CISS, an attitude-satisfaction survey, and a measure of leadership characteristics. Two other instruments, a team development survey and a community survey, are being developed and will complete this integrated battery. The CISS, developed for individuals 15 years and older with a 6th-grade reading level, has 200 interest and 120 skill items on a 6-point response scale. The results yield parallel interest and skill scores: orientation scales (e.g., influencing, organizing, helping, creating, analyzing, producing, and adventuring); basic scales (e.g., leadership, supervision, counseling, and international activities); occupational scales (e.g., financial planner, translator/interpreter, and landscape architect). Special scales measure academic comfort and extroversion.

Goal 5: Discovering Personality Variables

Major career theorists have emphasized personality development as a major factor to be considered in career development. For example, Roe (1956) postulated that early personality development associated with family interactions influences vocational direction. Super (1990) devoted considerable attention to self-concept development. Tiedeman and O'Hara (1963) considered total cognitive development in decision making. Holland's (1992) system of career selection was directly related to personality types and styles. The case for the use of personality inventories in career counseling programs seems well established; however, there is a lack of evidence that personality inventories are being widely used in career counseling programs.

The development of the *Sixteen Personality Factor Questionnaire* (16 PF) by Cattell, Eber, and Tatsuoka (1970) led the way for integrating personality inventories into career counseling programs. Vocational personality patterns and occupational fitness are considered major components of this questionnaire. The 16 factors measured by the 16 PF are "source" traits or factors, which are derived from distinct combinations of an individual's personality traits (Cattell, Eber, & Tatsuoka, 1970). These traits are compared with occupational profiles and provide vocational observations and occupational fitness projections. Vocational observations include information concerning the individual's potential for leadership and interpersonal skills and potential benefits from academic training. Occupational fitness projections rank how the individual compares with specific occupational profiles from extremely high to extremely low. Specific source traits are recorded for each occupational profile available (currently there are 24), providing a comparison of characteristic traits common to individuals employed in certain occupations. The 16 PF is singled out because a major portion of the inventory development was devoted to vocational personality patterns and occupational fitness projections. Throughout this text, references are made to the importance of satisfying individual needs associated with work, family, and leisure. As we assist individuals in career exploration, we must consider the individuality of each person we counsel. Within this frame of reference, individual personality patterns greatly assist in identifying and clarifying each individual's needs. As needs change over the life span, our goal is to help individuals clarify their needs for effective planning and goal achievement. Personality inventories provide valuable information for identifying needs and providing a stimulus for career exploration. The following examples demonstrate the use of personality inventories in career counseling programs.

- Ahmed reports that he is quite frustrated in his present working environment and is considering changing jobs. His unhappiness has caused family problems and social problems in general. His performance ratings by his superiors were high until the last two years, when they dropped to average. Assessment results indicate that he is interested in his current job as accountant. A personality inventory indicated a strong need for achievement. Group discussions that followed brought about a consensus that Ahmed was still interested in the field of accounting, but in his current position, he was not able to meet his needs to achieve. Earlier, these needs were apparently met from positive reinforcement received from high ratings by his superiors. At this point in his life, he is searching for something more than "just doing a good job of bookkeeping." Recognizing his source of frustration, he decided to stay in accounting but moved to another division in the firm.

- Shayna had definitely decided that she was interested in an occupation that would provide her with an opportunity to help people. A personality inventory indicated that she was very reserved and nonassertive and deferred to others. She agreed with the results of the personality inventory and further agreed that these characteristics would make it difficult for her to accomplish her occupational goal. Shayna became convinced that she would have to modify these personality characteristics through a variety of programs, including self-discovery groups and assertiveness training.

In these cases, personality inventory results provided the impetus and stimulation for action to meet individual career needs. In the first example, Ahmed recognized a motivational drive that he had repressed for years as the major source of his frustrations. Fortunately, he was able to meet his needs to achieve in another division of the firm in which he was employed. In the second example, Shayna chose to keep her career goal but increased her chances of success in that career with further training. These examples provide only two illustrations of the use of personality inventories in career counseling but clearly establish their potential usefulness. Personality inventories provide important information that can be incorporated into group or individual counseling programs to assist individuals with career-related problems.

Following are representative examples of personality inventories.

California Test of Personality
CTB-Macmillan-McGraw-Hill
20 Ryan Ranch Road
Monterey, CA 93940
800-538-9547
Fax 800-282-0266
www.ctb.com

Five levels of the test are available: primary, elementary, intermediate, secondary, and adult. The test assesses personal and social adjustment. Subscale scores are provided for the two major categories. The test is used primarily in career counseling to assess measures of personal worth and of family and school relations.

Minnesota Counseling Inventory
The Psychological Corporation
P.O. Box 708912
San Antonio, TX 78270-8912
800-872-1726
Fax 800-232-1223
www.psychcorp.com

This inventory was designed to measure adjustment of boys and girls in grades 9 through 12. Scores yield criterion-related scales as follows: family relationship, social relationship, emotional stability, conformity, adjustment to reality, mood, and leadership. Scales are normed separately for boys and girls. These scores provide indexes to important relationships and personal characteristics to be considered in career counseling.

Sixteen Personality Factor (16 PF)
Institute for Personality and Ability Testing Inc.
P.O. Box 1188
Champaign, IL 61824-1188
800-225-4728
Fax 217-352-9647
www.ipat.com

This instrument measures 16 personality factors of individuals 16 years or older. A major part of this questionnaire has been devoted to identifying personality patterns related to occupational fitness projections. These projections provide a comparison of the individual's profile with samples of occupational profiles. The instrument is hand-scored or computer-scored. Four forms have an average adult vocabulary; two forms are available for low-literacy groups.

Temperament and Values Inventory
Charles B. Johansson
Interpretive Scoring Systems
A Division of National Computer Systems, Inc.
P.O. Box 1416
Minneapolis, MN 55440
800-627-7271
www.ncs.com

This inventory has two parts: (1) temperament dimensions of personality related to career choice, and (2) values related to work rewards. The inventory has an eighth-grade reading level and is not recommended for use below the ninth grade. The inventory is untimed and computer-scored. Scores help determine congruence or incongruence with an individual's career aspirations.

Myers-Briggs Type Indicator
Consulting Psychologists Press, Inc.
3803 East Bayshore Road
Palo Alto, CA 94303
800-624-1765
Fax 650-969-8608
www.cpp-db.com

This inventory measures individual preferences by personality types: extroversion or introversion; sensing or intuition; thinking or feeling; and judging or perceiving. Scores are determined according to the four categories. The publisher's manual provides descriptions of the 16 possible types (combinations). Occupations that are attractive to each type are presented in the appendixes. This inventory provides direct references to occupational considerations based on one's personality type.

Goal 6: Determining Values

During the last three decades, much has been written about beliefs and values. Some argue that we have experienced significant changes in our value systems during the last 20 years. There is the ongoing debate about differences in values between the so-called establishment and the younger generation. Much of the concern has centered on lifestyle and the work role. Questioning the social worth of one's work has motivated many to reformulate their life goals. As career counselors, we must be concerned with individual beliefs and values in the career decision-making process. An important function is to act as agents who provide methods for clarifying values. In this frame of reference, we are concerned not with work values only but also with values per se as we help others find congruence with the inseparables—work and life.

For counseling purposes, we classify values inventories into two types: (1) inventories that primarily measure work values, and (2) inventories that measure values associated with broader aspects of lifestyle. Work value inventories, as the name implies, are designed to measure values associated with job success and satisfaction (achievement, prestige, security, and creativity). Values found to be high priorities for the individual provide another dimension of information that can be used in career exploration. In our second category, values are considered in much broader terms but can be related to needs and satisfactions associated with life and work. Thus, both types of inventories provide information that can be especially helpful for clarifying individual needs associated with work, home, family, and leisure. Two examples of the use of a value measure follow.

- Ngo, a middle-aged, married man with five children, was employed for five years as a salesman in a local furniture store. He is currently seeking a change in employment and sought out a state agency for assistance. As part of the assessment program, he took the *Survey of Personal Values* (Gordon, 1967). The results of the inventory clearly indicated that Ngo was very goal-oriented; that is, he preferred to have definite goals and plan precisely for the future. However, he felt that he had no real control over his life, particularly because in his past job as a salesman his commissions had fluctuated greatly from month to month. He expressed frustration and despair. The alert counselor further evaluated Ngo for depression and suicide ideation. He was able to continue career counseling when it was determined that Ngo was not clinically depressed, but counselor and client agreed to include solutions to depression in future counseling sessions.

  The major focus of the group discussions that followed centered on identifying those variables through which individuals can exert control over their lives. Ngo was encouraged to recognize his past experiences as assets for his future in the job market. Exploring potential careers by identifying skills from previous work experiences gave him the confidence he lacked in the past. More important, Ngo learned of several jobs for which he was qualified that gave him the opportunity to set goals and plan for the future.

- Rosa was considered an outstanding student in high school and was very active as a member of the student council. She expressed a deep concern to the career counselor about her inability to identify a working environment in which she felt she could find satisfaction. There were no particular role models, organizations, or occupations that seemed to have the potential to satisfy her needs. In the *Work*

Values Inventory (WVI) (Super, 1970) administered to her, she rated intellectual stimulus, creativity, and job placement very high. These values were incorporated into further discussions that provided her with a starting point from which she was able to launch a career exploration. Potential occupations were evaluated in part to determine how they could satisfy her work values identified by the WVI.

In the first example, a values inventory identified Ngo's major difficulty in career planning as stemming from a need to identify sources of discontentment with his past job. Once the unsatisfied value was revealed—a desire to have control over his life—Ngo was encouraged to identify past job skills that were applicable to new jobs over which he could have more control. In the second example, the identified work values served as a stimulus in launching a study of careers from the perspective of finding a career that could meet Rosa's needs. Once one is able to consider careers from an individual viewpoint, more realistic decisions usually follow. Following are representative examples of work values inventories.

Work Environment Preference Schedule
The Psychological Corporation
P.O. Box 708912
San Antonio, TX 78270-8912
800-872-1726
Fax 800-232-1223
www.psychcorp.com

This inventory measures an individual's adaptability to a bureaucratic organization. It is untimed and self-administered. A total score reflects the individual's commitment to the sets of attitudes, values, and behaviors found in bureaucratic organizations. Separate norms by sex are available for high school, college, and Army ROTC students.

Work Values Inventory (WVI)
Houghton Mifflin Company
222 Berkeley Street
Boston, MA 02116
800-225-3362
www.hmco.com

This inventory measures sources of satisfaction individuals seek from their work environments. Scores yield measures of altruism, aesthetics, creativity, intellectual stimulation, independence, prestige, management, economic returns, security, surroundings, supervisory relations, value of relationship with associates, way of life, and variety. Norms are provided by grade and sex for students in grades 7 through 12. The scores provide dimensions of work values that can be combined with other considerations in career counseling.

Following are representative examples of broader values inventories.

Study of Values
Houghton Mifflin Company
222 Berkeley Street
Boston, MA 02116
800-225-3362
www.hmco.com

This is a self-administered inventory that measures individual values in six categories: theoretical, economic, aesthetic, social, political, and religious. Norms are provided by sex for high school, college, and various occupational groups. The measured strength of values (indicated as high, average, or low) provides points of reference for individual and group counseling programs.

Survey of Personal Values
SRA-McGraw-Hill
220 East Daniel Dale
De Soto, TX 75115
800-843-8855
www.sraonline.com

This inventory measures values that influence how individuals cope with daily problems. Scores yield measures of practical-mindedness, achievement, variety, decisiveness, orderliness, and goal orientation. The inventory is self-administered. National percentile norms are available for college students, and regional norms are available for high school students.

The Values Scale
Consulting Psychologists Press, Inc.
3803 East Bayshore Road
Palo Alto, CA 94303
800-624-1765
Fax 650-969-8608
www.cpp-db.com

This scale measures 21 values: ability utilization, achievement, advancement, aesthetics, altruism, authority, autonomy, creativity, economic rewards, lifestyle, personal development, physical activity, prestige, risk, social interaction, social relations, variety, working conditions, cultural identity, physical prowess, and economic security. The measures are designed to help individuals understand values in relation to life roles and evaluate the importance of the work role with other life roles. Scores are interpreted by using percentile equivalents. Norms are available for high school and university students and adults.

Goal 7: Exploring Career Maturity Variables

Career maturity inventories—also referred to as career development inventories—measure vocational development as specified dimensions from which one is judged to be vocationally mature. The dimensions of career maturity are derived from career development concepts. That is, vocational maturity, like career choice, is a continuous development process that can be segmented into a series of stages and tasks (Crites, 1973, pp. 5–7; Super, 1957). Super put the process of career choice on a continuum, with "exploration" and "decline" as endpoints (as discussed in Chapter 2). Career maturity is considered the degree of vocational development measurable within this continuum. Super measured career maturity within several dimensions: orientation toward work (attitudinal dimension), planning (competency dimension), consistency of vocational preferences (consistency dimension), and wisdom of vocational preferences (realistic dimension). These dimensions identify progressive steps of vocational development and determine the degree of development relative to normative age levels.

Thus, career maturity inventories are primarily measures of individual career development. For example, attitudinal dimensions reveal individual problems associated with career choice. Competence dimensions provide measures of an individual's knowledge of occupations and planning skills. Career maturity inventories provide a focus for individual or group programs. They also evaluate the effectiveness of career education programs and curricula and help identify other career guidance program needs. Following is a list of representative career maturity inventories.

Career Development Inventory
D. E. Super, A. S. Thompson, R. H. Lindenman, J. P. Jordaan, and R. A. Myers
Consulting Psychologists Press, Inc.
3803 East Bayshore Road
Palo Alto, CA 94303
800-624-1765
Fax 650-969-8608
www.cpp-db.com

This inventory is a diagnostic tool for developing individual or group counseling procedures; it can also be used to evaluate career development programs. Scores yield measures of planning orientation, readiness for exploration, information, and decision making. The reading level is 6th grade, and the inventory applies to both sexes. Both cognitive and attitudinal scales are provided.

Career Maturity Inventory (CMI)
Psychological Assessment Resources, Inc.
P.O. Box 998
Odessa, FL 33556
800-331-8378
Fax 800-727-9329
www.parinc.com

The 1995 edition of the CMI yields three scores: Attitude Scale, Competence Test, and overall Career Maturity. The test can be both hand-scored and machine-scored. The CMI is designed to be used with students from grades 6 through 12 and with adults.

Cognitive Vocational Maturity Test (CVMT)
B. W. Westbrook
Center for Occupational Education
North Carolina State University
Raleigh, NC 27607
www.ets.org/testcoll/pdflist.html

This test is primarily a cognitive measure of an individual's knowledge of occupational information. Scores yield measures of knowledge of fields of work available, job selection procedures, work conditions, educational requirements, specific requirements for a wide range of occupations, and actual duties performed in a variety of occupations. This inventory provides important information about career choice abilities and can be used as a diagnostic tool for curricula and guidance needs.

Adult Career Concerns Inventory
Consulting Psychologists Press, Inc.
3803 East Bayshore Road
Palo Alto, CA 94303
800-624-1765
Fax 650-969-8608
www.cpp-db.com

Three major purposes are listed for this inventory: career counseling and planning; needs analysis; and measuring relationships between adult capability and previous, concurrent socioeconomic and psychological characteristics. Scores are related to career development tasks at various life stages as follows: exploration, establishment, maintenance, disengagement, retirement planning, and retirement living. Norms are available by age, starting at 25, by combined sexes, and by age groups and sex.

The Salience Inventory
Consulting Psychologists Press, Inc.
3803 East Bayshore Road
Palo Alto, CA 94303
800-624-1765
Fax 650-969-8608
www.cpp-db.com

This instrument, a research edition in developmental stage, is designed to measure five major life roles: student, worker, homemaker, leisurite, and citizen. Inventory results provide counselors with an evaluation of an individual's readiness for career decisions and exposure to work and occupations.

Goal 8: Using Computer-Assisted Career Guidance (CACG) Assessment

During the last three decades, the use of CACG assessment has steadily increased. One primary reason for the growth is that results are immediately available to clients. Computer-based assessment programs also interpret results to clients by occupational fit with lists of career options. However, some concerns about the validity of instruments in computer-based assessment have been expressed by independent researchers (Sampson, 1994; Sampson & Pyle, 1983) and by professional organizations such as the American Psychological Association (1985). In this section, we will review some of the advantages and disadvantages of six computer-based assessment processes.

The six different assessment processes associated with CACG (Sampson, 1994) are as follows:

1. Responding to an online instrument. This process increases validity of the instrument but also increases the time clients must spend online.
2. Inputting scores from an instrument completed offline. The obvious advantage is that clients spend less time online. The distinct disadvantage is that clients might not be fully aware of how assessment results relate to occupations.
3. User-controlled online self-assessment. Clients using this system may judge variables they consider most important. However, considerable online use is a disadvantage.

4. A system-controlled online self-assessment. Simplifying assessment by reducing options is considered an advantage for some clients. The disadvantage is a significant reduction in the client's control of the system.

5. Prestructured offline self-assessment. More students will have access to the system, but they may be overwhelmed with the comprehensive nature of some guidebooks used with this program.

6. User-controlled online sequence of self-assessment, clarification, and reassessment. The goal of this system is to improve the client's acceptance of using self-assessment, especially with clarification material available. However, more online time is needed for this process.

Counselors can also locate and recommend free or low-cost options that give credible information to clients as a way to structure continued self-exploration between counseling sessions. Self-exploration can encourage self-reflection for clients who have limited resources and also provide structure to discovering self.

Other problems associated with CACG assessment include various forms of instrument validity, scoring, search, and interpretative functions. Be aware that validity of CACG assessment systems should meet the same set of standards used for other psychometric measures. For instance, the validity of scoring standardized instruments includes weighting items into scales and ensuring error-free scoring. However, errors in these two processes are difficult to identify in computer-based assessment. Thus, career service providers might not be aware of potential errors and subsequent misleading results.

Finally, interpretative statements generated by computer-based testing systems should be evaluated carefully for their validity; one must ask for some proof that they are indeed valid results that clients can understand fully and apply to their search processes.

As computer-based assessment continues to grow, career service providers must insist that system developers and independent researchers meet the testing standards that have been clearly defined by the American Psychological Association. Evidence of valid testing standards should be clearly delineated in promotional materials, as well as in professional manuals.

Information About Assessment Instruments

Numerous publications can help you gather information about career assessment instruments, including these:

Kapes, J. T., & Whitfeld, E. A. (Eds.). (2001) *A Counselor's Guide for Career Assessment Instruments* (4th ed.). Tulsa, OK: National Career Development Association. http://ncda.org

Mental Measurements Yearbook
The Buros Institute of Mental Measurements
The University of Nebraska Press
135 Bancroft Hall
Lincoln, NE 68588-0348
www.unl.edu/buros

Test in Print
The Buros Institute of Mental Measurements
The University of Nebraska Press
135 Bancroft Hall
Lincoln, NE 68588-0348

Tests
Psychological Assessment Online
nww.wso.net/assessment

ERIC Clearinghouse of Assessment and Evaluation
http://ericae.net/testcol.htm

Summary

1. Standardized tests and assessment inventories have been closely associated with career counseling. Skills, aptitudes, interests, values, achievements, personality characteristics, and vocational maturity are among the assessment objectives of career counseling.
2. The use of standardized assessment procedures in career counseling provides the client with increased options and alternatives, subsequently encouraging greater individual involvement in the career decision process. In career counseling programs, assessment scores are used with other materials to stimulate and enhance career exploration.
3. There is a growing concern about the appropriate use of assessment results for diverse groups that were not included in a test's standardization and validation. Professional groups have issued guidelines to assist test users and developers.
4. Reliability and validity are two psychometric concepts that counselors must evaluate when selecting assessment instruments.
5. Issues involved in achieving equity in assessment include a wide range of variables that must be considered in test selection and use for diverse groups. Test manuals containing technical information should be reviewed carefully to make certain all assessment information is appropriate for each client.
6. The goals of assessment include evaluating traits for career exploration and career decision making. It is most important to establish a client–counselor relationship of collaboration to select tests and set goals for using them. Inventories that measure career beliefs are used as measures of dysfunctional thinking.
7. Aptitude tests primarily measure specific skills and proficiencies or the ability to acquire a certain proficiency. Measured aptitudes provide a good frame of reference for evaluating potential careers.
8. Achievement tests primarily assess present levels of developed abilities. The level of basic academic skills such as arithmetic, reading, and language usage is relevant information that should be included in planning for educational or training programs.
9. Interest inventories are relevant counseling tools because individuals having interest patterns similar to those of people in certain occupations will probably find satisfaction in those occupations. Interest inventories can effectively stimulate career exploration.

10. Personality development is a major factor in career development because the individuality of each counselee must be considered. Personality patterns are integral in identifying and clarifying the needs of each individual.

11. Assessment and clarification of beliefs and values are important components of career counseling. Two types of values inventories are (a) inventories that primarily measure work values and (b) inventories that measure dimensions of values associated with broader aspects of lifestyles.

12. Career maturity inventories measure the dimensions from which one is judged to be vocationally mature. Super identified dimensions of career maturity as orientation toward work, planning, consistency of vocational preferences, and wisdom of vocational preferences. Career maturity inventories have two basic purposes: (a) to measure an individual's career development and (b) to evaluate the effectiveness of career education programs.

13. Computer-assisted career guidance assessment has steadily increased. Validity of instruments and the proper reporting of meeting usual testing standards has been a chief concern of researchers and professional organizations.

Supplementary Learning Exercises

1. Visit a state rehabilitation office to determine the assessment programs used for rehabilitation programs. Summarize the purpose of assessment in this context.

2. Administer and interpret one or more of the tests and inventories discussed in this chapter. Summarize the results and discuss strategies for using the results in career counseling.

3. Interview a personnel director of an industrial company and discuss the company's assessment program for placement counseling. Identify the rationale for each assessment instrument used.

4. Review AAC's Multicultural Assessment Standards: A Compilation for Counselors. Present your review to the class.

5. Interview a high school or a college counselor concerning his or her assessment programs for career counseling. Identify the counseling strategies underlying the use of assessment instruments.

6. Request permission from a university counseling center to take (or self-administer and interpret) its battery of tests and inventories used in career counseling. Summarize the results.

7. Review the evaluations of an aptitude test; an achievement test; and one interest, values, personality, and career maturity inventory in the Mental Measurements Yearbook.

8. Write an essay defending this statement: Assessment results can be used effectively in career counseling programs for diverse groups.

9. Choose one or more of the following situations and develop an assessment battery that can be incorporated in career exploration programs:
   a. middle school in a socioeconomically deprived neighborhood
   b. senior high school from which 70 percent of the graduates enter college
   c. community college in a large city
   d. small four-year college
   e. large university

      f. community agency providing career counseling for adults

      g. rehabilitation agency

      h. private practice in career counseling

10. Select at least two of the references for evaluating assessment instruments and compare the information obtained.

For More Information

American Psychological Association. (1985). *Standards for educational and psychological testing.* Washington, DC: Author.

American Psychological Association. (1986). *Guidelines for computer-based tests and interpretations.* Washington, DC: Author.

Betz, N. E., & Fitzgerald, L. F. (1995). Career assessment and intervention with racial and ethnic minorities. In Frederick T. L. Leong (Ed.), *Career development and vocational behavior of racial and ethnic minorities* (pp. 263–277). Mahwah, NJ: Erlbaum.

Brown, D., & Brooks, L. (1991). *Career counseling techniques.* Boston: Allyn & Bacon.

Fouad, N. A., & Spreda, S. L. (1995). Use of interest inventories with special populations. *Journal of Career Assessment, 3,* 453–468.

Harris-Bowlsbey, J., Dikel, M. R., & Sampson, J. P. (1998). *The Internet: A tool for career planning.* Columbus, OH: National Career Development Association.

Lowman, R. L. (1991). *The clinical practice of career assessment: Interests, abilities, and personality.* Washington, DC: American Psychological Association.

Sandoval, J., Frisby, C. L., Geisinger, K. F., Scheuneman, J. D., & Grenier, J. R. (1998). *Test interpretation and diversity: Achieving equity in assessment.* Washington, DC: American Psychological Association.

Whiston, S. C. (2000). *Principles and applications of Assessment in Counseling.* Pacific Grove, CA: Brooks/Cole-Thomson Learning.

Zunker, V. G., & Osborn, D. (2002). *Using assessment results for career development* (6th ed.). Pacific Grove, CA: Brooks/Cole.

Suggested InfoTrac College Edition Topics

Assessment counseling	Interpreting assessment
Assessment diagnosis	Multicultural assessment
Assessment use	Reliability
Career assessment	Validity
Disability assessment	

Self-Assessment and a Model for Using Assessment

Chapter Highlights

- Using self-assessment as an alternative in career counseling

- Learning how to self-assess

- Self-assessment through self-observations

- Autobiography

- Focused questions to uncover specific variables

- Nontraditional interest identification

- Card sorts

- Lifeline—A career life planning experience

- Guided fantasy exercise to increase self-awareness

- Self-assessment of skills

- Using assessment results, including standardized tests

- Seven-stage model for using assessment results

- The future of assessment

IN THE PRACTICE of career development a key goal is for each client to realistically and appropriately evaluate self. Traditionally, individuals were administered a variety of *standardized tests* that were designed to measure aptitudes, intelligence, interests, values, and personality, among other traits. The primary purpose was to empower clients for making rational decisions. As discussed in the previous chapter, however, standardized tests may not be appropriate for all members of a diverse society. Hence, self-assessment techniques discussed in this chapter provide *alternative methods* for fostering self-knowledge. The use of self-estimates techniques is not new to the counseling profession. Examples of current programs that include self-estimates of traits are by Harrington and O'Shea (1992) in their career decision-making package, McKinlay (1990), who developed a questionnaire for identifying skills and interests, and Bolles (2000), who recommends self-estimates of developed skills as a vital step in career decision making, especially for adults in transition. Currently, several computer-assisted career guidance programs contain self-estimates of abilities and interests, for instance, that are used in career exploration modules.

In this chapter, we focus on assisting individuals to self-assess by using nontraditional methods of self-estimates. We also focus on assisting individuals in recognizing how their personal traits were shaped and developed within environmental and contextual interactions. Clients therefore are made aware of both internal and external variables as interacting influences in their career development (Savickas, 2002). Finally, clients who are actively involved in the process of self-assessment are empowered to determine the direction assessment takes in a career counseling model (Healy, 1990). The rationale here is that involved clients are in a better position to ask for more in-depth information about their personal traits and characteristics.

This chapter explores the rationale for self-assessment, which includes support information from career theorists. In the second section, some examples of self-assessment are described. Learning to self-assess is introduced in the third section. In the fourth section a model for using assessment results that includes both standardized tests and self-assessment through self-estimates is discussed. Finally, future assessment is briefly described.

Rationale of Self-Assessment as an Alternative

In this section some theoretical perspectives reinforce the importance of self-assessment in the practice of career development. We offer some background information to help counselors recognize that each client's ability to self-assess is most relevant to her or his career development and maintenance. Career and human development theory research suggests that each client's unique development evolves from internal and external interacting influences of life events, and experiences. We influence and are influenced by our environment. It is a life-span process. Those individuals who can accurately and realistically project self into changing environments and situations more than likely will increase their chances to make optimal decisions.

In his seminal work in social learning theory, Bandura (1986) emphasizes the role of thoughts and images in psychological functioning. One of his major positions is that as we learn from environmental interactions, we also learn to evaluate or estimate a sense of self. This process is known as a triadic reciprocal interaction system that includes (1) contextual environmental interactions with (2) an individual's beliefs, self-perceptions, memories, prediction, anticipation, and (3) behavioral actions. At the core of this triad is the *self-system*—composed of cognitive structures and self-perceptions—that directs behavior. The self-system includes self-awareness, self-inducements, self-reinforcements, and self-efficacy. A most important point to contemplate here is that development of self is a multidimensional and multifaceted process.

In a related study, Sigelman and Rider (2003) suggest that the goodness of fit between an individual and environment greatly influences such factors as self-awareness and self-efficacy. For instance, if an individual perceives that he or she is valued by society, that is, there is a goodness of fit to social expectations, certain behaviors are reinforced. Hence, the individual is conditioned to believe that these behaviors, such as sex-typed activity and the level of prestige of an occupation, are appropriate. However, if messages from environmental variables change, the individual might reevaluate beliefs.

In another study, Newman and Newman (2003) suggest a list of interacting factors that affect sex-role socialization and the career decision-making process as shown in Figure 7-1. Although several factors are involved in the schemata, they could be grouped under the Bandura triadic interaction system. The point here is that there appears to be solid agreement that cognitive, situational, and behavioral factors are involved in forming a sense of self that influences an individual's career development and subsequent choice process.

In most career development models discussed in Chapter 3, self-knowledge is frequently mentioned as a key concept in the career choice process. The term *self-knowledge,* in this context, is often reflected in other frequently mentioned constructs such as self-concept, self-awareness, self-perceptions, self-efficacy, and self-esteem. These terms represent a sense of self that we are interested in assessing for career counseling. In the following summations of career development research, we observe more evidence to support the importance of discovering the foundations from which one's self-knowledge influences career choice and maintenance.

Closely related to our discussion of self-knowledge is the social-learning model, as discussed in Chapters 2 and 3, which emphasizes the importance of learning experiences and their effect on occupational selection. Krumboltz and Nichols (1990) suggest that self-knowledge is accumulated over time through complex cognitive systems that involve information processing and memory processes. From a learning theory perspective, self-observation generalizations and task approach skills are fundamental to constructing individuals' belief systems about themselves. These beliefs are the foundation from which individuals set goals and make choices; beliefs are formed primarily from the individual's unique learning experiences, genetic endowments, and environmental conditions and events.

Within this conception of learning, individuals form self-generalizations based on numerous experiences. Some may be fairly accurate whereas others are faulty and harmful to the individual's development. Individuals also develop work habits, performance standards and values, problem-solving methods, and emotional responses that are referred to as task approach skills. The key point is that individuals construct new self-generalizations and task approach skills over time as they learn from new and different experiences (Mitchell & Krumboltz, 1996; Savickas, 2002). The important point here is that self-knowledge can change over time, hence, self-assessment is viewed as a means to evaluate the validity of one's rationale in making occupational choices and/or to change career directions.

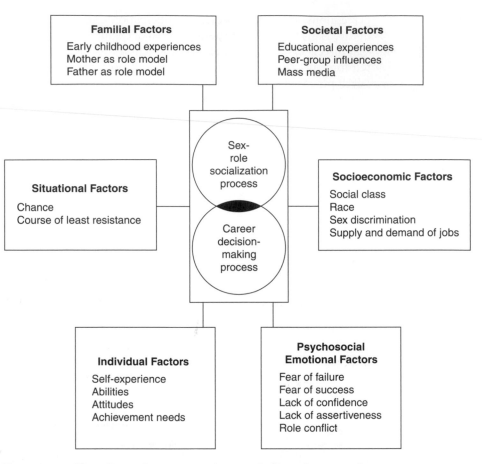

Figure 7-1   **Factors affecting the sex-role socialization and career decision-making process**

SOURCE: From *Development Through Life: A Psychological Approach,* by Newman-Newman. Copyright © 1999. Reprinted with permission of Brooks/Cole, a part of The Thompson Corporation.

In the cognitive information approach to career counseling discussed in Chapters 2 and 3, self-knowledge is considered a significant element in cognitive information processing. Self-knowledge involves interpretation and reconstruction. The interpretation process is based on matching current situations with episodes stored in long-term memory. Similar to the learning theory approach, reconstruction occurs according to existing schemata; individuals reconstruct past events to accumulate new data (Sampson, Reardon, Peterson, & Lenz, 2004).

Self-concept theory, according to Super (1957) and Super, Starishesky, Matlin, and Jordaan (1963), suggests that self-concept plays an important role in occupational selection. Super's position has been that individuals go through developmental stages in which the self-concept is cultivated. According to Krumboltz and Nichols (1990), Super did not specify how self-concept was refined, but he did recognize that the development of self-concept was a result of experiences. Thus, there appear to be significant similarities between Super's self-concept theory and learning theory by Krumboltz and Nichols (1990); both theories support the proposition that learning evolves from contextual interactions.

In Holland's (1985a) typology theory, discussed in Chapter 2, self-evaluation is a broader and more general assessment that is used to find congruence with a work environment characterized by six general orientations. He has emphasized, however, that a satisfactory occupational choice depends on an individual's self-knowledge and accurate occupational knowledge. Those clients who possess a high degree of self-awareness generally are viewed as having a greater chance of finding congruence in a work environment.

Similar to Holland's approach, accurate self-knowledge improves one's chances of finding congruence with a work environment and its reinforcement potential in the trait-and-factor and person-environment-fit model. An in-depth analysis of one's abilities, interests, values, and personality style is needed to match congruent work environments. The individual projects self into the work environment in search of fulfillment and to satisfy achievement needs. The greater one's knowledge and understanding of one's unique traits, the better one's chance of meeting personal goals.

Tiedeman and O'Hara (1963) developed a career decision-making model that refers to self-in-situation from the earliest awareness of self to when an individual becomes capable of evaluating experiences, anticipating and imagining future goals, and storing experiences in memory for future reference. The logic of the Miller-Tiedeman (1988) model is that one must view life as a learning process; let life teach you (Wrenn, 1988). The "inner wisdom" implied is the driving force of optimal career selection.

Gottfredson (2002), as reviewed in Chapter 2, especially stressed the importance of self-concept as gender self-concept that develops into a strong need that influences career choice. In general, both sexes develop self-sophistication and discrimination through cultural and socioeconomic conditions learned in their environments. Although Gottfredson did not describe how people learn, she points out that career choices are limited as a result of environmental situations and contextual interactions such as quality of education, availability of libraries, neighborhood, and family background (Krumboltz & Nichols, 1990).

Understanding human development in an ecological system and contextual theory, introduced in Chapter 2, suggests that development is ever changing and an ongoing interplay of forces. Thus, self-assessment provides clients with a greater understanding of forces that have influenced the development of skills and interests and at the same time can provide direction of future learning and growth needs. Assisting clients to improve their self-assessment techniques will enhance their abilities and desires to assess who they are and the dynamic interactions within contexts that influenced them.

In a multicultural career counseling model, discussed in Chapter 3, contextual issues receive a high priority. Self-generalizations may be limited because of a lack of experiences, exposure to learning opportunities, and discrimination. Living under oppressive conditions can restrict career development and exposure to activities and events that promote growth. Clients who through self-assessment focus on limitations they have experienced therefore should be encouraged to use this information to develop strategies for more exposure to a variety of occupations and to foster self-improvement. Multicultural counseling encourages clients and counselors to evaluate each client's environmental background thoroughly, including unique contextual variables that have contributed to career development.

In sum, self-assessment can enhance a client's understanding of assessment's purpose and empower clients to manage the appraisal process as well as a career search (Healy, 1990). Two important questions that can aid in placing career search in greater perspective to an individual's needs are (1) how and why certain skills were developed, and (2) what lifestyle events influenced the development of interests. Self-assessment is a process of seriously evaluating one's traits and characteristics. It requires a realistic appraisal of current self, self-in-situations, and one's future self in the context of multiple life roles. It enhances active participation in determining self-knowledge, readiness, and committed involvement in the decision process. Finally, clients should recognize that numerous variables should be considered in making a choice. The logic associated with self-assessment provides a pathway for clients to assume an active role in a collaborative client–counselor relationship that, in turn, enables clients to become more involved in the entire counseling process.

Learning to Self-Assess

The prevailing goal here is how to learn to effectively self-assess. The initial step is to recognize that self-assessment is a means of learning more about oneself through self-observation of current and previous learning experiences and/or through nontraditional measuring instruments and exercises. For example, learning from experiences involves numerous sources, such as family (nuclear or extended), school, peers, work experiences, hobbies, religious affiliation, leisure activities, community involvement, media, role models, and many life events and activities. One's interests in an occupation may be traced to a combination of these influence variables. Knowledge of this link provides a basis for evaluating how an interest is developed and its validity. For instance, when a student was asked why he chose geology as a major, he replied, "Because my friends did." When he recognized that he chose geology for the wrong reasons he was now prepared to begin a career choice process based on his interests and abilities. In most cases clients can find significant relationships from salient messages received from their environment. Some of the messages one receives may limit career choice, some may positively influence one's career choices, and some may contribute to indecisiveness. Self-assessment through self-observation should be focused to increase one's self-awareness and to provide direction for expanding its growth.

Self-observation has been used in a variety of counseling programs to enhance one's self-awareness. Self-monitoring, for instance, is used in self-management strategies as a means of identifying problems that can interfere with an individual's ability to appropriately maintain a self-managed lifestyle (Beck, 1976; Brammer, Abrego, & Shostrom, 1993; Cormier & Cormier, 1991; Cormier & Hackney, 1987; Cormier & Nurius, 2003). The overarching goal of self-management is to promote enduring client changes through self-directed behavior. Clients are taught to self-monitor certain key behaviors by self-observation and self-recording. Clients who self-assess or self-observe and record their behaviors have been found to develop a greater sense of awareness of those focused behaviors and more concrete information about their frequency and influence (Kanfer, 1980). The outcomes of self-management through self-monitoring therefore are quite relevant to the objectives and goals of career counseling models.

To strengthen clients' involvement in the career counseling process, self-management strategies can be adapted in a self-assessment process designed to provide clients with skills to manage career life changes. The potential of increasing awareness of significant events, conditions, and traits from a client's contextual interactions, however, has not been fully appreciated in career counseling models (Bingham & Ward, 1996; Healy, 1990; Subich, 1996). There appears to be general agreement about the potential benefits for clients who maintain a daily log that charts information about activities, situational antecedents and consequences, and thoughts and feelings recorded during these experiences. There are multiple uses of this information including problem identification and a means of developing a baseline for evaluating certain traits such as interests, abilities, values, and personality style.

Counselors are directed to assist clients in identifying any themes that emerge from self-observation and self-assessment. Such themes can be confirmed through further assessment. During the review of relevant themes, counselors guide the client to observe which identified events and influences were dominant. For example, Aldo, a legal resident for two years, was working part time and wanted a full-time job, but was undecided. His daily log contained such activities and statements as these:

"The boss asked me to arrange the shelves so that the workers could find what they need."

"I wish the boss would tell me more about what he expects."

"I don't like for him to change my work assignment."

"My father told me to get a regular job with regular hours so you know what to expect."

(next day)

"I am happy!"

"Today I do what I usually do and I like to have everything ready for the crew to pick up the materials they need."

"I look at the list and count the number of things they want and I put exactly that amount in the bag."

"Tonight we did what we usually do each week—we go to hear some music and then we ate at Lugi's."

"I feel good tonight."

The pattern of some statements and observations recorded by Aldo for an entire two-week period reflected an interest and a need for work environments and leisure time to be well organized, precise, and routine and in which the work tasks and time commitments are clearly defined. Aldo confirmed these observations; however, the counselor was concerned that Aldo had not been exposed to many other work environments and informed him that work could change in the future. The counselor and Aldo agreed that he would observe several different jobs by job shadowing. The counselor and Aldo also agreed that it would be helpful to evaluate his educational achievement level for the possibility of training for targeted work environments in the future.

Another example illustrates Aya's frustration with deciding on an occupation. Her statements reflected an interest in music, with several log entries about attending musical concerts and listening to musical programs. Her favorite place to go during free time was the record and music store; however, she never mentioned any musical-related careers as possible choices. When asked about her musical interests, she replied that she had learned to play the piano from her uncle but never considered music as a career. Further probing indicated that Aya did not believe a musical career was appropriate for her because her family considered it as amusement only and not appropriate work for a woman. She also mentioned that a music career would require college and that "my family does not go to college." She also confided, however, that she would be thrilled to be a music teacher.

The counselor's first session addressed gender stereotyping. The counselor carefully approached this subject in a discussion with Aya concerning her perception of gender roles and was delighted to find that Aya was particularly interested in the interaction of gender and culture. She was extremely interested in their discussion of traditional gender roles that collide with modern society. The counselor recognized that Aya had been socialized to think of work in terms of traditional gender stereotypes and that she would need further information, time, and discussions before she rearranged her priorities. In the meantime, the counselor would also proceed with career counseling.

Using this information, counselor and client approached the family for a meeting to discuss Aya's future. Both realized the family must give their blessing to a career that would require a college degree and a significant change in their perception of what was appropriate work for a female member of their family. Another hurdle would be to convince her family that college is for everyone who is capable, including women.

These two cases illustrate the importance of clients' participation in self-assessment through self-observation. By recording their self-observations Aldo and Aya were actively involved in resolving their problems. Counselors are in a much better position to assist clients in understanding personal preferences and unique experiences that influence and limit career choice when clients present their own interpretations of their behavior. Self-assessment provides an entry into understanding the significance of salient messages each individual receives from a social ecology.

In a related discussion of environmental influences, Healy (1982) suggests that counselors should lead clients to realize the importance of personal connections with others, and also family and social support systems. Current personal associations can be compared with past ones from different periods in an individual's life span. Feelings about relationships per se can be explored further by having the client reflect on work-related associates, such as a mentor, respected supervisor, and a subordinate. As the client's history unfolds, other important information can be discussed, such as skill development of strengths and accomplishments that can be used in the career search.

Self-assessment through self-observation can also assist clients in recognizing dysfunctional beliefs. Clients, for example may become aware of distortions in their thinking processes as they discuss situational events. Be aware that counselors need to fully prepare clients for such exercises. Meichenbaum (1977) suggests that two critical factors in self-observation are the client's willingness to participate and his or her ability to do what Meichenbaum refers to as "listen to themselves." Sampson, Reardon, Peterson, and Lenz (2004) suggest that clients should be presented with both negative and positive data about themselves and about occupations that challenge their modes of thinking. Counselors can also use examples of faulty cognitions, such as those by Nevo (1987) and Doyle (1998) found in Chapter 5, as examples for recognizing how irrational thinking can limit and hamper career search. Finally, clients learn a new internal dialogue through self-talk, referred to as cognitive restructuring. As clients refocus their self-talk from negative to positive thoughts and statements about themselves, they continue to observe themselves and assess outcomes.

In sum, self-assessment involves clients in self-observations that focus on their unique learning experiences and environmental conditions and events. Salient messages that influenced or limited career choice are the central focus of such an exercise. Counselors should fully inform clients of the purpose and techniques of self-observation and self-assessment. The outcome of this process should enable clients to have greater control and direction of the career counseling process.

Self-Assessment Procedures for Career Counseling

This section will provide some examples for encouraging and stimulating self-assessment. Counselors should use these methods as examples from which they can develop their own procedures to meet the unique needs of each client. Clients who can conceptualize the purpose of self-assessment should be more willing to participate in the process. Counselor and client agree to the purpose of and need for each procedure; therefore, clients also collaborate in the selection process of nontraditional assessment measures.

Autobiography

Counselors may find that an autobiography helps to complement the intake interview. The autobiography is usually written, but can be given orally. Counselors instruct clients to simply "write an autobiography of your life," with no further instructions. The unstructured autobiography has the advantage of leaving the subjects of the response up to the client. The disadvantage is that clients may choose to avoid subjects that could be significant. In that case, a counselor can draw on his or her Gestalt training to facilitate awareness of these gaps, once the autobiography is shared in the counseling session. Counselors may also suggest a structured outline to follow in composing the autobiography, or they may suggest that the client write a work autobiography.

Focused Questions to Uncover Specific Variables

Counselors may develop specific questions that can be used to tap subjects of importance revealed in the interview or from other background information. Counselors can introduce clients to such questions by pointing out the value of discussing significant influences from contextual variables. Some examples follow:

How did you become who you are?

What does your family want you to do?

Father? Mother? Siblings? Uncle and aunt? Others?

Who has been the most influential person in your life? How?

What do you predict will be your career (job) (work) in the future?

What have others (friends, family, teachers, etc.) told you your career should be?

In outline format, trace the development of your interests and abilities.

What were some major events in your life?

Make a list of your likes and dislikes and relate them to your experiences.

Compose a list of your most significant problems. Circle those that are most troublesome.

Such probing questions and exercises were designed to focus attention on relevant contextual interactions and the messages the client received from them. Clients self-assess the major influences and relate them to interests, skills, personality, and vocational identity for further evaluation.

Interest Identification

Goodman (1993) presents an intriguing method of assessing interests adapted from Simon, Howe, and Kirschenbaum (1972). Goodman suggests that activities she has devised stimulate clients to want to know more about their interests.

Clients are instructed to write down 20 things they like to do. They can list activities done at work; leisure activities, such as movies, parties, and reading; or taking classes. The following code is assigned to each interest listed.

1. Put a T next to the activities that you would enjoy with additional training.
2. Put an R next to each item that involves risk—physical, emotional, or intellectual.
3. Put a PL beside those items that require planning.
4. Indicate with an A or a P or an A/P whether you prefer to do the activity alone, with people, or both.
5. Next to each activity, put the date when you last engaged in it.
6. Star your five favorite activities.

SOURCE: From "Using Nonstandardized Appraisal Tools and Techniques." Presentation to Michigan Career Development Association Annual Conference. April 29, 1993 at Kalamazoo, MI. Reprinted by permission of J. Goodman.

Each activity provides counselor and client with relevant subjects for discussion and evaluation of its significance. Clients are encouraged to draw conclusions from each statement through self-assessment and relate them to interests. Other examples of techniques used to encourage clients to self-assess interests include the following:

1. Develop a list of at least 10 role models. Explain why you selected each model and relate your choices to interests.
2. List five occupations you like and five you do not like.
3. List the types of activities you enjoy.
4. List the school subjects you like most and least.
5. List your favorite TV programs, magazines, and books.

In sum, interests can be identified through a variety of questions and exercises that require clients to be active participants. Many of the suggested exercises can be done in groups and have the advantage of group interactions; however, some clients may be more comfortable when relating environmental contextual interactions to counselors who have established a trusting relationship with them.

Card Sorts

Card sorts are another method of determining interests. Clients sort cards that have the name and description of an occupation on them into three categories: "Would Not Choose," "Would Choose," and "No Opinion." Counselor and client discuss all categories and identify common themes that emerge. Clients relate interests and common themes to their backgrounds.

Counselors should be aware that card sorts are also available for identifying values, hobbies, skills, and personality characteristics.

Lifeline—A Career Life Planning Experience

This exercise requires the client to draw a line from birth to death and indicate on it key life experiences and present position. The major purpose of this exercise is to actively involve clients in concentrating on future tasks and life planning. The following exercise was used at Colorado State University to prompt self-awareness and the recognition that each individual has certain responsibilities in developing his or her future.

Exercise	Purpose
Lifeline	To identify past and current situations in life
Identifying and stripping of roles	To become free of all previous roles by temporarily discarding them
Fantasy time	To develop more self-awareness when free of identified roles
Typical day and a special day in the future	To further crystallize self-awareness and individual needs for the future when free of identified roles
Life inventory	To identify specific needs and goals with emphasis on identifying each individual's positive characteristics.
News release	To further clarify specific interests and future accomplishments desired
Resume goals	To clarify or reformulate goals while reassuming originally identified roles
Goal setting	To set realistic short-term and long-term goals

This exercise has been recommended for use with groups primarily for the purpose of group interaction. An example of this lifeline exercise with a hypothetical group is discussed in Chapter 17.

Guided Fantasy—An Exercise to Increase Self-Awareness

Brown and Brooks (1991) point out that guided fantasy is not to be used with all clients, who may be unwilling to participate for a variety of reasons. In a literature review, however, Skovholt, Morgan, and Negron-Cunningham (1989), as cited in Brown and Brooks (1991), report that guided fantasy has been used successfully for more than sixty years with clients of different age levels, sexes, and cultural groups.

One major purpose of guided fantasy is to uncover subconscious material that can be used in career decision making (Cormier and Nurius, 2003; Skovholt, Morgan, & Negron-Cunningham, 1989). Spokane (1991) suggests that mental imagery does increase self-awareness and encourages expressions of aspirations that could go undetected. The purpose and procedure for this exercise suggests that clients will express their needs and desires openly when they are free of perceived restraints. The procedures for guided imagery include the following:

1. Induce relaxation through Jacobson's (1938) relaxation techniques.
2. Establish the fantasy itself, such as a day on the job or my workplace in the future.
3. Discuss the reactions to the fantasy.

Skills Identification

Skills identification through self-assessment techniques has received renewed attention (Bolles, 2000; Brown & Brooks, 1991; Holland, 1992). The focus is on identifying skills from previous experiences in a number of activities including work, hobbies, and volunteer work. The rationale for this objective is that clients may fail to recognize developed skills and also do not know how to relate them to occupational requirements (Bolles, 2000).

The Self-Directed Search (Holland, 1992) includes a section in which clients evaluate themselves on 12 different traits based on previous experience. In addition, Brown and Brooks (1991) suggest several methods involving self-assessment of skills. Specific skills identification encourages clients to consider skills developed from a variety of experiences as important factors in career exploration. Most intervention strategies stress skill identification from the individual's total lifestyle experiences.

Some computerized career counseling programs are designed to identify client skills by having clients self-rate their abilities according to well-constructed scales such as top 10% as high, upper 25% as above average, middle 50% as average, and bottom 10% as low. Thus, users rate a variety of skills according to this scale. Be aware that clients who have limited opportunities to use skills could have some difficulty in ranking themselves. In these cases, counselors can provide opportunities for clients to try out and improve their existing skills and to learn new ones.

In sum, counselors may personalize numerous nontraditional methods of self-assessment to meet the unique needs of their clients. These procedures do provide an alternative assessment process when standardized assessment is not appropriate. Nontraditional methods also can be used as an initial assessment to assist clients in recognizing additional evaluation needs. Finally, self-assessment results should help focus clients' self-knowledge and career awareness.

Model for Using Assessment Results

Flexibility is the key to a successful assessment model. A model should be structured to meet the needs of all clients and have the flexibility to blend with traditional career counseling models. Both standardized and self-assessment techniques can be used and, in fact, are to complement each other. Assessment is one of many tools that can foster career development, but it does not dominate the career counseling process: Client and counselor negotiate its use together.

The use of an assessment model that is built on a collaborative client–counselor relationship, however, does not decrease counselors' responsibilities; in fact, it requires counselors to sharpen their knowledge of assessment standards for instrument selection and use. Counselors should be proficient in effectively relating the purpose of assessment and in interpreting the results in a meaningful manner. Clearly, the effective use of assessment results in career counseling requires a knowledge base of psychometric theory and practice. Counselors should be prepared to evaluate psychometric evidence of validity, reliability, and appropriate norms for each standardized test. The following are some guidelines for effectively using an assessment model in career counseling:

1. Counselors are to be aware of current references that evaluate standardized instruments. Counselors can also consult with test publishers and consultants for advice on selecting and using assessment instruments.

2. Counselors should use caution when using nonstandardized assessment instruments or exercises that are used to complement or replace standardized instruments. For example, guided fantasy should not be used by counselors who have not been trained or supervised in its administration and use. The rule to follow is that all instruments and exercises require training and supervision.

3. Counselors should have a working knowledge and understanding of the theoretical concepts from which career counseling models were developed. A flexible assessment model can be adapted to enhance the agenda of career counseling models and complement their purpose. The point here is that counselors should be able to explain how assessment is to be used and what the client's role will be in the process. Clients who understand and are active in the counseling process are empowered to participate in setting the counseling agenda.

4. Counselors need to inform clients how to self-assess. The increasing diversity of backgrounds of clients requires that counselors evaluate contextual interactions in an attempt to make assessment use and interpretation meaningful. From this vantage point, clients assess what they have and have not learned, what human traits they have or have not cultivated, what advantages and limitations they have experienced, and how and why they have or have not set goals for the future. Of course, there are many other reasons for clients to evaluate contextual interactions, but these examples provide viable opportunities to focus on problem identification and subsequent purposes of assessment.

A model designed to incorporate both standardized and self-assessment is conceptualized as a useful tool within the purposes, goals, and procedures of a career counseling model. The pathway of a career counseling model determines the overall role of assessment; however, assessment is prescribed and tailored when client and counselor establish its purpose. Thus, career counseling does not begin with a battery of tests that are automatically administered to all clients; rather, assessment enhances a major focus of problem identification emphasized in career counseling models. Although assessment is an important component of career counseling models, it should not detract from other important counseling steps and stages (Healy, 1990).

A model for using assessment results has seven stages that are outlined here, followed by an explanation of each step.

Stage 1: Client and counselor should maintain a collaborative relationship.

Stage 2: Client and counselor should negotiate the client's role in assessment.

Stage 3: Counselors should describe the principles and purpose of standardized tests and self-assessment techniques.

Stage 4: Client and counselor should specify client's assessment needs from information in the intake interview.

Stage 5: Client and counselor should select appropriate assessments instruments.

Stage 6: Client and counselor should reevaluate and identify client's problems.

Stage 7: Client and counselor should formulate goals.

The first stage in this model is designed to maintain the collaborative client–counselor relationship that was established in the intake interview. The major focus of assessment is determined by its role in the career counseling model selected. Career counseling models that call for precounseling inventories, such as the multicultural model, actually begin with assessment. Precounseling inventories should receive the same evaluation as any other assessment instrument, that is, client and counselor discuss the purpose and agree that these instruments could be helpful.

The client's role in assessment as negotiated in Stage 2 should be characterized as a partner who collaborates and negotiates need, purpose, selection, and use of each instrument or exercise that follows the script of the career model being used. Obviously, some clients will be able to assume a greater responsibility in this process than others will; however, an informed client should be more responsive and active in the entire counseling process. In any case, counselors should inform clients of the purposes of career counseling and the role of assessment. In most assessment models reviewed in Chapter 3, assessment results are used to plan for further evaluations and to develop intervention strategies.

Stage 3 introduces the principles and purposes of assessment, especially self-assessment. A review of goals of standardized assessment in Chapter 6 will provide some suggestions for principles and purposes of standardized instruments. Self-assessment in this context begins by involving the client in developing tentative conclusions about self-identity from background data, especially contextual interactions. Clients assess their identities as they recall observations of self-in-situation and how they learned to refine and cultivate such traits as interests, values, personality, and skills. The salient messages that were received from contextual interactions are very important. Clients might not be aware that they have unwittingly eliminated certain career paths by assimilating contextual influences. Through self-assessment, clients filter out these problems and prepare themselves for their roles in career counseling, that is, to be open to considering all careers of interest. Self-assessment measures and exercises are an extension of this process. Self-assessment becomes a means of identifying and confirming client's observations, and these findings can be used as data to identify significant problems.

Client and counselor may opt to use standardized instruments, self-assessment instruments, or both in the process of exploration and discovery. For example, standardized assessment instruments may be used to verify or confirm tentative conclusions reached by means of self-assessment. Obviously, all assessment instruments must be appropriate for each client.

Stage 4 includes the important role of specifying client needs. Motivated clients should help develop a list of concerns that will help identify barriers and reach goals. Specifying concerns means just that; for example, client and counselor agree that a client's level of reading and math skills will provide a starting point for improving them. A criterion-referenced test, for example, can be used to inform both client and counselor of specific deficiencies in reading and math. In addition, client and counselor may agree that a measure of interests would assist the client in an exploration exercise.

Once concerns have been established, client and counselor review standardized instruments and self-assessment procedures in Stage 5 to determine the appropriate type and kind to be used. Counselors must make certain that a collaborative relationship is maintained. Clients should be encouraged to express their opinions and be active in the selection process; clients advance their careers by taking charge of actions that offer promising directions. Appropriate assessment instruments should equip them with information that illuminates pathways to career exploration and direction. A client who suddenly discovers a work environment that appears to be amiable, for instance, might also be interested in finding other work environments of interest. Clients who are equipped to understand the importance of assessment results can initiate appraisals they believe to be important.

In Stage 6, client and counselor identify any problems that surfaced during the initial appraisal. Some problems may require additional assessment whereas others can be processed through career interventions. Identified problems are dissected into concerns or needs, and those requiring further assessment are to be recycled in the assessment model. Outcomes of some intervention strategies may also require further evaluation.

Finally, client and counselor formulate goals as designated by Stage 7. This stage refers to possible future assessment of intervention outcomes. For example, after a client has completed an intervention strategy designed to develop certain skills, an appropriate assessment instrument may be used to evaluate progress.

Formulating goals is an important next step for clients who have successfully completed the assessment stage and are moving on to the next stage in the career counseling model. The client's objective is to complete the career decision process. Counselors and clients should recognize that the use of assessment is one step in a career counseling model and, most important, not necessarily the dominant step. A major focus of future career counseling research may involve assessment, but surely will involve the effectiveness of intervention strategies and other model components.

In sum, an assessment model should be flexible enough to blend with career counseling models built from different career development orientations. An assessment model should be designed to meet the needs of all clients, including those from diverse groups. Assessment is one step or stage in the career counseling process; it should not dominate career counseling. An assessment model suggests that both standardized tests and self-assessment instruments can be used in combination to complement each other. Assessment should be personalized, that is, it is used when established needs or concerns have been discovered by client and counselor. In fact, client and counselor must maintain the collaborative counselor–client relationship established in the intake interview. Counselors equip clients to become active agents in the assessment process and empower them to establish goals and the directions career counseling should take to meet their needs.

A Glimpse at the Future of Assessment

The first edition of this book was written by hand in 1981, then dictated onto tape that a secretary used to produce the first draft. This process was tedious, expensive, and time-consuming. A typing error often required the retyping of a complete page, and making corrections to a manuscript was costly!

The differences in how we produce books today compared with yesterday may mimic significant changes observed in assessment in the intervening thirty years. Paper-and-pencil tests are being replaced by computer-based assessment. Computerized test administration and interpretation and inventories available on the Internet are expected to increase. Computer adaptive testing is now online; Graduate Record Examinations are most often administered in computer format. Test questions are selected from a bank of items stored in the computer according to how the test taker responds to items. For example, if a question is answered incorrectly, the new item selected may have the same degree of difficulty and measures the same construct. When enough information has been collected about a construct, the program selects items designed to measure another construct. Thus, two individuals may take the same test but respond to different items. The advantage is shorter testing time, accessibility, and immediate feedback (Sandoval, 1998a).

Factors involved in computer-assisted career guidance assessment programs were briefly mentioned in the last chapter. We anticipate the evolution of assessment options via the Internet. Multimedia will make a wider range of test items available. Sandoval (1998a) suggests that computerized administration and scoring of performance assessments are being developed. Being able to respond to videotapes of current and changing work environments explained in the language of your choice has some exciting possibilities. Assessment by multimedia virtual reality offers options never before available.

Ideally, the development of additional assessment techniques will increase client control over his or her assessment plan. Let us hope that equity of assessment interpretation will be a major focus of future instruments. Finally, our future clients may be able to create their ideal careers through multimedia exposure that is appropriate for their use and be offered potential congruent work environments. Such a program may no longer just be a futuristic dream. No doubt there should be many new formats for assessment in the future; however, counselors also need to be aware of safeguards and seek the approval of their professional associations for all future assessment instruments.

Summary

1. Self-assessment has been used in a variety of ways in the career counseling process. Healy (1990) has called for reforming career appraisals by using more self-assessment in career counseling.
2. Several career development theories refer to self-knowledge as an important ingredient for selecting a work environment. Self-assessment attempts to uncover the contextual interactions that have influenced individuals in both selecting a career and in limiting careers considered.
3. Self-assessment also empowers clients to negotiate with counselors to determine the benefits of assessment and the direction career counseling will take. Clients become personal agents for developing their careers.
4. Self-assessment includes autobiographies, lifeline exercises, focused questions, interest identification exercises, guided fantasy, and skills identification.
5. A seven-stage model for using assessment may be used in traditional career counseling models. This model is designed to enhance a collaborative client–counselor relationship.

6. Advancing technology should provide new and different formats for future assessment. Computer-adaptive and computer-scored and interpreted assessment will continue to expand. Multimedia and virtual reality provide opportunities for developing innovative assessment techniques.

Supplementary Learning Exercises

1. What do you consider to be the major advantages and disadvantages of (a) standardized tests and (b) self-assessment instruments?
2. Develop a rationale for using self-assessment in career counseling. Explain your major points.
3. Develop a list of reasons that you would support evaluating a client's environmental contextual interactions. Compare them with those of your classmates.
4. Explain the importance of self-knowledge in career counseling.
5. Develop at least five focused questions to uncover developed skills.
6. Search the career counseling literature for at least five exercises that provide interest evaluations.
7. Research the advantages and cautions of using guided fantasy.
8. Give as many reasons as you can for maintaining client–counselor collaborative relationships in an assessment model.
9. Describe the principles and purposes of standardized tests and self-assessment.
10. Outline the client's role in the assessment process.

For More Information

Comas-Diaz, L. (1996). Cultural considerations in diagnosis. In F. W. Kaslow (Ed.), *Handbook on relational diagnosis and dysfunctional family patterns* (pp. 159–160). New York: Wiley.

Comas-Diaz, L., & Grenier, J. R. (1998). Migration and acculturation. In J. Sandoval, C. L. Frisby, K. F. Geisinger, J. D. Scheuneman, & J. R. Grenier, *Test interpretation and diversity* (pp. 213–241). Washington, DC: American Psychological Association.

Fouad, N. A. (1995). Career behavior of Hispanics: Assessment and career intervention. In F. T. L. Leong (Ed.), *Career development and vocational behavior of racial and ethnic minorities* (pp. 165–187). Mahwah, NJ: Erlbaum.

Geisinger, K. F. (1998). Psychometric issues in test interpretation. In J. Sandoval, C. L. Frisby, K. F. Geisinger, J. D. Scheuneman, & J. R. Grenier (Eds.), *Test interpretation and diversity* (pp. 17–31). Washington, DC: American Psychological Association.

Kapes, J. T., Mastie, M. M., & Whitfield, E. A. (1994). *A counselor's guide to career assessment instruments* (3rd ed.). Alexandria, VA: National Career Development Association.

Peterson, G. W., Sampson, J. P., & Reardon, R. C. (1991). *Career development and services: A cognitive approach.* Pacific Grove, CA: Brooks/Cole.

Sandoval, J. (1998). Testing in a changing world: An introduction. In J. Sandoval, C. L. Frisby, K. F. Geisinger, J. D. Scheuneman, & J. R. Grenier, *Test interpretation and diversity* (pp. 3–17). Washington, DC: American Psychological Association.

Sandoval, J. (1998). Test interpretation in a diverse future. In J. Sandoval, C. L. Frisby, K. F. Giesinger, J. D. Scheuneman, & J. R. Grenier, *Test interpretation and diversity* (pp. 387–403). Washington, DC: American Psychological Association.

Whiston, S. C. (2000). *Principles and applications of assessment in counseling.* Wadsworth/Thomson Learning.

Zunker, V. G., & Osborn, D. (2002). *Using assessment results for career development* (6th ed.). Pacific Grove, CA: Brooks/Cole.

Suggested InfoTrac College Edition Topics

Ability estimates	Mental imaginary
Assessment model	Self-assessment
Estimating interests	Self-estimates
Focused questions	Self-generalization
Guided fantasy	Self-report
Interest identification	Skill identification

Technology
in the New Millennium

8

Chapter Highlights

- Guidelines for using computer-assisted career guidance systems

- Cautions about and advantages of computer-assisted career guidance systems

- Development of career information systems

- Brief review of DISCOVER and SIGI PLUS

- Steps in using computer-assisted career guidance programs

- How to use the Internet appropriately for career guidance

- Examples and Web locations of current programs

- New technology to develop skills

- Review of innovative learning delivery systems

- Implementing a computer-based program

NEW TECHNOLOGY, automation, computer science, the Internet, and increased specialization have brought about numerous changes in occupational structure and job demand in the last three decades. The pace of change is ever increasing; jobs that existed a few years ago no longer exist. Knowledge and use of technology head the list of prerequisites for the future worker. In the meantime, there has been an explosion of career information in printed materials, computerized career information programs, and an abundance of career information systems on the Internet. Counselors are now faced with an overwhelming amount of career information that must be organized to be useful—always requiring an enormous time commitment. In addition, career counseling has broadened in scope to include personal problems and more emphasis now is placed on multiple choices over the life span. Hence, the traditional primary role of occupational information provider is now only a part, albeit a most important tool, in comprehensive career counseling programs. By necessity, the time once allocated to organizing, editing, and classifying occupational information has been reduced by the increasing demand for broad-scope career-related programs. Nevertheless, the effective career counselor must focus on how to provide each client with *useful information* that includes resources reflecting the ever changing labor market.

Today's sophisticated clientele demands up-to-date projections about the workforce, then uses this information as a major factor in making career decisions and transitions. Current job search strategies must include labor market projections as well as current job descriptions. Therefore, keeping abreast of changing occupational trends remains a very important part of career counseling. It should not be surprising that counseling professionals have for the most part emphatically endorsed the development of computer-assisted career guidance systems. The fast-paced development of both hardware and software systems has created very attractively designed programs for different populations and for different purposes. The easily accessible, up-to-date career information on computer-based programs gives counselors a very powerful tool to help meet the needs of many clients. Other developments such as online assessment and interactive career guidance software systems have added greatly to the flexibility of programming. Clearly, counselors periodically need easily accessible information to help clients anticipate future developments.

Technology has also provided the tools for innovative learning delivery systems designed for developing skills and increasing and broadening general and industry-specific knowledge. The worker who assumes a self-directed, career-managed program will seek out learning programs that are accessible and individualized. New technology and prototype learning systems are being refined and fine-tuned to meet the learning needs of the 21st century workforce. Counselors who provide relevant information about new learning technologies available to most clients will be in a good position to help clients maintain a lifelong learning position.

We begin by discussing some relevant research about computer-assisted career guidance systems. Included are a brief description of system components, the development of Career Information Delivery Systems (CIDS), an overview of the college and adult versions of DISCOVER and SIGI Plus, and suggestions on how to use and implement a computer-assisted career guidance system. Next, some Internet sources of labor market and job information are provided. The importance of skill development then is discussed. Finally, some learning delivery systems are reviewed.

Computer-Assisted Career Guidance Systems (CACG)—Some Implications of Research

Evaluating the effectiveness of computer-assisted career guidance systems is an ongoing process undertaken by many counseling professionals and universities, including the Center for the Study of Technology in Counseling and Career Development at Florida State University. The purpose of this center is to provide continuing support for the improved professional use of computer applications in counseling and career guidance. In recent years, the center has contributed a great deal of research for this effort.

In a study comparing the effectiveness of three computer-assisted career guidance systems—DISCOVER (American College Testing Program, 1984), System of Interactive Guidance and Information (SIGI) (Katz, 1975), and SIGI PLUS (Katz, 1993)—the center found that clients who used these systems responded favorably to the career options generated (Peterson, Ryan-Jones, Sampson, Reardon, & Shahnasarian, 1987). In a related study, Kapes, Borman, Garcia, and Compton (1985) compared user reactions to DISCOVER and SIGI. Specifically, the researchers evaluated the reactions (ease of use, quality of information provided, and total effectiveness) of undergraduate and graduate students and found no significant differences among the ratings of the two systems. Perhaps more important, both systems were rated as highly useful.

In a study of general satisfaction regarding computer-assisted career guidance among undergraduate students at a medium-size southern university, Miller and Springer (1986) found that students rated DISCOVER as a worthwhile counseling intervention that helped them meet their career exploration needs. In another study analyzing the effectiveness of SIGI, Maze and Cummings (1982) found that the users needed very little assistance with various components. Splete, Elliott, and Borders (1985) have successfully used DISCOVER II and SIGI in their Adult Career Counseling Center at Oakland University.

A study by Roselle and Hummel (1988) compared the effectiveness of using DISCOVER II with two groups of college students, who were separated according to levels (high versus low) of intellectual development as measured by a standardized instrument. To evaluate how effectively they used the system, the students were observed and audiotaped as they interacted with DISCOVER II. The evaluation criteria included how well they learned about career possibilities, integrated career information, reached a career decision, and took appropriate action. The results supported the hypothesis that effective interaction with DISCOVER II is related to intellectual development. As a result of these findings, the research team suggested that students with low intellectual development need more structure and opportunities for discussion with a counselor during and after their interaction with computer-assisted career guidance systems.

In a related study, Kivlighan, Johnston, Hogan, and Mauer (1994) posed the question, Who benefits most from computer-assisted career guidance systems? This group of researchers used vocational identity to evaluate the effects of SIGI PLUS on 54 college students. They discovered that those students who had a sense of direction and purpose benefited most when exposed to a computer-based career program. These results suggest that strategies used to address clients' purpose and directions are productive methods of assisting them to gain maximum benefits from computer-assisted career guidance systems.

In a study of user evaluation of computer-assisted career guidance system effectiveness, Peterson, Ryan-Jones, Sampson, Reardon, and Shahnasarian (1994) had 126 university students evaluate a career guidance system they had completed. Students filled out a career guidance evaluation form that measured effectiveness of information about occupations, including occupational rewards and demands. The general attractiveness of the system that was used was also evaluated. The results indicated that significantly more students rated systems positively on all dimensions of the evaluation form.

In another study, Zmud, Sampson, Reardon, Lenz, and Byrd (1994) examined responses from 112 university students who used a computer-assisted career guidance system. More specifically, the students' attitudes toward computers, user satisfaction with human–computer interface, satisfaction with decision and task support, and general satisfaction with computer-assisted career guidance systems were evaluated. The results revealed that the students' attitudes toward computers are favorable; students perceived computers to be enjoyable, nonthreatening, and easy to use. Students were also very satisfied with the computer systems' quality, information on occupational recommendations, and increased self-knowledge they experienced.

In general, these studies indicate that users react positively to computer-assisted career guidance systems. Moreover, it is suggested that these systems are worthwhile counseling tools that can help clients meet career exploration needs. Therefore, counselors should be computer literate enough to understand the development, rationale, and purpose of computer-assisted career guidance systems and be able to use them on a daily basis.

Some Cautions When Using Computers

A major concern with the use of computers in career counseling is that of confidentiality (Harris-Bowlsbey, Dikel, & Sampson, 1998; Sampson, 1983). Confidentiality abuses are more likely with electronic data storage systems than with traditional approaches. Velasquez and Lynch (1981) maintained that this problem can be solved with identification codes, passwords, and general restrictions on individuals who may access client information, but counselors must assure each client of the specific methods used to maintain confidentiality.

When using the Internet the potential for violation of confidentiality is increased through inappropriate access to client records, e-mail correspondence, client case notes, and client assessment information. Solutions include encryption programs, changing passwords frequently, and converting messages into code (Harris-Bowlsbey, Dikel, & Sampson, 1998). The law and professional ethics require sufficient security measures in a computer-based practice.

An example of federal government programs designed to promote security of individuals' information on the Internet is the Health Insurance Portability and Accountability Act of 1996 (HIPAA). This legislation addresses many goals and objectives including guaranteed security and privacy of health information. It provides new protection for workers and their families who may have preexisting medical conditions and could suffer discrimination when seeking health coverage. Employers and other health care providers are required to incorporate privacy provisions. Much more information on HIPAA currently can be obtained online at the following Web sites:

http://hipaaplus.com/abouthippa.htm
www.hep-c-alert.org/links/hippa.html

Counselors also should be aware that computer-assisted career guidance assessment instruments should meet the same standards used to evaluate traditional psychometric measures. Validity and reliability must be established for the instruments' use within the computer career guidance system. In particular, scrutiny should be given to the possibility of scoring errors and subsequent weighting of psychometric scales that can lead to misleading results. Most important, the counselor must have substantial evidence that the interpretative statements generated by computer-based testing are valid. Finally, counselors should be certain that each client fully understands the implications of computer-generated interpretative statements when applying them to the career search process (Zunker & Osborn, 2002).

Another fear among some career counseling professionals is that computerized systems will be the sole source of career guidance programming. Computer-assisted career guidance systems should supplement, but not replace, the counselor. Although software programs are becoming more user-friendly, the career counselor must structure and sustain the client throughout the career guidance sequence, especially in choosing career-related programs on the Internet. Computers do allow for independent and individualized courses of action but do not remove the counselor's responsibility for direction and structure. Finally, the counselor must address the problem of user anxiety. Inadequately prepared users can easily become discouraged with computerized systems. Personnel must be available to instruct users during the initial stages, assist users through various phases of the system, and follow up with users who have used the system (Sampson & Pyle, 1983).

Advantages of Computer-Assisted Career Guidance Systems

The interactive capability of computerized systems allows users to become more actively involved in the career guidance process. It is hoped that this active involvement will encourage users to ask more questions of the process itself. Second, user motivation is sustained through the unique use of immediate feedback. Third, the opportunity to individualize the career exploration process provides opportunities to personalize career search strategies. Fourth, computer-assisted career guidance systems provide systematic career exploration and career decision programs that may be accessed at any given time. Fifth, access to large databases of up-to-date information for local, state, national, and international locations is immediately available. The availability of service to remote locations, cost-effectiveness, and rapid turnaround for assessment results has distinct advantages.

Types of Computer-Assisted Career Guidance Systems

The most common types of computer-assisted career guidance systems are information systems and guidance systems. Information systems provide users with direct access to large databases on such subject areas as occupational characteristics (work tasks, required abilities, work settings, salary) and lists of occupations, educational and training institutions, military information, and financial aid.

Guidance systems typically are much broader in scope. They contain a variety of available modules, such as instruction in the career decision process, assessment, prediction of future success, assistance with planning, and development of strategies for future plans. Many computer-assisted career guidance systems contain an information system as well as a guidance system. Many systems are directed toward certain populations, such as students in junior high school, high school, and college; some systems are for people who work in organizations; and some address the needs of retirees.

Computer-assisted career guidance systems have undergone vast changes during the last decade. Future modifications could come even more quickly as these systems are designed to meet the needs of an ever changing work environment and the skills associated with rapid technical change. Understandably, many of the computer-assisted career guidance systems have similar components and are accessed through menus that provide some flexibility for individual needs. The following components are found in most systems:

- Occupational information
- Armed service information
- Information about postsecondary institutions of higher learning
- Information on technical and specialized schools
- Financial aid information
- Interest inventories
- Decision-making skills

Other common components include the following:

- Local job information files
- Ability measures
- Value inventories
- Methods of predicting academic success in college
- Job search strategies
- Resumé preparation information
- Information on job interviews
- Components for adults

Development of Career Information Delivery Systems (CIDS)

The growth of CIDS was a direct result of funding from a now defunct National Occupational Information Coordinating Committee (NOICC) through its State Occupational Information Coordinating Committees (SOICCs). Improved microcomputer technology in the 1980s resulted in a movement away from mainframe delivery systems and significantly reduced the cost of implementing such a system. Career information is organized in most systems on a national and state basis. Some of the national commercial systems include options to develop state and local information (McCormac, 1988).

Since its beginning in the late 1980s, CIDS has become a very popular tool that has been used effectively within comprehensive counseling programs in schools and colleges and by adults seeking further training, education, or different jobs. It is estimated that in 1994, more than 40 states had CIDS users as official state systems, and more than 9 million people used them at about 20,000 different sites (Mariani, 1995–96).

The four components common to most CIDS are assessment, occupational search, occupational information, and educational information. Online assessment includes instruments that measure values, interests, skills, aptitudes, or experiences as they relate to career choice. Many systems will accept results from additional assessment instruments, such as *The Self-Directed Search, ASVAB, Strong Interest Inventory,* and *GATB* (discussed in Chapter 6).

Skills assessment is a tool to help students and experienced workers identify skills desired and needed in the current workforce. The *American College Testing Program's Work Keys System* is designed to help learners make transitions from school to work or from job to job. It assesses the skills individuals possess, determines the skills that jobs require, and provides instructional support to help learners improve their skills. The process includes a comparison of skill levels required for particular jobs with learners' skill levels (American College Testing Program, 1996a).

The CIDS occupational search is very innovative. Users can generate lists of occupations from assessment results. As users choose search variables from a list, the level of congruence users give to each variable is processed by the computer to generate lists of occupations. If a user is not satisfied and wishes to explore other occupations, the system allows him or her to change the criteria selected in the original search. Finally, a user may simply select an occupation for review.

The occupational information component contains key information about a large number of occupations, such as the nature of the work, working conditions, numbers employed, job outlook, education and training requirements, recommended school courses, earnings, related occupations, physical demands, common career ladders, and sources for more information. Many CIDS programs include state and local information about occupations.

The educational component includes information about vocational and technical schools, two- and four-year colleges, and, in some systems, graduate schools. Included in this component are admission requirements, programs of study, types of degrees offered, school affiliation, community setting, tuition and fees, financial aid information, total enrollment, housing information, athletic programs and other student activities, student body characteristics, military training opportunities, special programs, and sources for more information (Mariani, 1995–96).

Career development programs in schools use CIDS in many innovative ways. For example, counselors use printouts of occupational descriptions in grades 3 and 4 to illustrate the kind of information that can be found in their local CIDS. In a related type of program, students in elementary schools are asked to make a list of occupations that interest them. The counselor then provides printed descriptions of the requested occupations. Both programs serve as an introduction to CIDS that primes the students to use the career exploration program individually when it is available to them. The extent of CIDS use in secondary schools often depends on the number of staff or computers available. In some schools, peer counselors or adult volunteers introduce students to CIDS.

CIDS is also integrated into the curriculum in some junior and senior high schools. Some schools offer career exploration programs that include CIDS. Others infuse career exploration into existing courses, such as a major writing project in an

English class on one's career choice. Universities and colleges usually incorporate CIDS in their career center as a part of a total career exploration system. Credit courses in career exploration also are offered at some postsecondary institutions. Some instructors require that students do a career search as a part of a course requirement or assign projects that include the use of CIDS. CIDS are also used at other sites, such as employment and training offices, vocational rehabilitation offices, state job services, public libraries, prisons, and public businesses. Also, the federal government has established one-stop career centers in several states. As Mariani (1995–96, p. 22) put it, "Some people may find themselves choosing a career, getting a job, and buying a new wardrobe all at the local mall." More information can be obtained from state CIDS directors and from the following sources.

Association of Computer-Based Systems for Career Information
c/o National Career Development Association
5999 Stevenson Avenue
Alexandria, VA 22304-3300
703-823-9800, ext. 309
www.acsci.org/acsci_states.asp

Center for the Study of Technology in Counseling and Career Development
Florida State University Career Center
5408 University Center, 4th Level
Tallahassee, FL 32306-1035
904-644-6431

Two Early Computer-Assisted Career Guidance Systems

The original DISCOVER system was designed to assist high school and college students in making career choices. DISCOVER for colleges and adults, published by the American College Testing Program (1987), contained the following modules:

1. Beginning the career journey
2. Learning about the world of work
3. Learning about yourself
4. Finding occupations
5. Learning about occupations
6. Making educational choices
7. Planning next steps
8. Planning your career
9. Making transitions

Although users were advised to proceed through the modules in a sequential order, certain modules can be accessed on demand. A user, for example, seeking information about educational institutions can access two-year or four-year college lists in 2000 or the 2000 version. A different version of the DISCOVER program for Colleges and Adults depicts a world-of-work center directory, a building containing four halls (modules). The first hall is designed to help users learn more about self and career through self-assessment, and by evaluating life roles and transitions. The second hall is devoted to choosing an occupation using a variety of inventories, a world-of-work map, and then comparing one's characteristics with job demands and work environment. Hall three assists the user in planning for an education with the use of lists of majors, educational institutions, and available financial aid. In hall four, the user develops methods for finding work by using suggestions about ways to learn and to earn money, defining the ideal job, preparing a job search, and reviewing interview tips. Users can save their program results on a disk for future use or to share them with other helpers.

DISCOVER provides meaningful interactive tasks and information modules to help users in making career decisions. The online assessment program provides an effective method of evaluating interests, abilities, and values. The flexibility of this program makes it possible to access relevant tasks and data as needed, such as job descriptions and education-training information. Counselors should be aware that computer-based programs are changing rapidly. We can expect to find significant changes in programs and methods of delivery in future systems.

DISCOVER Multimedia

DISCOVER Multimedia is a version of DISCOVER in compact disc–interactive (CD-i) format. It should not be confused with CD-ROM. This new system does not require a computer, as it can be used on a color TV and a disc player. This system consists of three discs. Disc 1 is entitled "Learning about Yourself" and allows users to visually identify occupations that match specific interests and abilities. Six video sequences that illustrate the World-of-Work Map are also available. Disc 2 contains detailed information about approximately 500 different occupations through a slide show that enhances the text for each occupation. There is a 15- to 20-second narrative for each occupation, accompanied by color photographs. Disc 3 contains a two-year and four-year college search sequence. A narrative is accompanied by two photographs of most four-year institutions. The publishers of this program suggest that it will encourage young people, especially those who are accustomed to playing video games, to learn more about career information. The major rationale for this program is that photographs and full-motion video will make career planning not only more enjoyable but also more realistic.

System of Interactive Guidance and Information (SIGI) and SIGI PLUS

Another major computerized system is SIGI and SIGI PLUS, developed by Katz (1975, 1993, and published by Educational Testing Service, 1996). There are five SIGI subsystems as follows: Values, Locate, Compare, Planning, and Strategy. These subsystems were developed to assist college students by clarifying values, locating and identifying occupational options, comparing choices, learning planning skills, and developing rational career decision-making skills.

SIGI PLUS contains the following components: Introduction, Self-Assessment, Search, Information, Skills, Preparing, Coping, Deciding, and Next Steps. This system was developed to include adults in general and those who are seeking information about organizations. Katz (1993) suggests that individual needs determine the level of motivation in the career search and, as such, are considered as domains of self-understanding. Thus, needs are centered around values, interests, temperament, and attitudes that should be assessed as important variables in the search process. One outstanding feature of this program is the special needs of adults in transition; it is designed to assist adults who may be changing occupations, moving into new occupations, or reentering the labor force. Reardon, Peterson, Sampson, Ryan-Jones, and Shahnasarian (1992) found that students liked both systems, SIGI and SIGI PLUS, but preferred the latter because of its greater flexibility. Evidently, students opted for more control of a system that is user-friendly to their individual needs. For more information see www.ets.org.

Steps in Using Computer-Assisted Career Guidance Programs

Throughout this chapter, several direct references have been made about the use of computer-assisted career guidance programs. The primary purpose of this discussion has been to emphasize the computer's role in meeting the career exploration needs of individuals and groups. Structured procedures that use components of computerized programs as a career counseling assistant are a major advantage. Computer-assisted career guidance programs can be a major component of a total career guidance program. As such, they are coordinated with other components, materials, and procedures; they are not the sole delivery system. Individual needs may dictate the use of several components including computerized systems, or in some cases, computerized systems alone may meet client needs. Within this framework, I advise following these steps for using computer-assisted career guidance programs:

1. Assessment of needs. Individualized needs of each student should determine the direction of program use and the components accessed. For example, one student might need information on financial aid programs only. A client moving to a distant state could be seeking information on two-year and four-year colleges within driving distance of his or her future residence.
2. Orientation. Each client or group of clients should be given a thorough orientation to the purpose, goals, and demonstrated use of computerized systems.
3. Individualized programs. Each individual should follow a preconceived plan based on needs. This plan can be modified as needed; the flexibility of computerized programs can be a distinct advantage when plans change.
4. Counselor intervention. The individualized plan should provide for counselor intervention. For example, it may be appropriate to discuss the results of one of the inventories. Providing sources of additional occupational information and discussing tentative occupational choices are good strategies in the career exploration process. The point is that individuals should not be "turned over to the computer" without any planned intervention from a counselor.
5. Online assistance. Provisions should be made to assist individuals in various stages of career exploration. How to return to the main menu or how to access various components can be frustrating experiences for the computer novice. The following questions can be anticipated: "How can I get this printed?" "I need to stop now and go to class—what should I do?" "I hit the wrong key, can you help me?"

6. Follow-up. As in all phases of career exploration, individual progress should be monitored. Career counselors should help individuals sustain their motivation, evaluate their progress, and evaluate the effectiveness of programs.

In sum, many computer-based modules are designed primarily to develop the individual's decision-making skills. The counselor should assist clients at various stages, however, including helping access different functions of a system. Most important, the counselor demonstrates how computer-based programs can be helpful in the practice of career development.

Using the Internet

The Internet is a significant resource that is actively used by both counselors and clients. The future use of the Internet will continue to be an important subject for professional counseling associations, as well as practicing counselors. The Internet may be described as a proverbial sleeping giant that has enormous potential for the career counseling profession. We are beginning to tap the resources that are available now, but the future use of the Internet will be an important subject of the career counseling profession in the generations to come.

Harris-Bowlsbey, Dikel, and Sampson (1998) have developed a guide for using the Internet in career planning. This guide contains sample Web sites for assessment, searching databases, education and training opportunities, financial aid, internship opportunities, job openings, career information, education and training information, military information, and career counseling programs. In sum, Web sites can assist individuals with self-assessment of such traits as interests, skills, abilities, values, intelligence, and personality. Web sites also provide information for (a) exploring occupations, (b) educational institutions, (c) scholarships, (d) financial aid opportunities, and (e) job openings. Some Web sites provide free information whereas others charge a fee. Still other Web sites provide information resources that link occupations, educational institutions, and other opportunities with trade journals, government agencies, professional organizations, and so on. You can also locate chat rooms and support groups, or post a resumé for job placement. Many other networking possibilities can be used to meet individual needs.

The growth of the Web resources and their use by both counselors and clients is an indication of their value. Counselors should be aware of the counseling competencies of Internet providers, especially their training experiences. Second, in Chapters 6 and 7, the necessity of using valid and reliable assessment instruments is clearly stated. But the problem does not stop there; one must also interpret the results according to the prescribed use of the instrument. Invalid interpretation of results can lead to invalid conclusions and subsequently to invalid decisions. Most important is the readiness of the client for decision making in terms of his or her focus on unique individual concerns that may require individual counseling. This precaution is directed not just to clients who may need psychotherapy but also to those individuals who require counselor direction to overcome barriers that prohibit appropriate career-decision techniques. A major point is the availability of user support when needed (Harris-Bowlsbey, Dikel, & Sampson, 1998).

Figure 8.1 illustrates an appropriate use of the Internet in career planning and in the decision-making process. Six steps are illustrated: In the first step, individuals

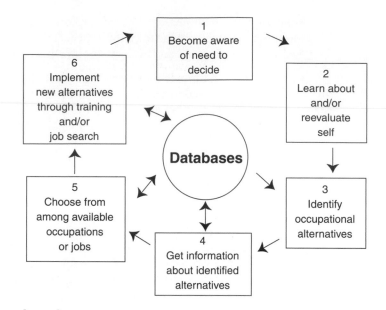

Figure 8-1   Career planning process

Source: From *The Internet: A Tool for Career Planning,* by J. Harris-Bowlsbey, M. R. Dikel, & J. P. Sampson, 1998, p. 2. Copyright 1998 by the National Career Development Association. Reprinted with permission of NCDA.

realize a need to decide. Learning about and/or reevaluating self, step two, suggests that clients be alert to their personal attributes and limitations. In step three, occupational information is presented in a manner "that facilitates the transition of self-information into occupational alternatives" (Harris-Bowlsbey, Dikel, & Sampson, 1998, p. 2). The next three steps are used to refine the identified alternatives into possible tentative choices by using the vast database of information available on the Internet. Finally, the individual decides to seek more information and eventually selects the new alternative (Harris-Bowlsbey, Dikel, & Sampson, 1998).

Examples of Web Locations

To assist counselors in providing services appropriately through Internet-based career resources and services, the National Career Development Association (NCDA) and the National Board for Certified Counselors (NBCC) have published guidelines. (See Appendix I for NCDA Web sites that list guidelines.) The following book is a valuable resource for Internet use by counselors:

The Internet: A Tool for Career Planning by Harris-Bowlsbey, J. H., Dikel, M. R., & Sampson, J. P. National Career Development Association. 4700 Reed Road, Suite M, Columbus, OH 43220. Phone (888) 326-1750, Fax (614) 326-1760.

Following are some examples of current programs:

America's Job Bank
www.ajb.dni.us

Currently one of the most widely used sites, this is a computerized network that links 2000 state employment offices and contains a national pool of active job opportunities.

Labor market information and training resources for federal and state employment can also be obtained here. In addition the replacement for the Dictionary of Occupational Titles (DOT), O'NET can be accessed.

U.S. Department of Education
www.ed.gov

This site is designed to help parents, teachers, and students. Information on such topics as financial aid, grants, and educational software packages can be reviewed, and some of it can be downloaded.

Occupational Outlook Handbook
www.bls.gov/oco/

Career Resources
http://careerresource.coedu.usf.edu/linkcareerlab/Careerlab.htm

This brief introduction to the Internet suggests that computerized career-related programming has only begun to surface. We can expect to see a growing list of innovative ideas that will build to a comprehensive linked system of the future. One goal of the Internet is to build a nationwide talent bank to help employers and prospective employees make initial contacts (Woods & Ollis, 1996). The unique career-related programs developed at this time should serve as the foundation for the continuing evolution of computerized career-related programming.

Implementing a Computer-Based Program

It has often been said that the first steps in implementing new programs are the most important ones. This cliché certainly applies to implementing a computer-assisted system for career guidance. Systematic planning for computer-assisted systems is related directly to their effectiveness and acceptance by students, faculty, and community (Sampson, 1994). In this section, we will review an implementation model, but first we will discuss implementation problems.

The information contained in Box 8-1 identifies problems associated with implementing a computer-assisted career guidance (CACG) program. Some of these identified problems suggest a lack of effective planning, whereas others are associated with inadequate staff training and a lack of integration with other career services. For instance, staff must be aware that CACG does not take the place of counselor intervention with clients and that some clients need assistance with linking information found on CACG to their career search and other assistance. The significant danger here is the false assumption that CACG is the sole career service component!

Sampson (1994) makes a very important point that implementation problems could very easily limit CACG's long-term effectiveness. Furthermore, all parties must be educated to the effective use of CACG before it is selected and put online. Proper implementation ensures that CACG is an important component of career services.

Box 8-1	CACG Implementation Problems

Inadequate planning
- Use of "ad hoc" or "no planning" approaches
- Inadequate linkage between computer use and organizational needs
- Inadequate needs assessment prior to computer use
- Adoption of systems overly influenced by funding or administrators
- Piecemeal rather than systematic adoption of systems
- Limited staff participation in decision making about CACG

Poor integration of CACG systems within career services
- Lack of suitable context for clients to process their use of information resources
- Lack of counselor intervention for clients who need assistance
- Lack of evaluation data for demonstrating accountability and for improving CACG integration
- Scheduling problems
- Inconsistent support from CACG developers

Inadequate staff training
- Imbalance between training expenditures and hardware/software expenditures
- Inadequate training with respect to
  hands-on experience with systems
  a conceptual basis for comparing and selecting systems
  integrating CACG with various service delivery models
- Unrealistic expectations about the performance of computer applications
- Unrealistic expectations about the time needed for implementation
- Confusion regarding the role of the counselor and the role of the computer

Staff anxiety and resistance concerning CACG
- Concern over changes in the workplace
- Negative staff attitude as a result of implementation problems

Note: Staff anxiety and resistance are negatively influenced by planning, integration, and training problems described above.

Source: From *Effective Computer-Assisted Career Guidance: Occasional Paper Number 2*, by James P. Sampson, 1994. Center for the Study of Technology in Counseling and Career Development, Florida State University. Reprinted by permission.

The process of implementing CACG includes the following seven-step implementation model developed by Sampson (1994):

1. Begin with a program evaluation to determine how well current guidance services meet clients' needs. If the evaluation discloses unmet needs, the staff should highlight the purpose and goals regarding how a computer-based system can close the gap. To accomplish this goal, establish a selection committee.

2. Have the committee identify desired software products that will meet clients' needs. After reviewing systems, the committee should determine appropriate software and hardware.

3. Software integration involves comprehensive plans for how a system will be implemented. This implies that committee members have become very knowledgeable about the chosen system. Plans include how to mesh the system with the overall guidance program and to specify roles of staff members, operational procedures, and evaluation systems.

4. The next step involves comprehensive staff training. The effectiveness of a computer-assisted guidance program is strongly related to a working knowledge of the system.

5. The trial use determines how well the staff has done its homework and how students react to using the system. The system begins operation after successful trial evaluations.
6. The system becomes operational.
7. Evaluation of service delivery is seen as an ongoing process. Evaluation feedback suggests that there should be continual refinement. Fast-paced development of hardware and software probably means that computer-assisted programs could change every year.

The seven-step implementation program was developed by Sampson (1994) of Florida State University, Center for the Study of Technology in Counseling and Career Development. Anyone seeking information about computer-assisted career guidance programs should contact this center.

Technology: A Lifelong Learning Tool

In this book's final chapter we discuss adults in career transition and the counseling challenges they present. A major emphasis in that chapter and here is that lifelong learning is a means by which one fosters all life roles, and especially the work role. This position suggests that each worker is to seek out training programs offered by employers and at other sites, such as educational institutions, as well as skill development programs that are computer-based and available on personal computers. Implied here is that each worker is responsible for managing his or her career development; in this context, career management is viewed as self-directed activities to increase career options (Stamps, 1999).

Counselors play an important role in helping clients build an understanding of why career management is best driven by activities that are self-directed. Those who take full responsibility for their career development recognize the necessity of lifelong learning and how skill development influences their career direction. When there is fit between individual (interests, abilities, skill acquisition) and occupation, there is a greater likelihood of job satisfaction and tenure (Ostroff, Shin, & Feinberg, 2002). Hence counselors provide *reasons* for self-directed skill acquisition activities as well as information about delivery systems of learning.

How important is skill development? In the 1990s, Bynner (1997) conducted a longitudinal study of individuals from childhood through age 21 and found that poor basic skills (literacy and math) made it difficult to acquire broader work-related skills such as the ability to work in teams, adaptability, and establishing interpersonal relationships. Not surprisingly, basic skills were most important in gaining employment in school-to-work transition. Basic skills are not only essential in finding employment, therefore, but also provide the individual with the foundation to develop more-universal skills valued by employers (Cappelli et. al., 1997; U.S. Department of Labor, 1992). The ability to work with others, however, may be more important than specific skills in many occupations, with the exception of those jobs that require specific technical skills, such as computer programming, engineering, and some medical-related careers (Ryan, 2000; Werbel & Gilliland, 1999). The recommendation here is that individuals are to develop both general skills (adaptability, flexibility, dependability) and industry-specific skills. Very essential for most all employees is a solid foundation in basic skills.

Career development theorists have pointed out numerous variables that determine career progression leading to initial career choice and multiple choices over the life span. Abilities, interests, values, and personality often are mentioned as personal characteristics that influence individual choice. Of this group of variables, interest patterns have been emphasized, especially in the research of Holland's typology, that is, congruence between one's interests and occupational types makes for a good fit (Holland, 1985). The importance of this research has been underscored by individuals who discover careers that fit their interests and remain in those occupations (Feldman, 2002). In addition, emphasis on skill development in the current job market suggests that counselors give this variable equal attention. Keep in mind that it was Mitchell and Krumboltz (1996), among others, who emphasized skill development through learning programs as a key ingredient in one's career development. Drucker (2002), who suggests that the next society will be dominated by knowledge workers, clearly endorses educational and training programs that develop skills and increase knowledge.

In assessing the dynamics among interests, abilities, skill acquisition and fit, Ostroff, Shin, and Feinberg (2002) suggest that initial choice of career goals is indeed influenced by interest patterns but, as workers are exposed to work requirements and on-the-job experiences, they gravitate to occupations that are commensurate with their abilities over time. What we have here is a relationship that develops largely through demands, requirements, and activities different occupations make. Career interests and abilities crystallize at various times during career development (Worthington & Juntunen, 1997), thus, workers experience congruence with requirements of certain work activities and develop skills accordingly. Those who learn new skills, however, may change career direction, meaning initial career choice may not result in a longtime commitment for everyone. Skill development therefore is a continuous lifelong learning commitment that can significantly influence one's career transitions.

The obvious key to assisting clients in skill development is knowledge of emerging learning technologies. Many organizations have a variety of training methods and learning experiences for developing employees. There are also many self-directed learning programs available through a variety of resources. Such programs include readings, workbooks, and correspondence courses. Of greatest interest, however, have been the emerging training technologies. We begin with on-site training programs offered by employers.

Some On-Site Training Methods

On-the-job training is one of the oldest methods used by organizations. Beginnings workers are trained on the work site by experienced workers. They learn by imitating instructors. *Job rotation* is a process of rotating workers through a variety of jobs, with the expectation of learning by experience. *Apprentice training* is a method that involves an established worker tutoring a novice worker and is common in skilled trades. After a lengthy period of time an individual is promoted to a journeyman.

Some Off-Site Training Methods

Off-site training programs are considered to be those learning activities at a place removed from the work site such as a community college, an organizational training facility, or in one's home. These methods of training are often referred to as *distance learning.* Some courses offered through distance learning programs are referred to generally as computer-aided instruction. Instruction is videotaped and made available for viewing on personal computers without regard to time. Prepackaged programs are often referred to as courseware. Instructor assistance and peer support is available through television, telephone, e-mail, or fax (Muchinsky, 2003).

Colleges and universities in most states also offer distance learning programs. Likewise, some Fortune 500 companies are spending considerable sums developing delivery of distance courses; for example, Federal Express offers 4,000 courses through interactive video (Martin, 1996; Morgan & Hawkridge, 1999). The major advantage of these training programs is that they can be individualized, are available at any time, and they eliminate traveling to an educational institution. Also, some learners appreciate the quality of instruction from professors that would not otherwise be available to them. Students also appreciate and learn from interacting with other students in multiple locations. The downside of some distance learning programs includes a rather sterile classroom atmosphere at remote sites, slow transmissions, and poor video (Goldstein & Ford, 2002).

CD-ROM and Interactive Multimedia

As the name implies, this form of learning involves interactive media through action video, animation, graphics, text, and audio. Multimedia programs using CD-ROM technology have been enhanced by videodiscs and computer-based programs that add to the flexibility of how and what is learned. The one program usually selected to represent the best of this technology is PLATO (Programmed Logic for Automated Teaching Operations). This interactive media system consists of over 5,000 assignable learning activities that are self-paced. Workers can upgrade their basic skills of reading, math, and writing; learn problem-solving skills; and/or upgrade their skill in workplace communication through interactive media. Some prominent companies offer PLATO-driven programs to employees for continuous learning to enhance their positions and effectiveness (Goldstein & Ford, 2002).

Preliminary results of the effectiveness of PLATO programs have been promising. Learners have improved their math scores and higher scores were recorded on mastery tests when compared with results from traditional classroom instruction (Johnston, 1995). The high cost of developing learning programs for PLATO delivery, however, limits its flexibility when variations of a particular learning program are needed. One of the most impressive aspects of PLATO is the number of self-paced programs available and the effectiveness of improving basic skills.

Web-Based Instruction

Of all training programs, Web-based instruction is probably the most flexible in that users can access programs at any time through widely available Web browsers. Web training is easily updated and is enhanced by hyperlinks to additional training material, exercises, and feedback, allowing users to determine the level and depth of information needed. There appears to be endless possibilities for learning opportunities through linking to other Internet sites or corporate intranet sites (sites within an organization, for instance). Users also can share information and ideas and discuss problems with an expert and/or other trainees. Brown, Milner, and Ford (1998) have suggested that Web-based instruction include a guidance component. Guidance usually would include information about purpose of learning, and how to learn the material effectively. Thus, such guidance programs can help learners make more effective decisions about what to learn and how to learn it effectively. At this time we know relatively little about the effectiveness of Web-based training; however, we can expect many more innovations that should be of interest to all counselors who offer career-related counseling.

Intelligent Tutoring Systems (ITS)

This learning platform is a computer-based program that is highly individualized and is considered to be an improved-tech version of programmed instruction (Steele-Johnson & Hyde, 1997). This system is designed to diagnose a user's level of understanding, performance, and types of errors made in performing a task. Using the data collected from each user, the system provides guidelines for more appropriate procedures and learning activities. Thus, the system individualizes training experiences that are developed from individual needs. More specifically, a writing process tutor component that focuses on developing writing process skills identifies errors and presents solutions. Likewise, a scientific inquiry skills component presents errors and suggestions for accurate data analysis. Interactive systems have the distinct advantage of allowing users to ask questions about particular tasks. Feedback may first come in the form of hints about correct procedures but, eventually, direct analogies are given, followed by explicit instructions. Although the individualized approach of this system makes it most attractive, the cost of developing programs is very high. The following extract is a good example of this system's current use and suggests the potential of the future use of ITS.

> Thus, these high end systems respond adaptively to both learning level and learning style, making judgments about student knowledge and learning needs. For example, NASA has employed ITS to train flight dynamics officers how to deploy satellites in space a complex task that requires performing the correct sequence of activities (Steele-Johnson & Hyde, 1997). The ITS presents a deployment problem with information based on the types of errors committed in performing the task. The trainees can also engage in dialog with the system by querying the system with help messages. The success of the trainee in navigating these sequences of activities affects the type of feedback and tutoring the trainee receives. (Goldstein & Ford, 2002, p. 262)

Although this system offers many possibilities for developing skills that can be applied in a variety of work environments, it is still being developed and refined. It could be a stand-alone system in the future or it could be combined with other systems that would complement each other. At this time, counselors should be aware of ITS and consider it to be an example of what the future may bring in terms of training programs for skill development. This observation holds true for our next system as well, virtual reality training.

Virtual Reality (VR) Training

This learning system is a hi-tech version of work simulations through virtual reality. Work simulation in this case, however, is viewed in a three-dimensional (3-D) world that workers will encounter. It purports to be a captivating experience that takes advantage of visual learning and experiential engagement that is highly motivating. It is a very flexible system that permits control of time in its simulations, that is, it can move faster, slow down, reverse, or halt. It is designed to present different levels of detail. Learning modules can be updated and/or integrated with other modules.

In 1999, an animated person named Steve was placed in a 3-D mock-up of a work environment (Rickel & Johnson, 1999). Users can ask Steve to demonstrate how to perform tasks, and provide assistance while they are practicing certain tasks. One advantage of VR training systems is clear: They are flexible enough to demonstrate a variety of work environments and interactions within different work environments. Groups of virtual people can be used to simulate work environments and significant interactions between workers. VR will more than likely become available on the Internet and will expand its programs, for instance, to include negotiation skills in a room full of virtual people (Gunther-Mohr, 1997).

Goldstein and Ford (2002) have compiled applications of VR systems and some are summarized here. The military has been quite involved in virtual reality training; for instance, the U.S. Air Force trained aircrews in how to use emergency parachutes by simulating different conditions they may encounter. Using virtual reality they created different weather conditions, hostile locations, day and nighttime environments, and examples of different wind conditions. The U.S. Army, HOPE, and the Center for Advanced Technologies developed VR training for traditional skill trades (HOPE in Focus, 2000). In the private sector, Motorola has offered VR training in how to use machines on the manufacturing line in several of its locations. Again, VR training is individualized in that learners can stop and start machines they will use and become actively involved in solving problems that may occur. Finally, VR systems are being developed at Penn State to train surgeons to perform a very delicate microsurgical procedure of joining two blood vessels. In sum, VR is used in a variety of training programs ranging from learning how to parachute in emergencies, develop skills for traditional skill trades, operate machinery on manufacturing lines, and perform microsurgical procedures. In all cases, simulated conditions in 3-D were created to represent real problems that may be encountered in performing certain tasks. Learners have the advantage of setting their own pace and are able to ask for help and directions whenever needed.

In conclusion, it is not certain at this time which of the current training delivery systems will emerge as the leader. It is also not certain what kind of new and different technologies will emerge that may prove to be even more effective than the ones that currently are being developed. More than likely we will experience a mixture or blend of systems that prove to be effective with certain training goals and modules. The focus of future training models could be integrated learning systems that are designed to meet specified requirements and needs of the workforce in the 21st century (Goldstein & Ford, 2002). Finally, skill development should be available for all clients. There appears to be an increasing number of programs that focus on developing basic skills. We can expect that *broadband technology* will increase the ease of accessing educational/training programs in the near future. (See Chapter 18.) The message here is that counselors are to recognize that, in a knowledge society, continuous career development requires one to effectively read, write, and do basic math. On the other end of the knowledge spectrum, continuous development requires the fine-tuning of developed skills through a variety of training programs. For all clients, technology may offer opportunities to learn and develop skills determined by each individual's needs and interests.

Summary

1. The rationale for computerized career counseling stems from the need for up-to-date information and the unique capabilities of the computer to satisfy this need. A number of computerized counseling systems with different combinations of computer hardware and software and different sets of objectives have been developed.

2. Some research indicates a positive reaction to computer-assisted guidance systems by users. Moreover, the results suggest that the systems evaluated are worthwhile for counseling intervention and help individuals meet career exploration needs.

3. The most common types of computer-assisted career guidance systems are information systems and guidance systems.

4. Career Information Delivery Systems (CIDS) were developed with the assistance of NOICC and the SOICCs. One of the major purposes was to give states the opportunity to develop state and local data.

5. The DISCOVER program and SIGI and SIGI PLUS for colleges and adults are examples of systems that include online assessment programs, job descriptions, and educational information, all of which are easily accessible.

6. A seven-step implementation model should be followed when implementing a computer-based program.

7. The Internet has tremendous potential for the career counselor. Currently, information on the Internet includes self-assessment programs, search databases, and career development resources.

8. Skill development is an important factor in determining occupational fit. Innovative learning systems include simulated training, CD-ROM and interactive multimedia, intelligent tutoring systems, and virtual reality training.

Supplementary Learning Exercises

1. Visit a school, college, or agency that has a computer-based career information system. Request a preview of the system, and identify the major components in a written report.

2. Outline and discuss the advantages of having a computer-assisted career guidance system in one or more of the following: a high school, a community college, a four-year college, and a community agency providing career counseling to adults.

3. Form two groups and debate the issues relating to the following statement: Computer-assisted career guidance systems will replace the career counselor.

4. Develop a local visit file (individuals in selected occupations who agree to visits by students) that could be included as a component in a computer-assisted career guidance system. Describe the advantages of a visit file.

5. Interview a career counselor who has substantial experience in using computer-assisted career guidance systems. Write a report on the systems used and summarize the counselor's evaluation of the systems.

6. Describe the advantages of having a statewide occupational information data bank of job openings and labor forecasts. How could you incorporate this information in career counseling programs in high schools, community colleges, four-year colleges or universities, and community programs for adults?

7. Decide what is meant by an interactive computer-assisted career guidance system. Illustrate your description with your own version of an example script.

8. Explain your conception of the future role of the Internet as a counseling tool. Focus on the advantages and limitations.

9. Describe why skill development is so important in the current work environment. How would you help a client access learning and developmental programs?

10. Choose two hi-tech learning delivery systems and explain how they could be integrated to meet individual needs.

For More Information

Gati, I. (1994). Computer-assisted career counseling: Dilemmas, problems, and possible solutions. *Journal of Counseling and Development, 73,* 51–57.

Goldstein, I. L. & Ford, J. K. (2002). *Training in organizations* (4th ed.). Belmont, CA: Wadsworth.

Harris-Bowlsbey, J., Dikel, M. R., & Sampson, J. P. (1998). *The Internet: A tool for career planning.* Columbus, OH: National Career Development Association.

Healy, C. C. (1990). Reforming career appraisals to meet the needs of clients in the 1990s. *The Counseling Psychologist, 18,* 214–226.

Jones, L. K. (1993). Two career guidance instruments: Their helpfulness to students and effect on student's career exploration. *School Counselor, 40,* 191–200.

Kivlighan, D. M., Johnston, J. A., Hogan, R. S., & Mauer, E. (1994). Who benefits from computerized career counseling? *Journal of Counseling and Development, 72,* 189–192.

Mariani, M. (1995–96, Winter). Computers and career guidance: Ride the rising ride. *Occupational Outlook Quarterly, 39,* 16–27.

McCormac, M. E. (1988). Information sources and resources. *Journal of Career Development, 16,* 129–138.

Muchinsky, P. M. (2003). *Psychology applied to work.* Belmont, CA: Wadsworth/Thomson Learning.

Sampson, J. P. (1994). *Effective computer-assisted career guidance: Occasional paper number 2.* Center for the Study of Technology in Counseling and Career Development, Florida State University.

Sampson, J. P., Kolodinsky, R. W., & Greeno, B. P. (1997). Counseling on the information highway: Future possibilities and potential problems. *Journal of Counseling and Development, 75,* 203–212.

Wilson, F. R. (1995). Internet information sources for counselors. *Counselor Education and Supervision, 34* (4), 369–387.

Zunker, V. G., & Osborn, D. (2002). *Using assessment results for career development.* Pacific Grove, CA: Brooks/Cole.

Suggested InfoTrac College Edition Topics

Career information	Job shadowing
Computer counseling	Simulation
Computer-based counseling	Skill training
Computer-based training	Virtual reality
Distance learning	Web-based training

9 On Being an Ethical Career Counselor

Chapter Highlights

- Some ethical standards from several professional organizations

- Ethical competency issues

- Some boundaries of confidentiality

- Some responsibilities of informed consent

- Some boundaries of measurement and evaluation

- Some Internet user ethical issues

- Ethical responsibilities with peer counselors

- Examples of violations

LEADERS OF PROFESSIONAL helping organizations prudently have spent considerable effort and time on developing ethical standards for their members. In this chapter, we examine some ethical issues, principles, and standards that were developed by the National Career Development Association (NCDA) (1997). Because career counselors may be members of two or more professional associations, our discussions often include examples of ethical codes from other professional associations.

In counseling encounters, counselors often are faced with crucial decisions concerning the welfare of their clients and so they may ask the following questions: Is this in the best interest of my client? Which test should I use in this case? Is this intervention strategy appropriate? Is the information on this Web site accurate? Should I get the client's consent to confer with others? Do I have the necessary training to handle this case? These questions illustrate the nature of concerns among counselors for appropriate materials, techniques, and counseling competencies. There are, however, many more ethical issues that have surfaced in the last three decades that underscore the need for counselors to fully comprehend the boundaries implied in ethical standards (Welfel, 2002).

Ethical standards and codes of ethics are designed to be very inclusive. They address moral dimensions of counselor relationships and behavior as well as competency requirements, confidentiality, informed consent, misconduct, and violations of trust and care. As with most laws and rules, ethical guidelines cannot possibly include each and every circumstance and situation that involves ethical behavior. Thus, ethical standards offer solutions for counselors in a wide range of categories in which the *intent* of standards are to be followed. More important, however, is the position that counselors are to establish patterns of action that help them respond appropriately to all client needs. In the diverse society of the 21st century, client concerns and needs can be quite complex. In this chapter we present some examples of major ethical issues for counselors regarding competence, confidentiality, informed consent, measurement and evaluation, Internet user issues, and use of peer counselors. Examples of violations do not include sensational cases such as sexual exploitation. This chapter introduces readers to examples of subtle situations and consequences that can lead to misconduct.

Some Boundaries of Ethical Competence

We begin our discussion of competence by emphasizing the importance of the client's welfare. Client welfare should be the counselor's ultimate concern, suggesting that professional counselors practice within the boundaries of their competence. Counselors' competence usually is determined by an evaluation of their education, training, supervised experience, credentials, and appropriate professional experiences. Every counselor should be able to present evidence of qualifications for the counseling position they occupy or the position they seek. What matters are principles of integrity, professional and social responsibility, and respect for individuals' rights and dignity. Counselors therefore are to strive to maintain the highest standards of competence in their work. In essence, counselors have a moral and professional responsibility to insure that each client receives appropriate guidance.

Two general guidelines from the National Career Development Association (NCDA) (2003), underscore the competency issue as follows:

> 6. NCDA members seek only those positions in the delivery of professional services for which they are professionally qualified.
> 7. NCDA members recognize their limitations and provide services or only use techniques for which they are qualified by training and/or experience. Career counselors recognize the need, and seek continuing education, to insure competent services. (p. 2)

SOURCE: All quotations from the *National Career Development Association Ethical Standards* (2003) are reprinted by permission. Copyright © 2003 by the National Career Development Association. Reprinted by permission.

Within these boundaries there are many important considerations. For example, a counselor encounters a new, highly touted standardized measurement instrument that he or she has not used. It turns out that this is a very complex instrument that measures personality variables that are indicative of levels of career maturity and career choice indicators. Even after reading the technical manual carefully, the counselor is not certain of this instrument's appropriateness and the most effective method for interpreting the results. In this case the counselor correctly decides to not use this instrument until more information about its use is received and supervised training is available.

Another counselor uncovers a severe thinking disorder in a client who has a history of impulsively acting out, with little thought given to the consequences of his actions. His ability to function on a job has been impaired by his impulsive and hostile actions. Although good rapport has been established, the counselor decides treatment will require a long-term commitment and counseling skills that she is only beginning to develop. The counselor decides to refer this client for treatment of a potential thinking disorder but will delay career counseling until it is more appropriate. Counselors will find that decisions of this kind are ongoing ones that challenge professionals to continue their training and upgrade their competence.

The American Counseling Association (ACA) (1995) also clearly points out that new specialty areas require education, training, and supervised experience. In Section E: Evaluation, Assessment, and Interpretation, E.2 is stated as follows:

> a. Limits of Competence. Counselors recognize the limits of their competence and perform only those testing and assessment services for which they have been trained. They are familiar with reliability, validity, related standardization, error of measurement, and proper application of any technique utilized. Counselors using computerized-based test interpretations are trained in the construct being measured and the specific instrument being used prior to using this type of computer application. Counselors take reasonable measures to ensure the proper use of psychological assessment techniques for persons under their supervision. (p. 7)

Example of a Violation

Counselor A accepts a position in a mental health agency to provide career-related counseling to a client population that is primarily from Asian families. Counselor A has no previous experience in counseling or assessing Asian clients. The issue of competence here addresses the need for supervised training with the particular client population being seen by the mental health agency, as stated by the American Psychological Association (1992):

> 1.08. Human Differences: Where differences of age, gender, race, ethnicity, national origin, religion, sexual orientation, disability, language, or socioeconomic status significantly affect psychologists' work concerning particular individuals or groups, psychologists obtain the training, experience, consultation, or supervision necessary to ensure the competence of their service, or they make appropriate referrals. (p. 4)

The NCDA (2003) ethical standards addresses this situation within the major heading of B. Counseling Relationships, Number 13, stated as follows:

> NCDA members who counsel clients from cultures different from their own must gain knowledge, personal awareness, and sensitivity pertinent to the client populations served and must incorporate culturally relevant techniques into their practice. (p. 5)

Other professional associations usually address this issue of competence in more general terms, stating that counselors are to offer only those counseling services for which they are qualified. In our example, Counselor A could accept such a position if arrangements were made for him to receive supervision that could be completed during training (Gelso & Fretz, 2001).

Example of a Violation

Counselor B, who has specialized in career counseling of adults, has been in private practice for several years. One of her most lucrative referral sources, a local business organization, requested that she administer a specific individual intelligence test to one of its employees. She was told that the results were to be used in a high-stakes decision concerning the promotion of the client to an important position in the organization. Counselor B informed the organization that she has not given an individual intelligence for several years and did not take a graduate course in individual testing. The organizational representative sent back word that the results were needed immediately and she was to do her best. Realizing that she might lose a most important referral source, she agreed to administer the test.

The violations of competence are quite clear in this case. Counselor B violated ethical codes by performing functions in which she had not received appropriate training. Second, she did not address the issue of promotion based on results from a single standardized test of intelligence. The following codes of ethics from two professional groups apply. NCDA (2003) ethical standards in section C: Measurement and Evaluation, number 4 states: "Because many types of assessment techniques exist, NCDA members must recognize the limits of their competence and perform only those functions for which they have received appropriate training" (p. 6). Likewise, the ACA (1995) code of ethical standards , Section C: Professional Responsibility, C 2 states: "a. Counselors practice only within the boundaries of their competence, based on their education, training, supervised experience, state and national professional credentials, and appropriate professional experience" (p. 4).

Counselor B could have approached this situation by offering assistance in developing valid criteria that can be used in the promotion process. She also could be prepared to offer alternate testing for which she had been trained. Counselors who accept referrals also must be in a position to inform clients of rights to information about the purpose and anticipated courses of action in the use of any and all assessment results.

Some Boundaries of Confidentiality

The principle of the client's rights to privacy is a key element in a counseling relationship, thus counselors usually begin counseling with a reinforcement of the privacy principle. The rationale is that clients expect that discussions of private events and thoughts revealed to counselors will not be shared with others without their consent. All professional counseling associations stress the importance of the client's right to privacy. In section B entitled Counseling Relationship of the NCDA (2003) ethical standards, it is clearly stated that "the counseling relationship and information resulting from it remains confidential, consistent with legal obligations of the NCDA member. In a group counseling setting, the career counselor sets a norm of confidentiality regarding all group participants' disclosures" (p. 7).

Example of a Violation

Counselor C shows a client's personality inventory profile to a student worker in the high school counseling center and remarks that this case is going to be difficult. This obvious violation is serious—one that could be damaging to the client even though the counselor in this case did not intend harm and considered his actions as "small talk."

Ethical standards for school counselors were developed by the American School Counselor Association (ASCA) (1998) and clearly identify ethical codes relating to confidentiality as follows:

A. 2. Confidentiality
   The professional school counselor:
   b. Keeps information confidential unless disclosure is required to prevent clear and imminent danger to the counselee or others or when legal requirements demand that confidential information be revealed. Counselors will consult with other professionals when in doubt as to the validity of an exception. (p. 1)

Counselor C's remark is a good example of how casual conversation about clients can result in ethical misconduct. In a counseling center where there is good rapport between staff and professional counselors, one may be tempted to share some bits of confidential information about a client, which could lead to damaging results. Information about an individual's personality profile, for example, can be grossly misconstrued by an untrained staff member who then shares this information with someone who makes further misinterpretations and shares his or her own conclusion with yet another person. The end result can be quite damaging to a client who has asked for help.

Example of a Violation

In a large community college, Counselor D is very busy overseeing and providing career counseling services to a steady stream of students. The large number of students using career services attracted the attention of a university professor, who asked for permission to use student files to gather data that was to be used in a research project. The counselor was thrilled to work with the well-known professor and offered to provide access to student records. The data was promptly collected by student workers from open files without the consent of the students who had used career services.

NCDA (2003) ethical standards, Section D. Research and Publication, 9 states:

NCDA members who supply data, aid in the research of another person, report research results, or make original data available, must take due care to disguise the identity of respective subjects in the absence of specific authorization from the subject to do otherwise.

The implications of the above ethical standard are very clear in directing counselors and researchers to the importance of keeping client records confidential. In this case the counselor should only make data available with the student's permission or by providing essential data in a manner that would disguise the identity of each student. Likewise, researchers should make certain that the identity of all subjects studied in research projects is protected and their privacy is maintained. Research projects are most important in the search for answers to improve career counseling effectiveness but should not be accomplished in a way that would not intrude on the individual client's rights of confidentiality and informed consent.

The Code of Ethics of the American Mental Health Counselors Association (AMHCA) (2000) Principle 3 on Confidentiality states:

> Mental Health counselors have a primary obligation to safeguard information about individuals obtained in the course of practice, teaching or research. Personal information is communicated to others only with the person's written consent or in those circumstances where there is clear and imminent danger to the client, to others or to society. Disclosure of counseling information is restricted to what is necessary, relevant and verifiable. (p. 3)

The client's rights to privacy have far-reaching implications for counseling practice. First, the client must be assured that confidentiality will be maintained. Second, effective counseling practices have focused on gaining client rapport and trust in order to freely exchange information. The legal implications of a client's rights to privacy, however, are much more complex and inclusive. It is therefore in the best interest of every professional counselor to review the many issues involved in the confidentiality code of ethics of their professional associations carefully, particularly the boundaries of informed consent.

Example of a Violation

Because of a client's serious personal problems, Counselor D decides to refer this client to another professional located in a nearby mental health agency. Thus, the counselor received written permission to give another professional information gathered in the interview and subsequent counseling sessions. Some contents of the confidential information sent to the mental health agency were leaked to a relative of the client by a part-time clerk. An investigation of the agency revealed that security for confidential information was meager at best and there were no clearly defined policies on maintaining confidential records. In fact, information about clients could be accessed by a number of workers at the agency. In addition to the violation committed at the mental health agency, the referring counselor violated client confidentiality by not making certain that defined policies were in place that effectively insured the confidentiality of client information in the agency to which the client had been referred. The lesson here is that you do not assume client confidentiality when you refer clients but in fact have an obligation to the client to see that confidentiality will be maintained.

The ACA Code of Ethics (1995) also addresses confidentiality of records as follows:

> Section B. Consultation, b. Cooperating Agencies
> Before sharing information counselors make every effort to ensure that there are defined policies in other agencies serving the counselor's client that effectively protect the confidentiality of information, confidentiality of any counseling records they create, maintain, transfer, or destroy, whether the records are written, taped, computerized, or stored in the other medium. (p. 4)

Some Boundaries of Informed Consent

Informed consent involves disclosure by the counselor of important information the client needs in making the decision as to whether she or he is to start counseling. *Free consent* is when a client agrees to engage in counseling without coercion (Welfel, 2002). In informed consent the counselor informs the client of the purpose, goals, and procedures of engaging in a counseling relationship. The counselor and counselee roles should be defined clearly enough that the client is empowered to make informed decisions during the counseling process. In other words, the client is not to be coerced into a counseling relationship but, on the contrary, will have the freedom to choose to participate in certain counseling activities. Free consent also implies that clients have the right to refuse to engage in certain counseling activities; it is imperative therefore that a collaborative counseling partnership be established and effectively maintained. In this kind of counseling relationship, clients and counselors *both* agree on goals and counseling interventions and jointly share in the selection of materials and procedures.

The APA (1992) code of ethical standards, Section 4.01, is one of the most inclusive examples of how to build a counseling relationship (Welfel, 2002).

Section 4.01 Structuring the Relationship

(a) Psychologists discuss with clients or patients as early as is feasible in the therapeutic relationship appropriate issues such as the nature and anticipated course of therapy, fees, and confidentiality.

(b) When the psychologist's work with clients or patients will be supervised, the above discussion includes that fact and the name of the supervisor, when the supervisor has legal responsibility for the case.

(c) When the therapist is a student intern, the client or patient is informed of that fact.

(d) Psychologists make reasonable efforts to answer patients' questions and to avoid apparent misunderstandings about therapy. Whenever possible, psychologists provide oral and/or written materials, using language that is reasonably understandable to the patient or client. (p. 9)

In the process of establishing and structuring a counseling relationship, the counselor communicates basic information concerning the parameters of informed consent. Welfel (2002) has compiled the following list of information that is recommended and should be communicated when applicable.

Goals, techniques, procedures, limitations, risks, and benefits of counseling.

Ways in which diagnoses, tests, and written reports will be used.

Billing and fees

Confidentiality rights and limitations

Involvement of supervisors or additional mental health professionals

Counselor's training status

Client's access to records

Client's right to choose the counselor and to be active in treatment planning

Client's right to refuse counseling, and the implications of that refusal

Client's right to ask additional questions about counseling and to have questions answered in comprehensible language. (p. 109)

Although this list appears to be very inclusive, there are many more situations in which informed consent is necessary. For example, the use of experimental counseling techniques and electronically recording or observing counseling sessions should be added to the list of information communicated. In sum, what we have here is the *intent* of providing clients with all information about what is to take place in counseling, the materials used, other professionals who may assist or observe, alternative programs, and goals of the counseling process itself. Finally, counselors are to be alert to the methods of obtaining informed consent with special populations such as minors, clients with diminished capacity, and court-mandated counseling (Welfel, 2002).

Finally, we mention that there is increasing concern among professionals of violations of informed consent that are related to telecommunication in psychological practice. Counselors may not be able to verify ages and the mental capacity of individuals who access a counselor's home page and submit e-mail questions. Consequently, there is no adequate way at this time to verify that the recipient of personal advice is a responsible adult and understands the parameters of informed consent.

Some Boundaries of Measurement and Evaluation

Career counselors frequently use standard assessment instruments to measure traits such as interests, personality, and ability, among many others. Computer-generated assessment has also been a popular means of measuring traits that are integral to the counseling process. It should not be surprising that the NCDA has developed ethical codes that foster the use of assessment results. In Section C: Measurement and Evaluation of the NCDA Ethical Standards (2003), there are fifteen statements concerning topics such as selection, use, limitation, and interpretation of assessment instruments. They begin by stating the ethical importance of informing the client of the purpose and explicit use of test results. Some other ethical standards include the recommendations that counselors are to recognize the limits of their competence with assessment instruments and all assessment instruments used must meet the standards of validity, reliability, and appropriateness. The administration of tests should follow directions in the test manual and one is not to use tests that contain obsolete data. The following selected ethical standards are quoted in full for emphasis; they contain references to the release of test data and the use of computer-generated assessment.

> 8. An examinee's welfare, explicit prior understanding, and agreement are the factors used when determining who receives the test results. NCDA members must see that appropriate interpretation accompanies any release of individual or group test data (e.g., limitations of instrument and norms).
>
> 9. NCDA members must ensure that computer-generated assessment administration and scoring programs function properly, thereby providing clients with accurate assessment results. (pp. 6–7)

Example of a Violation

Groups of community college students are invited to the career center for help in choosing a major. During the course of the discussions, students are invited to take an interest inventory to help them decide on a college major. They are told to drop by the counseling center to pick up the results the next day. Those who want more advice at that time can make an appointment to see a counselor or join a group for more information.

All test results, including interest inventories, should be "placed in proper perspective with other relevant factors" in the career counseling process (NCDA, 2003). The release of test data to clients without the benefit of interpretation of the results and the meaning and proper perspective of those results is a serious violation of ethics. Assessment results are used most effectively when their purpose is clearly established through a review of its applications for the individual, its limitations, and how the results specifically will assist in goal attainment.

Example of a Violation

A student in a university psychology class obtains an appointment with a career counselor. He tells the counselor that after reading about personality disorders in his textbook, he thinks that he has a personality disorder that has "bothered me for a long time." Although he has made a definite career decision, he has doubts about his ability to accomplish his goal since "I might have a personality disorder." The counselor explains that verifying a personality disorder will require extensive testing and interview time. He suggests to the client that he should return after semester break for an appointment but if there is an emergency he should find a professional near his home. The counselor also offered to help find a qualified person. The student was insistent, however, about finding some other way of checking out his problem before he returns. Because the semester was over and he was on his way home, the counselor suggested that he take a personality inventory on the Internet and bring the results for interpretation when he returned from semester break.

The APA (1992) on ethical principles Section 2.08: Test Scoring and Interpretation Services states:

> (b) Psychologists select scoring and interpretation services (including automated services) on the basis of evidence of the validity of the program and procedures as well as other appropriate considerations.
> (c) Psychologists retain appropriate responsibility for the appropriate application, interpretation, and use of assessment instruments, whether they score and interpret such test themselves or use automated or other services. (p. 7)

Several ethical principles were violated by the counselor in our example. The exact number of sites on the Internet that offer psychological and career assessment is unknown but there is evidence that the number has increased significantly (Sampson & Lumsden, 2000). Counselors are to use only test administration and interpretation services for which there is sufficient evidence of their validity and reliability and evidence of appropriate application and interpretation. Many unanswered questions remain about the marketing and availability of psychological testing on the Web. Counselors are advised to exercise extreme caution with such services at the present time. In the case of a suspected personality disorder, the counselor had insufficient information about the client's problems. He was in no position to suggest any standardized testing, much less a personality test administered on the Internet in which the client was to interpret his results.

Some NCDA Guidelines for Using the Internet

The use of the Internet for the delivery of career-related services has been carefully scrutinized by the NCDA (1997) and other professional organizations. It is quite evident that the capabilities of Internet delivery services will expand rapidly with the onset of sound and video. We can expect that the NCDA will monitor online career-related services very carefully in the future; more ethical standards and codes should follow. In the meantime we review guidelines approved by the NCDA in October 1997.

Some distinctions are made between career planning and career counseling services when clients are using the Internet. When clients are involved in specific planning needs such as identification of occupations based on interests, skills, and experiences, or support for job-seeking, they are engaging in career planning. Even though these same services are a part of career counseling, this term implies a more in-depth procedure in a counseling relationship. Client Y, for example, is majoring in accounting and is looking in a specific location for a future job. Client Y is considered to be a career planner, although if client Y becomes discouraged and considers a career change, he or she will take part in a systematic career counseling process. Thus, there are multiple needs of clients that may involve the use of the Internet. In all cases, however, the counselor has a significant ethical responsibility.

Here are some general suggestions based on NCDA (1997) guidelines for the use of the Internet for provision of career information and planning services as paraphrased:

1. Counselors are to evaluate Web sites and other services to make certain they have been prepared by professional career counselors; the developer's credentials and qualification should be carefully evaluated.
2. Counselors are to have knowledge of free public access points to insure that all clients have the advantage of Internet career-related services.
3. The appropriateness of the content on the Web site should be carefully scrutinized. Each Web site should state the kinds of client concerns its programs can address.
4. Counselors should screen each client's career counseling needs and determine if those needs can be addressed appropriately on the Internet.
5. Counselors are to monitor each client's progress periodically and be prepared to offer referrals in the client's geographical location. A review of client progress should be thorough and, if there is doubt about the client's progress, a referral to face-to-face services should be made.
6. The provider of Internet services should present credentials to the user; develop individual counseling goals for each user; inform the user of costs, how to report unethical behavior, security measures used, information about electronically stored data, how privacy is maintained; and provide easily accessed pathways to career, educational and employment information.
7. The Web site should also include information and services available through linkage with other Web sites.
8. The use of assessment guidelines includes (a) the need to assure that psychometric properties of assessment instruments on the Internet are the same as printed

forms, (b) the ethical standards of administering and interpreting the printed form of a test used must be maintained, (c) assessment results are to be confidential, (d) clients who do not fully understand the meaning of assessment results should be referred to a qualified counselor, and (e) all measurement instruments used that require interpretation by the user must be validated as self-help instruments.

Finally, unacceptable counselor behavior on the Internet was identified by NCDA (1997) as follows:

1. Use of false e-mail identity when interacting with clients and/or other professionals. When acting in a professional capacity on the Internet, a counselor has a duty to honestly identify him/herself.

2. Accepting a client who will not identify him/herself and be willing to arrange for phone conversation as well as online interchange.

3. "Sharking" or monitoring chat rooms and bulletin board services, and offering career planning and related services when no request has been made for services. This includes sending out mass unsolicited e-mails. Counselors may advertise their services but must do so observing proper "netiquette" and standards of professional conduct. (p. 5)

Concerns about Internet counseling relationships have also been expressed by the National Board of Certified Counselors, Inc. and Center for Credentialing and Education, Inc. (2001). Some concerns are difficulty in identifying Internet clients, need for parental/guardian consent of a minor, confidentiality of Internet counseling, identification of local assistance in case of emergencies, and lack of visual cues during the counseling process. These and other concerns should occupy the research efforts of many professionals in the future. Clearly, there is much to be learned about the use of the Internet for career-related assessment and counseling. Also see Ethical Standards for Internet On-Line Counseling approved by the ACA governing council in October 1999.

Some Ethical Implications of Using Peer Helpers

In the 1960s, Zunker and Brown (1966) published a study involving the use of trained peer counselors to deliver academic adjustment guidance to entering college freshmen students. The purpose of the student-to-student counseling program was to assist students in adjusting to the changes in academic demands and requirements from high school to college. In small groups of three to five students, trained peers, usually juniors and seniors, presented a very carefully structured program that included examples of how to plan a class schedule, take class notes, choose a college major, and improve study habits. Discussions focused on the give-and-take of college life and the discipline and skills necessary to be a successful student. The program was successful both in terms of student survival after one semester in college and in that many peer counselors became interested in counseling as a result of their peer counseling experiences.

When this study's results were reported in several presentations at professional association conventions, ethical concerns regarding peer helping programs surfaced. There was general concern, and rightly so, that peer helping programs could pose some potential ethical risks such as confidentiality concerns, the client's rights of privacy, and competency issues of peer helpers. Over the years, peer counseling programs have grown and expanded to include such issues as suicide, drug and alcohol abuse, and depression. It is not unusual to find peer helpers or facilitators in high school counseling centers as well as universities and in community mental health programs. In career counseling programs, peer counselors are used in a variety of helping positions such as discussion leaders, career information facilitators, and in outreach programs. Lenz (2000) has published an outstanding review of the use of paraprofessionals in career services.

Welfel (2002) suggests that in career counseling programs that use peer counselors, clients are to be informed of issues of confidentiality. More specifically, clients should be informed that peer counselors have been thoroughly informed of ethical standards of confidentiality. Secondly, clients are also to be informed of the responsibility and oversight of professional directors of peer counseling programs on all issues of confidentiality. The implications of a well-informed peer helper suggests to clients that they are well trained for their helping roles and are regularly supervised. Peer counselors who are well trained also are aware of their limitations as a helper and therefore have explicit instructions on how and where to refer students who may express personal concerns that require professional help. The roles and limitations of peer helpers should be thoroughly defined. The dedication of a professionally trained and certified counselor to the administration and supervision of peer counseling programs is an essential part of what makes peer counselors effective and ethical.

On Becoming Ethical

In this brief review of ethical standards that included some ethical codes from several professional associations, we find that there are reminders of conduct that is considered ethically correct and that which constitutes a violation of professional ethics. Be aware that only a small number of ethical violations have been discussed. There are general themes, however, that permeate the ethical position of most counseling associations. One theme suggests that counselors must be dedicated to the welfare of their clients. This dedication includes not only the development of counseling knowledge and skills to address presenting problems from clients, but also the desire and knowledge of how to appropriately accomplish counseling goals in an ethical manner. What is suggested here is that counselors not only expand and sharpen their skills to meet a variety of client needs but that they also increase their knowledge of ethical codes and standards.

The intent of the counselor to do what is ethically appropriate in a counseling relationship is an essential part of a moral obligation of most professional counseling associations. Counselors are to fully understand that there are severe legal ramifications of misconduct. As with most standards, codes, rules, and laws, ignorance of the law does not excuse anyone from committing a violation. Counselors are to recognize that in the 21st century it is most important to learn the general principles of ethical standards and codes that have been developed by their professional associations. In addition, counselors should find a source or sources that are easily accessible for advice and consultation concerning appropriate ethical practice.

In sum, we have only introduced some principles of ethical codes and standards. Our purpose was to inform readers of the importance of ethics in counseling practice.

Secondly, there are indications that counselors can expect to find that the appropriateness of their methods, procedures, and counseling materials will be carefully scrutinized. All professional counselors therefore must be prepared to show evidence of their training and credentials as well as continued training to update their skills to use new and different procedures and materials. An increased sensitivity to potential ethical problems that could arise from certain counseling encounters should be fostered through workshops and by reviewing the details of ethical codes and standards of your professional associations. Finally, ethical complaints by NCDA members can be filed by any individual or group of individuals to this address:

ACA Ethics Committee
Executive Director
American Counseling Association
5999 Stevenson Avenue
Alexandria, VA 22304

Summary

1. Ethical standards and codes address moral dimensions of counseling relationships.
2. Counselors are to practice within the boundaries of their competence.
3. Counselors only seek positions for which they are qualified.
4. Counselors are to recognize their limits of competence.
5. Information associated with a counseling relationship is to remain confidential.
6. Disclosure of information to another professional requires a signed written consent.
7. The client's rights to privacy must be upheld.
8. Free consent suggests that a client agrees to engage in a counseling relationship without coercion.
9. Informed consent suggests that clients are informed of the purpose and goals of counseling.
10. Clients are also to be informed of the purpose and explicit use of assessment instruments.
11. Counselors are to select scoring and interpretation services, including automated services, only on the basis of information of their validity.
12. The use of the Internet in career counseling requires a careful and thorough evaluation that is very inclusive.
13. Peer counselors must be thoroughly trained in the ethics of counseling, especially regarding issues of confidentiality and competency.

Supplementary Learning Exercises

1. Write a brief essay on what it means to be an ethically professional counselor.
2. Under what conditions could a counselor accept a position for which they are not qualified? Defend your answer.
3. Investigate professional associations to determine what is considered to be appropriate training for you to incorporate a newly developed counseling technique or assessment instrument in your practice. Share with classmates.

4. List and discuss the conditions under which you could disclose information about a client without his or her consent.
5. Discuss the importance of a client's rights to privacy in a counseling relationship.
6. Research the literature to determine the most frequent ethical violations of counselors in your state of residence and nationwide.
7. Discuss the similarities and differences between free consent and informed consent. Explain their importance.
8. What is the counseling significance of informing clients about the purpose and use of assessment results. Identify at least five reasons for this suggestion.
9. How would you investigate the appropriateness of an Internet career-related counseling program? List your resources.
10. Under what conditions can counselors be assured that peer counselors are following appropriate ethical standards? What do you consider to be the greatest ethical risk with the use of peer counselors?

For More Information

Codes of ethics for the helping professions (2003). Pacific Grove, CA: Brooks/Cole. Author.

Corey, G., Corey, M., & Callanan, P. (1998). *Issues and ethics in the helping progressions* (5th ed.). Pacific Grove, CA: Brooks/Cole.

Welfel, E. R. (2002). *Ethics, counseling, psychotherapy.* Pacific Grove, CA: Brooks/Cole.

See Web sites for professional associations in appendix I.

Suggested InfoTrac College Edition Topics

Codes of ethics	Standards of ethics
Counseling ethics	Unethical behavior
Ethical counseling	Unethical practice
Responsible practice	

10 Career Counseling for Multicultural Groups

Chapter Highlights

- Definitions of culture

- Four major cultural groups: Asian Americans, African Americans, Hispanic Americans, and Native Americans

- Cultural variability

- Cultural differences in work-related activities

- Learning how to be culturally competent

- Review of immigrants' problems and adjustments to a new and different culture

- Living and working in a culturally diverse society

THE NEED TO DEVELOP career counseling strategies for multicultural groups will increase throughout this century. An article, "Minority Numbers" (U.S. Bureau of Census, 1993), based on a report from the Population Reference Bureau of the U.S. Census Bureau, suggested that by the middle of the 21st century, the United States will no longer be a predominately white society. The more appropriate reference will be "a global society," in which half of all Americans will be from four ethnic groups: Asian Americans, African Americans, Hispanic Americans, and Native Americans. These projected demographics containing the potential of an increasingly diverse society will present significant challenges to all the helping professions. As more multicultural groups gain access to opportunities for education and higher-status jobs, the career counseling profession should be prepared to assist them.

Career counselors are intent on developing career counseling objectives and strategies that will assist individuals of various ethnic groups to overcome a multitude of barriers including prejudice, language differences, cultural isolation, and culture-related differences. Because this group is composed of persons from a wide variety of ethnic backgrounds, counselors are being challenged to become culturally aware, evaluate their personal views, and understand that other people's perspectives may be as legitimate as their own (Brammer, 2004; Sue & Sue, 1990).

We begin this chapter with an introduction to the meaning of culture as it relates to career counseling. Second, four major cultural groups are briefly discussed. Cultural variability and worldviews are examined in the third section. In the fourth section, culturally related work values are explored. Fifth, the challenge of becoming culturally competent is presented. Immigration and its sequelae is reviewed in the sixth section. Finally, we offer some suggestions on how to help clients live and work in a culturally diverse society.

What Is Culture?

Cultural diversity is an important topic for all counselors, and especially for the career counselor. In many respects, we have not addressed the issue of culture in the counseling profession. For example, researchers are in the early stages of studies to determine appropriate intervention strategies and assessment instruments for specific ethnic groups (Betz & Fitzgerald, 1995; Slattery, 2004), which are among the many issues and questions to be resolved. Because of the variety of ethnic groups found in the United States today, we may find the answer to these issues and questions to be very evasive and quite complex. To deal with this subject in greater depth, readers are provided with a list of references at the end of this chapter. In the meantime, the career counselor must give high priority to cultural variables that influence career development.

Returning to the question of identifying culture, perhaps each of us could offer an explanation of what culture means. We would be able to illustrate our definitions with examples of cultural aspects, variables, customs, and perceptions of different individuals from a variety of "cultures." We could describe activities associated with a culture, we could refer to heritage and tradition of cultures, we could describe rules and norms associated with cultures, we could describe behavioral approaches associated with cultures, and we could describe the origin of cultures. These are examples of different meanings associated with the definition of culture and the different interpretations we use to identify people of different cultures. Thus, culture is a complex concept that can refer to many aspects of life and living. Matsumoto (1996) defines culture "as the set of attitudes, values, beliefs, and behaviors shared by a group of people, but different for each individual, communicated from one generation to the next" (p. 16).

Ogbu (1990) defines culture as follows: Culture is an understanding that a people have of their universe—social, physical, or both—as well as their understanding of their behavior in that universe. The cultural model of a population serves its members as a guide in their interpretation of events and elements within their universe; it also serves as a guide to their expectations and actions in that universe or environment (p. 523).

These definitions, although leaving a lot to be said about culture, provide a good fit for the career counselor's use of the word. For example, sharing implies the degree to which an individual holds the values, attitudes, beliefs, norms, or behaviors of a particular group. Furthermore, the emphasis is on cognitive processes of psychological sharing of a particular attribute among members of a culture. Although culture can be conceptualized in different ways, there appears to be agreement that language, family structure, environment (social context), and traditions are most influential in determining group differences (Lum, 2003; Okun, Fried, & Okun, 1999). The lesson to be learned is that even within cultures, each individual should be treated as such rather than from a stereotypical viewpoint that one has about a particular culture. We must be alert to cultural diversity among members of any ethnic group; for instance, Wehrly (1995) points out that 56 ethnic groups identify with their own culture and have their own language in Mexico. The point is that one should not assume that any ethnic group is homogenous.

Culture is a learned behavior. Therefore, two people from the same race may share some values, attitudes, and so on, but might also have very different cultural makeups. How much has been acculturated from racial heritage through socialization varies even within the dominant cultural group of a country (Triandis, 1992, cited in Matsumoto, 2000). Therefore, we must not make assumptions from cultural stereotypes—as we have heard so often in counseling, we enter into counseling relationships with individuals. In this chapter, references will be made to one or more of the major cultural groups briefly identified in the following section.

Four Major Cultural Groups

Governmental agencies have grouped individuals by culture for a variety of reasons but especially for the national census. Our discussion will include the most recent groupings as African Americans (black is often used), Asian, Southeast Asian, Asian Indian, and other Asian, Hispanic (Latino/a is often used), and Native Americans (First Nations People is often used). The data in Figure 10-1 reveals percentages of our total population by race from 1990 and projected to 2050. It is estimated that almost 50% of the population in the United States will be minorities by the year 2050 (U.S. Department of Commerce, 1996). More specifically, there will be an estimated increase from 12% to 15% in African Americans, from 0.8% to 1% in Native Americans, from 3% to 10% in Asian and Pacific Islanders, from 9% to 22% in Hispanics, and a decrease from 76% to 52% in white Americans. These data indicate that we must continue to rethink our counseling theories, models, and materials to meet the needs of this increasingly diverse population. Even though there appears to be justification for the construct of human universal issues common to all people, we must also remember that each individual is shaped by unique contextual experiences. This message has been repeated often throughout this text.

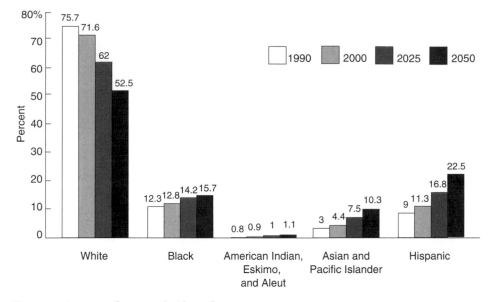

Figure 10-1 Percentage of population by race

SOURCE: Adapted from U.S. Department of Commerce, Bureau of Census 1996.

African Americans

The second largest racial minority group in this country is African Americans. Most African Americans live in urban areas and have assumed a moderate position in our society. For the most part, they have been wage earners rather than being self-employed. Almost half of all African Americans own their home and about 1.5 million are employed as business executives, managers, and professionals. African American men have achieved greater career mobility than African American women have. Some of both sexes have achieved upward mobility to professional occupations as the overall success of African Americans' upward movement increases. Those who have attained middle-class status are also in position to take advantage of educational opportunities and career mobility. About 35% of African Americans are considered to be middle class or higher (Sue & Sue, 2003). Others, particularly those classified as underclass—primarily from three generations of families on welfare—are without job skills and experience both internal and external resistance to changing their status (Axelson, 1993; Smith, 1983).

McRoy (2003) reports that from 1940 to 1990 the unemployment rate of African American males has been twice that of White males. In recent times, however, even though African American males have made progress in comparison to White males, there continues to be significant differences in employment rates, especially in the large inner cities. The good news is that at the turn of the century there were indications that the poverty rate for African Americans was the lowest ever measured by the U.S. Census Bureau (2000b). When compared with Whites, however, their poverty rate continues to be higher. The U.S. Census Bureau (2000b) data collected for the latest census indicated that the median income for African Americans was the lowest among the four major groupings used by this agency. Asian American groups had the highest median income followed by Whites and Hispanics.

Over the last two decades we have witnessed a growing diversity within African communities. A rising number of African American upper-class professionals live in predominately white communities and work as doctors, engineers, lawyers, and computer scientists. In the Atlanta area, however, there are upscale communities that are primarily inhabited by affluent African Americans professionals who seemingly prefer to blend into the larger sociocultural group but also wish to maintain their cultural heritage.

Some African American families, however, continue to struggle. In the 1970s there was a sharp increase in African American families that were primarily maintained by women. In 1999, for example, 45% of African American families were maintained by a woman with no spouse present. Also, African American families tend to be larger than White families (U.S. Census Bureau, 1999). Counselors should be aware that these families primarily need help to survive before addressing other relevant needs.

African Americans graduated from high school at approximately the same rate as White Americans of European descent (U.S. Bureau of Census, 2002). In most African American homes, education is viewed as a means of improving one's economic status. More African Americans are finding ways to attend colleges and universities. In a survey completed in 1994, 13% of African Americans who were age 25 or over obtained a bachelor's degree, compared with only 8% in 1980 (Bennett & DeBarros, 1995). In 1996, 16% of African American females and 11% of African American males had at least a bachelor's degree. Furthermore, 18% of African males and 15% of African American females between the ages of 35 to 44 had obtained a bachelor's degree (Bennett & DeBarros, 1998). These data are encouraging but counselors should continue to reinforce the counseling objective of lifelong learning.

Achievement and motivation among African Americans in college have been found to be equally high for both men and women. This finding suggests that African American women have high expectations for work and a sense of responsibility to contribute to family income. They tend, however, to choose the more traditional feminine professional occupations at about the same rate as white women do (Woody, 1992). The message to the counselor is twofold: Encourage and enhance the high level of achievement motivation of African American women and encourage more to consider nontraditional, professional occupations.

The loss of jobs in the manufacturing sector has reduced job opportunities for many minority workers, including African Americans. Many of these jobs were filled by unskilled and semiskilled workers. It is therefore critical to connect minority groups with training and educational opportunities. Counseling interventions that encourage skill development to compete for the more attractive jobs in the workplace are most desirable; however, occupations that are available to African Americans continue to be relatively constricted.

In a related study, Woody (1992) researched work patterns of African American women and found that many lack requisite skills to compete for technical work and will fail to qualify for higher-level jobs. She argued that African American women have severe job limitations, and many are restricted to low-end jobs because of discrimination. She suggested that there is a "women's work subculture" that may be alleviated only through an improved national employment policy.

Finally, in order to be effective helpers of African Americans, McRoy (2003) suggests that counselors should be aware of their competence to work effectively with members of a culture different than their own. Specifically, they are to evaluate the following:

Level of cultural competence in relation to African Americans.

How racism, oppression, and discrimination have affected the worker both personally and professionally.

Worker's own racial and cultural heritage as well as how the worker's interpersonal style can affect his or her personal and professional relationships with African American clients.

How power and privilege have differently affected African Americans and Whites in the United States. (p. 231)

These recommendations suggest that counseling someone of a different cultural background will require preparation designed to understand culture-specific variables in order to appropriately address their needs. In the case of African Americans, counselors can build an understanding of their needs by becoming familiar with their unique history, and the impact of contemporary racism and oppression. More suggestions follow later in this chapter.

Asian and Pacific Americans

Before the 2000 census, Asian and Pacific Islanders were the two major groups used to classify and compile the number of Asian Americans living in this country. In the last census, four major groups emerged as a means of identifying the incredibly diverse Asian population that now resides in the United States: Asian, Southeast Asian, Asian Indian, and other Asian. These groups are further divided as follows:

Asian Americans	Chinese, Japanese, Filipino, Korean
Southeast Asians	Cambodian, Hmong, Vietnamese, Laotian, Thai, Malaysian, Singaporean
Asian Indian	Bengalese, Bharat, Dravidian, East Indian, Goanese
Other Asian	Bangladeshi, Burmese, Indonesian, Pakistani, Sri Lankan

It is not surprising that among these groups there are vast differences in ethnicity, language, religion, and cultural values. Each group has a distinct history and there are also within-group differences. It is therefore most important to view each Asian client as a unique individual whose status, characteristics, and traits have been shaped in a unique environment. Counselors may need to call on other helpers or individuals known to be familiar with certain populations of Asians.

We should also expect to find significant differences in educational achievement, occupation, wages earned, and standards of living among Asian Americans. D. Sue (1998) suggests that there is a myth about Asians being a "model minority group." There is no doubt that some Asians have excelled in educational achievement, earn high wages, and are employed in prestigious jobs and professions but there are also Asians Americans who are undereducated, receive public assistance, live in crowded urban areas, are unemployed, and are involved in juvenile delinquency. Similar to other culturally diverse groups, there are indeed within-group differences.

We do know, however, that many Asian American groups place high value on education. Sue and Okazaki (1990) suggested that Asian Americans perceive education as a means of upward mobility and are highly motivated to remove barriers that could limit them. However, Leong and Serafica (1995) argued that Asian Americans are often victimized by discriminatory employment practices. Asian women are given especially low status and are exploited in the working world (Chu, 1981; Kumata & Murata, 1980; D. Sue, 1998). Hsia (1981) argued that Asian Americans are hindered in the job market because of poor communication skills, which accounts for their tendency to choose jobs such as engineering, computer science, business, and economics.

In evaluating counseling processes as a source of conflict for Chinese Americans, Sue and Sue (1990) made several pertinent observations: (1) Chinese American students inhibit emotional expression and do not actively participate in the counseling process, (2) Chinese Americans are discouraged from revealing emotional problems by their cultural conditioning, and (3) Chinese American students react more favorably to well-structured counseling models. Sue's conclusions emphasize the importance of understanding cultural influences when counseling Chinese Americans.

Fernandez (1988) argued that Southeast Asian students should be counseled using behavioral approaches. She considered it inappropriate to use counseling techniques that require clients to verbalize excessively. Evanoski and Tse (1989) have successfully used bilingual materials and role models in workshops directed toward parents of Chinese and Korean children that exposed them to methods of accessing a variety of occupations. The basic assumption was that these parents have a tremendous influence on their children.

The following special needs and problems associated with Asian Americans in counseling are summarized from suggestions by Kaneshige (1979), Sue (1992), and Ivey (1986).

1. Asian Americans are very sensitive about verbalizing psychological problems, especially in group encounters.
2. Asian Americans tend to be inexpressive when asked to discuss personal achievements and limitations.
3. Asian Americans tend to misinterpret the role of counseling in general and the benefits that may be derived from it.
4. Asian Americans can be perceived as very passive and nonassertive with authority figures, but in reality they are reacting to cultural inhibitions that discourage them from being perceived as aggressive.
5. Asian Americans may strongly resist suggestions to modify behavior that is unassuming and nonassertive.

Vietnamese clients presented particular problems for career counselors who assisted them in relocating in this country following the Vietnam War. The needs and problems of this adult cultural group illustrate the limitations of employment for first-generation Asian Americans. In addition to the need to learn English, other problems and difficulties were (1) recognizing the importance of transferable skills, (2) considering past work history as relevant, (3) understanding the concept of career ladders, (4) locating information about unemployment, and (5) recognizing the importance of resumé preparation and interview skills training.

As a group, Asian Americans are known to have a strong work ethic. In general, Asian Americans are very industrious workers, seem to value education, and have taken advantage of higher education to enhance their career development. They are also known to do well in business administration, engineering, and sciences. However, the stereotype of the Asian American as being good in sciences but lacking in verbal skills could limit their access to careers that require communication skills. Even though the most recent immigrants from Asia are employed mainly in service occupations, many Asian Pacific Americans can be found as workers in the professions, in office and clerical jobs, and as service workers.

Finally, among traditional Asian cultures, offering what is considered to be desirable help includes giving advice and suggestions but avoiding confrontation and direct interpretation of motives and actions. When discussing personal issues, it is more appropriate to be indirect, and the counselor should do most of the initial verbalization with a rather formal interactive approach (Sue, 1994). Be aware that Asian Americans may resist help from a counselor or mental health worker because they often rely on a "natural healing" process (Leung & Cheung, 2001). According to Fong (2003) Asian Americans may not seek help because they:

1. Do not recognize or acknowledge there is a mental health problem
2. Are afraid of being stigmatized if they seek help
3. Do not want to address negative comments about their traditional healing practices
4. Do not have access to bilingual bicultural services
5. Assume the provider will not be culturally competent. (p. 270)

Hispanic (Latinos/as) Americans

The Hispanic population has grown much faster than predicted and as a result is currently the largest minority group in this country. According to Axelson (1999) they will easily reach more than 39 million by the year 2025. Cohn and Fears (2001) point out that the largest subgroup of Hispanics is of Mexican ancestry. Other significant subgroups are from Central and South America, Puerto Rico, and Cuba. According to Ivey and Ivey (2003), some groups of Hispanic Americans prefer to be recognized as Mexican American, Cuban American, and Puerto Rican American.

There appears to be solid evidence that Hispanics underuse counseling services in both mental health and academic settings (Axelson, 1999). Counselors need to encourage the use of services and advocate that there is good evidence that they could benefit from services, especially when intervention strategies are designed to meet their special needs. Rodriguez and Blocher (1988), for example, found that interventions with academically and economically disadvantaged Puerto Rican women produced positive results by raising their levels of career maturity and developing beliefs that they can control their own destinies.

Social factors such as social-class membership, environment of the home and school, and the community in which the individual resides significantly influence career perspectives and attitudes toward work (Cormier & Nurius, 2003; Osipow, 1983; Pietrofesa & Splete, 1975). Arbona (1995) supported this conclusion by debunking the idea that cultural traits have restricted Hispanics in career choices. Instead, socioeconomic status and lack of opportunity have restricted Hispanics from access to higher education and subsequently to their occupational aspirations. Hispanics, however, are not a homogeneous group; there are important differences between subgroups and between Hispanics from different socioeconomic backgrounds (Arbona, 1995; Fong, 2003).

It is not a good idea, however, to overgeneralize about the Hispanic students in our schools today; many are acculturated and fit into the mainstream of society. One can expect, for example, to find diverse value systems among Hispanics. There are, however, those Hispanics who cling to their traditional heritages and, consequently, may have difficulty in adjusting to an Anglo-dominant school and culture. Caught between conflicting cultures, the adolescent Hispanic seeks the support of peers who are experiencing similar conflicts. As a result, there is usually less interaction with other groups of students and, typically, school becomes a low priority.

The Mexican American family, in particular, has been characterized as a closely knit group that greatly influences the values of its members. For example, Axelson (1999) suggested that Spanish-speaking children generally are taught to value and respect family, church, and school as well as masculinity and honor. Families are primarily patriarchal (as far as the center of authority is concerned) with a distinct division of duties; that is, the father is the breadwinner, and the mother is the homemaker. Spanish is the primary language spoken in the home and in the barrio. However, it appears that traditions, including family solidarity, are breaking down among younger Hispanics (Axelson, 1999).

Fouad (1995) recommends several career intervention strategies for Hispanics. Researchers are encouraged to assess these recommendations and to aim their research efforts toward examining the career behavior of Hispanics. The following career counseling recommendations have been paraphrased from Fouad (1995, pp. 186–187).

1. Consider the cultural context of all clients, including Hispanics. Some Hispanics have retained traditional value systems, whereas others may not be traditional. When we are not certain about the client's cultural background, we need to be creative or, as Leong (1993) has labeled it, to have "creative uncertainty." Using this approach, we are to guide our counseling efforts toward the client's willingness to inform us of how culture has influenced his or her life.
2. Be flexible in the career counseling process, especially when we incorporate familial and environmental factors in decision making.
3. Choose assessment instruments with care relative to what is appropriate for Hispanic cultures.
4. Use immediate intervention to retain Hispanic students in school. Career information should include reasons for taking math and science courses.
5. Develop strategies to include self-efficacy as a key to future career success.
6. Provide Hispanic females with a wide variety of career information, including information on nontraditional careers.

The following suggestions for developing effective interventions for Hispanic Americans are adapted from Zuniga (2003, pp. 257–258):

Respond to cultural preferences of client rather than imposing your own.

Include natural support networks.

Address stress-related immigration issues.

Attend to survival issues and personal needs of client and client's family.

Use techniques to assist clients make adaptations to new and different living conditions.

Utilize client's religion or belief system in strategy planning.

Use narrative therapy, metaphor, and family system approaches.

Act as an advocate for client's needs.

Native Americans

Weaver (2003) suggests the use of several terms for identifying Native groups such as Native American, Native Indigenous, and First Nations People. In our discussion we will continue to use the general term Native American as there is no consensus as to which better describes or identifies Native people. We do know, however, that Native Americans are quite diverse. Within the United States, there are more than 500 distinct Native American nations that significantly differ in language, religious beliefs, and social characteristics among other aspects of their cultures. Almost two thirds of Native Americans live in urban areas for training, college, or employment. Many keep close contact with their families and friends who live on reservations. Of those Native Americans who live outside the reservation, the largest concentrations are in Los Angeles, San Francisco, and Chicago, but Minneapolis, Denver, Tulsa, Phoenix, and Milwaukee also contain significant numbers. The states with the highest numbers of Native Americans are Oklahoma, California, Arizona, New Mexico, Alaska, Washington, North Carolina, Texas, New York, and Michigan (Johnson, Swartz, & Martin, 1995).

On the reservations, many are involved in farming, ranching, fishing, and lumber production. Off the reservations, Native Americans work in factories, on farms, and as skilled craftpersons. Some tribes engage in various enterprises, such as motel management; others offer bingo and lottery games to the general public (Axelson, 1993). Gambling casinos on reservations have also emerged.

An important variable in the career development of Native Americans is the degree to which they adhere to cultural customs, language, and traditions (Johnson, Swartz, & Martin, 1995). The degree of cultural heritage is described on a continuum by Ryan and Ryan (1982, cited in LaFromboise, Trimble, & Mohatt, 1990), as follows:

1. Traditional: Speak only native language and observe traditions.
2. Transitional: Speak both native language and English and may question traditions of the past.
3. Marginal: Speak of themselves as Indian but identify with roles in dominant society.
4. Assimilated: Have generally embraced the dominant society.
5. Bicultural: Are accepted by dominant society but also identify with tribal traditions and culture.

As with other ethnic groups, we should not stereotype Native Americans but, rather, focus on the degree to which each client adheres to cultural customs, language, and traditions. Significant differences between individuals within cultural groups must be addressed in the career counseling process. But we should also remember that old traditions should be respected, and some may be used to foster career development; the use of role models and experientially related activities are recommended (Johnson, Swartz, & Martin, 1995).

Martin (1995) has developed the following initial intervention strategies for Native Americans that include cultural and contextual variables.

1. Obtain information about the Native American client. For instance, the counselor should have information about the client's tribe and reservation community and should visit the reservation, if possible. Relevant information includes tribal history, customs, and family systems. As in all career counseling strategies, the counselor should have up-to-date educational and career information and as much information about workplace affiliates as possible.

2. Establish communication with the client. The counselor should use what is referred to as cultural/environmental/contextual focusing; this "includes not only knowledge of and respect for the values of other cultures, but comfort with and knowledge of one's own values and ethnicity" (Betz & Fitzgerald, 1995, p. 263). Perspectives of presenting problems are better understood by both counselor and client within this context.

3. Be aware that extended families play an important role in the decision-making process. A major goal is to gain the family's support and provide clients with specific methods that will assist in the career development process.

4. Obtain an evaluation of the client's English ability, preferably from an educational institution that offers courses in English for Native Americans.

5. Use strategies to increase the client's knowledge of the world of work. Recommended are structured reading-discussion techniques using current occupational resources. Video resources may also be used, and group guidance can be an effective technique with Native Americans.

6. Help your Native American client to obtain firsthand knowledge of an occupation: job shadowing (spending time in the workplace with an individual engaged in a particular occupation), interviewing individuals on job sites, or enrolling in an on-the-job training program are recommended.

Most of the counseling strategies discussed in this chapter are often referred to as specially focused interventions (Betz & Fitzgerald, 1995). The name certainly applies to ethnic groups who have special needs that counselors must become increasingly aware of, especially for Native Americans. Bowman (1995) argues that it is impossible for career counselors to be aware of all variables within a culture and we acknowledge that fact, but the proper attitude is to be open to continued learning about cultural diversity.

Another variable to be considered in counseling approaches is that tribes differ in value orientations and individuals differ within tribes. Thus, as in all minority groups, general recommendations for counseling have to be modified to meet individual needs. Thomason (1991, 2000) pointed out that a major consideration is the degree of acculturation in the dominant society. Furthermore, he suggested that the client's set of beliefs about how changes occur is an important consideration for developing intervention strategies for Native Americans.

Herring (1990) argued that there are many career myths about Native Americans; he believes that we simply do not have the necessary research results to draw many conclusions about their career development. Like other minority groups, Native Americans have not been exposed to a wide range of careers and have limited opportunities to attend college because of high unemployment rates. He suggested that Native Americans be introduced to more nontraditional occupations and be provided with career information using Native American role models to expand their career considerations.

Many Native Americans have a strong desire to retain the symbolic aspects of their heritage, much of which is different from the dominant culture. The challenge for counselors is to assist Native Americans in preserving the positive aspects of their heritage while encouraging them to modify some behaviors. For example, the ability to enjoy the present should be combined with planning skills, and the ability to share with others should be combined with assertive behavior. The value orientation of Native Americans is a sensitive issue for career counselors.

Native American resistance to counseling in general is exemplified by the under-use of existing mental health services. According to Manson (1982) and Weaver (2003), Native Americans are the most neglected group in the mental health field. Miller (1982) suggested that more Native Americans would take advantage of counseling relationships if appropriate counseling strategies were used. Trimble and LaFromboise (1985) summarized Miller's strategies that remain on target in current times as follows:

1. Personal ethnic identity in itself is hardly sufficient for understanding the influence of culture on the client.
2. The client's history contains a number of strengths that can promote and facilitate the counseling process.
3. The counselor should be aware of his or her own biases about cultural pluralism—they might interfere with the counseling relationship.
4. The counselor should encourage the client to become more active in identifying and learning the various elements associated with positive growth and development.
5. Most important are empathy, caring, and a sense of the importance of the human potential (p. 131).

In sum, be aware of the diversity, history, culture, and contemporary problems of Native Americans. Display patience and listen intently. Remaining silent when major points are discussed communicates an understanding of Native American traditions of the time necessary to reason and think through problems (Shulman, 1999).

Cultural Variability and Worldviews

In general terms, worldview refers to the individual's perception and understandings of the world (Slattery, 2004; Sue & Sue, 1990). Okun, Fried, and Okun (1999) point out that worldviews include, among other variables, perceptions of basic human nature, the roles of families, relationships with others, locus of control, orientation of time, work values, and activities. Worldviews, in this context, are developed both through individual experiences that are nonshared and through shared experiences and events. Nonshared experiences account for much of the variability within cultures, whereas shared experiences reflect worldviews that are common among members of a specific culture. For instance, individualism and collectivism are often used to explain cultural differences (Triandis, 1994). In individualistic cultures such as those in Europe and North America, a great amount of value is placed on individual accomplishment. The individual strives for self-actualization. The rugged individualist is revered for his or her autonomy and independence; individuals are empowered to achieve and become individually responsible.

In collectivist cultures such as those in Africa, Asia, and Latin America, the individual's major function is focused on the welfare of the group for their collective survival. Individuals strive to build group solidarity. In these societies, individual uniqueness is not rejected, but more emphasis is placed on being identified with one's social group. The needs of the group take precedence over self-interest. What is important here is sharing, cooperation, and social responsibility. For example, an individual may conceptualize a career choice from the perception of what is best for the family group rather than from an individualistic perspective. In many collectivist cultures, family is more important than the individual.

When counseling individuals from different ethnic groups, counselors should evaluate the degree and nature of acculturation by how it has affected the client's worldview. For instance, Axelson (1999) suggests that some cultural values break down as the younger generations assimilate the values of the dominant white culture. In this context, acculturation refers to the extent to which a client has assumed the beliefs, values, and behaviors of the dominant white society. It is not unusual for some clients to make an attempt to adjust to local environments whereas others live biculturally or multiculturally; that is, they adopt some behaviors of the white dominant culture and retain values from their own culture and the cultures of others they have come to know. Many experience conflicts, especially between generations, when older members of a family want to retain cultural rules, scripts, and roles, while the younger generation adopts those of the dominant white society. For example, the concept of family honor conditions one to never oppose collective family decisions, but members of the younger generation might prefer that the locus of control shift from a collectivist to an individualist position. They wish to express themselves independently and make decisions based on their individual needs and self-interest.

Among some cultures, differences in time orientation from the dominant society can present barriers to effective career planning and other time commitments that are normally assumed in career counseling. In traditional career counseling, the client is expected to be on time for appointments and abide by a set of time rules to complete certain counseling interventions. In cultures of color, individuals are not as obsessed with being on time and maintaining a strict time commitment. A Navajo Indian woman asked me if the next meeting would be "Indian time" or "American time." She explained that "Indian time" is "whenever we get together that is convenient." Being on time for most counselors is viewed as a positive value, and lateness is often misunderstood as a symptom of indifference or a lack of basic work skills. In this case, I learned that time orientation has different meanings for different cultural groups.

Hall's (1971) theory on concept of time has often been cited. In his conceptualization, time is divided into polychronic and monochronic categories. People engage in and are highly involved in tasks at any given time in the polychronic time category. Activities are rather unstructured, and individuals are more spontaneous and consider appointments as easily changed. In the monochronic category, time is viewed as fixed, and one task is undertaken at a specified time. Schedules are considered very important, and appointments are viewed as almost sacred (Okun, Fried, & Okun, 1999). Collectivistic cultures tend to favor polychronic time whereas individualistic cultures opt for monochronic time.

Another worldview perspective, how different groups view human nature, is an important concept for counselors to understand when working with multicultural groups. African Americans and European Americans consider human nature as both good and bad. In African American cultures, good and bad behavior is determined by their benefits to the community. European Americans judge good and bad as a part of each individual; good and bad are two sides of human nature that are in opposition and conflict (Diller, 1999).

The belief that human nature is basically good and that human beings can be trusted to have positive motives is shared by Asian, Native, and Latino/a American cultures. Following this logic has subjected these groups to being judged by the dominant society as naïve and gullible in the workplace. The perception is that individuals who follow such logic need to "wise up" to reality. Counselors should assist individuals from different cultures to be aware of and alert to workplace associations, which might require them to modify their conceptualizations of human nature.

Finally, personal space and privacy are also considered to be culturally oriented. Individuals from different cultures tend to invade each other's personal space without being aware of it. Triandis (1994) suggests that you invade personal space by walking into it, staring into it, and even through smell by wearing a strong perfume. This invasion is culturally determined; for instance, North American and Arabic cultures expect others to look them in the eye when talking whereas Asians consider direct eye contact to be insulting. Hall (1982) claims that Arabs expect to stand very close to each other when engaged in a serious conversation. Thus, conversational distances are often determined by language and culture; for example, Latino/as usually stand closer to each other than Anglo-Americans do when conversing. Counselors need to be alert to any signals of discomfort with regard to space and adjust distances accordingly.

In sum, individuals are socialized and shaped by their societies and contextual interactions within their environments. Thus, it is not surprising that one cultural group generally may view a behavior as being appropriate, but members of a different culture may view that same behavior as gross or insulting. The point here is that we as counselors must attempt to understand our clients in terms of their origins, assimilation, and acculturation; we should learn to appreciate differences that exist in the way others think and behave. We must resist stereotyping clients by their culture. It is important to recognize that there are different worldviews within cultural groups. In essence, worldviews are to be considered as unique for each individual. Worldviews basically are developed within each individual's ethnic and racial heritage. Finally, worldviews can be modified through experiences with other cultures.

Cultural Differences in Work-Related Activities

Many clients have different work values, including people from different cultural backgrounds. Value orientations to work can be sources of serious conflict and misunderstanding in the workplace. One of the most provocative studies of work-related values was done by Hofstede (1984). His study included 50 different countries in 20 different languages and 7 different occupational levels (Matsumoto & Juang, 2004). His aim was to determine dimensions of cultural differences of work-related values. His findings are paraphrased as follows:

1. *Power distance.* This dimension attempts to answer the basic hierarchical relationship between immediate boss and subordinate. In some countries, such as the

Philippines, Mexico, Venezuela, and India, individuals tended to maintain strong status differences. In countries such as New Zealand, Denmark, Israel, and Austria, status and power differentials were minimized. In the United States, there was some degree of minimizing power differences.

2. *Uncertainty avoidance.* This term is used to describe how different cultures and societies deal with anxiety and stress. On a questionnaire designed for this study, countries that had low uncertainty avoidance indexes differed significantly from countries that had high scores. Examples from those with low scores were that workers had lower job stress, less resistance to change, greater readiness to live by the day, and stronger ambition for advancement. Examples of high uncertainty avoidance scores were fear of failure, less risk taking, higher job stress, more worry about the future, and higher anxiety.

3. *Individualism/collectivism.* This dimension attempted to answer the question about which cultures foster individual tendencies rather than group or collectivist tendencies. In this study, the United States, Great Britain, Australia, and Canada had the highest scores for individualism. Peru, Colombia, and Venezuela were most collectivistic. People in highly individualistic countries were characterized as placing more importance on employees' personal lifestyle, were emotionally independent from the company, found small companies attractive, and placed more importance on freedom and challenge in jobs. People in countries with low individualism were emotionally dependent on companies, frowned on individual initiative, considered group decisions better than individual ones, and aspired to conformity and orderliness in managerial positions.

4. *Masculinity.* This dimension is thought to be an indicator of which cultures would maintain and foster differences between sexes in the workplace. However, most employees who answered the questionnaire were men, so the conclusions drawn here should be considered tentative. People in countries that had high scores on this variable were characterized as believing in independent decision making, having stronger achievement motivation, and aspiring for recognition. People in countries that had low scores on this variable were characterized as believing in group decisions, seeing security as more important, preferring shorter working hours, and having lower job stress.

These results appear to suggest that culture does have an important role in work-related values. Moreover, we can conclude that employees' perceptions of work roles—as well as of other life roles—are influenced by culture-related values. Differences between cultures help us understand employee attitudes, values, behaviors, and interpersonal dynamics. Nevertheless, we must remember that differences between countries, as outlined in this study, need not necessarily correspond with similar differences on the individual level. The cultural differences found in this study suggest that we use them as general guidelines to understand how cultural dimensions influence work-related values, to see that they can lead to conflicts in the workplace, to be aware that cultural differences are legitimate, and to challenge us to recognize that individual differences exist within cultures (Matsumoto, 1996, 2000; Matsumoto & Juang, 2004).

The Challenge of Becoming Culturally Competent

During the last two decades, an increasing number of publications have addressed the need for counselors to become culturally competent, that is, to develop the ability to provide appropriate services cross-culturally. Sue, Arredondo, and McDavis (1992) have developed nine competence areas as basic for a culturally skilled counselor. The three overarching dimensions are (1) understanding one's assumptions, values, and biases; (2) understanding the worldview of the culturally different client; and (3) developing appropriate intervention strategies and techniques. The three dimensions are broken down into subgroups of beliefs and attitudes, knowledge, and skills, and each of the subgroups are delineated in self-explanatory statements. Information about competencies can be obtained from the American Counseling Association Web site listed in Appendix I.

In another publication addressing cultural competence, Cross, Bazron, Dennis, and Isaacs (1989) developed individual cultural competence skills. They suggest five skill areas that have some overlap with the nine competence areas reported in the previous paragraph. Growth in each of the five skill areas can be measured separately, but growth in one area tends to support growth in the others. They include (1) awareness and acceptance of differences, (2) self-awareness, (3) dynamics of difference, (4) knowledge of the client's culture, and (5) adaptation of skills. Each skill area will be discussed separately in the paragraphs that follow.

The first skill area, awareness and acceptance of differences, is essential for counselors to begin the process of becoming culturally competent. In addition to recognizing individual and unique differences with every client, counselors are to become more aware of cultural differences that exist in worldviews and work-related activities that were discussed earlier. This first step is essential for developing an appreciation of cultural diversity.

When discussing awareness of differences, Sue and Sue (1990) suggested that Western-oriented mental health practices cannot be applied universally to culturally different populations without recognition of significant cultural differences. Sue and Sue implied that counselors who are unaware of different worldviews (psychological orientation, manners of thinking, ways of behaving and interpreting events) are essentially ineffective; counselors must learn to accept the worldviews of others. The following characteristics are necessary to be a culturally effective counselor (Sue, 1978):

1. An ability to recognize which values and assumptions the counselor holds regarding the desirability or undesirability of human behavior
2. Awareness of the generic characteristics of counseling that cut across many schools of counseling theory
3. Understanding of the sociopolitical forces (oppression and racism) that have influenced the identity and perspective of the culturally different
4. An ability to share the worldview of his or her clients without negating its legitimacy
5. True eclecticism in his or her counseling (p. 451).

Sue and Sue implied that counselors can use their entire repertoire of counseling skills as long as they accept different views and are cognizant of the experiences and lifestyle of the culturally different. These researchers emphasized that counselors must be alert to the influences of different views and environmental factors. Finally, counselors must be cautious not to impose their values on others.

The second skill area, self-awareness, requires the counselor to recognize any prejudice that would make it difficult to empathize with people of color. Counselors are to view the role of culture in their own lives as a backdrop for appreciating how and why others may be different. The recommended outcome is for an appreciation of how a variety of cultural variables shapes human behavior. To develop this skill area, one is required to develop sufficient self-knowledge of culture-specific factors that influence behavior and a personal awareness of one's own cultural background. In short, counselors must recognize their limitations and expertise. An evaluation of racial attitudes, beliefs, and feelings may well be assessed by a white racial identity developmental model such as the one built around the work of R. T. Carter (1995) and Helms (1990b). Their conceptualizations of an identity model that represents that of a white member of the dominant society contains five stages as follows:

1. Contact stage: Is unaware of any biases associated with his or her race and racial identity.
2. Disintegration stage: Acknowledges a white identity that often results in confusion and conflict.
3. Reintegration stage: Devalues other races and idealizes whiteness.
4. Pseudo-independent stage: Intellectualizes the understanding and acceptance of other races and is somewhat tolerant.
5. Autonomy stage: Becomes nonracist and internalizes a multicultural identity.

This model enlightens counselors to the behavioral characteristics that occur at various stages of identity development for both the counselor and the client. The process should not be conceived as a linear progression but, rather, as continuous and cyclical, involving interactions with individuals from diverse cultures that lead to adaptive changes. Counselors should continually evaluate their progress of awareness as racial and cultural beings.

Axelson (1993) suggested basic points of self-awareness for improving counseling in a multicultural society, including cultural–total awareness, self-awareness, client awareness, and counseling procedure awareness. These basic points of awareness lead to focusing on the client's needs. Needs are most appropriately conceptualized from a broad base of human experiences to more discrete distinctions. The broad base of human experiences includes common human experiences, specific cultural experiences, individual experiences, and the unique individual. This approach to counseling in a multicultural society consists of the following four steps:

1. Recognize that all human beings possess the like capacity for thought, feeling, and behavior.
2. Be knowledgeable in several cultures; study differences and similarities among people of different groups and their special needs and problems.
3. Gain an understanding of how the individual relates to important objects of motivation, what his or her personal constructs are, and how they form his or her worldview.
4. Blend steps 1, 2, and 3 into an integrated picture of the distinctive person as experienced during the counseling process (p. 18).

The third skill area, the dynamics of difference, also relates to self-awareness. This skill is seen as a counselor's knowledge of subtle differences between cultures in the way they interact and communicate. For instance, eye contact has different meanings; some cultures avoid eye contact and others may expect it while conversing. Counselors can communicate an awareness of differences between cultures by adopting appropriate cultural counseling techniques.

The fourth skill area, knowledge of the client's culture, suggests that counselors be prepared for counseling by familiarizing themselves with the client's cultural orientation. Suggested topics include country of origin, sociopolitical context, preferred language, religion, family role, gender roles, cultural assumptions of appropriate behavior, cultural values and ideologies, class definitions if any, power in relationships, work roles, customs, and traditions. Knowledge of the client's culture is most relevant in the counseling process, especially in the development of appropriate collaborative relationships between client and counselor that are essential for productive counseling outcomes.

The adaptation of skills, the fifth skill, is the process of altering counseling programs and intervention strategies to better fit the client's cultural values. Again, the counselor must be familiar with the client's cultural background. For example, clients from collectivistic cultures may expect their families to participate in all decisions, and counselors who ignore this basic need may be quite ineffective. Counselors need to evaluate the counseling process carefully from the perspective of how methods, procedures, and materials can be adapted to make certain they are culturally appropriate.

Counselors who become familiar with the terms *etics, emics,* and *ethnocentrism* will fully appreciate the need to adapt their counseling methods, materials, and procedures. The term *etic* suggests that there are universal truths across cultures. The basic assumption, for example, is that one can evaluate behavior and motivation by universal cultural norms. Thus, counselors' own culture has relevance for people of all cultures. In essence, the etic perspective is from outside the group (Wehrly, 1995). The term *emic* considers truths as culture specific. The basic assumption is that we should judge an individual's behavior by the values, beliefs, and social mores of his or her particular culture. The emic perspective is from within the culture (Wehrly, 1995). When counselors insist on strictly using their own background of biases, values, and beliefs to interpret culturally different actions and behaviors, they are suggesting that their race is superior, and that is known as ethnocentricism (Matsumoto, 1996, 2000). As Okun et al. (1999) point out, we expect all others to think and act as we do.

In a provocative publication on multicultural counseling, Speight, Myers, Cox, and Highlen (1991) suggest that counselors will be overwhelmed with current approaches to counseling individuals from different cultures if they are expected to base counseling only on culture specific differences. Furthermore, these researchers suggest that culture-specific counseling is impractical and results in fragmentation of efforts. This research team has suggested a much broader approach to multicultural counseling that includes not only cultural specificity but also human universality and individual uniqueness. Human universality involves constructs applicable to all cultures. For example, counselors would explore a variety of worldviews from different cultural groups for the purpose of discovering common themes among them. Such themes would be used with specific cultural information as a backdrop for incorporating individual uniqueness as a third dimension in career counseling.

Self-knowledge is emphasized in optimal theory as a means of understanding and appreciating others. Awareness of one's worldview is important for recognizing feelings, assumptions, and biases from which one views others. The major task of this process is to become alert to personal and sociopolitical meaning of one's culture and ethnicity. Thus, counselors discover themes that are universal in scope and are common to racial, ethnic, and cultural groups. Figure 10-2 illustrates the development of worldview from the perspective of a more holistic approach that includes individual uniqueness, cultural specificity, and human universality.

In sum, the optimal theory approach is multidimensional in nature and differs from culture-specific approaches by stressing the influences that shape worldviews as being more holistic. Therefore, counselors would build an understanding of how (a) specific cultures influence the development of worldview, (b) the human universality of themes cut across cultures, and (c) the uniqueness of the individual is developed. Within this theory, interrelationships are interconnected from which emerge values, beliefs, and actions. This redefinition of multicultural counseling should attract research and debates that will take time to delineate.

In a related publication, Diller (1999) argues that our traditional counseling services have been based on Northern European cultural values, ideals, and beliefs that are referred to as *Eurocentric*. Duran and Duran (1995) strongly suggest that we cannot meet the needs of individuals who are culturally different by the exclusive use of Eurocentric-based counseling theories, practices, and materials. The call is for counseling to not be culture-bound, that is, we must move away from only using Eurocentric approaches and be more sensitive to different cultural values and assumptions. Again, we can adapt our counseling approaches to gain more relevant culture-specific information and develop culturally appropriate interventions as demonstrated by the Multicultural Career Counseling Model for Ethnic Women in Chapter 3.

Skill and competency development are most important in meeting the challenge of becoming culturally competent. However, counselors must also evaluate their basic assumptions about career counseling, that is, can contemporary theory and practices meet the needs of an increasingly diverse population? What is implied here is that counselors not only need to build skills for cultural competency, but they must also rethink the underlying principles of current theories and practices. The following paragraphs, which outline the assumptions for a multicultural counseling theory, suggest that we use both Western and non-European systems of helping.

Recognizing that a theory for multicultural counseling and therapy was long overdue, Sue, Ivey, and Pedersen (1996) proposed a multicultural counseling and therapy theory (MCT). These authors have suggested that contemporary theories of counseling and psychotherapy do not deal adequately with the complexity of culturally diverse populations, and we assume that this conclusion includes career development theory and counseling. Specifically, current theories do not describe, explain, or predict current cultural diversity. But even more important, the shortcomings in current contemporary theories and practices will not prepare the mental health profession adequately to meet the needs of an increasingly diverse population, in which current minorities will become a numerical majority within several decades.

Following is a summary of other underlying assumptions that prompted the development of MCT:

1. Individualism should not dominate the mental health field. (Consider self-in-situation and people-in-context discussed in Chapter 2.)

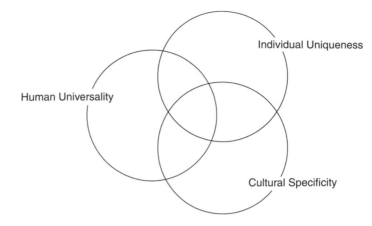

Figure 10-2   Influences on worldview

SOURCE: From "A Redefinition of Multicultural Counseling," by S. Speight, L. Myers, C. Cox, & P. Highlen, 1991, *Journal of Counseling & Development, 70,* 29–35. Reprinted with permission. No further reproduction authorized without written permission of the American Counseling Association.

2. Learning occurs within a cultural context.
3. Cultural identity is changing.
4. Culture should be defined inclusively and broadly.
5. Counselors must possess an understanding of the culture and sociopolitical context of a client's behavior before they can develop appropriate intervention strategies and use appropriate assessment instruments.
6. To develop multicultural competence, the counselor must increase his or her own self-awareness.
7. Multicultural training will be necessary to increase the skills and perspectives needed in the future.

The comprehensive nature of this metatheory should promote a large body of research well into the 21st century. In fact, Sue et al. (1996) have developed suggestions for various research approaches for their theory. They have suggested that past researchers focused on social biases of Eurocentric society and subsequently have not addressed the positive attributes and characteristics of racial and ethnic minority groups.

The MCT theory has many implications for the future of counseling, but its main focus is on changing conventional counseling. As we learn from the research that this theory will certainly promote, we will be in a better position to consider counseling strategies to meet the needs of culturally diverse groups. Here are some of the suggested changes at this point (Sue et al., 1996):

1. Balance the focus of counseling. We are to move away from the traditional focus on the individual and pay more attention to family and cultural issues. Thus, a balance is needed between self-oriented help and self-in-relation help.
2. Expand the repertoire of helping responses. Some of the helping responses that counselors now use—and, in fact, their approach to helping responses—may be

inappropriate for culturally different clients. For example, passive attending and listening skills could confuse some clients from different cultures.

3. Identify indigenous helping roles. Dealing with human problems is quite different from one culture to another. Counselors should be trained to understand different culturally based roles and that traditional healers found in some cultures are viewed with high credibility.

4. Develop alternatives to the conventional counseling role. New and different counseling roles may require that counselors practice outside of their offices, such as in the community or in organizations. Counselors should become more externally focused—that is, advocate changes in the community, enhance job opportunities, and intervene on behalf of the client. In sum, counselors need to become advisors, advocates, facilitators of indigenous support systems, consultants, and change agents.

Immigration and Its Sequelae

Immigrants have arrived in this country under a variety of circumstances. Some are exiles, such as recent immigrants from Southeast Asia, parts of Central America, and Cuba. Some immigrants have come to find work and enjoy the privileges of a free society, and many have come for both political and financial reasons. The first great wave of immigrants came from Northern and Western Europe circa 1820 to 1880, and the second wave came from Southern and Eastern Europe circa 1881 to 1929. After World War II, the current increase in immigrants began and continues into the 21st century. The largest numbers have come from Mexico, Asia, Cuba, Central and South America, and the Middle East (Axelson, 1999).

That migration experience can be a very stressful one is probably a gross understatement of what some individuals have experienced. Adjustment to a new culture involves multiple factors that include transitions and transformations. Transition involves reconstructing social networks and adjusting to a new socioeconomic system and a different cultural system (Rogler, 1994). The transformation process, although similar to transition, encompasses ethnic identity issues of acculturation and assimilation or gradual inclusion of values and social mores from the dominant culture. Some modify their ethnic identities; others strive to maintain cultural beliefs shaped in their homeland.

Counselors evaluate an immigrant's migration experience to uncover such information as country of origin, sociopolitical context, education experiences, socioeconomic status, belief systems, types of migration, occupational history, culture shock, support systems, and medical history. The postmigration evaluation process should include level of acculturation, language skills and preferred language, level of adjustment, and impact on identity (Comas-Diaz & Grenier, 1998). The postmigration adjustment process is greatly affected by the host country's attitudes toward the immigrant, the level of family adjustment, the geographical region of relocation, and acculturative stress experienced by individuals and the family as a group.

The most pressing need for most immigrants is finding work for their financial support. Those who cannot speak and understand English and lack job skills usually are forced to accept low-level work and the minimum wage scale. More educated and sophisticated immigrants have found successful careers in a variety of occupations and professions; however, recent immigrants are usually found in low-paying service and manufacturing jobs. Not surprisingly, skill and educational level of immigrants greatly determines their job placement and their experiences in assimilation.

A common experience among immigrants is cultural shock, especially for those who locate in geographical areas where they are isolated. As they confront a different cultural environment they face isolation, loneliness, and loss of support from their families. Those who relocate in enclaves where they live with other members of their culture who have recently migrated collectively experience the angst of a different cultural environment. According to Okun et al. (1999), minorities are tolerated if they conform to the dominant culture and are expected to assimilate white values and lifestyle.

Development of children and adolescents is especially interrupted and may remain in a discontinuous state for long periods. Their self-identity is challenged severely by new and different peer groups. Learning a new language for many immigrants poses significant problems for obtaining work, in educational programs, and in social activities. Counselors should evaluate the acculturation level to determine the degree of adoption of beliefs, values, and lifestyle of the host culture. Developmental issues of adjustment to cultural differences and the host cultures' sex roles are important variables related to developmental tasks of immigrant children and adolescents. As immigrants lose some of their original cultural identity and acquire a new identity in a second culture, they may alternate between wanting to "belong" and resistance to "belonging"; their developmental process can be most difficult.

The need to assimilate values and lifestyle of the host culture has become a growing conflict. Multiculturalists suggest that there should be a model of partial assimilation in which immigrants retain some of their customs, beliefs, and language. There is pressure to conform rather than to maintain their cultural identities, however, and these conflicts are determined largely by the community to which one migrates (Okun et al., 1999). These experiences are not new; many Europeans experienced exclusion and poverty during the first two waves of immigration in the 19th and 20th centuries. Eventually, these immigrants transformed this country with significant changes that included enlightenment and acceptance of diversity. People of color, however, continue to struggle for acceptance. Once again, the challenge is to recognize that other cultures think and act differently and that they have the right to do so. Perhaps, in the not too distant future, immigrants will no longer be strangers among us (Suro, 1998).

Evaluating and understanding an immigrant's identity development can be at least partially assessed by a Minority Identity Development model developed by Sue (1981) and Atkinson, Morten, and Sue (1993). This model describes the psychosocial development of minority group members. Stages of development and transitions between stages are expressed in terms of the minority members' attitude toward self, others of the same minority, others of a different minority, and the dominant society or groups.

Stage 1: Conformity. The individual is self-deprecating and prefers to be identified with dominant cultural values.

Stage 2: Dissonance. The individual develops conflicts about the dominant system and is in a state of cultural confusion.

Stage 3: Resistance and immersion. The individual is more self-appreciating and rejects the dominant society.

Stage 4: Introspection. The individual carefully evaluates his or her attitude toward self and the dominant society.

Stage 5: Synergetic articulation and awareness. The individual accepts his or her cultural identity and develops selective appreciations of the dominant culture.

In addition to providing guidelines for career counseling activities, this model also provides counselors with a greater understanding of the stress and adjustment problems of immigrants. Excerpts from an interview described in Box 10-1 illustrate a migrant's acculturation and adjustment to the dominant society.

Helping Clients to Live and Work in a Culturally Diverse Society

You have seen numerous references to the fact that projections of population growth in this country clearly indicated a growing culturally diverse society. Stated in another way, the next society will be composed of an increasing number of individuals who will be culturally different than the dominant society that exists today. Our role is to assist all clients to adjust to living in the United States as well as helping Americans adapt to new and different cultural traditions and beliefs. It seems reasonable to suggest that we begin by attempting to understand and assist the immigrant to resolve adjustment problems in a new society, as well as address one's own beliefs associated with cultural bias, racism, and stereotypical thinking. There appears to be agreement among experts in multicultural counseling that helpers are to thoroughly uncover and evaluate their cultural beliefs before attempting to counsel clients who are culturally different. Using this same logic we can offer suggestions to all clients on how to effectively live and work in a culturally diverse society.

In this chapter we have only touched on what it really means for someone to fully understand their cultural bias, racism, and stereotypical thinking. We have learned that culture is a learned behavior. Within our own ecological system we have learned and accepted beliefs, traditions, and developed worldviews. Human development theorists inform us that an individual's developmental process is both continuous and discontinuous over the life span. In other words we make gradual progress to comprehend the world we live in or we stagnate. In this context, there are periods in our lives when we choose to take the time and "back away" so to speak, in order to think through a situation that has emerged as a critical incident—for example, coming face-to-face with cultural differences that are difficult to comprehend. The time we spend during these periods of critical thinking are most important, primarily because we have chosen to not act emotionally, with little thought given to the consequences of our actions. On the contrary, we search for solutions and answers that include different approaches, an enlightened perspective of the past and the future, and in the end a means to live our life more fully.

Matsumoto (2000) suggests that we recognize that culture is the "degree to which a group of people share attitudes, values, beliefs, and behaviors" (p. 499). It is not a race, nationality, or birthplace! From this perspective, we view culture as a psychological construct or a learned worldview and a way of thinking and living. We approach each person, therefore, as a unique individual who has learned customs and traditions from contextual interactions in a unique environment. Differences in behavior and

Box 10-1	An Immigrant's Experiences

During the pre-interview stage, the counselor and Zoila agreed that the Multicultural Career Counseling Checklist (Ward & Bingham, 1993) and the Career Counseling Checklist (Ward & Tate, 1990) would be helpful for organizing background information and identifying problems. After discussing several items on both checklists, the counselor was encouraged that rapport had been established. Both counselor and client felt comfortable with discussing racial issues and differences in cultural groups.

Zoila was raised a Catholic and noted that all members of her family in Mexico were Catholics. She became a Protestant when she married her Mexican-American husband about one year after arriving in this country and has been active in church work. She has been married for 20 years and has two children, ages 19 and 15. The oldest child, a girl, is attending college, and the youngest is in his sophomore year in high school.

When she arrived in this country, Zoila could not speak a word of English. She attended an adult education program for three years before she became proficient. Thus, in her early years she could only socialize with other Hispanics. She felt that this was the limiting problem she faced as an immigrant. She did not feel that the local Hispanic community was prejudiced and did not experience overt discrimination in the community. However, she does harbor the feeling that many people "think that those who come from Mexico are not good." She remembers being "homesick" for her family, especially her mother. She also missed holiday celebrations and traditions in Mexico. She occasionally returned to Mexico to visit her family but plans to remain in the local community and make a life for her family in this country.

Zoila left Mexico primarily because there was little work for women in Mexico, especially where she lived. She claims that she has always wanted to work in a situation where she could

advance. She felt that her chances in Mexico for such an opportunity were practically nil. She recognized early that upward mobility meant education or training, and she set out to get it. She took several jobs in local industries and also worked as a caregiver in a home for the mentally retarded and saved her money for an education. After receiving a GED Certificate she enrolled in college to take business courses. She feels that the course that helped her the most was public speaking during which she was able to improve her English skills.

In the meantime, she raised two children who have also done quite well in their educational programs. She speaks English in her home except, as she put it, "when I get angry." Her daughter has a greater link to Mexican traditions and customs than does her son, who Zoila characterizes as being "Americanized."

Zoila now owns and operates a small business that employs three other individuals. Her business has been successful for seven years. She has managed to purchase the building in which her business is located and rents out part of it to a retail outlet. She is mostly accepted by both Hispanics and members of the white community. She is a member of the local Chamber of Commerce. Her friendly and pleasing personality attracts many to her business.

When Zoila was asked about her lifestyle here, she replied that she had been raised to believe that the man of the house was to make the living while she raised the children. "This is the way in Mexico," she stated. However, she felt the need to work in this country to provide more opportunities for her children. Even though she enjoys her work and interactions with the public, she would prefer to be "just a housewife." She stated, "If you want to get ahead here, you don't have the choice."

In sum, the story of Zoila illustrates a relatively successful process to immigration. This true story continues to unfold.

Figure 10-3   Steps to interpersonal and intercultural success or stagnation

SOURCE: From *Culture and Psychology*, 3rd ed., by Matsumoto/Juang. © 2004. Reprinted with permission of Wadsworth, a part of The Thomson Corporation.

thinking are the result of individual development and not meant as an insult or confrontation to others. Understanding how one's beliefs have been developed is the key to understanding why differences exist between cultures and individuals from different cultures. From this perspective we can move away from negative stereotypes on to a more comprehensive viewpoint that recognizes that cultural differences are legitimate. We are indeed the product of a unique multidimensional developmental process. As a result we just happen to think and behave differently.

In Figure 10-3, two alternatives to resolve cultural differences are provided by Matsumoto and Juang (2004). The "voyager" is one who is willing to learn more about cultural influences and ready to resolve negative emotions. The "vindicator," on the other hand, is one who remains stagnant by refusing to debunk stereotypical thinking. Finally, what we learn about cultural differences is not something we have to agree with or accept as our own. Our mission is to give others who differ from us the benefit of the doubt and to make an attempt to understand their worldview and lifestyle (Matsumoto & Juang, 2004).

Summary

1. Culture is a very complex concept that can refer to many aspects of life and living. Culture is a learned behavior. Two people from the same race could share some values, attitudes, and so on, but might also be very different in their cultural makeup. Counselors should be alert to value orientation when working among different cultural groups.

2. Four major cultural groups are African Americans, Asian Pacific Americans, Hispanic Americans, and Native Americans. Currently, the largest racial minority group in this country is Hispanics. Culturally different African Americans tend to

remain social isolates in church, school, and employment. Many Asian Americans place a high value on education. Asian Americans tend to inhibit emotional expression, and so many do not actively participate in counseling programs. In general, Asian Americans are reluctant to admit personal problems because of their cultural conditioning. Asian Americans tend to misinterpret the role of counseling and its potential benefits. The second largest minority group in this country is Hispanic Americans. General cultural characteristics of Hispanic Americans appear to distinguish them as the least "Americanized" of the ethnic groups. The Hispanic family typically is a closely knit group that greatly influences the value systems of its members. Native Americans are culturally conditioned to view life from a different perspective than that of the dominant white culture. Native Americans generally are not motivated to achieve status through the accumulation of wealth. The lifestyle of most Native Americans is extremely democratic, and their culture promotes egalitarianism.

3. Culture variability of worldviews includes constructs of individualism and collectivism. Examples of other differences in cultures are time orientation, view of human nature, and personal space and privacy. Worldviews should be considered unique for each individual.

4. Culture does have an important role in work-related values. Differences between cultures help us understand employee attitudes, values, behaviors, and interpersonal dynamics.

5. Effective counselors have knowledge of and are sensitive to different cultural orientations when establishing rapport in counseling relationships. To be effective with populations of different cultures, counselors must be aware of different worldviews (the psychological orientation of thinking, behavior, and interpretation of events). Counselors must be careful not to impose their values on others. Necessary skill areas include awareness of differences, self-awareness, knowledge of client's culture, and adaptation of counseling method, materials, and procedures.

6. Optimal theory is multidimensional in nature and emphasizes how (a) specific cultures influence the development of worldviews, (b) the human universality of themes cut across cultures, and (c) the uniqueness of the individual is developed.

7. A multicultural counseling and therapy theory (MCT) was developed because, as the authors suggest, contemporary theories of counseling do not deal adequately with the complexity of culturally diverse populations. We must balance the focus of counseling, expand the repertoire of helping responses, identify indigenous helping roles, and develop alternatives to the conventional counseling role.

8. Immigrants have special needs that involve the premigration process as well as the adjustment process in a new and different culture. Adjustment to a new culture includes transitions of reconstructing social networks, adjusting to a new socioeconomic system, and learning a different cultural system.

9. Counselors must develop a greater sensitivity to culturally diverse clients when conducting an interview. Technique issues include eye contact, touch, probing questions, space and distance, verbal style, restrictive emotions, confrontation, self-disclosure, and focus on self-in-relation and self-in-context.

Supplementary Learning Exercises

1. Define your cultural background and that of a classmate. Compare differences and similarities.
2. How would you explain the differences between individualism and collectivism? What socialization variables influenced the differences between them?
3. Do you believe the multicultural counseling and therapy theory (MCT) is necessary? Support your conclusion.
4. Take one or more of the four major cultural groups discussed in this chapter and develop culture-specific issues that should be addressed in career counseling.
5. Write an essay about how cultural worldviews are developed. Include differences between other cultures and the white dominant culture.
6. Describe how different cultural work values can be sources of conflict and misunderstanding in the workplace. Develop appropriate interventions.
7. Debate the pros and cons of counselors becoming culturally competent.
8. What do you consider to be the most difficult culturally competent skill to learn? Explain.
9. Interview a culturally different person. Share your experience with the class.
10. Which of the following two methods do you consider to be the most effective for career counseling? Support your conclusions.
    a. Use culture-specific information.
    b. Use human universality information.

For More Information

American Psychological Association. (2002). *Guidelines on multicultural education, training, research, practice and organizational change for psychologists.* Washington, DC: American Psychological Association.

Atkinson, D.R., Morton, G., & Sue, D. W. (1998). *Counseling American minorities: A cross-cultural perspective* (5th ed). Boston: McGraw-Hill.

Axelson, J. A. (1999). *Counseling and development in a multicultural society* (4th ed.). Pacific Grove, CA: Brooks/Cole.

Bingham, R. P., & Ward, C. M. (1996). Practical applications of career counseling with ethnic minority women. In M. L. Savickas, & W. B. Walsh (Eds.), *Handbook of career counseling theory and practice* (pp. 291–315). Palo Alto, CA: Davies-Black.

Brammer, R. (2004). *Diversity in counseling.* Belmont, CA: Brooks/Cole-Thomson Learning.

Chun, K. M., Balls-Organista, P., & Marin, G. (Eds). (2003) *Acculturation: Advances in theory, measurement, and applied research.* Washington, DC: American Psychological Association.

Comas-Diaz, L. (1996). Cultural considerations in diagnosis. In F. W. Kaslow (Ed.), *Handbook on relational diagnosis and dysfunctional family patterns* (pp. 159–160). New York: Wiley.

Comas-Diaz, L., & Grenier, J. R. (1998). Migration and acculturation. In J. Sandoval, C. L. Frisby, K. F. Geisinger, J. D. Scheuneman, & J. R. Grenier, *Test interpretation and diversity* (pp. 213–241). Washington, DC: American Psychological Association.

Diller, J. V. (1999). *Cultural diversity: A primer for the human services.* Pacific Grove, CA: Wadsworth.

Hays, P. A. (2001). *Addressing cultural complexities in practice: A framework for clinicians and counselors.* Washington, CD: American Psychological Association.

Hofstede, G. (1984). *Culture's consequences: International differences in work-related values.* Newbury Park, CA: Sage.

Ivey, A. E., & Ivey, M. B. (1999). *Intentional interviewing and counseling* (4th ed.). Pacific Grove, CA: Brooks/Cole.

Lum, D. (Ed.). (2003). *Culturally competent practice: A framework for understanding diverse groups and justice systems.* Pacific Grove, CA: Brooks/Cole-Thomson Learning.

Matsumoto, D., & Juang, L. (2004). *Culture and psychology* (3rd ed.). Belmont, CA: Wadsworth-Thomson Learning.

Nagayama, H., & Okazaki, S. (Eds). (2003). *Asian American psychology: The science of lives in context.* Washington, DC: American Psychological Association.

Okun, B. F., Fried, J., & Okun, M. L. (1999). *Understanding diversity: A learning practice primer.* Pacific Grove, CA: Brooks/Cole.

Sternberg, R. J., & Grigorenka, E. L. (2004). *Culture and competence: Contexts of life success.* Washington, DC: American Psychological Association.

Sue, D. W., Arredondo, A., & McDavis, R. J. (1992). Multicultural counseling competencies and standards: A call to the profession. *Journal of Counseling and Development, 70,* 477–486.

Sue, D. W., Ivey, A. E., & Pedersen, P. B. (1996). *A theory of multicultural counseling and therapy.* Pacific Grove, CA: Brooks/Cole.

Sue, D. W., & Sue, D. (1999). *Counseling the culturally different: Theory and practice* (3rd ed.). New York: Wiley.

Suro, R. (1998). *Strangers among us: How Latino immigration is transforming America.* New York: Knopf.

Suggested InfoTrac College Edition Topics

Acculturation

Cultural competence

Culture and gender

Culture and power distance

Culture and social behavior

Culture and work values

Diversity in counseling

Multicultural counseling

11 Gender Issues in Career Counseling

Chapter Highlights

- Career development theories for women

- Multicultural perspectives when working with women and men

- Factors that influence gender development

- Shared work roles

- Special needs of women and men

A FEW SHORT YEARS AGO, career counseling programs for women consisted of exploring the traditionally held working roles. The choices were narrowed to such occupations as clerk, teacher, or nurse. One of the first questions asked was, "How will this job fit into your husband's occupational goal?" The message to women was quite clear: You have only a few jobs to choose from, and your career is secondary to your husband's or other family obligations. Currently, career counselors find that women are rearranging their career priorities—planning for a lifelong career in a wide range of occupations has become the highest priority for many. A career first and marriage maybe or later is the new order of preference for those who aspire for a career outside the home. In this post–women's movement era, women continue to look beyond the traditional feminine working roles. The women who embark on this career course will find that many barriers still remain. First, the bias associated with gender stereo-types in the working world still exists (Galliano, 2003; McBride, 1990; Rider, 2000; Wentling, 1992; Wood, 1994). Second, the woman who gives her career development equal status with her husband's will find acceptance of her role personally challeng-ing, with little support from many men and women (Betz & Fitzgerald, 1987; Matlin, 2004). Male and female counselors might also resist accepting women's changing career priorities (Harway, 1980; Unger & Crawford, 1992). In essence, resistance to women's role in the working world continues in our society—albeit somewhat less strongly since the women's movement—from men and women at all levels of the workforce, from managers and professionals to blue-collar workers.

In response to the women's movement, men have rallied with movements of their own in the form of several organizations with a variety of agendas. The Society for the Psychological Study of Men and Masculinity, Division 51 of the American Psycholog-ical Association, was formed to focus research on men's lives, including gender role socialization and gender role conflict. Another group, considered to be pro-feminist, is the National Organization for Men Against Sexism, formed as an activist group to promote less discrimination against women. Other men's groups represent various positions on gender role and masculinity. The mythopoetic movement, for instance suggests that men are to endorse a different and new masculinity that does not oppress women and children. Built on religious beliefs that men are to head house-holds, several groups have formed to promote traditional feminine and masculine roles. Yet other groups endorse a men's rights movement and suggest that men are the real victims of sexism (Matlin, 2004). We have groups of men who endorse and sup-port the feminist movement and some groups who have organized to uphold tradi-tional roles. One can only speculate about the future of gender issues but we can be certain that career counselors will deal with problems and concerns of femininity and masculinity in the foreseeable future.

This chapter begins with a discussion of career development theories for women. Be aware that many of the career development theories discussed in Chapter 2 were based primarily on studies of white males. Second, multicultural perspectives when working with both women and men will be discussed. Third, gender issues in the workplace will be summarized. Fourth, some special needs for women and men will be highlighted.

Career Development Theories and Women

Women's career development has received only cursory attention by career develop-ment theorists (Herr, Cramer, & Niles, 2004; Osipow, 1983). Super (1957, 1990) is one of the major career development theorists (discussed in Chapter 2) who addressed women's career development patterns, which he classified into seven categories: stable homemaking, conventional, stable working, double track, interrupted, unstable, and multiple trial. Super among others viewed career development of women as different from men, suggesting multidimensional patterns of development that should be delineated. His double-track career pattern, which establishes homemaking as a sec-ond career, recognizes that an increasing number of women are career oriented.

Ginzberg (1966), another theorist, considered three lifestyle dimensions for women that may be used in career counseling approaches: (1) traditional (homemaker oriented), (2) transitional (more emphasis on home than on job), and (3) innovative (giving equal emphasis to job and home). These dimensions reflect lifestyles found among some working women; however, he also recognizes that an increasing number of women place the highest priority on the development of a career. Some women may be reluctant to become more career oriented for fear of losing the stereotypical female identity so readily accepted by our society. For many, the loss of this identity has indeed been threatening and deters a serious focus on career development.

In the 1960s, Zytowski (1969) denoted the vocational development patterns of women as (1) mild vocational, (2) moderate vocational, and (3) unusual vocational. These patterns closely follow the lifestyle dimensions developed by Ginzberg in that each category is progressively more occupationally oriented. According to Zytowski, the modal life role for women in our society is that of homemaker. Through vocational participation, a woman may change her modal lifestyle. Patterns of vocational participation for women are determined by age at entry, the length of time the woman works, and the type of work undertaken. Further determinants of vocational patterns for women are individual motivation, ability, and environmental circumstances, such as financial needs. Of significance to our considerations is that women do differ and have special needs to be included in career development programs.

In the 1980s, Betz and Fitzgerald (1987) suggested that social class, attitudes generated by marriage, financial resources, educational level, and general cultural values of past and immediate families, are major determinants influencing occupational choice. Furthermore, occupational choices of both genders are not made independently of other variables in our society. Women, like men, do indeed have special needs that must be addressed in career counseling programs.

In a related research study that began with 3,000 sixth-graders in southeast Michigan and tracked 2,000 of them well into early adulthood, Eccles, Barber, and Jozefowicz (1999) report some interesting findings. They suggest that numerous mediators developed from contextual interactions are involved in career choices among women. For instance, occupational aspirations are mediated by expectancy beliefs and values that are referred to as achievement-related choices. Women who expect to do well in particular occupational environments tend to aspire to such careers. Furthermore, gendered socialization experiences lead to the development of core personal values and self-identity, which are instrumental in establishing long-range goals. Gender roles influence the kind of activities women want to participate in regarding an occupation and lifestyle. Career roles for women are also influenced by a culture's definition of female roles, which include parenting and spouse-support. Finally, mediation developed from individual experiences of cultural interactions can modify career aspirations.

In the late 1970s, Sanguiliano (1978) emphasized the theme of different and special needs of women. Although she agreed that women do follow a serial life pattern, there are unique times of hibernation, renewal, postponement, and actualization. She contended that life-stage theorists such as Erikson (1950), Havighurst (1953), Kohlberg (1973), and Levinson (1980) reveal significant shortcomings in describing the development of women. Stage theorists do not account for the unexpected, critical events and the myriad of unusual influences that shape feminine life patterns. Sanguiliano suggested that a woman's life cycle does not follow a rigid progression of developmental tasks but is similar to a sine curve representing the impact of unique experiences and critical events.

According to Sanguiliano, the formulation of self-identity is one fundamental difference between men's and women's developmental patterns. Women's self-identification is significantly delayed because of the conflicting expectations ascribed to feminine identity. Men learn their masculinity early and are better prepared to adapt to changes, but women do not have comparable, clearly defined boundaries and images of appropriate gender-linked roles. Men are reinforced in their efforts to attain clearly defined masculine roles; women depend on loosely defined feminine roles and have few support systems.

Sanguiliano's principal argument is that women's individual life patterns require special consideration. Attention should focus on unique paths women take to break away from gender-role stereotyping. Individual progress toward self-identity is germane to Sanguiliano's approach to determining counseling components for women.

Spencer (1982) supports Sanguiliano's denial that women's development follows the rigid progression suggested by life-stage theorists. Spencer contends that feminine developmental tasks are unlike masculine tasks and that women follow unique patterns of development. Using Levinson's life-cycle sequence and transitional periods of men, Spencer compared women's development with the men's model: early transitions (ages 17–28), age-30 transitions (ages 28–39), midlife transitions (ages 39–45), and late-adult transitions (ages 65–?).

The early transitional period, the time when one reappraises existing structures, begins the search for personal identity (Erikson, 1950; Levinson, Darrow, Klein, Levinson, & McKee, 1978). Spencer contended that separating from the parental home is more difficult for the young woman than for the young man; women receive less encouragement and experience less social pressure to become independent. Furthermore, women do not have adequate support systems to encourage self-expression in a society that presents conflicting messages. In essence, women have a more difficult time developing self-identity.

During the age-30 transitions, marital conflicts are prevalent in women who look for new directions. For example, women who want to spend time in career development often find forming egalitarian marital relationships difficult. The frustrations women face in dual family/career commitment are often misunderstood. On one hand, women are socialized to think of themselves only as homemakers, but, on the other hand, they have a strong need to express themselves in a career. Women have to struggle to realize that greater freedom and satisfaction are options.

Midlife transitions are periods of reappraising the past and of continuing the search for meaning in life. This period is marked by an increased awareness that some long-held beliefs might not be valid. For women, successful appraisal of life accomplishments is usually reflected in what others (husband and children) have done. Therefore, when their children leave home, women have difficulty creating new identities and new life purposes.

The late-adult transitions are a continued reappraisal of self in society. According to Spencer, the primary task of this period is to gain a sense of integrity in one's life. Spencer (1982) concluded that women rarely achieve the developmental goal of ego autonomy—"They are doomed from the start" (p. 87).

Spencer (1982) and Sanguiliano (1978) suggested that women have different developmental patterns than men do: (1) Women experience intense role confusion early in their development; (2) women are more inhibited in their self-expression; (3) women tend to delay their career aspirations in lieu of family responsibilities; and

(4) women's developmental patterns are more individualized. These unique and individualized developmental patterns may present significant problems in career decision making. Among many variables, counselors should carefully consider self-concept development and value assessment in career decision-making programs for women.

Chusmir (1983) identified characteristics and background traits of women in nontraditional vocations (construction trades, skilled crafts, technical fields, science, law, engineering, and medicine). He suggested that women who choose nontraditional occupations have personality characteristics usually attributed to men. For example, they tend to be more autonomous, active, dominant, individualistic, intellectual, and psychologically male-identified than are women who choose traditional careers (social work, nursing, teaching, and office work). Motivational characteristics of women who choose nontraditional occupations are also similar to those attributed to men: achievement orientation, status seeking, and strong need for self-regard and recognition. Examples of background traits of women in nontraditional occupations are better education; better mental health; fewer or no children; eldest or only child; postponed marriages; had fathers who were younger, in management roles, and well-educated; and took women's studies courses.

Chusmir suggested that personality and motivational traits of women who choose nontraditional occupations are formed by the time they are teenagers. Clearly, the research focuses on the importance of early feminine developmental patterns. These findings suggest that intervention strategies designed to expand occupational choices for girls should be introduced during elementary school years.

In each of the career developmental patterns of women briefly reviewed, emphasis was placed on the woman's role as homemaker, and the special needs of women interested in developing careers were stressed. Women who give at least equal emphasis to job and home were considered "innovative" (Ginzberg, 1966) or "unusual" (Zytowski, 1969) because they differed in lifestyle from the "typical" homemaker. These terms are very misleading today, however, as predictions from the U.S. Department of Labor suggest that women job seekers will slowly increase (Matlin, 2004; Peterson & Gonzalez, 2000). Even more important are the considerations we should give to women as individuals, free of gender-role stereotyping, in an expanding job market.

The general developmental patterns of women suggest that a woman's life cycle does not follow life-stage models developed from the study of men. Compared with men, self-identity is slower to develop, primarily as a result of gender-role stereotyping. Our society accords a secondary priority to career choice as well as to career development for women. Women's difficulty with career decision making is closely associated with role confusion and the lack of role models and support systems.

Currently, career development theorists have given more attention to women's career development. For example, some gender issues are addressed in the individual developmental constructs in the theory of work adjustment and person-environment-fit counseling (Dawis, 1996) discussed in Chapter 2. Although gender is not considered as a defining variable in the theory, gender becomes important when it influences work skills and work needs that have not been identified. The point here is that women have not been given an opportunity equivalent to that of men to develop the full range of work skills required in the world of work. Therefore, what reinforces women in a number of work environments is unknown. However, this theory considers gender as an important "background" variable that could account for personality structure, style, and adjustment style of workers. Therefore, when more gender variables are identified in the world of work, more emphasis can be given to gender as a defining variable.

Gottfredson (1996) makes an interesting observation about gender concerning group differences, for instance, how gender, ethnic, and social groups and how group membership per se might shape career aspirations (see Chapter 2). Gottfredson asserts that group-based identities influence and shape one's preference for place and fit in the social order. Moreover, the theory of circumscription and compromise "assumes that most young people orient to their own gender and social class when contemplating careers" (p. 202). Gottfredson stresses that orientation to sex roles in early childhood (ages 6 to 8) results in a concern for individuals to do what is considered appropriate for one's sex, particularly in vocational aspirations.

In the theory of sociological perspectives on work and career development Hotchkiss and Borow (1996) suggest that long-standing social inequities constrain females' work-related achievements. Although there is some evidence of decline in gender segregation of occupations (Matlin, 2004; Roos & Jones, 1993), there is much more to do to reduce gender barriers in the work world.

In an outstanding article, Fitzgerald and Betz (1994) suggest that women's career development is affected by discrimination and sexual harassment, cultural constraints as occupational gender stereotypes, and gender-role socialization, in addition to the "motherhood mandate." One point well taken is that women's abilities are not being fully used either in education and in occupations; thus, many women are functioning in jobs for which they are overqualified. Fitzgerald and Betz suggest that, first, each career development theory should determine its applicability to particular groups, such as gender and ethnic groups. Second, information should be given about the applicability of a theory for groups or how people's characteristics affect the predictive validity of a theory. Third, each theory should be scrutinized for its conceptualization of structural and cultural factors and how they relate to important theory variables. Using structural and cultural factors as a measure of a theory's effectiveness will provide new perspectives for career theories, particularly for greater insights into women's career development.

Finally, the fact that men and women differ in many dimensions gives credence to a multifaceted model of development. After more than 30 years of gender research, Spence (1999) concludes that numerous sets of dimensions determine masculinity and femininity. Furthermore, even though males and females of any given age differ by identified gender-related behaviors, these attributes vary among individuals within each gender; they are thought to be influenced by contemporary contextual interactions. What Spence and other researchers are emphasizing is that gender roles are most complex in development; they are multidimensional and multifaceted with no overarching unitary or single dimension or sets of dimensions that determine masculinity or femininity. There are, however, numerous factors whose interaction is extremely complex in determining one's gender role identity development. What is most important to recognize is that one's gender-related behaviors can be modified or sustained by contemporary experiences.

The answer to the question of why men and women differ in their choices is viewed as differences in values, goals, and self-perceptions. Thus, educational and occupational choices are guided by the following according to Eccles, Barber, and Jozefowicz (1999):

> (a) one's expectations for success on and sense of personal efficacy for various options, (b) the relation of the options to both one's short- and long-range goals and one's core self-identity and basic psychological needs, (c) one's gender-role-related schemas, and (d) the potential cost of investing time in one activity rather than another. All these psychological variables are influenced by one's experiences, cultural norms, and the behaviors and goals of one's socializers and peers. (pp. 158–159)

Thus, a much broader multifaceted and multidimensional approach to women's development has the promise of unearthing more information about career aspirations of women.

Multicultural Perspectives When Working with Women and Men

On several occasions in this chapter and more often in the previous chapter, the point has been made that women and men are socialized in a particular culture. By incorporating ethnicity in career development of both sexes we gain a greater understanding of multiple facets of influence that shape values, beliefs, actions, and worldviews. A most important point to remember is that one's development does not take place in isolation but is greatly influenced by salient messages received within the environment. Hence, ethnic-related messages are integrated with other variables that greatly affect gender role development. We will briefly examine ethnicity and gender of African Americans, Southeastern Asians, Hispanics, and Native Americans.

African American women have a long history of doing menial labor as cooks, housemaids, nannies, and other low-pay-scale jobs (Galliano, 2003; Harley, 1995). More recently, African American women are found in professions largely as a result of federal legislation and affirmative action policies (Higginbotham, 1994; Matlin, 2004). An increasing number of African American women have been successful in owning their own businesses (Ballard, 1997). Most overall career growth appears to be in the public sector, however; women of color continue to be subjected to discrimination in the private sector.

The collective strengths of African American women are in social networks of other women and relatives such as sisters. Many regularly participate in sororities, church women's groups, and women's social clubs. In essence, female friendship is a strong support system for African American women. Women support each other in difficult times and remain loyal to their churches. African American women have a strong spiritual commitment that is used to counteract the unfairness and hardships of oppression and racism. Some of the challenges facing African American women are health problems associated with poverty and isolation. Teenage pregnancy among African Americans is declining, but the problem remains a challenge.

Career counseling for ethnic women was discussed and illustrated in Chapters 3 and 10. We cannot overemphasize the point that career counselors must recognize that there is diversity in any subgroup. Thus, African American women are not to be considered as a homogeneous group. Winbush (2000) suggests, however, that job training and child care are two primary needs of many African American women.

Parham (1996) makes the point that African American men value treating others with respect, kindness, and decency. He infers that African American men have not received reciprocal treatment in this country by the white dominant society. He suggests that counselors become active advocates to change discriminatory practices in communities. Furthermore, he suggests that counselors address the oppressions associated with racism and white supremacy directly with clients. A most important counseling goal is for counselors to assist African American men to develop self-awareness or self-knowledge. Counselors, for example, are to assist African American men in developing a self-identity that underscores their ability to express themselves openly and freely. Strongly suggested here is that we must "help African-American clients more fully understand, appreciate, and express, their Africanness" (Parham, 1996, p. 188). Finally, some developmental strategies to help African Americans include assisting self-concept development, developing more internally directed behavior, becoming more aware of job opportunities, clarifying motivational aspirations, and dealing with ambivalence toward whites.

Southeastern Asian American women have received little attention in research literature. This population consists of a variety of groups including women from Vietnam, Laos, and Cambodia. Since 1975, more than one million Southeastern Asian refugees have migrated to the United States (Zaharlick, 2000). Of this group, the Vietnamese are thought to be the best educated and most fluent in English and have the most experience in professional and technical occupations. There is much diversity among this subgroup of people, however, although some values are shared. Southeastern Asian women feel a strong devotion to their children and to family continuity, they strive to avoid actions that would bring shame to the family, and they strongly embrace self-control (Zaharlick, 2000).

A couple I know owned and operated a restaurant and both worked on the midnight shift in a local weaving plant. Their goal was to provide the necessary funds for their son's educational expenses. Their devotion to their child's education is a good example of their values and family commitment. When I expressed this to them, their response was simply that they expected him to spend most of his time studying. They did not seem to feel that what they were doing was anything special and showed great pride in their son's achievement. Obviously, in this case, family and devotion to their child was of major importance.

Southeastern Asian women have difficulty in witnessing current breakdowns in family honor as their children adopt more of the values and lifestyle of the dominant culture (Axelson, 1999). Their children are learning from a new and different peer group that individualism is the contemporary lifestyle. A pervasive problem for Southeastern Asian women is the growing trend of children who disobey family rules. Conflicting information experienced by all family members in a new and different society can result in family discord. Counselors can expect to find that some Asian clients have serious conflicts about their future work and life role.

When the needs of Asian American men are addressed, the tremendous diversity within and between groups should be kept in mind. According to Leong (1996b), however, individualism and collectivism are key variables for understanding differences between Asian Americans and Euro-Americans. This is especially true for Asian Americans who are less acculturated. Asian American men consider family honor more important than personal goals, hence, decisions are based on what is best for the family.

Client–counselor relationships, especially among less acculturated men, must be carefully balanced. Asian Americans, for example, expect a hierarchical relationship with counselors. More specifically, Asian American men expect a professional relationship rather than an egalitarian one. Balancing the roles of counselor and counselee is essential, therefore for effective interviewing and intervention strategies. Some suggested developmental strategies for Asian American men are learning to understand organization systems and bureaucracies, improving communication skills, and learning to understand the give-and-take of work environments. Counselors may find that using Asian Americans as role models will enhance the effectiveness of counseling goals.

Hispanic women, a very diverse group who have migrated from many different countries, have some common background variables such as religion preference. Most are Christian and members of the Catholic Church, although in recent years some have joined Protestant groups. Hispanic women learn from their religion that they are to view their chief roles as mothers and wives (Burgos-Ocasio, 2000). They are primary caregivers and center their lives around family needs. Career, therefore, may not be a very meaningful term.

Traditionally, the health needs of some Hispanic women are taken care of by home remedies and other women in the family, and they use indigenous healing systems by referring individuals to a currandismo (Mexican folk healer). Counselors are to approach this subject carefully because some Hispanics strongly support indigenous healing systems. Although more information about the benefits of current medical practices may be needed, all nontraditional methods, remedies, and healers should be recognized (Sue, Ivey, & Pedersen, 1996).

Ortiz (1996) points out more Hispanic women are migrating and joining the U.S. labor force. Most have few skills, little education, and end up finding work as maids, factory workers, or in nonskilled jobs. Their major goal is to send their earnings back to their country of origin to support their families. Short-term goals include finding a place to live and a job. Long-term goals usually include becoming legal citizens and bringing their children, if any, and families to join them.

All Latino subgroups, such as Mexican, Cuban, and Puerto Rican, are quite nationalistic. Gender identity for men is associated with the term *machismo,* which generally stands for arrogance and sexual aggression in Latino/Latina relationships. Machismo is also associated with men having firm control of their families. This stereotyped portrayal of men suggests that more value is placed on boys than on girls in Latino/a culture. However, the reverence for motherhood has influenced the trend toward equalization of sexes in the Hispanic cultures (Arredondo, 1996).

Because of the great diversity among Hispanics, counselors should spend considerable time learning about specific cultures. Suggested developmental strategies for Hispanic American males include learning about effective communication skills, work environments and organizations, the use of career information, job search strategies, and interpersonal relationships. Other suggestions include learning goal-setting and problem-solving skills, developing working parent skills, and improving financial management of resources.

Neal (2000) also reminds us that there is great diversity among the customs and cultures of Native Americans. "The roles of women vary from tribe to tribe and geographical region to geographic region" (p. 166). Native American women historically have been influential within their tribes. This tradition continues in many tribes; for instance, Wilma Mankiller was the Chief of the Cherokee Nation of Oklahoma in 1985 (Mankiller & Wallis, 1993). Other Indian nations have also elected women as chairpersons or chiefs. Some tribes have a council of women elders that has control of ceremonial life and businesses operated by the tribe. However, the traditional primary role for Native American women, similar to so many other cultures, is care of the family.

Of most significance to Native American women as homemaker and caregiver is that Native American families are the poorest socioeconomic group (Neal, 2000). The most impoverished families in this country are Native American families with no husband present. The source of strength among Native Americans, however, is their biological family and the extended community family. They also find spiritual strength from their traditional ancestral homelands.

Native Americans are also a very diverse group of people who have been grossly misunderstood. Native American men have very often been stereotyped as drunkards who sit around the reservation and do little work. This reputation unfortunately has been widespread in this country and in Canada. The most devastating aspect is that the blame for alcoholism has been placed completely on the Native American. One needs to investigate the historical relationship between the U.S. government and Native Americans to understand the full extent of their losses individually and collectively.

LaFromboise and Jackson (1996) suggest that we return the principle of empowerment to the Native Americans so that they can control their own lives: "People are capable of taking control but often choose not to do so because of social forces and institutions that hinder their efforts" (LaFromboise & Jackson, 1996, p. 196). The following strategies are designed to help Native American men maintain their cultural heritage while introducing concepts of career development of the dominant society:

1. Use parents and relatives as counseling facilitators. The rationale for this approach is embedded in the strong family ties of Native Americans.
2. Use Native American role models. They should assist in helping break down resistance to counseling objectives. Native Americans should react more favorably to other Native Americans.
3. Emphasize individual potential in the context of future goals. Identity conflicts that make it difficult for Native Americans to project themselves into other environments, including work environments.

In sum, counselors must be prepared to meet the needs of clients who have been shaped and influenced by their cultural heritage. This brief review of gender issues from different cultural groups suggests that much is to be learned about diversity issues in career counseling. Chapter 10 provides an overview of the culturally related gender issues counselors will face in the 21st century.

Some Factors That Influence Gender Development

It should not be surprising that most researchers seem to agree that gender development is a continuing process over the life span. Gender development does not stop when you graduate from high school, tech school, or college or even when and if you get married. It is a continuous process in which behavior is modified and reinforced by contextual and situational factors in one's entire life. From this viewpoint, one can observe some stages in life during which a script of appropriate gender behavior is established that will serve as reference points as one grows older. Counselors should recognize, however, that people modify their behavior and adapt to changes brought on by situational conditions. Second, the sociocultural context of environment determines to a large extent the character and uniqueness of each individual's gender development. Hence, gender socialization is a multidimensional process that includes cognitive, intrapsychic, and social learning factors (Camilleri & Malewska-Peyre, 1997).

In the meantime, feminist counseling theory introduced in Box 11-1 suggests strategies for addressing the special concerns of women. Currently, women's psychology has been integrated into mainstream psychology and especially into several academic disciplines, including human development, counseling, and sociology. In the last three decades, gender differences have been the primary focus of research efforts among several academic disciplines. After reviewing significant research findings on gender differences, Galliano (2003) concluded that researchers should address the position that men and women are more similar than different. She suggests that we should not view men and women as "separate spheres" but observe gender behavior in shared contextual relationships. This does not mean that we do not continue to point out differences between women and men. What is suggested is observing and evaluating contextual interactions between men and women as in a systems approach, in order to build a greater understanding of the gender socialization process.

A significant amount of research has focused on interacting influences on gender development. More specifically, do the environmental and relational gender role influences from early childhood and adolescence carry over to adulthood? The general consensus is that, because of the complexity of factors involved in the gender developmental process, it is difficult to determine the degree and significance of influences from early childhood that are related to the way an adult thinks and behaves. Parental influence on gender development in early childhood and adolescence are good examples of this problem. Is a young adult male who behaves very aggressively on the job the result of a very aggressive father? Does a young married female choose a career rather than having a family because her mother was a very successful lawyer? It seems plausible to assume that a father's aggressive behavior may influence his son's perception of how to approach work tasks and associates; however, there can be other, stronger influences in adolescence such as belonging to a gang of peers who promote aggressive acts among its members. Likewise, the young married female who opts for a career could have experienced situational conditions that reinforced her mother's example of career orientation. The point here is that each individual is indeed influenced by a number of specific cultural and situational factors that contribute to the development of preferred gender roles (Martin & Ruble, 1997).

There are, however, some general themes of childhood gender socialization that have been compiled by Galliano (2003) in abridged form and summarized here:

Boys
1. May avoid being identified with anything feminine.
2. May want to develop physical abilities and competencies associated with masculinity.
3. May feel the need to be more aggressive.
4. May want to be free of adult supervision.
5. May project self into adult work roles.

Box 11-1	Feminist Therapy

Feminist therapy was developed from the work of women in several academic disciplines whose goal was to provide social change that values women. They particularly challenged the social forces that restrain women from achieving equality of opportunities in work and lifestyle. Feminist therapists have focused on differences between men and women in life-span development, social and sexual development, work roles, and decision-making. One important goal was to develop an understanding of the impact of gender roles and power differences in society (Sharf, 2000).

Over twenty years ago, Sturdivant (1980) suggested that the goals of feminist therapy are to address problems that interfere with a woman's development, reinforce self-esteem, address the quality of interpersonal relationships, help women fulfill life roles, accept their body as it is and not what media says it should be, and become involved in political action about women's issues. When conceptualizing women's problems, counselors are to acknowledge power differences between men and women and the pervasive nature of interpersonal relationships. Finally, the impact of sociocultural variables on each client's development is to be closely scrutinized.

Excerpts from an intake interview illustrate the pervasive and inclusive nature of a female client's problems. Judy has limited the career choices she will consider because she has been socialized to believe that women are not capable of competing for certain jobs. Her family was very traditional and believed that women should choose such jobs as teacher, nurse, and secretary. Her family's beliefs were reinforced by some of her teachers, schoolmates, extended family, and members of her community. In this case, the counselor chose to use feminist-oriented strategies that focus on the reasons the client is not realistic about obstacles, primary reference groups, and what family circumstances influenced her (Gottfredson, 1996).

This example illustrates that Judy's problems primarily emerged from internalizing values from important adults in her environment. She had been socialized to believe that women did not have the freedom to choose and she was, therefore, limited in job choice. In this case, the counselor was able to select strategies that attacked the root of the problem of gender socialization and advocated empowerment and action. Feminist therapy focuses on consequences of women's experiences in home, school, and community.

SOURCE: See Worell, J., & Remer, P. (1992). *Feminist perspectives in therapy: An empowerment model for women,* New York: Wiley.

Girls

1. May expand and continue connection with maternal role.
2. May project self in social and domestic roles.
3. May recognize the importance of physical appearance.
4. May be aware of lower social status as a female.
5. May reflect gender role flexibility in behavior and attitudes.

The tentative gender boundaries one would expect for both girls and boys can be well developed during childhood. For girls, the domestic and maternal role has been reinforced by a number of factors including television ads and programs, and books. Boys are encouraged to be aggressive, to avoid being identified as feminine, and to feel they should prepare for an occupational role. Girls, on the other hand, are more attuned to appearance and social roles.

In adolescence, gender role development is intensified. There is pressure to assume roles associated with femininity and masculinity. Boys step up their efforts to develop a strong, sturdy body whereas girls are more concerned with how their body compares to the ideal female model. Boys' self-concept identity is more intrapersonal whereas girls are more interpersonal and more emotionally connected with others. Finally, be aware that the forces of a changing society could alter influences on gender socialization for both men and women and there are distinct differences within groups (Galliano, 2003).

The study of gender development in childhood and adolescence also has focused on a number of factors, including influence from parents, siblings, school, teachers, classmates, other peer groups, and media (television and books). The study of adult gender development, however, has focused on the degree to which early influences have affected an adult's worldview, personality characteristics, thinking process, and behavior. The rationale here is that stable gender differences in characteristics and traits have been internalized. In this scenario the individual would view the world from a position of inflexible gender differences even though a changing society sends the opposite message. According to Unger (2000) and Galliano (2003) study of stable gender differences among adults have been mixed and are inconsistent, especially when one attempts to objectively observe and measure individual traits. We cannot always be certain of the behavioral and environmental sources that affect an adult's worldview. Therefore, an individualized, contextual approach to gender development, especially with culturally diverse clients, is most appropriate.

Finally, the implications for counseling include an approach that is broadly focused on both internal and external factors. Because gender socialization is a complex process that is multidimensional and multifactorial, each client is to be viewed as a unique individual. Counselors may find similar traits and opinions between individuals from the same cultural background, for example, yet individual differences are to be recognized within groups. The contextual approach to gender development suggests that it is ever changing; views can be modified by a variety of experiences and situational conditions in one's environment. The need for an individual approach to counseling is underscored by unique interpretations one makes of multiple life experiences, situations, and conditions.

Gender in the Workplace

In early human existence women and men worked side by side and shared home responsibilities. Together they gathered food, worked in fields, hunted, and raised livestock. In the home, both contributed to caring for children, completing household chores, and making and mending household items. Generally, this type of sharing continued for thousands of years and in some remote areas of the world remains the modus operandi today (Carnoy, 1999; Galliano, 2003). One contributing factor to the division of labor by gender was the industrial revolution.

The rise of industrialism in the late 18th century created vast social changes, including restructuring of how we work and live in most industrialized nations today. A most significant change was the relocation of the workplace. As urban areas grew, generating job opportunities in manufacturing, work was divided between those who worked in a factory (mostly men) and those who stayed home for household tasks (mainly females). The division of labor by gender during the industrial revolution that placed women in a secondary position in society was a pervasive element that eventually led to calls for equality and set the stage for the first women's movement to gain the right to vote. It should also be mentioned that in some nations at the beginning of the 21st century, women continue to be treated as second-class citizens with few rights.

The division of labor by gender became an accepted way of life in the 20th century and still exists today, as women continue to be viewed as primary caregivers and homemakers. Men, on the other hand, are the breadwinners and head of the household. In effect, women were relegated to a lower status or, as some prefer, a lower position identity. Some women did work in factories and some were employed as secretaries, teachers, and nurses, jobs which met the approval of society as appropriate for women. Men, however, identified more strongly with their work role and forged ahead in leadership roles in industry, government, and civil service. Before World War II, middle-class America endorsed the concept of division of labor by gender (Galliano, 2003).

Shortly after World War II began, however, jobs that were primarily considered as men's work were now being done by females of all ethnicities. Women worked on the production line in manufacturing plants, helped build ships and aircraft, and held management positions as well. But after the war was over in 1945, most women were sent home to resume their household tasks. The prewar trends of gender ideals had been established and were reinforced by white middle-class families that centered their attention on the success of the father's career. The ideal family of the 1950s was portrayed as the attractive housewife appropriately dressed, wearing a neat apron while joyfully involved in household chores. The father in suit and tie returns triumphantly to the ideal suburban home after a day on the job (Coontz, 1997).

Three influential social movements that culminated in the 1970s brought a large number of women back to the workforce: The civil rights movement, anti–Vietnam War protests, and the second wave of the women's movement—all contributed to socioeconomic change. During this period, many families found it necessary to have two paychecks to pay their bills. As a result, women returned to the workforce with career goals of their own. Women workers in other countries also continued to grow; in 1996, women occupied 40% of the industrialized countries' paid workforce. According to the U.S. Bureau of Census in 1998 approximately 60% of the paid workforce in the United States were women (Galliano, 2003).

At the beginning of the 21st century, women continue to struggle for work identity. Phillips and Imhoff (1997), for example, suggest that women have lower career aspirations than do men and take longer to choose a career path, and that men advance faster, further, and earn more pay than do women. According to Wajcman (1998), career-type barriers in the corporate world are perceived differently by men and women. It should not be surprising that women are more concerned about prejudices of colleagues, sexual discrimination and harassment, inflexible work patterns, and difficulty in being accepted in the senior management "club."

On the other hand, women have made progress in pursuing medical degrees. In 2002, 40% of entering medical students in the United States were women compared to only 5.5% in 1950. In the corporate world, however perceptions of effective leadership styles and management approaches have remained solidly masculine (Wajcman, 1998).

Matlin (2004) suggests that the number of women entering professional schools for the study of law and veterinary medicine is increasing but it will be well into the

21st century before they are equally represented. In the meantime we find that women continue to be employed in traditionally female occupations. The U.S. Bureau of Census (1997) reports that the percentage of secretaries who are women is 99%; dental hygienists, 98%; registered nurses, 93%; elementary school teachers, 83%; and social workers, 69%.

In this brief historical summary of gender and work we can gain a fuller understanding of the significant role of gender in career development of both women and men. Although we have emphasized the need for research on shared work roles, differences in gender roles between men and women are significant variables to consider in career choice and in work-related behavior. Currently, we have witnessed some progress for women in the work world but gender stereotyping has remained a deterrent for many.

Special Needs of Women and Men

This section is devoted to some special needs of women and men that currently are relevant in the work environment. Equalization of job opportunities continues to be the goal of contemporary society but women still face significant workplace barriers associated with bias and status level. Men share some special needs with women but both women and men must deal with their own sets of needs. Both shared needs and the somewhat different needs of women and men in contemporary society will be the focus of discussion. First, gender stereotyping will be discussed as a core element that affects behavior of both women and men in multiple roles, including the work role. Next, we summarize fear of femininity and restrictive emotionality associated with men. Third, we discuss sexual harassment in the workplace. Fourth, we summarize problems associated with achievement, competition, and self-destructive behavior. Dual roles for both men and women are covered in the next chapter.

In career counseling, gender role issues often determine the content of intervention strategies. Fear of femininity, for instance, may influence some men to overcompensate by exaggerated masculine behavior. A woman who has been sexually harassed in the workplace may experience periodic episodes of depression. Problems experienced by these clients suggest sets of concerns that require a holistic counseling approach. Counselors not only address situational gender issues but cognitive and behavioral issues as well. In addition counselors may also assume an advocacy role for some situational problems such as sexual harassment in the workplace.

In the following example, a male worker was reported to be experiencing severe symptoms of stress and tension. In the interview the counselor discovered that he was a very aggressive individual who felt he had failed in his job performance because "I am not a good enough man to be successful." His poor self-concept was reinforced when he was not promoted and received a less than average appraisal from his supervisor. After several counseling sessions, it was apparent that this man's work identity and masculinity were being threatened by his interpretation of events and real events in the current work environment. The client admitted that working with others was difficult for him and he may be perceived as someone who would do most anything to get recognition from his supervisor. In essence, he was overly aggressive to the point that he ended up being isolated at work. There were several issues addressed, including fear of femininity, as the driving force behind his actions, his behavior in general, and his need to overcompensate when he felt threatened.

Clearly, men are socialized to identify strongly with their work, thus, failure on the job attacks the core of their masculinity. Be aware that we do not suggest that this is the only need to be addressed in this case, but the root of this client's current problem may be best understood from what he perceives as an appropriate male role. When he was faced with the possibility of not rising to his level of expectation, he was not able to cope with a competitive work environment. His interpersonal skills and cognitive functioning were diminished by his faulty thinking to the point that his behavior became intolerable. The lesson for counselors here is that both external and internal factors are to be evaluated for sources that influence thinking and subsequent behavioral patterns.

The influence of gender socialization is also a most relevant factor in career choice as well as in working relationships and interactions. The next society as identified by Drucker (2002) suggests an increase of shared working roles among women and men. It appears that women and men will continue to have different and same status levels in the workplace in contemporary society. In a future knowledge society, however, more work tasks can be done equally well by both sexes. Gender stereotyping is a significant obstacle in the workplace that needs to be removed to promote shared work roles.

Gender Stereotypes

Gender stereotypes are beliefs that one holds about the characteristics and traits of women and men. Gender stereotypes are also what one perceives as appropriate roles for women and men, whether they are accurate or not. It is a belief system that has been largely internalized by sociocultural contextual interactions. The important point here is that one's beliefs about gender stereotypes are a pervasive influence in the everyday give-and-take of human existence. Matlin (2000), who captures the essence of bias associated with gender stereotyping, states:

> We know that stereotypes simplify and bias the way we think about people who belong to the social categories of female and male. Because of gender stereotypes, we exaggerate the contrast between women and men. We also consider the male experience to be "normal" whereas the female experience is the exception that requires an explanation. We also make biased judgments about females and males—for instance, when we judge whether they are feeling emotional or stressed. (p. 67)

Stereotypical thinking can indeed bias one's perception of appropriate work roles for women and men. Because women and men are once again working side by side in jobs that were once considered for men only, more emphasis needs to be placed on shared roles in counseling approaches. One would not expect such work environments to be completely free of discrimination and sexual harassment even though some progress for equality has been made: Much more needs to be done to debunk stereotypical thinking in the workplace. Very often, bias against women is most prevalent when their competence is evaluated in traditional masculine roles (Eagly, Karau, & Makhijani, 1995).

In the corporate world, for instance, women have difficulty achieving leadership roles. In a survey completed in 1998, only 10% of senior management jobs in the Fortune 500 companies were occupied by women. Only 4% of CEOs and other executive officers were women (Martell, Parker, Emich, & Crawford, 1998). It appears that women continue to be viewed as strong in personal and family roles and are not meant to assume leadership roles, and so the glass ceiling remains in place in corporate America. This so-called glass ceiling is the invisible barrier that blocks women from high-level positions; "sticky floor" is a metaphor for women that are not promoted from low-level assignments (Matlin, 2000). Barriers consist of subtle attitudes and prejudices that have blocked women and minorities from ascending the corporate ladder (Galliano, 2003; Reskin & Pakavic, 1994).

In essence, gender stereotyping promotes the belief that women should be traditionally feminine and men are to be traditionally masculine. In contemporary society, there are inconsistent and mixed messages about traditional roles, but a different message seems to be emerging. The facts are that many women are working outside the home to help maintain a family and others are working because they choose to. We have witnessed a dramatic increase in the number of women who are actively pursuing a career and women who are employed in traditionally male-dominated jobs. Organizations and institutions are searching for ways to promote cooperative working relationships between men and women. The question is how to debunk gender typing and move toward building working relationships in which all participants can experience self-fulfillment (Galliano, 2003; Matlin, 2004).

Gender stereotyping beliefs can be addressed through the medium of faulty conceptions. Counselors should focus on the source of thinking scripts of gender typing and try to restructure and modify cognitive beliefs. Some suggestions are Meichenbaum's (1977) cognitive behavioral modification and cognitive methods used in rational-emotive therapy (Ellis, 1994). Group counseling may include social-skills training, including role play and homework. The primary goal is to have clients examine their beliefs and work through practical problems of gender stereotyping.

Fear of Femininity

Researchers seem to agree that men's fear of being perceived as feminine has been indoctrinated through gender role socialization (Matlin, 2004; O'Neil, 1982, 1990; Solomon, 1982). Some refer to differences in gender role development as a masculine/feminine polarity (Levinson, 1996; Levinson et al., 1978). O'Neil (1982) summarized the roles associated with masculine/feminine polarity. Masculinity is associated with the following:

1. Power; exercising control over others; (being recognized as) a person of strong will; a leader who "gets things done"
2. Strength, bodily prowess, toughness, and stamina to undertake long, grueling work and to endure severe bodily stress without quitting
3. Logical and analytical thought, intellectual competence, understanding of how things work
4. Achievement, ambition, success at work, getting ahead, earning one's fortune for the sake of self and family

Femininity is associated with the following:

1. Weak, frail, submissive, and unassertive behavior; victimized by others who have more power and are ready to use it exploitatively; limited bodily resources to sustain a persistent effort toward valued goals
2. Emotions, intuition; likelihood of making decisions on the basis of feelings rather than careful analysis
3. Building a nest, taking care of needs of husband and children
4. Homosexuality (pp. 21–22)

According to the Levinson research team (Levinson, 1996; Levinson et al., 1978), the integration of masculine/feminine polarity usually is achieved during midlife because younger men tend to identify strongly with the stereotypic masculine characteristics, which are reinforced by cultural conditions. The Levinson studies suggest that evolving tasks in early adulthood make it difficult for men to deviate from learned masculine roles.

Other investigators who have concentrated on problems associated with fear of femininity (Cochran, 1994; O'Neil, 1982, 1990; O'Neil, Good, & Holmes, 1995) suggested that the fear of femininity among men contributes to their obsession with achievement and success and is associated with (1) restrictive self-disclosure (fear their thoughts and actions will be associated with femininity), (2) health problems arising from conflicts, and (3) stress and strain.

Studies of gender differences in self-disclosure in the early 1990s revealed that men tend to avoid emotional intimacy with one another. Furthermore, it was suggested that women were more willing than men were to disclose to intimates. Another conclusion was that fear of femininity is one of the major factors that contributes to men's avoidance of emotional intimacy (Skovholt, 1990). Clearly, the fear of femininity is an appropriate topic for helping men and women to understand effects of their gender role socialization.

Restrictive Emotionality

The fear of being perceived as unmanly makes many men resist being open, honest, and expressive, for such expressions are considered an open admission of vulnerability and loss of the control so important to the masculine role (Matlin, 2004; Rabinowitz & Cochran, 1994). O'Neil, Good, and Holmes (1995) believed that restrictive emotionality is one of the leading causes of poor interpersonal relationships between men, between men and women, and between men and children. These authors suggest that men and women have developed two different styles and levels of communication: Men de-emphasize interpersonal relationships in communication, whereas women tend to be more expressive and more concerned with interpersonal processes. Different levels and styles of communication can lead to misunderstandings and conflicts in many social situations, including interactions at home and in the workplace.

Emotional expression and self-disclosure have long been viewed as serious problems for some men (Matlin, 2004; Skovholt, 1990). The expression of grief, pain, or weakness is perceived to be especially unmanly. It appears that some men have been socialized to believe that restricting their display of emotions is a signal to others of their strong masculinity. In numerous situations, however, it sends a different and disturbing message of not caring, a lack of interest or commitment, and/or complete disregard for others. Relationships typically are built on trust, caring, and sharing among other involvements and commitments. The inability to communicate emotional feelings can have an adverse affect on interpersonal relationships.

Fear of femininity and emotionally restrictive behavior are primarily attributed to gender role socialization. Being perceived as weak, frail, or emotional suggests that one is not manly enough to achieve and be successful. Suggestions to help men modify effects of socialization include cognitive-behavioral techniques such as restructuring, reframing, and modeling. Men also may benefit from group counseling with focus on expressive and assertiveness training. The primary goal here is to change rigid gender role masculine behavior.

Sexual Harassment

The issue of sexual harassment has been well documented in the workplace for several years. For example, in 1980 the Working Women's Institute concluded that sexual harassment was the single most widespread occupational hazard women face in the workforce (Lott, 1994). The attention given to sexual harassment was dramatically increased by (1) the 1991 Senate hearings involving Supreme Court nominee Clarence Thomas and his accuser, Anita Hill; and (2) the U.S. Navy Tailhook scandal involving the mistreatment of women by U.S. Navy personnel.

What constitutes sexual harassment has been the central issue of several court cases. The "reasonable woman" standard was applied as the appropriate legal criterion for determining whether sexual harassment had occurred: If a reasonable woman would consider behavior offensive even though a man would not, the court would rule that sexual harassment had occurred (Fitzgerald & Ormerod, 1991). Sexual harassment does indeed occur, according to Barnett and Rivers (1996) (cited in Peterson & Gonzalez, 2000); more than 50% of working women will experience sexual harassment in their jobs. Other factors used to determine when a behavior is considered offensive are (1) if the behavior was judged extreme, (2) if the victim was responsible for what happened, (3) if the perpetrator was a direct supervisor of the victim, and (4) if there was significant frequency of occurrence (Kail & Cavanaugh, 1996, 2004).

In a *Newsweek* poll in October 1992 (Lott, 1994), 21% of women respondents claimed they had been harassed, and 42% said they knew someone who had. Rider (2000) suggests that roughly two thirds of women report some form of sexual harassment at work. Some descriptions of harassment are sexual remarks, suggestive looks, deliberate touching, pressure for dates, letters and calls, pressure for sexual favors, and actual or attempted rape. Beginning more than two decades ago, many large organizations developed policies, procedures, and programs to define sexual harassment, to decide what to do about it, and to determine how to prevent it. In June 1992, 81% of Fortune 500 companies offered their employees sensitivity training programs designed to make them more aware of acts that constitute sexual harassment (Lott, 1994).

In the late 1990s, Fernandez (1999) developed training programs that are needed to enhance gender relations in corporate America. Aamodt (1999) and Galliano (2003) also suggested that sensitivity training to eliminate sexual harassment in the workplace should be a primary target of employers. These recommendations are based on data that reveals that sexual harassment affects all levels of the workforce. In a national survey completed in 1996, for example, 79% of female physicians reported being sexually harassed in medical school (Dickstein, 1996). In blue-collar jobs, women of color consider harassment to be a major problem (Ragins & Scandura, 1995). It appears obvious that sexual harassment continues to be a problem in the workplace that must be addressed to make certain women have equal access to employment and career advancement.

In essence, sexual harassment consists of unwelcome sexual overtures or requests for sexual favors. A legal term used in sexual harassment is *quid pro quo,* which indicates some type of reward is offered for sexual favors. This kind of behavior creates an offensive and hostile work environment and is most demeaning to women. In many organizations today, sexual harassment awareness and prevention is a part of incoming training for new staff. In addition, ongoing sensitivity training programs include such topics as how people respond to being touched when engaged in a conversation, what is considered as offensive physical contact, cultural differences in physical contact, and inappropriate verbal statements and comments about physical appearance. The major goal here is to promote appropriate interactions between women and men in the workplace (Muchinsky, 2003).

Achievement, Competition, and Self-Destructive Behavior

In the contemporary workforce, men and women will both face events and conditions that are stressful. The fact is they are likely to experience some of the same problems and concerns in the workplace. Some examples include the need to achieve and succeed, deal appropriately with competition, and be able to relax while participating in leisure activities. The rationale here is that when women and men experience highly competitive and demanding work environments, they will develop similar stressful conditions and reactions. Men, however, have been the main focus of research dealing with achievement, competition, leisure, and self-destructive behavior. More recently, women have been studied to determine their reactions to these factors (Schafer, 2000).

As early as the 1990s, Russo, Kelly, and Deacon (1991) suggested that men are conditioned to perceive career success and achievement as primary measurements of manhood and masculinity. These researchers suggested that a man's work represents his status in society and is the primary base for measuring success over the life span. Basow (1992) pointed out that men are conditioned to be overly competitive, ambitious, and status-seeking because these are the qualities associated with successful men. In other words, men validate their masculinity through competition at work. Intense competition among men in the workplace can result in some men being very reluctant to be honest with their peers, and subsequently they have difficulty in developing interpersonal relationships. Hence, intense competition among men and between men and women may be highly related to stressful work environments and work anxiety (Lowman, 1993; O'Neil, 1982; O'Neil, Good, & Holmes, 1995). The point here is that both men and women experience work-related stress including occupational insecurity, especially during economic downturns.

Closely related to issues of dealing with competition are behaviors that lead to health care problems. One pattern of work overcommitment is the widely studied Type A behavioral pattern. Friedman and Rosenman (1974), and in the 1990s Strube (1991), conceptualized a model of how men behave in the workplace and designated the two masculine styles of functioning as Type A and Type B. Type A persons have an accelerated overall lifestyle, with involvement in multiple functions. They are over-committed to their vocations or professions, have an intense drive to achieve, and develop feelings of guilt when relaxing. Other characteristics include excessive drive, impatience, competitiveness, restlessness; abrupt speech; nervous gestures; and rapid walking, eating, and moving. Type B persons are the opposite. They are characterized as being serene, having the ability to relax, and lacking a sense of time urgency.

According to Thompson, Grisanti, and Pleck (1987), there is more Type A behavior in males than in females. Greenglass (1991), however, found that professional women were predominantly Type A. Type A behavior has been linked to cardiovascular problems; workers who experience stress may have a higher rate of heart disease than non–Type A workers (Baker, Dearborn, Hastings, & Hamberger, 1988; Houston & Kelly, 1987). A five-year study at the Duke University Medical Center found that mental stress could hold the key to future heart problems. The major conclusion was not surprising—reducing abnormal responses to mental stress can lead to a reduction of cardiac problems (Jiang et al., 1996).

In the workplace, Type A individuals have an intense sense of time urgency and attempt to participate in most tasks, job assignments, and events that are ongoing in the work environment. Type A individuals give the impression that they can meet all challenges and successfully cope with any challenge, especially at work. Schafer (2000) suggests that a Type A personality pattern includes most of the following: Insecurity status, time urgency, hyperaggressiveness, free-floating hostility, and the drive toward self-destruction. In addition, Type A behavior characterizes women as well as men in our society. He points out that there has been a sharp rise in Type A behavior among women since the 1970s.

In the 1980s, Braiker (1986) suggested that contemporary women who work and live under excessive stressful conditions are more accurately described by what she coined as Type E. She distinguishes Type A from Type E by suggesting that achievement-oriented women experience stressful conditions not only in their career but also in their personal life. Type E women have the tendency to become involved in numerous activities to the point of role overload. Braiker (1986) characterizes Type E women as needing to do things perfectly, being overly concerned to please others, having a strong need to prove self to everyone, wanting to have it all, striving to get people to need them, having difficulty in relaxing, and demonstrating a strong desire to be everything to everybody.

Cognitive restructuring is often suggested as an effective intervention to modify Type A behavior. The following recommendation could also be used as an intervention strategy for women who are identified with Type E behavior patterns. In cognitive restructuring, individuals learn to recognize behaviors that are self-destructive by acknowledging unrealistic and irrational beliefs that have reinforced their Type A and Type E behavior patterns. Counseling sessions, designed to promote cognitive restructuring, help individuals identify anxiety-arousing situations so they can take steps to modify their behavior (Doyle, 1998). Relaxation training, developed by Wolpe (1958), is another method of helping Type A individuals deal with anxieties. Other suggestions include stress-management methods related to time management, use of constructive self-talk for building self-esteem and reducing anger, and redefining role requirements (Braiker, 1986; Schafer, 2000).

In sum, this chapter introduces some sets of problems and concerns associated with gender issues that influence behavior of women and men in multiple life roles. The focus of concerns has been devoted to career development, career choice, and work-related issues. Career counselors, however, recognize that they are to address the needs of the total person, including multiple roles. Gender issues do indeed represent a very pervasive influence in the lives of clients who seek counseling. One core element of gender concerns is gender stereotyping. One's beliefs about gender typing greatly influences career identity, interpersonal relationships, how one communicates, and one's worldview in general. The fear of being perceived as feminine is a driving force behind exaggerated masculinity. Men also fear being perceived as emotional and some have difficulty when interacting with women. Sexual harassment creates offensive and hostile work environments. Organizations provide sensitivity training in an attempt to build more cohesive work relationships. In contemporary workplaces men and women face stressful conditions. The need to achieve, outdo competition, and be considered successful is a driving force for both women and men in the current work world. Closely related to these issues are self-destructive behaviors that can lead to health problems. Learning to deal with stress is an essential task in order to manage all life roles in contemporary society.

The call is for a counseling approach that is sensitive to gender and recognizes that behavior should be studied in gendered contexts (Denmark, 1994). Galliano (2003) also suggests that gender-related norms are best evaluated in situational and contextual interactions between women and men. Of particular interest to counselors are shared work roles and different and same status levels in the workplace. A psychology of gender approach in workplace environments could play a most important role in the future workforce. As Spence (1999) indicated, gender development is a complex process that is both multifaceted and multidimensional.

Intervention Strategies

Intervention strategies should focus on multiple factors associated with gender typing and its effect on career development and multiple life roles. A number of cognitive-behavioral techniques can be used to modify gender stereotypes. Group counseling composed of both women and men can include an almost endless number of components. The following group interventions are representative of activities that can be used to address gender issues.

Intervention Component I—Working Climate

The purpose of this intervention strategy is to prepare both men and women for challenges they may face in work environments. Each individual will face a different set of circumstances, especially those who are required to work in different sites, but there are some general guidelines that are relevant for all. They include: (1) learn effective methods of communicating in work environment that is free of gender role stereotyping, (2) recognize that positions of authority may include both males and females, (3) be prepared to interact with members of both sexes in decision-making groups, (4) develop skills that contribute to good worker-supervisor relationships,

(5) understand the role of the informal group in a typical organization, and (6) learn effective methods of establishing rapport with all peer affiliates.

A combination of role-playing exercises, discussion groups, and effective use of audiovisual material is recommended for accomplishing the specific tasks of this intervention. Some specific tasks are as follows:

1. Identify typical stereotyping of female and male workers in the workplace and illustrate how stereotyping affects work relationships.
2. Clarify competitive nature of working environment especially among knowledge workers of both sexes.
3. Identify and clarify interpersonal skills needed by both men and women in the work environment.
4. Discuss a variety of potential interactions in work settings including shared work roles and power relationships.

Intervention Component II—Expressiveness Training

The two goals of this component are to help clients identify situations in which it is appropriate to express their emotions and to learn that it is acceptable to freely express emotions in those situations. Inexpressiveness can become highly dysfunctional in many relationships, including those with peer affiliates in the work environment, children, spouse, and friends. Self-disclosure may be difficult for some participants who may be especially guarded and not want to reveal any real or imagined weakness to fellow workers. Men as well as women may resist certain cooperative tasks that could expose their vulnerability.

Counselors should recall that some cultural groups, especially Asian Americans and Native Americans, believe that someone who publicly displays emotional responses to be weak or immature. Special consideration should be given to these groups by explaining differences between cultures and American workers who have a European background.

Specific tasks of this intervention strategy follow.

1. Clarify how individual behavior has been shaped through contextual situations and conditions. Explore differences and similarities between men and women.
2. Discuss and illustrate the advantages of expressive behavior and disadvantage of inexpressive behavior.
3. Identify rigid gender roles that affect one's resistance to disclose followed with examples and illustrations.
4. Clarify potential problems of inexpressive behavior at work, in the home, with colleagues, and with friends.
5. Identify and discuss factors that prohibit expressive behavior.
6. Clarify the differences between self-control and inexpressive behavior.
7. Role-play/rehearse expressive behavior.

Intervention Component III—Dual-Career Roles

In this chapter, we acknowledged that an increasing number of women are planning lifelong careers in a wide range of occupations. The fact is, women are giving career development a higher priority than—or at least equal status—to other priorities, such as marriage and family. Dual-career families are becoming less novel in the 2000s, but the increased prevalence of this lifestyle has not been accompanied by changes in values, beliefs, or behavior of many of the men or women in these marriages. Men may have difficulty making the transition from traditional attitudes of man-at-work/woman-at-home to that of negotiating dual-career and family roles. These entrenched attitudes and perceptions of appropriate masculine roles will die slowly because of the long-standing socialization process that has stereotyped gender role models. The process of change requires one to recognize deeply rooted patterns of masculine role behavior and attitudes toward women in general. However, research in the early 1980s and 1990s indicates that when men are challenged to modify their behavior in dual-career families, they change their attitudes and actions (Biernat & Wortman, 1991; Wilcox-Matthew & Minor, 1989). The recent shift of roles in dual-career families gives this intervention component credibility for helping husbands make adjustments in their attitudes toward their wives' career aspirations, demonstrating advantages of fathers' being able to participate in their children's lives more directly, and encouraging men to assume a greater role in household management responsibilities. Women as well as men should learn to understand that modifying gender role behaviors and the thinking process that drives behavior will take cooperation between both spouses.

The specific tasks in this strategy are designed to clarify the concept of dual-career families and to introduce changes in male role models. Special consideration should be given to the task of identifying and clarifying dual-career family problems. Rapoport and Rapoport (1978) captured the essence of dual-career family problems in the 1970s that continue to be relevant: (1) overload dilemmas (the management of household and child-rearing activities), (2) personal norm dilemmas (conflicts arising from what parents consider proper lifestyle and what other individuals consider proper), (3) identity dilemmas (intrinsic conflicts associated with life roles), (4) social network dilemmas (conflicts associated with relatives, friends, and other associates), and (5) role cycle dilemmas (conflicts associated with family life cycles such as birth of a child, a child leaving home, and other domestic issues that produce stress on career development). Suggested solutions include shared responsibility exercises, time-management techniques, and effective planning between parents who have discussed and established individual and family priorities. Shared responsibility and role-coping exercises also can be used in this component.

Specific tasks include:

- Clarify the concept of dual earners and dual careers.
- Clarify how socialization has determined gender roles in our society.
- Clarify the concept of an egalitarian marriage.
- Identify and discuss methods of sharing household management and tasks.
- Clarify how husband and wife can visualize multiple life roles as a joint family effort.
- Identify and clarify changing styles of interaction between spouses who both support dual-career concepts.
- Identify changing attitudes in relation to work and responsibilities in dual-career families.

Intervention Component IV—Lifestyle Skills

To learn that every person is unique and should be considered as an individual who has certain aptitudes, interests, and aspirations is the primary purpose of this intervention strategy. Women especially in developed countries have more control over their lives than ever before. Men are also to determine their lifestyle orientation and preferences in regard to career, family, leisure, place of residence, work climate, and overall style of life. We have not yet reached the ultimate androgynous society and probably never will, but we have taken giant steps away from gender role stereotypes. Specific tasks include the following:

- Explore lifestyle factors of financial orientation including independence and social prominence.
- Discuss benefits derived from participation in community activities and community services.
- Clarify work-related needs of achievement, career development, and commitment.
- Clarify orientation toward family life.
- Explore the reasons for a commitment toward self-improvement through lifelong learning.
- Identify how life roles are interrelated and intertwined.

In sum, what should be communicated is that every person is an individual who has certain strengths and weaknesses and, like everyone else, is unique. The challenge is to clarify individual uniqueness (self-image, skills, and aspirations) and to project those characteristics into all life roles. In this intervention component, special attention is directed toward goal setting from an individualized frame of reference. Clarifying work identity, free of sex-role stereotyping, along with individual strengths and weaknesses is to be fostered. Learning to be assertive and not overly aggressive is an important lifestyle skill. One's individuality could be explored through discussing background experiences, including those contextual interactions involving family, peers, school, and other life events. Finally, gender issues are to be viewed as important constructs to be addressed in one's worldview.

Summary

1. Women are reassessing their career priorities and are looking beyond the traditional feminine working roles. Even though women are being given greater opportunities to expand their career choices, barriers to the changing role of women in the working world still exist.

2. In response to the women's movement, men are reexamining their roles, beliefs, and relationships with women. The Society for the Psychological Study of Men and Masculinity, Division 51 of the American Psychological Association, was formed to study gender role and masculinity. Other groups with a variety of agendas have formed.

3. Super was one of the major career development theorists who addressed career development patterns of women. Ginzberg denoted three lifestyle dimensions—traditional, transitional, and innovative—in career counseling approaches for women. Zytowski labeled vocational developmental patterns of women as mild vocational, moderate vocational, and unusual vocational. Sanguiliano suggested that a woman's life cycle does not follow a rigid progression of developmental tasks and that attention should focus on unique paths women take to break away from gender role stereotyping. Spencer supported Sanguiliano's denial that

women's development follows the rigid progression suggested by life-stage theorists. Spencer contended that feminine developmental tasks are unlike masculine tasks and that women follow a unique pattern of development. Chusmir suggested that personality and motivational traits of women who choose nontraditional occupations are formed by the time they are teenagers. Spence views women's development as multifaceted and multidimensional.

4. Counselors must be aware of unique influences that shape gender role development. Cultural groups have some special needs that must be addressed and individual differences within groups must be recognized.

5. Each individual is influenced by a number of specific cultural and situational factors that contribute to gender stereotyping. Tentative gender boundaries are established in childhood. Gender role is intensified in adolescence. It is not certain how and to what extent gender differences remain stable among adults.

6. The division of labor by gender is attributed to the industrial revolution. Men became the primary breadwinner and women caregivers. In World War II women took over jobs that traditionally were reserved for men. After the war they were sent home to continue as primary caregivers. The second wave of the women's movement paved the way for women to return to the workforce in large numbers. Currently, women have made great progress but gender stereotyping has remained a deterrent for many.

7. Some special needs of women and men are gender stereotyping beliefs; fear of femininity and restrictive emotionality among men; sexual harassment of women in the workplace; and problems for both men and women associated with achievement, competition, and self-destructive behavior.

8. Counseling approaches should be free of gender role typing. Counseling strategy components include working climate, expressiveness training, dual-career, and lifestyle skills.

Supplementary Learning Exercises

1. Develop a scenario that demonstrates gender role stereotyping in a work setting. Present it to the class for critique.

2. Interview a woman and a man who currently hold nontraditional jobs. Summarize the problems they have faced and their recommendations to others

3. While observing several television programs, develop a list of characters that represent dimensions of gender role appropriate behavior.

4. List your experiences in school and home that influenced gender role appropriate behavior. Compare and discuss your list with classmates.

5. Develop a counseling component that is designed to help women and men recognize stereotyping in the work environment.

6. Visit a women's and men's center and obtain descriptions of career-related counseling programs. Summarize your findings and point out the potential use of these centers as a referral source.

7. Interview a self-employed woman and man. Focus on the problems they have encountered. Compare responses and draw conclusions.

8. Develop an intervention that focuses on gender typing that could be used in group counseling programs composed of women and men.

9. Make a list of barriers that currently block minorities from advancing to higher-level jobs. Compare and discuss results with classmates.

10. Develop counseling strategies that could be used to help women and men deal with self-destructive behavior.

For More Information

Bronstein, P., & Quina, K. (2003). *Teaching gender and multicultural awareness: Resources for the psychology classroom*. Washington, DC: American Psychological Association.

Eccles, J. S., Barber, B., & Jozefowicz, D. (1999). Linking gender to educational, occupational, and recreational choices: Applying the Eccles et al. model of achievement-related choices. In W. B. Swann, J. H. Langlois, & L. A. Gilbert (Eds.), *Sexism and stereotypes in modern society* (pp. 153–192). Washington, DC: American Psychological Association.

Foote, W. E., & Goodman-Delahunty, J. (2004). *Evaluating sexual harassment: Psychological, social, and legal considerations in forensic examinations*. Washington, DC: American Psychological Association.

Galliano, G. (2003). *Gender: Crossing boundaries.* Belmont, CA: Wadsworth/Thomson Learning.

Geary, D. C. (1998). *Male, female: The evolution of human sex differences.* Washington, DC: American Counseling Association.

Hansen, L. S. (1997). *Integrative life planning: Critical tasks for career development and changing life patterns.* San Francisco: Jossey-Bass.

Matlin, M. W. (2004). *The psychology of women.* Belmont, CA: Wadsworth/Thomson Learning.

Nelson, D. L., & Burke, R. J. (Eds.) (2002). *Gender, work stress, and health.* Washington, DC: American Psychological Association.

Rider, E. A. (2000). *Our voices: Psychology of women.* Pacific Grove, CA: Wadsworth.

Spence, J. T. (1999). Thirty years of gender research: A personal chronicle. In W. B. Swann, J. H. Langlois, & L. A. Gilbert (Eds.) (1999). *Sexism and stereotypes in modern society* (pp. 255–290). Washington, DC: American Psychological Association.

Suggested InfoTrac College Edition Topics

Counseling men	Masculinity
Counseling women	Men's movement
Feminist movement	Psychology of gender
Gender and work	Sexual harassment
Gender bias	Women and work
Gender stereotypes	Women's movement
Gendered society	

Special Issues in Family Systems Featuring Issues of Dual Careers

12

Chapter Highlights

- How to identify the nuclear and extended family

- Current trends of change in family systems and family relationships

- Case example of a dual-career couple in conflict

- Issues facing dual-career families

- Implications for career counseling

- Appropriate counseling interventions for the case example

THE FAMILY'S INFLUENCE on career development has been a significantly relevant issue for a number of career development theorists. Roe (1956) and Roe and Lunneborg (1990) stand out as pioneers in directing considerable attention to the developmental period of early childhood in their study of parent–child relations. Super (1990) projected the homemaker role as a major life role in the life-span, life-space approach to career. In the late 1990s, Gottfredson's (1996) treatise on sex role orientation emphasizes the role of family influence. Mitchell and Krumboltz (1996) suggest that environmental conditions and events are factors that influence career paths. In sociological perspectives on work and career development, family effects on career development are considered a major variable: "The focus is on how family structure (intact, not intact) and maternal work roles influence development of work-related attitudes and choices of youth" (Hotchkiss & Borow, 1996, p. 284). Goldenberg and Goldenberg (2002), Berns (2004), and Matlin (2004) among others continue to emphasize the family's influence on career and life role development.

Many other factors of parental actions and behaviors—such as parents' expectations for their children's success and parents' perceptions of their children's competence, interests, skills, and activities (Eccles, 1993)—are potential causal factors of career development. These examples, among others, suggest that more emphasis should be given to the study of familial variables to determine the degree to which these variables affect career development. As we begin the 21st century, we are encountering a different world in which traditional family systems have been altered, transformed, and reconstituted. Furthermore, determining the degree to which such variables as single parents, dual-worker parents, divorce, and remarriage shape career development is a challenge for professionals from several academic disciplines. Changes in family systems suggest that career development might also be changing its course. To fully delineate career development, the career counseling profession will likely require a closer alliance with other academic disciplines that view the work role as a pervasive variable in the lives of current and future generations.

In recent years, both parents often have to work to fulfill financial responsibilities, but it also should be recognized that many women choose to work and pursue a career. In greater numbers, women are assuming the dual role of homemaker and worker. Families in which both parents work are referred to as either dual-career or dual-earner households. Both types share some common goals and common issues. The term *dual-career* is usually reserved for families in which both spouses hold professional, managerial, or technical jobs. Most of our discussion will be devoted to dual-career families.

As more women have changed roles, men also have changed by assuming a larger share of the homemaker role. But sharing responsibilities, particularly in the home, has caused role conflicts. In this chapter, we will discuss some aspects of family dynamics in a changing world and the challenges that face couples in dual-career roles. More specifically, in the first part of the chapter we discuss the family as a system and some aspects of family relationships, including culturally different families. In the second part of the chapter, issues facing dual-career families, some of which relate to dual-earner families, are covered. Finally, implications for career counseling are presented.

The Family as a System

In this chapter, the family is conceptualized as a social system. Any system, whether a corporation, a city government, or a family, comprises interdependent elements that have interrelated functions and share some common goals. In this perspective, we view individuals in families as interconnected elements, each of whom contributes to the functioning of the whole. Thus, we cannot wholly understand the system by focusing on the component parts because each is affected by every other part; the relationships of those parts result in a larger coherent entity. Families are viewed as composites of many factors, such as genetic heritage from parents that are passed on to their children; members share common experiences and develop common perspectives of the future. The family system is embedded in larger social systems. The nuclear family, most common in the United States, consists of husband/father, wife/mother, and at least one child. The extended family, the most common form around the world, is one in which parents and their children live with other kin. The sequences of changes in families are referred to as family life cycles.

In this respect, the family itself is also a developing organism of roles and relationships that occur over the family life cycle (Kail & Cavanaugh, 2004; Shaffer, 2002). Rowland (1991) and Shaffer (2002) among others point out that an increasing number of people do not experience the traditional family life cycle; social changes have altered the makeup of the typical family in a changing world. Sigelman and Rider (2003) suggest that the following trends of change in family systems alter the quality of family experience.

1. More single adults. Although more adults are staying single, more than 90% of today's young adults are expected to marry eventually.
2. Postponement of marriage. More adults are delaying marriage. The average age at first marriage for men is 26 and for women, 24.
3. Fewer children. The average number of children in U.S. families is 1.8. Adults are waiting longer to have children, and increasing numbers of young women are choosing to remain childless.
4. More women working. About 12% of married women with children under age 6 worked outside the home in 1950; the figure increased by the early 1990s to 57% and to 62% in 2000.
5. More divorce. As many as 4 out of 10 newlyweds are expected to divorce.
6. More single-parent families. Twenty-three percent of children under the age of 18 in 1998 lived only with their mothers and 4% only with their fathers.
7. More children living in poverty. The increasing number of single-parent families has led to the increase in numbers of impoverished children. Today, nearly 1 in 5 children in the United States live in homes below the poverty level.
8. More remarriages. Most divorced individuals are remarrying. About 25% of U.S. children will spend some time in a reconstituted family, usually consisting of a parent, a stepparent, and children from another marriage.
9. More years without children. Adults are spending more of their later years without children in their homes for the following reasons: Some who divorce do not remarry, people are living longer, and couples bear children in a shorter time span.
10. More multigeneration families. Because people tend to live longer, more children establish relationships with grandparents, and some with great-grandparents. Parent–child relationships last longer, some for 50 years or more.

These trends of change in family systems pose some interesting questions concerning career development. For example, will perceptions of life roles, including the work role, be altered? What impact will family transitions have on career development? Several researchers found that some aspects of men's behaviors in the home appear crucial to a child's developing self-concepts. Moreover, fathers in dual-career families are likely to model less stereotypic behaviors, thus providing children with a more positive role of being involved in parenting. Also, observing women as economically independent and having more choices and opportunities influences children's perceptions of what women can do and become. The point is that although these trends might not have negative effects on images that children form about career and life roles, counselors need to remain aware of potential causal factors that contribute to and influence career development in these rapidly changing times (Galliano, 2003; Gilbert, 1993).

Family Relationships

Mothers traditionally have been the primary caregivers for children. But recent research indicates that mother–child relationships cannot be understood fully without considering the father's influence (Shaffer, 2002). Both parents indirectly affect their children through their own interactions—the way in which they influence each other. For example, mothers who experience a supporting relationship with their husbands tend to respond to children in a more sensitive manner (Cox, Owen, Henderson, & Margand, 1992; Newman & Newman, 2003). Fathers, on the other hand, are likely to become more involved with their children when their wives suggest that they have an important role in their children's lives (Goldenberg & Goldenberg, 2002; Palkovitz, 1984). Thus, as one would suspect, mothers, fathers, and children all affect one another in the socialization process.

The previous discussion of changing family systems suggests that U.S. children are being reared in a diversity of environments: in single-parent families, reconstituted families, and multigeneration families. Many other variables within family structures also account for more diversity, such as poverty or the number of children within a family system. Therefore, it is difficult to predict or develop a profile of a successful marriage for these diverse groups; however, longevity of marriage appears to have at least some relationship to marital satisfaction. Kail and Cavanaugh (2000) suggest that marital satisfaction is highest at the beginning, drops in satisfaction when children leave home, and rises in later life. Figure 12-1 illustrates the level of overall marital satisfaction from start of marriage to retirement from work.

Lauer and Lauer (1986) interviewed women and men who had been married at least 15 years and compiled their reasons for staying married. The first seven responses were the same for both men and women, and they are listed here in order of frequency: (1) My spouse is my best friend; (2) I like my spouse as a person; (3) Marriage is a long-term commitment; (4) Marriage is sacred; (5) We agree on aims and goals; (6) My spouse has grown more interesting; and (7) I want the relationship to succeed (p. 385).

In dual-career marriages the degree of marital satisfaction is related to agreement between the husband's and wife's attitudes and aspirations (Newman & Newman, 2003). The way conflicts are expressed and negotiated and the manner in which resources are shared appear to be strong binding forces. Not surprisingly, couples that have more traditional sex role attitudes tend to experience greater stress in a dual-career marriage. This conclusion supports Gilbert's (1993) and Matlin's (2004) findings on dual-career families. For instance, husbands who witnessed their fathers truly involved in family work were more comfortable in assuming family roles.

Culturally Diverse Families

Counselors also are to be sensitive to the values and traditions of culturally diverse families. Significant diversity among ethnic groups greatly contributes to attitudes, values, behavior patterns, and acceptable roles of family members. A historical conti-

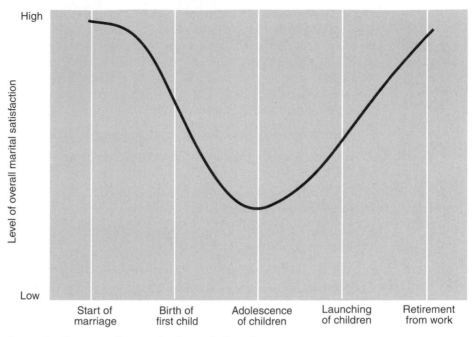

Figure 12-1   Level of overall marital satisfaction

Source: From *Human development: A lifespan view,* 3rd ed., by R. V. Kail/Cavanaugh. © 2004 Reprinted with permission of Brooks/Cole, a part of The Thomson Corporation.

nuity of unique roles by ethnic groups shapes family identities. Ethnicity therefore is a powerful driving force in determining the rules, rituals, and esprit de corps of family members. Understanding the family context provides clues for each individual's unique development.

The point is made several times in this text that there are significant differences within groups. This position is especially important when counseling members of culturally diverse groups. Counselors are to remain alert to a client's unique social system of rules and roles of her or his ethnic group. We can expect to find clients who have different levels and degree of assimilation into dominant middle-class society. Some will maintain their family roles, whereas others may alter their views of traditional roles. In essence, all families are not alike. The roles and rules of family life may differ from culture to culture and family to family.

The work role of culturally diverse individuals especially is shaped by differing worldviews. In collectivist societies of Africans, Asians, and Hispanics, it is expected and accepted that all members of a family contribute to its welfare and survival: Individual aspirations are secondary. Consequently, providing career counseling approaches that include family and family needs are often most effective. In other words, counselors may find it to be very productive to also discuss an individual's career concerns with some family members.

In Asian and Hispanic families, husbands typically are head of the family and the family usually maintains strong traditional gender roles, including stereotypical male–female relationships. There are more women who are head of the family in

African American homes and who assume the role of primary breadwinner. Behavior, conduct, and family roles in most culturally diverse groups are also influenced by religious issues. All of these factors can affect an individual family member's approach to work roles. To put their counseling needs in perspective, some problems members of culturally diverse families have and will face are listed here as adapted from Goldenberg and Goldenberg (2002). The following can serve as a check list when evaluating potential conflicts with members of culturally diverse families.

Effects of poverty (poor housing, lack of transportation, and health care)

Country of origin (language barrier, work role perceptions, and view of government)

Circumstances of immigration (political oppression and lack of trust for governmental agencies)

Degree of acculturation (worldviews, conflicting messages of appropriate behavior, and perception of work role)

Spiritual beliefs (family roles, health care issues, and social activities)

Skin color (discrimination and exclusion from some work roles)

Feelings of powerlessness (lack of direction and difficulty adjusting to new environment)

Poor self-esteem (depression, restriction of job choice, and interpersonal relationships)

Lack of trust of institutions (resist using agencies for assistance)

English fluency (restricted job choice and limited personal contacts)

Intergenerational family conflicts (conflicts over parents' view of appropriate behavior and contemporary views of the host country)

Lack of support in community (isolation and restricted community involvement)

Discrimination (feelings of oppression, isolation, and restricted career choice)

Socioeconomic status (exclusion of opportunities in life, work, and leisure)

In sum, families in cultural transition may experience stress associated with coping with the demands and mores of the dominant society. For immigrants, the first priority is to find work that will maintain their family. Many individual family members do not view career choice as their own. On the other hand, many culturally diverse families have resided in this country for several generations and have adopted some of the dominant society's rules and roles. They continue to struggle for acceptance and the opportunity for career advancement and recognition. Some still face discrimination and rejection from the dominant society. They often need support and direction for finding solutions to real-life problems. In dealing with complex issues of culturally diverse families, counselors may assume the role of teacher, coach, adviser, advocate, problem solver, and even role model (Goldenberg & Goldenberg, 2002).

In the next section, dual-career families will be discussed, but first we review a case example of a dual-career couple in conflict.

Case 12-1 A Dual-Career Couple in Conflict

A conversation between a hair stylist and her customer went something like this:

CUSTOMER: I just don't know how Jose and I can keep our sanity. He is gone most of the time, and now I have to leave for a few weeks. I hope the children will be okay.

STYLIST: Both of you sure travel a lot. I know Jose flies to New Orleans every week and now you are going overseas. When do you do fun things?

CUSTOMER: Fun things!! What's that?? All we ever do is argue about who is supposed to do what at the house and with the children.

STYLIST: You know, Maria, you have been telling me the same story every week. And I think you are depressed over the whole situation. I do hope you and Jose can work something out.

The customer, a married woman named Maria, has two children, ages 9 and 5. The family lives in a fashionable home in an exclusive neighborhood. Almost everyone but the stylist viewed Maria's and Jose's relationship as dynamic and exciting because of their prestigious career positions. Although their marriage situation is unusual in a number of ways, Maria was expressing typical problems associated with dual-career marriages.

Maria was reared on the West Coast with two siblings. Both parents were professionals. Her mother was a medical doctor specializing in internal medicine, and her father was an electrical engineer who had established his own consulting firm. Maria recalls that even though her parents were very busy with their careers, they made time for their children. They had a maid who also served as their nanny when they were small, but both parents shared in household tasks and driving Maria and her playmates to fun places.

Maria is now an internationally known architect employed by a prestigious international firm based in Phoenix. She is very pleased with her current position. Her husband, Jose, is a college professor currently employed at a university in a southern state more than 1,000 miles from their home. Jose flies to his job every week, leaving on Monday and returning on Friday. He now has tenure and does not want to give up his current position.

Jose and Maria moved to Phoenix when a position opened in an architectural firm. Jose decided that if someone had to travel on a regular basis, it should be him. When Jose is asked about this decision, he usually replies, "It's best for the kids to have their mother with them." Maria is not particularly pleased with this response, however, as it indicates that Jose doesn't recognize her achievements and the fact that she had been selected after a highly competitive search by the firm. By his response, Jose seems to ignore the fact that she receives more than three times his pay and that they had agreed that most of her earnings would be set aside for the children's education. Maria doesn't expect Jose to tell every casual acquaintance about all these details, but she does expect more of an appreciation for a mutual decision that had been thoroughly discussed and agreed on. Jose, on the other hand, feels that Maria overlooks his traveling time and the hardships associated with it. Maria seems to view his position as just another professor's job that is relatively unimportant.

The conversation in the salon continued:

STYLIST: I don't believe your husband gives you credit for all you have done.

MARIA: Well, sometimes he does, but it seems harder for him to express those kinds of feelings.

STYLIST: Why can't he do that? Why doesn't he just say it?

MARIA: Hmm . . . that's something I have to think about.

On the way home, Maria was worried. She was now having difficulty with her oldest son, who is losing interest in all school subjects. At home, he has refused to obey her on a number of occasions. When she discussed this situation with her mother by phone, Maria got the usual response: "Maybe you should give more attention to your children." Jose grew up in a midwestern state with three siblings. Jose's father was a corporate lawyer who had built a reputable practice. His mother was a homemaker who had no intentions of working outside the home. Jose recalls the scrumptious meals his mother would prepare and that she always seemed to be there when he needed her. Jose's relationship with his father was one of respect, but there was never much affection expressed between the two, and his father was often too busy to spend time with him and his siblings. Jose describes his family system as a traditional one.

Jose and Maria met in graduate school. After a courtship of two years, they became engaged and were married soon after graduation. They lived in the Northwest and on the Atlantic coast. They moved to Jose's New Orleans teaching location when a position opened. Each move was made to improve Jose's career. Maria had taken jobs in nearby cities in each location, and her growing reputation as an outstanding architect finally gave her the opportunity to take "the job of a lifetime," and so the family moved to Phoenix.

It was Friday, and Jose was on his way home for the weekend. He had invited one of his male colleagues, Bob, to join him. They had planned for time to prepare a research project.

BOB: Jose, this is a nice flight, but doesn't it get tiresome to do this every week?

JOSE: I'm used to it by now, but I have to admit that there are times I would much prefer to stay at home. Actually, it's not the flight as much as it is the nights away from home that bother me.

BOB: Well, I hated to see you move. I still don't know why you had to do it.

JOSE: Maria just had to have this job, and I guess I had to cave in just this once. But I hope you understand that I get my way most of the time. Anyway, let's start talking over our plans for this research project. You know, Bob, I think this project could get us an international reputation.

The first year in Phoenix was a relatively happy one, as Maria tried her best to take most of the responsibility of managing the household. During the second year, Jose began to argue about household tasks and spending time with the children on weekends, and he often refused to attend business-related events with Maria's firm. The small arguments seemed to get bigger, and Jose was often irritable. Both Jose and Maria felt they had reached a crucial stage in their marriage.

The next section addresses issues facing dual-career families. As you read this section, identify issues and potential sources of problems Maria and Jose were experiencing in their marriage. Following this discussion is a summary of Maria's and Jose's case.

Issues Facing Dual-Career Families

The following issues are representative of current problems found among dual-career families, some of which apply to dual-earner families as well. This relatively new family structure was brought to the attention of researchers by the studies of British university graduates in the 1970s by Rapoport and Rapoport (1978). Following their work, many studies involving dual-career families contained serious methodological limitations, such as focusing on women only and using only academics as samples (Herr & Cramer, 1996). Nevertheless, the following issues emerged as potential career counseling concerns and have been refined by a number of current studies of dual-career families by Galliano (2003), Goldenberg & Goldenberg (2002), Coltrane (2000), and Matlin (2004) among others.

Expectations and Intentions of Work and Family

In a study of university students, Gilbert (1993) found that young women and men reared in dual-career families were highly committed to a role-sharing marriage. In other words, children raised in dual-career families were more likely to develop positive views of integrating occupation and family work. This contrasts with the usual situation in traditional family structures, where the husband assumes the primary employment role and home roles are assumed by the wife.

These findings suggest that the kind and type of role sharing observed in the childhood home by both women and men greatly influence their expectations of roles in marriage. Silberstein (1992) and Goldenberg and Goldenberg (2002) argue that a lack of agreement between expectations of roles in marriage has the potential to create interpersonal tension. The point is that role overload typically occurs between spouses when family roles are not clearly defined. For example, if the husband's occupational role is assumed to be primary, or if a wife views the husband's employment as a less important career, there is a greater potential for minimal sharing of household work. Currently, men seem to be more willing to participate in household tasks than in the past. Partners appear to benefit from relationships of sharing, which contribute to feelings of equity in multiple roles.

Role Conflict

Role conflict is generally thought of as a system of competing demands from different roles; in the case of the dual-career family, the conflict is between family roles and work roles. Society generally has viewed the woman as the primary homemaker. The division of labor between spouses usually results in negotiating family roles, which are more complex when the family responsibilities include child care. When a husband neglects household tasks, his wife may experience role overload. Role conflict is likely when husbands or both husbands and wives believe that men should continue to fulfill the traditional role of family breadwinner.

Evidence in the 1990s suggests that role conflict and role overload were decreasing somewhat in dual-career families; men seemed to be increasingly willing to share in household tasks and in child care (Dancer & Gilbert, 1993). In the beginning of the 21st century, Goldenberg and Goldenberg (2002) report that men continue to assist in child care and household tasks in dual-career families. Some evidence also supports the position that, in heterosexual marriages, African American and Hispanic American men tend to spend more time doing household tasks than do European American men (Shelton & John, 1993). Although women have been somewhat relieved of household tasks during the past three decades, they continue to do the most work and assume the most responsibility for household tasks (Kail & Cavanaugh, 2004).

Klinger (1988) developed a model designed to delegate household tasks based on interests, aptitudes, and time available. This flexible model provides for changes in tasks and in who performs them as the situation or as economic factors change. It also addresses the fact that some tasks may be viewed as more desirable than others, so that the most-preferred and least-preferred tasks should be rotated between the spouses. The last part of the model provides for a "recycling" that ensures an equitable division of labor. Although this model was developed in the late 1980s, it appears to be relevant for dual-career families today.

Part I—Formulate list of household tasks.

Part II—Agree on the frequency of the tasks (daily, biweekly, weekly, monthly, annually).

Part III—Agree on the person(s) responsible for accomplishing the task (considering each person's available time, interest, abilities). Highly desirable or highly undesirable tasks are rotated.

Part IV—Review of the tasks to determine the following:

    a. Did the person(s) designated perform the task?

    b. Was the task viewed as satisfactorily completed?

    c. For "no" responses to questions a or b, what were the obstacles to completing the task?

    d. What additional resources (time, dollars, people, or other factors) are needed to complete the task successfully?

Part V—Recycle: Add or delete tasks, change person(s) responsible for completing task if changes are necessary to maintain the perception of both persons that the division of labor is equitable.

This model can also be adapted to include child care. When the couple begins using the model, both partners should go through all the stages on a weekly basis. As they become familiar with the model, and if they are generally satisfied, then they can cycle through less frequently. The main determinant in how frequently the process is reviewed should be the level of dissatisfaction: the greater the level of dissatisfaction, the greater the need for the couple to recycle through the process.

Matlin (2004) also suggests that a major problem of dual-earner families is the division of responsibility for a variety of household tasks. She suggests that couples are to develop a list of tasks, including shopping for food, cooking, washing dishes, doing laundry, and paying bills. When the list is completed, couples are to decide which partner has the primary responsibility for each task. This process not only provides a means of negotiating household tasks but also can build the perception of an equitable relationship of sharing family responsibilities.

Child Care

When both parents work, the care of children becomes a critical issue. Because more than half of the mothers in the United States work outside the home, child care has been an increasing concern. According to the National Commission on Children (1993, cited in Newman & Newman, 1995), there has been a steady increase in the use of day care since 1965. Forms of day care used include sitters, day care homes, and relatives. Day care facilities continue to be widely used by dual-earner families in the beginning of the 21st century (Sigelman & Rider, 2003) although the trend of home-based enterprise, which allows time for providing child care in one's home, has increased (Munk, 2000).

Organizations have also recognized the need to provide for child care, and some offer one or more of the following alternatives:

Emergency care: Companies provides temporary care when employees' regular arrangements fail.

Discounts: Organizations arrange for a discount from national day care chains or pay a small portion of the fees.

Vouchers: Some organizations pay subsidies or offer special assistance to some low-paid employees.

Referral services: Organizations may offer employees a list of approved day care centers.

On-site day care: Day care centers are located on the organization's site.

Flexible benefits: Money paid to day care centers is deducted from each employee's salary, thus, it is not considered taxable income.

Some organizations have developed family-oriented work policies that are designed to help dual-career families with child care responsibilities. Most are designed to help parents by offering flexible work policies as follows:

1. Telephone access is an organization's policy that permits parents to make personal calls to their children or receive them.
2. Parental leave is also provided by many organizations. This type of leave is different from maternity leave in that it is primarily for care of children who are seriously ill.
3. Flextime permits parents to choose arrival and departure times within a set range.
4. Flexible work arrangements permit arranging part-time work, job sharing, flexplace work (part of the day at home and part at the office), or telecommuting (work from home or satellite office) (Gilbert, 1993).
5. As reported earlier, home-based enterprises are increasing. One partner or both partners can remain at home to perform certain kinds of work for an organization. Technology has provided the means for home-based work through the use of e-mail, faxing capabilities, and teleconferencing (Munk, 2000).

One of parents' major concerns, however, is the potential negative effects on children who are placed in day care centers. Research in the early 1990s indicated that day care infants were no different from infants who were reared in their homes on mea-sures of cognitive, linguistic, and social development (Clark-Stewart, 1993). In fact, most studies at that time suggested that children benefited from their day care experi-ences (Sigelman & Shaffer, 1995). Because low-quality care was found to be associated with poor outcomes, researchers became more concerned about how to determine quality of care among day care centers (NICHD Early Child Care Research Network, 2000). Research focused on identifying the core elements of high-quality day care centers was reviewed by Shaffer (2002) and has been compiled into characteristics of high-quality infant and toddler day care as reported in Table 12-1.

The information in this table points out that a pleasant, nurturing environment and child care ratio is highly important. Care givers must also be well trained in child development and should be emotionally able to establish relationships with infants. Licensing groups also provide some assurance of the quality of care. A most interest-ing additional finding about child care is the importance of the mother's perception of dual-earner families and work per se. In essence, a mother's positive attitudes about work and mothering are most important to how a child will react to day care center activities. Rightfully so, the pressure of positive day care results should not wholly be the mother's responsibility. Fathers can enhance day care outcomes of their children by showing support and appreciation of their spouses' working and parenting role (Cabrera et al. 2000).

Relationship Factors

A pivotal point in dual-career families is a geographical relocation to enhance the husband's or the wife's career. Clearly, a move could represent a sacrifice by one spouse. According to Silberstein (1992) and Goldenberg and Goldenberg (2002) usu-ally the husband receives the major benefits from geographical moves; however, more couples are deciding to move to favor the wife's career. In some situations, a decision is made to commute so they can maintain their current residence.

Competition between partners in dual-career homes is usually associated with a need to achieve and be recognized. Competition usually emerges when one spouse develops feelings of insecurity or frustration associated with his or her career (Galliano, 2003; Silberstein, 1992). Feelings of competition might not be expressed directly but instead could result in debates about a variety of family or career concerns. For example, the tendency to address the issue of competition indirectly might lead to arguments about such issues as work schedules, vacation schedules, and child care commitments. The view that competition is largely inappropriate can cause dual-career partners to deny or avoid the issue.

Another very important aspect of dual-career relationships is the decision-making process within the family—more specifically, who is empowered to make decisions. This factor seems to boil down to the question of equity in the decision process. For dual-career families, it is particularly important to reach mutual agreement on both major and minor decisions. Otherwise, one partner may feel treated unjustly.

The sharing of decision making and subsequent agreement of common life goals can serve as a foundation of support for family roles. Likewise, the sharing of percep-tions of women's and men's roles in dual-career marriages is considered significantly relevant to how partners combine occupational and family roles (Gallino, 2003; Gilbert, 1993; Matlin, 2004).

Table 12-1	Characteristics of High-Quality Infant and Toddler Day Care
Physical setting	The indoor environment is clean, well-lighted, and ventilated; outdoor play areas are fenced, spacious, and free of hazards; they include age-appropriate implements (slides, swings, sandbox, etc.).
Child:caregiver ratio	No more than three infants or four to six toddlers per adult caregiver.
Caregiver characteristics/ qualifications	Caregivers should have some training in child development and first aid; they should be warm, emotionally expressive, and responsive to children's bids for attention. Ideally, staffing is consistent so that infants and toddlers can form relationships (even attachment relationships) with their caregivers.
Toys/activities	Toys and activities are age appropriate; infants and toddlers are always supervised, even during free play indoors.
Family links	Parents are always welcome, and caregivers confer freely with them about their child's progress.
Licensing	Day-care setting is licensed by the state and (ideally) accredited by the National Family Day Care Program or the National Academy of Early Childhood Programs.

SOURCE: From *Developmental Psychology: Childhood and Adolescence,* 6th ed., by Shaffer. © 2002. Reprinted with permission of Wadsworth, a part of The Thomson Corporation.

As early as the late 1970s, Hall and Hall (1979) suggested four distinct behavior patterns of two-career families: accommodators, adversaries, allies, and acrobats. Each pattern of behavior is distinguished from the other by priorities that partners establish for work and family involvements. Goldenberg and Goldenberg (2002) suggest that the following descriptions of two-career family behavior patterns continue to be relevant in contemporary society.

The *accommodator* relationship is one in which one partner's career involvement is the highest priority and home involvement is the lowest. The other partner has the opposite commitment. This type of relationship may be described as a more traditional one. In an *adversary* relationship both parties give their highest priority to career involvement and little to family and home involvement. This type of family relationship usually leads to competition to achieve and conflicts over child care and other family roles.

When both partners are strongly but equally committed to advancing their careers and their home roles their relationship is referred to as *allies*. Satisfaction and fulfillment, however, primarily comes from a happy family and home life. Finally, the *acrobats* are couples who are also actively committed to career and home roles. They want it all and go all out to become high achievers, have happy children, attend social events, and go to prestigious places for vacations. The acrobats work in harmony to achieve their goals but are not surprisingly subject to role overload.

In sum, in the accommodators' version of dual-career relationships, one partner assumes primary responsibility for family matters while the other focuses on the work role. In most accommodator families men are considered primary breadwinners and women contribute to family income with full- or part-time work outside the home. Their primary role is homemaker. Relationship conflicts are highly probable in an adversary dual-career family. Competition among partners for career advancement and conflicts over which partner assumes family roles can create friction among partners. Allies, however, view their careers as most important and support each other's work role. Family life has a lower priority and these couples may avoid having children. Couples who are described as having a relationship in which they are both highly involved in careers and in family roles are labeled acrobats. They seek the best for themselves and their family and can be subject to work overload.

Other Personal Factors

The need to dominate is a personality factor that influences how partners combine occupational and family roles. Typically, a dominating partner expects the other partner to take a secondary role in career aspirations and subsequent effort, thought, and time relegated to a career. For example, a dominating male may view his spouse as primarily responsible for raising children and the spouse's income as providing extra money. Or a deferring female may see her spouse as being the major breadwinner who must work full time, while she works part time and assumes the role of rearing children (Gilbert, 1993; Goldenberg & Goldenberg, 2002).

The attitudes, values, and subsequent views about women as professionals and about who should assume responsibility for which major role in dual-career marriage can largely determine the degree of the partners' "fit" in dual-career home environments. For instance, do both spouses have a favorable attitude toward a role-sharing marriage? Do both agree to work full time and share financial responsibilities? In essence, how interested and committed are both partners to an egalitarian marriage?

The stages of career development of both partners are also important considerations. For example, one partner might have reached the point where career has become rather secondary in life's priorities and, as a result, might not support the other partner's career advancement. Second, personal factors could make one partner resist accepting nontraditional roles to provide time for the other partner's career efforts. In this case, one partner debunks the other partner's career aspirations and offers little in the way of role sharing for the other partner's career growth and productivity.

Implications for Career Counseling

Clearly, one major problem of dual-career marriages is gender equity. The subtleties of male dominance often present in dual-career marriages lead couples to deal indirectly with their anxieties. Instead of attacking the underlying reasons for their frustrations, couples might resort to arguments over role assignments, child care, or other surface problems. In many instances, women might be searching for equity, while men might fear giving up power. The gap between expectations and reality for both spouses could be a productive intervention strategy, particularly if it is designed to clarify disparate expectations between spouses (Goldenberg & Goldenberg, 2002; Silberstein, 1992).

The major decision points in any marriage are crucial, but in dual-career marriages specific decision points can be identified. When to have children can be a particularly perplexing problem. This question usually arises during early career stages when women can more easily have children, which makes this decision a complex one. One method of resolving this issue is through negotiated compromises. Each spouse must share not only in this decision but also in actions and responsibilities that follow the decision.

Another major decision point that can provoke anxiety and stress in dual-career marriages is the necessity of moving to another location to foster one spouse's career. Again, who has the major role in being a breadwinner? Decisions of this type highlight underlying questions that might have been avoided in the past. Counselors should be prepared to develop strategies that would prompt a reexamination of individual and collective priorities for both partners. The issues and individual feelings about work and family are indeed complex, and many couples may not be fully aware of personal issues involved in a geographic move to benefit one spouse's career. The counselor's task is to illuminate these issues for clarification. So far we have dismissed concrete issues such as management of household tasks and sharing of duties as if they have little relevance to the welfare of dual-career marriages. But it appears more appropriate to address the possibility of underlying and unresolved issues before the more concrete ones can be effectively dealt with. The idea of role sharing, planning for children, making time for leisure, and offering support to one's spouse are examples of viable topics for the career counselor. Finally, it is important to recognize that some couples may need to be referred to a marriage counselor to enhance marital satisfaction. Marital relationships might best be addressed in couples therapy.

Case 12-1 (continued)

The case of Jose and Maria illustrates some of the stress associated with dual-career marriages. Both have highly advanced career positions that are quite demanding. Their high income level permits them to hire domestic help, but the responsibilities of managing the household and rearing children cannot be completely relegated to others outside the family system. The task of managing a two-career household has caused some of the following problems for Maria and Jose.

Gap Between Marital Expectations and Reality

For Maria and Jose, the gap between expectations and reality has led to some of their frustrations. Perhaps Maria, who was reared in a dual-career home, had not fully realized that family responsibilities cannot be fully delegated the way she had envisioned from her childhood experiences. It may have appeared easy for her mother, but in reality her mother was in a much better position than Maria is to control the demands of her workload and to keep a firm hand on household and family-related tasks.

Jose was not reared in a dual-career home; in fact, he was the product of a typical traditional system in which family roles were sex-role stereotyped. For the first years of marriage, Jose was happy; his expectations of married life, the roles of husband and wife, were mostly being met. Even though Maria was working full time, most attention was directed to his work role advancement through geographical moves. And even though he had agreed to the fourth move for Maria's benefit, he expected the traditional roles of husband and wife to continue, though perhaps with some modifications. When Maria had to ask for more of his support for household and child care activities, as well as support for her work, he felt betrayed.

Role Overload

For her part, Maria was an aggressive worker. She had multiple abilities and creative talents that needed to be expressed. Her work was now a challenge to her previously unused creativity, and it required that she devote most of her energy and cognitive skills to several ongoing projects. She would often arrive at home feeling fulfilled but also drained of energy. She also felt guilty when she was unable to devote more time to her children.

Competition and Empowerment Issues

Jose also experienced high levels of frustration associated with his career and his home life. The reality was that Jose was away from home and from his children on a regular basis. He also blamed commuting to work for his lack of productivity (research projects) in his academic discipline. Jose could very well have developed a fear of losing empowerment in his home. These two assumptions on Jose's part were troublesome ones. Being away from home four days a week can be stressful for all family members. However, Jose had not let any distractions interfere with his academic productivity in the past.

Jose's high anxiety level was a product of fear associated with losing control over family matters. He had developed a strong need to be empowered to make decisions, and, more important, he expected most family decisions to agree with his perceived role as head of the family. When his family position was threatened, Jose fought back by competing with his spouse for career recognition.

Problems identified in this dual-career relationship are complex but typical of dual-career marriages. A closer look at the identified problems suggests that there was no significant indication of dysfunctional work, unsatisfactory work environments, or unstable peer and supervisory relationships. In fact, both spouses were well satisfied with their career positions. There were indications that some role sharing had been successful, and the family had functioned relatively well for several years. Their financial future was very promising.

Many of the identified problems also reveal a gender equity battle between a highly successful wife and a successful husband. Some identified problems are typical of equity disagreements. For instance, their expectations of marriage were quite different. Jose foresaw a more traditional marriage, with the husband assuming the primary work role, the wife working only for extra income, and the wife assuming the primary responsibility for house and child care. Maria had quite a different view of marriage—an egalitarian one of sharing and appreciating each other's independence.

When these two different perspectives began to collide, stress, anxiety, and frustration were predictable outcomes. The reactions of partners in conflict can vary considerably, but in this case—other than both being identified as having conflicting expectations of marriage—Maria's other problem was role overload. On the other hand, Jose's multiple problems are clearly a part of expectations of marriage and his views of gender roles.

Couples Counseling

The recommendations for intervention strategies in this case could include couples counseling designed to illuminate conflicting expectations of marriage and resulting conflicts. The major goal would be to address marriage roles of sharing and gender equity. The needs and problems of the children also need to be addressed.

In conjunction with couples counseling, the career counselor can provide (1) role-sharing strategies; (2) leisure time commitments, including family leisure time; (3) restatement of career goals, which center on agreement of plans for the future; (4) career development of children as a sharing venture; and (5) reformulation of life-span goals.

A number of outstanding counseling models are available for dual-career marriages, including integrative strategies by Stoltz-Loike (1992). This integrative approach is based on the following assumptions:

1. A family has a variety of responsibilities that must be performed to function properly. How they are performed depends on the couple's skills, talents, and preferences.
2. Couples must communicate attitudes toward responsibilities. Conflicts need to be discussed and resolved.
3. Dual-career couples can effectively serve as models to help other couples balance career and family roles.
4. Communication, negotiation, and problem solving are to be viewed as ongoing processes over the life span.
5. Interventions are to be tailored to meet a variety of presenting problems among dual-career couples.
6. A spouse must balance his or her own family and work responsibilities with those of the other spouse.
7. Solutions to issues must be contextual to include each spouse's life, workplace, and community setting.

The major goal of this approach is to achieve balance of family and career equity. Helping couples recognize that role conflicts can occur at any time over the life span is another major goal. Because of overlapping roles and responsibilities, basic relationship skills of communication, negotiation, conflict resolution, and life-span success are stressed.

It should not be surprising that there are multiple views of family counseling (Goldenberg & Goldenberg, 2002). The variety of and growing number of intervention models for family counseling suggest that there is a diversity in counseling outlook primarily driven by varied professional backgrounds. Secondly, family counseling is offered in a variety of settings including churches and synagogues, hospitals, universities and colleges, community mental health clinics, social agencies, and in private practice. There are also a wide range of family configurations such as gay parents, cohabiting couples, stepfamilies and teenage parents. Counselors, therefore, may choose from a variety of intervention procedures that requires a careful appraisal of couple and family functioning.

Summary

1. The families' influence on career development has been a significantly relevant issue for a number of career development theorists.
2. The family is conceptualized as a social system. The nuclear family is the most common in the United States. The extended family is the most common form around the world.
3. Current trends in family systems include increased number of single adults, postponement of marriage, decreased childbearing, more female participation in the labor force, more divorce, more single-parent families, more children living in poverty, more remarriage, increased years without children, and more multigeneration families.
4. The example presented of a dual-career couple in conflict is typical of issues involving struggles for gender equity of household and child care tasks and of work recognition.
5. Issues facing dual-career couples are expectations of work and family, role conflict, child care, geographic moves, competition, relationship factors, and a number of personal factors. Counselors are to be sensitive to the needs of culturally diverse clients.
6. Implications of career counseling include illuminating underlying issues of gender equity, couple communication, sharing exercises, family and career status, and conflict resolution.

Supplementary Learning Exercises

1. Does the nuclear family or the extended family have more influence on a child's career development? Defend your position.
2. What strategies would you suggest for a single parent who is concerned about a child's career development?
3. Defend the following statement: Mother–child relationships cannot be fully understood without the addition of the father's influence. Explain how your position would relate to culturally diverse families.
4. Which two trends in changing family systems do you consider to be the greatest threat to the traditional U.S. family system? Defend your choice.
5. What are the major differences between dual-career and dual-earner families? Of the two, which would have the greater difficulty with role conflicts?
6. Explain how expectations of marriage influence behaviors in dual-career marriages. Give at least five examples.
7. Give three examples of how parents in a traditional marriage influence their children's perceptions of dual-career marriages.

8. How can agreement on life-span goals affect a dual-career marriage? Give at least three examples.
9. Explain how you could assist a dual-career couple negotiate a geographic move that will benefit the wife's career.
10. Interview one couple in a dual-career marriage and one in a dual-earner marriage. Explain the similarities and differences.

For More Information

Barnett, R. C., & Rivers, C. (1996). *She works, he works: How two-income families are happier, healthier, and better off.* San Francisco: Harper.

Dreman, S. (1997). *The family on the threshold of the 21st century: Trends and implications.* Mahwah, NJ: Erlbaum.

Frone, M. R., Russell, M., & Barnes, G. M. (1996). Work-family conflict, gender, and health-related outcomes: A study of employed parents in two community samples. *Journal of Occupational Health Psychology, 1,* 57–69.

Galliano, G. (2003). *Gender: Crossing boundaries.* Belmont, CA: Wadsworth/Thomson Learning.

Gilbert, L. A. (1993). *Two careers/one family.* Newbury Park, CA: Sage.

Goldenberg, H., & Goldenberg, I. (2002). *Counseling today's family* (5th ed.). Pacific Grove, CA: Brooks/Cole.

Matthews, L. S., Conger, R. D., & Wickrama, K. A. S. (1996). Work–family conflict and marital quality: Mediating processes. *Social Psychology Quarterly, 59,* 62–79.

McHenry, P. C., & Price, S. J. (1994). *Families and change: Coping with stressful events.* Thousands Oaks, CA: Sage.

Rider, E. A. (2000). *Our voices: Psychology of women.* Pacific Grove, CA: Wadsworth.

Silberstein, L. R. (1992). *Dual-career marriage: A system in transition.* Hillsdale, NJ: Erlbaum.

Taylor, R. J., Jackson, J. S., & Chatters, L. M. (1997). *Family life in black America.* Thousands Oaks, CA: Sage.

Suggested InfoTrac College Edition Topics

Child care and work	Gender and house work
Dual-career family	Gender and power
Dual-earner family	Gender and relationships
Flextime	Gender and work
Gender and career choice	Household husbands

13 Career Counseling for Individuals with Disabilities

Chapter Highlights

- The Americans with Disabilities Act

- Special problems and needs of individuals with disabilities

- Implications for career guidance

- Rehabilitation programs

- Case study: client at a state rehabilitation center

- Career education and a module for individuals with disabilities

- Group counseling program for individuals with disabilities

CAREER COUNSELING PROGRAMS for individuals with disabilities have elements in common with traditional career counseling programs; however, the diversity of needs requires specially designed assessment instruments (see Osborn & Zunker, 2006), career counseling techniques, materials, and career-related educational training programs. The overarching counseling goal for persons with disabilities is to maximize each individual's potential for life and work in the 21st century. It will be emphasized throughout this chapter that persons with disabilities are a very diverse group that share some common elements of thinking and behaving and yet have very unique special needs. Once again, helpers are to recognize within-group differences in order to effectively meet the needs of their clients.

The terms used to describe people with disabilities have been changed to negate stereotypes and false ideas. The major objection was labeling individuals with demeaning names. For example, a spastic does not describe a person but refers to a muscle with sudden involuntary spasms. It is much more acceptable to think of a disability as a condition that interferes with an individual's ability to do something independent such as walk, see, hear, or learn. Thus, it is preferable to say "people with disabilities," rather than "the disabled"; "Joe is a wheelchair user," rather than "confined to a wheelchair"; "has a hearing impairment," rather than "is deaf-mute"; and "persons with mental retardation," rather than "the mentally retarded." The focus should be on the unique identity of a person rather than on a label that implies that everyone with that particular label is alike and has a separate status from the general population. A person's identity should be an individual matter that focuses on a unique condition, and the words we use should convey this message (Matlin, 2004).

In this chapter, we first focus on the Americans with Disabilities Act (ADA). The second section describes special problems and needs of individuals with disabilities. Implications for career counseling and the role of state rehabilitation agencies are then discussed. An actual counseling case of an individual with a disability who sought services from a state rehabilitation agency is described in the next section. Finally, a career education program for students with disabilities is briefly reviewed, followed by a description of a group counseling program for individuals with disabilities who have been hospitalized.

The Americans with Disabilities Act

The ADA, signed into law on July 26, 1990, is a comprehensive law. For example, Title III regulations require public accommodations (including private entities that own, operate, or lease to places of public accommodation), commercial facilities, and private entities to make reasonable modifications of policies, practices, and procedures that deny equal access to individuals with disabilities. Box 13-1 provides an overview of requirements in public accommodations.

The ADA identifies individuals with disabilities as follows: An individual with a disability is a person who has a physical or mental impairment that substantially limits one or more "major life activities," or has a record of such impairment, or is regarded as having such an impairment. Examples of physical or mental impairments include, but are not limited to, such contagious and noncontagious diseases and conditions as orthopedic, visual, speech, and hearing impairments; cerebral palsy; epilepsy; muscular dystrophy; multiple sclerosis; cancer; heart disease; diabetes; mental retardation; emotional illness; specific learning disabilities; HIV disease (whether symptomatic or asymptomatic); tuberculosis; drug addiction; and alcoholism. Homosexuality and bisexuality are not physical or mental impairments under the ADA. "Major life activities" include functions such as caring for oneself, performing manual tasks, walking, seeing, hearing, speaking, breathing, learning, and working. Individuals who engage in the illegal use of drugs are not protected by the ADA when

Box 13-1	Americans with Disabilities Act Requirements in Public Accommodations Fact Sheet

General

- Public accommodations such as restaurants, hotels, theaters, doctors' offices, pharmacies, retail stores, museums, libraries, parks, private schools, and day care centers may not discriminate on the basis of disability. Private clubs and religious organizations are exempt.
- Reasonable changes in policies, practices, and procedures must be made to avoid discrimination.

Auxiliary Aids

- Auxiliary aids and services must be provided to individuals with vision or hearing impairments or other individuals with disabilities, unless an undue burden would result.

Physical Barriers

- Physical barriers in existing facilities must be removed, if removal is readily achievable. If not, alternative methods of providing the services must be offered, if they are readily achievable.
- All new construction in public accommodations, as well as in "commercial facilities" such as office buildings, must be accessible. Elevators are generally not required in buildings under three stories or with fewer than 3,000 square feet per floor, unless the building is a shopping center, mall, or a professional office of a health care provider.
- Alterations must be accessible. When alterations to primary function areas are made, an accessible path of travel to the altered area (and the bathrooms, telephones, and drinking fountains serving that area) must be provided to the extent that the added accessibility costs are not disproportionate to the overall cost of the alterations. Elevators are required as described above.

SOURCE: U.S. Department of Justice, Civil Rights Division, 1991. Americans with Disabilities Act Handbook, Coordination and Review Section.

an action is taken on the basis of their current illegal use of drugs (U.S. Department of Justice, 1991, pp. 3–4).

Of interest to helpers are the ADA's requirements concerning employment of individuals with disabilities and transportation accessibility. Box 13-2 includes a fact sheet prepared by the U.S. Department of Justice on employment and transportation requirements and the effective dates of these requirements. One major issue covered in this act is employment discrimination. The ADA prohibits discrimination in all employment practices including job application, hiring, firing, advancement, compensation, training, and other terms and conditions of employment. Also included are advertising for employment, fringe benefits, and tenure. Employers are free, however, to select the most qualified applicant available and to make decisions based on reasons unrelated to a disability. For example, two individuals apply for a typist job and one is able to accurately type more words per minute. Thus, the employer can hire the better typist even though that particular person does not have a disability and the other does. The key to such decisions appears to center around job performance needs, and in this case, typing speed is needed for successful performance of the job.

Other subjects covered in the ADA that interest helpers are job descriptions, job application forms, job application process, interviews, testing and medical examinations, hiring decisions, benefits, working conditions, raises and promotions, and rea-

Box 13-2	Americans with Disabilities Act Requirements Fact Sheet

Employment

- Employers may not discriminate against an individual with a disability in hiring or promotion if the person is otherwise qualified for the job.
- Employers can ask about one's ability to perform a job, but cannot inquire if someone has a disability or subject a person to tests that tend to screen out people with disabilities.
- Employers will need to provide "reasonable accommodation" to individuals with disabilities. This includes steps such as job restructuring and modification of equipment.
- Employers do not need to provide accommodations that impose an "undue hardship" on business operations.

Who Needs to Comply

- All employers with 25 or more employees must comply, effective July 26, 1992.
- All employers with 15 to 24 employees must comply, effective July 26, 1994.

Transportation

- New public transit buses ordered after August 26, 1990, must be accessible to individuals with disabilities.
- Transit authorities must provide comparable paratransit or other special transportation services to individuals with disabilities who cannot use fixed route bus services, unless an undue burden would result.
- Existing rail systems must have one accessible car per train by July 26, 1995.
- New rail cars ordered after August 26, 1990, must be accessible.
- New bus and train stations must be accessible.
- Key stations in rapid, light, and commuter rail systems must be made accessible by July 26, 1993, with extensions up to 20 years for commuter rail (30 years for rapid and light rail).
- All existing Amtrak stations must be accessible by July 26, 2010.

SOURCE: U.S. Department of Justice, Civil Rights Division, 1991. Americans with Disabilities Act Handbook, Coordination and Review Section.

sonable accommodations. More information about ADA and the Individuals with Disabilities Education Act of 1992 (IDEA), discussed later in this chapter, can be obtained from the following:

Office on the Americans with Disabilities Act
Civil Rights Division U.S. Department of Justice
P.O. Box 66118
Washington, DC 20035-6118
www.usdoj.gov/crt/ada/

Special Problems and Needs of Individuals with Disabilities

The problems and needs associated with disability can be very inclusive and pervasive. Using a holistic counseling approach, counselors are to address interrelationships of personal and career concerns as well as adjustment problems associated with disability. Matlin (2004) captures the essence of how counselors should view their role when she states that "disability is an additional factor that creates variability" (p. 366). Implied here is that disability is multifaceted and a diversity of strategies are needed, for example, to address self-concept, social status, life roles, and especially the work role. The severity of functional limitations and the individual's adjustment to his or her limitations are most important factors to consider in counseling. The special problems and needs of individuals with disabilities discussed in this section should be considered as representative examples from a diverse population.

Adjusting to Physical Trauma

To begin we recognize that individuals whose disabilities result from physical trauma might have difficulty adjusting to and accepting disability. Adjusting to the label of a person who has a disability can be a long and painful journey. The process of adjustment can interfere with motivation to seek retraining and employment. Some individuals might experience the feeling that what has happened is their fault in that they have done something wrong and even sinful and are being punished. This kind of faulty thinking can result in shock, depression, and denial before one is ready to accept and start the adjustment process. The fact is that psychological denial of a disability is discussed frequently in rehabilitation literature. Failure to accept one's limitations can impede counseling assistance; the individual will not be open to retraining or to experiences provided by rehabilitation agencies or educational institutions (Salsgiver, 1995).

Feelings of Inferiority and Negative Stereotypes

People with disabilities can also experience a sense of rejection from others. Some researchers have contended that individuals with physical disabilities are given an inferior status position in our society. The frustrations produced from a physical disability can be accompanied by shame and feelings of inferiority. The acceptance of one's physical condition is often linked to all facets of one's self-esteem. Careful consideration should be given to interrelated sources of poor self-concept, ways of reacting to physical disability, and ways of adjusting to it. Counselors need to assist clients in dealing with prejudice and discrimination and especially how it affects self-image (Brammer, 2004; French, 1996; Wright, 1980).

Individuals who are labeled handicapped or disabled can also face negative stereotypes from work associates and supervisors as well as from others in their environment. Negative stereotypes can lead to discrimination in employment, housing, schooling, and social interactions (Corrigan et al., 2000). In addition, employers are reluctant to hire individuals with disabilities because of erroneous assumptions: increased sick leave will be required, insurance rates will be affected, safety on the job will be endangered, and plant modifications will be mandatory. People with mental retardation especially are considered to need constant supervision and are perceived as incapable of learning. In general, employers have negative stereotyped views of individuals with disabilities, which can result in discrimination (Corrigan et al., 2000; Daniels, 1981; Mackelprang & Salsgiver, 1999). For example, the label amputee might conjure up an image of someone who is severely restricted. Another individual who has had successful open heart surgery might be perceived as sickly and weak. Such generalizations inhibit opportunities for employment, especially for individuals who have minor functional limitations. The point here is to debunk the faulty thinking that links all persons with a disability together into one category of handicapped or disabled rather than viewing each person as an individual with unique characteristics.

An advocacy role through personal contact with potential employers is one effective method for building positive attitudes about people with disabilities. The importance of the advocacy role is underscored by Neff (1985), who contended that individuals with disabilities face an impressive array of negative social attitudes, prejudice, and other social barriers. Some examples of successful placement of individuals with disabilities are an effective method that may break down an employer's stereotypes. Noble (1992) suggests that a disability should be seen as a diversity and not a deficiency; thus, clients are viewed as individuals rather than patients. Employers are to base an individual's ability to perform on the nature of the work rather than dismissing an individual's application for a job simply because he or she is "disabled or handicapped" (Brammer, 2004). See Box 13-3.

Focusing on School Dropouts

In schools we find a high dropout rate of students who are in special education classes. Adolescents who are diagnosed as having an attention deficit hyperactive disorder (ADHD) also have a high dropout rate (McWhirter et al., 2004). There can be many reasons why students drop out of school, however, social alienation of students with disabilities is an important contributing factor. People with a disability often are excluded from the mainstream of society and, in schools, experience a lack of acceptance by fellow students and even teachers. Some students may be openly defiant while others are more subtle in their rejection.

One way to counter rejection from the mainstream is by legitimate examples of role models. Individuals who have overcome their disability and are now considered successful, for instance, can be a source of hope and encouragement. Theatrical interventions in schools with children has produced some positive results in changing the way 84 children (ages 9 to 13 years) viewed individuals with disabilities (D'Amico et al., 2001). A musical that incorporated individuals with different disabilities was presented to these children. The reaction to this musical was as expected: Children responded more positively to people with a disability and in fact thought they were able to sing, act, work, and be friends. The lesson here is that counselors, teachers, and all school personnel should be united to confront prejudice against students with disabilities.

Goals of Helpers

As mentioned earlier, disabling conditions have the potential to create a poor self-concept (Humes, Szymanski, & Hohenshil, 1989; Mackelprang & Salsgiver, 1999). Individuals with disabilities tend to report lower self-esteem and self-awareness. A life associated with constant rejection and being labeled as different can potentially create a poor self-image. "Who am I?" may indeed be a difficult question to answer positively. Helper's goals in this context are to assist individuals in accurately assessing strengths and weaknesses to help them modify their self-perceptions. Programs that include components to help develop positive self-images are very important in meeting the needs of these individuals.

Box 13-3	A Disabled Person's Story

I am now officially classified as a 44-year-old person with a disability. About ten years ago I was diagnosed as having multiple sclerosis (MS) but continued with my job as a sales and account representative with a large international company until 2002. Since then my life has changed dramatically!

I have difficulty visualizing life without a job or a workplace to go to each day. I continue to wrestle with this problem. After all, I am only in my mid-forties, married to a woman I deeply love, and have a strong desire to do what I always thought I would do—develop a career. Work has been a major focus in my life since graduating from a major university in the Midwest with a degree in business administration.

When I look back at my life I realize that my work ethic was greatly influenced by my parents. My father was employed by the same major organization for 33 years. My mother not only managed household duties but when she was young operated a beauty shop in our basement. Later she went to work for a bank and spent 23 years on that job. Work in the lives of family members has always been very important!

My first job after college was with a large international firm as a customer sales representative. My primary responsibilities included all aspects of customer service. During a four-year span I received several promotions and honor awards. Since my first job I have worked in two other major organizations as a key account manager and market development representative. I considered my career to be going in the right direction. I enjoyed the work and especially the interaction with clients and fellow workers.

Over ten years ago I suddenly experienced blurred vision in my left eye and pain in my right toe and heel. Little did I know that this was the initial warnings of MS. Later I was told that this neurological disorder turns the immune system against the body's protective nerve coating and disrupts transmission signals to the brain. Eventually functions such as walking and cognitive abilities are affected. I started using a cane several years ago but now use an electric wheelchair.

Currently I am on disability, unemployed, and daily contend with muscle spasms and a burning sensation in my legs and feet. One positive note, my wife fully supports me in every way she can.

Despite all the above problems I still would like to be involved in some kind of work. Work was a major part of my life and without it I feel empty and unsatisfied. I am currently investigating some possibilities of volunteer work. My recommendation to other people who have a disability is to aggressively seek out available help and assistance. Keep a positive outlook and strive toward goals, put your health first, and realize that you are differently "abled."

I advise counselors to stay current with employment laws and regulations concerning people with disabilities. Also develop a list of companies that have a good track record for employing and mentoring people with disabilities. When you counsel persons with a disability, address personal problems as well as career ones. People with disabilities can use all the help they can get!

Note: This is a real life story of an individual who prefers to remain anonymous.

It is clear that people with disabilities will likely have personal concerns that are interrelated to career choice and development. For example, individuals can be deficient in assertiveness and in independence if they have experienced early onset of a disability which in turn may lead to indecisiveness when attempting to make a career choice. Onset of disability in adulthood often requires that career counselors reintroduce the process of career redevelopment. By assessing the realities of their functional limitations, for example, individuals may be required to change career direction. In sum, later onset of disability has interrelated elements of career and personal adjustment. One not only is required to adjust to a different work role, but also to other life roles as well.

Finally, the lack of visibility of individuals with physical disabilities working successfully in a broad spectrum of career fields reinforces low self-esteem and negative attitudes about labor market potential. Negative attitudes about potential work environments can also be reinforced by employment personnel who exhibit feelings of discomfort when interviewing individuals with a disability (Bryan, 1996). In addition, some standardized tests and inventories used for employment selection can result in conflicting or misleading assumptions concerning employment potential (Osborn & Zunker, 2006).

In sum, people with disabilities face barriers that are developed from negative stereotypes and generalizations that may limit their potential for employment. They are also confronted with social alienation in schools and mainstream society. Onset of disability is an important factor in determining strategy interventions. Personal concerns of individuals with disabilities are often generated by poor self-concept and the inability to accept and adjust to their disability. Rejection, inferior status, discrimination, and prejudice lead to low self-esteem and negative attitudes. Counselors are to assume an advocacy role and examine each client's individual needs to determine intervention strategies.

Multicultural Issues

We have learned in our discussions about other special populations in the immediate preceding chapters that diversity is multifaceted and multidimensional, hence females who are African American and have a disability are labeled as having a triple (gender, culture, and disability) minority status. On the other hand, an Asian man who is disabled would be considered to have a double minority status. Peterson and Gonzalez (2000) suggest that these individuals more than likely will have to overcome double and triple minority status in their job searches, thereby reducing their chances of obtaining employment. Clearly, helpers are to develop effective strategies to overcome all barriers that clients face in the work world and in all life roles.

In this context, helpers are to focus on the interrelationships of double and triple minority status with other variables that affect career development. For example, onset of disability, severity of disability, self-image, support networks, and so on are variables that interact with cultural and gender factors that are interrelated and interconnected. All variables are unique individual characteristics that provide direction or pathways to intervention strategies and goals of counseling. In a holistic counseling approach all sets of concerns are addressed. Counselors especially need to be advocates in their communities to help individuals who are considered to have double and triple minority status by focusing on effective integrated strategies to help them find employment.

Finally, it is generally agreed that career counseling of individuals with disabilities is very challenging, especially for culturally diverse clients (Brammer, 2004). In the case example presented later in this chapter, a rehabilitation counselor goes through the steps of developing an individualized plan of employment for a Latino female who has a disability. This carefully designed, comprehensive program included problem identification, psychological and physical evaluations, a comprehensive plan, financial assistance, college enrollment, job search counseling, and follow-up evaluation. Postemployment services are also discussed.

Implications for Career Counseling

The problems associated with the career development of individuals with disabilities exemplify the often expressed need for counselors to adopt proactive roles. In addition to directly assisting the client with physical disabilities, counselors should support community education and training programs to foster acceptance in the work world. Programs that assist educators, families, and employees in working with individuals with disabilities can be invaluable in reducing the physical and psychological barriers that currently exist.

People with disabilities face negative attitudes, prejudice, discrimination, and other social barriers. As a consequence, holistic-oriented counseling programs should provide more positive roles and role models. Developing positive self-images and interpersonal relationship skills are important intervention strategies. Finally, a proactive role implies considerable dedication to removing social barriers and to providing supportive counseling. Above all, counselors are to help persons with disabilities develop self-directed plans, actions, and behaviors in order to become self-advocates (Blotzer & Ruth, 1995; DePoy & Gilson, 2004; Tower, 1994). This section focuses on programs for individuals with disabilities sponsored by state rehabilitation agencies and on rehabilitation centers sponsored by the private sector.

State Rehabilitation Programs

The purpose of state rehabilitation agencies is to provide counseling and other services to individuals who have a disability or disabilities. Each individual with a disability is evaluated to determine if they meet the general criteria adopted by the agency that determines eligibility for services. Eligibility is generally determined by two criteria: (1) Each person must have a disability that results in a substantial handicap to employment, and (2) vocational rehabilitation services must reasonably be expected to benefit the person relative to employability. Disabling conditions among populations served by state agencies are extensive and inclusive. Rehabilitation services have been extended to individuals with mental illness, orthopedic problems, mental retardation, visual and hearing problems, circulatory problems, amputation of limbs, and other disabling conditions such as alcoholism, cancer, epilepsy, kidney disease, multiple sclerosis, muscular dystrophy, and cerebral palsy. To meet the needs of such a diverse group of individuals, state rehabilitation agencies have developed numerous and varied programs designed to assist individuals reentering the workforce or maintaining their chosen occupations.

In the early 1980s, Parker and Hansen (1981) compiled a list of services provided by state rehabilitation agencies that are generally in vogue today: (1) counseling and guidance; (2) medical and psychological evaluation; (3) physical and mental restoration services; (4) prevocational evaluation and retraining; (5) vocational and other training services; (6) expense allowances; (7) transportation; (8) interpretive services for the deaf; (9) reader, orientation, and mobility services for the blind; (10) prostheses and other technical aids and devices; (11) work adjustment and placement counseling; (12) job placement services; (13) occupational license, tools, equipment, and so forth; and (14) other goods and services to benefit the client in achieving employability.

Rehabilitation agency programs are designed to emphasize inclusion of their clients (Berns, 2004). Epps & Jackson (2000) present a broad view of services for individuals with disabilities to include evaluation, special education, financial assistance, counseling, vocational training, recreation and referrals for addressing various needs. Sciarra (2004) suggests that school counselors are to work with teachers as partners by responding to in-class behaviors, address concerns of parents of children with disabilities, and to provide solution based counseling procedures directly to students with disabilities.

Privately Supported Rehabilitation Agencies

Among the most widely known, privately sponsored, nonprofit rehabilitation agencies are Goodwill Industries, Salvation Army, Jewish Vocational Services, St. Vincent De Paul Society, National Society for Crippled Children and Adults, United Cerebral Palsy Association, Volunteers of America, and Deseret Industries. Although these organizations and other national, state, and local private rehabilitation agencies sponsor a diversity of programs, Goodwill Industries of America serves as a good example of a national network of programs for individuals with disabilities. Goodwill Industries of America is generally recognized as the world's leading privately sponsored agency for training individuals and with facilities for individuals with disabilities.

Local Goodwill Industries are autonomous, having their own boards of directors, and are affiliated with the national organization, Goodwill Industries of America of Bethesda, Maryland. Goodwill Industries conducts a wide range of activities, including classroom instruction, sheltered workshops, encounter sessions, therapy (physical, occupational, or speech), counseling, and placement.

Many local Goodwill Industries collect donated clothing, furniture, household goods and appliances, books, art objects, radios, and televisions for repairing, refurbishing, and rebuilding by individuals with disabilities. These items are sold in a network of bargain retail outlets. Another method Goodwill Industries uses to provide jobs is to subcontract with private industries and with state and federal government agencies for assembling and manufacturing of goods, janitorial services, grounds maintenance, and other services.

Goodwill Industries also provide educational skills training programs. For example, Goodwill Industries of San Antonio provides the following services: psychological testing, vocational evaluation, personal and social adjustment, work adjustment, prevocational training, special academic instruction, therapeutic recreation, skills training, and job placement. The individualized services offered by this agency are funded from service fees charged to referring agencies, such as the Texas Rehabilitation Commission, the Commission for the Blind, local independent school districts, the City of San Antonio Manpower Consortium, the Veteran's Administration, and private insurance firms.

Most age groups can be served by privately supported, nonprofit rehabilitation agencies. Services include provisions for assistive devices such as artificial limbs, braces, wheelchairs, glasses, and hearing aids. Assistance is also given to help individuals develop independent living skills through programs in which individuals share supervised apartments. The Salvation Army and Volunteers of America have emphasized programs for homeless individuals with alcohol or psychological problems.

Career services providers need to be aware of the goals, objectives, and services of private rehabilitation agencies in their community or local area. Programs that help prepare individuals with disabilities for employment (such as work-adjustment seminars, prevocational classes, personal counseling, medical management, and mobility training) are valuable referral resources for helpers. Sheltered workshops, supported by a number of private rehabilitation agencies, provide a workplace for individuals who are unable to meet work requirements in the competitive job market. Counseling for disabled individuals is greatly enhanced through a wide variety of programs offered by rehabilitation programs supported by the private sector.

Case 13-1 Counseling Program

The following is an actual case of an individual who received rehabilitation services from a state agency. Names, dates, and other information have been changed to protect client confidentiality. This example illustrates rehabilitation services provided by a state agency in a small town of about 25,000 people. The following steps in the rehabilitation process are covered in this case: (1) initial contact, (2) diagnostic workup, (3) evaluation and certification, (4) vocational assessment, (5) service planning, (6) placement, and (7) postemployment services.

Initial Contact

The purposes of the initial contact are to establish a counseling relationship, provide the client with information about the state agency, and obtain information from the client to determine eligibility for rehabilitation services. In this case, Sam, the rehabilitation counselor, interviewed the client to obtain personal/social information, educational background, past work experiences, physical limitations, and financial needs. Excerpts from the case file are used to illustrate examples of information recorded from the initial contact.

Dora was a self-referred high school graduate and had never received rehabilitation services. She was 40 years old, divorced approximately three years ago, and had two children. Her older child was married and living nearby, but the younger child had chosen to live with her. Dora had married at age 18 and had lived in several cities and states with her salesman husband. Sam noted in his report that her mood was very flat and that she seemed remorseful and lethargic. She became extremely emotional when she referred to her marriage, stating, "I resent that my husband left me because of my arthritis."

Dora reported that she had suffered serious problems with arthritis for the past ten years, requiring five surgical procedures on her hands. During the interview, she demonstrated lack of finger flexibility and restricted hand mobility. She was taking two prescribed medications.

Dora's only source of income was $800 monthly child support, and she had no savings. She was unable to insure her five-year-old car, and her current rent and utility bills totaled $510. Dora's work experience was very limited; she had worked as a teacher's aide for approximately nine months but was unemployed at the present time.

Sam decided that Dora was a good candidate for rehabilitation services and had her fill out an official request form. She was then scheduled for a medical and psychological evaluation. Sam had to verify reported physical problems, and he wanted a full report on potential psychological disturbances associated with the emotional instability he had observed. Sam also requested reports of previous medical diagnosis and treatment.

Diagnostic Workup

The orthopedist's report indicated that Dora had a severe case of rheumatoid arthritis. After carefully studying the medical report, Sam arrived at the following functional limitations and vocational handicaps.

1. Can stand for short periods of time only (Orthopedic report from Dr. Bone)
2. Unable to lift anything over 10 lbs. on a repetitive basis (Orthopedic report from Dr. Bone)
3. Unable to push or pull (Client's statement)
4. Cannot bend for prolonged periods (Client's statement)
5. Has limited finger dexterity (Orthopedic report from Dr. Bone)

The psychological report discussed results of intelligence, academic achievement, personality, and several aptitude tests. Sam summarized Dora's assets from the psychological evaluations as follows:

1. Normal intelligence
2. Good clerical skills
3. Ability to learn and retain new information
4. Good reading skills
5. Good oral expressive skills
6. Average academic achievement for her educational level
7. Potential for college-level training

In addition, Sam summarized Dora's limitations:

1. Diagnosed as depressive reaction
2. Poor self-concept
3. Lacks confidence
4. Subject to mood swings
5. Limited work history
6. Poor manual dexterity
7. Easily fatigued

Evaluation and Certification

After reviewing medical and psychological reports, Sam approved Dora's request for rehabilitative services. The results of her disability as well as the degree of her handicap were evaluated. In this case, her physical disability was considered severe enough to merit services. Psychological problems associated with the depressive reaction would also be considered in planning services for her. In developing a rehabilitation plan, Sam was required to address all services that would help Dora reach her rehabilitation goal.

Dora was notified of her acceptance, and an appointment was set for the following day. In preparation for the next counseling appointment, Sam carefully reviewed the material that had accumulated in Dora's file. He paid particular attention to medical problems resulting in functional limitations. The psychological report clearly indicated that Dora would need supportive counseling; however, he decided that his first goal was to establish a vocational objective.

Vocational Assessment

In the counseling sessions that followed, limitations and assets were thoroughly discussed. Although Dora had strongly considered teaching as a vocational objective, she agreed that an interest inventory would help verify her interests and introduce other career considerations. Dora was given a computer-scored inventory, and a date was set for the next counseling session.

The vocational assessment phase of the rehabilitation process continued with an interpretation and discussion of interest inventory results and the test data contained in the psychological report. Dora decided that she would like to explore a career in either elementary school teaching or social work. With these two careers in mind, Sam directed her to references describing these occupations in detail. Dora spent considerable time reviewing job descriptions and requirements. At Sam's suggestion, she made on-site visits to a school and a social welfare agency. Shortly after these visits, Dora decided that she would prefer a career as an elementary education teacher.

Service Planning

Sam developed a comprehensive vocational plan for Dora. This plan, known as the Individualized Plan of Employment (IPE), contains the following aspects of action:

1. The rehabilitation goal and immediate rehabilitation objectives
2. Vocational rehabilitation services
3. The projected date of initiating services and the anticipated duration of services
4. Objective criteria, evaluation procedures, and schedules for determining whether the rehabilitation goal and intermediate objectives are being achieved
5. Explanation of availability of a client assistance program (Roessler & Rubin, 1982, p. 132)

Sam postulated that Dora would need assistance with medical and emotional problems during the course of her college training. He also recognized that he would have to assist Dora in obtaining grants and other benefits that might be available to her. Excerpts from Sam's service plan suggestions follow: (1) enrollment in a local college with financial assistance for tuition, fees, and transportation; (2) other financial assistance through grants and Social Security benefits; (3) physical treatment to be continued as necessary; and (4) regular counseling sessions necessary to address reported psychological problems. Sam was especially concerned that arthritis patients often develop depression. He recommended that an assessment be done and suggested some prevention options such as teaching Dora to self-monitor for depression. Sam decided to provide supportive counseling and, if necessary, refer Dora to the university counseling center or local mental health agency.

Thomas and Butler (1981) and Mackelprang and Salsgiver (1999) suggested that rehabilitation clients often need extensive personal counseling designed to assist them in accepting their disabilities, adjusting to reactions of others to their disabilities, reintegrating their self-concepts, and adjusting to changes in relationships with family and others in their lives. Counselors need to evaluate different counseling theories and techniques in meeting the needs of different types of clients through an integrative counseling approach. In essence, individuals with disabilities may require extensive personal adjustment counseling that focuses on the interrelationships of personal and career concerns and life roles.

During the next four years, Dora made remarkable academic progress despite recurring physical and psychological problems. She had three operations on her hands to improve flexibility, and the regular supportive counseling provided by Sam helped her overcome depressive reactions and pointed out the importance of support systems such as family and close friends. Sam and Dora would evaluate the possibility of family counseling in the future. Financial assistance provided by the state and other agencies helped Dora maintain subsistence. During her final year in college, Sam directed Dora to attend seminars on resumé preparation and job interview skills.

Placement

In a conference with Sam, Dora decided that she wanted to remain in the area. Sam evaluated the local job market for teachers and found it to be keenly competitive for elementary school teachers; however, he decided that he could improve Dora's chances of obtaining a position by assisting her in job interview preparation. Sam also helped Dora develop a list of alternate school systems to which she could apply.

Postemployment Services

Sam plans to follow Dora's work for at least 60 postemployment days. He will focus on her adjustment to her new job and adaptations she must make in her daily schedule. Finally, Dora will be notified that if services are needed in the future, he can reopen her case.

Dora's case illustrates the comprehensive nature of rehabilitation counseling for individuals with disabilities. The services offered involved considerable client contact and coordination of functions provided through training programs, financial assistance resources, and medical treatment. Although state rehabilitation programs follow a general pattern, there are variations in services given. Nevertheless, rehabilitation counselors must possess numerous skills and considerable knowledge to foster client career development.

Career Education for Students with Disabilities

Brolin and Gysbers (1989) developed the Life-Centered Career Education Curriculum (LCCE) for individuals with disabilities that continues to be relevant in the 21st century. This program has been widely adopted in school systems in several states and in some foreign countries. This innovative curriculum focuses on 22 major competencies that students need to succeed in daily living, personal/social, and occupational areas after leaving school. For daily living, competencies include buying and preparing food, managing finances, and caring for personal needs. For personal/social skills, competencies include achieving self-awareness, achieving independence, and making adequate decisions. Finally, for occupational preparation, competencies include selecting and planning occupational choices and obtaining a specific occupational skill. This model is competency based and specifies counselor time for carrying out guidance activities in each component.

Counselors are provided with a trainer/implementation manual, activity books, and an inventory to assess competency levels. The suggested competencies for this model are infused into the kindergarten through grade 12 curriculums. Some school systems have used this model to facilitate and improve community awareness of students' needs and to increase parent participation in learning activities. The LCCE has also been used for staff in-service training to make staff aware of the model's structure and purpose.

Brolin and Gysbers (1989) suggest that career awareness, career exploration, and preparation are major benefits of this model. These benefits are similar to procedures and practices by Berns (2004) and Sciarra (2004). The career awareness phase is very important during the elementary years. Programs that focus on helping students with disabilities should emphasize developing self-worth, socially desirable behaviors, communication skills, positive attitudes toward work, and desirable work habits.

The career exploration phase includes guidance activities that explore abilities, needs, and interests. The use of work samples, simulated job tasks, and community jobs are important hands-on experiences. In addition, this phase includes experiences with the work roles of homemaker, family member, and volunteer, and with individuals engaged in productive avocational/leisure activities.

The preparation phase includes guidance activities that help clarify personal/ social and occupational competencies. Interests, aptitudes, and skills are further clarified. Lifestyle and career choices are more clearly delineated. It should be noted that many students with disabilities require more than the usual amount of time to prepare for an occupation.

One issue that needs to be addressed in the 21st century is the place of proficiency tests required for graduation in many states. Should all students with disabilities be required to take and make acceptable scores on these tests? Perhaps more important, what kind of criteria should be used for students with disabilities to determine high school graduation? Finally, can the stereotypes and negative attitudes toward individuals with disabilities be erased from many professionals, including some members of the counseling profession? No doubt, some students with disabilities need individual attention, but counselors need to view these students' needs in perspective rather than in a stereotypic manner. As with other special populations, students with disabilities should receive counseling, first, by identifying their individual needs and, second, by building programs to meet them (Brolin & Gysbers, 1989).

Educating and Counseling Individuals with Disabilities in Public Schools

Public schools have not always been involved in the education of students with disabilities. The following brief historical summary presents a reflection of how mainstream society has viewed people with disabilities and the changes in thinking of how their needs should be met by public education.

In the early 1800s some states established residential schools for the education of students with disabilities. In this protective environment, however, some residents spent their entire life in these schools because there were no provisions for educating individuals with disabilities in public schools. It was not until the latter part of the 19th century when special classes in public schools became available. The movement that led to public funds for special classes was primarily driven by parents of children with disabilities who banded together and lobbied for legislation. This movement also influenced research aimed at providing better teaching methods and materials for special classes. In 1975 the Education for All Handicapped Children Act was passed by Congress. This act required that all children with disabilities between the ages of 3 and 21 will receive education in regular classrooms whenever possible. In an effort to serve children from birth to age three the 1975 Act was updated to Individuals with Disabilities Education Act (IDEA) of 1990. This act provides a special category of "developmental delay" for children who are in need of early interventions and special services. Each state is required to develop specific criteria and evaluations for identifying children who need early interventions (Berns, 2004).

An important provision of IDEA allows states to use the category "developmental delay" for preschool children. For example, children with special needs that have been diagnosed with cerebral palsy or spina bifida can be provided with special interventions and special services. Other children who have been exposed to environmental variables such as abuse, disease, or poverty can also receive special services under this act.

Goals for children with disabilities are conceptualized via an Individualized Education Program (IEP) written for each child by the beginning of the school year. This written plan is communicated to key school personnel and family. Included in the plan are the child's level of education performance, goals and objectives, related services provided to the child, evaluation procedures, and transition services for school-to-work or continuing education, usually by the age of 14 to 16.

Students with disabilities are also provided with tutors, interpreters, transportation, speech pathology and audiology, occupational and physical therapy, medical, and counseling services among others. They also receive hearing aids, wheelchairs, Braille dictionaries, and other supplementary aids. Innovative programs continue to be developed across the nation, including integrated classrooms and using peers as socialization agents (Berns, 2004).

What we see here is a movement from no provisions of funds for students with disabilities to a growing recognition that people with disabilities have unique needs that can and should be fostered in public education. Although many citizens recognized the need for funds before 1975, it was not until around this time that general funding was provided. Sadly, before 1975, people with disabilities were isolated and had little interaction with others. This point is made to underscore the importance of viewing each student as a unique individual rather than as someone who is disabled or handicapped, a narrow stereotypical view. Helpers are to take heed—the general public is in need of a greater understanding of students with disabilities, their potentials, individual problems, and what these students are capable of accomplishing and what they can contribute to society. Counselors should recognize that we are only in our infancy in educating the general public about people with disabilities. Counselors are in a good position to develop a unified community effort to support and underwrite programs that provide opportunities for students with disabilities to live and work, and more important, be accepted in a community.

To serve students with disabilities effectively counselors should consider the development of a cooperative plan that involves school personnel and members of the community. Ideally, a cooperative effort between teachers and counselors promotes an effective school program that is supported and recognized by the community. Community leaders are to be encouraged to contribute to special classes in a variety of ways including visitations to work sites. School-to-work transitions require a proactive school effort and strong community involvement.

School counselors have a vital role in assisting teachers with building career development plans for students with disabilities. A major focus is on career information that provides an understanding of work roles, responsibilities, and the realities of the workplace. Counselors should be prepared to offer suggestions for evaluating and teaching information processing skills and strategies to enable students to comprehend critical information they will need in the work world. One key to helping teachers is a current comprehensive list of materials and teaching aids that are available in a variety of media formats.

Counselors will also want to provide prevocational skills training specifically tailored for students with a disability. Prevocational skills may include learning to accept responsibility, care of materials, being punctual, and learning to take initiative. In many cases this information is included in classroom instruction and counselors act as a consultant to teachers. Counselors should also make available appropriate measurement tools for specific needs of individual students. What is stressed here is the necessity to use standardized tests that are designed and standardized for students with disabilities or alternate forms of testing similar to methods discussed in Chapter 7.

Counselors can also lend a hand with life skills training. Such intervention strategies may include a number and variety of topics that deal with everyday living including purchasing goods, budgeting, banking, health care, home management, and interpersonal relations training. Understandably, the functioning level of each individual will greatly affect the content and level of life skill training. In other words, intervention strategies should be individualized.

Other career development interventions are also affected by the functioning level of each client. In general terms, however, clients should be taught interviewing skills, how to relate with authority figures and fellow workers, social skills, and experiences that one usually finds in the give-and-take of working and living. Finally, the transition from student to employee provides the counselor with the opportunity to help students learn to effectively change roles. As Ettinger (1991) long ago pointed out, change in environment is sometimes very difficult for people with disabilities.

A Group Counseling Program for Adult Individuals with Disabilities

The following counseling program illustrates a group counseling procedure for individuals with disabilities. The descriptions include excerpts that illustrate relevant counseling techniques. The counseling activity sequence consisted of four highly structured meetings, shown in Table 13-1. The clients were hospitalized male patients who were accepted as clients for a vocational rehabilitation project. John had been injured in a car accident and was almost totally paralyzed. The other clients had been injured in industrial accidents. Rex's right leg was amputated below the knee. Roberto had lost three fingers and developed a serious infection. Harold's injury prevented him from bending his left leg. Several days before the first counseling meeting, each client completed a vocational counseling inventory that was to be used as a counseling tool for each of four group meetings.

Table 13-1	Vocational Rehabilitation-Counseling Activity Sequence
Title	**Activity**
Personal/social adjustment counseling	Briefing on the purpose of counseling session; discussion of problems of workers with disabilities, personal/social adjustment problems, and factors influencing work performance
Peer group affiliation	Counseling session on the importance of good peer relations, factors influencing peer group affiliation, the give-and-take of working with others, and the influence of the working environment on job satisfaction
Worker–supervisor affiliation	Counseling session on the factors determining good relations with a supervisor, the role of the supervisor, and the influence of good worker–supervisor relations on work proficiency and job satisfaction.
Job attitude	Counseling session on factors determining vocational success, factors influencing attitudinal development, and the influence of job attitude on work proficiency and job satisfaction

Session I: Personal/Social Adjustment Counseling

The counselor began the first session with the usual self-introductions. The counselor briefed the clients on the purpose of the counseling session.

COUNSELOR: We're going to have four meetings to talk about some problems that you might experience when you return to the workforce. Today we're going to cover some personal problems that you might experience in readjusting to a work role and general factors that influence the performance of workers who have similar problems.

The next excerpt illustrates the use of the previously completed vocational counseling inventory and the importance of group interaction. The counselor selected items to stimulate discussion. For example, the item, "Now that I have a disability, life is going to be difficult," generated considerable discussion.

HAROLD: I've thought about this a lot since I've been in this hospital, and things are really going to be different when I get out.

ROBERTO: Well, I've been here for almost two months, and I've learned to accept the fact that I probably will be doing a different kind of work than I did before. By the way, what kind of work did you do? (looking at Harold)

HAROLD: I was a foreman on a construction job, and I had to go around the different jobs for this contractor I worked for.

ROBERTO: Well, you might be able to do the same kind of thing.

During this meeting, it was difficult for John to enter into the discussion, for he had been recently injured and was almost completely paralyzed. However, toward the end of the session he spoke.

JOHN: I used to play in a band before I had this car accident, but I don't know what I am going to be able to do now. Anyway, I'm going to this Warm Springs Foundation, and I hope I will get some feeling back in my body and I will find out something.

John's response had a great impact on the entire group because his message was quite clear; here was someone who still had hope even though his injury had the potential of being much more restrictive than those of the other members of the group.

Session II: Peer Group Affiliation

The next excerpt illustrates how group interaction enhanced Session II. This meeting began with the counselor's question, "What kind of people did you like to work with on previous jobs?"

During the course of exchanging ideas, several opinions were expressed. It became apparent to the counselor that all but one member of the group seemed to have a fairly healthy attitude toward peer workers. The counselor used several key questions and phrases to stimulate discussion: "Are most people you work with easy to talk to during breaks?" "Some people feel like an outsider on the job." "A friend of mine prefers working alone." "Are most of the people you have worked with friendly?"

Through group interaction, the point was made that good peer relations are most important for the worker with a disability. Examples of statements from group members follow:

JOHN: Some people are going to try to pity me because I've got a disability, while some are going to be very uncomfortable when I'm around.

REX: To have a friend, you have to be a friend, and you can also do that as a disabled person.

HAROLD: Not everybody you work with is going to be friendly, but it sure helps if you try.

Session III: Worker–Supervisor Affiliation

The excerpts from this session illustrate how the counselor took advantage of the experiences of one group member to enhance the discussion. Harold had been employed in a supervisory position before his accident but was rather hesitant in communicating his viewpoint as a supervisor. The counselor began this session by having each member of the group discuss his relationships with a past supervisor or a boss. Each client stated that he had very little difficulty with worker–supervisor relationships. However, the counselor suspected that the relationships between employee and supervisor were not as compatible as expressed by the clients. Therefore, the counselor introduced several topics, hoping to elicit further responses from the group. An example of the exchange among group members follows:

COUNSELOR: I've had some bosses that I would have worked harder for had they been more friendly. How about the rest of you?

ROBERTO: I remember a few guys like that, and we used to really chew them up during our bull sessions.

JOHN: Yeah, sometimes bosses give too many orders and are not really interested in you.

HAROLD: (Finally responding) Well, when I was the boss, sometimes I had to get on people to make them work. Look at it this way, bosses have bosses, and they also have pressure to get the job done.

REX: Hey! How about that, I guess so.

JOHN: Yeah, I guess everybody has to answer to someone.

The discussion continued, centering on how one's perception of a supervisor influences personal reactions to the work environment.

Session IV: Job Attitude

The following excerpt illustrates how the counselor continued with the very productive previous counseling session and related the previous topic of discussion to the purpose of this final meeting.

COUNSELOR: Well, last time we raked bosses over the coals, but we finally agreed that bosses and supervisors do have a pretty tough job, and they are generally good guys if you act like you want to work with them and do a good job. This will be especially important for a worker with a disability.

The counselor then asked each group member to restate what he had learned from the previous meeting.

COUNSELOR: Each of you has illustrated how your attitudes about a supervisor influenced how you viewed the work environment. Now, let's direct our attention to how your attitudes will affect your return to the workforce as a worker with a disability.

ROBERTO: If you have a good attitude about your boss and people you work with, you will probably like your job, too.

JOHN: We have gotta think positive or we'll lose hope.

HAROLD: Sometimes it's going to be hard to have the right attitude—but you only hurt yourself.

This group counseling program was designed to encourage group interaction by sharing concerns about new and different lifestyles as persons with disabilities. Programs like this one emphasize (1) personal/social adjustment problems that might be encountered by each member of the group when he or she returns to the workforce, (2) retraining that could be necessary for a different occupation, (3) peer affiliation and supervisor relationships as a person with disabilities, and (4) the influence of one's attitudes on work proficiency and job satisfaction.

Summary

1. The terms used to describe people with disabilities have changed to negate stereotypes and false ideas.
2. The passage of the ADA has focused more attention on career counseling programs designed especially to meet the needs of individuals with disabilities. The ADA is a comprehensive document that covers several subjects significant to the rights of individuals with disabilities, including fair employment practices and access to public accommodations and transportation.
3. Special problems and needs of persons with disabilities include difficulty adjusting to and accepting physical disabilities, attitudinal barriers, being labeled "disabled," lack of role models, onset of disability, social/interpersonal skills, self-concept, skills for independent living, and architectural barriers. Educational programs that develop a better understanding of the special problems are needed by both employers and families.
4. State rehabilitation agencies provide numerous and varied programs for persons with disabilities. An actual case of an individual who received rehabilitation services from a state agency included the following steps: initial contact, diagnostic workup, evaluation and certification, vocational assessment, service planning, placement, and postemployment services.
5. Privately supported rehabilitation agencies provide educational, work, and counseling programs. Among services offered are psychological testing, vocational evaluation, personal/social adjustment counseling, work adjustment, prevocational training, special academic instruction, skills training, job placement, and sheltered workshops.

6. A career education program for students with disabilities uses a Life-Centered Career Education Curriculum. Included are a career awareness phase, a career exploration phase, and a preparation phase.

7. A group counseling program that promotes the vocational rehabilitation of individuals with disabilities included activities in (a) personal/social adjustment, (b) peer group affiliation, (c) worker–supervisor affiliation, and (d) job attitude counseling.

Supplementary Learning Exercises

1. Interview a rehabilitation counselor and obtain program descriptions for individuals with disabilities.

2. Make several observations of a special education class. Compile a list of common problems based on your observations. Relate these problems to job placement.

3. Develop a list of rehabilitation journals that publish articles concerning career counseling programs for individuals with disabilities.

4. Visit an industry that employs individuals with disabilities. Compile a list of jobs performed and worker function activities.

5. Survey your campus to find physical barriers that restrict individuals with disabilities. Discuss how these barriers and others contribute to psychological barriers.

6. Interview an individual who has a disability and is currently employed. Report your results to class.

7. Compile a list of audiovisual materials that can be incorporated in career counseling programs for individuals with disabilities. Review and report on at least two.

8. Develop counseling components designed to meet two or more special problems and needs.

9. Survey a community to determine programs available for individuals with disabilities. Using the survey results, develop plans for using these programs in a high school or community college counseling program.

10. Interview a personnel director of an industry that employs individuals with disabilities to determine common problems experienced by these workers. Develop counseling components to help individuals overcome the problems commonly reported.

For More Information

Brammer, R. (2004). *Diversity in counseling.* Belmont, CA: Brooks/Cole-Thomson Learning.

DePoy, E., & Gilson, S. F. (2004). *Rethinking disability: Principles for professional and social change.* Belmont, CA: Brooks/Cole-Thomson Learning.

Frank, R. G., & Elliott, T. R. (Eds.). (2000). *Handbook of rehabilitation psychology.* Washington, DC: American Psychological Association.

French, S. (1996). The attitudes of health professionals towards disabled people. In G. Hales (Ed.), *Beyond disability: Towards an enabling society* (pp. 151–162). London: Sage.

Mackelprang, R., & Salsgiver, R. (1999). *Disability: A diversity model approach in human service practice.* Pacific Grove, CA: Brooks/Cole.

Scherer, M. J. (2004). *Connecting to learn: Educational and assisting technology for people with disabilities.* Washington, DC: American Psychological Association.

Szymanski, E. M., & Parker, R. M. (Eds.) (1996). *Work and disability: Issues and strategies in career development and job placement.* Austin, TX: PRO-ED.

Suggested InfoTrac College Edition Topics

Americans with Disability Act

Assessment for disabled persons

Career for disabled persons

Counseling disabled persons

Needs of disabled persons

Onset of disability

Rehabilitation programs

Career Counseling for Gay, Lesbian, and Bisexual Clients

14

Chapter Highlights

- Sexual orientation as a factor in career counseling approaches

- Negative stereotypes attributed to homophobia

- Forms of discrimination at work: blackmail, ostracism, sexual harassment, exclusion, the lavender ceiling

- Identity issues and a homosexual identity formation model

- Holistic approach to identity development

- Cultural differences in sexual orientation

- Special needs of youth with same-sex orientations

- Six-stage model for career counseling gay, lesbian, and bisexual individuals

IN OUR FINAL CHAPTER on special populations it seems appropriate to reflect on some statements made in several chapters concerning the needs of diverse groups. On several occasions the point was made that a single career development theory cannot fully account for all needs of all clients. Thus, career counseling models should be flexible enough to incorporate special provisions for special populations or groups that have unique needs. For instance, practitioners need intervention strategies that focus on meeting the needs of individuals who are experiencing multiple identities and multiple oppressions. Moreover, accounting for the needs of special groups is good reason for developing minitheories for building counseling models. The previous four chapters in this section support that position and, with the addition of this chapter, we suggest even more consideration be given to the needs of special populations.

As we develop as a nation in the 21st century, the chances are that an even greater number of groups of individuals with special needs will emerge. Thus, what began as a humble counseling program in the 20th century to help immigrants with special needs should continue to expand its focus to include appropriate counseling models for other groups with special needs. The groups discussed in this chapter are no exception to that position.

First, the special needs of gay, lesbian, and bisexual persons (g/l/b) will be discussed. Gelberg and Chojnacki (1996) suggest this grouping to provide fluidity to the discussion of individuals who have special needs because of their sexual orientation. Two other ways of referring to this population is gay, lesbian, bisexual, and transgendered (GLBT) and/or simply sexual minorities (Barrett & Logan, 2002). The term g/l/b and sexual minorities will be used interchangeably. This grouping does not imply that g/l/b needs are the same and does not suggest a greater priority for any one group. Distinctions between groups and within groups will be highlighted throughout this chapter. In the first sections some general trends and counseling issues of sexual minorities will be introduced. The sections that follow will include discrimination in the workplace of g/l/b individuals, identity issues, cultural differences in sexual orientation, counseling concerns of sexual minority youth, and career counseling suggestions for g/l/b clients.

Gay, Lesbian, and Bisexual Persons

It is difficult to arrive at a precise number of g/l/b persons living in this country; however, estimates have ranged between 5 and 25 million individuals (Henderson, 1984; Kinsey, Pomeroy, & Martin, 1948; Michael, Gagnon, Lauman, & Kolata, 1994) and 7.5 to 25 million (Elliot, 1993). In 1999, however, Sprague (1999) estimated that there are 26 million sexual minority Americans. One problem in determining more precise numbers is the methodologies and definitions used for defining sexual orientation preference. We are safe in assuming, however, that there are a significant number of potential g/l/b clients who need career counseling.

There appears to be a growing trend for more open discussion about the effects of sexual orientation on career development. Kronenberger (1991) and Barrett and Logan (2002) reported that more lesbian women and gay men are coming out of the closet and discussing issues they face, especially in the workplace. Evidence suggests that more companies are supporting gay and lesbian associations and networks, including Xerox, AT&T, Lockheed, Rand Corporation, Hewlett-Packard, Sun

Microsystems, U.S. West Communications, and Levi Strauss. Many of these organizations have regarded gay men and lesbian women as another diverse group in the workforce and are dealing with this group just as they do with multiethnic groups; they have added a sexual-orientation component to diversity training programs. However, the issues surrounding homosexuality in general and its effect on career development and bias in the workplace are far from being settled.

One major objective of sexual minorities is to find acceptance in the workplace by removing barriers that discriminate and inhibit their career development. Hudson (1992) suggested that counselors should prepare for counseling g/l/b clients by building an extensive body of resources including specific information on those organizations and companies that support them as employees and a list of g/l/b professionals who could provide support and information. Several years ago Eldridge (1987) provided the following recommendations for counselors that remain relevant in contemporary society: (1) keep in mind the subtle, insidious nature of heterosexual bias and use this knowledge as a reminder for reflection; (2) use gender-free language; (3) become familiar with models of g/l/b identity formation; (4) identify a consultant who can provide helpful information or feedback from sexual minorities; and (5) become familiar with local support networks.

Counselor Checklist

A counselor checklist by Goldenberg and Goldenberg (2002) containing myths regarding g/l/b clients is provided in Box 14.1. There are many purposes for this list but one of the most relevant is the need for counselor preparation for counseling sexual minorities. As mentioned on several pages in this text, stereotypes need to be debunked when dealing with the needs of special groups, and there are many common myths regarding g/l/b clients that have led to g/l/b identity issues and self-criticism. It is therefore the responsibility of counselors who counsel sexual minorities to build an understanding of their unique development as well as the basic issues they face in contemporary society.

Some General Counseling Issues

The purpose of this section is to focus on problems and concerns sexual minorities face in career counseling and in the workplace. The first issue that generally surfaces is that of stereotyping about the kind of jobs gay men and lesbian women commonly hold. For example, gay men are thought to occupy traditional female jobs such as interior decorator or hair stylist; lesbians are firefighters, truck drivers, and auto mechanics. As has been emphasized throughout this text, clients should feel free to explore all occupations of interest. Clients who have had their career aspirations limited because of stereotyping—that is, the jobs they consider appropriate because of their sexual orientation—especially need encouragement to consider all career options. Counselors need to take an active role in challenging stereotypes in an effort to expand a client's perception of what is an appropriate career, and in this context, sexual orientation should be viewed as only one factor to consider in career exploration and decision.

Box 14-1	A Counselor Checklist of Common Myths Regarding Homosexuality

Do you believe these statements?

- Most gay men are effeminate, and most lesbians are masculine in appearance and behavior.
- Most gay couples adopt male/female (active/passive) roles in their relationships.
- All gay men are sexually promiscuous.
- Gay men believe that they are women in men's bodies, and gay women believe that they are men in women's bodies.
- Most gay people would have a sex-change operation if they could afford it.
- Most gay people are child molesters.
- People choose to become homosexual.
- Most gay people are unhappy with their sexual orientation and seek therapy to convert to heterosexuality.
- Counselors report high success rates in converting homosexuals to heterosexuals.
- Most gay people are easily identifiable by their dress and mannerisms.

- Homosexual behavior is unnatural because it does not occur in other species.
- Homosexuality is the result of a hereditary defect.
- Homosexuals have hormone abnormalities.
- All homosexual males have dominant, overbearing mothers and weak, passive fathers.
- Homosexuality threatens the continuity of the species.
- All male hairdressers, interior decorators, and ballet dancers are homosexuals.
- Homosexuality is an illness that can be cured.

SOURCE: Gartrell, 1983.

SOURCE: From *Counseling Today's Families*, 4th ed., by Goldenberg/Goldenberg (Belmont, CA: Brooks/Cole, 2002), p. 250. This box is reprinted with kind permission of Springer Science and Business Media from N. Gartrell, "Gay Patients in the Medical Setting," in C. C. Nadelson and D. B. Marcotte (eds.), *Interventions in Human Sexuality*, p. 396. Copyright © 1983 Plenum Publishing Group.

Homophobia has been described as "an irrational fear, hatred, and intolerance of g/l/b persons" (Gelberg & Chojnacki, 1996, p. 21). This feeling of fear, hatred, and intolerance has led to violence, discrimination, and rejection of sexual minorities in society in general and the workplace in particular. This fear enhances negative stereotypes and is deeply embedded in our society and in many societies around the world. Currently, there are frequent reports of extreme violence resulting in physical and psychological harm to sexual minorities (Brammer, 2004).

Internalized homophobia refers to how g/l/b individuals are affected by societal beliefs as they react to salient messages received in their environments. In early identity development some sexual minorities who are greatly affected by internalized homophobia reject themselves as appropriate individuals and form a dislike for self and a self-hatred for their feelings of attraction to members of the same sex. This is particularly true during early stages of awareness of their sexual orientation. Adolescents, for instance, might not fully understand the precise meaning of their differences in sexual identity but quickly learn that it is negatively regarded. They may be described as highly anxious, fearful, guilty, and self-loathing (Barrett & Logan, 2002; Gelberg & Chojnacki, 1996). Gay and lesbian adolescents are particularly vulnerable to internal conflicts in coming to terms with their sexual orientation and challenges and threats from their peers and others in society.

Heterosexist assumptions are based on a culture that is biased toward heterosexuality (Eldridge & Barnett, 1991; Goldenberg & Goldenberg, 2002). In our society and in many others throughout the world, heterosexism is considered the only viable lifestyle (Galliano, 2003). The point here is that counselors must be aware of their own homophobic and heterosexist bias when counseling sexual minorities. Those counselors who want to become g/l/b affirmative must challenge their own assumptions when trying to understand the complexity of a sexual orientation different than their own. For instance, two same-sex partners who live together in many states do not have the same rights as legally married individuals of the opposite sex do. Sexual minorities are not welcome in some work environments. The stigma associated with being a g/l/b person might continue over the life span. These examples suggest that sexual minorities might view career life planning much differently than heterosexual individuals do.

The American Psychological Association (1991) has issued a published set of guidelines for avoiding heterosexual bias in language. Counselors should carefully choose proper words, especially gender-free nouns such as partner or significant other. Avoid the term *homosexual,* which could imply a diagnostic category of mental illness. Use the term *sexual orientation* rather than *sexual preference.*

Discrimination of G/L/B Persons at Work

There are many forms of discrimination of sexual minorities at work. One example is overt discrimination, which can lead to violence directed at g/l/b individuals. "Gay bashing," which is not always work-related, has been documented in newspaper articles in various geographical regions. Many incidents of "gay bashing" are not reported, however, primarily because the victim is reluctant to call attention to his or her sexual orientation. In many cases, violence is simply threatened as a means of harassing sexual minorities at work.

"Hidden discrimination" is typically involved in hiring, promotion, and compensation (Barrett & Logan, 2002; Friskopp & Silverstein, 1995). Known sexual minorities are treated differently than are their peers and are given diminished opportunities for advancement. This form of discrimination is subtle but effectively relays the message that this person is not wanted in an organization. Overt and hidden discrimination in a work environment obviously discourages sexual minorities from making their sexual orientation known.

Other forms of discrimination are blackmail, ostracism, sexual harassment, exclusion or avoidance, termination, and the so-called "lavender ceiling." Openly gay managers may not have access to higher-level corporate positions because of their sexual orientation, and as a result, plateau early in their careers when they reach the "lavender ceiling" (Friskopp & Silverstein, 1995). The "lavender ceiling" for sexual minorities, like the "glass ceiling" for women, is a discrimination method that is often hidden.

Because discrimination at work, especially in a hostile work environment, has the potential of being very threatening to sexual minorities, support groups may be helpful. Clients may find that networking provides important and relevant information to help determine if one should leave an organization or transfer to another, more friendly and amiable division. For instance, when interviewing a gay man who had experienced threats of violence in an organization, Friskopp and Silverstein (1995) found that by networking he discovered that a different division in the organization was more g/l/b affirmative and friendly. Counselors should provide a list of company-based g/l/b employee groups that can provide information about specific organizations. Statewide gay professional organizations are another valuable resource. Clients also can be directed to resources that provide the names and addresses of g/l/b friendly organizations as listed in the final section of this chapter. Finally, a resource file of individuals who have experienced workforce discrimination as a sexual minority and are willing to help others is a most valuable referral source.

Identity Issues

Concepts of identity development have a long-standing relationship with career counseling. Career development theorists such as Super (1957, 1990), have emphasized the importance and pervasive nature of self-concept development in career counseling. More recently, identity development literature has involved racial-ethnic and sexual orientation identity models. Barrett and Logan (2002) and Reynolds and Pope (1991) argue, however, that there is a scarcity of research on issues of multiple oppressions and identities; Latina lesbians, for example, face more complexities in the identity development process than do white, middle-class females. Unearthing identity issues involved in developing g/l/b sexual orientations will take considerable extensive research in the future.

Model of Homosexual Identity Formation

Cass (1979, 1984) has developed a gay identity model entitled Model of Homosexual Identity Formation (HIF). There appears to be empirical evidence to support its constructs (Levine & Evans, 1991). The HIF contains six stages and is discussed in the following paragraphs.

> Stage I: Identity Confusion
>
> Stage II: Identity Comparison
>
> Stage III: Identity Tolerance
>
> Stage IV: Identity Acceptance
>
> Stage V: Identity Pride
>
> Stage VI: Identity Synthesis

Identity Confusion, Stage I, may be described as an awareness stage in which the individual recognizes that his or her feelings and behaviors indicate a same-sex orientation. This is a period of soul-searching and internal conflicts and a process of clarifying self-concept in adolescence (Erikson, 1963) during which coming to terms with sexual identity is an integral part of development. In Stage II, Identity Comparison, the individual acknowledges the possibility of being attracted to the same sex, feels different, and develops a sense of social alienation; the individual has difficulty in identifying with family and peer groups. During Stage III, Identity Tolerance, the individual tolerates rather than accepts an identification of an individual whose sexual orientation is different; however, the individual begins to contact other g/l/b persons to counter isolation. Identity Acceptance, Stage IV, is characterized by continued contacts with other g/l/b persons to validate a new identity and a new way of life. The individual accepts a g/l/b sexual orientation as an alternate identity. In Stage V, Identity Pride, the individual takes pride in disclosing an identity as a g/l/b person and rejects heterosexuality as the only appropriate lifestyle. In the final stage, Stage VI, Identity Synthesis, the individual is able to integrate a g/l/b identity with other aspects of self and develops compatibility with both heterosexual and g/l/b worlds.

This model provides points of reference for many factors that are significant to career counseling and career decision making, starting with problem identification during the intake interview. Individuals who have not fully developed their sexual orientation identity might have difficulty in projecting their self-concept into a work environment. They might limit their occupational choices or appear indecisive during times of anxiety, confusion, and instability. For instance, those who have reached Stage IV of identity acceptance might not be fully prepared or able to integrate their unfinished identity development within a career. Role confusion, emotional instability, irrational thinking, and indecisiveness can all be related to identity formation suggested in the HIF model. A word of caution—more than likely other related variables and factors also warrant consideration in problem identification, including examples that are discussed in the following paragraphs.

When using this model as a framework for career counseling, the counselor should be aware of the following four points: (1) some sexual minorities may recycle through the model depending on experiences and encounters within contextual interactions in the environment and particularly in the work environment; their progress might not be continuous; (2) the time it takes to move through the different stages in the identity model can vary enough that there are significant differences and might involve other factors not accounted for in the model; (3) there appear to be developmental differences between g/l/b persons, that is, gay men, lesbian women, and bisexuals could have different patterns of identity development; and (4) sexual orientation is only one variation in human development and other variables might account for individual variation (D'Augelli, 1991; Fassinger & Schlossberg, 1992; Fox, 1991; Gelberg & Chojnacki, 1996; Pope & Reynolds, 1991; Reynolds & Hanjorgiris, 2000; Sophie, 1986).

Some related issues that point out the limitations of stage identity models are relevant to developing career counseling interventions. First, stage identity models suggest that sexual identity development has only one outcome; these models fall short of accounting for diversity of experiences during the developmental process (L. S. Brown, 1995). Individuals develop multiple identities that must be integrated with other group memberships and identities. A bisexual person, for instance, who is uncertain about how to interpret his or her sexual attractions to both men and women might be very apprehensive about making a career commitment. Second, individuals from different ethnic backgrounds could reflect a completely different viewpoint of sexual concepts and identity. Some cultural groups may inhibit certain forms of sexual expression and prescribe others (Brammer, 2004; Rust, 1996).

Also, as suggested in Chapter 10, identity development is not a segmented process and should therefore be considered more comprehensive and inclusive (Myers, Speight, Highlen, Cox, Reynolds, Adams, & Hanley, 1991). As a more holistic approach, identity development is viewed as a multidimensional process that includes multiple oppressions based on race, ethnicity, sexual orientation, sex, and age. For an ethnic minority lesbian, all oppressions must be considered to fully understand the process of identity development. This comprehensive viewpoint suggests that we should not isolate variables but, rather, assist individuals in conceptualizing the totality of the process of self-identity development. For example, individuals are not to be socialized into a worldview that leads to a fragmented sense of self. Furthermore, for an individual to feel positive about being a sexual minority requires that individual to repudiate external stereotypes of g/l/b individuals. Although an optimal theory of identity development suggests that current identity models have limitations, the HIF model does provide some guidelines for relevant information that can be included in the career counseling process.

In sum, unique development can account for differences among each type of sexual orientation. For instance, the unique needs of lesbian women could result in different patterns and timing of development than would be typical of gay men or bisexual individuals (Barrett & Logan, 2002; Sophie, 1986). Etringer, Hillerbrand, and Hetherington (1990) suggest that lesbians are less uncertain about making a career decision when compared with gay men, heterosexual men, and women. The researchers conclude, "the degree of uncertainty regarding one's career choice and degree of dissatisfaction with that choice vary by sex and by sexual orientation" (p. 107). The causes of uncertainty among g/l/b populations have not been fully determined but are thought to be associated with employment discrimination and self-disclosure of sexual orientation. Hence, lesbian women, for example, might be more reluctant to self-disclose in career decision making than gay men are.

A good characterization of sexual minority identity development is a gradual process of discovery rather than a sudden awakening during childhood. Children might sense a feeling of being different, and this perception can provide sexual meaning during puberty. Periods of confusion might be followed by anxiety that usually takes years to resolve. Progress from one stage to another is usually not orderly, but individuals move to and from stages of development sporadically as they struggle with self-awareness (Barrett & Logan, 2002; Brammer, 2004; Coleman & Remafedi, 1989). Thus, counselors who can identify a client's progress in the HIF model have significant information concerning self-awareness and other important factors relevant to career decision making.

Some research identifies when the awareness of same-sex feelings and attractions takes place. For gay males, this is during early to mid-adolescence and for lesbian women, around the age of 20 (Anderson, 1994). Other findings include a survey of 13 Japanese American gay males in which half of them reported that they began to experience same-sex feelings during the early teens and the remainder in their late teens and early twenties (Wooden, Kawasaki, & Mayeda, 1983).

A survey of onset of sexual orientation of 120 lesbian women and gay adolescents suggested they experienced same-sex feelings between 4 and 18 years of age (Telljohann & Price, 1993). Finally, a study by Uribe and Harbeck (1992) reported same-sex experiences for gay males occurred at an average age of 14, but much later for lesbian women. These studies suggest that onset of same-sex attractions can vary for individuals but it usually begins during adolescence. Gay males experience same-sex activities earlier than lesbian women do. The amount of time that it takes an individual to progress through stages does not appear to be clear-cut nor is the age when gay men and lesbian women reach the final stage of identity in Cass's model. One could conclude that progress through the HIF is not necessarily linear but could be characterized as cyclical as individuals cycle-regress-recycle through stages. This argument is supported by Barrett and Logan (2002) and McCarn and Fassinger (1996) who suggest that the developmental process of gay men and lesbian women could extend well into adulthood.

Cultural Differences in Sexual Orientation

In this section, we focus on differences in sexual orientation by culture. The research in this area is very sparse; counselors should watch for more in-depth research and analysis in the near future. More than likely new themes and patterns of cultural differences in sexual orientation will emerge early in the 21st century. In the meantime, this discussion of cultural differences in sexual orientation provides a means of discovering special needs of Asian Americans, African Americans, Latina and Latino Americans, and Native Americans.

According to Chung and Katayama (1999), there are significant differences between Asian and American cultures toward acceptance of the different sexual orientation of g/l/b individuals. Chung and Katayama point out that heterosexism and homophobia are more prominent and intense in Asian cultures and suggest three overarching reasons why homosexuality is not accepted in Asian cultures: First is the philosophy of harmony and complementary parts of the Chinese *yin-yang,* which has counterparts in other Asian cultures such as Korea and Japan. This philosophy represents a natural order of life that prescribes that persons of the opposite sex are to be unified; thus, it is against nature to have a same-sex orientation. Second, because traditional gender roles and family systems in most Asian cultures are so highly honored, same-sex orientations are unacceptable. As a result, sexual minority activities and relationships are closely censored. Third is the prominence of agrarian societies in Asian countries, in which farmlands are passed down from one traditional family to the next. Same-sex orientation works against this long-established tradition. These traditions and the philosophy of a "natural life," according to yin-yang, does not allow for an open same-sex orientation lifestyle. Because the consequences of disclosing a same-sex orientation are so severe, most sexual minorities remain in the closet. As a result, the concept of g/l/b identity is not recognized in many Asian cultures (Chung & Katayama, 1999).

Asian American g/l/b persons have found a somewhat more compatible environment in America, especially in certain geographic regions. Being aware of the mores, traditions, and lifestyles of the sexual minorities' mother country and its society, however, provides counselors a greater understanding of identity development and contextual messages individuals receive from their environment in this country. Evidence also indicates that Asian lesbians and gays have difficulty in being accepted in white and middle-class-oriented gay communities (Chan, 1989; Newman & Muzzonigro, 1993). In this context they are considered, like other minority ethnic groups, to have a double minority status. As Chung and Katayama (1999) put it, their "efforts involve the parallel psychological processes of developing integrated ethnic and sexual identities" (p. 166).

In a study by Chan (1989), 19 women and 16 men between the ages of 21 and 36 who identified themselves as lesbian, gay, and Asian Americans were interviewed and filled out a questionnaire. Most of the sample was Asian Americans who were born in Asia. The results suggested that most of these first-generation individuals preferred to identify themselves as lesbian and gay rather than as Asian Americans, but others in the sample refused to identify as one or the other, preferring instead to identify with both. This latter group felt that it was as difficult to be accepted by the gay and lesbian community as by the Asian community. Chan (1989) concluded that the stage of identity development largely determined whether an individual was identified more closely with being lesbian or gay or Asian American. Disclosure as lesbian or gay in this sample usually occurred by informing a sister rather than parents. It appeared that most felt their parents would not accept their sexual orientation and feared rejection.

In another study, Chan (1997) suggests that modern homosexual identities are Western constructs. East Asian cultures have no comparable sexual identities. Discussions about sexuality are taboo and considered highly embarrassing even among friends. An individual's sexual orientation is considered to be private. Sexuality issues are not usually expressed in public. Moreover, the concept of individual identity does not exist; there is only group identification as a family member. Thus, cultural differences in identity development, especially among Asian Americans, need further exploration and analysis.

In a study of gay issues among black Americans, Loiacano (1989) found similar results to those reported by Asian sexual minorities. Black American lesbians are largely considered incompatible with role expectations in a black community (Greene, 1997; Lorde, 1984; Smith 1997). Furthermore, gay and lesbian communities do not offer the same level of affirmation to blacks that they do to their white members. Black gay men were viewed as inferior as members of gay communities and do not receive the same level of affirmation that white members do (Icard, 1986). Loiacano (1989) confirmed these findings in an interview with a small sample of three males and three females. Later, he suggested that three themes emerged from his interview: (1) finding validation in the gay and lesbian community, (2) finding validation in the black community, and (3) needing to integrate identities (Loiacano, 1993). Although his study is considered as only providing tentative data, it seems to verify the idea of a double minority status among black gays and lesbians.

A study of 20 older African American gay men living in New York City, whose average age was 56, presents some interesting data. The authors of this study conclude that being an African American gay was different than being white and gay primarily because of the interpretation of race and color in our society (Adams & Kimmel, 1997). In the African American community, gay men are perceived negatively as wanting to be female, as being cross-dressers, and as threatening family child-rearing responsibilities. Gay men are also perceived as traitors to African American families and their race. The lesbian and gay community is viewed as a white establishment that ignores the needs of people of color. These attitudes and stereotypes make it difficult for African American gay men to feel accepted in both the African American community and the gay and lesbian community (Adams & Kimmel, 1997). The results of this study should be interpreted as characteristic of this sample only; however, similar conclusions were reached by Barrett and Logan (2002), Icard (1986), Lorde (1984), and Loiacano (1993).

Finally, a study of the results of an anonymous questionnaire of 1,400 African American gay men and lesbian women from various geographic regions in the continental United States was reported by Peplau, Cochran, and Mays (1997). Significant conclusions of relevant information for career counseling include the findings that interracial partners were relatively common among the respondents and that same-sex activities are often more hidden in the African American community than in white gay and lesbian communities. These conclusions suggest that African American gay and lesbians have little support for their sexual orientation within their communities, which makes it more difficult to integrate identities for career development and to focus on traditional career and life planning issues.

Barrett and Logan (2002) and Espin (1987) found similar results among Latina lesbian women. This group of lesbians also feared rejection in the Hispanic community and received marginal support in the gay and lesbian community. Espin found that it was difficult to determine if ethnic identity or sexual orientation identity was considered most important by the women studied. She concluded that her respondents had varying degrees of success as identifying as both lesbian and Latina.

Morales (1992) depicts the Latino and Latina community as being excessively homophobic and thus having little tolerance for gay and lesbian lifestyle. He suggests that Latino gay men and Latina lesbians exist in three worlds: the gay and lesbian community, the Latino and Latina community, and the white heterosexual mainstream society. Choosing which of the three to identify with presents challenges and conflicts that are indeed complex. In the beginning of the choice process Latino gay men and Latina lesbians might resort to denial of conflicts. Using the unrealistic logic of denial, they might naïvely choose a gay and lesbian lifestyle with the hope that they will find a utopian lifestyle free of discrimination and conflicts they encounter in their own communities and in the dominant culture.

A second choice might focus on coming out as a bisexual rather than as gay or lesbian. This choice avoids being labeled and categorized as gay, or in Spanish, *maricón* and thus, might be more acceptable to individuals who have difficulty in identifying with gay and lesbian communities. In a third choice, Latino gay men and lesbian women choose to live independently in all three communities and not "mix" the three. The conflicts in allegiances that soon develop usually lead to high levels of anxiety and fears of betrayal and most come to the conclusion that some form of unity is desirable (Morales, 1992).

In the final stages of establishing priorities, the integration process becomes the central focus. Being identified within three communities as gay or lesbian, however, can result in fear and anxiety about the future and lead to the recognition that such an identity will be a constant challenge. These circumstances expose Latino gay men and Latina lesbians to risks of loosing career opportunities that are already limited because of their minority status (Morales, 1992). Like other minority groups, Latino gay men and Latina lesbians should be helped throughout this entire process by support groups and relevant information about prospective employers and their hiring policies (Barrett & Logan, 2002).

To understand the gay and lesbian world of Native Americans, we must digress in a few sentences to the mid-18th century. French missionaries at that time report finding Native American men who dressed in women's clothing, assumed female roles, and accepted other men as sexual partners. The French word *berdache,* meaning male homosexual, was given to these men and also to women who assumed the role of warrior and hunter and wore male attire.

Among the Native Americans in whom this behavior was observed, the berdache were not only tolerated, but well accepted in some tribes. The berdache phenomenon was evidently widespread in the major cultural groups in North America, in some tribes in Mexico and South America, and among the Alaskan Eskimo (Mondimore, 1996).

According to Tafoya (1997) and Brown (1997), the berdache phenomenon is a part of a Native American's worldview of a "Two-Spirited tradition." In this context, Native Americans are not comfortable with identifying themselves as g/l/b persons but, rather, as individuals who possess both male and female spirits. As Tafoya (1997) explains, "gay can be seen as a noun, but Two-Spirit as a verb. . . . This is meant as a metaphoric statement, meaning that a noun is a person, place, or thing, whereas a verb deals with action and interaction" (p. 5). What is emphasized here is that the Native American tradition stresses transformation and change that is too flexible to fit the categories of gay or straight. Masculine and feminine concepts of Native Americans are quite different from European concepts. There is a greater spectrum of acceptable sexual behavior among Native Americans, and there is less stigma associated with women who assume male roles and men who assume female roles (Brammer, 2004; Brown, 1997; Highwater, 1990).

The berdache phenomenon and the Two-Spirited person might not be well known among many young Native Americans, especially those who have attended federal boarding or missionary schools. However, a visit to the Lakotas and Sioux in the Northern Plains in 1982 found that the berdache tradition was still practiced although modified from what was described as the "old ways" (Williams, 1993). Contemporary practices are more secretive and are not enthusiastically endorsed by young Native Americans; however, Native Americans in general have great tolerance and respect for personal choice. In this context, the Native American community might be more accepting of individuals who identify as Two-Spirited in Native American terms or as g/l/b in the dominant society. Nevertheless, g/l/b individuals must also face a dominant society that is less tolerant and discriminates against individuals who are identified as having a same-sex orientation. Native Americans are also subject to stereotyping as discussed in Chapter 10.

In sum, one could conclude that ethnic minority gays indeed have a double minority status. A lesbian ethnic minority could be given a triple minority status. Both ethnic minority gays and lesbians struggle with parallel psychological processes of identity; ethnic identity and sexual orientation identity development complement or complicate self-awareness and self-concept development. In addition, lesbians must also overcome gender role socialization that can limit career development.

Throughout this text it has been emphasized that we must identify unique individual needs for career counseling direction. In this section some needs have been identified that can be generalized to most ethnic minority g/l/b groups. In other words, ethnic minority g/l/b persons share some general needs such as protection against discrimination, but each group of ethnic minorities also has special needs. Within these groups, individual needs must also be unearthed. In essence, all the unique needs of individuals who seek career counseling should be addressed.

Counseling G/L/B–Oriented Youth

Counselors have often been reminded that adolescents most need their services. In the context of working with g/l/b–oriented youth, the complex task of sexual identity can be very disruptive. A counselor who is aware of the issues surrounding the development of self-concept in career development must also be alert to the special problems brought about by sexual minority status during adolescence. Many g/l/b adolescents Coleman and Remafedi (1989) interviewed had abandoned their friends, were rejected by their families, had failing grades, and were involved in substance abuse. Furthermore, half of the sample had run away from home, had been arrested, or had a sexually transmitted disease. A smaller minority of the group had attempted suicide, accepted money for sexual favors, or been sexually victimized. Other studies in the 1970s by Bell and Weinberg (1978), Saghir and Robins (1973), and Jay and Young (1979), found that sexual orientation was a precipitating factor in suicide attempts among sexual minorities and that most attempts at suicide occurred before the age of 21. More recently, Barrett and Logan (2002) and Remafedi (1999) suggest that suicide rates are indeed higher for sexual minority youth.

Counselors should also recognize that overall health is a most important component of career counseling and that it is not unusual for many adolescents to take health for granted in a rather cavalier way. Their attitude about HIV infection might be reflected as a gay's problem; however, we now know that the risks of becoming HIV infected among sexually active adolescents have increased significantly for both heterosexual and g/l/b persons. The point here is the need to inform all adolescents, including sexual minorities, of the probability of HIV infection through sexual activity and the sharing of needles. Moreover, the risks appear greater for all adolescents who have not received instructions of risk-reduction guidelines (Ryan & Futterman, 1998). What we must make clear here is that HIV/AIDS is not solely a g/l/b disease.

Winfeld and Spielman (1995) have proposed an HIV/AIDS education program for the workplace that could be modified and used for other groups as well, including adolescents. Some topics that are relevant to our discussion here are the following:

- Theories of the origin of AIDS
- What are HIV and AIDS?
- How are HIV and AIDS transmitted?
- How are HIV and AIDS not transmitted?
- Who is at the greatest risk?
- Risk-reduction guidelines

Counselors who recognize the influence of sexual orientation on career development will create an atmosphere in which sexuality can be openly discussed. Counselors must be prepared to convey full acceptance of g/l/b clients. Counselors are not to assume that every client is heterosexually oriented or that certain clients are sexual minorities on the basis of stereotypical suggestions. The adolescent especially needs to feel comfortable in expressing sexual orientation issues. The counselor should convey a nonjudgmental attitude. Uncertainty, ambiguity, cultural stigma, and fears of the future are viable topics to be integrated in preparing adolescents for career decision making. A summary of other suggestions for counseling g/l/b youth is adapted from Barrett and Logan (2002) as follows:

1. Allow adolescents to explore their sexuality by avoiding premature labeling. Counselors are to encourage clients to seek out social and recreational opportunities. Be aware that at this age clients are immersed in a period of exploring and searching for answers.
2. Do not assume that all clients are heterosexual. Be prepared to provide accurate information regarding sexual minorities.

3. Ensure respect and confidentiality. Be prepared to discuss private sexual matters with clients. Make it clear that each client's rights to privacy and confidentiality are legally protected.
4. Be willing to mentor a gay/straight support group. Invite other professionals to become a part of the group's activities.
5. Be prepared to counsel both gay youth and their families. Be aware that families may react in a hostile manner. Be prepared to help adolescents and their parents with a wide range of feelings and reactions, including shock, denial, anger, and rejection.

Career Counseling for G/L/B Persons

Although sexual minority clients bring unique issues to career counseling, these issues can be resolved in integrative career counseling models that adapt and fuse personal and career counseling approaches to meet specific needs of all clients. The multicultural career counseling model for ethnic minority women outlined and discussed in Chapter 3, provides some guidelines for meeting the special needs of the sexual minority population. Within that model, steps designed to meet the special needs of ethnic minority groups provide examples for meeting the special needs of g/l/b persons. For instance, g/l/b persons locate their stage of identity development. Counselors explore their biases of sexual minorities. The contextual interactions of sexual minorities should be fully explored. Standardized tests that have not included sexual orientation as a variable in their development should be used with caution. Some g/l/b individuals might have limited their career choices because of stereotyped perceptions of what is considered appropriate work for gay men and lesbian women. The use of allies as mentors in the career decision process and job search is a viable option. All these issues should be resolved with holistic counseling models that meet the unique needs of g/l/b individuals.

The following six stages are designed for sexual minorities, and most important, can be included within contemporary career counseling models. Stage 1, precounseling preparation, requires the counselor to evaluate his or her awareness of the g/l/b worldviews and cultures. Counselors must challenge their own assumptions about g/l/b sexual orientation. Counselors may want to use consultants to assist them in the preparation process. The basic assumptions of counselors who are affirmative sexual minority helpers are characterized by an adaptation of the work of Schwartz and Harstein (1986) and quoted from Gelberg and Chojnacki (1996, p. 17) as follows:

1. Being gay, lesbian, or bisexual is not a pathological condition.
2. The origins of sexual orientation are not completely known.
3. G/l/b persons lead fulfilling and satisfying lives.
4. There are a variety of g/l/b lifestyles.
5. G/l/b persons who attend counseling without a desire to change their sexual orientation should not be forced into change.
6. G/l/b–affirmative individual and group counseling should be available.

Individuals who are g/l/b ethnic minorities should be perceived as having double or triple minority status. Counselors may also want to include steps that are a part of the multicultural career counseling model for ethnic minority women discussed in

Chapter 3. For example, in Stage 1, counselors may want to self-administer the *Multicultural Counseling Checklist* (Ward & Bingham, 1993) and have their client take the *Career Counseling Checklist* (Ward & Tate, 1990), both of which are displayed in Appendix B and C. Gender issues may also be included for female clients who are considered as having a triple minority status.

Stage 2, establishing an affirmative trusting relationship, may require considerable time and effort beyond one counseling session. Counselors can expect g/l/b clients to be reluctant to express themselves freely until a trusting relationship has been established and maintained. A collaborative relationship in which the counselor is an ally is recommended as a viable affirmative approach. To be an effective ally, counselors need to become knowledgeable about sexual minority issues, limitations of career choice, and the influence of homophobic attitudes expressed by important others in a sexual minorities' career development. Affirmative career counselors not only assist g/l/b persons with career decision making but remain as allies and resources if and when discrimination is encountered in hiring and in the workplace.

As discussed in Chapter 3, a culturally appropriate counseling relationship also consumes time and is most necessary for effective counseling with ethnic minority g/l/b persons. Counselors should also create a counseling environment that is conducive to discussing worldviews that may be quite different than their own. The client–counselor relationship can be facilitated by early discussions of ethnic/racial information (Bingham & Ward, 1996).

Stage 3, client identity issues, involves the client's place of development on the six stages of the Cass (1979) HIF model. This information is to be used with career development issues to evaluate the readiness of the client to make career decisions. It is also a point of reference for counseling interventions of personal counseling or psychotherapy. For instance, some clients may need further assistance with developing their identities before beginning career counseling or in conjunction with it. Client identity issues can also be related to problems with irrational thinking and emotional instability. Difficulty with progression through identity stages also can result in client indecisive behavior. The following excerpts from a case of a female senior high school student illustrated how identity problems interfere with career decision making.

In her senior year in high school Liz was asked by her parents to see a career counselor. Her speech patterns were very stilted, and she was hesitant to express herself openly, seemingly saying only what was absolutely necessary. Her counselor changed the subject to a known interest of Liz's, horseback riding, and spent the major portion of the first counseling session discussing this topic. On her next visit to the counseling center, Liz was much more relaxed and warmly greeted the counselor. After a few minutes of small talk, the counselor suggested that they begin the interview. This session and the following session were productive as they discussed demographic information and educational attainment. When future plans were introduced, Liz stated that her parents want her to follow a lifestyle pattern that she is not sure she wants. "Go to college and meet a nice boy you can marry," she stated as she mocked her parents. This was the beginning of a long story Liz told that focused on her confusion with sexual identity, rebellion, and a general indecision about what the future holds for her. The more she expressed her thoughts, the more certain the counselor became that Liz was greatly confused about her identity as a woman and was far from being ready to make career choices. The counselor proceeded with personal counseling directed at identity development.

Counselors need to create a counseling climate in which the client feels free to express identity development issues. Counselors should encourage discussion of contextual interactions that may assist the client in understanding sources of confusion and negative feedback. Specific issues that are ethnically/racially related are most appropriate for multicultural groups. Counselors may want to use a mentor who can participate as an ally in helping the client resolve issues. Counselors should offer support and be an affirmative confidante. The following case illustrates the use of an ally in the career counseling process with an ethnic minority gay man.

Julio was born in Texas to immigrant parents from Mexico. He often visited Mexico and was fluent in both English and Spanish. His stated need for career counseling went something like this: "I need a steady job so I can go to college for a better one." As Julio discussed his background, he revealed that he was openly gay, which made him the subject of jokes on the job. He needed advice about how to manage his sexual orientation with his family and fellow workers.

Julio had not met many gays in his new community and felt uncomfortable talking to "straight" men about his problem. The counselor took this opportunity to tell Julio of a gay Mexican man who would be willing to act as an ally to help solve Julio's problems.

After several visits with the ally, Julio informed the counselor he felt much more at ease when talking about his personal problems to an interested gay man. He felt that he had gained a better understanding of what to expect when he is identified as a gay person from members of the local Mexican American community. He also was given the names and addresses of local business places and organizations that were considered gay and lesbian friendly.

In this case the counselor felt that Julio would react most positively to someone who could realistically share his problems and provide him with advice from real-life experiences. The counselor had learned that it is most difficult to convince an ethnic minority who is gay that the counselor understands the minority's problems. Clearly, one who has experienced similar problems as an ethnic minority and who also has a gay sexual orientation can help clients by sharing personal experiences.

Stage 4, identify variables that may limit career choice, suggests that discrimination, bias, and stereotyping are negative influences that limit career choices for all sexual minorities, including ethnic minority individuals. A thorough discussion of these three variables should center on how each might have influenced clients to not consider certain careers. The major basis for their decisions to eliminate certain careers could be flawed such that appropriate careers seem to be only those that are stereotyped for gay men, lesbian women, and ethnic minorities. Obviously, clients should conclude that any and all careers can be considered in the choice process. In essence, the client takes back what has been taken away.

Stage 5, tailored assessment, should follow the assessment model described in Chapter 7 and outlined as follows:

Step 1: Maintain a client–counselor collaborative relationship.

Step 2: Maintain the role of assessment in the counseling model used.

Step 3: Negotiate the client's role in assessment.

Step 4: Describe the principles and purposes of standardized tests and self-assessment procedures.

Step 5: Client and counselor specify the client's assessment needs from information in the intake interview.

Step 6: Client and counselor select appropriate assessment instruments.

Step 7: Client and counselor reevaluate and identify problems.

Step 8: Client and counselor formulate goals.

In the next stage, career counseling models typically proceed to problem identification and the establishment of counseling goals. After client concerns are listed as sets of needs, appropriate intervention strategies are suggested. Client concerns, therefore, may include problems that are interrelated to career needs. In these cases interventions may address personal and career concerns simultaneously. Counselor and client can also develop a learning plan similar to the one used in the Cognitive Information Processing model (Sampson, Reardon, Peterson, & Lenz, 2004). During this process resources for sexual minorities should be provided. A list of Web sites that contain locations of organizations with nondiscrimination policies, addresses for employer policies, gay employee groups, and gay professional organization are listed at the end of the next stage.

Stage 6, job search strategies, prepares clients for developing their resumés and the job interview and locating sexual minority affirmative organizations. Counselors should emphasize to clients the importance of assessing work environments. This process for sexual minorities involves more than finding job opportunities. In some respects the process adds another dimension to the person-environment-fit constructs; sexual minority individuals should locate a work environment that is actively g/l/b affirmative. Counselors can help g/l/b clients avoid many problems they could face in a hostile work environment by providing direction for locating a friendly environment in the job search process. The key is having up-to-date resources.

Resources should provide the criteria to determine if an organization is g/l/b affirmative, has antidiscriminatory policies that include sexual orientation, domestic partner benefit policies, diversity training that includes sexual orientation, and existence of sexual minority employee groups. Clients should also be able to evaluate overall "gay friendliness" of a potential work site. Finally, a most important resource is the networks that provide advice for g/l/b persons. Counselors would be wise to compile a list of local available networks that offer assistance to sexual minorities. In addition, counselors should recruit and train local gay men and lesbian women to assist other g/l/b persons who need help in locating an affirmative workplace.

The following list of Web pages should offer helpful resources for sexual minority clients.

For health problems:

http://gmhc.org

For families:

www.pflag.org

For education and career resources:

Gay, Lesbian, Straight Education Network (GLSEN): www.glsen.org

Public Education Regarding Sexual Orientation Naturally: www.personproject.org

National Gay and Lesbian Task force: www.ngltf.org

YouthResource: A Project of Advocates for Youth: www.youthresource.com

Queer Resources Directory: www.qrd.org

National Youth Advocacy Coalition (NYAC): www.nyacyouth.org

Gay and Lesbian Association of Retiring Persons: www.gaylesbianretiring.org

The American Counseling Association: www.aglbic.org/resources/rt07.htm

The American Psychological Association: www.apa.org/pi/l&bres.html

The National Career Development Association: http://ncda.org

Another unique issue for g/l/b persons involved in the job search process is the question of whether the client should reveal his or her sexual orientation. This decision has many implications for sexual minority clients. Brammer (2004), Winfeld and Spielman (1995), Gelberg and Chojnacki (1996), Friskopp and Silverstein (1995), and Pope, Prince, and Mitchell (2000) suggest that coming out is a multidimensional process involving a number of factors and variables that include the following: the client's identity development; the g/l/b affirmative status of the employing organization; the knowledge of the client's sexual orientation by family, friends, and associates; the status of the client's partner and what "coming out" would mean to him or her; and the readiness of the client to face the workplace as a known sexual minority. Keep in mind that identity development is an ongoing, continuous process that is more cyclical than linear as individuals move up and down the parameters of the HIF model. Counselors can assist clients in making this decision through discussions of the implications of many variables that are both external and internal. Clients may be helped by other g/l/b persons who have gone through this process. Counselors may also suggest that clients network with g/l/b employees in the organizations of interest.

Some suggestions for coming out at work include extensive planning. One must lay the foundation for a positive reception, which includes having an outstanding job performance and building credentials that support and enhance job assignment. Supportive allies also need to be identified. Clients who also recruit heterosexuals as allies will usually have a stronger support base. Clients may also be instructed to test the waters by dropping clues about their sexual orientations, for example, by suggesting they support gay people and their rights. Reactions to such statements provide clues about what one might encounter in coming out (Friskopp & Silverstein, 1995).

Vargo (1998) and Barrett and Logan (2002) suggests that gay men and lesbian women must be prepared for coming out at work by being fully aware of the reasons why one should take this step. Relevant questions include what the client's short-term and long-term goals for coming out are and how these goals can be reached. For instance, should one come out to only a few selected workers and gradually inform other key persons? Will coming out enhance the chances of advancement or detract from it? Clients should be encouraged to anticipate problems that might emerge and how these problems can be solved.

There appears to be strong supporting evidence from professional gay men and lesbian women that the benefits of coming out at work are far greater than are those of remaining in the closet (Brammer, 2004; Friskopp & Silverstein, 1995; Vargo, 1998; Winfeld & Spielman, 1995). Some problems reported that arise from remaining in the closet are fear of exposure, problems in socializing, lower self-esteem, and vulnerability to harassment such as blackmail. In addition, gay men and lesbian women resented having to censor thoughts, even words, and, of course, actions that might reveal one's sexual orientation. Professional gay men and lesbian women who experienced coming out strongly suggested that being in the closet is a very painful and disturbing experience. For instance, Ike felt relieved that he could now be honest and "above board" with his fellow workers. Ann was tired of a double life and felt much better about herself and her relationships at work after coming out. The major personal benefits derived from coming out appear to be self-acceptance and self-actualization (Barrett & Logan, 2002; Friskopp & Silverstein, 1995; Signorile, 1993). However, each individual should be encouraged to thoroughly evaluate his or her work environment for the consequences of coming out as well as for his or her ability to manage pressure and discrimination that could result from coming out.

Coming out at lower-level jobs or nonprofessional work might be more perilous and risky, especially in highly conservative environments. Clients should be encouraged to evaluate each work environment for its openness shown by other gay employees and the advantages and disadvantages of announcing one's sexual orientation in that environment. It appears there is a growing trend for more sexual minorities to come out at work primarily because of formal policies that protect them from discrimination (Vargo, 1998). Being closeted at work or coming out at work are viable topics for sexual minorities; however, more research is needed with an in-depth analysis of the psychological antecedents and subsequent consequences of this process.

In sum, g/l/b persons have special needs that are to be addressed in the career counseling process. Career counseling can proceed within existing career counseling models for sexual minorities with some adaptations and modifications. Special needs may be included in career counseling models as additional components that are relevant to the stages and steps of existing models. Counselors must also account for individual differences and subsequent needs of individuals within groups. For instance, an ethnic minority lesbian should be viewed as an individual with a triple minority status. All ethnic minority g/l/b persons receive an additional minority status that may reflect unique needs of their ethnic minority identification.

Summary

1. G/l/b persons have special needs because of their sexual orientation that should be addressed in career counseling.
2. There are estimates of between 5 and 25 million g/l/b persons in this country.
3. More organizations and companies are supporting gay and lesbian associations and networks. Many regard gay men and lesbian women as another diverse group in the workplace.
4. Individuals with a sexual orientation of g/l/b continue to be stereotyped as to the kinds of jobs they should hold; are threatened by violence often resulting from homophobia; form a dislike for themselves through internalized homophobia; and generally receive negative feedback from a society that views heterosexuality as the only viable lifestyle.

5. Discrimination in the workplace can involve threats, lack of promotions, black-mail, ostracism, sexual harassment, exclusion or avoidance, termination, and the "lavender ceiling."

6. Sexual orientation is considered an important component of identity development. Identity development may follow a six-stage process that varies by sex and race, sexual orientation, and other developmental factors associated with individual environments. Some g/l/b clients progress through stages at different rates, and the age when g/l/b persons reach the final stage in an identity model varies.

7. Ethnic minority gay men have a double minority status. A lesbian ethnic minority may have a triple minority status. Ethnic minorities suggest that they are only marginally received in g/l/b communities.

8. Adolescents who are g/l/b oriented face a complex task of developing a sexual identity. They might be abandoned by friends and rejected by their families. Among major problems are suicide ideation and HIV infection.

9. Unique issues g/l/b persons bring to career counseling can be resolved in current career counseling models with some adaptations and modifications. Six stages that can be included within current career counseling models are precounseling preparation, establishing an affirmative trusting relationship, client identity issues, identify variables that can limit career choice, tailored assessment, and job search strategies.

Supplementary Learning Exercises

1. Develop an informative program about HIV/AIDS that could be used in schools at all levels.
2. Choose three special needs of g/l/b clients and develop appropriate intervention strategies.
3. Develop a list of topics that could be used with adolescents who are in the process of developing a sexual orientation of gay, lesbian, or bisexual.
4. Develop a list of publications that could be used by g/l/b clients in conjunction with career counseling.
5. Develop a career counseling program that would specifically meet the needs of a triple minority status woman.
6. Visit an organization that is g/l/b affirmative. Obtain published materials that state the organization's policies. Share this with your class.
7. Interview a gay, lesbian, or bisexual person. Make note of his or her workplace experiences.
8. Identify the topics you would use in an intake interview with g/l/b persons. Specify how you would introduce selected topics.
9. What are some methods you would use to inform the public that you are a g/l/b affirmative counselor? List some problems you might experience.
10. Debate the following issues as either pro or con:
    a. G/l/b persons should have equal rights.
    b. G/l/b persons do not choose their sexual orientation.
    c. G/l/b persons should be restricted from choosing certain occupations.

For More Information

Barret, B., & Logan, C. (2002). *Counseling gay men and lesbians: A practice primer.* Pacific Grove, CA: Brooks/Cole-Thomson Learning.

Brammer, R. (2004). *Diversity in counseling.* Belmont, CA: Brooks/Cole-Thomson Learning.

Cass, V. C. (1984). Homosexuality identity formation: Testing a theoretical model. *Journal of Sex Research, 20*(2), 143–167.

Chan, C. S. (1997). Don't ask, don't tell, don't know: The formation of homosexual identity and sexual expression among Asian American lesbians. In B. Greene (Ed.), *Ethnic and cultural diversity among lesbians and gay men* (pp. 240–249). Thousand Oaks, CA: Sage.

Chung, Y. B., & Katayama, M. (1999). Ethnic and sexual identity development of Asian American lesbian and gay adolescents. In K. S. Ng (Ed.), *Counseling Asian families from a systems perspective* (pp. 159–171). Alexandria, VA: American Counseling Association.

Friskopp, A., & Silverstein, S. (1995). *Straight jobs, gay lives.* New York: Scribner.

Gelberg, S., & Chojnacki, J. T. (1996). *Career and life planning with gay, lesbian, & bisexual persons.* Alexandria, VA: American Counseling Association.

Mondimore, F. M. (1996). *Homosexuality.* Baltimore: Johns Hopkins University Press.

Rust, P. C. (1996). Managing multiple identities: Diversity among bisexual women and men. In B. A. Firestein (Ed.), *Bisexuality* (pp. 53–84). Thousand Oaks, CA: Sage.

Vargo, M. E. (1998). *Acts of disclosure: The coming-out process of contemporary gay men.* New York: Haworth.

Winfeld, L., & Spielman, S. (1995). *Straight talk about gays in workplace.* New York: AMACOM.

Suggested InfoTrac College Edition Topics

Counseling and sexual orientation

Resources and sexual orientation

Cultural differences and sexual orientation

Sexual identity formation

Discrimination and sexual orientation

Work and sexual orientation

15 Career-Related Programs and Counseling in Elementary Schools

Chapter Highlights

- Career educational goals and competencies

- Building support for career-related programs

- National career guidelines

- Career competencies by grade level

- Role of elementary school counselors

- Strategies for integrating career development concepts

- Resources for career development

- Counseling culturally different children

CAREER-RELATED PROGRAMS in elementary schools have come to be viewed by many as essential ingredients in the educational process of all students (Berns, 2004; Sciarra, 2004). Comprehensive career-related programs that are currently in vogue are intentional and sequential. They begin in prekindergarten with the assumption that career development is considered to be a lifelong process; comprehensive career programs are to be age-appropriate and should include experiential activities. Effective career-related programs in schools require a cooperative effort that usually includes planning, oversight, and operational procedures that are a product of a joint effort by administrators, teachers, counselors, parents, and community volunteers.

Career-related programs in elementary schools require the development of model programs, resources, and strategies, and most important, carefully planned methods of curriculum integration. Obviously, counselors play an extremely significant role as proactive agents promoting, developing, and evaluating career development programs. In addition to counseling duties, counselors assume multiple roles such as coach, leader, consultant, coordinator, teacher, team facilitator, career-related information specialist, and promoter of community involvement.

Our public schools are universal in that they are open to all and they are considered prescriptive by providing standards of achievement primarily based on the needs of an ever changing society (Berns, 2004). First and foremost are academic goals of mastering basic skills that prepare learners to embark on a lifelong journey of learning. Students are expected to master numerous skills and understand concepts that will equip them with the ability to solve problems, think rationally, and accumulate general knowledge. Social, civic, cultural, and personal goals are to be enhanced and promoted as an important part of interpersonal understanding, social enculturation, and emotional and physical well-being (Berns, 2004; Goodlad, 1984). Finally, vocational goals are considered to be the product of the total educational experience, which includes career education programs designed to prepare students for career choice and subsequently make a successful transition from school-to-school and/or school-to-work. Although these goals may be listed as separate categories, they are inherently interrelated. A deficiency in basic skill development, for example, could affect one's progress in all educational programs. Hence our focus in this chapter will be on vocational goals for students in elementary schools that reflect interrelationships of all educational goals.

In this chapter we begin with building support for career-related programs. Second, we present implications for career development programs. Third, career development goals and competencies are provided. Next, representative examples of specific classroom activities are presented, followed by an example of integrating career development concepts in the classroom. Finally, we provide suggestions for counseling children from different cultures.

Building Support for Career-Related Programs— Keys to Success

Counseling programs at all school levels usually require counselors to justify program content and materials. Building support for career-related programs in the elementary school requires a sophisticated approach to justify time and effort in an already crowded curriculum. A critical step in establishing elementary school career-related programs, therefore, is to convince teachers, administrators, and parents of the need for career education. Counselors are to base their recommendations on a background of accepted academic findings and research as well as straightforward information that provides a connection between learned basic skills and work requirements. The information contained in the following paragraphs provides points of reference that counselors may use to underscore their recommendations.

Building support and developing career-related programs requires an academic foundation and background in a number of disciplines. One important academic discipline for elementary school counselors is developmental psychology. Development in this context usually refers to systematic changes of physical, cognitive, and psychosocial development as interactive influences that shape individuals. How children learn, their ways of responding, and their readiness for learning provide an essential foundation for program planning and counseling children.

Human development is not an isolated, detached, or unrelated series of events in life; rather, it is a blend of diverse elements, including psychosocial and economic variables. These interacting elements formulate life stages and cover the entire life span. Understanding human development is one essential ingredient leading to a greater comprehension and interpretation of career development stages and tasks.

Piaget (1929), noted for his work in cognitive development, has provided a description of how humans think and the characteristics of their thinking at different stages of development. In early development, children cultivate "schemes" through their senses and motor activities. During the years from ages 2 through 5, children begin to develop conceptual levels but do not yet have the ability to think logically or abstractly. By the time children reach elementary school age, they have developed the ability to apply logic to thinking and can understand simple concepts. Through concrete experiences, children learn to make consistent generalizations. For example, children learn to classify persons or objects in more than one category (the Little League coach can also be a police officer).

Encouraging and directing concrete experiences to promote increasingly abstract conceptual operations during this stage of development is a vital part of educational and career guidance programming in elementary schools. A sample exercise to illustrate this process would be asking students to identify one type of skill necessary for good schoolwork and then asking them to identify a job that requires a specific school subject.

Learning by Observation

Observation is also a contributing element to early cognitive development. Krumboltz's learning theory of career choice and counseling, discussed in Chapter 2, emphasizes the importance of observation learning attributed to reactions to consequences, observable results of actions, and reactions to others (Mitchell & Krumboltz, 1996). Children are particularly prone to adopting the behavior models they observe (Fagot & Leinbach, 1989). According to Bandura (1977, 1986), there are five stages of observable learning: (1) paying attention, (2) remembering what is observed, (3) reproducing actions, (4) becoming motivated (to reproduce what is observed), and (5) perfecting an imitation according to what was observed. Within this frame of reference, parents, teachers, teachers' aides, and classmates are potential models that elementary school children will imitate. Of course, models may come from other sources, such as television, movies, and books. The potential benefits of observational learning for career development of elementary school children are very important. Directed observable learning experiences involving work roles are an important component of early career guidance programs.

Self-Concept Development

In Chapter 2, we briefly mentioned Super's self-concept theory and its pervasive nature (Super et al., 1963). In a later publication, Super (1990) clarified his position on the nature and scope of self-concept in career development. Individuals, in Super's view, have constellations of self-concepts, or "self-concept systems," that denote sets or constellations of traits. In an elementary school setting, for example, an individual might have a different view of self as a student and as a member of a peer group. An individual might see himself or herself as gregarious but also as a weak student or not very intelligent. Elementary students are formulating sets of self-concepts as they focus on class requirements; interrelationships with peers, teachers, and important adults; and the social structure in which they live and function.

In her theory of circumscription and compromise, discussed in Chapter 2, Gottfredson focuses on the development of self-images and occupational aspirations in four stages. In the first stage, orientation to size and power (ages 3 to 5), children recognize adult occupational roles and exhibit same-sex preferences for adult activities, including employment. During stage two, orientation to sex roles (ages 6 to 8), children focus on what is appropriate for one's sex; they now recognize that adult activities are sex-typed. As a result, children tend to dismiss occupations that are considered appropriate for the other sex. In stage three, orientation to social valuation (ages 9 to 13), children rule out low-status occupations as preferences. As Gottfredson (1996) puts it, "they reject occupational alternatives that seem inconsistent with those new elements of self" (p. 193). Stage four is characterized as an orientation to the internal unique self beginning at age 14. Individuals gain self-awareness and project self, sex role, and social class into their perceptions of vocational aspirations.

Self-concept development is not a static phenomenon but an ongoing process, which changes sometimes gradually and sometimes abruptly as people and situations change. In elementary school, children experience for the first time many aspects of existence in an adult world, such as competition and expectations of productive performance. In play, they interact with peers and also assume roles in supervised and unsupervised situations. Self-esteem for some will be enhanced through academic achievement, whereas others will experience both positive and negative feedback in peer-socialization activities. Enhanced self-esteem encourages development of personal ideas and opinions of a positive nature; accurate self-concepts contribute to career maturity (Super, 1990).

Development by Stages and Tasks

Stage theorists have concentrated on developmental patterns of accomplishments, events, and physiological and sociological changes in human development. During the transition process from one stage to another, developmental tasks provide a description of requirements or actions that are necessary to pass successfully through a stage of development. This perspective suggests a foundation for building effective career-related programs.

According to Havighurst (1972), the developmental tasks expected of students before leaving the sixth grade reveal a set of physical and academic skills, social role development, and personalized values. Almost all of these tasks can be related to Super's (1990) concept of career development tasks (see Chapter 2). For example, during the growth stage (to age 14), according to Super's scheme of developmental stages and tasks, individuals go through numerous experiential learning activities while developing greater self-awareness. Directed experiences in elementary school that promote physical and academic growth, interpersonal relationships with members of the same and the opposite sexes, and self-concept development are important components of career development. Students who fail to achieve the developmental tasks in both Havighurst's and Super's steps could require special attention and direction.

Erikson (1963) suggested that the stage of development from ages 6 to 11 emphasizes industriousness; that is, children learn that productivity brings recognition and reward. In Erikson's view, children develop a sense of industriousness through their accomplishments, but they might be intimidated by the requirements of success and develop a sense of inferiority. Expressing success through academic achievement, for example, is a major contributor to establishing industriousness in work role and self-concept development. A sense of inferiority at this stage of development calls for individualized intervention strategies.

Differences in growth and physiological changes between girls and boys in elementary school greatly influence social relationships and emerging self-perceptions. Learning appropriate masculine or feminine roles, according to Havighurst (1972) and Gottfredson (1996), among others, precludes greater equality between sexes, especially in occupational behavior. Particularly important are perceptions of appropriate behavior patterns—that is, patterns regarded as acceptable for a given sex. Sex role stereotyping is fostered through observation and imitation of male and female models. Other influences come through textbooks, other books, and popular television programs that describe and depict differences in rules for boys and girls.

Influence of Family Interactions

Early relations within the family and their subsequent effects on career direction have been the main focus of Ann Roe's work (1956). Her main thrust was analyzing differences in personality, aptitude, intelligence, and background as related to career choice. She studied several outstanding physical, biological, and social scientists to determine whether vocational direction was highly related to early personality development.

Roe (1956) emphasized that early childhood experiences play an important role in finding satisfaction in one's chosen field. Her research led her to investigate how parental styles affect need hierarchy and the relationships of these needs to later adult lifestyles. She drew heavily from Maslow's hierarchy of needs in developing her theory. The need structure of the individual, according to Roe, is greatly influenced by early childhood frustrations and satisfactions. For example, individuals who desire to work in contact with people are drawn in this direction primarily because of their strong needs for affection and belongingness. Those who choose the nonperson-type jobs are meeting lower-level needs for safety and security. Roe hypothesized that individuals who enjoy working with people were reared by warm and accepting parents and those who avoid contact with others were reared by cold or rejecting parents.

Roe (1956) classified occupations into two major categories: person-oriented and nonperson-oriented. Examples of person-oriented occupations are (1) service (concerned with service to other people); (2) business contact (person-to-person contact, primarily in sales); (3) managerial (management in business, industry, and government); (4) general culture (teaching, ministry, and journalism); and (5) arts and entertainment (performing in creative arts). Examples of nonperson-oriented jobs are in the arenas of (1) technology (production, maintenance, and transportation); (2) the outdoors (agriculture, forestry, mining, etc.); and (3) science (scientific theory and application).

Within each occupational classification are progressively higher levels of functioning. Roe (1956) contended that the selection of an occupational category was primarily a function of the individual's need structure but that the level of attainment within the category depended more on the individual's level of ability and socioeconomic background. The climate of the relationship between child and parent was the main generating force of needs, interests, and attitudes that were later reflected in vocational choice.

Roe modified her theory after several studies refuted her claim that different parent–child interactions result in different vocational choices (Green & Parker, 1965; Powell, 1957). She currently takes the position that the early orientation of an individual is related to later major decisions—particularly in occupational choice—but that other variables not accounted for in her theory are also important factors. The following statements by Roe (1972) express her viewpoint on career development:

1. The life history of any man and many women, written in terms of or around the occupational history, can give the essence of the person more fully than can any other approach.
2. Situations relevant to this history begin with the birth of the individual into a particular family at a particular place and time and continue throughout his or her life.
3. There may be differences in the relative weights carried by different factors, but the process of vocational decision and behavior do not differ in essence from any others.
4. The extent to which vocational decisions and behaviors are under the voluntary control of the individual is variable, but it could be more than it sometimes seems to be. Deliberate consideration of the factors involved seems to be rare.
5. The occupational life affects all other aspects of the life pattern.
6. An appropriate and satisfying vocation can be a bulwark against neurotic ills or a refuge from them. An inappropriate or unsatisfying vocation can be sharply deleterious.
7. Because the goodness of life in any social group is compounded by and also determines that of its individual members, the efforts of any society to maintain stability and at the same time advance in desired ways can perhaps be most usefully directed toward developing satisfying vocational situations for its members. But unless the vocation is integrated adequately into the total life pattern, it cannot help much.
8. There is no single specific occupational slot that is a one-and-only perfect one for any individual. Conversely, there is no single person who is the only one for a particular occupational slot. Within any occupation, there is a considerable range in a number of variables specifying the requirements.

Roe's theory is usually referred to as a needs-theory approach to career choice (Bailey & Stadt, 1973; Zaccaria, 1970). According to Roe, combinations of early parent–child relations, environmental experiences, and genetic features determine the development of a need structure. The individual then learns to satisfy these developed needs primarily through interactions with people or through activities that do not involve people. Thus, Roe postulated that occupational choice primarily involves choosing occupations that are person-oriented, such as service occupations, or nonperson-oriented, such as scientific occupations. The intensity of needs is the major determinant that motivates the individual to the level hierarchy within an occupational structure (Zaccaria, 1970).

Roe's theory has generated considerable research but little support for her theoretical model (Osipow, 1983). Roe's postulated effect of the parent–child interactions on later vocational choices is difficult to validate. Differing parental attitudes and subsequent interactions within families present such an overwhelming number of variables that no study could be controlled sufficiently to be considered empirical. The longitudinal requirements necessary to validate the theory present another deterring factor. Notwithstanding, Roe made a great contribution to career counseling in having directed considerable attention to the developmental period of early childhood.

Involving Teachers and Parents in Career-Related Programs

The developmental period of early childhood is a most relevant concern of the elementary school counselor. Planning strategies and joint activities with teachers and parents that meet the approval of administrators is an awesome task and requires a solid academic background and relevant professional experience. The following example underscores this recommendation.

An elementary school counselor who moved to a different location in a large city discovered that her new school did not have a parent–teacher organization. The school was located in what was considered to be a very poor area of the city. It soon became apparent that parents had little understanding of what they could do to help their children learn. The counselor approached the school's principal for permission to solicit teachers' help in organizing group meetings with parents to inform them of how they could be advocates for helping children learn and to understand the important role parents play in career development. From these beginnings and with the support of the teaching staff, programs were established to involve parents in their children's education, including career-related projects. Specific goals included the need for parents to collaborate with teachers in program development, to support career-related programs by precept and example in the home, to become involved in developing their children's self-concept, and to encourage their children to explore many career opportunities. A major goal was to encourage family members to provide needed support for career development learning activities and to ensure that their children will come to school to learn. Box 15-1 contains suggestions for involving parents in learning activities.

The lesson here is that counselors are to be prepared to appreciate and understand the ecological system of the community in which they are working. With this knowledge, counselors are in a better position to approach parents, secure their support, and identify community resources. Developing an understanding of contextual issues and the current political climate helped the counselor in our example obtain the endorsement of community members. Cooperative efforts among teachers, counselors, and parents are usually developed through collaborative relationships. In many

---

Box 15-1   **Strategies for Involving Families in Learning**

1. Recognize and show that parents are significant contributors to their child's development. Call on parents for advice, help, support, and critical evaluations.
2. Present a realistic picture of what the child's program is designed to accomplish.
3. Maintain ongoing communication with parents. Provide written information regarding due process procedures and parent or parent–teacher organizations, as well as oral and written information about the child's progress.
4. Show parents you care about their child. Call, write notes, and spend time listening to parents' concerns.
5. Keep parents informed as to how they can help their child at home. Enable parents to enjoy their children.

6. Use parents' ideas, materials, and activities to work with their child.
7. Be familiar with community services and resources so you can refer parents when necessary.
8. Be yourself. Don't pretend to know all the answers when you don't; don't be afraid to ask for advice or refer parents to other professionals and resources.
9. Recognize that diverse family structures and parenting styles influence parental participation.
10. Help parents grow in confidence and in self-esteem. (Gargiulo & Graves, 1991; Heward, 1999)

Source: From *Child, Family, School, Community: Socialization and Support* by Berns, p. 283. © 2004. Reprinted with permission of Wadsworth, a part of The Thomson Corporation.

---

instances there are community resources that can be used to support school programs. Counselors can play an important advocacy role in gaining community cooperation and support.

Finally, career development involves a series of competencies by area and level according to national guidelines. Students are to achieve specific competencies that are evaluated by indicators of competence that demonstrate their knowledge and skills. One important outcome of this process is the development of a sense of life purpose. This objective may appear to be overwhelming and indeed it is a very pervasive goal; however, children search for a connectedness with others and the world around them as they develop a sense of the future. One way to help children begin their lifetime journey is to provide them with the means to become involved in their own development, encouraged and reinforced by collective efforts of family members (McWhirter et al., 2004). The importance of a compassionate, involved caregiver cannot be overemphasized. A significant work role is one route that can lead to a sense of life purpose. Be aware that we do not suggest that all educational goals are to be directed to establishing a work role. On the contrary, purpose of life is a pervasive concept that is very inclusive. The position here is that the work role is relatively easy for elementary school children to observe and comprehend. They can make connections and identify with work roles of their parents and other important adults. They can make concrete connections between workers and individuals as they become self-aware and develop self-image and self-concepts. Thus, the broader and more sophisticated conceptualization of career life perspective and the interrelationships of all life roles have roots that are firmly embedded in observations and experiences in early childhood.

National Career Development Guidelines

Broad vocational goals such as learning about the world of work, developing self-knowledge, and equating school achievement with work roles provide the bases for goal development but not the specifics needed for career infusion interventions. In 1976 the National Occupational Information Coordinating Committee (NOICC) was established. It had many functions including projects that led to national career counseling and development guidelines. Implementing national guidelines in states and local communities helped facilitate (1) achievement of career development competencies by all students; (2) improved career guidance and counseling programs that are comprehensive and integrated within the total guidance and counseling program; (3) clearly defined staff roles, increased teaming with teachers and other school and district staff, and improved counselor expertise; (4) greater program accountability; and (5) improved articulation of career-related programs across educational levels (NOICC, 1989, p. 30). NOICC is no longer a functioning committee but the national career development guidelines have remained as the major guidelines for effective career counseling over the life span.

National career development guidelines in the elementary school include three areas, as follows:

1. **Self-knowledge**
   a. Knowledge of the importance of self-concept
   b. Skills to interact with others
   c. Awareness of the importance of growth and change

2. **Educational and occupational exploration**
   a. Awareness of the benefits of educational achievement
   b. Awareness of the relationship between work and learning
   c. Skills to understand and use career information
   d. Awareness of the importance of personal responsibility and good work habits
   e. Awareness of how work relates to the needs and functions of society

3. **Career planning**
   a. Understanding of how to make decisions
   b. Awareness of the interrelationship of life roles
   c. Awareness of different occupations and changing male/female roles
   d. Awareness of the career planning process

Career Goals and Competencies for Kindergarten through Sixth Grade

Following a review of suggested K–6 goals and competencies, we will return to these national career guidelines with representative examples of classroom interventions. In the meantime we examine the American School Counselors Association (Campbell & Dahir, 1997) recommended functions of elementary school counselors as paraphrased:

• Implement effective classroom guidance activities such as fostering peer relationships, understanding of self, communication skills, decision-making skills, study skills.

- Develop effective individual and small group counseling addressing such topics as self-image, self-esteem, interpersonal concerns, family issues, personal adjustment, and behavior problems.
- Use assessment instruments as measures of ability, interests, academic achievement, and skills.
- Foster the developmental process through career awareness of lifelong growth of values, interests, and skills that will influence their future work roles.
- Coordinate programs that will involve school and community resources, all school career-related activities, and other programs that promote students' self-knowledge and skill development (p. 69).

These counselor functions suggest that elementary school counselors are completely challenged to fulfill a variety of professional tasks. They infer that establishing goals for local career-related programs are carefully planned and tailored after reviewing goals and competencies established locally, statewide, and from national programs. Table 15-1, by Paisley and Hubbard (1994), provides a sample of career goals and competencies for kindergarten through sixth grade. The overall goals are similar to the national career goals established by the NOICC (1992) of self-knowledge, educational and occupational exploration, and career planning. However, the specificity of the competencies by grade level found in this table is unique and valuable information for all school professional personnel. Special attention should be given to the overall goals listed in this table that emphasize awareness of self or self-knowledge, knowledge of the diversity of the world of work, the relationships between school performance and career choice options, and the development of a positive attitude toward work.

Career-related objectives and goals should be integrated and infused in classroom instruction. It is therefore essential that classroom teachers support the development of career-related competencies as an important part of their instructional program. Elementary school counselors should be prepared to assist classroom teachers create career-related modules including supplementary materials, and serve as a proactive consultant for community resources. What we have here is a need for elementary school counselors who have a good background in curriculum development and teaching methods. An overarching goal is to focus on classroom learning activities that address vocational competencies and foster career development. Within this context, elementary school counselors become a part of curriculum development through consultation. Thus, counselors' ability to work with classroom teachers is essential. To enhance the effectiveness of career-related programs counselors should have a working knowledge of effective classroom instruction and supplementary materials that address specific career development goals.

Representative Strategies for Classroom Activities

Career development competencies for elementary school students were developed from national career guidelines and are provided in Appendix E. These competencies are designed as strategies to promote self-knowledge, educational and occupational exploration, and career planning. Competencies provide specific objectives that counselor and teacher use as indicators of a student's comprehension of a strategy or tasks that represent mastery and understanding of career development goals. Both

Table 15-1	Sample K–6 Career Goals and Competencies

Overall Goals
- Become aware of personal characteristics, interests, aptitudes, and skills
- Develop an awareness of and respect for the diversity of the world of work
- Understand the relationship between school performance and future choices
- Develop a positive attitude toward work

Competencies

Kindergarten students will be able to:
- Identify workers in the school setting
- Describe the work of family members
- Describe what they like to do

First-grade students will be able to:
- Describe their likes and dislikes
- Identify workers in various settings
- Identify responsibilities they have at home and at school
- Identify skills they have now that they did not have previously

Second-grade students will be able to:
- Describe skills needed to complete a task at home or at school
- Distinguish which work activities in their school environment are done by specific people
- Recognize the diversity of jobs in various settings

Third-grade students will be able to:
- Define what the term future means
- Recognize and describe the many life roles that people have
- Demonstrate the ability to brainstorm a range of job titles

Fourth-grade students will be able to:
- Imagine what their lives might be like in the future
- Evaluate the importance of various familiar jobs in the community
- Describe workers in terms of work performed
- Identify personal hobbies and leisure activities

Fight-grade students will be able to:
- Identify ways that familiar jobs contribute to the needs of society
- Compare their interests and skills to familiar jobs
- Compare their personal hobbies and leisure activities to jobs
- Discuss stereotypes associated with certain jobs
- Discuss what is important to them

Sixth-grade students will be able to:
- Identify tentative work interests and skills
- List elements of decision making
- Discuss how their parents' work influences life at home
- Consider the relationship between interests and abilities
- Identify their own personal strengths and weaknesses

Source: From *Developmental School Counseling Programs: From Theory to Practice,* by P. O. Paisley and G. T. Hubbard (American Counseling Association, 1994), pp. 218–221. Reprinted with permission. No further reproduction authorized without written permission of The American Counseling Association.

teacher and counselor are to develop strategies to enhance career development. In some cases community resources can also be used. Representative examples of specific classroom activities follow:

Self-Knowledge Strategies

1. In a group discussion, ask students to use open-ended sentences, such as
   I'm happy when _____.
   I'm sad when _____.
   I'm afraid when _____.
2. Have students compile a list or draw pictures of people they talked to during the week. In groups, discuss types of relationships students have with the people they talked to.
3. Ask students to describe a friend and then themselves. Discuss and describe individual differences.
4. Play "Who Am I?," with one student playing a role and others trying to guess the role.
5. Have students select magazine pictures of events, places, and people that interest them. Share interests.
6. Ask students to summarize ways in which individuals may be described. Then, ask students to select and describe self-descriptions.
7. Ask students to answer the following questions in writing or orally: What do I do well? What goals do I have? What do I do poorly? Who am I like? What makes me different from others?
8. Have students make lists of "Things I like" and "Things I don't like." Compile the lists and discuss the variety of interests.
9. Form a "Who Am I?" group and meet once a week, during which each student describes a personal characteristic of an individual who performs a specific job. Compile a list for future discussions.
10. Ask students to list several interests and to describe how they became interested in an activity.

Educational and Occupational Exploration Strategies

1. Arrange a display of workers' hats that represent jobs in the community. Have each student select a hat that indicates a job he or she would like to do someday and explain why the job is appealing.
2. Assign students to develop a list of skills for their favorite jobs and describe how these skills are learned.
3. Ask each student to pretend that a friend wants a certain job, and ask each to describe the kinds of skills the friend would need.
4. Have students develop a list of activities their parents do at home and have them identify those that require math, reading, and writing.
5. Have students make a list of school subjects and identify jobs in which the skills learned from the subjects are used.
6. Refer to a list of occupations and have students describe what kind of person might like a particular occupation.
7. Have students make a list of occupations involved in producing a loaf of bread.

8. Ask students to find a picture from a magazine or newspaper that depicts a female and a male in nontraditional jobs.
9. Have students interview their parents about their work roles and discuss these roles with the group.
10. Ask each student to adopt the identity of a worker and list work roles. Discuss how work has a personal meaning for every individual.

Career Planning Strategies

1. Ask students to make a list of jobs/occupations they would use to describe their neighbors or acquaintances. Share with others.
2. Have students identify the kinds of people who work in a selected list of occupations. Emphasize likenesses and differences.
3. In a self-discovery group, discuss how people have different interests and enjoy different or similar activities.
4. Have students describe how workers in different activities are affected by weather.
5. Ask students to collect newspaper and magazine photos of different people and describe likenesses and differences.
6. Have students identify workers who visit their homes. Identify differences of work and occupations.
7. Assign students to write a short paragraph answering the question, "If you could be anyone in the world, who would it be?" Follow with a discussion.
8. Divide the class into groups of boys and girls and ask each group to make a list of jobs girls can and cannot do. Compare lists and discuss how women are capable of performing most jobs.
9. Have students describe in writing, orally, or both "someone I would like to work with." Make a list of positive characteristics that each student describes.
10. Discuss how people work together and demonstrate using the example of three people building a doghouse together. What would each person do?

Career Infusion

The idea of integrating career development concepts into existing curricula is referred to as *infusion*. This technique requires that teachers expand their current educational objectives to include career-related activities and subjects. For example, teaching decision-making skills can be infused with traditional academic courses. Planning a class project with a designated time limit involves certain decisions, such as specifying the goals of the project, determining the possible approaches to the project, selecting the best one, and actually following through. Decision-making and planning skills are applicable to many—if not all—subjects and should be consciously taught as skills to be developed and refined. Infusion of career objectives requires that formal attention be given to career-related skills and tasks. An example of an infusion model for the elementary school follows.

The following career infusion module is designed to improve career awareness. This module was developed in the 1970s during the heyday of the career education movement and still remains viable as a learning module today. This module provides rationale, objectives, description, location of activity, personnel required, cost, time, resources, and evaluation measures.

Subject: Math, reading, language
Concept: Career awareness
Answering a Job Advertisement
Rationale: Students should have an understanding of the jobs described in want ads in order to develop an awareness of various occupations. Students should also learn about the requirements of various occupations and draw conclusions of whether they would like to work in the environment described by a want ad and during follow-up.
Objective: Students will describe in writing how different occupations are described in terms of salary, hours of work, training, and educational requirements.
Description:

1. Discuss various ways people find out about openings in the job market.
2. Present a page from the local newspaper with want ads listed.
3. Have students select three careers in which they are interested and research the requirements, salary, training, and education necessary for the job being advertised.
4. Have the students write a description of the job that appeals to them the most and explain their choices.
5. Have students share their findings with classmates in a 3–5 minute report.

Where activity occurs: Classroom
Personnel required: Teacher
Cost: Cost of newspaper
Time: Discussion, one-quarter period; research and select careers, one and one quarter periods; share with classmates, one-quarter period
Resources: Newspaper
Evaluation measures: Oral and written report

SOURCE: *Project Cadre: A Cadre Approach to Career Education Infusion,* by C. C. Healy and O. H. Quinn, 1977. Unpublished manuscript. Reprinted by permission.

Another important part of the elementary school counselor's role is that of keeping up-to-date career resources that effectively address career development goals. Materials that provide interactive programs can be very effective. For example, an interactive career CD-ROM program for grades 3 and up combines animation, photography, voice interviews, and music. Included in the package is a very simple self-assessment that matches answers by referring students to occupational clusters.

In another resource, students from grades 2 to 6 can take a video field trip in their classroom. Topics could include Timber! From Logs to Lumber, The Fire Station, The Airport, The Dairy, and others. For many such activities, complete lesson plans are available along with suggested additional activities. Also, a Children's Dictionary of Occupations is available on CD-ROM and in print. Student's activity packages for these publications are opportunities for interactive participation. These examples suggest that an abundance of relevant materials is available to assist teachers and counselors in meeting the goals of career development in the elementary school. The materials mentioned here are published by:

MERIDIAN Educational Corporation
236 East Front Street
Dept. K8-F98
Bloomington, IL 61701
800-727-5507

Another very important resource is listed as follows:

Center on Education and Work
964 Educational Sciences Building
1025 W. Johnson St.
Madison, WI 53706-1796
800-446-0399
Fax 608-262-9197
www.cew.wisc.edu
E-mail cewmail@education.wisc.edu

The above facility has numerous resources for teachers, counselors, administrators, and employers that are designed for student programs K–12, college level, and for adults. They also sponsor an annual series of career conferences designed to assist with implementing career-related programs.

Counseling Children from Different Cultures

Beginning in Chapter 3, different approaches to counseling multicultural groups were illustrated. In Chapter 10, which was devoted entirely to multicultural counseling, the point was made repeatedly that individuals from different cultures may share some common beliefs, but the significant differences within groups suggest each client be treated as an individual. Counselors should, however, be aware of culture-specific traits, beliefs, and customs from which counselors can vary their approaches. For instance, emotional boundaries of closeness of relationships are most difficult to observe (Thompson & Rudolph, 2000; Thompson, Rudolph, & Henderson, 2004). Indo-Chinese, for example, only discuss problems with family members. In this context, counseling relationships might have to be carefully delineated to client and family.

Of utmost importance, counselors must evaluate the client's level of acculturation when determining how counseling will proceed. For instance, a fifth-generation Latina girl might aspire to a professional career, whereas a Latina immigrant female might be conditioned to consider her role only that of a homemaker. The point here is not to stereotype individuals because of their cultural backgrounds, but, rather, to remain alert to modifying counseling to meet individual needs.

A review of Chapters 3 and 10 should assist counselors in preparing for delivery of individual and group career counseling programs for children from different cultures. Counselors often might have to offer nontraditional means of services to some clients. For instance, children who have been negatively affected by racism and oppression might react positively to spiritually oriented counseling programs to gain self-respect. Richardson (1991) suggests that counselors may find that African American churches can be a good resource for helping some students.

In sum, people of color might be reluctant to seek counseling because of a lack of understanding of its purpose and perhaps fear of its consequences. Some children, particularly Native American children, might feel that going to a counselor is a sign of weakness (LaFromboise & Jackson, 1996). And some children from Asian American cultures might view going to a counselor as shameful and embarrassing or as an action that is indicative of failure (Thompson & Rudolph, 2000). In general, children from different cultures have different worldviews from which they interpret relationships. For some, there is a need to avoid loss of face; for others, subtle forms of communication are preferred (Leong, 1996a). Thus, it is essential that counselors learn about culture-specific variables in the lives of children from different cultures.

In sum, the elementary school counselor is challenged with the responsibility of developing and promoting very pervasive career development programs that include specific competencies. These competencies foster self-knowledge, introduce educational and occupational exploration and career planning. In the process, students discover the relationship between education and work role, learn more about themselves, and the interrelationships of all life roles. Teachers, counselors, and parents are to foster positive attitudes toward work. Ideally, students become actively involved in their own career development and learn to involve their families in the process. Family members can serve as representatives of certain occupations, but more important, can support and reinforce student career-related activities. Finally, students learn that educational competencies are necessary to survive in an ever changing work environment (Herring, 1998). This process is viewed as a joint effort of school personnel, parents, and community. In this context, the elementary school counselor is a teacher, counselor, consultant, planner, and an expert resource person.

Implications for Career Development Programs in Elementary Schools

The preceding recommended three areas of career development for students in elementary school, combined with other research reported, suggests many ideas that can be applied to career guidance programs in elementary schools. Following is a representative list.

1. Self-concepts begin to form in early childhood. Because of the influence of self-concept formation on career development, there is strong evidence to support directed experiences in enhancing self-concept.
2. An important aspect of career development is building an understanding of strengths and limitations. Learning to identify and express strengths and limitations is a good way to build a foundation for self-understanding.
3. Elementary school children imitate role models in the home and school. Both parents and teachers can provide children with positive role models through precept and example.
4. Children learn to associate work roles by sexual stereotyping at an early age. Exposure to career information that discourages sex role stereotyping will broaden the range of occupations considered available by children of both sexes.

5. Community resources provide a rich source of career information, models, and exposure to a wide range of careers. Students from families whose parents did not attend high school have a special need for community opportunities.

6. Self-awareness counseling is a major goal of the growth stage in elementary schools. Methods used to enhance self-awareness encourage development of the ability to process and interpret information about self and others and about differences among people.

7. Learning to assume responsibility for decisions and actions has major implications for future career decisions. Some beginning steps include skills development that enables children to analyze situations, to identify people who can help them, and to seek assistance when needed.

8. Understanding the relationship between education and work is a key concept for enhancing career development. Skills learned in school and during out-of-school activities should be linked to work-related activities.

9. The idea that all work is important builds an understanding of why parents and others work. Reflection on the reasons for working fosters awareness that any productive worker should be respected.

10. Learning about occupations and about people who are actually involved in occupations builds an awareness of differences among people and occupations.

Summary

1. Career-related programs in elementary school require the development of model programs and carefully planned strategies for curriculum integration.

2. Elementary school counselors assume multiple roles such as teacher, coach, consultant, team facilitator, career information specialists, and advocate for community involvement.

3. Career-related programs are considered as an essential part of elementary school education.

4. National career guidelines for elementary schools were established by the NOICC.

5. Self-knowledge, education and occupational exploration, and career planning are overarching goals of elementary school guidance programs.

6. Integrating career development concepts into existing curricula is referred to as infusion.

7. Counselors may be required to modify career-related programs for children from different cultures.

8. Elementary school counselors should acquire an extensive background in several academic disciplines including career and human development, learning theory, and a knowledge of effective teaching strategies for children.

Supplementary Learning Exercises

1. Defend the following statement with examples to prove your point: Individuals have a profound adaptive capacity at various stages of development.

2. Construct at least two activities/strategies in which concrete experiences promote abstract conceptual operations.

3. Construct at least two activities/strategies of observational learning that would promote career development of elementary school-age children.
4. Survey a sample of elementary school students to determine their perception of appropriate career roles for their sex.
5. Describe your development from childhood. Identify significant transitions and their influences on your career.
6. Give as many reasons as you can for the significance of Roe's needs theory of career development for elementary school counseling.
7. Present several examples of how worldviews of children from different cultures affect their career decisions.
8. Explain how human and career development is interrelated. Give at least five examples.
9. Why is it important to involve parents and other community members in the elementary school career guidance program? Give examples.
10. Using one or more of the implications for career counseling in the elementary school, identify specific career guidance needs and develop activities and strategies to meet them.

For More Information

American School Counselor Association. (2003). *The ASCA national model: A framework for school counseling programs.* Alexandria, VA: Author.

Berns, R. M. (2004). *Child, family, school, community: Socialization and support.* Belmont, CA: Wadsworth/Thomson Learning.

Herr, E. L., Cramer, S. H., & Niles, S. G. (2004). *Career guidance and counseling through the life span: Systematic approaches.* New York: Pearson Education, Inc.

Sciarra, D. T. (2004). *School counseling: Foundations and contemporary issues.* Belmont, CA: Brooks/Cole-Thomson Learning.

Shaffer, D. R. (2002). *Developmental psychology: Childhood and adolescence* (6th ed.). Belmont, CA: Wadsworth/Thomson Learning.

Sharf, R. S. (2002). *Applying career development theory to counseling* (3rd ed.). Pacific Grove, CA: Brooks/Cole.

Thompson, C. L., Rudolph, L. B., & Henderson, D. (2004). *Counseling children* (6th ed.). Belmont, CA: Brooks/Cole-Thomson Learning.

Suggested InfoTrac College Edition Topics

Career competencies and children

Career education

Career infusion

Circumscription of careers

Cognitive functioning and children

Directed learning

Early relations with parents

Ecology systems

Learning gender roles

Social status and children

16 Career-Related Programs and Counseling in Secondary Schools

Chapter Highlights

- Comprehensive school guidance programs, including planning for life strategies

- Exemplary comprehensive school guidance programs in public schools

- Sample career goals and competencies

- Examples of integrating career development concepts through classroom infusion

- Sources of career videos for educational purposes

- Integrating academic and vocational education

- Goals of tech-prep programs

- Apprenticeship and future work

- School-to-work programs

- Role of placement in the high school

THIS CHAPTER COVERS SAMPLES of competencies and selected strategies for career-related programs and counseling in middle/junior and senior high school. First, we discuss a comprehensive school guidance program (K–12), then planning for life strategies that are a part of the comprehensive school guidance program. We provide current career guidance goals and student competencies by area and school level. Some examples of career infusion modules are outlined. In the next section, school-to-work programs and related programs of integrating academic and vocational education, tech-prep strategies, apprenticeships, and the future workforce are examined. Finally, we discuss placement in the secondary school.

Comprehensive School Guidance Programs

Gysbers and Henderson (1988, 2001) have created detailed plans for developing, designing, implementing, and evaluating a comprehensive school guidance program. In an earlier conceptual treatise on comprehensive guidance programs, Gysbers and Moore (1987) pointed out that a comprehensive guidance model is not an ancillary guidance service; rather, it is a model in which all staff members are involved, including administrators, community members, and parents. Furthermore, these groups are involved in a common objective whose goal is the total integrated development of individual students. According to Gysbers and Henderson, guidance programs should be viewed as developmental and comprehensive in that regularly scheduled activities are planned, conducted, and evaluated and comprehensive guidance programs feature a team approach. In essence, this means a full commitment to surveying current guidance programs within a district; establishing students' needs; establishing plans, activities, and staff to meet those needs; and recognizing that a comprehensive guidance program is an equal partner with other educational programs.

Human growth and development forms the foundation on which comprehensive guidance programs are built, especially within the domain of lifetime career development. The focus is on the interrelationship of all aspects of life. For instance, the family role is not treated separately from other life roles. The life career developmental domains are characterized as follows: (1) self-knowledge and interpersonal skills (self-understanding and recognizing the uniqueness of others); (2) life roles, settings, and events (roles such as learner, citizen, and worker; settings such as community, home, and work environment; events such as beginning the work role, marriage, and retirement); (3) life career planning (decision making and planning); and (4) basic studies and occupational preparation (knowledge and skills found in various subjects typically offered in school curricula).

Counselor involvement and commitment in this approach is extensive. Counselors are involved in teaching, team teaching, and supporting teachers. A major innovation in this program is the development of student competencies and the methods used to evaluate them. For example, at the perceptual level, the acquisition of knowledge and skills related to selected aspects of community and self are evaluated as environmental orientation and self-orientation. The conceptual level emphasizes directional tendencies (movement toward socially desirable goals) and adaptive and adjustable behavior. The generalization level is the level of functioning exhibited by students throughout the mastery of specific tasks. Each of these competencies is broken down into specific goals with identified competencies; student outcomes are specified by grade level and activity objectives.

Monitoring is accomplished using an individualized advisory system; each advisor has 15 to 20 students. The allocation of the counselor's time during the school day is suggested in percentages for participation in curriculum, individual planning, responsive services (recurring topics such as academic failure, peer problems, and family situations), and system support (consulting with parents, staff development, and compensatory programs).

Comprehensive school guidance programs are a means of systematically implementing a program concept for guidance activities in kindergarten through grade 12. The value of this model is its comprehensive nature and the involvement of school professionals, selected members of the community, and parents. The program's flexibility allows for local development of needs. Another major advantage is the evaluation of student outcomes, professional effectiveness, and program design. The program is driven by a life career development theme. The profound message to the career counseling profession is to recognize the importance of the interrelatedness of all life roles.

Planning for Life Strategies

A program called Planning for Life has been sponsored by the U.S. Army Recruiting Command with the support of the National Consortium of State Career Guidance Supervisors and the Center on Education and Training for Employment at Ohio State University. This comprehensive guidance program provides a framework for improving the effectiveness of elementary, secondary, and postsecondary programs; counselor education; and supervision and administration of career guidance programs. The special objectives of the National Consortium of State Career Guidance Supervisors are quoted as follows:

1. Provide a vehicle to enable states to join together in supporting mutual priorities, ongoing programs, and career development and prevocational services.
2. Promote the development and improvement of career guidance at all levels of education.
3. Involve business, industry, and government in creating and evaluating quality career guidance programs.
4. Serve as a clearinghouse through which states can seek assistance from public and private sources for program improvement and expansion.
5. Offer technical assistance to states in developing their annual and long-term plans related to career guidance and counseling. (National Consortium of State Career Guidance Supervisors, 1996, p. iv)

The Planning for Life Program complements comprehensive guidance programs. First, this program places career planning within the framework of the total school guidance program; career planning for all students is emphasized as in comprehensive guidance plans. More specifically, elements of the Planning for Life Program are identified by the "seven C's":

1. Clarity of purpose shares the program's purposes with school, family, business, and community.
2. Commitment suggests that an investment of resources from all parts of the community is essential.

3. Comprehensiveness ensures that the program addresses all participants in the community with all career and educational opportunities.
4. Collaboration refers to the degree to which schools, family, business, and community share program ownership.
5. Coherence is the term used to make certain that there is a documented plan for all students and to see that specific assistance and program assessment is provided.
6. Coordination is the degree to which the program is interdisciplinary and career planning is developmental.
7. Competency is proof of student attainment.

Each year, outstanding programs are given national awards: The Omaha, Nebraska, public school system, one of 1994's winners, is a good example. The program is outlined in Box 16-1.

One outstanding feature of the Omaha public schools plan is collaboration. The schools obviously have the support of the community, which is an important part of any comprehensive guidance program. The comprehensive nature of this program is also impressive. Parental involvement in career education programs offers tremendous opportunities for supporting the school's efforts in career guidance. As is the case with most comprehensive career guidance programs, all students graduate with a career plan. Follow-up data on implementing these plans would provide yet another measure of overall effectiveness.

Finally, planning for life suggests that career and life are both ongoing processes that require individual and community commitment. Because of the very nature of our society, individuals must periodically reevaluate their circumstances to achieve a more productive life and career. The connections and links between lifestyle and career are clearly interwoven; we can hardly separate one from the other in program development. Thus, life planning programs suggest an important lesson: Planning for the future involves the interrelationship of both lifestyle and career.

Be aware that there are many outstanding career-related programs in public schools. Most statewide public instructional programs contain provisions for career development standards, goals, and objectives for all grade levels. In addition, the National Standards for School Counseling Programs (Campbell & Dahir, 1997) have been published under the direction of the American School Counselor Association in which developmental guidance programs are included. The point here is counselors have at their disposal a number of references to standards, examples of program content, goals, objectives, and techniques for career development programs in schools. Local planning should include a review of one's statewide program and of others that could add depth and innovation to developing local goals and objectives.

Middle/Junior School

Students in middle/junior school should continue the career development goals that were initiated in the elementary school of self-knowledge, educational and occupational exploration, and career planning. The essential tasks are learning about and exploring career-related information. A summary of career guidance goals for middle/junior school students has been compiled by Herring (1998), paraphrased as follows: (a) decision-making skills, self-awareness by recognizing strengths and weaknesses;

| Box 16-1 | Omaha Public Schools Comprehensive Guidance and Counseling Program |

Grade Levels Kindergarten Through Twelve: Rural, Urban, Suburban

Overview

The Omaha Public Schools Comprehensive Guidance and Counseling Program provides a curriculum-based approach to address the career domain of student development.

- *Clarity of Purpose:* The career curriculum includes an agreed-upon written statement of purpose, philosophy, goals, and outcomes. All materials were developed by program committee members who include counselors, teachers, administrators, community agencies, and industry.
- *Commitment:* Teachers, community agency representatives, the business community, and counselors deliver the career program to all students. Personnel specializing in career planning are assigned to provide support and coordination for career planning in grades kindergarten through twelve. Advanced education planning specialist counselors are available in each high school.
- *Comprehensiveness:* The career planning guidance curriculum is delivered to all students beginning in kindergarten. All students graduate with a career portfolio. Assessments are utilized throughout the

program. At least two advanced career education evening programs for parents and students are provided each year in all district high schools.

- *Collaboration:* Career planning program partnerships include: Urban League, University of Nebraska–Omaha, Metro Community College, Chamber of Commerce, Explorers, Nebraska Educational Planning Center, Gifted Education Instruction, vocational education and community relations agencies. The program has received over $100,000 in foundation grants each year for the past two years.

All goals and materials are designed and developed by committees representing various school departments, industry representatives and educational agencies. Advisory committees include parents/guardians, community and industry representatives, and counselors who monitor, evaluate, assess, and improve the career planning program. Parents have access to the student portfolio for comment and review.

- *Coherence:* All students begin to develop career/educational plans in seventh grade. Students annually update their portfolios each year through grade twelve. They use the portfolio to prepare a resumé and

---

(b) educational awareness by recognizing the relationship between educational and work skills; (c) economic awareness by understanding how supply and demand influence job availability; (d) occupational awareness by learning about the content of jobs; and (e) work attitudes by recognizing the role of work in society. In middle/junior school, students are encouraged to gain a greater depth of information about the work world and its relationship to life roles. Students also link skills learned in school with work requirements.

During the middle/junior school years students are to make tentative plans and explore occupations on their own. The timing of learning modules coincides with student development of more conscious recognition of their self-characteristics and the importance of relationship skills. Their increasing awareness of self suggests more focus on their personal attributes and how they could fit an occupational environment. Ideally, students should also learn more about the decision-making process and develop their career education plan for after high school. All students graduate with a career planning portfolio.

- *Coordination:* A written career planning curriculum is delivered to all students in grades K through 12. Specified outcomes and activities are developmentally sequenced for each grade level. Activities are delivered in conjunction with the academic curriculum. Career counselors formulate written plans that include activities, resources, and evaluation.
- *Competency:* All students complete a career planning portfolio that includes goals, outcomes, and academic progress. Each component of the program is evaluated.

Commercial materials used:
- IDEAS Interest, Determination, Exploration & Assessment System (IDEAS)
- Self-Directed Search (SDS)
- The Harrington-O'Shea Career Decision Making (CDM)
- Myers-Briggs Type Indicator (MBTI)
- True Colors
- Guidance Information System

Noncommercial/local materials used:
- *Look to the Future* Curriculum Guide for elementary school
- Growing Through Development Guidance K–6

- Growing Through Transitions: Career and Educational Planning Grades 7–12
- Growing Through Counseling Curriculum Guide
- Educational/Career Planning Portfolio
- Parent Information Envelopes
- Career Educational Planning Brochures

Program Features

The Omaha career program is an integral component in a total, comprehensive, competency-based guidance program. The inclusion of career planning in a total program emphasizes the importance of career development in the student's total development. The K–12 career guidance curriculum provides comprehensive, extensive activities to provide students with a developmentally appropriate classroom-based approach to career development and career planning.

For more information contact:
Stan Maliszewski, Guidance Supervisor
Omaha Public Schools
3215 Cuming Street
Omaha NE 68131
402-557-2704

Source: From *Planning for Life: 1995 Compendium of Recognized Career Planning Programs.* National Consortium of State Career Guidance Supervisors, Center for Education and Training for Employment, 1900 Kenny Road, Columbus, OH 43210.

potential career paths and/or work environments. Discussion with students about job requirements should be designed to foster an appreciation of the role of work in their futures. As they learn how to interpret information about career opportunities, students should also become aware of skills needed to find a job. In sum, career-related programs should foster more awareness of local occupations, their requirements, and opportunities they offer (Drummond & Ryan, 1995; Sciarra, 2004).

We pause here to point out that not all students will react positively to career-related programs; on the contrary, counselors should expect to find a wide range of attitudes about future goals and work opportunities among students. It should not be surprising that some students have very limited views of their ability to obtain certain jobs. To gain a more inclusive perspective of different views of career development, we briefly explore a sociological perspective of work and career development that is certainly not new, but still relevant in current society.

Sociologists' View of Work Roles

Work per se is viewed as being more inclusive from a sociologist's point of view than is generally perceived; the status hierarchy of occupational structure, power and authority in the workplace, work socialization processes, labor unions and collective bargaining, operation of the labor market, and sociology of professions are examples. Second, career development theories assume that individuals have at least a moderate degree of control in the career decision-making process. In contrast, sociological theory strongly suggests that institutional and impersonal market forces constrain decision making and greatly impede satisfaction of career aspirations. Third, sociologists have done much more significantly relevant research than have career development theorists on institutional factors that determine and shape workplace environments. According to sociologists, forces such as formal rules and supply and demand determine the nature and scope of work activities. Although sociologists appreciate the constellation of personal attributes that influence job performance and satisfaction, sociological research has been directed to other determinants of career development that should concern the career counselor (Blau, Gustad, Jessor, Parnes, & Wilcox, 1956). The following topics are used to represent some sociological perspectives of work and career development.

Status Attainment Theory

The hypothesis is that parental status greatly affects the occupational level their children attain. More fully, parental status influences attitudes concerning appropriate levels of education and career plans (including educational level) of their children.

Sociology of Labor Markets

In taking this position, sociologists argue that institutional practices rather than individual career aspirations shape career outcomes. For example, in the structure of organizations, a satisfying career is not necessarily one that has been planned but is more a matter of obtaining a preferred position when the opportunity presents itself. In a much broader sense, individuals are assigned to job slots or work positions, rather than obtaining them from personal planned choices.

The structure of some business and government organizations is characterized by the institutional career ladder of promotions. Some ways institutional management policies affect career development are as follows: (1) those who work in the core sector of an industry make higher wages than do those in the periphery sector; (2) level of education and experience have a greater influence on wages in the core sector than in the periphery; and (3) minorities and women have limited access to jobs in the core sector.

Race and Gender Effects

Ongoing research indicates that minorities are concentrated in low-status occupations and earn less than whites do (Newman & Newman, 2003; Saunders, 1995). Some evidence suggests that there is a decline in gender segregation of jobs, but women tend to be concentrated in a narrow band of occupations that pay less than men earn (Kail & Cavanaugh, 2004; Reskin, 1993). Interestingly, men and women both earn less in jobs that are culturally defined as "women's work." One also can observe that when women enter traditionally male jobs, salaries seem to go down, but when men enter traditionally female jobs, the salaries tend to go up. Some practical solutions for counselors:

1. Career counselors need to be aware of sociological research that informs them of how individuals choose and are selected for work roles. In the career choice process, the sociologist stresses that choice is restricted by a number of variables, including status of parents, labor market demands, and structures in organizations. Thus, counseling strategies need to be developed to assist clients to cope with the social environment they encounter.
2. Career counselors should inform clients about the complexities of the work world and the difficulties they may experience when they encounter the labor market. Counselors need to develop strategies to enhance realism about the work world.
3. Career counselors need to assist clients in combating gender stereotyping, which limits career options.
4. Minority groups can be assisted in career planning by improving their chances for completing educational programs, enhancing attitudes about work, providing career information, and developing skills. Finally, clients should be offered assistance in using community resources.
5. Career counselors should provide assistance for raising educational aspirations. Counselors can display evidence of the close relationship between years of schooling and status level of parents and between years of schooling and success at work (Hotchkiss & Borow, 1996).

In sum, counselors need to provide the means by which middle/junior high school students learn to make tentative choices. Such strategies that foster self-knowledge, exploration of careers, and career planning involve the counselor not only in individual and group counseling, but also in teaching, mentoring, consulting, and providing appropriate resources. Infusion of career development learning opportunities in the classroom should continue. The following example for a geography class is designed to include planning, decision making, and awareness of career opportunities while completing a lesson in geography.

Career Infusion Module

Subject: Social studies, geography
Concept: Planning and decision making
Career awareness
Chamber of Commerce Exercise
Rationale: Students should be exposed to different ways in which different groups make decisions, in order to improve their own decision making.
Objectives:

1. Students will be able to describe their part in the project to accord with teacher observation.
2. Students will list all the Republics of South America and at least one feature from the tourist bulletin for each.

3. Students will identify at least two ways in which their project activity corresponds to duties in two specific occupations.

Description: During a unit on South America, divide the class into six groups. Each group will be a Chamber of Commerce for a Republic of South America. Each group can plan a tourist bulletin with articles and drawings.

1. Students will tell how their group decided who would research information, write articles, draw pictures, and so on.
2. Students will describe their responsibilities in preparing the tourist bulletin and tell how they think those responsibilities were like some they might have on a job.
3. Students will answer the question, "Can you see how assuming responsibility for something in this project might help you assume responsibilities in an adult occupation?"

Personnel required: Teacher
Cost: None
Time: 3 or 4 periods, estimated
Resources: Maps of and information about South America
Impact on regular offering/curriculum goals: Complement regular unit on South America; help students remember important information about the area
Evaluation measures: Paper/pencil test

SOURCE: *Project Cadre: A Cadre Approach to Career Education,* by C. C. Healy and O. H. Quinn, 1977. Unpublished manuscript. Reprinted by permission.

The geography module encourages middle/junior high school students to expand their career development competencies as they learn more about self, self-in-situation, and that learning is a lifelong process. More sophisticated and insightful responses are expected, especially in describing changes in physical, psychological, social, and emotional development. Students are to continue relating school subjects to work roles and describing the importance of improving and enhancing their skills in high school courses. Self-knowledge becomes more individualized as students are able to draw more in-depth conclusions from classroom experiences and standardized test results. There is an increased emphasis on effectively locating and using career information. In general, students are to expand their vision of the future while developing an appreciation of the importance of work in our society.

National Career Development Guidelines

The competencies for middle/junior school students described in Appendix F suggest some excellent learning objectives. These competencies focus on self-knowledge, educational and occupational planning, and career planning. Counselors and teachers are to plan for strategies that enhance competencies as a part of classroom instruction. What, for example, is an effective intervention strategy for identifying environmental influences that are associated with students' attitudes, behaviors, and aptitudes? And more important, how can career-related skills become a part of academic achievement of basic skills? These examples only represent the numerous challenges that teachers, counselors, and parents can jointly address. The infusion model described in preceding paragraphs is a good example of an innovative strategy. Some other strategies for addressing specific career development goals follow.

The following suggested activities are strategies designed to meet the objectives of self-knowledge, education and occupation information, and career planning. This continuation of what has been learned in the elementary school requires middle/junior school students to explore career information in greater detail, gain greater insight into self-concept and self-knowledge, and apply planning skills. Some representative strategies follow:

Self-Knowledge Strategies

1. Introduce the concepts of self-image, self-worth, and self-esteem. Assign small groups to discuss the relationship of these concepts to educational and occupational planning. Compile a list from these groups.
2. Ask students to complete a standardized or original personality inventory. Using Holland's (1992) classification system, have students relate personality characteristics to work environments.
3. Have students list courses in which they have excelled and those in which they have not. Ask students to relate skills learned to their personality characteristics and traits and interests.
4. Assign students to construct a life line in which they designate places lived in and visited, experiences in school and with peer groups, and major events. Have them project the life line into the future by identifying goals.
5. Have students discuss how different traits are more important for some goals than for others. Compile a list of jobs and corresponding traits.

Educational and Occupational Exploration Strategies

1. Ask students to write a description of the type of persons they think they are, their preferences for activities (work and leisure), their strengths and weaknesses, and their desires for a career someday. Discuss.
2. Have students list several occupations that are related to their own interests and abilities. Discuss.
3. Lead a class discussion by identifying relationships of interest and abilities to various occupations. Each student should explore one occupation in depth, including reading a biography, writing a letter to someone, or conducting interviews. The student should research training requirements, working conditions, and personal attributes necessary for the job.
4. Ask each student to visit a place in the community where he or she can observe someone involved in a career of interest. Have students discuss their observations, such as type of work, working conditions, or tools of the trade.
5. Have the students make a list of the school subjects that are necessary to the success of persons whose careers are being investigated. Discuss.
6. Ask students to research preparation requirements for several selected occupations. Have them identify one similarity and one difference in preparation requirements for each of the occupations listed. Discuss.
7. Assign students to write short narratives explaining why certain jobs have endured and others have disappeared. Discuss.

8. Have students classify ten occupations by abilities needed, such as physical, mental, mechanical, creative, social, and other. Have students select three occupations that match their abilities and interests.

9. Have students do a mini-internship program where they shadow a worker. Discuss and share with other students.

10. Have students write a story about the many jobs involved in producing a hamburger. Discuss.

Career Planning Strategies

1. Present steps in a decision-making model and discuss the importance of each step. Ask students to identify a problem and solve it by applying steps in the model.

2. Organize students into groups and have them construct a list of resources and resource people who could help solve a particular problem.

3. In a group discussion, compare a horoscope from a daily newspaper with other ways of solving problems and making decisions.

4. Assign students to select three occupations and then to choose one using a decision model. Share and discuss in groups.

5. Have students prepare an educational plan for high school. Share and discuss in groups.

Developmental Tasks and Cognitive and Physiological Development in Junior and Senior High School

Adolescence has been described as a period of turmoil resulting in a transition from childhood. Continuity of development is, for some, sporadic and chaotic. The key characteristic of this stage of development, according to Erikson, is the search for identity as one subordinates childhood identifications and reaches for a different identity in a more complex set of conditions and circumstances. The major danger of this period is role confusion; thus, this stage is often designated "Identity versus Confusion." In Erikson's (1963) view, this is a critical period of development. As he put it,

> These new identifications are no longer characterized by the playfulness of childhood and the experimental zest of youth: with dire urgency they force the young individual into choices and decisions which will, with increasing immediacy, lead to commitments for life. (p. 155)

Role Confusion

According to Erikson, the choice of career and commitment to a career has a significant impact on identity. Given the current difficulty surrounding occupational choice because of rapidly changing job markets and impersonal organizations, Erikson suggested that many careers pose a threat to personal identity; as a result, some individuals avoid a firm career choice. Many adolescents delay commitment or place a psychological moratorium on the decision until further options are explored. Excerpts from an interview with Ted illustrate this point:

TED: My parents want me here so that I can choose a career. They don't like it that I haven't picked one.

COUNSELOR: As I said, we should be able to help you, Ted, but first, tell me more about jobs or careers you have considered.

TED: I thought about a few, like photography, but I really don't know what I want.

COUNSELOR: Tell me more about your thoughts on photography.

TED: A photographer like Mr. Brown is not what I want to be. I guess I'd like to work for a magazine.

COUNSELOR: You mentioned Mr. Brown. What don't you like about his job?

TED: I don't want to take pictures of weddings and things like that. To tell the truth, I don't really know much about what a photographer or any other worker does. I just wish my parents would leave me alone until I have more time. I'm planning on going to community college when I finish school and I want to decide while I'm there.

A young person unable to avoid role confusion might adopt what is referred to as a "negative identity," assuming forms of behavior that are in direct conflict with family and society. Those who develop a more appropriate sense of direction can find this experience positive, but for others, the negative identity is maintained throughout adulthood. Identity diffusion, according to Erikson, often results in lack of commitment to a set of values and, subsequently, to occupations.

Career Maturity

Likewise, Super (1990) and Crites and Savickas (1996) suggest strong relationships between identity and career commitment as variables of *career maturity*. Career maturity implies a stabilized identity that provides individuals with a framework for making career choices, a crystallized formation of self-perceptions, and developed skills. Career maturity is a continuous developmental process and presents specific identifiable characteristics and traits essential to career development. Characteristics of career maturity are decisiveness and independence, knowledge of occupational information, and in planning and decision-making skills. (Chapter 6 reviews career maturity inventories that provide specific information about other dimensions of career maturity.)

Finally, defining appropriate sexual roles and achieving relationships with peers are crucial developmental tasks for adolescents (Havighurst, 1972). Success in accomplishing these tasks is essential to social adjustment at this stage of life. Socially responsible behavior implies that the first steps have been taken in achieving emotional independence from parents and other adults. According to Havighurst, social relationship patterns learned during adolescence greatly affect an individual's adjustment to rules and life roles, including the work role, of the dominant society.

Cognitive Development

Cognitive development, according to Piaget and Inhelder (1969), is the transition from concrete operational thinking to formal thought that is a gradual process beginning at approximately 12 years of age. During early adolescence, patterns of problem solving and planning are quite unsystematic. Near the end of high school, however, the adolescent has the ability to deal with abstractions, form hypotheses in problem solving, and sort out problems through mental manipulations. Linking observations and emotional responses with a recently developed systematic thinking process, the adolescent reacts to events and experiences with a newly found power of thought. In formal thought, the adolescent can direct emotional responses to abstract ideals as well as to people. Introspective thinking leads to analysis of self-in-situations, including projection of the self into the adult world of work (Elkind, 1968; Gillies, 1989; Kail & Cavanaugh, 2004; Keating, 1980; Piaget & Inhelder, 1969).

The cognitive development of formal thought introduces sets of ambiguities. On one hand, the adolescent is developing a systematized thinking process to solve problems appropriately. On the other hand, there is unrestrained theorizing, extreme self-analysis, and more-than-usual concern about the reactions of others. By virtue of concern for others, the peer group influence is particularly strong during adolescence. Self-analysis can lead to what Miller-Tiedeman and Tiedeman (1990) refer to as "I-power" as a means of self-development. Increased self-awareness is an essential part of the adolescent's development, particularly in clarifying self-status and individualized belief systems in the career decision-making process.

In the *development of formalized thinking,* adolescents do not simply respond to stimuli but also interpret what they observe (Bandura, 1977, 1986). In this connection, they will perceive stimuli in the environment as having positive and negative associations. An example of a negative association is a junior high student who believes that lawyers "rip you off because they are all crooks." In this sense, perceptions and values associated with occupations are developed through generalizations formed by experience and observations. Brown, Mounts, Lamborn, and Steinberg (1993) and Newman and Newman (2003) found that parents have the greatest influence on the long-range plans of adolescents, but peers are more likely to influence immediate identity or status. Occupational stereotypes as perceived in career decision making may be generalized from interactions with both parents and peers as well as gained through other stimuli, such as films and books.

Sexual Maturity

A dramatic physiological change, sexual maturity, takes place for most boys and girls during middle/junior and senior high school. Accompanying or preceding sexual maturity are dramatic bodily changes, such as increased muscle tissue and body stature, which permit the adolescent to perform adult physical tasks for the first time. Particularly important to the adolescent is physical appearance. In middle/junior and high school, concern for appearance reaches its peak as girls compare themselves to movie and television stars, females appearing in commercials, and professional models. Boys use the standards of physical strength and facial and body hair for judging early maturity (Biehler & Hudson, 1986; Kail & Cavanaugh, 2004). Feeling comfortable within the dominant peer group is highly related to being judged as "grown-up" or mature.

Reflecting on sexual maturity, Cal related the following incident:

> I wanted to do everything I could to be grown up, but I was just a little twerp. I even tried to imitate how men walked. I guess I was 12 or 13 when I lit my first cigarette. Even though I coughed until I almost choked, I kept on smoking that cigarette! Yes sir, I

wanted to be one of those "cool cats" with all the know-how. But the worst of it was P.E. I didn't want to undress in front of anybody. I made up all kinds of excuses until the locker room was clear, and then I went home and showered. You know, it was important then to be accepted by my friends. I guess I ended up being liked by most of them. Now when I look back, it seems we were all trying to fool each other.

Quiang, an early-maturing junior high school student, reflected on her experiences:

All of a sudden it seemed I had outgrown everyone—especially the boys. Some of the girls seemed as physically mature as I was, but they usually acted uneasy around me, and I certainly felt awkward around them. It was during this time that I made friends with some older girls. As far as the boys were concerned, there were mixed feelings. The older boys didn't accept me because I was "too young," while the younger ones were too little for me. I just felt out of place for a few years until everybody caught up.

The effects of early and late sexual maturity provide a frame of reference for counseling intervention. Evidence suggests that early-maturing males are more than likely to receive approval and reinforcement for their behavior among male peer groups and adults. Late-maturing girls also enjoy acceptance and popularity (Livson & Peskin, 1980; Sigelman & Rider, 2003). Simmons and Blyth (1987) confirm early- and late-maturity differences and their related benefits and costs, and they report some additional special effects:

- Early-maturing boys had more dates and dated more often than did late-maturing boys. Furthermore, early-maturing males were more positive about physical development and athletic abilities.
- Early-maturing girls had poorer grades in school and had more discipline problems. Also, they were more negative about their physical development.

Sexual maturity may be one basis for differentiating career guidance activities. Late-maturing males and early-maturing girls might experience a greater need for counseling intervention than do their peers. It seems that junior/middle and high school students benefit from guidance programs that inform them of the extent, type, and variation of physiological changes in early adolescence and that specifically address anxieties related to bodily changes (Richards & Larson, 1993; Williams & Currie, 2000).

In sum, human development is viewed as both continuous and discontinuous. Developmental stages provide a sound basis for the identifying needs and concerns of students in both middle/junior and high school. Ginzberg, Ginsburg, Axelrad, and Herma (1951) are generally considered to be the first to approach a theory of occupational choice from a developmental standpoint. This team, consisting of an economist, a psychiatrist, a sociologist, and a psychologist, set out to develop and test a theory of occupational choice. Their original study was part of a more comprehensive study of the world of work.

Developmental Stages by Ginzberg Group

In developing their theory, Ginzberg and associates undertook an empirical investigation of a carefully selected sample of individuals who would have reasonable freedom of choice in selecting an occupation. Their sample comprised males from upper-middle-class, urban, Protestant or Catholic families of Anglo-Saxon origin, whose educational level ranged from sixth grade to graduate school. Because of the highly selective nature of the sample, the study's conclusions have limited application. Specifically, female and ethnic minority career developmental patterns were not considered, nor were those of the rural or urban poor. Therefore, be aware that the conclusions this study reached do not necessarily apply to other than the identified sample. This study's value, however, is in its emphasis on career development during the middle/junior and high school years.

The Ginzberg group concluded that occupational choice is indeed a developmental process and their focus generally covered a period of six to ten years, beginning around age 11 and ending shortly after age 17 or in young adulthood. There are three distinct periods or stages in the occupational choice process: fantasy, tentative, and realistic. Table 16-1 outlines these steps.

According to Ginzberg and associates, during the fantasy period, play gradually becomes work-oriented and reflects initial preferences for certain kinds of activities. Various occupational roles are assumed in play, resulting in initial value judgments about the world of work.

The tentative period is divided into four stages. First is the interest stage, during which the individual makes more definite decisions concerning likes and dislikes. Next is the capacity stage of becoming aware of one's ability as related to vocational aspirations. Third is the value stage, when clearer perceptions of occupational styles emerge. During the final transition stage, the individual becomes aware of the decision for vocational choice and the subsequent responsibilities accompanying a career choice.

The realistic period is divided into three stages. The first stage is the exploration stage, which, for the group studied by Ginzberg and associates, centered on college entrance. During this stage, the individual narrows the career choice to two or three possibilities but is generally in a stage of ambivalence and indecisiveness. However, the career focus is much narrower in scope. During the second stage, crystallization, the commitment to a specific career field is made. Change of direction for some— even at this stage—is referred to as pseudocrystallization. The final stage, specification, is when the individual selects a job or professional training for a specific career.

The Ginzberg group recognized individual variations in the career decision process. Individual patterns of career development that lacked conformity with age-mates were identified as deviant—that is, deviant from the highly selected sample that comprised white males from upper-middle-class, urban families. Two primary causes for individual variations in career development were suggested: (1) early, well-developed occupational skills often result in early career patterns, deviant from the normal development; and (2) timing of the realistic stage of development may be delayed significantly because of such variables as emotional instability, various personal problems, and financial affluence.

From this study emerged a distinctive, systematic process based primarily on adolescent adjustment patterns that lead individuals to occupational choice. More specifically, the occupational choice process was the gradually developed precept of occupations subjectively appraised by the individual in the sociocultural milieu from childhood to early adulthood. As one progresses through the stages outlined by this study, vocational choice is being formulated. As tentative occupational decisions are made, other potential choices are eliminated. In the original study, Ginzberg and

Table 16-1	Stages or Periods in the Ginzberg Study	
Period	**Age**	**Characteristics**
Fantasy	Childhood (before age 11)	Purely play orientation in the initial stage; near end of this stage, play becomes work-oriented
Tentative	Early adolescence (ages 11–17)	Transitional process marked by gradual recognition of work requirements; recognition of interests, abilities, work rewards, values, and time perspectives
Realistic	Middle adolescence (ages 17 to young adult)	Integration of capacities and interests: further development of values; specification of occupational choice; crystallization of occupational patterns

Source: Adapted from Ginzberg, Ginzburg, Axelrad, and Herma (1951).

associates stated that the developmental process of occupational decision making was irreversible in that the individual could not return chronologically or psychologically to the point where earlier decisions could be repeated. This conclusion was later modified to refute the irreversibility of occupational decision making; however, Ginzberg (1972) continued to stress the importance of early choices in the career decision process. The work of Ginzberg and associates has greatly influenced occupational research, particularly for developmental tasks related to career development. In a later review of his theory, Ginzberg (1984) reemphasized that occupational choice is lifelong and coextensive with a person's working life:

> Occupational choice is a lifelong process of decision making for those who seek major satisfaction from their work. This leads them to reassess repeatedly how they can improve the fit between their changing career goals and the realities of the world of work. (p. 180)

In sum, this theory is more descriptive than explanatory in that it does not provide either strategies for facilitating career development or explanations of the developmental process. Not surprisingly, some evidence supported the major tenets of the theory in that some concepts of vocational development do indeed occur but not necessarily in timing and sequence postulated (Hollender, 1967). This theory did provide a framework for the study of career development.

Implications for Career-Related and Counseling Programs in Middle/Junior Schools

The three recommended areas of career development for students in middle or junior high school, combined with research, yield numerous implications for career development programs.

1. In many respects, middle/junior school is an educational transition from structured classroom settings to more specialized educational programs. Learning to

relate acquired skills to educational and occupational goals promotes exploratory reflection and activities.

2. There appears to be a strong need to increase junior high school students' abilities to realistically appraise their own abilities, achievements, and interests. Minority students and students from homes where parents' education level is low need special assistance in understanding their strengths and limitations.

3. Students in middle/junior school have difficulty identifying and evaluating their interests in relation to total life experiences.

4. A limited knowledge of occupations makes it difficult for middle/junior school students to relate in- and out-of-school activities to future jobs. Exposure to jobs and career fields should be expanded to provide a basis for linking various activities to work.

5. The naiveté and limited knowledge of the factors necessary for evaluating future work roles suggest the desirability of introducing informational resources and teaching the necessary skills for their use. Learning about career options, for example, increases awareness of exploration opportunities.

6. Physiological development and sexual maturity during middle/junior school involve individual changes in self-perceptions and social interactions. Opportunities to explore, evaluate, and reflect on values seem to be very desirable activities for promoting a better understanding of self during this stage.

7. Middle/junior school students will greatly benefit from hands-on experience with skill activities associated with occupations. Basic and concrete experiences provide a means of learning skills used in work.

8. Because middle/junior school students should begin to assume responsibility for their own behaviors, they would benefit greatly from improved knowledge of planning, decision-making, and problem-solving skills.

9. Increased awareness of sexual differences among junior school students suggests that emphasis be placed on learning how sex role stereotyping, bias, and discrimination limit occupational and educational choices.

10. Students in middle/junior school who continue the process of awareness initiated in elementary school will recognize the changing nature of career commitment. The skills and knowledge learned to evaluate initial career choices will be used to evaluate multiple choices over the life span.

High School

Rites of passage are most relevant to this age of transitions. The high school years are truly a time of learning to prepare for and make important decisions about the future. A listing of career goals and competencies by Paisley and Hubbard (1994), displayed in Table 16-2, suggests that students have now reached a time when they are expected to take more independent actions and accept responsibility for their decisions. A greater sense of awareness and knowledge of the world of work are guiding principles for the next great step in life. Moreover, students who have developed a positive attitude concerning the idea of a lifetime of learning will recognize that a variety of options await them.

Table 16-2	Sample of Grades 10–12 Career Goals and Competencies

Overall Goals
- Become aware of personal characteristics, interests, aptitudes, and skills
- Develop an awareness of and respect for the diversity of the world of work
- Understand the relationship between school performance and future choices
- Develop a positive attitude toward work

Competencies
Tenth-grade students will be able to:
- Clarify the role of personal values in career choice
- Distinguish educational and skill requirements for areas or careers of interest
- Recognize the effects of job or career choice on other areas of life
- Begin realistic assessment of their potential in various fields
- Develop skills in prioritizing needs related to career planning

Eleventh-grade students will be able to:
- Refine future career goals through synthesis of information concerning self, use of resources, and consultation with others
- Coordinate class selection with career goals
- Identify specific educational requirements necessary to achieve their goals
- Clarify their own values as they relate to work and leisure

Twelfth-grade students will be able to:
- Complete requirements for transition from high school
- Make final commitments to a career plan
- Understand the potential for change in their own interests or value related to work
- Understand the potential for change within the job market
- Understand career development as a life-long process
- Accept responsibility for their own career directions

SOURCE: From *Developmental School Counseling Programs: From Theory to Practice*, by P. O. Paisley and G. T. Hubbard (American Counseling Association, 1994), pp. 218–221. Reprinted with permission. No further reproduction authorized without written permission of the American Counseling Association.

National Career Development Guidelines

The role and scope of the high school counselor includes a continuation of preparing students for a variety of life roles. As discussed earlier in the comprehensive career guidance programs, planning for life becomes more relevant for students in high school. The understanding of life roles and their interrelationship is a good perspective to foster. The national career guidelines also include three areas of career development for students in high school: self-knowledge, educational and occupational exploration, and career planning. Specific competencies for career development goals are included in Appendix G. These competencies require a more sophisticated understanding of purpose and scope of career development goals. There is also a practical bent stressed in competencies that hopefully lead students to connect the purpose of lifelong learning with requirements of the work world.

The following strategies are designed to meet the goals of self-knowledge, educational and occupational exploration, and career planning in the high school. Many of these strategies were developed in the 1970s and 1980s but continue to be relevant in the 21st century.

Self-Knowledge Strategies

1. Have students list five roles they currently fill. Discuss in small groups and identify future roles, such as spouse, parent, and citizen. Discuss.
2. Discuss or show films on sex-role stereotyping. Have students identify how sex role stereotyping prohibits many individuals from becoming involved in certain events, including work roles.
3. Assign students to select newspaper and magazine pictures and articles that illustrate societal perceptions of appropriate behavior and dress. Discuss.
4. Have students discuss physical differences among their peers. Emphasize how differences could affect individuals.
5. Discuss the value of cooperative efforts in the work environment. Have students develop a project in which cooperation is essential. Discuss.
6. Have students observe workers performing specific tasks and make notes of skills and time required to complete tasks. Discuss.
7. Have students discuss employer expectations compared with their own. Develop a consensus about how both are justified and can be attained.
8. Have students role-play a supervisor reacting to an employee's work performance. Discuss reactions of supervisors in a variety of situations.
9. Have students research the various causes of tardiness and absenteeism among workers. Discuss.
10. Ask students to interview at least three workers and three supervisors of workers on the subject of good work habits. Discuss.

Educational and Occupational Exploration Strategies

1. Have students identify geographical factors that can affect career choice (Geary, 1972). Obtain newspapers from urban and rural areas. Compare employment opportunities and contrast differences.
2. Have students identify high school courses required for entry into trade schools, colleges, or jobs (Walz, 1972). Discuss elements of required courses and develop brochures that list jobs and corresponding high school courses required.
3. Help students understand how human values are significant in career decision making (Bottoms, Evans, Hoyt, & Willer, 1972). Develop a list of values that could influence selection of a career. Each student selects two values of importance and locates a career that would be congruent with those values. Discuss.
4. Help students understand the principles and techniques of life planning (Brown, 1980). In small groups, in eight 1-hour meetings, six components are presented and discussed: "Why People Behave the Way They Do," "Winners and Losers," "Your Fantasy Life," "Your Real Life," "Setting Goals," and "Short- and Long-Term Planning."

5. Help students prepare for entrance into colleges and universities (Hansen, 1970). A college-bound club discusses in weekly meetings such topics as how to read a university catalog, how to visit a campus, and how to evaluate universities and colleges.
6. Discuss the value of leisure activities. Have students report on the benefits involved in five leisure activities of their choice. Discuss.
7. Have students develop a list of leisure activities they enjoy and estimate the amount of time necessary to participate in each. Form groups to decide which occupations would most likely provide the necessary time and which ones would not.
8. Ask students to debate the pros and cons of selected leisure activities.
9. Assign students to develop a list of leisure activities they enjoy now and project which of these can be enjoyed over the life span. Have students collect and discuss brochures from travel agencies and parks.
10. Have students discuss the concept of lifestyle in terms of work commitment, leisure activities, family involvement, and responsibilities and share their projections of future life roles and lifestyle.

Career Planning Strategies

1. Ask students to review several job search manuals. Discuss the steps suggested in the manuals and develop strategies for taking these steps.
2. Assign students to visit a state employment agency and describe its functions. Discuss.
3. Have students research newspaper want ads and select several jobs of interest. Discuss and identify appropriate occupational information resources.
4. Have students demonstrate the steps involved in identifying an appropriate job, filling out an application, and writing a resumé. Discuss.
5. Have students participate in a mock interview. Critique and discuss appropriate dress and grooming.
6. Help students develop planning skills (Hansen, 1970). A one-year course, taught as an elective, covers six major areas of study: (a) relating one's characteristics to occupations; (b) exploring manual and mechanical occupations; (c) exploring professional, technical, and managerial occupations; (d) relating the economic system to occupations and people; (e) exploring clerical and service occupations; and (f) evaluating and planning ahead.
7. Help students evaluate careers relative to standards of living and lifestyle (Sorapuru, Theodore, & Young, 1972a; Steidl, 1972). Students project themselves 10 to 15 years in the future and identify the kind of lifestyles they would like to have. Each student selects four careers and conducts research to determine if the projected lifestyle can be met through these careers.
8. Provide good job search procedures (Sorapuru, Theodore, & Young, 1972b). Students who have had part-time jobs explain how they got them. Groups investigate local organizations that help people find jobs. Students investigate telephone directories, school placement center files, and state employment agencies for leads to jobs. Students write resumés and "walk through" steps for applying and interviewing.
9. Help students understand the stressors of work responsibility (Bottoms et al., 1972). Students identify individuals who recently attained a position of prominence and compare changes in lifestyle (work, leisure, and family).

10. Involve parents in career planning and decision making in high school (Amatea & Cross, 1980). Students and parents attend six 2-hour sessions per week and discuss the following at school and at home: self-management and goal setting, elements in career planning and decision making, comparing self with occupational data, information gathering skills, and training paths.

Career Infusion Module

Developing planning skills for future educational and vocational choices also involves a multitude of learning activities and guidance programs. Decision-making skills and knowledge of occupations and job placement are key factors to emphasize in career development infusion. The following infusion module for a high school English class should help students become more aware of the importance of decision making. Following this module is an example of an intervention strategy for understanding gender role stereotyping.

Subject: English
Concept: Planning and decision making
Decision making exemplified in literature
Rationale: Students should become more aware of the importance of decision making.
Objectives:

1. Students will arrange in order the steps in the systematic decision-making model discussed in class.
2. Students will analyze either a personal decision or a decision made by a literary character by listing the steps taken in making the decision; students will write in one page how that decision followed the steps in the model or, if it didn't, how it could.

Description: Read and hold a class discussion on Robert Frost's poem, "The Road Not Taken," having students express their thoughts about the importance of decision making and talk about experiences that led them to make an important decision or to change their minds after making one. Bring out the following points in the discussion:

1. It is important that the student make a decision systematically and participate in its formulation.
2. Before making a decision, one must examine the consequences of the decision, both pro and con.
3. To do this, one must try to get accurate information about each decision.
4. Decision making can be thought of as a series of steps: (a) set the goal; (b) figure out alternative ways of reaching the goal; (c) get accurate information to determine which alternative is best; (d) decide on an alternative and carry it out; (e) figure out if the choice was correct and why; and (f) if you did not reach the goal, try another alternative or start the process over again.

Personnel required: Teacher
Cost: None

Time: One period
Resources: Robert Frost's poem, "The Road Not Taken"

SOURCE: *Project Cadre: A cadre approach to career education infusion,* by C. C. Healy & O. H. Quinn, 1977. Unpublished manuscript. Reprinted by permission.

Sex Role Stereotyping

All students need to be prepared for self-sufficiency in the future. One major challenge is to assist both boys and girls in overcoming the problems associated with gender role stereotyping. Counseling-component modules for the classroom present one method of accomplishing this objective. The following case example uses a counseling module for junior high school.

Jane, Sari, Bart, and John are in a junior high school self-discovery counseling group. The counselor asks each member to study an advertisement that uses a man or a woman on television and also to locate one in a magazine. Each will record the product being advertised and describe the individual in the ad.

Sari and John recorded the information for two ads, which were discussed in the next group session. Sari's notes included the following: "This woman was beautiful on television, in a long flowing dress with gorgeous hair blowing in the wind. She was advertising a soap to be used for the face and hands for keeping them soft and pretty."

John's notes were taken on a magazine ad: "This ad was on a full page in a magazine. It showed a man advertising cigarettes who had a tattoo on his hand. He looked like a cowboy with a weather-beaten face."

The counselor asked the group to discuss the characteristics of each character in the two ads. The adjectives used to describe each character were recorded. For the woman in the ad, the list included beautiful, graceful, clean, dainty, and sexy. The list for the man included macho, handsome, outdoorsman, self-assured, and rugged.

The counselor asked the group to discuss the appropriate roles in life for men and women implied by these advertisements. The apparent differences in roles were then extended to typical gender role stereotypes such as women are to be pampered, dependent, and pretty, whereas men are strong, free to do as they please, and independent. The group discussed how these ads and other types of gender role stereotyping have influenced their own perceptions of lifestyles for men and women and, subsequently, the careers they find appropriate for men and women. The counselor summarized the influence of gender role stereotyping found in advertising and elsewhere in society. Finally, the changing role of women in general and in the workforce in particular was emphasized.

Role models may also be used as a counseling component that can effectively emphasize the occupational potential of girls. Examples of women who have enjoyed successful careers provide girls with concrete evidence that women do have opportunities to develop careers in a working world thought to be dominated by men. Numerous techniques apply to such a component. One method is to have students interview working women and write a summary of their work-related experiences.

Biographies of women may also be reviewed and discussed. These examples should emphasize how women can overcome gender role stereotyping and find equal opportunity in the job market. They also illustrate that women can effectively assume leadership roles in the world of work. Finally, role models provide support for girls seriously considering a career-oriented lifestyle and may also provide some potential mentors.

Locating a mentor from whom one can learn the skills of a given career directly is usually highly productive. Therefore, career education and career counseling programs that instruct girls on the values of mentor relationships are very useful. A mentor is usually an older person who is admired and respected and has tremendous influence on the young. The point here is that women who aspire to professional careers have fewer opportunities to find a mentor than do men, primarily because there are fewer female mentors available. There is some evidence that cross-gender mentoring can be of value, but because some men have a tendency to not take career women seriously, there is the danger of increasing the chances of gender role stereotyping.

Career Videos for Individual and Group Counseling

Some excellent career videos are available for educational purposes. Feller (1994) has collected a list of 650 career videos, 161 of which have been reviewed and rated by career development specialists. More information and a complete list of videos by Feller (1994) can be obtained in Zunker (1998) and from the following address:

Dr. Rich Feller
Colorado State University
School of Education
222 Education Building
Fort Collins, CO 80523-1588
970-491-6897
Fax 970-491-1317
E-mail feller@condor.cahs.colostate.edu

Some Significant Career-Related Programs

Since the 1980s there have been a number of career-related programs designed to enhance the career development of high school students. Even apprenticeship programs have been revisited and projected into the future workforce. Recognizing changing workforce needs, especially the need for technical skills, the U.S. Department of Labor established a committee on apprenticeship in the 1980s. Like other work-based learning, training under the supervision of a master worker is a desirable learning experience. Building technical skills and observing how technical tasks relate to theoretical knowledge and interpretation was viewed as a major advantage of apprenticeships.

Apprenticeships

The *Federal Committee on Apprenticeship* suggests training strategies with the following eight essential components:

- Apprenticeship is sponsored by employers and others who can actually hire and train individuals in the workplace, and it combines hands-on training on the job with related theoretical instruction.
- Workplace and industry needs dictate key details of apprenticeship programs: training content, length of training, and actual employment settings.

- Apprenticeship has a specific legal status and is regulated by federal and state laws and regulations.
- Apprenticeship leads to formal, official credentials: a Certificate of Completion and journeyperson status.
- Apprenticeship generally requires a significant investment of time and money by employers or other sponsors.
- Apprenticeship provides wages to apprentices during training according to pre-defined wage scales.
- Apprentices learn by working directly under master workers in their occupations.
- Apprenticeship involves both written agreements and implicit expectations. Written agreements specify the roles and responsibilities of each party; implicit expectations include the right of program sponsors to employ the apprentice, recouping their sizable investment in training, and the right of apprentices to obtain such employment (Grossman & Drier, 1988, pp. 28–63).
- Apprenticeships are independent of vocational-technical education programs, tech-prep programs, and cooperative education. This distinction is made because only apprenticeship produces fully trained journeypersons with the skills needed to perform effectively in the workplace. The concept of apprenticeships is important in a work-based program that was designed to meet the ever- and fast-changing technical needs of the workplace.

Tech-Prep Programs

At about the same time apprenticeship programs were revisited, tech-prep programs were emphasized. Tech-prep is a national strategy designed to ensure that students exit high school or a community/technology college with marketable skills for job placement, have academic credentials to pursue higher education, or both. In this context, tech-prep means integrated academics and technical training for secondary, postsecondary, and apprenticeship students, plus curriculum development to meet the skills requirements of advanced technology jobs. Also included was an innovative career counseling program that provided information about high-demand occupations, a comprehensive assessment program for students in middle/junior school, and an individualized career and educational plan for high school graduates.

To accomplish the goals of tech-prep programs, school systems and cooperating colleges and universities formed consortiums with industry. Through such organizations, education and industry can effectively address and coordinate work-site-based training. In addition, follow-up assessment of graduates is enhanced.

One major goal of tech-prep programs was to encourage vocational education students to take more advanced, academically oriented courses. Typically, schools devise a variety of two-year technical curricula that include such subjects as applied mathematics, applied biology/chemistry, and principles of technology. There is often a working relationship with cooperating colleges that have agreed, by prior arrangement, to accept these courses for college credit or as entrance requirements.

Operationally, students concentrate on basic concepts during their first year and learn more about applications of the concepts during the second year. In principles of technology, for example, first-year students examine principles of force, work, energy, and power; in the second year, they apply these concepts in optical systems, radiation, and transducers. Many colleges that accept the principles of technology courses count them as a laboratory-science requirement (Cetron & Gayle, 1991).

Reinforcing the idea of integrating academic and vocational education, Grubb, Davis, Lum, Plihal, and Mograine (1991) describe the following models:

1. Incorporate more academic content in vocational courses. (Vocational teachers modify vocational courses to include more academic content.)
2. Combine vocational and academic teachers to enhance academic competencies in vocational programs. (A cooperative effort involves more academic content in vocational courses.)
3. Make academic courses more vocationally relevant. (Academic teachers modify courses or adopt new courses to include more vocational content.)
4. Modify both vocational and academic courses. (Change content of both vocational and academic courses.)
5. Use the senior project as a form of integration. (Teachers collaborate in developing new courses around student projects.)
6. Implement the Academy model. (Use team teaching of math, English, science, and vocational subjects for two or three years and then require other subjects in regular high school.)
7. Develop occupational high schools and magnet schools. (Occupational schools have been more successful in integrating vocational and academic education than the magnet schools have.)
8. Implement occupational clusters, "career paths," and occupational majors. (Students are encouraged to think about occupations early in high school.)

The major goal of the above recommendations is to encourage vocational education students to take more rigorous academic courses. In an ever changing society, quality of life and work options will largely be determined by one's basic skills and commitment to be a lifelong learner.

School-to-Work Programs

The U.S. Department of Education and the U.S. Department of Labor have jointly sponsored a work-based program known as school-to-work. This is considered a new approach to learning for all students in which students apply what they learn to real life and to real work situations. In 1994, the School-to-Work Opportunities Act was signed into law, offering the possibility for all sectors of a community to work together in making education a more meaningful experience. Every school-to-work system must contain the following three core elements (U.S. Departments of Education and Labor, 1996):

1. School-based learning: Classroom instruction based on high academic and business-defined occupational skill standards.
2. Work-based learning: Career exploration, work experience, structured training, and mentoring at job sites.
3. Connecting activities: Courses that integrate classroom and on-the-job instruction; matching students with participating employers, training mentors, and

building other bridges between school and work. (See Appendix H for a summary of a student's work experience in her own words.)

The major educational focus of this act is to assist students in making the transition from school to work. A work-based learning approach is designed to develop skills in critical thinking, problem solving, communications, and interpersonal relations. These skills are considered vital for all work roles.

Another major objective is to have students learn about job possibilities by shadowing existing workers and discussing work life and the workplace with someone while on a job. Experiencing multiple workplaces is stressed.

To apply academics to real tasks on a specific job, workplace mentors collaborate with classroom teachers. This rationale suggests that students will become more motivated in all academic programs when they are able to experience the connections and links between their schoolwork and what is required on a job.

Quality school-to-work programs must be expertly coordinated between the work site and the classroom. Thus, teachers must also be convinced of the program's benefits. Teachers, supervisors, and students must cooperatively plan academic content and skill development to ensure an appropriate learning experience. Finally, it must be pointed out that school-to-work programs are not just another program for noncollege-bound students. On the contrary, this program allows students to participate in advanced academic courses while developing workplace skills. This national program recognizes that we are now part of a technological society that requires technical skills for practically all careers, including professional ones.

A comprehensive qualitative study of the effectiveness of school-to-work programs was conducted by Bluestein, Phillips, John-Davis, Finkelberg, and Roarke (1997). Their findings suggest that counselors, teachers, and mentors are to be prepared to offer a significant amount of support and attention to students struggling in the process of transitional changes and making connections between life and work. It appears that a significant number of students had difficulty in comprehending and understanding the concept of career. Work for these students may be seen as a series of events that lead to work opportunities over which they have little control. Prudent planning and its value are at best vague concepts that need to be fostered. These students are in need of positive job experiences to encourage planning for a future work life. Positive experiences in the workplace can be effectively reinforced by supervising teachers, supervisors at work, and counselors. Ironically, it was found that family member involvement often had a negative impact on student's progress.

The counseling challenges here are very significant ones! Work-bound students have significantly different problems than do students who are college-bound. The point here is that school-to-work programs should address the issues of the culturally diverse who have limited access to jobs. Keep in mind that status attainment theory suggests that parental status greatly affects the occupational aspirations of their children (Blau, Gustad, Jessor, Parnes, & Wilcox, 1956). Fouad (1997), who observed school-to-work programs, pointed out that many students who were irregular in school attendance continued this pattern of irregular attendance in the workplace. Work-bound students therefore may need assistance in restructuring their faulty thinking and behavior: Patterns of behavior that reflect a lack of discipline and responsibility will need to be addressed as part of a career development agenda. These problems suggest a broad scope of professionally challenging counseling needs that call for integrative intervention strategies (Gelso & Fretz, 2001).

Placement as Part of Career Planning

In this section, we cover the role of placement officers in secondary schools and also the role of the state employment agency. The integration of career planning and placement services in many educational institutions has evolved gradually during the last three decades. A current suggestion is to eliminate the word *placement* as a part of the name of the center where career services are offered (J. K. Carter, 1995). This name change is the result of changing missions in educational institutions. For instance, many career centers have focused more on preplacement services, such as general information about educational programs, outreach programs, cooperative education and internships, part-time jobs, and computerized career guidance and information systems. Placement should remain as a primary service offered by educational institutions, but in institutions where career planning and placement services have been combined into career centers, the services include a wide variety of programs that have received equal and in many cases more attention than placement has. Thus, a more appropriate name for locations that provide career-related services, including placement, is the more generic term *career centers.*

The Purpose and Rationale for Career Centers

Career centers have been developed as a major component of career guidance programs. The management of programs and the use of occupational information material are major responsibilities of the career counselor. The counselor's knowledge of how to use occupational information relates closely to the effectiveness of the career center. Counselors must also be well acquainted with the content of the various sources of career information. Program development for individual and group use of the center must be carefully planned.

Presentation of materials will vary according to the differing needs of groups and individuals. For example, a senior high school freshman class may be given an overview demonstration of the various resources in the center, whereas a group of high school juniors are presented with specific resources needed for a class project. Or a group of high school seniors may be given the assignment of researching the various careers in their declared majors.

Individual use of career information is highly personalized, and the counselor must recognize that different learning styles among clients call for flexibility in the use of career information resources. Moreover, Sharf (2002) pointed out that information-seeking behavior will vary from client to client. As counselors help individuals sort and assimilate information, they must also provide direction by generating questions concerning specific information that can be obtained from available resources. Just as career decision making is an individualized process, so too is the use and assimilation of career information. In sum, the career center is used by individuals who are in various phases of career decision making; some are seeking information to narrow down choices, whereas others are searching for answers in the beginning phases of decision making. It is also a place where instructors can meet with groups of students or entire classes for a variety of career guidance objectives. Finally, the entire professional staff is encouraged to use the center as a resource for ongoing projects.

Several advantages of career centers are worth considering. First, a centralized location provides the opportunity to systematically organize all career materials into more efficient and workable units. The centralized facility also allows counselors to monitor materials on hand and simplifies the task of maintaining and selecting additional materials. Second, students and faculty are attracted to centrally displayed materials that are easily accessed. Thus, a wider use of materials is usually assured, and in addition, attention is directed to programs offered by the career center. In essence, the career center brings into focus career-related programs and career resources offered by an institution. A third consideration is the methods of promoting coordination and acceptance of career-related programs among faculty, staff, administration, students, and community. A well-organized and well-operated career center will encourage a variety of members of an institution to participate in development, programming, and evaluation of career center materials and facilities. A commitment from a cross-section of individuals will greatly enhance the career guidance efforts an educational institution offers.

A final consideration is programming innovations for the use of career materials and outreach activities, which are usually generated within the career center or sponsored by the career center. A well-planned facility can become the focal point in planning new programs and innovative activities for career guidance and career education. In essence, the career center should facilitate a wide variety of program development opportunities among staff and faculty.

The Role of Placement in High School

A major component of the placement part of career planning involves job listings from local, state, regional, national, and international sources. The numerous federal and state programs that provide job placement for high school graduates and dropouts are valuable referral sources for secondary schools. A cooperative venture between the school, the business community, and federal and state agencies is essential in developing local sources of job listings. One of the most effective approaches is through a community advisory committee (Gysbers & Henderson, 1988, 2001). Local service clubs, chambers of commerce, federal and state agencies, and professional and personnel organizations are excellent resources for developing a local career advisory committee. As demand for hands-on experience increases, local career opportunities will be essential to the success of these programs. A viable listing of local part-time and full-time jobs will also enhance the popularity of the career planning and placement office.

Programs that enhance the transition from school to work should also be offered in senior high schools. In this respect, placement should be viewed as a vital function and a continuation of career guidance programs (Herr, Cramer, & Niles, 2004). Some suggested program topics include how to prepare for an interview, write a resumé, locate job information, apply for a job, learn if you are qualified for a job, and find the right job.

Finally, computer-assisted career guidance programs (discussed in Chapter 8) provide vital, timely information about the current job market. The ability to generate local job information on available computer programs is extremely helpful to the job seeker. In fact, the fast-changing job market very well may require that computer capabilities be up-to-date.

Placement services also can provide a vital link between academics and the working world. Career planning and placement services offered early in secondary programs should provide the student with knowledge of career skills to be developed in secondary education. Such programs should be established not to discourage future formal academic training but to provide relevance and added motivation for learning per se. Career planning and placement in this sense should be an ongoing program for students in various levels of secondary education, with the placement function playing a vital role in student services.

Placement by State Employment Agencies

State employment agencies consist of a network of local offices in cities and rural areas across the nation. This network is based on federal and state partnerships with the U.S. Employment Service, providing broad national guidelines for operational procedures in state and local employment offices. One principal source of job information has been compiled into what is referred to as a job bank. The job bank is a listing of all job orders compiled daily within each state. Those offices with computer terminals have direct access to the job bank. This up-to-the-minute job information is available to all job seekers, who are required to fill out an application and be interviewed before they are given access to the job bank.

The functions of state employment agencies, which have very active placement programs, are to help the unemployed find work and to provide employers with qualified applicants for job orders. Many state agencies divide their services into two categories: (1) placement for job seekers and (2) services to employers. For job seekers, state agencies offer the following services:

1. Job listings in professional, clerical, skilled, technical, sales, managerial, semiskilled, service, and labor occupations
2. Personal interviews with professional interviewers
3. Assistance with improving qualifications
4. Referral to training
5. Testing
6. Counseling
7. Service to veterans
8. Unemployment benefits (for those who qualify while they are looking for work)

Services offered to employers are as follows:

1. Screening for qualified applicants
2. Professional interviews
3. On-site recruitment and application taking
4. Computerized job listing in most areas of the state
5. Aptitude and proficiency testing
6. Labor market information on technical assistance
7. Technical assistance with job descriptions, master orders, and turnover studies
8. Unemployment insurance tax information

Job placement is the focus of state employment agencies, but career counseling is available when requested. State employment agencies also administer assessment instruments that typically are used in career counseling, such as aptitude and achievement tests. Individuals are regularly referred to state employment agencies by other state agencies. For example, rehabilitation agencies refer clients who have had extensive career counseling and are in need of job listings. The placement function is enhanced by computerized job banks and lists of qualified job applicants that provide a readily accessible matching system. Employment opportunities are quickly available to job seekers who need immediate placement.

Summary

1. Comprehensive school guidance programs are a means of systematically implementing a program concept for guidance activities in grades K–12. The value of this model is its comprehensive nature and the involvement of school professionals, selected members of the community, and parents.
2. The Planning for Life Program complements comprehensive guidance programs. "Planning for life" suggests that career and life are ongoing processes that require individual and community commitment.
3. Oregon educational reform includes real-work experiences based on student's interests and in the final two years of high school school-to-work or school-to-school is emphasized.
4. Middle/junior and high school counselors provide guidance activities based on self-knowledge, educational and occupation exploration, and career planning. Counselors must be creative and innovative in developing a variety of strategies.
5. Intervention strategy for understanding sex role stereotyping, career videos, and career development guidelines are resources that are available to assist school counselors.
6. Government-sponsored programs address changes in vocational education that place a greater emphasis on technology. Work-based programs and apprenticeships are being stressed.
7. Models for integrating vocational and academic education are designed to encourage vocational education students to take more rigorous academic courses.
8. Tech-prep programs have stressed the need to integrate academics and technical training. Students who opt for tech-prep would also qualify for higher education.
9. A work-based program, known as school-to-work, assists students in making the transition from school to work. The rationale for this program suggests that students will become more motivated in all academic programs when they are able to experience the connections between schoolwork and what is required on a job.
10. Secondary placement offers a variety of programs to assist high school students in transition to work and entering college.

Supplementary Learning Exercises

1. Interview a representative from the business community for suggestions about how to establish collaborative efforts to meet school-to-work objectives. Summarize your recommendations.

2. Interview a school counselor to determine the role and scope of his or her career guidance program. Evaluate your findings and offer suggestions.

3. Develop objectives and strategies for introducing life planning concepts in the elementary school.

4. What strategies would you use to convince a middle/junior high class that life and career planning are important goals?

5. Develop a format that could be used annually to evaluate the career planning progress of high school students.

6. Interview at least two parents of school-age children who are willing to participate as career infusion models. Develop a format for presenting a program to a class.

7. Develop course objectives and goals for a minicourse on decision making for junior and senior high school students.

8. Visit a local industry to determine the kinds of on-site job experiences available. Write a description of at least five possible on-site jobs.

9. Develop at least five counseling strategies for middle/junior high school students to promote opportunities for reflecting on self-in-situation.

10. Develop at least five counseling strategies for senior high school students designed to help them choose a training program or a college.

11. Visit a senior high school placement office. Report your findings to the class.

For More Information

Beymer, L. (1995). *Meeting the guidance and counseling needs of boys.* Alexandria, VA: American Counseling Association.

Gysbers, N. C., & Henderson, P. (2001). Comprehensive school guidance and counseling programs: A rich history and bright future. *Professional School Counselor, 4,* 246–256.

Gysbers, N. C., & Henderson, P. (1988). *Developing and managing your school guidance program.* Alexandria, VA: American Association for Counseling and Development.

Henri, C., Schouwenburg, C. L., Pychyl, T. A., & Ferrari, J. R. (Eds.) (2004). *Counseling the procrastinator in academic settings.* Washington, DC: American Psychological Association.

Herr, E. L., Cramer, S. H., & Niles, S. G. (2004). *Career guidance and counseling through the life span: Systematic approaches* (6th ed.). New York: Pearson Education, Inc.

Herring, R. D. (1998). *Career counseling in schools.* Alexandria, VA: American Counseling Association.

Nastasi, R. K., Berstein-Moore, R., & Varjas, K. M. (2004). *School-based mental health services: Creating comprehensive and culturally specific programs.* Washington, DC: American Psychological Association.

Newman, B. M., & Newman, P. R. (2003). *Development through life: A psychological approach* (8th ed.). Belmont, CA: Wadsworth/Thomson Learning.

Paisley, P. O., & Hubbard, G. T. (1994). *Developmental school counseling programs: From theory to practice.* Alexandria, VA: American Counseling Association.

Suggested InfoTrac College Edition Topics

Adolescence and career

Career competencies in secondary schools

Career education

Career infusion

Career maturity

Cognitive functioning and adolescence

Developmental tasks

Placement and secondary schools

Physiological changes

School-to-school programs

School-to-work programs

Status attainment theory

Tech-prep programs

Work-based programs

17 Career Services and Counseling in Institutions of Higher Learning

Chapter Highlights

- Characteristics of college students

- How college affects career choice and development

- National goals for college career guidance programs

- Implications for career guidance programs in institutions of higher learning

- Career prep program at a community college consortium

- Module model of a curricular career information service

- Metroplex model for career counseling

- Life-planning workshops, including example case

- Work- and experience-based programs for college and university students

- Role of college and university placement offices

NOT TOO MANY years ago, the general opinion of university graduates was that they were now fully prepared for a lifetime of work. The training period was finally over! One had learned everything that was necessary to make a living. The major challenges of career counseling in this context were to help students find a specific career path and prepare them for placement. Although universities and colleges continue to assist students in career decision making and placing them in a job, the current general consensus is that career development is never over! Students are to sustain their careers through a lifelong learning plan that includes the development of all life roles. This position presents some intriguing challenges to career-related and counseling programs in institutions of higher learning.

In this chapter, several career counseling and guidance programs will be introduced as examples of current programs designed to meet the needs of students in colleges and universities. Keep in mind that college students are a diverse group of individuals who are from different cultural backgrounds, and range in age from recent high school graduates to older adults. Counselors therefore need to be well grounded in counseling practices that address a wide spectrum of needs from a diverse group of individuals. It should not be unusual for counselors to integrate marriage counseling with career concerns, for example, and/or to discover a wide range of personal problems that limit and hinder academic progress and career choice. Comprehensive career services are offered at many colleges and universities. Some offer credit for career-related courses and many offer seminars presented by counselors, faculty members, paraprofessionals, and/or business leaders. The content of career-related services vary and may include seminars on career options and alternatives, programs for undeclared majors, the connection between college majors and work roles, job search strategies, how to do an interview and prepare a resumé, and making an effective transition from college-to-work (Morrison, 2002). More program content currently used in colleges and universities is introduced in the paragraphs that follow.

We begin this chapter with a brief review of how the university and college experience affects students' career choice and development. We also introduce national career guidelines and competencies for adults. Examples of career counseling programs in institutions of higher learning include representative models of innovative career counseling programs, such as a career prep program at a community college consortium, a curriculum module model, a metroplex model, a life-planning workshop, and work-experience models. Finally, the role and function of college placement services is discussed.

How College Affects Students' Career Choice and Development

An outstanding and often-quoted comprehensive study of research findings on how college affects students was completed in 1991 by Pascarella and Terenzini. This study covered a survey of college students over a twenty-year period. The following conclusions were paraphrased from the chapter reporting career choice and development.

1. Students frequently change their career plans.
2. Significant occupational status differences between high school and college graduates are sustained over the life span.

3. Individuals with bachelor's degrees are more likely to obtain high-status managerial, technical, and professional jobs.
4. College graduates are less likely to be unemployed than are high school graduates.
5. College graduates are less likely to suffer the effects of prolonged periods of unemployment.
6. Employers see college graduates as possessing requisite skills and values that make them more desirable for employment and advancement.
7. College graduates enjoy significantly higher levels of career mobility and advancement.
8. College experiences tend to produce conflicting influences on satisfaction with one's work. College tends to develop a capacity for critical judgment and evaluation that in turn provides sensitivity to shortcomings of jobs.
9. Maturity of career thinking and planning can be modestly improved through various career development courses.
10. Socialization in college increases student occupational aspirations.
11. College may enhance occupational success by facilitating development of traits that describe a psychologically mature person, such as symbolization (reflective intelligence), allocentrism (empathy and altruism), integration (ability to combine a variety of views), and stability and autonomy.
12. For reducing unemployment, a college education was more important for nonwhites than for whites.

The results of this study suggest that the benefits of a college education were quite significant for student transitions to the world of work. Most of this study's conclusions remain relevant, although periods of high unemployment experienced by many college graduates in a struggling economy are not fully accounted for. These conclusions should not be surprising: They give credence to recommendations counselors have made for years about the influence of higher education on lifestyle and future opportunities for career development. Not only does the college experience provide for career mobility and advancement, but it also increases occupational aspirations. In essence, the benefits of higher education help improve the quality of life and the capacity to make the most of it but cannot guarantee making appropriate judgments over the life span.

National Goals for Career Services and Counseling Programs in Higher Education

We include the national competencies and indicators for adults (Kobylarz, 1996) in Table 17-1 to underscore the necessity of preparing students for the work world and integrating life roles into a future lifestyle. These competencies and indicators present a significant challenge to institutions of higher learning and point out the importance of and need for effective career development programs. These competencies and indicators not only suggest the importance of educational and occupational exploration, but also the importance of work as it affects values and lifestyle. The far-reaching influences on college students suggested by these guidelines are quite apparent. National competencies and indicators are very inclusive, suggesting that career development is indeed a comprehensive process. Students who recognize the pervasive nature of career development will be better prepared to make a series of transitions over the life span. Career services foster a foundation to view career development and its influence on other life roles from a broader perspective.

Counselors are to be advocates for counseling services that address student career concerns and development. Students in the 21st century will continue a career journey after graduation that will present significant challenges. Concerns and needs will likely include decision-making and information-seeking skills, interpersonal relationships, how to adapt to situations and circumstances, forging a new identity, and maintaining a strong academic background that provides a foundation for lifelong learning. The specification of competencies of self-knowledge, educational and occupational exploration, and career planning continue and are excellent examples for programming at college and university counseling centers.

Examples of Career-Related Services in Institutions of Higher Learning

Counselors will find that there are numerous career-related programs in institutions of higher learning. Some institutions offer credit for 1- or 3-hour courses that are built around some aspect of career development. An undergraduate career course at Florida State University, for example, has been offered since 1974 and approximately 6,200 students have taken it (Reardon, Lenz, Sampson, & Peterson, 2000). This course covers a variety of topics including career planning, self-knowledge information, decision making, information about the global economy and the work world, career and family roles, job hunting techniques, and discussions about one's first job and early career moves.

University career centers also offer seminars or workshops on a variety of career-related subjects including the interrelationship of life roles, benefits of a college education, the connection between majors and work roles, self-help programs, and availability of internships, among many other topics. In some institutions, instructors assign career-related projects that are to be done in the university career center. Individual and group counseling is available at most institutions, and most institutions have a placement office or an employment services office available to students. One can expect to find computerized career guidance systems and internships at most institutions of higher learning. Finally, some institutions offer career-related services to alumni.

In the following sections, examples of strategies designed to meet the needs of some students are presented. The first example is a tech-prep consortium that has assembled a career prep handbook. The second is a curricular career information service module that covers a wide range of needs and contains modules for special population groups. The third is a career counseling program at a large metropolitan university that must serve not only its large student enrollment but also its alumni. Another exemplary program is a career life planning approach. Finally, work-based educational opportunities for students are briefly discussed.

Career Prep at a Community College Consortium

In central Nebraska, 38 high schools have formed a consortium known as Central Nebraska Tech Prep Consortium. This consortium uses the combined expertise of its professional staff to develop materials and counseling strategies that are designed to

Table 17-1   Adult Competencies

Self-Knowledge

COMPETENCY I: Skills to maintain a positive self-concept.

    Demonstrate a positive self-concept.

    Identify skills, abilities, interests, experiences, values, and personality traits and their influence on career decisions.

    Identify achievements related to work, learning, and leisure and their influence on self-perception.

    Demonstrate a realistic understanding of self.

COMPETENCY II: Skills to maintain effective behaviors.

    Demonstrate appropriate interpersonal skills in expressing feelings and ideas.

    Identify symptoms of stress.

    Demonstrate skills to overcome self-defeating behaviors.

    Demonstrate skills in identifying support and networking arrangements (including role models).

    Demonstrate skills to manage financial resources.

COMPETENCY III: Understanding developmental changes and transitions.

    Describe how personal motivations and aspirations may change over time.

    Describe physical changes that occur with age and adapt work performance to accommodate these.

    Identify external events (e.g., job loss, job transfer) that require life changes.

Educational and Occupational Exploration

COMPETENCY IV: Skills to enter and participate in education and training.

    Describe short- and long-range plans to achieve career goals through appropriate educational paths.

    Identify information that describes educational opportunities (e.g., job training programs, employer-sponsored training, graduate and professional study).

    Describe community resources to support education and training (e.g., child care, public transportation, public health services, mental health services, welfare benefits).

    Identify strategies to overcome personal barriers to education and training.

COMPETENCY V: Skills to participate in work and lifelong learning.

    Demonstrate confidence in the ability to achieve learning activities (e.g., studying, taking tests).

    Describe how educational achievements and life experiences relate to occupational opportunities.

    Describe organizational resources to support education and training (e.g., remedial classes, counseling, tuition support).

COMPETENCY VI: Skills to locate, evaluate, and interpret information.

    Identify and use current career information resources (e.g., computerized career information systems, print and media materials, mentors).

    Describe information related to self-assessment, career planning, occupations, prospective employers, organizational structures, and employer expectations.

    Describe the uses and limitations of occupational outlook information.

    Identify the diverse job opportunities available to an individual with a given set of occupational skills.

    Identify opportunities available through self-employment.

    Identify factors that contribute to misinformation about occupations.

    Describe information about specific employers and hiring practices.

COMPETENCY VII: Skills to prepare to seek, obtain, maintain, and change jobs.

    Identify specific employment situations that match desired career objectives.

    Demonstrate skills to identify job openings.

    Demonstrate skills to establish a job search network through colleagues, friends, and family.

    Demonstrate skills in preparing a resume and completing job applications.

    Demonstrate skills and attitudes essential to prepare for and participate in a successful job interview.

    Demonstrate effective work attitudes and behaviors.

Table 17-1 **(continued)**

Describe changes (e.g., personal growth, technological developments, changes in demand for products or services) that influence the knowledge, skills, and attitudes required for job success.

Demonstrate strategies to support occupational change (e.g., on-the-job training, career ladders, mentors, performance ratings, networking, continuing education).

Describe career planning and placement services available through organizations (e.g., educational institutions, business/industry, labor, community agencies).

Identify skills that are transferable from one job to another.

COMPETENCY VIII: Understanding how the needs and functions of society influence the nature and structure of work.

Describe the importance of work as it affects values and lifestyle.

Describe how society's needs and functions affect occupational supply and demand.

Describe occupational, industrial, and technological trends as they relate to training programs and employment opportunities.

Demonstrate an understanding of the global economy and how it affects the individual.

Career Planning

COMPETENCY IX: Skills to make decisions.

Describe personal criteria for making decisions about education, training, and career goals.

Demonstrate skills to assess occupational opportunities in terms of advancement, management styles, work environment, benefits, and other condition of employment.

Describe the effects of education, work, and family decisions on individual career decisions.

Identify personal and environmental conditions that affect decision making.

Demonstrate effective career decision-making skills.

Describe potential consequences of decisions.

COMPETENCY X: Understanding the impact of work on individual and family life.

Describe how family and leisure functions affect occupational roles and decisions.

Determine effects of individual and family developmental stages on one's career.

Describe how work, family, and leisure activities interrelate.

Describe strategies for negotiating work, family, and leisure demands with family members (e.g., assertiveness and time management skills).

COMPETENCY XI: Understanding the continuing changes in male/female roles.

Describe recent changes in gender norms and attitudes.

Describe trends in the gender composition of the labor force and assess implications for one's own career plans.

Identify disadvantages of stereotyping occupations.

Demonstrate behaviors, attitudes, and skills that work to eliminate stereotyping in education, family, and occupational environments.

COMPETENCY XII: Skills to make career transitions.

Identify transition activities (e.g., reassessment of current position, occupational changes) as a normal aspect of career development.

Describe strategies to use during transitions (e.g., networks, stress management).

Describe skills needed for self-employment (e.g., developing a business plan, determining marketing strategies, developing sources of capital).

Describe the skills and knowledge needed for preretirement planning.

Develop an individual career plan, updating information from earlier plans and including short- and long-range career decisions.

SOURCE: From *National Career Development Guidelines: K–Adult Handbook,* by L. Kobylarz, 1996. Stillwater, OK: National Occupational Information Coordinating Committee Training and Support Center.

accomplish their collective career guidance mission. Each spring, career guidance staff selected from the consortium meet to revise their plans and materials. Counselors bring new ideas and materials that are evaluated and eventually distributed to the consortium members.

Each member of the consortium uses a student career preparation handbook that is designed to be used with all high school students. This handbook can be considered an extension of a comprehensive career guidance system that students have participated in during elementary, middle/junior, and high schools. The handbook is designed to continue the development of self-knowledge, educational and occupational exploration, and career planning. For example, a section entitled "Career Prep" is designed to help students make intelligent decisions about acquiring skills needed for careers in the 21st century. An informative section of the handbook describes the variety of two-year programs that are offered at local community colleges as well as four-year university programs in Nebraska.

Other interesting topics include employability skills, how education enhances employability, and 20 "Hot Track Jobs." As students proceed through the handbook they self-administer a career path assessment, identify their interests, and self-rate their abilities while reflecting on working conditions. On the basis of these results, students can investigate career clusters of Arts and Communication, Business, Management, Technology, Human Services, Industrial and Engineering Technology, Natural Resources and Agriculture, or a combination of these. Each cluster is divided into specific jobs, for example, the Health Services section contains Laboratory Technology with listings of Pharmacists, Clinical Laboratory Technicians, Medical Laboratory Technicians, Pharmacy Technicians, and Ultrasound Technologists.

Academic expectations in community and technical schools, four-year institutions of higher learning, and a directory of most Nebraska postsecondary educational institutions are also provided. Internet addresses are given for Web sites that contain related information such as American Job Bank, National Career Search, Peterson's Education Center, Employment Opportunities, and many more. Students also can review high school educational planning suggestions that include samples of curriculum requirements for different tech-prep plans. Also included are postsecondary entrance test requirements, a senior year planning checklist calendar, postsecondary visitation features, application process, financial and scholarship information, budgeting tips, sample student resumés, and an example letter of application.

In sum, this program suggests that students have important decisions to make concerning their futures. What is stressed here is that intelligent educational decisions are going to be necessary now and in the future. In fact, students are informed that they need to be prepared for a lifetime of learning new skills for new and different jobs in a global society. Students are encouraged to recognize the relationship between high school courses and the work world. Students are also to recognize that they have choices that include two-year associate degrees, vocational/technical training, and attending a four-year university. Moreover, it is pointed out that a planning strategy is essential for meeting individual short- and long-term goals. This handbook supports the principles of what students have learned about themselves thus far in the educational process and suggests that much more is to be learned about the future. Finally, a lifelong learning approach is strongly endorsed and students are encouraged to continue career planning.

Curricular Career Information Service (CCIS): A Module Model

An innovative program for delivering educational and vocational information was initiated at the Florida State University career center in 1975. The program emphasizes an instructional approach to career planning services. It has been updated and modified periodically since its inception and continues to be a major delivery system of career services and a support network for other career-related programs the university offers. The CCIS is self-help-oriented, uses instructional models, and is multimedia-based; the program is delivered by paraprofessionals. The CCIS is an outreach program used in residence halls and the university student center. In addition, the modules have been used as the nucleus of a three hour-credit course in career planning offered by two academic departments at Florida State University. The instructional modules were conceptualized to meet specific counseling goals and are structured around behavioral objectives.

Modules I through V are shown in Table 17-2; modules VI through XVI can be found in Sampson, Reardon, Peterson, and Lenz (2004) and/or obtained from the following address:

> Dr. Robert Reardon
> Florida State University
> The Career Center
> Tallahassee, FL 32306-1035
> 904-644-6431
> Fax 904-644-3273

After a brief interview, a typical student is directed to the first module, which begins with a 10-minute slide presentation outlining the goals and purposes of the CCIS. The second module provides an overview of variables considered desirable in career planning using slides and selected materials. The third module requires self-assessment, primarily accomplished through self-administration and self-interpretation of the SDS (*Self-Directed Search*) interest inventory (Holland, 1987b). The fourth module consists of a slide presentation of career information resources. The fifth module assists the student in locating careers related to academic majors. Other modules include employment outlooks, leisure planning, career planning for African Americans, career decision making for adult women and students with disabilities, and career interest exploration through work and occupational skills. The instructional approach to career planning used in the CCIS has potential application for many career-related programs. The overall effectiveness of each module is evaluated according to behavioral objectives. Major and minor components of each instructional unit can be effectively evaluated through a systematic review process. Thus, CCIS provides the opportunity for continuous modification and upgrading of each instructional component. As career-related materials and programs change rapidly in the future, the opportunity to systematically evaluate and subsequently upgrade them will be a major asset. Additional modules can also be developed as needs are identified.

One major advantage of instructional modules is that they are very flexible. Once a system of instructional modules has been established, the building of additional

Table 17-2	Curricular Career Information Services (CCIS) Modules

Module Title	Objectives	Activities
I. Everything You've Always Wanted to Know About CCIS	1. To introduce you to the CCIS. 2. To help you select activities that will assist you in solving your career problem.	a. Examine a Career Center brochure located on the yellow rack near the Career Center entrance to learn more about CCIS services and programs. b. Ask a Career Advisor to explain CCIS and the career advising process to you. c. Attend a Career Center tour. d. Browse the remaining module sheets on the yellow rack to learn more about some of the common concerns addressed through the career advising process.
II. What's Involved in Making a Career Decision?	1. To dispel common misconceptions about career planning; 2. To help you identify areas that are important to consider development; and 3. To help you establish some guidelines for the process of career decision making.	a. Review the "What's Involved in Career Choice" sheet to gain a greater awareness of the career decision-making process. b. Review "A Guide to Good Decision Making" sheet to explore more effective ways to make career decisions. c. Review the "Career Choice Resources in CCIS" and/or books catalogued IA in The Career Center Library. d. Review materials in the Module II folder in the Mobile file (File 1). e. Attend a "Choosing a Major/Career" workshop in CCIS. f. With the assistance of a Career Advisor, complete the "Guide to Good Decision Making Exercise." g. Register for Units I and II of the Introduction to Career Development Class. A course syllabus is available for your review in the Module XVI section of the Mobile File (File 1).
III. Looking at You	1. To help you examine some of your interests, values, and skills. 2. To help you identify some occupations or fields of study for further exploration.	INTERESTS a. Complete the Self-Directed Search (SDS). b. Complete the "Career Areas" topic in the Explore section of the CHOICES computer program. c. Complete the Internet Inventory in the "Learning About Yourself" module of the DISCOVER computer program. d. Complete the "Self-Assessment" section of SIGI PLUS. VALUES a. Interact with the SIGI PLUS computer program. b. Complete the Values Card Sort. c. Complete the Values inventory in the "Learning About Yourself" module of the DISCOVER program. SKILLS a. Complete the aptitudes section in the CHOICES Guidebook. b. Interact with the Micro Skills computer program. c. Complete the Motivated Skills Card Sort. d. Complete the Abilities Assessment in the "Learning About Yourself" module of the DISCOVER computer program.

Table 17-2 (continued)

Module Title	Objectives	Activities
IV. Information: Where to Find It and How to Use It	1. To help you locate all Career Center information related to your educational and career planning needs.	a. Perform a search using Career Key for the topic of interest to you. b. Review the diagram on the back of this sheet to locate various multimedia resources available in The Career Center Library.
V. Matching Majors and Jobs	1. To help you learn how specific job titles relate to college majors or fields of study.	a. Review printed materials in the Module V "Matching Majors and Careers" folders in the Mobile File (File 1), specifically the "Match-Major" sheets. b. Read sections in these books or others found in Area IIC of The Career Center Library.

Within activity b. (Module V):

IIC AA C7	The College Board Guide to 140 Popular College Majors
IIC AA M3	What Can I Do With a Major in . . . ?
IIC AA N3	College Knowledge and Jobs
IIC AA P4	College Majors & Careers
IIC AA O2	The Occupational Thesaurus (Vols. 1 & 2)
IIA 025	Occupational Outlook Handbook

c. Perform a search on Career Key under the topic *Occupations by Major* to get a list of relevant CCIS resources. Ask a Career Advisor for assistance.

d. Use the *College Majors Card Sort* to find majors and occupational opportunities.

e. Review employment information in the *Undergraduate Academic Program Guide* for FSU majors.

f. Use the SDS code assigned to a particular FSU major to search for occupations in the *SDS Occupations Finder* or the *Dictionary of Holland Occupational Codes* (IA G6).

g. Examine materials on FSU academic programs in File 3.

h. Review selected Employer Directors that list organizations by major, career, or geographical areas.

i. Consult with Career Center staff members in Placement Services and Career Experience Opportunities (CEO).

j. With assistance from a Career Advisor, explore opportunities on Career Key for informational interviews, extern experiences, and networking assistance with participating professionals and FSU alumni.

SOURCE: From *Curricular Career Information Service,* by R. C. Reardon, 1996. Unpublished manuscript, Florida State University. Reprinted by permission.

modules is encouraged by a review of needs that are identified by staff members. Also inherent in this process is the identification of additional career materials. What we are stressing here is that instructional modules provide independent learning experiences that are self-paced and can be delivered effectively by paraprofessionals. The diversity of learning activities provided through a series of career planning modules allows individuals greater variety of options and effective means of choosing a point of entry for career exploration. The development of modules for specific groups (such as older adults, females, minority groups) represents a multifaceted approach to career counseling that eliminates the necessity of prescribing the same program for everyone. A diversity of programs also provides an attractive means of creating interest in career exploration activities.

In sum, colleges and universities are searching for methods to effectively deliver career-related programs to groups of students, such as the career prep programs in Nebraska and CCIS at Florida State. The rationale is that there are simply not enough counselors to provide individual counseling; however, students can be referred for individual assistance when necessary. CCIS programs use highly trained paraprofessionals for online supervision at various outreach locations. A relatively small professional staff commitment is needed for module development and evaluation. The attraction of this type of career service is that it is cost effective and meets the needs of many students (Colozzi, 2000). Comprehensive career counseling programs, however, generally use both group and individual counseling. A major point here is that individual counseling has been found to be the most effective career intervention therefore it should be available in all college and university career centers (Colozzi, 2000; Rayman, 1996; Sexton, Whiston, Bleuer, & Walz, 1997).

Career Counseling at a Large University: A Metroplex Model

A large university located in a metropolitan area may have the added responsibility of satisfying heavy alumni demand for career-related services. Not only is the career center faced with a large volume of currently enrolled students choosing from diverse academic programs, but the center must also respond to a wide variety of alumni requests for career counseling. Alumni contemplating career changes with subsequent reentry into the workforce represent a unique dimension of career counseling. The following examples of unique client needs exemplify the complexity of programs needed in such a career center: (1) individuals (young adults through middle age) anticipating a change of career direction; (2) individuals seeking relocation within their career field; (3) individuals desiring mobility within their career field through further educational training; (4) individuals seeking information about specific, current job market trends; (5) individuals seeking college reentry planning; and (6) individuals seeking second careers after early retirement from a primary career. In addition, many adults residing in the metropolitan area will seek assistance for career education planning before university enrollment. Thus, a career center metroplex model must be able to provide a wide range of services for currently enrolled students as well as for alumni and others in the community seeking assistance and/or career redirection.

The UCLA Placement and Career Planning Center is a good example of a metroplex model. This center offers career planning and placement services to students and alumni from all University of California campuses. Along with several in-house programs, this center also offers outreach programs on a number of subjects. For example, in conjunction with the alumni association and various academic departments, the center offers specific career panels on a broad spectrum of career fields such as mental health, allied health, banking and investments, motion pictures, advertising, and marketing and sales. Many seminars and other career-related programs are videotaped and are available on request. Other programs of interest that could be offered in heavy populated areas include direct job referral services, seminars on job search strategies, assistance with resumé preparation, interview skills training, job clubs (individuals engaging in similar job searches), life/work relationships, seminars on career decision making and problem solving, career information resources, graduate school selection, and retraining for a different or related career.

Before leaving this discussion we must acknowledge that inadequate funding for career providers has been a consistent problem at many universities and colleges. Counselors are often restricted and limited in what they can provide in the way of effective career-related programs. Nevertheless, institutions of higher learning can make a dramatic impact on communities through collaborative career-related programs with local business and industrial organizations. Universities and colleges can also offer tremendous support for career services in local schools and community agencies. Finally, a working relationship that is designed to foster educational transitions from high school to college or university or college to university will underscore the importance and need for students to adopt a lifelong learning commitment.

Life-Planning Workshops

Life-planning workshops for college students have been conducted at Colorado State University since the early 1980s. These workshops were designed primarily to actively involve individuals in developing life plans through a highly structured step-by-step program. One key goal of these workshops is to promote self-awareness and the recognition that each individual has certain responsibilities in developing his or her future. Even though these programs were developed for college students, the format could easily be adapted for other groups, including adults who have finished or dropped out of college.

Life-planning workshops are usually conducted in one-day sessions lasting approximately seven hours. Each group of four persons has a facilitator. The program is highly structured, but each group may progress at its own pace. Because the structure of the program is set, facilitators need only minimal training. Group members remain together through the entire program.

The workshop format consists of eight structured exercises, as follows. Each exercise is shared in the group, and interaction is strongly emphasized. The first exercise, *life line,* requires that an individual draw a line from birth to death (life line) and indicate on it key life experiences and present position. Keep in mind that exercises are designed to involve participants actively in concentrating on future tasks and life planning.

Exercise	Purpose
1. Life line	To identify past and current situations in life
2. Identifying and stripping of roles	To identify individual roles in life and share stripping of roles, individual feelings as one strips roles
3. Fantasy time	To develop more self-awareness when free of identified roles
4. Typical day and a special day of the future	To further crystallize self-awareness and individual needs for the future when free of identified roles
5. Life inventory	To identify specific needs and goals with emphasis on identification of each individual's positive characteristics
6. News release	To further clarify specific interests and future accomplishments desired
7. Reassume roles	To clarify or reformulate goals while reassuming originally identified roles
8. Goal setting	To set realistic short-term and long-term goals

Identifying and stripping of roles, the second exercise, requires that each individual identify and rank in importance five different roles currently occupying his or her life. Each participant is encouraged to identify positive as well as negative roles. The next step is to start with the least important role and "strip" that role (no longer assume the role) and express feelings associated with freedom from that role. In this manner, each role is stripped until the person is role free and subsequently able to freely express personal life-planning needs.

The third exercise, *fantasy time,* is a continuation of the second exercise, in which the individual is encouraged toward further introspection while being role free. More specifically, the individual considers the influence of roles when developing future plans.

Once roles have been stripped, in the fourth exercise the individual outlines *a typical day and a special day of the future.* Now that the individual is able to visualize his or her life without the restrictions of roles, he or she subsequently can consider ideal circumstances. This exercise is designed to provide an opportunity to consider how identified roles influence or actually block present and future need fulfillment.

The fifth exercise requires that each individual fill out a *life inventory,* which includes questions asking for greatest experiences, things done well and poorly, and desired future accomplishments. Each individual is directed toward developing specific needs and values while focusing attention on desired changes in the future. This exercise is designed to be a rebuilding process through identification of specific needs.

During the sixth exercise, *news release,* each individual considers his or her life line, as drawn in an earlier exercise, in relation to what the future should be. Each person writes a sketch of his or her life, projecting into the future while focusing on accomplishment and predominant roles. The major purpose is to promote the development of realistic future needs.

In the seventh exercise, *reassume roles,* the focus is on reassuming the roles that were stripped in earlier exercises. Each individual now must decide which roles should be kept and which should be discarded to reach his or her life goals. Reassumed roles may be rearranged in priority or replaced with new roles that provide greater opportunity for meeting goals. The emphasis is on the factors that can be changed to gain greater control of future life planning.

The final exercise, *goal setting,* requires that each individual describe specific behaviors that can bring about desired changes in his or her life. Again, the emphasis is on the individual's ability to make changes to meet life-planning goals.

Case 17-1 Life-Planning Workshop Exercises

The following example demonstrates more specifically the activities involved in this program. Liang has been married for six years, has two children, and currently is employed as a high school biology teacher. Her family life has been stable for most of her marriage, but she has recently felt a need to change her career and life direction. As she stated to her counselor, "I'm not sure of what's happened; I just feel frustrated. I love my husband and children, but I am unhappy." After several counseling sessions, the counselor recommended that Liang participate in a life-planning workshop.

After being introduced to staff and members of the group, she heard an explanation of the purpose and goals of the exercises. The first exercise required that Liang construct a life line in which she included the results of important decisions and events, such as the birth of her brother, death of her father, meeting her husband, marriage, the births of her children, and so on. She jotted down her age at the time of each event and drew an arrow next to the more significant decisions. Valleys and peaks indicated the ups and downs in life.

Then Liang shared her life line with Chris, another participant.

LIANG: We have some similar experiences, I see.

CHRIS: Yes, but you have more work experience than I have. I wish I had more experiences so I could figure out what to do.

LIANG: I have worked since I was married and before, and yet I am confused. Come to think of it, I guess working helps you figure out some things.

CHRIS: Yeah, I would hope so.

LIANG: Mainly, what you learn is what you don't want to do.

CHRIS: Oh, look, the major events in your life line are like mine; they center around family.

A general discussion of a life line's purpose was led by the group leader, whose major focus was the value of previous experience in determining future goals.

The next exercise, identifying and stripping of roles, created considerable tension for Liang because she was not prepared to strip her roles as parent, spouse, teacher, homemaker, and friend.

LIANG: I don't want to dump my husband and children; it's hard for me to think of myself without them.

CHRIS: I know, but remember, this is make-believe.

LIANG: That's so, but I still feel it is difficult.

CHRIS: Go on, tell me what you would do.

LIANG: Well, I've always wanted a higher degree, but with the children, I don't have time for college.

CHRIS: Go on. I bet you would like a different job too!

LIANG: This sounds like bragging, but my college profs encouraged me to consider college teaching.

As Liang and Chris continued to strip away roles, they recognized the ambiguities associated with the exercise as well as the benefits of imagined freedom.

LIANG: I've wound up with quite a different lifestyle, and you have too.

CHRIS: If only I could do it. How many jobs do you have listed?

LIANG: Let me see. College professor, model, business owner, chief executive officer. Oh yeah, I want to live on the West Coast! But really, how could I realistically accomplish any of these?

After the third exercise, fantasy time, Liang outlined a "typical day" and a "special day" in the future.

Typical day

Breakfast between 8:00 and 9:00

Go to campus for class preparation 9–11

Teach classes 11–12

Have lunch at faculty lounge 12–1:30

Office hours 2–3

Play tennis 3–5

Shop 5–6

Dinner 7–8

Attend play 8–10

Bedtime

Special day (no time commitments)

Wake up whenever I want in a plush room in a resort hotel

Breakfast in bed

Hike in the mountains

Go skiing

Meet friends around the fireplace at Happy Hour

Dine and dance

As Liang fantasized a role-free lifestyle, she also recognized the meaningfulness of her current roles. She cared deeply for her husband and children and did not want to give them up under any circumstances, but she also came to the conclusion that something was missing from her life. Perhaps, she thought, it was the desire for more freedom with fewer time commitments. But everyone likes that, she mused, so what's new?

As she filled out the life inventory for Exercise 5, she was now faced with having to make significant decisions about the future. As she listed her greatest experiences and things she had done well and poorly, the items seemed to center around academic achievements and her family. Surprisingly, after considerable thought, Liang listed some of her teaching activities under tasks done poorly. "This is awful," she almost stated out loud, but it was true. She had to face it. Her heart had not been in it. What a mess; she loved her students, and yet, she was not giving them her best.

When Liang focused on changes for the future, she came to the conclusion that a career change was necessary, but accompanying this thought was the chilling reality of what this would mean. Her entire lifestyle and routine would have to be changed, she concluded. Is it worth it? How would her husband react? Liang's list of specific needs included the following:

- A greater commitment to my work
- A change to pursue my interest of more academic training
- A higher-level job in education
- More and better communication with my family—let my family know how I feel.

During this exercise, Liang heard the following exchange in her group.

DANTE: What's the sense of all this? These needs I have would disrupt my current lifestyle tremendously.

JIM: It might take that, Dante.

TED: It's not that simple. I would like to follow through on my needs, but I have to consider the needs of my family, too. I think we gotta negotiate.

As Liang listened to the members discuss the problems of implementing their needs list, she realized that she was not the only one experiencing frustration. It was comforting to know she was not alone in wanting something different, but she also realized that different personal situations required personal solutions. The conversation in the group continued.

JEAN: I never thought of getting older as an advantage, but my perspective of the future has fewer complications since my children left home.

LIANG: Would you follow through on your need list if your children still lived at home?

JEAN: Yes, I think so; in fact, I know I would, but everyone's situation is different.

Liang performed the sixth exercise, news release, while observing her life line. By looking at her life as a series of peaks and valleys, she realized that it was more important now to live a more directed life with a balance between life roles. She recognized that it was her choice to devote the major part of life to her family, but she also wanted more out of life at this point. Perhaps, she thought, there would be fewer valleys and more peaks in the future for everyone in the family.

As the group continued this discussion, Jean made another point.

JEAN: Being older also makes you realize that life goes by quickly. Just look at your life line—if it tells you anything at all, it is that opportunities are there for the taking. But if you don't, well, the line just keeps on moving.

As Liang began Exercise 7, she felt no aversion to reassuming roles and, in fact, realized that she wanted to retain her current life roles.

LIANG: There is no way I would give up my family. Through all of this, they still come first.

JEAN: I don't see that as a negative; in fact, I think it's great.

In the final exercise, goal setting, Liang felt that she had gained the confidence to follow through on some specific goals. It would take courage, she thought, to change career direction. It would disrupt everyone's lifestyles to do it, but the chances were that it would be worth it in the future. She would use negotiation as a means of restructuring family life while she attended the university. Putting some money aside each month for the next year would help finance graduate school, and meanwhile she could attend evening classes.

LIANG: I have decided that going back to the university is best for me and my family!

DANTE: That's not good enough, Liang. You're supposed to give specific behaviors to change things.

JEAN: Yes, that's too general.

LIANG: OK, let me see. I will have a meeting with my husband on Monday at 6:30. We will discuss the following topics: advantages of going to graduate school, financial arrangements, family arrangements, sharing household duties, and options for time of enrollment.

Liang's case points out the value of delineating and specifying the consequences of life roles. Individuals often become so involved in fulfillment of a particular role that other roles are ignored, and frustrations and stressful conditions that evolve are often left unidentified and unresolved. The interaction of group members often provides support for individuals to discover their own needs for career development.

The concept of career life planning as illustrated suggests that career programs should be constructed from a broad-based framework of life events, conditions, and situations over the life span. The major goal of career life planning is to help individuals cope with changing events and accomplish the tasks and transitions of developmental stages successfully.

Although the experiences of life teach us how to cope with certain events, the future is always challenging and unpredictable. Lazarus (2000) suggested that past experiences can help one cope with future events. Calling this process "anticipatory coping," he proposed that skills learned through successfully coping with experiences can help when encountering future events, and unsuccessful experiences can provide a basis for identifying behaviors that should be modified. Though all experiences are useful for future encounters, successful experiences tend to have a snowball effect by providing indexes to appropriate behaviors. The purpose of career life planning is to provide skills that may be applied in coping effectively with a variety of future events. Teaching clients skills that help them meet future events is one of the developmental goals of career life planning.

Work- and Experience-Based Programs

A growing trend in all levels of education is to provide students the opportunity of work experience as a vital part of their educational programs. Although student teaching and a variety of intern and extern experiences are not novel ideas in institutions of higher learning, some innovations should interest the career counselor. One such innovation is the extern experience.

The extern model provides the student with an opportunity to observe ongoing activities in his or her major field of study and to interact with individuals on the job. The extern model differs from an internship in two ways: (1) the extern experience is of short duration, usually during semester breaks, and (2) students usually do not receive course credit for an extern experience as most of their experiences involve observation and job shadowing. Generally, during senior year, students submit a proposal of their career goals with a statement of how the extern experience would help them meet these goals. Career centers or other administrative entities have agreements with host agencies to offer such experiences. Selected students will spend a specified time with a host agency during midsemester break or during an interim semester.

Intern models, on the other hand, provide students with the opportunity to spend more time in a workplace and are more work-experience-oriented than are extern models. Interns actually do the work they are being trained to do. For example, junior-level students planning to become accountants may be chosen by an accounting firm to intern in one of its offices. Actual accounting work will be done under the supervision of a member of the firm. The time spent in this experience is usually negotiated so that it doesn't interfere with the student's progress toward a degree.

Job shadowing also gives college students a window to view future work environments. In this program, college students explore an occupation by observing at a job site. As they observe, they ask questions and practice working with people while making valuable contacts for future use. This program requires colleges and universities to make certain that work observation will be meaningful and constructive. Formal programs include orientation (briefing students on program requirements), matching (students are matched with volunteers who have agreed to serve as a host), shadowing (students spend several hours on the job with the host and may do hands-on work), and after shadowing (students write letters of thank you and reflect on what they have learned). Job shadowing usually takes place during semester breaks (Mariani, 1998).

The practice of providing college students with actual work experience related to their college majors should proliferate during the 21st century. The length of the experience also should increase; students will find an expanded time frame more beneficial than current extern programs allow. As colleges attempt to help students make more realistic career choices, more experience-based models will certainly emerge. We can expect to find that more students will spend a significant part of their university experience in the workplace.

Implications for Career Services and Counseling

A review of national career development guidelines leaves little doubt that young adults must be prepared to make a number of major decisions. Selecting a work role and understanding the impact of work on other life roles are very pervasive goals that emerge on the horizon during school-to-work transitions. Even though these tasks seem almost insurmountable they actually represent the beginning of a life of transitions in an ever changing society. Some career counseling goals develop during this specific period of transitions but many are a continuation of early attempts of empowering individuals to overcome obstacles and make appropriate decisions based on their own needs and choice of lifestyle. For some, the unresolved issues of adolescence will continue to affect their ability to function, adapt to changes, and make rational decisions. Problematic personal issues must be resolved along with career issues in a holistic approach to counseling interventions.

An overarching goal prepares students to understand that career development is a lifelong process, one is inextricably intertwined with other life roles. Students are encouraged to search for and maintain a balanced lifestyle. In this context, career decision making is viewed as a complex task that is very inclusive. The context of decisions therefore is an important part of rational decision making; individual situations can result in a variety of circumstances that may influence career decision. Dual-career couples, for example, will need to consider the decision's impact on two careers before making the next transition. Thus, making decisions now and in the future requires a careful evaluation of many factors in the context of one's life.

Finally, we attempt to incorporate the concept of and understanding of socialization processes in our interventions. According to Muchinsky (2003), socialization in the work environment "is the process of mutual adjustment between a team and its members, especially new members" (p. 290). Ideally, one finds a work environment in which there is stability, rapport with others, and common goals and objectives. Students must be prepared to go through a socialization process that may require them to modify their behavior in order to find acceptance and subsequent feelings of well-being in a work environment. Students therefore can benefit from learning about interpersonal processes in teams and how to enhance interpersonal relationships at work.

Several career development strategies in the senior high school are applicable at postsecondary institutions. For example, career guidance must meet the needs of students at various stages of career development. Understanding the relationships between career choice and educational requirements is essential. College students are to be encouraged to relate their personal characteristics to occupational requirements. Each student should be given the opportunity to identify and use a wide variety of resources to maximize his or her career development potential.

In sum, college students should be assisted in systematically analyzing college and noncollege experiences and in incorporating this information into career-related decisions. In addition, career-related programs should help students select major fields of study and relate these to career fields. Career life planning that focuses on factors that influence career choices over the life span is a valuable concept to incorporate in counseling interventions. Placement programs should provide a wide range of services and information, including projected job markets and overall employment statistics, job search strategies, interview skills training, and job fairs.

College Placement

The traditional placement service in our educational institutions has evolved into a career planning center. As suggested in the previous chapter, some professionals believe that the use of the word *placement*, such as the "Career Planning and Placement

Center," has become obsolete (Carter, 1995). The major argument centers around the students' perception of such a center as the place where you interview for a job, and not much else. Thus, students overlook the fact that placement is only one of several career services offered. The current philosophical stance is that placement is subsumed in a center that offers a wide variety of career services that are of at least equal status with placement; therefore, the name of the center should reflect this change. What has been suggested are more generic names, such as Career Planning Center, Career Service Center, or simply Career Center. Regardless of the name, such centers should be student-service-oriented and should indeed offer a wide variety of services to all students—and in some cases, to alumni or individuals in the community. In this context, placement continues to be an important part of services offered.

Partially to emphasize a changing philosophical position, national, regional, and local placement organizations have also undergone name changes. The national organization formerly called the College Placement Council is now the National Association of Colleges and Employers (NACE), a name change that reflects the broad-based approach of career service centers. Employers are now an important part of national, regional, and local organizations, and their participation in planning and sharing in all organizational matters has distinctly improved services to students. For instance, college representatives and employers have found a tremendous arena for exchanging information, such as salary surveys, job market information, internship programs, and workshops.

Don't be surprised, however, if you continue seeing the term *placement* used in the names of centers and programs being offered, at least until students and faculty become more familiar with the current changes that are taking place. In the meantime, many of the following programs may be found at typical career planning and placement offices:

1. Full-time employment listings
2. Temporary-work files
3. Full-time vacation jobs
4. Job-search strategy meetings
5. Resumé-preparation workshops
6. Interview practice sessions
7. Career interest testing
8. Career exploration workshops
9. Individual and group counseling in career searching
10. Special programs such as minority recruiting opportunities for employers
11. Follow-up studies of previous graduates

Many colleges and universities have installed automated placement services. For a moderate fee students can send resumés to regional, national, and international employment networks. Also, students can access information 24 hours a day to learn about full-time vacancy listings, to schedule interviews, and to receive information on part-time jobs, summer job vacancies, and internships (Herr & Cramer, 1996).

Technology may change how college students market themselves! Most college career centers are online and resumés can be sent to prospective employers through cyberspace. Telephone interviewing is a growing industry. Recruiters may use telephone interviews to narrow down a list of potential employees. Likewise, video conferencing is another way to interview even in remote areas. The increasing costs of travel could encourage the use of video conferencing technology in the future as a means of selecting applicants and screening them.

Interview Skills Training

The importance of training programs designed to improve interview skills is underscored by the fact that employers' decisions are often heavily based on their impressions of the interviewee. Also, many college students are, at best, only moderately experienced with interview procedures. Instruction has primarily been through role playing, videotape feedback, and mock interviews with personnel directors.

Using videotape has become a popular method of preparing individuals for an interview. Feller (1994) has compiled a list of commercial videos produced in the last decade, including ratings, reviews, and descriptions of 650 videos, some of which assist individuals in preparing for an interview. Some videotapes that discuss interview preparation illustrate poor interview techniques and then follow with suggested changes and demonstrations of interviewee skills. Others demonstrate techniques, including establishing good eye contact; assuming the appropriate posture, voice level, and projection; closing the interview; following up; negotiating; and making a decision.

Videotapes can be used for individual training or in a workshop format, and they are also effective for group viewing—with or without discussion. For large groups, individuals can be divided into dyads or triads for practice interviewing. This procedure provides individuals with role-playing opportunities that can be videotaped for immediate feedback. One advantage of using videotape is that segments of the interview can be replayed and analyzed to afford greater flexibility of training.

Resumé Writing

As jobs become more competitive, personnel managers rely more heavily on resumés to select individuals for further evaluation. The resumé is the first criterion of the selection process, and its importance cannot be overstressed. The primary purpose of a resumé is to obtain an interview for the desired position. An effective resumé is one that "sells" the candidate's qualifications to the employer and thus provides the candidate the opportunity for an interview. Most effective resumés relate the candidate's skills, experiences, education, and other achievements to the requirements of the job. Resumés are essential for individuals seeking professional, technical, administrative, or managerial jobs and are often needed for clerical and sales positions. Preparation of a good resumé is an essential part of the job search sequence.

A functional resumé is designed to emphasize an individual's qualifications for a specific job. This type of resumé is often used by individuals who have had extensive work experience, particularly if they are applying for jobs in the same area in which they have had experience or for a job that is related to their experience. The functional resumé stresses selected skill areas that are marketable, and it allows the applicant to emphasize professional growth. Individuals can select guidelines from the following outline to prepare their resumés.

I.   **Personal data**
    A. Name, address, and telephone number
    B. Other personal data are optional, such as date of birth, marital status, citizenship, dependents, height, and weight.

II. **Job or career objectives**
   A. Prepare a concise statement of job objective and the type of position desired.

III. **Educational history (If the previous work experiences are more closely related to the job objective, list them before educational history.)**
   A. In reverse chronological order, list the institutions attended for formal education.
   B. High school can be omitted if a higher degree has been awarded.
   C. List dates of graduation and degrees or certificates received or expected.
   D. List major and minor courses related to job objectives.
   E. List scholarships and honors.

IV. **Employment history**
   A. In reverse chronological order, list employment experiences, including
      1. Date of employment
      2. Name and address of employer and nature of firm or business
      3. Position held
      4. Specific job duties
      5. Scope of responsibility including most relevant experiences
      6. Accomplishments and highlights of background

V.   **Military experience**
   A. List branch and length of service, major duties, assignments, rank, and type of discharge.

VI. **Achievements related to job and career objectives (optional)**
   A. List other assets, experiences, and skills significant to job objective. For example, knowledge of foreign language, volunteer activities, and special skills.

VII. **References**
   A. It is often not necessary to list references on the resumé. One may state that references are available on request.
   B. If references are listed, the name, position, and address of at least three persons is usually sufficient.

Here are some additional suggestions:

1. Because of affirmative action laws, many employers prefer that optional personal information (with the exception of citizenship) be deleted from the personal data section (I).
2. The job objective section (II) is designed to bind the parts of the resumé together into a common theme or direction and should be carefully stated.
3. The educational history section (III) should relate academic skills and achievements to the requirements of the job objective. Specific, relevant courses and experiences as well as degrees or specializations of formal education should be recorded.
4. The employment history (IV) should relate previously acquired working skills and accomplishments to the requirements and duties of the job objective. Voluntary as well as paid experiences should be included.
5. The military experience section (V) should relate skills and accomplishments acquired during military duty to the requirements and duties of the job objective.

6. The achievements (VI) listed should relate to the job objective, delineating any relevant special skills or accomplishments that were not recorded previously.

Examples of resumés are an important teaching instrument. Counselor will want to accumulate copies of resumés from former students who have applied for different types of positions. A good model will help the novice write a resumé. There are many possible formats, and a number of publications on the market today provide examples of them. Such publications should be included in the counseling center's bibliography on job search strategy.

Computer-Assisted Career Guidance Programs

As discussed in Chapter 8, computer-assisted career guidance programs provide up-to-date information on the job market. Many systems contain local information about jobs. Computer-assisted programs also have components that provide information to students and notify them of other vital information that can be used in the job search. Employers can register job vacancies, salary, interview schedules, and so forth. Computer-assisted programs also provide a quick method of matching qualified students and requests for job orders from prospective employers. For instance, an employer asks the placement office by phone or fax printouts for junior-level accounting majors who have at least a 3.0 grade point average and have plans to graduate in two semesters. Through prearranged agreements with students, the placement office can fax a list of students who meet the requirements. Speed of response may be important in the competitive job market, and placement offices that can quickly provide information to students as well as to prospective employers could have a significant advantage. Second, computer-assisted programs make current information easily accessible to the placement office staff. This is only one method of assisting students and employers through computer-assisted career guidance programs, but it points out the potential of these programs. Finally, see Chapter 8 for information available on the Internet.

The Follow-Up

Follow-up information provides a valuable resource for multiple use by the career center. Here, however, we only cover the use of follow-up data as an aid in assisting college students in career planning. The overall employment status of graduates paints a realistic picture of the variety of jobs available to graduates from a particular institution. In addition, information on the current employment status of graduates according to majors can be most useful to the prospective graduate. Thus, follow-up is a very important resource that indicates employment trends and employment potential according to specific educational goals offered at the university level.

Follow-up is an important function of career centers, especially given the competitiveness of the job market. The information obtained from following up is valuable in helping students plan their education and careers. Even though the labor market may make abrupt changes, the follow-up has many implications for the job search strategy: (1) This information should aid the student in thinking about the type of organization in which he or she is likely to find employment with a particular degree; (2) a realistic salary is usually listed according to field of study; (3) the employment potential is better understood by field of study; and (4) the job satisfaction of working in a particular field is known. In essence, follow-up information should aid the individual in clarifying values and subsequently establishing goals; it also provides practical information concerning initial career search activities and probable geographical location of prospective jobs.

Most college and university career centers conduct an annual follow-up of the most recent graduating class. Some surveys report data in seven areas: (1) plans after graduation, (2) job commitment, (3) type of organization, (4) field of employment, (5) job satisfaction, (6) helpfulness of degree in employment, and (7) salary. Using this data, career center staff can compile information about jobs that graduates currently hold, including the graduates' field of study and employer, the nature of the job (part- or full-time), job satisfaction, salaries, plans for the future, and the satisfaction with the academic institutions' program.

Summary

1. College affects students' career choices and development by providing career mobility and advancement and by increasing career aspirations. The benefits of higher education can also lead to a fulfilling lifestyle and the capacity to make appropriate judgments over the life span.
2. National competencies and indicators are designed to enhance self-knowledge, educational and occupational exploration, and career planning for adults. These guidelines can be used to develop career guidance programs at institutions of higher learning.
3. Members of a consortium of community colleges in Nebraska have designed a handbook that continues and extends the career counseling activities of comprehensive career guidance program in schools. Students are given more information about principles of self-knowledge, educational and occupational exploration, and career planning.
4. The CCIS developed at Florida State University uses an instructional approach to career planning. The model is self-help-oriented, uses instructional models, and is multimedia-based. Several modules have been developed to help students perform a career search sequence; several other modules have been developed for special groups such as minorities and blind students. The diversity of learning activities provided through a series of career planning modules allows the individual a greater variety of options and a more effective means of choosing a career.
5. Career counseling centers located in metropolitan areas have heavy alumni demands for educational and career planning. The UCLA Placement and Career Planning Center is a good example of a metroplex model. This center is divided into several units to meet demands of currently enrolled students in undergraduate and graduate programs, as well as alumni and others in the community requesting educational and career planning assistance.
6. Life-planning workshops for college students have been conducted at Colorado State University for several years. The workshops are designed primarily to help students develop a life plan. Life-planning workshops (usually one-day sessions) consist of highly structured, step-by-step exercises.

7. The demand for work- and experience-based programs for college students is increasing. Extern models provide the opportunity to observe ongoing activities in a major field of study. Intern models are more work-oriented and cover a longer time.

8. Implications for career-related programs include a wide variety of resources to maximize each student's career development potential.

9. The typical college placement office has drastically changed its image during the last 20 years. The intensification of the job search has led college placement centers to assume a wider scope of responsibilities. The placement office is no longer just an employment agency; it offers a variety of seminars and programs that assist students in planning for careers as well as in searching for a job.

10. Typical programs being offered in two- and four-year college career centers include career search strategies, interview skills training, and instructions on writing resumés.

11. Computer-assisted career guidance programs provide career centers with a wide range of options that allow staff to react quickly to employers' requests and student needs.

12. Follow-up studies serve as important resources for students when they include (a) types of job opportunities available by geographical areas, (b) general employment patterns and fields of employment of graduates with specific majors and degrees, (c) employment potential within specific industries, and (d) current salary schedules. Follow-up information is often incorporated into career planning programs.

Supplementary Learning Exercises

1. Using the CCIS model, develop a module to introduce high school students to career information resources.

2. Develop a philosophical statement that includes the placement office as a vital part of the career counseling efforts in postsecondary schools.

3. Develop a strategy that would justify adult career centers as an extension of career-related services offered in universities.

4. Write to several large universities located in metropolitan areas and request descriptions of their career counseling programs. Compare the programs for commonalities and innovative components.

5. Visit an industry to determine potential extern and job shadowing experiences available for college students. Compile the available experiences with recommendations for college majors that could benefit through an extern experience.

6. Survey a community to determine the number and kinds of agencies that are actively involved in career planning and placement activities. Develop plans to involve all agencies in a cooperative career planning and placement effort.

7. Develop plans and strategies that would focus on career-related services for college dropouts. Include in your plans the strategies you would use for encouraging dropouts to continue in an educational or training program.

8. Defend the following statement: Career-related programs are essential in secondary schools and in two- and four-year institutions of higher learning.

9. What is the purpose of career life planning? Is it relevant in today's world? Will changes in scope be necessary in the 21st century?

10. Describe what you consider to be the major advantages of life-planning workshops.

For More Information

Herr, E. L., Cramer, S. H., & Niles, S. G. (2004). *Career guidance and counseling through the life span: Systematic approaches* (6th ed.). Boston: Pearson Education, Inc.

Luzzo, D. A. (Ed.). (2000). *Career counseling of college students: An empirical guide to strategies that work.* Washington, DC: American Psychological Association.

Marcia, J. E. (1991). Identity and self-development. In R. M. Lerner, A. C. Peterson, & J. Brooks-Gunn (Eds.), *Encyclopedia of adolescence:* Vol. 1. New York: Garland.

Pascarella, E. T., & Terenzini, P. T. (1991). *How college affects students: Findings and insights from twenty years of research.* San Francisco: Jossey-Bass.

Reardon, R. C. (1996). A program and cost analysis of self-directed career advising services in a university career center. *Journal of Counseling and Development, 74,* 280–285.

Reardon, R. C., Lenz, J. G., Sampson, J. P., & Peterson, G. W. (2000). *Career development and planning: A comprehensive approach.* Pacific Grove, CA: Brooks/Cole.

Spokane, A. R. (1991). *Career intervention.* Englewood Cliffs, NJ: Prentice-Hall.

Suggested InfoTrac College Edition Topics

Career centers and colleges

College majors and careers

Career choice and college students

College students and intern programs

Career development and college students

Computer-assisted career-guidance programs

Career planning workshops and courses

Placement services

18 Work in Our Lives

Chapter Highlights

- Changing organizations and new concepts in career development

- Postbureaucratic organizations have advantages for multicultural groups

- How work has changed

- Basic skills needed for work in the future

- The rise of the knowledge worker

- The rise of the temporary worker

- Knowledge as the key resource

- Stress at work

- Aging workers

WORK IN AMERICA has a fascinating, extensive history. Work is at the heart of our concerns as professionals and individuals fortunate enough to live in a free society. Work can involve the most simple step-by-step procedures or be physically and mentally demanding, complex, interesting, boring, creative, or menial; or it can involve all the descriptions listed and many more. Throughout our history, work has fascinated researchers who have attempted to delineate the complexities of the labor itself and the problems of individuals who do it. Today, work has prevailed as a most viable subject within the scientific community and has occupied scholars from a variety of disciplines who dared venture into the complex arena associated with work.

In this chapter we cover the vast changes in the workplace, how work is being restructured, and how the nature of work is changing. First, we discuss the changing workplace that many Americans are currently experiencing and the potential of working in multiple sites. Next, we discuss how work has changed, what has happened to work in America, the rise of the temporary workforce, and, finally, the emerging number of knowledge workers. Throughout these discussions a balance between work and other life roles is emphasized as a major career development goal. (See Box 18-1.)

Changing Organizations and New Concepts in Career Development

In the 1970s and 1980s, career development in organizations was related to upward mobility with predictable promotions and job descriptions. An employee aspired to reach the top of the pyramid in an orderly progression of steps. Numerous forecasts, however, predicted the replacement of the pyramidal organizational structure with a "flat" model, in which workers move laterally and use their skills for different projects. In this environment, workers are expected to learn new skills and adapt to the requirements of working with a team. Workers are to be flexible and prepared to adapt to the requirements of new and different tasks. Workers rotate to different projects and are required to initiate objectives that meet goals through innovation and learning. Management coordinates projects and participates directly in achieving these objectives. There appears to be a partnership between workers and managers and between workers and workers. Greater cooperation—sharing skills and mentoring—is encouraged. In sum, structural changes have been accomplished, accompanied by closer relationships between employees and employers and the reshaping of careers.

Tomasko (1987) and Aamodt (2004) suggested that organizations' structure will have the following components: (1) a lean headquarters (limited staff); (2) networks, not conglomerates (workers can be rotated); (3) vertical disintegration and decentralization (no superstructures); (4) staff services that can be sold to others (once an efficient staff has been assembled they can be marketed to other users); (5) expert systems rather than experts (development of computer-based expert systems); and (6) greater human resource planning (switch from personnel administration).

Changing Organizational Patterns

The old models of organizational structure are compared with the new evolving models in Table 18-1. Included among the changes for workers are broader roles and an increased demand for multiple skills. The previous models had numerous job

Box 18-1	The Meaning of Work

Why do people work? This seemingly simple question has been debated for centuries from many perspectives, including religion, economics, psychology, and philosophy. Some religious doctrine taught that work was a form of punishment for our original sin. Work was an obligation or duty toward building God's kingdom. Work was thus good and hard work even better. Work was noble because of its taxing nature and because it is a hardship that strengthens our character. Religious teachings also emphasized work as a means of controlling and restraining our passions. Lack of work, or idleness, fosters unhealthy impulses, which deflect us from more admirable pursuits. Thus work is thought of as an arduous process, deliberately filled with hardships, a means of facilitating our personal development. The view from an economic perspective is that work provides us with the financial resources to sustain life and the aspiration to improve the quality of our material life. The

most common accepted definition of work, the exchange of labor services for pay, clearly reflects an economic viewpoint. Work has psychological meaning as well, giving us a source of identity and union with other individuals, in addition to being a source of personal accomplishment. Work also has the effect of providing a temporal rhythm to our lives. Our work gives us our time structure—when we have to leave for work and when we are off work to pursue other activities. Finally, work even provides a philosophical explanation of our mission in life—to derive meaning from creating and giving service to others. As can be inferred, there is no one answer to the question of why we work, but its multiple meanings provide a basis to understand why work is so important.

Source: From *Psychology Applied to Work* (7th ed.), by P. M. Muchinsky, p. 340. Copyright 2003 Wadsworth, a division of Thomson Learning, Inc.

classifications that were narrowly focused. Currently, the term *multiskilling* is used to reflect the notion that many skills are to be learned in a lifelong learning program that may involve formal training as well as on-the-job training and job rotation. Organizational training programs now cover a variety of skills, including the basic skills of reading, writing, and computation; interpersonal skills; problem-solving skills; and leadership skills. (See Chapter 8.)

A smaller core of full-time employees is supplemented with part-time, temporary, or contract workers. The work environment is highly automated, and workers who have learned several skills are used selectively. When necessary, short training programs for the core workers are used to improve quality practices.

The overall strategy of the evolving organizational model is lowering costs of operations while improving product quality. Organizations have increased the purchase of quality components and services from proven products and management procedures in other organizations. For example, if a component can be produced better and cheaper elsewhere, the organization will contract for this component with another organization, which could be located in a foreign country. We currently have many multinational organizations that produce some or all their products in foreign countries such as Mexico, India, Thailand, South Korea, and many others. In a global web of organizations, products become international composites. Reich (1991) clearly illustrates this point:

When an American buys a Pontiac Le Mans from General Motors, for example, he or she engages unwittingly in an international transaction. Of the $20,000 paid to GM (at that time), about $6,000 goes to South Korea for routine labor and assembly operations,

$3,500 to Japan for advanced components (engines, transaxles, and electronics), $1,500 to West Germany for styling and design engineering, $800 to Taiwan, Singapore, and Japan for small components, $500 to Britain for advertising and marketing services, and about $100 to Ireland and Barbados for data processing. The rest—less than $8,000—goes to strategists in Detroit, lawyers and bankers in New York, lobbyists in Washington, insurance and health-care workers all over the country, and General Motors shareholders—most of whom live in the United States, but an increasing number of whom are foreign nationals. (p. 113)

Organizations have also decentralized to speed up the process of taking action on relevant issues, such as making transactions with different entities in the manufacture of a Pontiac Le Mans. These evolving models emphasize simultaneous product and process development to get new products on line. There is a greater reliance on suppliers and contract firms, which has drastically changed working environments in organizations and the skills required of workers.

The implications for career development in restructured organizations are quite significant. Kanter (1989) and Muchinsky (2003), among others, have suggested that organizations will no longer provide highly structured guidelines for careers; the individual must be more assertive in developing his or her destiny. Self-reliance and the ability to adapt to new and different work circumstances are key factors in career development. The new workplace will require greater flexibility from employees and the ability to do several jobs; that is, in some cases, to be more of a generalist than a specialist. Competency in new skills—and, more important, the ability to anticipate future skills—will make individuals more marketable and secure. Although technical competence is extremely important, people skills and the ability to create synergy within a team also has a high priority.

Reengineering the Corporation

The standard pyramidal organizational structure has been replaced recently by what was earlier referred to as "flat models." New organizational structures currently are being developed from evolving operational changes to effectively meet the demands of doing business in a world that is also experiencing rapid and significant changes. There seems to be agreement that the massive bureaucracies of yesterday's organization were not structured to keep up with the fast pace of competitiveness U.S. corporations are facing today.

In bureaucratic organizations, labor was fragmented into specialized work. In reengineered corporations, work is more integrated and has shifted to teams of employees. Instead of just one worker performing a particular task, now teams of workers as generalists complete the total process—assembling an automobile, for example. The following illustration is an example of what influenced leaders to rethink standard organizational procedures: One company discovered that it took seven days to process an order; several steps in the process passed through layers of bureaucracy. It was quickly discovered that the person who took the order could "walk" it through this process in just a few hours, thus delivering the product to the customer in one day instead of seven. In developing organizations today, the renewed interest in serving the customer has caused changes in standard practices.

According to Hammer and Champy (1993), the following "three C's" are the driving force behind the changing organizations: customers, competition, and change.

Table 18-1	Changing Organizational Patterns in U.S. Industry

Old Model: Mass production, 1950s and 1960s	New Model: Flexible decentralization, 1980s and beyond
OVERALL STRATEGY • Low cost through vertical integration, mass production, scale economies, long production runs. • Centralized corporate planning; rigid managerial hierarchies. • International sales primarily through exporting and direct investment.	• Low cost with no sacrifice of quality, coupled with substantial flexibility, greater reliance on purchased components and services. • Decentralization of decision making; flatter hierarchies. • Multimode international operations, including nonequity strategic alliances.
PRODUCT DESIGN AND DEVELOPMENT • Internal and hierarchical; in the extreme, a linear pipeline from central corporate research laboratory to development to manufacturing engineering. • Breakthrough innovation the ideal goal.	• Decentralized, with carefully managed division of responsibility among R&D and engineering groups; simultaneous product and process development where possible; greater reliance on suppliers and contract engineering firms. • Incremental innovative and continuous improvement valued.
PRODUCTION • Fixed or hard automation. • Cost control focuses on direct labor. • Outside purchase based on arm's-length, price-based competition; many suppliers. • Off-line or end-of-line quality control. • Fragmentation of individual tasks, each specified in detail; many job classifications. • Shopfloor authority vested in first-line supervisors; sharp separation between labor and management.	• Flexible automation. • With directs costs low, reduction of indirect cost becomes critical. • Outside purchasing based on price, quality, delivery, technology; fewer suppliers. • Real-time, on-line quality control. • Selective use of work groups; multiskilling, job rotation; few job classifications. • Delegation of shopfloor responsibility and authority to individuals and groups; blurring of boundaries between labor and management encouraged.
HIRING AND HUMAN RELATIONS PRACTICES • Workforce mostly full-time, semiskilled. • Minimal qualifications acceptable. • Layoff and turnover a primary source of flexibility; workers, in the extreme, viewed as a variable cost.	• Smaller core of full-time employees, supplemented with contingent (part-time, temporary, and contract) workers, who can be easily brought in or let go, as a major source of flexibility. • Careful screening of prospective employees for basic and social skills, and trainability. • Core workforce as an investment; management attention to quality-of-working life as a means of reducing turnover.

Table 18-1	(continued)
Old Model: **Mass production, 1950s and 1960s**	**New Model:** **Flexible decentralization, 1980s and beyond**

JOB LADDERS
- Internal labor market; advancement through the ranks via seniority and informal on-the-job training.

TRAINING
- Minimal for production workers, except for informal on-the-job training.
- Specialized training for craft and technical workers.

- Limited internal labor market; entry or advancement may depend on credentials earned outside the workplace.

- Short training sessions as needed for core workforce, sometimes motivational, sometimes intended to improve quality control practices or smooth the way for new technology.
- Broader skills sought for all workers.

SOURCE: Office of Technology Assessment, U.S. Congress, 1990. *Worker Training: Competing in the New International Economy.* Washington, DC: Government Printing Office.

Today's customers expect products to meet their individual needs and are no longer satisfied with what the seller may have mass-produced to be only "good enough." High-quality goods are what today's more sophisticated consumer wants. Price, selection, and service are three key words used to describe customer satisfaction. Reengineering is about "starting over" in organizational design. It is basically a search for new models of work and new approaches to process structure (Hammer & Champy, 1993). The old models of bureaucratic organizations must be rejected along with the assumptions of the past. Focusing on labor, reengineering casts out hierarchical controls and divisions of labor. While focusing on process structures, such as research and development of new products and accounting, reengineering stresses creative use of information technology. Following are two examples that illustrate process structures.

A few years ago a large U.S. camera manufacturing company discovered that its major rival in Japan had produced a 35-mm, single-use camera for which the U.S. company had no competitive offering. Traditionally, the product design process would take 70 weeks to produce a rival camera. Because this time lapse would give its competitor a huge advantage, the U.S. corporation's management team decided to reengineer its product-development process. In the old model of development, some groups waited for earlier steps to be completed before their work began (referred to as "fragmented work").

In another design process, parts were designed simultaneously and then integrated. The major problem with this process was that all subsystems did not mesh, and the newly designed product could be significantly delayed. In this division of labor, the groups were not adequately communicating with each other.

To solve the problem, the organization developed a computer-integrated product design database. The database collects each engineer's work and combines it daily for an overall design review by the contributing engineers. Each group or individual can resolve problems immediately, instead of facing weeks or months of delay. The organization succeeded in getting out its rival camera in 38 weeks.

Another example of reengineering is in the procurement process. In a large automobile manufacturing plant, the receiving clerk accepted deliveries of products without prior knowledge of an order for them. He had to assume they had been ordered, and he would let the accounts payable office handle any errors. Evidently, there were a large number of errors, for the accounts payable department had 500 employees.

The organization reengineered the procurement process that included the accounts payable function. Eventually, the procurement process produced three documents: the purchase order, the receiving document, and the invoice. Now the receiving clerk matches the three forms and is empowered to order payment. The organization currently has 125 people working in the vendor payment process (Hammer & Champy, 1993).

These two examples introduce changes that organizations have undertaken to successfully compete in the global marketplace. Even more changes are expected in the future. How many individuals will lose their jobs is unknown at this time. A better understanding of current organizational changes should assist counselors in developing a clearer perspective of this revolutionary process, which is expected to continue.

Will Postbureaucratic Organizations Have Advantages for Multicultural Groups?

According to Fernandez (1999), more members of organizations will have opportunities to advance and be recognized, including minorities, in postbureaucratic organizations. He views the bureaucratic organization as an intensely political organization that has promoted informal rules and relationships through political maneuvering. Furthermore, the bureaucratic organization is inflexible and promotes homogeneity; that is, everyone is treated as if they were the same. Differences in ambitions, needs, lifestyle, and worldview are ignored. Simply put, Fernandez suggests that the bureaucratic organizations' mode of operation constitutes unfairness and creates inequities.

Within the new and different organizational structure that has been discussed in the preceding paragraphs, individuals become more empowered to make decisions. There are fewer layers of management and fewer status distinctions. Communication will be more direct and more workers will be recognized for their unique contributions. Workers will also be given the opportunity to rotate jobs and satellite offices will shuffle staff to accomplish goals. Diverse work teams should develop trust, respect, and mutual accountability. In such a work environment, team accomplishment is rewarded. The individual worker is valued for what he or she contributes to the team's performance regardless of race, color, creed, gender, or sexual orientation.

In an environment where there are diverse groups, each person should reflect on his or her own culture, respect other cultures, develop relationships with people of diverse backgrounds, learn to know others by interacting with them, learn to communicate effectively, become flexible, learn how to adapt, and, finally, adjust to the behaviors of others. Fernandez (1999) strongly suggests that postbureaucratic organizations may provide the environment in which individuals from different cultures can learn to work effectively together.

Examples of How Work Has Changed

The following examples illustrate how work is changing in the workforce of the 21st century. These illustrations only scratch the surface of the vast changes in how work is organized and accomplished.

Case 18-1   The Secretary

Joan took a secretarial job that primarily required that she take shorthand, type, and make appointments. During most of her tenure of 15 years, the job requirements remained the same. But when the technology revolution arrived, the entire atmosphere of her office changed drastically. Joan was retrained to learn new skills, shorthand was no longer a requirement, typing was done on a computer, and appointments were made quite differently.

A person who filled a secretarial position 15 years ago may have been expected to type, take shorthand or dictation, manage files, make appointments, take telephone messages, and arrange for meetings, travel, or other appointments. Today, a secretary may be expected to perform all these tasks and, in addition, to use one or more software programs, usually including word processing, a spreadsheet, and list processing. The secretary may be expected to maintain an interactive calendar, posting the calendar to a network of linked associates. The secretary may be required to use electronic mail to communicate with clients at remote locations, to post and retrieve information from electronic bulletin boards, and to keep abreast of software changes to upgrade the office system. In many offices, the secretary is also expected to be familiar with the basic operating principles of high-speed copiers, laser printers, and fax machines, at least enough to serve as the first line of defense when the system fails (Newman & Newman, 1995, p. 576).

This example should serve as a point of reference for the work changes discussed in this chapter. It was chosen as an example of change because it is straightforward and easily understood. The complexity of changes in many areas of the workplace is somewhat difficult to comprehend, however, especially for clients who have not experienced industrial organizations. The next example represents a much broader scope of change in the future workplace.

Case 18-2   The Human Network Organization

Figure 18-1 illustrates how some future organizations may arrange their workplaces. Those individuals referred to as Front-line Generalists will use portable computers (PCs) to access information for field sales and services. Many front-line generalists may work out of a home office. The front-line support groups are located in local offices and have access to back-line specialists who have up-to-date information on products.

Central Management oversees the operation with a centralized database on mainframe or on supercomputers. This is referred to as a client-server model or, on the

Internet, as the browser-server model (Dent, 1998). This model emphasizes the importance of service and specialized expertise in the future workplace. Most significant in the future workplace is that Front-line Generalists are empowered to make critical decisions to meet the customers' needs; customer service is emphasized.

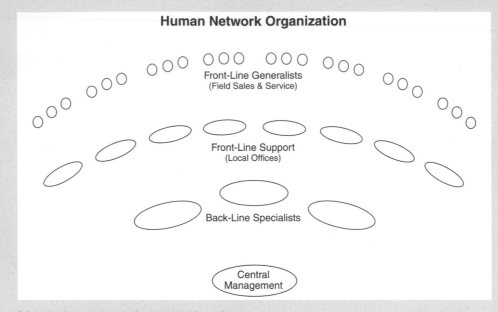

Figure 18-1   Human network organization

SOURCE: Reprinted with the permission of Simon & Schuster Adult Publishing Group from *The Roraring 2000's: Building the Wealth and Lifestyle You Desire in the Greatest Boom in History* by Harry. Dent. Copyright © 1998 by Harry Dent.

Case 18-3   Broadband Technology—The Wireless Office

A real estate agent decided some years ago that he would like a change of scenery from that of his central office. He wanted more flexibility and a change in atmosphere in the workplace so he set up a working office in his home and carried on business as usual by going online using a cable connection. Eventually, he wanted even more flexibility and another change of scenery: a wireless office made possible with Wi-Fi, shorthand for wireless fidelity. Broadband connections or "hotspots" allow subscribers to go online in various locations in a city to send e-mails or download files. This real estate agent found he could go online on a "hotspot" at the local coffee shop and, while enjoying a cup of coffee, transact some business. He frequently left his home office to meet with customers and a wireless localized network would allow him to use his laptop computer wherever he could find a T-Mobile Hotspot or a radio frequency that transmits a broadband connection.

Wi-Fi services have come to be known as the "waves of the future." Currently, subscribers usually pay fees according to their use and location. The Wi-Fi network's major advantage is it lets users access the Internet without a phone or cable hookup. Most "hotspots" are now found at nationally known coffee shops, some fast-food establishments, and colleges and universities. Wireless Local Area Networks (WLAN), however, are expected to grow rapidly in the near future. In addition, broadband technology should increase the ease of access to information and provide greater opportunities to access educational programs.

In sum, changes in how and where we work are illustrated by these three examples. The changes that will come in the future are not known, but as these examples illustrate, we should expect even more significant changes in work procedures and workplaces. This point emphasizes the growing need to address the pervasive nature of work in our lives. Changes in how and where we work can significantly affect other life roles and can be at the root of personal and career problems brought on by stress. The pressure to remain up-to-date and adapt to changes in the workplace has the potential of adversely affecting workers' feelings of well-being. Counselors can expect to find that their services will be needed to help individuals adapt to changes in work and maintain a life balance in an ever changing society in the 21st century.

What Has Happened to Work in the United States?

The majority of workers in developed countries a century ago worked with their hands at crafts, on farms, and performed domestic duties. During the industrial revolution of the late 1800s, factory workers became the largest single section (35%) of the American labor force. It is estimated that less than a quarter of American workers perform manual jobs at the current time and the total proportion of factory workers is at around 15% of the labor force. In the early 2000s, the American workforce had the smallest proportion of factory workers in all of the large developed countries (Drucker, 2002). Many of the lost manufacturing jobs have been "outsourced" to other countries where labor is much cheaper.

It should not surprise anyone that the American workforce will continue to make significant changes in the 21st century! To illustrate this point we once again return to the history of work in America. The U.S. Department of Labor estimates that 36 million jobs were eliminated in the United States between 1979 and 1993. In 1996, a *New York Times* poll put the number as high as 43 million through 1995. Although many of these jobs were eliminated by the development of new products and new procedures, the latest casualties were white-collar jobs that have been the victims of severe downsizing. A large percentage of total jobs lost were the result of contracting work with other companies. This type of job loss is referred to as "outsourcing" (Muchinsky, 2003; Uchitelle & Kleinfield, 1996).

An astonishing development in the 1990s was that far more jobs were added to the workplace than were lost! Many newly created jobs, however, offered fewer benefits and less pay and many were part-time positions. Individuals who were unable to find full-time work usually settled for temporary, part-time work. One of the country's largest employer was Manpower, Incorporated, which "rented out" 767,000 substitute workers each year (Uchitelle & Kleinfield, 1996).

A summary of what happened to two workers in the special report on downsizing by the *New York Times* written by Uchitelle and Kleinfield (1996) are good examples of what workers can expect during down times.

A loan officer, age 51, who made $1,000 weekly, was told when he returned from a family vacation that he no longer had a job. The news was devastating, but the worst of it was yet to come. He pumped gas, was a guinea pig in a drug test, drove a car for a salesman, and, at the time the story was written, was currently employed as a tour guide at $1,000 per month. His wife divorced him, and his children shunned him, ashamed of a father who had lost his job. This example might not be completely typical of all workers who lose their jobs, but it does point out the potential problems encountered by those whose jobs have been terminated by downsizing.

Next is the story of a woman who lost three jobs because of downsizing. More specifically, this is an example of a woman, still in her forties, whose pay dropped each time she experienced downsizing. Her first job was in a meatpacking plant at $8.50 per hour, her second job was in a bank mailroom at $7.25 per hour, and her third job was at $4.75 per hour loading newspapers. She was later employed at $4.25 per hour cleaning office buildings in Baltimore. She has not had a raise for three years. She has a high school diploma and enrolled in some courses for one year at a community college.

This exemplifies the difficulty workers face at the lower end of the economic ladder. In addition to the personal/social problems faced by these individuals, they need assistance to find resources for training programs to upgrade their skills.

What we have here is a scenario that has resulted in countless social and personal problems for working Americans. In addition, America and most other developed countries experience "up" and "down" times. When the economy falters, the obvious consequence is high unemployment, and if our past history turns out to be a good predictor of the future, we can expect to experience more of the same. To add to the confusion, organizations are reorganizing and abandoning fundamental assumptions that underlie previous operating procedures; they are making significant changes in operational procedures as well as in job requirements to prepare for 21st-century global competition.

Skills associated with organizational work grow more complex as advances in technology are usually followed by changes in the workplace. Organizations have had difficulty keeping job descriptions updated with the ever changing needs of operating and competing globally. *Job restructuring* is the term organizations prefer to describe these changing perceptions of work and skills organizations currently consider necessary for efficient operation.

Many have attempted to explain the ongoing changes in a variety of media, but the career counselor might have little information to pass on to the client about what is actually happening in the real world of organizational work. Part of this problem is that the change process in job requirements is ongoing. Second, the constant reconfiguration of the job market has been exacerbated by workforce reductions through downsizing and subsequent retraining programs and ironically, in the late 1990s, an increasing need for skilled workers. Finally, as corporations reengineer or restructure their workforces—a move to compete in the global market—the strategies emerging to meet their goals will, in effect, provide them with a more discernible definition of job requirements in the future. However, the likely continual evolution of new and different products in our current and future organizations will subsequently require new and different skills from employees (Drucker, 1992; 2002).

The Importance of Basic Skills

When the economy was as strong as it had been in the second half of the 1990s, unemployment remained low and there was greater competition among organizations for skilled workers. Thus, it is no surprise that economic conditions continue to be the driving force that determines labor demand and the increasing need for skilled workers. Rifkin (1995) and Muchinsky (2003) suggest, however, that technological advances may actually decrease the number of jobs available in the future. The lesson to be learned here is that career counselors should be prepared to assist clients in an ever changing job market.

In sum, the transformation of industries into smaller working units with vastly different operating procedures has created particular needs for individuals with certain types of skills. Meister (1994) identified six core workplace competencies employers require, as paraphrased here:

1. Learning skills: Organizations must adjust to new demands and improve their systems and processes to survive. Learning skills rank high in importance as organizations introduce changes. Employees must learn from a variety of sources, including coworkers, customers, suppliers, and educational institutions. The goal is for continuous improvement and to transform these skills into how an employee thinks and behaves.
2. Basic reading, writing, computation, and cognitive reasoning skills: Basic skills are a minimum requirement, but they are not narrowly defined as an ability to read, write, and perform mathematical computations. Employees must be able to apply information they read, for example, into action on a job.
3. Interpersonal skills: Good job performance in the past meant repeating tasks associated with each job. In current organizations, teams have become the vehicles of performance; thus individual performance is linked to well-developed interpersonal skills. The following skills are considered important: how to work in groups successfully and resolve conflicts, how to gain cooperation with creative peers, and how to network within the organization.
4. Creative thinking and problem-solving skills: The worker of today should be able to relate every phase of the production process, from obtaining raw materials to improving processes and procedures. Problem-solving skills should include being able to analyze situations, ask questions, seek clarification of what is not understood, and think creatively to generate options. The overall goal is for employees to develop skills that enable them to handle situations effectively without direction.
5. Leadership (and visioning) skills: In the emerging organizations, employees are encouraged to be active agents of change, rather than passive recipients of instructions. The employee today needs to develop abilities to envision improvement in work areas or establish a new direction and—perhaps most important—elicit the active commitment of others to accomplish his or her vision.
6. Self-development (and self-management) skills: These skills require that employees take charge of their careers and manage their own development. Employees must become aware of the changes in the workplace and be sure they have the requisite skills, knowledge, and competencies for their current assignments and potential future ones. The management of one's career is considered to be a learned competence and a necessary and important condition in the emerging corporation structure.

In sum, the future worker will need to continue learning new skills, methods, and procedures as well as build a knowledge base that provides a foundation for lifelong learning. The worker in the 21st century no longer works to "keep up with the Joneses" but to say abreast of changing technology and business trends. Promotions will be based on knowledge and skills not longevity! The key to the future is individual initiative that is knowledge driven.

The Rise of the Knowledge Worker

In Chapter 1, the point was made that the next society will be dominated by knowledge workers (Drucker, 2002). Knowledge workers, however, are not new to our workforce. Currently, knowledge workers are identified as doctors, lawyers, scientists, and psychologists among others. The new breed of knowledge workers will be a part of a growing trend of knowledge industries and knowledge work. As Meister (1994) pointed out, workers will be required to have vision and leadership skills, do creative thinking, and manage their individual development. Some of these skills are illustrated in the next paragraphs.

Reich (1991) also delineated worker skills that will be necessary for the effective operation of current and future organizations. He framed these skills in what he refers to as the "new web of enterprise" (p. 87). Such organizations are referred to as high-value enterprises that resemble a spider's web. New connections from multiple locations on the globe will be spun continuously. Teams of workers will generate concepts of new products, how to produce them, and how they will be marketed. During the give-and-take of debate among team members, mutual learning will occur through shared insights, experiences, and solutions. Workers will learn from each other, learn about each other, and learn how to help one another perform better. Each point on the web will be unique and will represent its own combination of skills.

Within this frame of reference, three different but related skills will be needed by each team member. First are problem-solving skills. *Problem solvers* continuously search for new combinations and applications that might solve all kinds of emerging problems. Team members must have intimate knowledge of, say, semiconductor chips and what can be expected of them if they are reassembled or redesigned for a new product.

The second skill is referred to as *problem identification* or, as team members, problem identifiers. This skill requires an intimate knowledge of a customer's business and how a new and different product can give this customer the competitive edge. Instead of using the art of persuasion to sell a product, the operational procedure here is identifying new problems and possibilities to which a product could be applied.

The third skill requires that the worker play the role of *strategic broker*. This high-value position requires knowledge of specific technologies and markets to the point of foreseeing the potential for new products. This individual must coordinate the role of the problem solver and problem identifier and raise necessary funds to launch projects. These people are characterized as being continuously engaged in managing ideas.

What we see here is a recognition that survival in the 21st century will, in large part, depend on a well-trained workforce. Newly acquired skills in problem solving and team building are designed to make improvements in job production, but work environments also must be redefined. The major goal appears to be the development of work environments that may be ever changing, where workers understand their work conceptually and look for methods to improve it. The ideal organizational work environment promotes a culture of lifelong learning and a working atmosphere that encourages all employees to want to learn (Meister, 1994). Finally, we must remember that not all organizations have been restructured or reengineered. Some organizations, particularly government ones, have retained a bureaucratic structure. Some clients may find congruence within these structures rather than in the emerging ones, although Reich (1991), Rifkin (1995), and Muchinsky (2003), among others, point out that these older, structured organizations are decreasing in number.

The Rise of the Temporary Worker

The temporary worker or "temp," often identified as part of the contingent workforce, is increasingly being used in organizations across the country. In the early 1990s about 100 temporary agencies and around 470,000 temporary employees existed in the United States. By the early 2000s we had 1,500 temporary agencies and over 1.6 million temporary workers (Cropanzano & Prehar, 2001). The major reason why organizations have adopted the strategy of hiring "temps" is to offset labor costs in response to an unpredictable economy. Many organizations have permanent jobs that are staffed by temporary workers. The irony is that the temporary worker is responsible to the employment agency. They are simply assigned to staff an organization and perform particular services. The use of temporary workers and contracting for special personnel and/or specialized services is likely to increase as a result of sudden and swiftly changing conditions that organizations are likely to experience.

Temporary workers come from several sources. Some are women who want more flexible work schedules. Workers who have been downsized and are seeking permanent employment are another source. Recent college graduates who could not find permanent jobs are yet another source. Finally, retired individuals who need to supplement their income also search for positions as temporary workers. According to Muchinsky (2003), temporary workers receive less pay than permanent workers and they have little job security or opportunity for growth. Furthermore, many temporary workers are dissatisfied with their employment relationship and feel a sense of powerlessness. The temporary worker is constantly faced with the uncertainty of how long he will be employed and the possibility of not having a regular paycheck. Temporary workers may have difficulty in finding work to be an important source of meaning in their lives, and the psychological costs to individuals could be heavy.

In keeping with the theme of this chapter, work in our life, it is suggested here that many in the American workforce are dissatisfied with work environments that have little in the way of security and offer very few opportunities for advancement and growth. In many working situations there are no promises for the future. It is no surprise that a "temp's" feelings of well-being are significantly affected and indeed he or she may be quite powerless to change his or her current situation.

The following is an example of one such situation in the global business world. A young business leader established a company that distributed plastic containers that he received from several Asian countries. His goal was to sell plastic containers to large companies that sold such products as facial creams, soaps, and medications. His home office employed a minimal number of workers and he was torn between enlarging his staff or keeping it lean in case of a downturn in sales. In the meantime, he was successful in locating quality containers that cost less than some major companies could find. Low labor costs at the manufacturing site were the key to his success. His major concern, however, was how long it would be before someone else found an even cheaper product. He was therefore hesitant to add personnel because in a global economy he had no control over product cost. He opted for temporary workers to meet his current needs.

This is an example of why organizations are diversifying into smaller units and moving manufacturing and production almost anywhere on the globe where the cost of doing business is the lowest. Along with the moves go American jobs, making the future of manufacturing work uncertain. As stated earlier by Drucker (2002), America has the smallest proportion of factory workers in its labor force than do all large developed countries.

Once again we return to the workers, the ones who are on the low end of the pay scale. Many low-paid jobs are in the service sector: janitors, home health care aides, hotel workers, child care workers, poultry and meat processors, security guards, maids, porters, cashiers, bank tellers, laundry and dry cleaning workers, clerks, waiters and waitresses, cooks, and pharmacist assistants. Many of these jobs are currently filled by temps. Typically, these workers have two jobs, live in low-cost housing, have limited health insurance, and limited resources. Their work hours are not standardized; for example, hotel workers are told not to come to work when hotel occupancy is down. Many of these workers, such as poultry and meat processors, are subject to repetitive tasks for long hours with short breaks that are strictly enforced. Many view the future with fear: Long-term planning is out or set aside for the more immediate goal of survival. It should not be surprising to counselors that workers at the low end of the pay scale experience stress-related problems that may be the source of depression, anxiety, relationship concerns, and physical problems such as frequent headaches, ulcers, and colitis (Shulman, 2003).

Many minority workers hold low-paid jobs and counselors are to be sensitive to their needs when addressing presenting problems they bring to counseling. Establishing trust may take time but is essential for effective counseling, especially with individuals who may have been taken advantage of and treated with disrespect. Be aware that these clients have been given little in the way of dignity; more than likely do not have a career identity; and have been denied some core areas of life such as stability, family life, respect, safety, and security. In sum, they have multiple needs including many things most Americans take for granted—a living wage, health care, transportation, a decent home, and most important, the ability to improve their current conditions. Some organizations do offer workers opportunities to receive training and basic educational instruction; however, low-end employees are less likely to have this opportunity. Counselors are to be aware of assistance resources that could provide aid for workers who hold low-paid jobs. As advocates, counselors support programs that educate the general public about the plight of families who are trying to survive on minimum wages. (See Box 18-2.)

What we have here are organizations that survive by cutting their operating and labor costs to meet global competition that in most cases has access to a low-paid labor force. Many organizations have outsourced their jobs to overseas sites and/or to temporary worker groups in order to market their goods at competitive prices. One only needs to read the daily newspaper to find that company X is closing its plants in several locations, reducing its labor force in this country, and restructuring in an overseas site. Be aware, however, that when there is a severe economic downturn or crisis, large-scale job loss is experienced both domestically and globally.

The most obvious affect of job reduction in organizations for the individual worker is the loss of earning a living. Many organizations offer outplacement counseling services to terminated employees. The major goal is to help employees assess individual strengths, evaluate career options, and learn effective job search strategies. The cost of this service is absorbed by the employer. What often may be overlooked, however, are the psychological effects of job loss, although some organizations are attempting to address these problems.

Knowledge as the Key Resource

Knowledge industries, knowledge work, and knowledge workers are the ingredients that will shape the future workforce. Be aware that the workforce will continue to consist of janitors, clerks, and maids, for example, but a growing number of workers will be known as professional knowledge workers. They will earn their position in the workforce through individual effort and dedication to learning. Collectively, knowledge workers will be the driving force behind the development and production of products. They apply their specialized skills and cooperate with other knowledge workers for product development as illustrated previously by a large camera manufacturing company.

Knowledge workers do and will continue to occupy positions such as x-ray technicians, paralegals, office technologists, dental technicians, and medical technologists among many others. What they all have in common is a formal education and they participate in continuing education. Knowledge workers prefer to identify themselves as "professionals" rather than as "craftpersons" or "workers." They may work in an organization but will identify themselves by their special skills, such as "I am an electrical engineer" (Drucker, 2002).

Knowledge work can provide a most important element to the meaning of work in one's life. It provides the individual with a career identity, for instance, and a social position in an ever changing society. It is not an inherited position but one that is earned through individual achievement. The potential for upward mobility is a means of hope for workers and an avenue to becoming successful, achieving respect and financial security. As in most work situations, however, the individual is challenged to maintain a balanced life that addresses all life roles.

Workers can also expect some opportunities for training offered by organizations. On-site training is usually conducted on the job site and involves the totality of the job. On-the-job-training is conducted by experienced skilled workers on the job site. Workers observe and imitate the behavior of the instructor. Job rotation is a process in which workers learn a number of skills and work requirements as they rotate through a variety of jobs. Off-site training methods include lectures, seminars, audiovisual material, computer-based training, Web-based training, simulation, and role playing (Muchinsky, 2003). (See Chapter 8.)

Stress at Work

One factor inherent in modern working life is stress, induced by work and the work environment. Stress in this context has been defined as a psychophysical response to various stimuli. Sources of stress have been the subject of research for several decades and in the early 1980s work-related stressor sources were compiled by a number of

---

Box 18-2   Workforce Centers—One-Stop Career Centers

One answer to assisting adults in career transition are state-sponsored workforce centers that are also known as one-stop career centers. This trend was initiated by the U.S. Department of Labor, and the Colorado Workforce Centers are a good example. Workforce centers have been designed to consolidate many components of state job services including employment and training services. A major goal of workforce centers is to assist job seekers as well as area employers. In some cases, adjoining counties have consolidated into multicounty workforce centers, while some larger populated areas and some isolated areas have single-county workforce centers.

Career development services offered at the workforce centers include the following:

Self-help service available:
- Career assessment
- Labor market information
- Information on training programs, education, and schools

- Information on scholarships, financial aid, and resources

Staff-assisted services are available to dislocated workers, displaced homemakers, older workers, economically disadvantaged youth, adults, and other special program recipients. Although most services offered in workforce centers could be listed as subheadings under career counseling, they are presented separately to inform prospective clients of a variety of services.

- Career counseling
- Basic education and GED remediation
- English as a second language
- Career management assistance
- Financial assistance for basic education and career programs
- Referrals to supportive services and other community-based organizations
- Career planning

---

researchers (Ivancevich & Matteson, 1980; Kasl, 1978; Levi, 1984; Shostak, 1980). Their results dramatize the complexity and variety of potentially stressful conditions most workers faced at that time:

1. Conditions of work: Unpleasant work environment, necessity to work fast, excessive and inconvenient hours
2. Work itself: Perception of job as uninteresting, repetitive, overloaded, and demanding
3. Shift work: Rotating shifts affecting bodily functions and role behaviors
4. Supervision: Unclear job demands, close supervision with no autonomy, scant feedback from supervisors
5. Wage and promotion: Inadequate income
6. Role ambiguity: Lack of clarity about one's job and scope of responsibilities
7. Career development stressors: Little job security, impending obsolescence, dissatisfaction over career aspirations and current level of attainment
8. Group stressors: Insufficient group cohesiveness, poor group identity in the organization
9. Organizational climate: Impersonally structured organizational policies
10. Organizational structure: Too bureaucratic or too autocratic

Most sources of stress uncovered in the 1970s and 1980s probably would be found in today's work climate, with the exception of organizational structure, which reflected a predominately different set of conditions than we currently find. By 1990,

- Supportive services to assist with training and program participation, based on need
- Computerized learning lab
- Internships and specialized work experience opportunities
- On-the-job training for permanent jobs with employers
- Workshops on goal setting, motivation, career planning, and employability skills
- Job searching in the 21st century
- Company information and profiles
- National job search sites via Internet
- Assistance with all stages of job search. In many of the workforce centers, the following technological help is available:
  - Self-help computer stations
  - Fax machine
  - Copier
  - Scanner
  - Phone room for professional inquiries
  - Typing tutorials

- Computerized self-assessment
- Internet access
- Microsoft Office Program staff assistance available for use of resources

Workforce centers have been structured through a partnership between private industry and public agencies to meet the challenge of the global economy.

What is viewed as a revolution in the workforce, education, and social policy has fueled changes that are driving American industry to search for ways to compete. A key element is the development of human resources. As American organizations integrate technology into all work processes, skill and job requirements will dramatically change. Thus, a workforce with technical expertise and the ability to analyze and solve problems, work in teams, and adapt to changes is crucial to the development of the future generation of organizations.

Magnuson (1990) offered the following indications of job-related stress among American workers:

- Low self-esteem
- Low motivation to work
- Poor concentration on work tasks
- Poor work relationships with peers and supervisors
- Poor communications with others on the job site
- Feelings of inadequacy and resentment
- Depression
- Excessive tardiness and absenteeism

In the late 1990s, Rice (1999) has suggested that job-related stress leads to dissatisfaction, burnout, and obsolescence. He considered psychological systems of work stress to include the following:

- Anxiety, tension, confusion, and irritability
- Feelings of frustration, anger, and resentment
- Emotional hypersensitivity and hyperactivity
- Suppression of feelings, withdrawal, and depression
- Reduced effectiveness in communication
- Feelings of isolation and alienation
- Boredom and job dissatisfaction

- Mental fatigue, lower intellectual functioning, and loss of concentration
- Loss of spontaneity and creativity
- Lowered self-esteem (p. 195)

Such symptoms, according to Rice (1999), can lead to several behaviors including lower performance, procrastination, work avoidance, aggression, depression, and increased alcohol and drug use and abuse. Work-related stress also can be the major source of family problems, poor relationships with other workers and friends, and in very severe cases might be one factor that leads to violence in the workplace.

Newman and Newman (2003) point out that stress is very pervasive—"one must enlist cognitive, affective, and behavioral strategies to manage stress" (p. 52). Cormier and Nurius (2003) suggest that self-management strategies designed to deal with stress can be very effective. These strategies include self-monitoring through recording thoughts, feelings, and behaviors when interacting within the environment. These recordings are to be reviewed for further insights into cognitive processes. Secondly, prearranged stimulus control that decreases disturbing reactions to certain events is another suggestion. Individuals learn to control or modify their disturbing reactions to certain stimuli. A third self-management strategy includes self-reward or a positive stimulus following a desirable reaction to target behaviors. Individuals learn to provide their own positive reinforcement for desirable behaviors. A fourth strategy suggests that individuals are to visualize how they could successfully perform a goal behavior. This strategy suggests projecting self as a model when performing in a desired manner. The major goal of these strategies is to build self-monitoring, self-directed procedures for managing stressful conditions and situations.

Types of interventions for coping with stress suggested by Sulsky & Smith (2005) include meditation, exercise, and relaxation techniques. In addition organizations are to evaluate job-design, selection and placement programs, and general working conditions. Job placement and demands are to consider person style fit including participation preferences, and coworker relationships. Clearly, both the individual and organization share the need to develop an awareness and recognition that stress at work should be systematically addressed.

There is a growing recognition among employers of the stressful conditions involving the interplay between work and family. The increased number of dual-earner families and the desire to hold on to effective knowledge workers has motivated organizations to become more family-role-oriented. Another driving force is the realization that material and socioemotional rewards are not mutually exclusive (Muchinsky, 2003). In other words, family life and the time to become involved in other interests and to be with friends also play an important role in individual happiness and satisfaction.

Progressive organizations have viewed family relationships as very inclusive. For example, family relationships now include multiple relationships including stepparenting, committed relationships between unmarried couples, and extended family responsibilities such as caring for nieces, nephews, grandchildren, and elderly relatives (Feldman, 2002). The point here is that increasing family responsibilities and subsequent conflicts may be the impetus that leads some individuals to work longer hours as a source of support and satisfaction (Hochschild, 1997). Under these circumstances the move to balance life roles focuses on family conflicts and the potential of a meltdown in the workplace, as family conflicts can also decrease an individual's ability to tolerate stress derived from the workplace (Stephens & Feldman, 1997).

Integrating work and life and finding a life balance are current subjects of interests to employers as well as employees (Fox & Spector, 2005). In response to work/family conflicts, organizations have established on-site or near-site child care centers and exercise facilities, and some have offered elder care assistance, such as arranging for transportation, medical schedules, and personal services. Flexible work schedules also are offered by many organizations.

The effects of stress are pervasive; work performance and interpersonal relationships are often affected. Stress has been linked to numerous physical problems, including cardiovascular diseases. Stress exists at all levels of the workforce, from executives to blue-collar workers (Muchinsky, 2003; Rice, 1999; Shostak, 1980). As organizations grow in complexity, potential stressor sources are expected to multiply.

The relationship between job stress and disease has also been exposed as an ongoing problem that has been ignored in many workplaces. The connection between work and health has focused attention on designing more healthful workplaces. The physical, psychological, and psychosocial consequences of work therefore are seen as significantly related to job design (Aamodt, 1999; Karasek & Theorell, 1990; Muchinsky, 2003). For example, bad job design fosters social isolation, little feeling of the social value of work, unrestrained job competition, sex role conflicts, little or no freedom or independence, long periods of intense time pressures, and little autonomy for workers.

Jobs designed for the future and considered healthful work—that is, beyond the material rewards of work—were described by Karasek and Theorell (1990) as follows:

1. More jobs are to be designed to make maximum use of every worker's skill and provide opportunities to improve and increase skills.
2. More work freedom exists when workers are able to select their work routines and peer affiliates. Some work may be done in the home.
3. Workers are given equal status in making decisions as far as work demands are concerned. Jobs may require routine tasks, but they also provide new learning challenges.
4. Social contacts are encouraged to promote new learning and prevent work isolation. Advanced technologies are made available to encourage new learning.
5. Democratic procedures are prevalent in the workplace. Grievance procedures protect workers from arbitrary authority.
6. Workers receive feedback from customers, and in fact, customers and workers are encouraged to work together to customize products.
7. All workers are to share in family responsibilities and tasks, especially in two-earner homes. Time is set aside for family activities. (pp. 316–317)

In sum, healthful work reduces the sources of job stress prevalent in current work environments primarily by giving the worker more freedom and autonomy. Social interactions are encouraged to reduce threats associated with job competition. New learning is encouraged by making new technologies accessible to workers. Finally, more freedom of choice concerning work roles and greater autonomy in the workplace are recommended as key ingredients for designing jobs for the future.

Aging Workers

A question often considered in the hiring process is, are aging workers more motivated to do good work than younger workers are? Research has shown that age per se is not a good predictor of how well a person will perform in either a blue-collar or a white-collar job. Older workers can be as competent as younger ones and typically have more positive attitudes toward their work. Furthermore, older workers seem to be more satisfied in their jobs, more involved in their work, and less interested in finding a different job (Warr, 1992).

As Sigelman and Rider (2003) point out, job performance of individuals in their fifties and sixties is not very different from that of younger workers. These authors note that performance of older workers is not hindered by age-related physical and cognitive declines that usually are significant when one is much older. Also, the American Council on Education (1997, as cited in Kail and Cavanaugh [2000]) report that older employees make up the largest percentage of individuals taking courses designed to improve their technical skills. Perhaps older workers are also successfully competing for jobs through what is referred to as *selective optimization with compensation* (Hansson, DeKoekkoek, Neece, & Patterson, 1997). In this process, the older worker focuses on the skills needed to compete (selection), practices to keep those skills sharp (optimization), and compensates for skills he or she lacks. One explanation for these findings is that older workers have found jobs that satisfy them, and they have accepted the downside of the job, realizing that it could be difficult to find a new job. The point here is that workers in their fifties and sixties can make good employees. We also can expect to find retired workers searching for work that will provide them with additional income and time to spend with their family.

Implications for Career Counseling

The purpose of this chapter was to illustrate the overwhelming need for career counseling of adults. The American workforce is facing changes in how and where they will work. Organizations are downsizing and outsourcing their workforce. The psychological concerns associated with job loss suggest that counselors make a significant effort to address these potential problems.

Advances in technology are challenging workers to stay abreast with the times. More training and formal education is necessary for the better jobs. Most workers will have to adopt a lifelong learning mind-set. The worker of today is surrounded by uncertainties, increasing competition for upward movement, and no promises for the future. Temporary workers are dissatisfied and feel insecure about the future as their job could be terminated at any time. Low-paid workers continue to struggle to survive. Many workers hold down two jobs or more.

All of the above can be sources of stress that adversely affect an individual's job performance and other life roles. Responses to sources of stress associated with work can be divided into three categories: physiological, psychological, and behavioral. In the physiological realm, consequences of stress can cause cardiovascular and gastrointestinal problems. Psychologically, clients may present depression, anxiety, and job dissatisfaction. Behaviorally, clients are subject to turnover, absenteeism, job performance, work maladjustment, and poor interpersonal relationship. In addition, all of these problems affect other life roles (Muchinsky, 2003).

Counselors are also to be cognizant of the possibility that client problems in other life roles can adversely affect performance and behavior in the work role. Warr (1987) supports this position by prudently pointing out that integrated functioning refers to the person as a whole when addressing mental health problems of reluctant workers. As far as work is concerned an individual's mental health is influenced by affective well-being, competence (success in performance), autonomy (self-regulation and independence), aspirations (establishes and maintains goals), and integrated functioning (whole person). What is suggested here is that counselors can isolate client career concerns, but should also address interrelationships of personal concerns in a holistic approach. Once again we make the point that personal and career concerns are inseparable. In the next chapter we cover adults in career transition.

Summary

1. Changes in work requirements and skills have evolved with the technological revolution. Jobs have been lost to downsizing and outsourcing while new jobs are being created. Workers are to be committed to lifelong learning in order to remain up-to-date. The term *multiskilling* is used to reflect the notion that many skills are to be learned in a lifelong learning program.

2. Organizations are reorganizing and abandoning fundamental assumptions that underlay previous operating procedures. Some skills individuals will need to compete are in the areas of reading, writing, computation, cognitive reasoning, interpersonal relations, creative thinking and problem solving, leadership, self-development, and self-management. In the "new web of enterprise," team members will function with problem solvers, problem identifiers, and strategic planners.

3. Organizations are changing from pyramidal structures to "flat models." Workers move laterally and use different skills for different projects. Organizations no longer provide structured guidelines for careers: Individuals must be more assertive in developing their destiny.

4. Multicultural groups may be given greater access to job advancement in postbureaucratic organizations.

5. Changes in the workplace have resulted in countless social and personal problems for working Americans.

6. The next society will be dominated by knowledge workers. They will be a part of a growing trend of knowledge industries and knowledge work. Knowledge will indeed be the key resource in the 21st century.

7. Temporary workers ("temps") are increasingly being used by organizations. Temps are given no promises for future employment.

8. Low-paid workers typically have two jobs or more, live in low-cost housing, and have limited resources.

9. Stress, defined as a psychophysical response to various stimuli, is inherent in modern working life. The effects of stress are pervasive: Work performance and interpersonal relationships are often affected. Stress affects all levels of workers, from executives to blue-collar work.

10. Workers in their fifties and sixties can be as competent as younger workers and typically have more positive attitudes. An increase in older workers is expected; some will commit to a second career whereas others will work part time.

Supplementary Learning Exercises

1. Describe your own work ethic and how it developed. Compare your description with a classmate's.
2. Develop a counseling component that is designed to help individuals overcome job stress.
3. Defend or criticize the following statement in writing or in a debate: Work ethics change because society changes.
4. How did teamwork displace assembly-line work that required one task to be repeated? Give an example.
5. What is the difference between the problem solver and the problem identifier? Which one has the most difficult task?
6. Explain the concept of a "new web of enterprise." How does it operate?
7. What is a knowledge worker? Give examples. How and why will they dominate the workforce of the future?
8. What is a temporary worker? Give examples. What would you tell a client about the advantages and disadvantages of temp work?
9. How would you assist an individual who has lost his or her job? Describe your procedures and their purpose.
10. Using the following resource, write an essay on the changes in organizations that will be experienced in the early part of the 21st century: Hammer, M., & Champy, J. (1993). *Reengineering the corporation: A manifesto for business revolution.* New York: HarperCollins.

For More Information

Drucker, P. F. (2002). *Managing in the next society.* New York: TalleyBooks/Dutton.

Feldman, D. C. (Ed.). (2002). *Work careers: A developmental perspective.* San Francisco: Jossey-Bass.

Fox, S., & Spector, P. E. (2005). *Counterproductive work behavior: Investigations of actors and targets.* Washington, DC: American Psychological Association.

Muchinsky, P. M. (2003). *Psychology applied to work* (7th ed.). Belmont, CA: Wadsworth/Thomson Learning.

Reich, R. B. (1991). *The work of nations.* New York: Knopf.

Rice, P. L. (1999). *Stress and health* (3rd ed.). Pacific Grove, CA: Brooks/Cole.

Rifkin, J. (1995). *The end of work: The decline of the global labor force and the dawn of the postmodern era.* New York: Putnam.

Suggested InfoTrac College Edition Topics

Burnout	Unemployment
Flextime	Work/family conflict
Occupational segregation	Work roles
Shift work	Work values

Career Counseling for Adults in Career Transition

19

Chapter Highlights

- Occupational transitions in the new millennium

- Job loss concerns

- Shift of risks from organization to individual

- Adults who want to change careers

- Establishment stage transitions

- Midcareer and maintenance stage transitions

- Late career and transition to retirement

- Interacting influences in career development

- Volatile behavior in the workplace

- Intervention components for adults in career transition

IN THIS CHAPTER, we concentrate on the growing need for programs and strategies to assist adults in career transition. In the last two decades more attention has been focused on the development of counseling programs for individuals who choose to make a career change and for those who are forced into it. Changing work roles appears to be inevitable and most certainly unavoidable for many in the workforce. As Drucker (1992, 2002) pointed out, we are in the middle of a transformation in this nation that is not yet complete. A major aspect of this transformation includes changing occupational structures and career patterns. This transformation is rapid and highly discontinuous in nature; changes can be quite drastic and pervasive in scope. We are living at a time of tremendous growth of knowledge through sophisticated research that has given us new technologies with vast potential for even more rapid changes in the near future. Billions-of-dollar mergers involving companies that can offer more programs through cable, for instance, are viewed by some as only temporary industry leaders, because even newer technological advances will provide better avenues to entertainment and the Internet. Access to the Internet, for instance, is being boosted by broadband technology discussed in the previous chapter. In the meantime our society is experiencing the conflicts associated with continuous change in how and where we work. Change in the world of work has been described as tumultuous, and its fallout will certainly have an effect on who will prosper in the future (Muchinsky, 1997, 2003).

Current speculation suggests that individuals who will prosper are those who are intelligent enough to learn new skills and, most important, those who are willing to experience new and different work situations. The flexibility to adjust and adapt to different work environments and the capacity to relate to other people are the qualities that will characterize future workers. Workers will no longer experience the luxury of a steady stream of continuous change but, on the contrary, will be required to adapt quickly to new and different ideas, goals, procedures, tools, and requirements. The reality of today's occupational world is that some individuals will be forced to make career transitions and others will choose to change careers to find satisfying work, proving there can be positive and negative consequences associated with adults in career transition.

The focus in this chapter is on the roles of the career counselor with clients who choose to change careers and with clients who are forced to make career transitions. We will address the special needs of adults including job insecurity, retraining, coping with unemployment, and adjusting to new and different work environments. The interrelationships of work with other life roles continues to be a focus. Finally, we offer career counseling intervention components for adults in career transition.

Occupational Transitions in the New Millennium

Many consider the changing organizational context discussed in the previous chapter to be the driving force that has changed the nature of unemployment and led to the loss of jobs for many, especially in the managerial and professional sector, and some identify it as the major cause for the erosion of traditional careers in organizations that once provided stable employment (Leana, 2002). The current practices of part-time and temporary employment, limited partnerships, and subcontracting provide little in the way of security and subvert promises that were once the trademark of traditional organizations' relationships with their employees. Within these growing changes, young adults are finding it difficult to select and launch a career, whereas older adults are having difficulty adjusting to decreased job security. In the following paragraphs, we will discuss job loss concerns, shift of risks from organizations to individuals, adults who want to change careers, establishment transitions, midcareer and maintenance transitions, late career and transitions to retirement, and volatile behavior in the workplace.

Job Loss Concerns

Adults who have lost their jobs due to "downsizing" and "outsourcing" and remain unemployed are likely to experience the psychological effects of job loss and the stress that is associated with job search. These individuals are often required to reevaluate their skills and goals, which may result in a completely different career direction. Beneath the surface of immediate career concerns, an individual's self-worth can be threatened by the loss of a regular paycheck and career identity. Moreover, there are often interrelated personal concerns associated with other life roles that need to be addressed. In essence, the psychological effects of unemployment can be very pervasive. There are, however, differences in the effects of unemployment by age and gender. Middle-age men tend to react more negatively to unemployment than do older and younger men (Vosler & Page-Adams, 1996). It appears that workers in their fifties tend to experience less stress because many of them had considered early retirement, changing to a different job, or assuming a consultant role (Leana & Feldman, 1992; Feldman, 2002). According to Kulik (2001), women who lose their jobs report a greater decline in general health than men do. In the next paragraphs we examine some concerns of individuals who have been forced to find a different job or change careers as the result of job loss.

The major intended outcome of employment is to earn a living wage; however, there are also important psychological consequences derived from work that are discontinued when one is out of work. More than twenty years ago, Jahoda (1981) captured the unintended consequences of work as summarized: (1) a daily time structure that is devoted to working, (2) shared experiences and interactions with cohorts and other individuals outside the nuclear family, (3) the opportunity to express purpose and goals of life, (4) reinforcement of personal status and identity, and (5) participation in activities associated with work that is viewed as a necessity in the give-and-take of daily life. Be aware that work's pervasive nature and complex meaning in one's life is not the argument here. What is being emphasized is the loss of valuable sources of support for one's psychological well-being (Muchinsky, 2003). Counselors will find that individuals differ in their reactions to loss of support; for example, some may become clinically depressed, some may experience increased difficulty with personal relationships, whereas others will present significant mood swings. Combinations of concerns are often presented.

Accompanying psychological problems associated with lack of support is the lack of available money, which has both practical and psychological consequences. The inability to provide funds for oneself and/or family can be a major source of stress. The loss of adequate housing, ample food, and other essentials can be devastating for families and is a major source of problems in maintaining relationships. As some see it, there is loss of control over one's life when the social contract for work has been broken (Rousseau, 1995). Along with the loss of job is the loss of a socially approved role and social contacts. Counselors should not be surprised to find that individuals as well as family members feel isolated, insecure, and experience a poor sense of well-being. In sum, the psychological effects of job loss vary by age and gender; can be the primary source of mental health problems, relationship concerns, and concerns involving multiple life roles; and negatively affect an individual's sense of well-being.

Shift of Risks from Organizations to Individuals

A significant change in employee relationships with organizations involves the management of employee careers. In the past, some organizations had elaborate systems for overseeing and planning each employee's career development, which led to advances up the career ladder. Currently, some organizations have limited programs for training employees that may include sensitivity training and such subjects as sexual harassment. Training for skill and knowledge development is being advanced as self-directed, continuous learning development through Internet-based delivery of self-managed resources, in-house computer-generated instruction, coaching, and mentoring (London, 2002). These training programs are directed primarily toward current needs of organizations. The primary responsibility of career planning, however, has been shifted to the individual employee. He or she now assumes the responsibility of taking appropriate steps to advance his or her career and develop skills that are marketable in the new work arena in an economy that is driven by global market forces.

Accompanying the loss of a career management partnership between organization and employee is the loss of job security and the promise of a regular paycheck. Highly valued job security and pay increases are no longer tied completely to longevity. Currently, many organizations endorse the concept of pay-for-performance (Rynes & Gerhart, 2000). Under these conditions the employee is challenged to assume the position that career planning will involve circular as well as linear moves. Once again we emphasize that learning to adapt and become flexible in the work role are important keys to success.

Associated with this shift of responsibility are significant risks and challenges for the individual. What we are stressing here is that work in our lives is taking a road less traveled and introducing unknowns and uncertainties that place greater responsibility on individual initiative and commitment to lifelong learning. Not only will individuals be required to make a series of career choices but they also must muster the personal strength and endurance to compete and learn new skills in multiple job roles and in different work sites. A life span of career development in the current organizational context suggests that fit will be accomplished through continuous learning that will test the individual's ability to make appropriate decisions while managing their own careers.

In the previous chapter, changes of organizational context were discussed to help counselors better understand the work world. We continue our discussion regarding why organizations have shifted responsibilities of career development to its employees. You may recall that the primary reason usually given for organizational changes is the global market: Market forces in the new millennium have been the main impetus behind the shift of risks from organizations to individuals in terms of managing employees' careers. Market forces can also determine levels of compensation, advancement, and the nature of work. Individual workers vary in their reaction to the loss of traditional organizational operational procedures that included work stability, advancement opportunities, training, and the possibility of a lifetime job. Some see this as an opportunity to become a free agent and take full control of their work role. Others are threatened by the uncertainties of the future and diminished availability of regular work. Yet others have reacted by being less committed to organizations. Because market forces are the primary determiner of who works and who doesn't, some employees have viewed the organization as being less important and have further reacted by expressing poor attitudes about work, delivering lowered performances, and displaying significantly less motivation about work per se (Leana, 2002).

Pressure on the worker to perform well has long been associated with how well one is compensated and how quickly one advances up the corporate ladder. In the new workforce, however, the predominate buzzwords are "pay-for-performance" and "pay-for-knowledge" (Drucker, 2002). Under these conditions, workers focus more on their career development and have less of a commitment to an organization. The performance-reward connection in the current work environment is not that different from past work environments. One could argue successfully that workers primarily have been rewarded for demand for their particular skills and their overall contribution to an organization, but many reached this point of competence through a partnership between worker and organization. Developing personnel for organizational purposes was a strong commitment in the traditional organization, but that commitment has shifted, leaving the individual responsible for staying abreast of new and different work requirements. It is not certain what effect the current position of self-development will have on an individual's career choice and development, but there is some evidence that more emphasis will be placed on the importance of skill development and continuous learning as predicators of career success (Feldman, 2002). Counselors, however, should be in a position to inform clients realistically about the nature of work in the 21st century and how their future may be determined greatly by their own initiative and actions.

Adults Who Want to Change Careers

There is a growing interest in research that addresses the sources that prompt some adults to change career paths. Career development theorists have suggested that there are some stable human characteristics, such as interests, personality traits, and values, that guide career development over the life span (Brown, 1996; Dawis, 1996; Holland, 1992). Yet some adults suggest that changes in these internal characteristics and traits have influenced them to consider a career change. Feldman (2002) among others believes that changes within people over time and person-in-environment interactions can persuade adults to change careers. Clearly, current organizational context and increasing environmental complexity has led many workers to reevaluate their career goals and make subsequent changes in career direction. Some opt for a boundaryless career that cuts across functions and workplaces and often requires multiple skills. As the name implies, a boundaryless career suggests that a worker is not bound to any organization or segment of an organization, but is prepared to use his or her expertise in different work sites and teams. Counselors should recognize that client concerns for career change can evolve from a number of internal and external factors or combinations of both, as briefly discussed in the following paragraphs.

Establishment Stage Transitions

One developmental perspective of career development is viewed as a multidimensional process that is both continuous and discontinuous. The career establishment years, age 25 to 44, are viewed by Super (1957) as a critical time when one struggles to form a unique identity in the work world. Individuals implement their self-concepts into careers that will provide the most efficient means of self-expression. Erikson (1950) suggests that during this period of time (early career), one is balancing intimacy and isolation while also attempting to maintain a unique identity in the process of developing relationships. What is being stressed here is that early career experiences provide individuals with opportunities to establish themselves in the workplace. There appears to be solid evidence that early encounters in the workplace will significantly influence the outcome of some of the most important socialization processes (Bauer & Green, 1994). Critical to the individual's career development are supervisor–worker and coworker relationships, especially in the current work environment that stresses teamwork. How individuals respond to authority figures may reflect a low concern for others or a more positive interdependent, cooperative orientation. The implications for counseling are simply that early work experiences may establish enduring positive and negative attitudes about work and relationships at work (Scandura, 2002). Thus, a negative experience in early career with a supervisor and/or peers may make it difficult to establish a working relationship with another supervisor and/or other coworkers. The obvious consequences of an individual who has poor relationships with other workers could be job loss or the desire to make a job change. Clearly, counselors are to evaluate the underlying reasons an individual wants to change careers and/or work sites.

During early career, individuals demonstrate their ability to function effectively on the job. For the beginning worker it can be an exciting time of entering the workforce. The novice, however, can be naïve about the complexities of the work environment and will expend considerable effort in learning how to function within its milieu. Although the pathway to a successful early career has pitfalls and stumbling blocks, there is a relatively well-defined direction. For example, building harmonious relationships in the work environment, becoming oriented to work rules and regulations, and demonstrating satisfactory performance are common concrete tasks of early career. The individual's personal reaction to advancement opportunities and acceptance of the values associated with organizational goals and peer affiliates are less tangible. Objective indexes (salary, merit pay, regulations, policies, etc.) and subjective indexes (meeting expectations, goal attainment, match between personal needs and organizational needs) are evaluative criteria the individual can use to determine a future direction in the organization or a change to another work environment.

In the following counseling session, Shanika, who has been with an organization for ten months, stated a need to withdraw and find another work environment as follows:

Counselor: Yes, we do have some information about the organization you asked about. But first I would like to know about the one you are leaving.

Shanika: As you know, it's a well-known organization, and I was excited about the opportunity of working there. But I don't seem to fit in.

Counselor: Could you be more specific?

SHANIKA: Well, the job assignment was not what I expected. The recruiter told me I would have a lot of responsibilities and interact with people at high levels, but in actuality there was little of either.

COUNSELOR: So it really wasn't the kind of job you expected?

SHANIKA: No, I was put off in a side office, and no one seemed to pay much attention to me. I did have a few assignments that seemed more like busywork than anything else.

COUNSELOR: Could this have been a part of the training program?

SHANIKA: Well, partly, but my supervisor hardly ever came around, and when he did, he seemed preoccupied.

In this case, reality shock and unused potential were frustrating experiences for Shanika. She had high expectations on the basis of what she was told about the job and had hoped to be challenged, but she experienced far less. There also appeared to be a communication gap between Shanika and her supervisor. The counselor recognized the potential effect of an early career encounter that could influence this client's future.

Reality shock and lack of appraisal and appropriate feedback while in early career are major causes of withdrawal from a work environment (Bauer & Green, 1994; Feldman, 2002; Wanous, 1980). In such cases, the career counselor must focus on the individual's perception of workplace situations, and more important, his or her level of sophistication in appraising them. Some individuals in early career will have unrealistically high expectations, whereas others may indeed find their jobs to be less than challenging and experience poor feedback from their supervisors.

On the other hand, work environments themselves can be very informative and educational; they provide a variety of learning experiences that are relevant to career development. For example, exposure to unknown jobs could expedite the desire to change career direction. Work experiences and skill development can provide a meaningful sense of direction in career development. Developing harmonious relationships, for example, means learning effective communication skills, interpersonal relationships, and general modes of behavior that are easily transferable to other work environments. Honing in on general and specific skills provides avenues that can lead to a change in career aspirations. Skill development itself can be a significant source for a desire to change careers in order to find a better fit. When there is congruence between interests, personality traits, and work skills fewer workers change jobs. In a study of beginning bank tellers, 45% of them left their job in the first four months; however, two-thirds of them took a similar job with another bank (Gottfredson & Holland, 1990). Looking for a better fit appeared to drive beginning bank tellers to search for another work environment rather than completely change careers (Ostroff, Shin, & Feinberg, 2002). The lesson here is that initial career choice and placement are not always right for everyone: Workers want to change careers or work sites for a variety of reasons. Counselors are to revisit the case for the individual that suggests each person is unique.

Career Anchors

Schien (1990), who followed the career patterns of alumni from the Massachusetts Institute of Technology (MIT), suggests that career anchors are formed during early career experiences and situations encountered in the workplace. He further suggests that career anchors develop over time and are not easily changed. Career anchors are considered to be core values, interests, and abilities that are developed during early career as follows: (1) technical functional competence—one's commitment to developing skills within a profession; (2) managerial competence—one's desire to assume responsibilities of leading others; (3) autonomy-independence—one's desire to work alone with little or no supervision; (4) security-stability—one's desire for stable employment; (5) service-dedication—a predisposition to help and assist others; (6) pure challenge—one's commitment to work that is continually challenging; (7) lifestyle integration—a need to have a balanced lifestyle; and (8) entrepreneurship—one's desire to work in environments that require creativity.

The concept of career anchors suggests that the formation of occupational self-concept is driven by talents and abilities developed in real work situations, motives and needs that are illuminated by work experiences, and attitudes and values learned from interactions in the workplace. What we have here are interactive influences from work situations that guide individual career choice in the establishment transitional process. Career anchors are thought to influence career choice and also to restrain it. Individuals therefore seek out work environments in which they have experienced success and avoid those that have the potential of resulting in failure. According to this theory, early work experiences and encounters are very influential in establishing a career direction (Scandura, 2002).

Midcareer and Maintenance Stage Transitions

Midcareer has been identified as the middle phase of an individual's work life, with its own set of tasks and social-emotional needs. In terms of Super's vocational developmental stages, midcareer may be thought of as the beginning of the maintenance stage, which is characterized by a continual adjustment process to improve working position and situation. Midcareer is also characterized by greater self-understanding and identification within the total system of a career field (Sterns & Subich, 2002; Tiedman & O'Hara, 1963). Feldman (1988) labeled the midcareer experience as "settling in," characterized by resolution of conflicts and conflicting demands within the work environment and in personal life. Midcareer is not necessarily age-related; individuals who make career changes may experience several midcareer stages.

The transitional process from early to midcareer has residual effects, as individuals establish themselves in a work environment. In early career, the major course of change is the socialization process, but in midcareer, changes are from diversified sources, such as new and different technology, product demand, market forces, and changes in the labor market. Developing a perspective of positive growth orientation in work environments and encouraging individuals to adapt to changes is a healthy attitude to promote. Also, finding a meaningful area of contribution is part of the process of establishing a career identity. Individuals must distinguish between real barriers (no growth, slow growth, and organizational decline) and perceived barriers (role confusion, poor career identity, nebulous perceptions of career success and direction) that affect their abilities to reach personal goals.

The following dialogue demonstrates some sources of career plateaus:

COUNSELOR: Tell me how you arrived at the decision to change jobs.

YING: Well, you know I've been with the company for twelve years, but I don't have the same enthusiasm for the job. I just can't put my finger on it.

COUNSELOR: Is the company doing well financially?

YING: That's a part of it; no promotion to speak of now.

COUNSELOR: Is this a company policy?

YING: No. John, a friend of mine, got one the other day. He's a lucky guy. He seems to always be in the right place at the right time.

COUNSELOR: Did you say that John was in your division?

YING: Yeah, he's always got something going. I don't understand how he does it. He went to this training program and six weeks later there he goes—up the ladder!

COUNSELOR: Tell me more about the training program.

YING: The company sponsored it. I could have gone, but I don't believe I like that kind of extra work. Besides, it would have interfered with the city golf tournament.

It appears from this conversation that Ying is not willing to be more assertive in his career development. The source of his plateau appears to be primarily a lack of a strong desire to advance. Perhaps Ying felt that he only needed to put in time for the next advancement. In midcareer, individuals may have difficulty balancing commitment to outside activities with intense competitiveness for promotions.

Mercedes, also in midcareer, tells how she discovered a career path in an organization:

MERCEDES: I kept looking in the want ads for a career in management after I finished college. I don't know how many times I was turned down. Finally, I took a temporary job in this company just to tide me over. As I kept looking at the want ads, I also started meeting more people in the company. I began to realize that this wasn't such a bad place after all. But what really did it for me was when I met Linda. When she told what she was doing in the company, I knew I wanted to know more about it. Well, you know the rest of the story. I found out about several jobs I never knew existed, and I landed one I liked very much. I have been here for 10 years now so I guess I'll stick around.

In Mercedes' case, she was exposed to occupations and career opportunities she had never known about before. A temporary job provided the means to discover unknown opportunities, and after a successful socialization period, she discovered a career path that appealed to her.

In a more preconceived manner, Al began his career in a high-tech organization with the goal of reaching the management level.

AL: I started out as a computer salesman. After a few years, the company offered me a retail store management job in the eastern part of the state. My wife didn't want to move. That was a tough decision; the kids didn't want to leave either. We spent eight years there, but made the best of it. Meanwhile, I took advantage of every career development opportunity through a variety of training programs. I got good feedback from my supervisor, which really helped. During that process, I became familiar with many aspects of the company. It finally paid off when I was made regional manager a few years ago. It worked out well. I live near a lake now and in a delightful part of the state.

COUNSELOR: What are your future plans?

AL: I like what I'm doing, but I have become more interested in civic organizations and church work.

COUNSELOR: Do you have as strong a commitment to the organization as you once had?

AL: Yes and no. It's different than before. My wife is happy that I devote more time to other things, but I still get excited about the future. I enjoy working with these young kids. They have good management skills, and I enjoy helping them.

As shown in this interview, midcareer is a time when individuals develop an increased awareness of the long-term dimensions of a career and shift their focus from the work world to personal roles. Attention is focused not only on career maintenance but also on life issues, such as parenting, joining civic organizations, and caring for aging parents. Priorities between work roles and personal roles fluctuate according to circumstances. A healthy attitude to promote is a balance of roles, as career and life changes become increasingly connected.

Midcareer is also a time when individuals become more aware of life stages in terms of time spans and begin to view career in terms of implementing future opportunities. Thus, loss of job is very disturbing to individuals at this point in their career development. The prospect of starting over to reach the point of establishment in career can be a significant problem for many individuals. Counseling may best be accomplished through a holistic approach that addresses both internal and external sources of stress and relationship concerns.

Late Career and Transition to Retirement

According to Fullerton (1999), the median age of the U.S. workforce in 2008 will reflect an increasing number of older workers. This growing proportion of older workers has many implications, including ones for counseling. Career issues for older workers include age-related changes in abilities and job performance, changing relationships, age discrimination, health concerns, family factors, and when and if to retire. *Bridge employment* is the term used to describe part-time employment in which the individual typically continues in the same work environment but with reduced responsibilities and time commitment. This arrangement allows workers to keep their career identity until they fully retire.

In late career, the major focus of an individual's life is on activities outside the organization. The individual builds outside interests and begins a gradual detachment from the organization. Activities within the organization may also shift from a power role to a minor role. Super refers to this stage as decline, characterized by preretirement considerations. Within the work environment, the individual is preparing to "let go" of responsibilities and pass them on to others. One major adjustment during late career is learning to accept a reduced work role and changing one's focus away from a highly involved work identity.

Emotional support in late career comes primarily from peers and particularly from old acquaintances. Moving away from the stress and turmoil associated with younger workers who are striving to move upward, late-career employees identify with peers and rekindle closer attachments to spouses. Having resolved many of the uncertainties of midcareer, they tend to focus on broader issues, such as the future of their profession or work. Some will retire and seek a job to supplement their income that also allows them to spend more time doing family activities (Drucker, 2002).

Throughout this book, career development has been presented as a continuous and discontinuous process over the life span. Career development is influenced by many variables: Some are externally generated (e.g., economic crisis and job loss), others are internally generated (e.g., perceptions of retirement), but all are integrated into the career development process. Nevertheless, retirement counseling is often overlooked as part of career development and as a career counseling objective. As we prepare to meet the challenges of individuals in the 21st century, demographic studies suggest that retirement counseling will be a major component in the practice of career development (Drucker, 2002; U.S. Bureau of Census, 2000a).

To meet this increasing need, some workplaces have developed preretirement programs that offer assistance in projecting pensions and other future benefits when the individual reaches retirement age. This type of preretirement program has often been referred to as a "probable inflation" model from which the individual can project his or her financial status at retirement. Other topics often addressed in organizational preretirement programs are optional retirement plans (such as partial retirement, which allows the individual to work part time), time management, financial planning, leisure alternatives, and marital and social relationships (Beehr & Bowling, 2002; Feldman, 1988).

Some organizations also offer planning services to individuals near retirement age. There are two types: limited and comprehensive. Limited retirement programs typically provide guidance in pension planning, social security and medicare information, health insurance options, and information on retirement benefits at various ages of retirement. Subjects and topics included in comprehensive programs commonly include those covered in the limited programs plus the following: maintaining good health, marital/emotional aspects of retirement, leisure activities, relocation advantages and disadvantages, legal concerns (wills, estate planning, inheritance laws), family relations, employment possibilities, and lifestyle change.

Interacting Influences

Throughout this text a holistic approach to career counseling has been emphasized. In the adult world of career transitions, the totality of interacting influences of personal and career concerns has significant relevance to career development. This position is especially meaningful if one accepts the proposition that an individual's career transitions over the life span are influenced by both internal and external factors. Earlier in this chapter, external factors of organizational context, downsizing, outsourcing, and economic downturns that lead to job loss and job insecurity were emphasized. There are, however, significant concerns that evolve from within the individual as suggested in Chapter 4, Table 4.1, including interrelated problems that overlap domains. Individual uniqueness therefore is influenced by interacting influences involving each individual's unique traits such as ability, culture, interests, personality, values, and person-in-environment experiences. Hence, career development is an ongoing process during which individuals develop new and different perspectives of life and subsequent short- and long-range goals.

Career development and uniqueness includes career maturity fostered through developmental tasks and stages (Super, 1957), experiences and learning in stages of psychosocial development as described by Erikson (1963), and the ability to make consistent generalizations and deal with abstractions through stages of cognitive development (Piaget, 1929). It is therefore likely that individuals will develop new interests, build new and different sets of skills, and explore different lifestyle options. As Feldman (2002) puts it, "The aging process itself creates incentives for individuals to modify their career interests, values, and skills across the life space" (p. 14). The point here is that adults make career transitions for a variety of reasons including ones that are stimulated by the maturation process. Thus, a career change in midcareer, for instance, may simply be an expression of a different set of interests and values.

The sources of a career change also could be influenced by mental disorders. Potential disruptions of cognitive clarity associated with mental health concerns could interfere with problem solving and the ability to appropriately evaluate experiences in one's ecological system, including the work role. Counselors play a vital role in these instances by helping clients determine if their reasoning and decision making is rational and realistic. A paranoid client, for example, may have difficulty with interpersonal relationships. An antisocial client may have difficulty in sustaining productive work, whereas a borderline client's impulsive behavior may interfere with work role functioning. These examples of interacting influences present significant challenges of potential concerns inextricably involved in career transitions.

A holistic approach to counseling suggests that the connection of presenting concerns that clients bring to counseling can be deeply rooted. They involve the uniqueness of an individual's personal development, such as the basis from which one interprets events, and situations in environment and numerous external influences, such as organizational context. This is not a simplistic matter. A case in point is a client whose feeling of well-being has been drastically disrupted. The interacting influences in this case may require extensive evaluation in order to determine its roots. More than likely, concerns overlap domains and will require interventions that address sets of concerns simultaneously. (See Box 19-1.)

In sum, it is essential that clients have the ability to rationally evaluate events and conditions in work environments that are changing, and subsequently, deal appropriately with career concerns. For example, an individual who has difficulty with processing information may have difficulty in appropriately conceptualizing current situations and future plans. Counseling objectives therefore must address both career and personal concerns. Individuals may need all the personal strength they can muster to address a crisis that threatens their livelihood. Counselors not only offer support but also assistance in developing rational and realistic plans and actions.

Volatile Behavior in the Workplace

An individual's history of volatile behavior may be exacerbated by job loss. In recent years, headlines in newspapers and top stories on newscasts have featured incidents of workplace violence. For instance, the following incidents have been compiled by Muchinsky (2003) and Aamodt (1999):

Box 19-1	Major Themes in Human Development

Human development research by a number of academic disciplines suggests that it is multidimensional as well as comprehensive in nature and scope (Kail & Cavanaugh, 2004). Career counselors should recognize that an abundance of published material suggests that human development is influenced by a number of factors and dimensions over the life span. In essence, human development is a unique process. Once again we stress that career counselors view each client as a unique person.

Following are some general themes of human development, adapted from Sigelman and Rider (2003):

1. We are whole persons throughout the life span. Physical, cognitive, personal, and social development intermesh throughout the life span, and each individual's development has a distinctive and coherent quality.

2. Development proceeds in multiple directions. Individuals experience significant changes in development over their life spans, but these are viewed as gains and losses, rather than by the old notion of progression that consisted of growth and improvement up to adulthood, stability into middle age, and decline in old age. Within this framework of development, for every gain there is a loss. For example, the amount of time spent on becoming an expert in a field means a loss of opportunity to develop other areas of specialization.

3. There is both continuity and discontinuity in development. The point here is that predicting the character of an adult from knowledge of the child is very risky. Continuity can continue from early childhood, but discontinuity can be fostered by events in one's environment, such as child abuse, inferior schools, or parental neglect.

4. There is much plasticity in human development. People can be adaptable throughout their life spans. Potentially harmful early experiences need not have a permanent effect on one's development.

5. Nature and nurture truly interact in development. There are multiple causal forces in human development; both nature and nurture interact in the change process. One or the other may be more influential in certain aspects of human development, but there are usually ongoing influences from both.

6. We are all individuals, becoming even more diverse with age. We do share common experiences with others, but we are indeed individuals and we accumulate our own unique histories of life experiences.

7. We develop in a cultural and historical context. We must recognize that human development takes place in different cultures, social classes, and racial and ethnic groups. Cultural variations in development should include contextual influences.

8. We are active in our own development. We create our own environment and influence those around us, but all participants are influenced in a reciprocal way.

9. Development is best viewed as a lifelong process. The linkages between early and late development are important connections to study. But it is also valuable to view behavior during each phase of life because development is a process. Understanding where we started from and where we are heading leads to an understanding of the processes involved.

10. Development is best viewed from multiple perspectives. Many disciplines have contributed to the understanding of human development. In this tradition, we must recognize that multiple theories are often integrated when we explain human development.

- In Tampa, a Florida man shot three men who were his supervisors while they were eating lunch. He then wounded two other workers before committing suicide.
- After a female coworker turned down his romantic advances, a Sunnyvale, California, man shot and killed seven people in an office.
- After a car mechanic was fired, he returned to his workplace and fired into a crowd of workers, killing two and wounding another.
- A Wendy's employee in Tulsa, Oklahoma, fired 12 shots from a .38-caliber handgun, wounding six people, including his supervisor. His boss had asked him to start work earlier.
- Four coworkers in the California Department of Transportation were killed by a fired former employee.
- In Houston, a supervisor was shot when he threatened to fire an employee.

These incidents point out workplace violence that centers around disgruntled employees and often involves individuals who have lost their jobs. Psychology of workplace violence is usually conceptualized as aggressive acts that are frequently retaliatory responses of individuals who see themselves as victims of injustice in the workplace. Such individuals conclude that they have been betrayed by organizations that have also violated the principles of procedural justice (Johnson & Indvik, 1994). In short, according to Aamodt (1999), violence against an employee or supervisor is considered to be an act of anger or vengeance.

The small amount of research on this topic has focused on studies of aggression and profiles of those who commit violence; however, violence in the workplace is indeed a complex phenomenon that contains many psychological antecedents. For example, many of the perpetrators of workplace violence have been known to have experienced interpersonal conflict and often have maladaptive personalities (Muchinsky, 2003). Moreover, aggression, especially in this context, should be conceptualized as a product of both individual and situational factors. For instance, such situational factors as noise, crowded conditions, heat, and alcohol usage can increase the likelihood of aggression (Pernanen, 1991). Clearly, the sources of inappropriate thinking and a lack of emotional control could be driving forces behind these volatile acts. A holistic counseling approach suggests that counselors be prepared to: (1) offer assistance to supervisors and line workers in recognizing symptoms of emotional, cognitive, and behavioral problems; (2) provide counseling services for career concerns as well as for problems that are considered personal, including those in the affective and cognitive-behavioral domains; and (3) offer assistance in developing good human relations, sensitivity training, and interpersonal skills to all employees and supervisors.

Implications for Career Counseling

The stages of adult career development provide guidelines for career guidance needs and program development. The need to assist individuals in career choice is apparent; however, the processes involved in organizational choice have not been clearly delineated by the counseling profession or by organizations. Thus, career counselors should encourage clients to carefully evaluate organizations on the basis of individual needs and realistic expectations. Assisting clients to learn about organizational life and the realities of the work world are important components of counseling.

The stages of entry in early career are highlighted by the socialization processes that take place in each work environment. The individual evaluates self-in-situation by observing the many facets of environmental working conditions, supervisor–worker relations, opportunities for advancement, and congruence with peer affiliates. During the socialization process, the individual may need support in developing a sense of direction in a workplace's social milieu, where he or she is also being observed and evaluated. Early career encounters are to be scrutinized carefully to determine their long-term effects. Helping individuals assess the complexities associated with multiple life roles are counseling goals of this stage. For those who decide to withdraw and try again in a different workplace, the decision process must include a careful analysis of the reasons for the desired change.

Counselors are to focus on the effects of job loss and/or job insecurity. Support and keying on the client's feelings of well-being are important counseling objectives. Counselors are encouraged to use a holistic counseling approach that integrates personal and career concerns. Loss of income can cause numerous problems including difficulty in maintaining relationships. Uncertainties in the 21st century work world suggests that clients may make several career changes and find jobs in new and different work environments. Adults should be encouraged to develop their skills through available learning and training programs, and to adopt a learning-for-living philosophy.

Learning to deal with competition is one of the major social-emotional needs of middle career, when individuals may need to reevaluate their career direction. As an individual integrates skills and becomes aware of potential career paths, help in establishing a set of new goals is a relevant counseling objective. The hazards associated with obsolescence and "career plateaus," downsizing, and outsourcing suggest that counseling programs encourage continuing education and training.

In late career, the individual is preparing to "phase out" or "let go" of major work responsibilities. Super (1990) used the term *decline* to indicate that a minor work role is imminent. Many people are reluctant to accept the fact that their work lives are almost over. Some may opt for a second career whereas others may choose a bridge employment arrangement that retains career identity but is also considered part-time employment with less responsibility. For others, this stage has been eagerly anticipated as a time of freedom from work and obligations. Counseling strategies that help all workers prepare for this phasing out should include preretirement and retirement programs. More specifically, career programs should be designed to help individuals assess future needs.

Interventions for Adults in Career Transition

Career counseling programs for adults in career transition have many elements in common with programs designed for initial career choice. However, there are enough different and distinct factors involved in career transition to merit the development of specific programs for adults considering career change. Major considerations are the individual adult experiences associated with work, leisure, family, and individualized lifestyle. Life's experiences provide both the counselor and the individual with a rich source of information from which to launch a career exploration. Identifying developed skills, interests, work experiences, and reformulated goals are examples of program strategies for the adult in career transition.

The intermeshing of physical, cognitive, personal, and social development that gives each period of the life span a distinctive quality should make us more aware of considering the overwhelming possibilities of an individual adult's development. Perhaps we have been guilty of attempting to oversimplify development into categories that appeared to be more manageable.

The concept of multiple directions of development, with its gains and losses, challenges the older view of development as consisting of continuous growth and improvement into adulthood, stability, and decline. We must recognize that we give up something in almost every step we take toward specialization. One suspects that many adults do not view choices in this manner. As humans, we have a remarkable capacity to change in response to experience. This translates into providing opportunities for growth even though an individual's past record is dismal.

The cultural and historical context in which one develops has enormous implications for counseling adults. This multicultural developmental position recognizes the centrality and primary importance of culture as an internalized subjective process that must be included in counseling programs developed for different ethnic groups.

There has been a greater recognition of individual agency in career development. We do indeed have an active role in our own development, and drawing adults' attention to this position will hopefully lead to more positive, assertive action. Finally, viewing development as a lifelong process reinforces the current importance placed on retraining and lifelong learning.

A counseling program for adults in career transition is outlined in Table 19-1. This program consists of seven intervention components referred to as strategies. Each intervention strategy has suggested technique options and specific tasks. The technique options suggested do not rule out other methods of accomplishing the specific tasks. In many instances, reference will be made to other chapters in this text. Following are brief explanations of each intervention component.

Experience Identification

Valuable assets often overlooked in career counseling are work and life experiences. One goal of this component is to evaluate past experiences carefully in relation to potential use in career selection. Typically, the adult overlooks the value of developed skills or only casually considers them in career exploration. This component is designed to provide the structure from which counselor and counselee can effectively evaluate an individual's background of experiences and relate them to interests, work requirements, and other variables associated with occupations.

The technique options suggested for this intervention strategy provide the counselor with alternatives to meet individual needs. In most instances, combinations of suggested options can be used. For example, after an individual writes an autobiography, the counselor can follow with an interview or work experience analysis or both. In other instances, only one of the options might be needed. This decision is often based on time availability and the educational level of the client.

The first technique option is the interview. An interview's primary purpose in this context is to assist the client in evaluating work and leisure experiences, training, and education in relation to potential occupational choices. In a holistic approach to counseling, personal and career concerns are viewed as inseparable, as discussed in Chapter 4. The suggestion here is to be sensitive to any work/family conflicts, faulty beliefs, and affective concerns. The interview should focus on (1) specific work experiences, (2) specific educational/training experiences, (3) specific leisure experiences and preferences, (4) specific likes and dislikes of former jobs, and (5) special recognitions. In general, the interview should provide the basis from which the next step in the counseling program is determined. (See Chapter 5.)

The format for the autobiography can be either structured or unstructured. In the latter approach, the individual is instructed to write an autobiography without being given any specific guidelines. In the structured approach, the individual may be instructed to follow an outline or answer specific questions or both. The structured approach has obvious advantages for our purposes in that we are attempting to identify and evaluate specific information.

An autobiographical sketch can be used to identify relevant information. First, the individual is instructed to describe a significant accomplishment, such as starring in a dramatic production, being a leader in a civic group, or teaching photography. Descriptions of the accomplishment are analyzed to determine the use of functional, adaptive, and technical skills. Each autobiographical sentence is analyzed and later compiled and related to Holland's six modal personal styles. The following sentence, for example, is taken from a description of teaching photography and is analyzed for functional, adaptive, and technical skills:

"I started each class by demonstrating the proper use of a number of different cameras."

Functional	**Adaptive**	**Technical**
teaching	leadership	knowledge of cameras
communication	articulate	
	orderly	

Skills that are easily identifiable are those that are explicitly stated, whereas other skills are only implied, such as those needed to accomplish the task. In this case, teaching, communication, and camera knowledge are fairly explicit, whereas being articulate, orderly, and showing leadership are only implied.

The next option, background information, requires that the individual fill out a specified form. The information requested includes demographic data; marital status and family size; a list of jobs held and duties, education, and training completed; armed services experiences; honors and awards; leisure preferences; hobbies; and other related information. A variety of approaches may be used to identify satisfaction and dissatisfaction variables associated with work and other experiences. One technique is to ask the individual to rank-order or to list likes and dislikes of each past job held. Another option is to provide spaces for free response reactions to work and other experiences.

Following the example of Bolles (1993), a work and leisure experience analysis form was designed (Figures 19-1 and 19-2), on which the individual lists specific work (Part I) and leisure experiences (Part II). In addition, the individual indicates likes and dislikes of the experiences listed. The objective is to identify tasks and experiences that may be considered in future career choices.

A review of the tasks for this intervention component suggests that the major

Table 19-1	Intervention Counseling Program for Adults in Career Transition	

Strategy component	Technique option	Specific tasks
I. Experience identification	1. Interview 2. Autobiography 3. Background information format and guide 4. Work- and leisure-experience analysis	1. Identify and evaluate previous work experience 2. Identify and evaluate life experiences 3. Identify desired work tasks and leisure experiences 4. Assess familial relationships 5. Identify reasons for job change 6. Identify career satisfaction variables 7. Identify factors that contributed to job changes 8. Identify reasons for current interest in career change
II. Interest identification	1. Interest inventories	1. Identify and evaluate occupational interests 2. Identify specific interest patterns 3. Relate interest to past experience 4. Compare interest with identified skills 5. Relate interest to potential occupational requirements 6. Relate interests to avocational needs
III. Skills identification	1. Self-analysis of developed skills 2. Self-estimates of developed skills 3. Standardized measures of developed skills	1. Identify and evaluate developed skills from previous work tasks 2. Identify and evaluate developed skills from leisure learning experiences 3. Identify and evaluate developed skills from formal learning experiences 4. Identify and evaluate developed functional, technical, and adaptive skills
IV. Value and needs clarification	1. Value and needs assessment through standardized inventories 2. Values clarification exercises	1. Clarify values in relation to life and work 2. Determine level and order of needs in relation to life and work 3. Identify satisfaction and dissatisfaction variables associated with work 4. Identify satisfaction and dissatisfaction 5. Identify expectations of future work and lifestyle 6. Identify desirable work environments, organizations, and peer affiliates 7. Realistically assess potential future achievements 8. Assess potential movement within current work environment 9. Identify work roles and leisure roles and how they interrelate with lifestyle 10. Relate values to factors that contribute to obsolescence 11. Identify personal factors associated with career decision

Table 19-1	(continued)	

Strategy component	Technique option	Specific tasks
V. Education/ training planning	1. Published materials 2. Locally compiled information resources 3. Computerized system 4. Internet	1. Identify sources of educational/training information 2. Identify continuing education programs 3. Identify admission requirements to educational/training programs 4. Investigate potential credit for past work experience and previously completed training programs 5. Evaluate accessibility and feasibility of educational/training programs 6. Identify and assess financial assistance and other personal assistance programs 7. Relate identified skills to educational/training programs for further development
VI. Occupational planning	1. Published printed materials 2. Internet 3. Computer information systems 4. Visit files	1. Identify sources of occupational information 2. Identify and assess occupational opportunities 3. Relate identified skills and work experience to specific occupational requirements 4. Evaluate occupations from a need-fulfilling potential 5. Relate identified goals to occupational choice 6. Relate family needs to occupational benefits 7. Identify educational/training needs for specific occupations
VII. Toward a life learning plan	1. Decision-making exercises 2. Life-planning exercises 3. Making the transition to self-development	1. Learn decision-making techniques 2. Clarify short-term and long-term goals 3. Identify original and reformulated career goals 4. Contrast differences between original and reformulated goals 5. Identify alternative goals 6. Clarify goals in relation to family expectations 7. Develop a flexibility plan for life learning 8. Develop life-planning skills 9. Identify lifestyle preferences 10. Identify attitude and beliefs of a self-directed approach

objective is to identify specific desired work tasks, leisure experiences, family/conflicts, lifestyle, and potential reasons for job change. Using this information, the counselor and client should be able to identify a partial list of career satisfaction variables. The tentative conclusions and outcomes of this component will usually provide information for the skills identification and development component, but will also be integrated into other components of the program.

Part I

Work experience
Bank Teller

General duties
Customer
accounts
Transactions

Specific tasks
O over number if liked
X over number if not liked

①Record + deposit
receipts
②Payout Withdrawals
✗Cash checks
✗Record transactions
✗Exchange Money

Figure 19-1   Work experience analysis form

Part II

Leisure experience
PTA Secretary

Specific tasks
O over number if liked
X over number if not liked

①Record Minutes
✗Call roll
③Read minutes

Figure 19-2   Leisure experience analysis form

Interest Identification

Career counseling and interest identification have had a close association in their respective developments. Measured interests have been used primarily in predicting job satisfaction in career counseling programs. In our efforts to assist the adult in career transition, we must also be concerned with interests and their relationship to potential occupational choices. Conceptually, it is thought that interest identification can broaden and stimulate adults' exploratory career options.

Adult clients should be in a relatively good position to identify individual interests, primarily from past experiences. Some are able, however, to identify uninteresting tasks and jobs but may not focus on positive interests. For these individuals, interest identification is essential; therefore, the suggested technique option for this component consists of interest inventories that cover a wide range of interests. As with the use of all assessment inventories, careful consideration should be given to the selection of the inventory. Briefly, the counselor should assess the counselee's educational level, expectations of the future, reading level, educational and training potentials, cultural background, and sexual orientation, among other factors. A number of inventories are also available for nonreaders. A list of inventories is provided in Chapter 6.

The task for Intervention Component II is to identify interest clusters or patterns as well as specific interest indicators. A major task is to relate identified interests to occupational variables and education/training opportunities in the following components to ensure that all components are well integrated.

Skills Identification and Development

Skills identification and particularly the development of new skills have received increasing attention in the workplace. We begin by focusing on three methods that can be used to identify each client's skills. The first method focuses on identifying skills developed from previous experiences in work, hobbies, social activities, community volunteer work, and other leisure experiences. (See examples of skills in Figures 19-3 and 19-4.) The rationale for this objective is that people, in general, fail to recognize developed skills and also do not know how to relate them to occupational requirements.

Bolles (1993) has long suggested that functional/transferable skills can best be identified by using a "quick job-hunting map." Holland provided a method to identify developed skills through self-estimates of ability. These methods along with career-related computerized systems concentrate on self-estimates of developed skills. The first technique option, self-analysis of developed skills, can be accomplished through the work and leisure experience analysis forms used in Intervention Component I. For example, the compiled specific tasks on this form provide sources for identifying developed skills. Following are some examples of this process.

Three steps are necessary to identify skills from the work and leisure analysis form: (1) list specific work tasks; (2) identify functional, adaptive, and technical skills for each work task; and (3) relate each functional, adaptive, and technical skill to one or more of Holland's six modal personal styles. For those skills that are difficult to identify using Holland's six modal personal styles, *The Occupations Finder* (Holland, 1987c) will help.

Skills used in tasks

a. Functional
1. Clerical
2. Communication
3. Editing
4. Organizational

b. Adaptive
1. Articulate
2. Leadership
3. Diplomatic
4. Courteous

c. Technical
1. Accounting
2. Knowledge of foreign money exchange

Figure 19-3 **Skills identification form**

Classification:
Conventional
1. Clerical
2. Bookkeeping
3. Teller

Rate yourself as:

Good   Average   Poor

(Clerical — Average ✓)
(Bookkeeping — Good ✓)
(Teller — Good ✓)

Figure 19-4 **Lifestyle identification form**

The second technique option, self-estimates of developed skills, can be accomplished by having the individual rate each functional, adaptive, and technical skill as good, average, or poor as illustrated in the previous example. These rankings provide self-estimates of skills within Holland's (1992) modal personal styles and corresponding work environments model.

A more traditional method of evaluating skills is through standardized testing, which is our third technique option. A variety of aptitude tests on the market today provide methods of evaluating skills based on normative data. Several aptitude tests were identified in Chapter 6.

The importance of specific skills identification is to encourage the client to consider skills developed from a variety of experiences as important factors in career exploration. By requiring that the individual identify skills in adaptive, functional, and technical groups, a more precise relationship to occupational requirements is understood, thus promoting a more realistic evaluation for future goals. This intervention strategy stresses the identification of skills from the individual's total lifestyle experiences.

Value and Needs Clarification

The emphasis thus far has underscored a holistic approach to counseling adults. This strategy correspondingly includes the adult's total lifestyle. Thus, this intervention component focuses on the individual adult's values and needs. More specifically, individualized values and needs are considered in relation to multiple life roles of work, leisure, and family. Each value and need must be considered in relation to the others. This approach recognizes that values are intertwined and interrelated.

The first technique option assesses values and needs through standardized inventories. Several inventories on the market today can be used for this purpose. Most inventories provide complete instructions for interpretation and counseling use. (See Chapter 6 for available inventories.)

Values clarification exercises are suggested as a second technique option. Values clarification may be accomplished in groups as well as in individual counseling programs. It is important to select strategies that emphasize skills that assist individuals in identifying and developing their value systems. See the *Life Values Inventory* (Crace & Brown, 1996) for suggestions of value clarification strategies.

The lifestyle component is indeed a broad, rather all-encompassing concept of career counseling. In this context, we consider the individual's entire system of values and needs associated with lifestyle. Individually developed values and needs may be thought of as an integrated system that determines satisfaction with life. We may dichotomize value systems for clarification, but eventually we must address the entire system of values. Our goal is to communicate to the adult in career transition that life is indeed multifaceted and that satisfactory solutions cannot be oversimplified. We must consider who we are, where we have been, and that our futures are relatively unpredictable.

Education and Training

With a major emphasis on lifelong learning it is safe to assume that education/training information is a high priority among adults in career transition. This intervention is designed to assist adults in identifying sources of educational/training information and making the most effective use of those sources. A greater variety of continuing education programs, which are discussed in Chapter 8, suggests that the working adult is in a much better position to improve his or her occupational skills. Exposure to educational/training opportunities should enhance the opportunities and options in career decision making.

This intervention strategy has four technique options. As with most intervention strategies, and particularly with this one, using all or combinations of options is recommended. The first option suggests using published materials. An important resource for working adults is locally compiled information, suggested as the second technique option. Educational/training programs within reasonable commuting distances and/or instructional programs on Internet Web sites provide opportunities for training while maintaining occupational and family obligations.

Counselors should encourage clients to evaluate any in-house training programs at their work site that may be available. On-site programs usually include on-the-job and job rotation training. Off-site programs include lectures, audiovisual material, computer-based training with the use of CD-ROM technology, Web-based training, simulation, and role playing (Muchinsky, 2003).

The third technique option for this intervention component is computerized career information systems. A number of interactive and information-oriented computer-assisted guidance programs are available today (as discussed in Chapter 8). Generally, three types of educational/training information files are available by computer: files containing programs for all states, files containing program information on a regional basis within states, and files of programs available nationally. Individual needs may dictate the need for localized programs.

The Internet, a fourth option, has the potential of providing relevant educational/training information files from local as well as state, national, and international sources. Read Chapters 8 and 9 carefully to determine the most appropriate use of the Internet.

The specific tasks for this component encourage a systematic approach to using educational/training information. Exposure to educational/training opportunities should encourage many adults to consider methods of upgrading their skills for higher level job opportunities. Second, many adults will be encouraged to consider educational/training programs to stay abreast with changing times. Possible educational credit from past work experiences should also provide the incentive for some clients to enter continuing educational/training programs. Finally, each client should be encouraged to adopt a lifelong learning commitment.

Occupational Planning

Occupational planning and the previously discussed educational/training component have many commonalities. Both focus on providing information to assist the adult in making the most effective use of occupational information. In fact, these two components are so closely related that they are often accessed at the same time. Consequently, resources often combine educational/training requirements with occupational information.

Three technique options for this component are using published materials, computer-assisted programs, and the Internet. Computer-assisted programs and the use of the Internet for career development are discussed in Chapter 8. Most computer-assisted programs contain national occupational information files, but many provide occupational information on a local or regional basis within states. International occupational information can be located on the Internet. Many state and federal agencies provide labor forecasts and occupational information that should be incorporated into this intervention strategy.

The fourth technique option, visit files, can be an important segment for delivering relevant occupational information. A visit file provides the names of individuals or organizations who agree to visits and interviews by people interested in obtaining firsthand information about certain occupations. This file is usually compiled locally through personal contacts, and in some cases may be available through purchased programs. Many computer-assisted programs that provide localized and regional data contain visit files.

The tasks for this component suggest that occupational information is more than just information about a job. For example, personal goal satisfaction, family/financial needs, and use of identified skills are just some of the variables to consider when accessing occupational information. Of major importance are the potential need-fulfilling opportunities available in each occupation under consideration. Finally, counselors are to help clients keep occupational information in perspective. Clients need to consider only as many options and choices as they can appropriately process to avoid information overload and subsequent indecision.

Toward a Life Learning Plan

This component assists in the development of a life learning plan that is self-directed. Decision-making techniques and life-planning exercises provide two methods of developing effective planning. The rationale for life learning is based on a continuing need to develop planning strategies to (1) meet technological changes, (2) stay abreast of the information explosion, (3) upgrade skills, and (4) reduce the chances of becoming obsolete. In addition, and perhaps more important, changing individual needs and reformulated goals also create a demand for effective planning. The techniques and skills developed in this component enhance decision-making techniques for meeting both occupational changes and changing individual needs associated with work, leisure, and lifestyle. Furthermore, these skills not only provide methods for formulating current plans but also encourage the development of strategies for long-range goals.

The first technique option, decision-making exercises, helps individuals effectively develop plans and decide on future options. The rationale here is that more adults are to assume a self-directed approach for career development. Learning to effectively process information to clarify future work requirements and identify relevant educational/training options should be fostered. Several examples of decision-making strategies are discussed in Chapter 3.

The second technique option promotes life-planning strategies. The specific task of establishing alternative plans for the future should be emphasized in this component. Skills identification and personal lifestyle preferences are integrated to provide the basis for alternative plans to meet future goals. Clarifying differences between original goals and reformulated goals is a counseling objective of this intervention; effective life-planning strategies help individuals to develop options and make effective decisions.

The third technique option suggests that adults can be greatly assisted by helping them make the transition to a self-development approach to career development. By identifying attitudes and beliefs that accompany a self-development mind-set, the counselor introduces rich sources of information that can be used in group as well as in individual counseling sessions. Clients must be reminded that they must take full responsibility for their career development, which can start with their willingness to learn new work requirements and relational skills.

Lifelong learning is an ongoing process that should be viewed as cyclic; individual changes and external conditions may require the individual to recycle through one or more counseling intervention strategies. A life learning plan therefore should be viewed as continuous, but with intermittent pauses. The important message is that the skills learned through these options will provide effective methods of finding and using resource information, clarifying individual needs, making decisions, and planning for the future.

Summary

1. Workers who will prosper in the 21st century are those who are intelligent enough to learn new skills. A lifelong learning commitment will be necessary for most workers.

2. The major causes for career erosion in traditional organizations are changing organizational context. Gone are the promises of traditional organization, including stable employment.

3. Psychological effects of unemployment are very pervasive and can be primary sources of mental health problems, relationship concerns, and a diminished sense of well-being. Counselors are to use an integrated approach to address multiple client concerns.

4. Career management has shifted from work organization to worker. Organizations are less willing to assume responsibility for employee's career development.

5. Career planning in the future will involve circular as well as linear moves. Workers can expect to work in multiple sites and be involved in new and different work requirements.

6. In the workforce, pay-for-performance and pay-for knowledge will predominate. Those workers who have the knowledge to perform well will more than likely get the best jobs.

7. Client concerns for career change can involve both internal and external factors. Counselors are to assume a holistic counseling approach when addressing adult career concerns.

8. Career counseling programs for adults in career transition have many elements in common with programs designed for initial career choice. There are enough different and distinct factors, however, to merit the development of specific programs for adults considering career change. Counseling intervention components that meet specific needs of adults include (a) experience identification, (b) interest identification, (c) skills identification, (d) values and needs clarification, (e) educational/training planning, (f) occupational planning, and (g) a life learning plan.

Supplementary Learning Exercises

1. Develop a list of the 10 most dominant needs in your life at the present time. Share these with a colleague and project how these needs may change over your life span. Identify major sources of dissatisfaction and how these factors can cause you to become an unfulfilled individual.

2. What are your suggestions for counseling programs that would meaningfully interpret the realities of working? Obtain your suggestions by interviewing workers and by observing working climates.

3. Develop an outline for writing a work autobiography. Using the outline, write your own work autobiography.

4. Using the experience-identification component strategy, develop a counseling program to accomplish two or more specific tasks.

5. Compile a list of your own skills developed through previous work, leisure, and learning experiences. Relate these skills to specific kinds of occupations. Why is skills identification important for adults in career transition?

6. Develop a set of counseling strategies to clarify values and needs associated with expectations of future work and lifestyle. Why is it important for the adult in career transition to clarify values and needs?

7. List at least four potential sources of work/family conflicts. Describe how you would address them in counseling.

8. Identify and list your personal goals and relate these to your career choice. Why is it important for adults to identify personal goals for career exploration?

9. How would you address the problems associated with an individual who has lost his or her job and is also depressed?

10. Explain how you would encourage a client to adopt a lifelong learning commitment? Outline the reasons you would provide.

For More Information

Feldman, C. C. *Work careers: A developmental perspective.* San Francisco: Jossey-Bass.

Feller, R., & Walz, G. (Eds.). (1996). *Career transitions in turbulent times.* Greensboro: ERIC Counseling and Student Services, University of North Carolina.

Hansen, L. S. (1997). *Integrative life planning: Critical tasks for career development and changing life patterns.* San Francisco: Jossey-Bass.

Muchinsky, P. M. (2003). *Psychology applied to work* (6th ed.). Belmont, CA: Wadsworth/Thomson Learning.

Niles, S. G. (Ed.). (2002). *Adult career development* (3rd ed.). Tulsa, OK: National Career Development Association.

Schlossberg, N. K. (1986). *Counseling adults in transition, linking practice with theory.* New York: Springer.

Suggested InfoTrac College Edition Topics

Adult development

Adult and self-development

Adult transitions

Boundaryless careers

Career anchors

Career transitions

Downsizing

Job loss

Knowledge workers

Outsourcing

Violence and the workplace

A Note Regarding Appendixes E, F, and G:

As this book went to the printer, the U.S. Department of Education Office of Vocational and Adult Education released new National Career Development Guidelines outlined at http://www.acrnetwork.org/ncdg.htm

Appendix A

Table of Basic Assumptions, Key Terms, and Outcomes

Theories	Basic Assumptions	Key Terms	Outcomes
Trait-Oriented Theories			
Trait-and-Factor	Individuals have unique patterns of ability or traits that can be objectively measured and correlated with requirements of occupations.	*Traits* primarily refer to abilities and interests. Parson's three-step model included studying the individual, surveying occupations, and matching the individual with an occupation.	The primary goal of using assessment data was to predict job satisfaction and success. Contemporary practices stress the relationships between human factors and work environments. Test data is used to observe the similarity between client and current workers in a career field.
Person-Environment-Correspondence Counseling	Individuals bring requirements to a work environment, and the work environment makes its requirements of individuals. To survive, individuals and work environments must achieve some degree of congruence.	*Personality structure* is a stable characteristic made up of abilities and values. *Ability dimensions* indicate levels of work skills. *Values* are considered as work needs. *Satisfactoriness* refers to clients who are more achievement oriented. *Satisfaction* refers to more self-fulfilled oriented clients. *Work adjustment* refers to a worker's attempt to improve fit in a work environment.	Client abilities (work skills) and values (work needs) are criteria used for selecting work environments. Work requirements determine reinforcers available by occupations. Knowledge of clients who are more achievement (satisfactoriness) or self-fulfilled (satisfaction) oriented enhances career choice.

Theories	Basic Assumptions	Key Terms	Outcomes
John Holland: A Typology Approach	Career choice is an expression of, or an extension of personality into the world of work. Individuals search for environments that will let them exercise their skills and abilities, express their attitudes and values, and take on agreeable problems and roles. There are six kinds of occupational environments and six matching personal orientations.	The six types of categories for individuals and work environment are *Realistic, Investigative, Artistic, Social, Enterprising,* and *Conventional. Consistency* refers to personality, i.e., those clients who relate strongly to one or more of the categories. *Differentiation* refers to those who have poorly defined personality styles. *Identity* refers to the degree in which one identifies with a work environment. *Congruence* is a good match between individual and work environment.	Individuals are products of their environment. Stability of career choice depends on dominance of personal orientation. Individuals who fit a pure personality type will express little resemblance to other types. Clients who have many occupational goals have low identity. Congruence occurs when client's personality type matches the corresponding work environment.
Social Learning and Cognitive Theories			
Krumboltz's Learning Theory Approach	Each individual's unique learning experiences over the life span develop primary influences that lead to career choice. Development involves genetic endowments and special abilities, environmental conditions and events, learning experiences, and task approach skills.	*Genetic endowments* are inherited qualities that may set limits on career choice. *Environmental conditions* are contextual interactions that influence individual choices. *Instrumental learning experiences* are those acquired through observation, consequences, and reaction of others. *Associative learning experiences* are negative and positive reactions to neutral experiences. *Task approach skills* are work habits, mental sets, emotional responses, and cognitive responses.	Learning experiences should increase the range of occupations in career counseling. Assessment is to be used to create new learning experiences. Clients need to prepare for changing work tasks. Career decision making is a learned skill. Clients need to be empowered as active participants in career search.

Theories	Basic Assumptions	Key Terms	Outcomes
Career Development from a Cognitive Information-Processing Perspective	Ten basic assumptions of this theory are outlined and explained in Table 3-1. Two overarching assumptions facilitating the growth of information-processing skills and enhancing the client's ability to solve problems and make career decisions.	CASVE involves the following generic processing skills: *Communication* (identifying a need), *Analysis* (interrelating problem components), *Synthesis* (creating likely alternatives), *Valuing* (prioritizing alternatives), and *Execution* (forming means-end strategies).	Career problem solving is primarily a cognitive process. Information processing can be improved through learning. Effective information processing skills can empower individuals to determine their own destiny. Making career choices is a problem-solving activity.
Career Development from a Social Cognitive Perspective	This theory is embedded in general social cognitive theory which blends cognitive, self, regulatory, and motivational processes into a lifelong phenomenon. Personal and physical attributes, external environmental factors, and overt behavior all interact as causal influences on individual development.	*Personal agency* reflects how a person exerts power to achieve a solution. *Triadic reciprocal interactions,* as explained in the basic assumptions, are from Bandura's (1986) social learning theory.	Self-efficacy is strengthened with success is experienced in a performance domain and is weakened with repeated failures; outcome expectations are shaped by similar experiences. Personal goals and/or personal agency act to sustain behavior. Career choice is influenced by environmental factors. Overcoming barriers to choice is a significant goal of this theory.
Developmental Theories			
Life-Span, Life-Space Approach	Career development is multidimensional. There are developmental tasks throughout the life span. Vocational maturity is acquired through successfully *(continued)*	Stages of vocational development are Growth, Exploratory, Establishment, Maintenance, and Decline. Developmental tasks are Crystallization, Specification, *(continued)*	Career development is a lifelong process occurring in stages. Self-concept is shaped through life experiences. Clients are involved in several life roles of child, student, leisurite, citizen, worker, spouse, homemaker, parent, *(continued)*

Theories	Basic Assumptions	Key Terms	Outcomes
Life-Span, Life-Space Approach (cont.)	accomplishing developmental tasks within a continuous series of life stages. Individuals implement their self-concepts into careers that will provide the most efficient means of self-expressions. Success in one life role facilitates success in another.	Implementation, Stabilization, and Consolidation. Self-concept is the driving force that establishes a career pattern. Attitudes and competencies are related to career growth and identified as career Maturity.	and pensioner. All life roles affect one another. In development societal factors interact with biological psychological factors.
Circumscription and Compromise: A Developmental Theory of Occupational Aspirations	A key factor in career decision is self-concept that is determined by one's social class, level of intelligence, and experiences with sex-typing. Individual's progress through four stages and learn to compromise based on generalizations of cognitive maps of occupations. Individuals are less willing to compromise job level and sex-type.	*Self-concept* is one's view of self. *Cognitive maps* of occupations reflect dimensions of prestige level, masculinity/femininity, and field of work. *Social space* refers to a zone or view of where each person fits into society. *Circumscription* is the process of narrowing one's territory of social space or alternative. *Compromise* suggests individuals will settle for a good choice but not best.	Individual development consists of four stages: Orientation to size and power, orientation to sex roles, orientation to social valuation, and orientation to internal unique self. Socioeconomic background and intellectual level greatly influence self-concept. Occupational choices are determined by social space, intellectual level, and sex-typing. Career choice is a process of eliminating options through cognitive maps. Individuals compromise occupational choices because of accessibility. Circumscription of occupations occurs through self-awareness, sex-type, and social class.
Person-in-Environment Perspective			
Career Construction: A Developmental Theory of Vocational Behavior	This theory focuses attention on contextual interactions over the life span. One's career development is constructed as individuals influence	Self-concepts guide and evaluate one's behavior. Career patterns are primarily determined by a combination of parental status, one's educational level, traits, and self-concepts.	Career construction theory focuses on assisting individuals with developmental tasks over the life span. It is a counseling process that helps clients construct and manage their careers. One overarching goal is to help individuals to increase

Theories	Basic Assumptions	Key Terms	Outcomes
	and are influenced within environmental systems. Clients are viewed as products of their environment. Vocational behavior is a core element in career construction theory.	Vocational maturity as a psychosocial construct is determined by one's level of vocational development. Life roles are interactive and are reciprocally shaped by each other. Developmental tasks in career construction include growth, exploration, crystallization, establishment, maintenance or management, and disengagement.	their realism in making career choices and transitions. To accomplish this goal one is to focus on understanding their vocational self-concept and validate their vocational identity. Each client's life story becomes a means of understanding self and subsequent focus for future growth.
A Contextual Explanation of Career	As people and their environments interact, development can proceed along many different pathways, depending on how one influences the other. A developmental-contextual life span assumes that interacting with a changing environment provides a foundation for individuals to form their own development.	*Contextualism* is a method of describing events or actions in an individual's life and a way in which counselors understand influences in career development from an individual's environmental interactions. *Actions* refer to the whole context in which an action is taken, how events take shape as people engage in them.	The study of actions is the major focus of the contextual viewpoint. Actions manifest behavior, they are internal processes, and they have social meaning. Environmental actions are to be observed from a "wholeness," that is, the influence of events that people engage in. Events take shape as people engage in them, and the totality of the actions and events influences participants.

Other Theories

Theories	Basic Assumptions	Key Terms	Outcomes
Ann Roe: A Needs Approach	Early childhood experiences and parental style affect the needs hierarchy and the relationships of those needs to *(continued)*	Examples of person-oriented occupations are service, business contact, managerial, teaching, and entertainment. Nonperson-oriented are *(continued)*	Original position was that individuals who enjoy working with people were raised by warm accepting parents and those who avoid contact with others were reared by cold or *(continued)*

Theories	Basic Assumptions	Key Terms	Outcomes
Ann Roe: A Needs Approach (cont.)	adult lifestyle. Those who choose nonperson-type jobs are meeting lower-level needs for safety and security. Those who choose to work with other people have strong needs for affection and belonging.	technology, outdoors, and science.	rejecting parents. Current position is that there are other important factors that determine occupational choice not accounted for in her theory.
Ginzberg and Associates	Occupational choice is a developmental process covering 6 to 10 years beginning at age 11 and ending shortly after age 17. As tentative occupational decisions are made, other choices are eliminated.	Stages of career development are Fantasy, Tentative, and Realistic. In *Fantasy,* play becomes work oriented. In *Tentative,* there is recognition of work requirements and one's traits. In *Realistic,* one narrows down occupational choices.	Career choice is a developed precept of occupations subjectively appraised in sociocultural milieu from childhood to early adult. There are three stages of development from before age 11 to young adult.
Sociological Perspective of Work and Career Development	Individual characteristics that are responsible for career choice are biologically determined and socially conditioned through family influences, social position and relations, and developed social role characteristics.	*Status Attainment Theory* suggests parental status greatly influences career choice. *Sociology of Labor Markets* refers to institutional practices that limit career aspiration such as jobs that have limited access for minorities and women. *Race and gender effects* refer to minorities being assigned to low-status jobs and women being given less status than men. Family status can limit educational aspirations.	Organizations and market forces constrain career choices. Clients are to learn to cope with social environments they encounter. Clients are to learn about the realities of the work world. Minorities are to be encouraged to complete educational programs and increase their educational aspirations.

Appendix B

Multicultural Career Counseling Checklist

If you have a client of a different ethnicity/race than yours, you may wish to use this checklist as you begin to do the career assessment with your client.

The following statements are designed to help you think more thoroughly about the racially or ethnically different client to whom you are about to provide career counseling. Check all the statements that apply.

My racial/ethnic identity: _____

My client's racial/ethnic identity: _____

I. Counselor Preparation

☐ 1. I am familiar with minimum cross-cultural counseling competencies.

☐ 2. I am aware of my client's cultural identification.

☐ 3. I understand and respect my client's culture.

☐ 4. I am aware of my own worldview and how it was shaped.

☐ 5. I am aware of how my SES influences my ability to empathize with this client.

☐ 6. I am aware of how my political views influence my counseling with a client from this ethnic group.

☐ 7. I have had counseling or other life experiences with different racial/ethnic groups.

☐ 8. I have information about this client's ethnic group's history, local socio-political issues, and her attitudes toward seeking help.

☐ 9. I know many of the strengths of this client's ethnic group.

☐ 10. I know where I am in my racial identity development.

☐ 11. I know the general stereotypes held about my client's ethnic group.

☐ 12. I am comfortable confronting ethnic minority clients.

☐ 13. I am aware of the importance that the interaction of gender and race/ethnicity has in my client's life.

II. Exploration and Assessment

- ❑ 1. I understand this client's career questions.
- ❑ 2. I understand how the client's career questions may be complicated with issues of finance, family, and academics.
- ❑ 3. The client is presenting racial and/or cultural information with the career questions.
- ❑ 4. I am aware of the career limitations or obstacles the client associates with her race or culture.
- ❑ 5. I understand what the client's perceived limitations are.
- ❑ 6. I know the client's perception of her family's ethnocultural identification.
- ❑ 7. I am aware of the client's perception of her family's support for her career.
- ❑ 8. I know which career the client believes her family wants her to pursue.
- ❑ 9. I know whether the client's family's support is important to her.
- ❑ 10. I believe that familial obligations are dictating the client's career choices.
- ❑ 11. I know the extent of exposure to career information and role models the client had in high school and beyond.
- ❑ 12. I understand the impact that high school experiences (positive or negative) have had on the client's confidence.
- ❑ 13. I am aware of the client's perception of her competence, ability, and self-efficacy.
- ❑ 14. I believe the client avoids certain work environments because of fears of sexism or racism.
- ❑ 15. I know the client's stage of racial identity development.

III. Negotiation and Working Consensus

- ❑ 1. I understand the type of career counseling help the client is seeking (career choice, supplement of family income, professional career, etc.).
- ❑ 2. The client and I have agreed on the goals for career counseling.
- ❑ 3. I know how this client's role as a woman in her family influences her career choices.
- ❑ 4. I am aware of the client's perception of the woman's work role in her family and in her culture.
- ❑ 5. I am aware of the client's understanding of the role of children in her career plans.
- ❑ 6. I am aware of the extent of exposure to a variety of career role models the client has had.
- ❑ 7. I understand the culturally based career conflicts that are generated by exposure to more careers and role models.
- ❑ 8. I know the client's career aspirations.
- ❑ 9. I am aware of the level of confidence the client has in her ability to obtain her aspirations.

❑   10.   I know the client understands the relationship between type of work and educational level.

❑   11.   I am aware of the negative and/or self-defeating thoughts that are obstacles to the client's aspirations and expectations.

❑   12.   I know if the client and I need to renegotiate her goals as appropriate after exploring cultural and family issues.

❑   13.   I know the client understands the career exploration process.

❑   14.   I am aware of the client's expectations about the career counseling process.

❑   15.   I know when it is appropriate to use a traditional career assessment instrument with a client from this ethnic group.

❑   16.   I know which instrument to use with this client.

❑   17.   I am aware of the research support for using the selected instrument with clients of this ethnicity.

❑   18.   I am aware of nontraditional instruments that might be more appropriate for use with clients from this ethnic group.

❑   19.   I am aware of nontraditional approaches to using traditional instruments with clients from this ethnic group.

❑   20.   I am aware of the career strengths the client associates with her race or culture.

Appendix C
Career Counseling Checklist

The following statements are designed to help you think more thoroughly about your career concerns and to help your assessment counselor understand you better. Please try to answer them as honestly as possible. Check all of the items that are true for you.

- ☐ 1. I feel obligated to do what others want me to do, and these expectations conflict with my own desires.
- ☐ 2. I have lots of interests, but I do not know how to narrow them down.
- ☐ 3. I am afraid of making a serious mistake with my career choice.
- ☐ 4. I do not feel confident that I know in which areas my true interests lie.
- ☐ 5. I feel uneasy with the responsibility for making a good career choice.
- ☐ 6. I lack information about my skills, interests, needs, and values with regard to my career choice.
- ☐ 7. My physical ability may greatly influence my career choice.
- ☐ 8. I lack knowledge about the world of work and what it has to offer me.
- ☐ 9. I know what I want my career to be, but it doesn't feel like a realistic goal.
- ☐ 10. I feel I am the only one who does not have a career plan.
- ☐ 11. I lack knowledge about myself and what I have to offer the world of work.
- ☐ 12. I do not really know what is required from a career for me to feel satisfied.
- ☐ 13. I feel that problems in my personal life are hindering me from making a good career decision.
- ☐ 14. My ethnicity may influence my career choice.
- ☐ 15. No matter how much information I have about a career, I keep going back and forth and cannot make up my mind.
- ☐ 16. I tend to be a person who gives up easily.
- ☐ 17. I believe that I am largely to blame for the lack of success I feel in making a career decision.
- ☐ 18. I have great difficulty making most decisions about my life.
- ☐ 19. My age may influence my career choice.

❑ 20. I expect my career decision to take care of most of the boredom and emptiness that I feel.

❑ 21. I have difficulty making commitments.

❑ 22. I don't have any idea of what I want in life, who I am, or what's important to me.

❑ 23. I have difficulty completing things.

❑ 24. I am afraid of making mistakes.

❑ 25. Religious values may greatly influence my career choice.

❑ 26. At this point, I am thinking more about finding a job than about choosing a career.

❑ 27. Family responsibilities will probably limit my career ambitions.

❑ 28. My orientation to career is very different from that of the members of my family.

❑ 29. I have worked on a job that taught me some things about what I want or do not want in a career, but I still feel lost.

❑ 30. Some classes in school are much easier for me than others, but I don't know how to use this information.

❑ 31. My race may greatly influence my career choice.

❑ 32. My long-term goals are more firm than my short-term goals.

❑ 33. I have some career-related daydreams that I do not share with many people.

❑ 34. I have been unable to see a connection between my college work and a possible career.

❑ 35. I have made a career choice with which I am comfortable, but I need specific assistance in finding a job.

❑ 36. My gender may influence my career choice.

❑ 37. I have undergone a change in my life, which necessitates a change in my career plans.

❑ 38. My fantasy is that there is one perfect job for me, if I can find it.

❑ 39. I have been out of the world of work for a period of time and I need to redefine my career choice.

❑ 40. Making a great deal of money is an important career goal for me, but I am unsure as to how I might reach it.

❑ 41. My immigration status may influence my career choice.

Appendix D
The Decision Tree

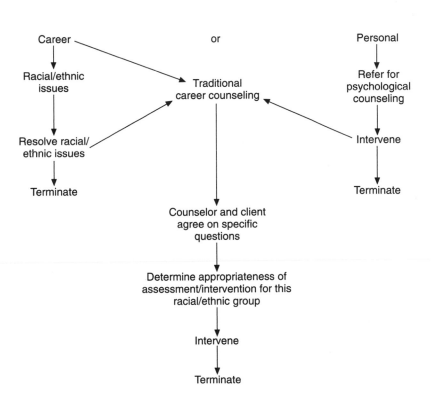

Appendix E

The National Career Development Guidelines: Competencies and Indicators for Elementary School Students

Competency I:
Knowledge of the importance of self-concept.

Describe positive characteristics about self as seen by self and others.
Identify how behaviors affect school and family situations.
Describe how behavior influences the feelings and actions of others.
Demonstrate a positive attitude about self.
Identify personal interests, abilities, strengths, and weaknesses.
Describe ways to meet personal needs through work.

Competency II: Skills to interact with others.

Identify how people are unique.
Demonstrate effective skills in interacting with others.
Demonstrate skills in resolving conflicts with peers and adults.
Demonstrate group membership skills.
Identify sources and effects of peer pressure.
Demonstrate appropriate behaviors when peer pressures are contrary to one's beliefs.
Demonstrate awareness of different cultures, lifestyles, attitudes, and abilities.

Competency III:
Awareness of the importance of growth and change.

Identify personal feelings.
Identify ways to express feelings.
Describe causes of stress.
Identify and select appropriate behaviors to deal with specific emotional situations.
Demonstrate healthy ways of dealing with conflicts, stress, and emotions in self and others.
Demonstrate knowledge of good health habits.

Competency IV:
Awareness of the benefits of educational achievement.

Describe how academic skills can be used in the home and community.
Identify personal strengths and weaknesses in subject areas.
Identify academic skills needed in several occupational groups.
Describe relationships among ability, effort, and achievement.
Implement a plan of action for improving academic skills.
Describe school tasks that are similar to skills essential for job success.
Describe how the amount of education needed for different occupational levels varies.

Competency V:
Awareness of the relationship between work and learning.

Identify different types of work, both paid and unpaid.
Describe the importance of preparing for occupations.
Demonstrate effective study and information-seeking habits.
Demonstrate an understanding of the importance of practice, effort, and learning.
Describe how current learning relates to work.
Describe how one's role as a student is like that of an adult worker.

Competency VI:
Skills to understand and use career information.

Describe work of family members, school personnel, and community workers.
Identify occupations according to data, people, and things.
Describe the relationship of beliefs, attitudes, interests, and abilities to occupations.
Describe jobs that are present in local community.
Identify the working conditions of occupations (e.g., inside/outside, hazardous).
Describe way in which self-employment differs from working for others.
Describe how parents, relatives, adult friends, and neighbors can provide career information.

Competency VII: Awareness of the importance
of personal responsibility and good work habits.

Describe the importance of personal qualities (e.g., dependability, promptness, getting along with others) to getting and keeping jobs.
Demonstrate positive ways of performing working activities.
Describe the importance of cooperation among workers to accomplish a task.
Demonstrate the ability to work with people who are different from oneself (e.g., race, age, gender).

Competency VIII: Awareness of how work habits relate to the needs and functions of society.

Describe how work can satisfy personal needs.
Describe the products and services of local employers.
Describe ways in which work can help overcome social and economic problems.

Competency IX: Understanding how to make decisions.

Describe how choices are made.
Describe what can be learned from making mistakes.
Identify and assess problems that interfere with attaining goals.
Identify strategies used in solving problems.
Identify alternatives in decision-making situations.
Describe how personal beliefs and attitudes affect decision making.
Describe how decisions affect self and others.

Competency X: Awareness of the interrelationship of life roles.

Describe the various roles an individual may have (e.g., friend, student, worker, family member).
Describe work-related activities in the home, community, and school.
Describe how family members depend on one another, work together, and share responsibilities.
Describe how work roles complement family roles.

Competency XI: Awareness of different occupations and changing male/female roles.

Describe how work is important to all people.
Describe the changing life roles of men and women in work and family.
Describe how contributions of individuals both inside and outside the home are important.

Competency XII: Awareness of the career planning process.

Describe the importance of planning.
Describe skills needed in a variety of occupational groups.

SOURCE: From *National Career Development Guidelines: K–Adult Handbook,* by L. Kobylarz, 1996. Stillwater, OK: National Occupational Information Coordinating Committee Training and Support Center.

Appendix F

The National Career Development Guidelines: Competencies and Indicators for Middle/Junior High School Students

Self-Knowledge

COMPETENCY I: Knowledge of the influence of a positive self-concept.

Describe personal likes and dislikes.
Describe individual skills required to fulfill different life roles.
Describe how one's behavior influences the feelings and actions of others.
Identify environmental influences on attitudes, behaviors, and aptitudes.

COMPETENCY II: Skills to interact with others.

Demonstrate respect for the feelings and beliefs of others.
Demonstrate an appreciation for the similarities and differences among people.
Demonstrate tolerance and flexibility in interpersonal and group situations.
Demonstrate skills in responding to criticism.
Demonstrate effective group membership skills.
Demonstrate effective social skills.
Demonstrate understanding of different cultures, lifestyles, attitudes, and abilities.

COMPETENCY III: Knowledge of the importance of growth and change.

Identify feelings associated with significant experiences.
Identify internal and external sources of stress.
Demonstrate ways of responding to others when under stress.
Describe changes that occur in the physical, psychological, social, and emotional development of an individual.
Describe physiological and psychological factors as they relate to career development.
Describe the importance of career, family, leisure activities to mental, emotional, physical, and economic well-being.

533

Educational and Occupational Exploration

COMPETENCY IV: Knowledge of the benefits of educational achievement to career opportunities.

Describe the importance of academic and occupational skills in the work world.

Identify how the skills taught in school subjects are used in various occupations.

Describe individual strengths and weaknesses in school subjects.

Describe a plan of action for increasing basic educational skills.

Describe the skills needed to adjust to changing occupational requirements.

Describe how continued learning enhances the ability to achieve goals.

Describe how skills relate to the selection of high school courses of study.

Describe how aptitudes and abilities relate to broad occupational groups.

COMPETENCY V: Understanding the relationship between work and learning.

Demonstrate effective learning habits and skills.

Demonstrate an understanding of the importance of personal skills and attitudes to job success.

Describe the relationship of personal attitudes, beliefs, abilities, and skills to occupations.

COMPETENCY VI: Skills to locate, understand, and use career information.

Identify various ways that occupations can be classified.

Identify a number of occupational groups for exploration.

Demonstrate skills in using school and community resources to learn about occupational groups.

Identify sources to obtain information about occupational groups, including self-employment.

Identify skills that are transferable from one occupation to another.

Identify sources of employment in the community.

COMPETENCY VII: Knowledge of skills necessary to seek and obtain jobs.

Demonstrate personal qualities (e.g., dependability, punctuality, getting along with others) that are needed to get and keep jobs.

Describe terms and concepts used in describing employment opportunities and conditions.

Demonstrate skills to complete a job application.

Demonstrate skills and attitudes essential for a job interview.

COMPETENCY VIII: Understanding how work relates to the needs and functions of the economy and society.

Describe the importance of work to society.

Describe the relationship between work and economic and societal needs.

Describe the economic contributions workers make to society.

Describe the effects that societal, economic, and technological change have on occupations.

Career Planning

COMPETENCY IX: Skills to make decisions.

Describe personal beliefs and attitudes.

Describe how career development is a continuous process with a series of choices.

Identify possible outcomes of decisions.

Describe school courses related to personal, educational, and occupational interests.

Describe how the expectations of others affect career planning.

Identify ways in which decisions about education and work relate to other major life decisions.

Identify advantages and disadvantages of various secondary and postsecondary programs for the attainment of career goals.

Identify the requirements for secondary and postsecondary programs.

COMPETENCY X: Knowledge of the interrelationship of life roles.

Identify how different work and family patterns require varying kinds and amounts of energy, participation, motivation, and talent.

Identify how work roles at home satisfy needs of the family.

Identify personal goals that may be satisfied through a combination of work, community, social, and family roles.

Identify personal leisure choices in relation to lifestyle and the attainment of future goals.

Describe advantages and disadvantages of various life role options.

Describe the interrelationships between family, occupational, and leisure decisions.

COMPETENCY XI: Knowledge of different occupations and changing male/female roles.

Describe advantages and problems of entering nontraditional occupations.

Describe the advantages of taking courses related to personal interest, even if they are most often taken by members of the opposite gender.

Describe stereotypes, biases, and discriminatory behaviors that may limit opportunities for women and men in certain occupations.

COMPETENCY XII: Understanding the process of career planning.

Demonstrate knowledge of exploratory processes and programs.

Identify school courses that meet tentative career goals.

Demonstrate knowledge of academic and vocational programs offered at the high school level.

Describe skills needed in a variety of occupations, including self-employment.
Identify strategies for managing personal resources (e.g., talents, time, money) to achieve tentative career goals.

Develop an individual career plan, updating information from the elementary-level plan and including tentative decisions to be implemented in high school.

SOURCE: From *National Career Development Guidelines: K–Adult Handbook,* by L. Kobylarz, 1996. Stillwater, OK: National Occupational Information Coordinating Committee Training and Support Center.

Appendix G

The National Career Development Guidelines: Competencies and Indicators for High School Students

Self-Knowledge

COMPETENCY I: Understanding the influence of a positive self-concept.

Identify and appreciate personal interests, abilities, and skills.

Demonstrate the ability to use peer feedback.

Demonstrate an understanding of how individual characteristics relate to achieving personal, social, educational, and career goals.

Demonstrate an understanding of environmental influences on one's behaviors.

Demonstrate an understanding of the relationship between personal behavior and self-concept.

COMPETENCY II: Skills to interact positively with others.

Demonstrate effective interpersonal skills.

Demonstrate interpersonal skills required for working with and for others.

Describe appropriate employer and employee interactions in various situations.

Demonstrate how to express feelings, reactions, and ideas in an appropriate manner.

COMPETENCY III: Understanding the impact of growth and development.

Describe how developmental changes affect physical and mental health.

Describe the effect of emotional and physical health on career decisions.

Describe healthy ways of dealing with stress.

Demonstrate behaviors that maintain physical and mental health.

Educational and Occupational Exploration

COMPETENCY IV: Understanding the relationship between educational achievement and career planning.

Demonstrate how to apply academic and vocational skills to achieve personal goals.

Describe the relationship of academic and vocational skills to personal interests.

Describe how skills developed in academic and vocational programs relate to career goals.

Describe how education relates to the selection of college majors, further training, and/or entry into the job market.

Demonstrate transferable skills that can apply to a variety of occupations and changing occupational requirements.

Describe how learning skills are required in the workplace.

COMPETENCY V: Understanding the need for positive attitudes toward work and learning.

Identify the positive contributions workers make to society.

Demonstrate knowledge of the social significance of various occupations.

Demonstrate a positive attitude toward work.

Demonstrate learning habits and skills that can be used in various educational situations.

Demonstrate positive work attitudes and behaviors.

COMPETENCY VI: Skills to locate, evaluate, and interpret career information.

Describe the educational requirements of various occupations.

Demonstrate use of a range of resources (e.g., handbooks, career materials, labor market information, and computerized career information delivery systems).

Demonstrate knowledge of various classification systems that categorize occupations and industries (e.g., *Dictionary of Occupational Titles*).

Describe the concept of career ladders.

Describe the advantages and disadvantages of self-employment as a career option.

Identify individuals in selected occupations as possible information resources, role models, or mentors.

Describe the influence of change in supply and demand for workers in different occupations.

Identify how employment trends relate to education and training.

Describe the impact of factors such as population, climate, and geographic location on occupational opportunities.

COMPETENCY VII: Skills to prepare to seek, obtain, maintain, and change jobs.

Demonstrate skills to locate, interpret, and use information about job openings and opportunities.

Demonstrate academic or vocational skills required for a full- or part-time job.

Demonstrate skills and behaviors necessary for a successful job interview.

Demonstrate skills in preparing a resume and completing job applications.

Identify specific job openings.

Demonstrate employability skills necessary to obtain and maintain jobs.

Demonstrate skills to assess occupational opportunities (e.g., working conditions, benefits, opportunities for change).

Describe placement services available to make the transition from high school to civilian employment, the armed services, or postsecondary education/ training.

Demonstrate an understanding that job opportunities often require relocation.

Demonstrate skills necessary to function as a consumer and manage financial resources.

COMPETENCY VIII: Understanding how societal needs and functions influence the nature and structure of work.

Describe the effect of work on lifestyles.

Describe how society's needs and functions affect the supply of goods and services.

Describe how occupational and industrial trends relate to training and employment.

Demonstrate an understanding of the global economy and how it affects each individual.

Career Planning

COMPETENCY IX: Skills to make decisions.

Demonstrate responsibility for making tentative educational and occupational choices.

Identify alternatives in given decision-making situations.

Describe personal strengths and weaknesses in relationship to postsecondary education/training requirements.

Identify appropriate choices during high school that will lead to marketable skills for entry-level employment or advanced training.

Identify and complete required steps toward transition from high school to entry into postsecondary education/training programs or work.

Identify steps to apply for and secure financial assistance for postsecondary education and training.

COMPETENCY X: Understanding the interrelationship of life roles.

Demonstrate knowledge of life stages.

Describe factors that determine lifestyles (e.g., socioeconomic status, culture, values, occupational choices, work habits).

Describe ways in which occupational choices may affect lifestyle.
Describe the contribution of work to a balanced and productive life.
Describe ways in which work, family, and leisure roles are interrelated.
Describe different career patterns and their potential effect on family patterns and lifestyle.
Describe the importance of leisure activities.
Demonstrate ways that occupational skills and knowledge can be acquired through leisure.

COMPETENCY XI: Understanding the continuous changes in male/female roles.

Identify factors that have influenced the changing career patterns of women and men.
Identify evidence of gender stereotyping and bias in educational programs and occupational settings.
Demonstrate attitudes, behaviors, and skills that contribute to eliminating gender bias and stereotyping.
Identify courses appropriate to tentative occupational choices.
Describe the advantages and problems of nontraditional occupations.

COMPETENCY XII: Skills in career planning.

Describe career plans that reflect the importance of lifelong learning.
Demonstrate knowledge of postsecondary vocational and academic programs.
Demonstrate knowledge that changes may require retraining and upgrading of employees' skills.
Describe school and community resources to explore educational and occupational choices.
Describe the costs and benefits of self-employment.
Demonstrate occupational skills developed through volunteer experiences, part-time employment, or cooperative education programs.
Demonstrate skills necessary to compare education and job opportunities.
Develop an individual career plan, updating information from earlier plans and including tentative decisions to be implemented after high school.

SOURCE: From *National Career Development Guidelines: K–Adult Handbook,* by L. Kobylarz, 1996. Stillwater, OK: National Occupational Information Coordinating Committee Training and Support Center.

Appendix H

A High School Student's Experience in a Cooperative Education Program

The following account of a student's participation in a high school cooperative education program points out the values of work experiences.[1] Experiential activities involved money management, cooperative work activities with regular work staff, coping with work-related stress, and responsibility for work tasks. This student credits the cooperative education program as the single most influential aspect of her career education.

During my high school years, I was enrolled in a cooperative education program—I was a co-op student. As many people know, a co-op program is where a high school or college student earns academic credit and sometimes wages by working in the "real world" as part of a specified vocational curriculum. For example, a student in a retail merchandise program can earn credit and money through working in a department store. A food services student can work in a restaurant, a welding student can work for a sheet metal company, and so on.

I attended a high school that contained an areawide vocational skill center. Because I planned to attend college, I enrolled in the typical college prep courses, but I was also able to combine a college prep track with a vocational course (two hours a day for two years) that led to vocational certification by the State of Michigan. Early in my high school career, I had chosen elective courses from business: typing, shorthand, general business. I did quite well in these courses, and although I had no aspirations of becoming a business tycoon, I thought that having a background in business could prove helpful in the future, so I planned to take the Stenographer/Secretarial vocational program in my junior and senior years.

Immediately after finishing my sophomore year I was told of a co-op job working in the County Treasurer's Office, which sounded more interesting than cleaning motel rooms (which I had done the previous summer). So I interviewed for, and subsequently landed, the position of clerk/"go-fer"/secretary in the Office of the County Treasurer of Chippewa County.

It was then that my real education began. As a 16-year-old, my work experience consisted of being a paper girl for two years, extensive babysitting, and cleaning motel rooms. I was now in an "adult" job, one full of responsibility and of learning a tremendous

[1]From *My Vocational Experience,* by M. K. Wiinamaki, 1988. Unpublished manuscript, Southwest Texas State University. Reprinted by permission.

amount of information. During the two-and-a-half years I worked in that office, I learned more about the world of work than I did in any class I have ever taken—in high school, college, or graduate school.

The first major concept I learned was responsibility. I was required to be on time, day-in, day-out, even if I did not feel like going to work. However, my responsibility did not end with punctuality. I also had to *perform,* usually in pressure situations, under legal deadlines imposed by the State. I was responsible for accepting delinquent taxes and penalties and had to figure out the charges. At certain times of the year the office would become extremely hectic, but I was still expected to be accurate. After all, I was dealing with public funds.

Another area of my on-the-job education involved money management. For the first time in my life I was receiving a substantial amount of money in the form of a regular paycheck. Granted, it was only minimum wage, but working 20 hours per week during the school semester and 40 hours per week during summer, even minimum wage looked good to a high school girl with few expenses. I began to buy all my own clothes, my own gas, and was responsible for all of my entertainment expenses. Looking back, I believe both my parents and I appreciated this step of "economic independence."

Another crucial concept learned through my co-op experience was decision making, particularly the idea that decisions do have consequences and should be weighed before plunging head-first into one. I learned this in a variety of ways: first, by watching the adults with whom I worked, and second, by becoming aware of the political process around me. Decisions I made during those years still affect my life today.

The most generalizable skills I learned through co-op were interpersonal skills. I worked in an office with three women; though all of us had vastly different personalities, we had to cooperate and learn to co-exist peacefully, even when we did not agree. I also dealt with the public, people who were often paying delinquent land taxes, plus penalties, and who were generally unhappy about having to do so. I learned to be tactful, diplomatic, patient, and above all, to have a sense of humor about myself and about people. Working in such a stressful environment also taught me the importance of dealing with stress in a productive manner.

Time management was another skill I learned in my co-op job. When I began working regular hours, I was forced to use free time in a more productive manner—suddenly I had less time to goof off, do homework, and participate in household chores. I gained respect for adults who dealt with their job, spouse, children, and home. Life was more complicated than it had previously seemed.

In my position in the County Treasurer's Office, I had many occasions to talk to and become acquainted with a variety of people who held various city and county positions, such as county clerk, registrar of deeds, district attorneys, judges, and county commissioners. While students my age were learning about local politics in government class, I knew the officials by name and discovered what they actually did in their respective positions. Also significant was the fact that I had greatly increased my job experience during the time I worked as a co-op student. Many of the skills, such as typing, interpersonal skill, and problem-solving proved invaluable in subsequent positions. While all these skills and concepts were worthwhile, I think the most valuable benefit was a very positive increase in my self-esteem. I was now capable of working in the real world, of earning a living, of sticking with something that was not always pleasant. And that is a tremendous benefit.

So what happened after I left the County Treasurer's Office? During the time I worked there, I discovered some things about myself and the kind of environment I wanted to work in, and office work as a career was not what I envisioned. I learned that I did not enjoy the rigid structure, the routine, the repetition, but I did like working with people rather than with things. I entered college as a psychology major and thoroughly enjoyed the world of concepts, ideas, theories, and speculation. Throughout my years in college, I worked as a typist, a secretary in the Admissions Office, and as a word processor. Upon receiving a B.A. in psychology and realizing that graduate school was a necessity, I moved to Texas and promptly got a job as a word processor in a large law firm in Austin. Once again I was using the skills learned first in my co-op job as a high school student. In fact, that word-processing job supported me throughout graduate school, and also confirmed my decision to work in the field of counseling. I am glad to say that I am now working as a counselor, and I think I appreciate it more due to the years I spent in various secretarial jobs.

In summary, I learned a great deal about working, life, and myself through my experiences in cooperative education, experiences that continue to influence my life. For me, being a co-op student was the single most influential aspect of any career education I received. It was most valuable not because it showed me what I wanted to do with my life, but rather what I did *not* want to do—at a time when I was not forced to make irrevocable decisions on majors, careers, and locations. It provided me with the opportunity to navigate the transition from adolescence to adulthood gradually, and it is an experience I will never forget.

Appendix I

Counseling Web Sites

The following professional associations and their Web sites provide an abundance of information about career counseling including competencies, ethical standards, and guidelines for using assessment.

American Counseling Association
http://www.counseling.org/

American Psychological Association
http://www.apa.org

American Psychological Association Code of Ethics
http://www.apa.org/ethics/code.html

American Psychological Association Healthy Lesbian, Gay, and Bisexual Students Project
http://www.apa.org/ed/hlgb/

Americans with Disabilities Act
http://www.usdoj.gov/crt/ada/

Association for Assessment in Counseling
http://www.aac.uc.edu/aac/index.html

Association of Computer-Based Systems for Career Information
http://www.acsci.org/

Association for Gay, Lesbian and Bisexual Issues in Counseling
http://www.aglbic.org/

Guidelines for the Use of the Internet for the Provision of Career Information and Planning Services
http://ncda.org/about/polnet.html

National Career Development Association
http://ncda.org

National Career Development Association Career Software Review Guidelines
http://ncda.org/about/polsrg.html

National Career Development Association Ethical Standards
http://ncda.org/about/poles.html

Services by Telephone, Teleconferencing and Internet: A Statement by the Ethics Committee of the American Psychological Association
http://www.apa.org/ethics/stmnt01.html

Standards for the Practice of Internet Counseling
http://www.nbcc.org/ethics/webethics.htm

References

Aamodt, M. G. (1999). *Applied industrial/organizational psychology* (3rd ed.). Pacific Grove, CA: Brooks/Cole-Wadsworth.

Aamodt, M. G. (2004). *Applied industrial/organizational psychology* (4th ed.). Belton, CA: Wadsworth/Thomson Learning.

Adams, C. L., & Kimmel, D. C. (1997). Exploring the lives of older African American gay men. In B. Greene (Ed.), *Ethnic and cultural diversity among lesbians and gay men* (pp. 132–152). Thousand Oaks, CA: Sage.

Amatea, E. S., & Cross, E. G. (1980). Going places: A career guidance program for high school students and their parents. *Vocational Guidance Quarterly, 28*(3), 274–282.

American College Testing Program. (1984). *DISCOVER: A computer-based career development and counselor support system.* Iowa City, IA: Author.

American College Testing Program. (1987). *DISCOVER.* Iowa City, IA: Author.

American College Testing Program. (1996a, Winter). *Activity, 34*(1). Iowa City, IA: Author.

American Council on Education. (1997). Many college graduates participate in training courses to improve their job skills. *Higher Education and National Affairs, 46*(19), 3.

American Counseling Association (ACA). (1995). Code of ethics and standards of practice. In *Codes of ethics for the helping professionals,* 1–17. Pacific Grove, CA: Brooks/Cole.

American Counseling Association. (1999). *Ethical standards for Internet on-line counseling.* Alexandria, VA: Author.

American Mental Health Counselors Association. (2000). *Code of ethics for mental health counselors.* Alexandria, VA: Author.

American Psychiatric Association. (1994). *Diagnostic and statistical manual of mental disorders* (4th ed., rev.). Washington, DC: Author.

American Psychological Association. (1990). Ethical principles of psychologists (amended June 2, 1989). In *American Psychology,* pp. 453–484. New York: Wiley.

American Psychological Association. (1991). Avoiding heterosexual bias in language. *American Psychologist, 46,* 973–974.

American Psychological Association. (1992). *Ethical guidelines of the American Psychological Association.* Washington, DC: Author.

American Psychological Association. (1999). *Standards for educational and psychological testing.* Washington, DC: Author.

American School Counselors Association. (1998). *Ethical standards for school counselors.* Alexandria, VA: Author.

Anderson, D. A. (1994). Lesbian and gay adolescents: Social and developmental considerations. *High School Journal, 77*(1/2), 13–19.

Anderson, J. R. (1985). *Cognitive psychology and its implication* (2nd ed.). San Francisco: Freeman.

Arbona, C. (1995). Theory and research on racial and ethnic minorities: Hispanic Americans. In Frederick T. L. Leong (Ed.), *Career development and vocational behavior of racial and ethnic minorities* (pp. 37–61). Mahwah, NJ: Erlbaum.

Arbona, C. (1996). Career theory and practice in a multicultural context. In M. L. Savickas & W. B. Walsh (Eds.), *Handbook of career counseling theory and practice* (pp. 45–55). Palo Alto, CA: Davies-Black.

Armstrong, P. I., & Crombie, G. (2000). Compromises in adolescents' occupational aspirations and expectations from grades 8 to 10. *Journal of Vocational Behavior, 56,* 82–98.

Arredondo, P. (1996). MCT theory and Latina(o)-American populations. In D. W. Sue, A. E. Ivey, & P. B. Pedersen, *A theory of multicultural counseling and therapy* (pp. 217–233). Pacific Grove, CA: Brooks/Cole.

Ashkenas, R., Ulrich, D., Jick, T., & Kerr, S. (1995). *The boundaryless organization: Breaking the chains of organizational structure.* San Francisco: Jossey-Bass.

Astin, A. W. (1984). Student values: Knowing more about where we are today. *Bulletin of the American Association of Higher Education, 36*(9), 10–13.

Atkinson, D. R., Morten, G., & Sue, D. W. (1993). *Counseling American minorities: A cross-cultural perspective* (4th ed.). Dubuque, IA: William C. Brown.

Axelson, J. A. (1993). *Counseling and development in a multicultural society* (2nd ed.). Pacific Grove, CA: Brooks/Cole.

Axelson, J. A. (1999). *Counseling and development in a multicultural society* (4th ed.). Pacific Grove, CA: Brooks/Cole.

Bailey, L. J., & Stadt, R. W. (1973). *Career education: New approaches to human development.* Bloomington, IL: McKnight.

Baker, L. J., Dearborn, M., Hastings, J. E., & Hamberger, K. (1988). Type A behavior in women: A review. *Health Psychology, 3,* 477–497.

Ballard, D. (1997). *Doing it ourselves: Success stories of African-American women in business.* New York: Berkley.

Bandura, A. (1977). *Social learning theory.* Englewood Cliffs, NJ: Prentice-Hall.

Bandura, A. (1986). *Social foundations of thought and action: A social cognitive theory.* Englewood Cliffs, NJ: Prentice-Hall.

Bandura, A. (1989). Regulation of cognitive processes through perceived self-efficacy. *Developmental Psychology, 25,* 729–735.

Barnett, R. C., & Rivers, C. (1996). *She works, he works: How two-income families are happier, healthier, and better off.* San Francisco: Harper.

Baron, S. A., Hoffman, S. J., & Merrill, J. G. (2000). *When work equals life: The next stage of workplace violence.* Oxnard, CA: Pathfinder.

Barrett, B., & Logan, C. (2002). *Counseling gays and lesbians.* Pacific Grove, CA: Brooks/Cole.

Barrett, R. C., & Hyde, J. S. (2001). Women, men, work, and family. *American Psychologist, 56,* 781–796.

Basow, S. A. (1992). *Gender: Stereotypes and roles* (3rd ed.). Pacific Grove, CA: Brooks/ Cole.

Bauer, T., & Green, S. (1994). Effect of newcomer involvement on work-related activities: A longitudinal study of socialization. *Journal of Applied Psychology, 79,* 211–223.

Beck, A. T. (1976). *Cognitive therapy and the emotional disorders.* New York: International Universities Press.

Beck, A. T. (1985). Cognitive therapy. In H. J. Kaplan & B. J. Sadock (Eds.), *Comprehensive textbook of psychiatry* (pp. 1432–1438). Baltimore: Williams & Wilkins.

Beehr, T. A., & Bowling, M. A. (2002). Career issues facing older workers. In D. C. Feldman (Ed.), *Work careers: A developmental perspective* (pp. 214–245). San Francisco: Jossey-Bass.

Bell, A., & Weinberg, M. (1978). *Homosexualities: A study of diversity among men and women.* New York: Simon & Schuster.

Bennett, C. E., & DeBarros, K. A. (1995). The Black population. In *U.S. Bureau of the Census, current population reports, series P23-189, population profile of the United States: 1995* (pp. 44–45). Washington, DC: U.S. Government Printing Office.

Bennett, C. E., & Debarros, K. A. (1998). *The Black population.* Washington, DC: U.S. Bureau of Census.

Bennett, G. K., Seashore, H. G., & Wesman, A. G. (1974). *Differential aptitude test.* San Antonio, TX: Psychological Corporation.

Berns, R. M. (2004). *Child family-select community: Socialization and support* (6th ed.). Belmont, CA: Wadsworth/Thomson Learning.

Betz, N. E. (1992b). Counseling uses of career self-efficacy theory. *Career Development Quarterly, 41,* 22–26.

Betz, N. E., & Corning, A. F. (1993). The inseparability of career and personal counseling. *Career Development Quarterly, 42,* 137–142.

Betz, N. E., & Fitzgerald, L. F. (1987). *The career psychology of women.* Orlando, FL: Academic.

Betz, N. E., & Fitzgerald, L. F. (1995). Career assessment and intervention with racial and ethnic minorities. In Frederick T. L. Leong (Ed.), *Career development and vocational behavior of racial and ethnic minorities* (pp. 263–277). Mahwah, NJ: Erlbaum.

Betz, N. E., & Hackett, G. (1986). Applications of self-efficacy theory to understanding career choice behavior. *Journal of Social and Clinical Psychology, 4,* 279–289.

Biehler, R. F., & Hudson, L. M. (1986). *Developmental psychology.* Boston: Allyn & Bacon.

Biernat, M., & Wortman, C. (1991). Sharing of home responsibilities between professionally employed women and their husbands. *Journal of Personality and Social Psychology, 60,* 844–860.

Bingham, R. P., & Ward, C. M. (1996). Practical applications of career counseling with ethnic minority women. In M. L. Savickas & W. B. Walsh (Eds.), *Handbook of career counseling theory and practice* (pp. 291–315). Palo Alto, CA: Davies-Black.

Blau, P. M., Gustad, J. W., Jessor, R., Parnes, H. S., & Wilcox, R. S. (1956). Occupational choices: A conceptual framework. *Industrial Labor Relations Review, 9,* 531–543.

Bloland, P. A., & Edwards, P. B. (1981). Work and leisure: A counseling synthesis. *Vocational Guidance Quarterly, 30*(2), 101–108.

Blotzer, M. A., & Ruth, R. (1995). *Sometimes you just want to feel like a human being: Case studies of empowering psychotherapy with people with disabilities.* Baltimore: Paul H. Brookes.

Blustein, D. L. (1990). An eclectic definition of psychotherapy: A developmental contextual view. In J. K. Zeig & W. M. Munion (Eds.), *What is psychotherapy? Contemporary perspectives* (pp. 244–248). San Francisco: Jossey-Bass.

Blustein, D. L., & Flum, H. (1999). A self-determination perspective of interests and exploration in career development. In M. L. Savickas & A. R. Spokane (Eds.), *Vocational interests: Meaning, measure, and counseling use.* Palo Alto, CA: Davies-Black.

Blustein, D. L., Phillips, S. D., John-Davis, K., Finkelberg, S. L., & Roarke, A. E. (1997). A theory-building investigation of the school-to-work transition. *The Counseling Psychologist, 25,* 364–402.

Blustein, D. L., & Spengler, P. M. (1995). Personal adjustment: Career counseling and psychotherapy. In W. B. Walsh & S. H. Osipow (Eds.), *Handbook of vocational psychology: Theory, research, and practice* (2nd ed.), (pp. 295–329). Mahwah, NJ: Erlbaum.

Bolles, R. N. (1991). *Job-hunting tips for the so-called handicapped or people who have disabilities.* Berkeley, CA: Ten Speed.

Bolles, R. N. (1993). *A practical manual for job-hunters and career changers: What color is your parachute?* (9th ed.). Berkeley, CA: Ten Speed.

Bolles, R. N. (2000). *A practical manual for job-hunters and career changers: What color is your parachute?* (16th ed.). Berkeley, CA: Ten Speed.

Bottoms, J. E., Evans, R. N., Hoyt, K. B., & Willer, J. C. (Eds.). (1972). *Career education resource guide.* Morristown, NJ: General Learning Corporation.

Bowman, S. L. (1995). Career intervention strategies and assessment issues for African Americans. In Frederick T. L. Leong (Ed.), *Career development and vocational behavior of racial and ethnic minorities* (pp. 137–161). Mahwah, NJ: Erlbaum.

Braiker, H. (1986). *The Type E woman.* New York: Dodd, Mead.

Brammer, L. M., Abrego, P. L., & Shostrom, E. L. (1993). *Therapeutic counseling and psychotherapy* (2nd ed.). Englewood Cliffs, NJ: Prentice-Hall.

Brammer, R. (2004). *Diversity in counseling.* Belmont, CA: Brooks/Cole-Thomson Learning.

Brems, C. (2001). *Basic skills in psychotherapy and counseling.* Belmont, CA: Wadsworth/Thomson Learning.

Bretz, R. D., Jr., & Judge, T. A. (1994). Person-organization fit and the theory of work adjustment: Implications for satisfaction, tenure, and career success. *Journal of Vocational Behavior, 44,* 32–54.

Brolin, D. E., & Gysbers, N. C. (1989). Career education for students with disabilities. *Journal of Counseling and Development, 68,* 155–159.

Bronfenbrenner, U. (1979). *The ecology of human development.* Cambridge, MA: Harvard University Press.

Brown, B. B., Mounts, N., Lamborn, S. D., & Steinberg, L. (1993). Parenting practices and peer group affiliation in adolescence. *Child Development, 65,* 467–482.

Brown, D. A. (1980). Life-planning workshop for high school students. *The School Counselor, 29*(1), 77–83.

Brown, D. (1996). Brown's values-based, holistic model of career and life-role choices and satisfaction. In D. Brown, L. Brooks, & Associates (Eds.), *Career choice and development* (3rd ed., pp. 337–338). San Francisco: Jossey-Bass.

Brown, D., & Brooks, L. (1991). *Career counseling techniques.* Boston: Allyn & Bacon.

Brown, D., Brooks, L., & Associates. (1990). *Career choice and development* (2nd ed.). San Francisco: Jossey-Bass.

Brown, D., Brooks, L., & Associates. (1996). *Career choice and development* (3rd ed.). San Francisco: Jossey-Bass.

Brown, D., & Associates. (2002). *Career choice and development,* (4th ed.). San Francisco, CA: Jossey-Bass.

Brown, K. G., Milner, K., & Ford, J. K. (1998). The design of asynchronous distance learning courses. Technical Report for the National Center for Manufacturing Sciences, Ann Arbor, MI.

Brown, L. E. (1997). *Two-spirit people.* Binghamton, NY: Haworth Press.

Brown, L. S. (1995). Lesbian identities: Concepts and issues. In A. R. D'Augelli & C. J. Patterson (Eds.), *Lesbian, gay, and bisexual identities over the lifespan* (pp. 3–24). New York: Oxford University Press.

Bryan, W. V. (1996). *In search of freedom: How people with disabilities have been disenfranchised from the mainstream of American Society.* Springfield, IL: Charles C. Thomas.

Burgos-Ocasio, H. (2000). Hispanic women. In M. Julia (Ed.), *Constructing gender: Multicultural perspectives in working with women* (pp. 109–139). Pacific Grove, CA: Brooks/Cole.

Bynner, J. (1997). Basic skills in adolescent's occupational preparation. *Career Development Quarterly, 45,* 305–321.

Cabrera, N. J., Tasmis-LeMonda, C. S., Bradley, R. H., Hofferth, S., & Lamb, M. E. (2000). Fatherhood in the twenty-first century. *Child Development, 71,* 127–136.

Camilleri, C., & Malewska-Peyre, H. (1997). Socialization and identity strategies. In J. W. Berry, P. R. Dasen, & T. S. Saraswathi (Eds.), *Handbook of cross-cultural psychology* (Vol. 2, pp. 41–67). Boston: Allyn & Bacon.

Campbell, C. A., & Dahir, C. A. (1997). *The national standards for school counseling programs.* Alexandria, VA: American School Counselor Association.

Campbell, R. E., & Cellini, J. V. (1981). A diagnostic taxonomy of adult career problems. *Journal of Vocational Behavior, 19,* 175–190.

Cappelli, P., Bassi, L., Katz, H., Knoke, D., Osterman, P., & Unseem, M. (1997). *Change at work.* New York: Oxford University Press.

Carnoy, M. (1999). The family, flexible work and social cohesion at risk. *International Labor Review, 138*(4), 411–429.

Carson, A. D., & Mowesian, R. (1993). Moderators of the prediction of job satisfaction from congruence: A test of Holland's theory. *Journal of Career Assessment, 1,* 130–144.

Carter, J. K. (1995, Winter). Applying customer service strategies to career services. *Journal of Career Development, 22*(2), 85–139.

Carter, R. T. (1995). *The influence of race and racial identity in psychotherapy: Toward a racially inclusive model.* New York: Wiley.

Carter, R. T., & Qureshi, A. (1995). A typology of philosophical assumptions in multicultural counseling and training. In J. G. Ponterotto, J. M. Casas, L. A. Suzuki, and C. M. Alexander (Eds.), *Handbook of multicultural counseling* (pp. 239–262). Thousand Oaks, CA: Sage.

Cass, V. C. (1979). Homosexuality identity formation: A theoretical model. *Journal of Homosexuality, 4*(3), 219–235.

Cass, V. C. (1984). Homosexual identity formation: Testing a theoretical model. *Journal of Sex Research, 20*(2), 143–167.

Cattell, R. B., Eber, H. W., & Tatsuoka, M. M. (1970). *Handbook for the sixteen personality factor questionnaire (16PF).* Champaign, IL: Institute for Personality and Ability Testing.

Cautela, J., & Wisock, P. (1977). The thought-stopping procedure: Description, application and learning theory interpretations. *Psychological Record, 2,* 264–266.

Cavanaugh, J. C., & Blanchard-Fields, F. (2002). *Adult development and aging* (4th ed.). Belmont, CA: Wadsworth/Thomson Learning.

Chan, C. S. (1997). Don't ask, don't tell, don't know: The formation of homosexual identity and sexual expression among Asian American lesbians. In B. Greene (Ed.), *Ethnic and cultural diversity among lesbians and gay men* (pp. 240–249). Thousand Oaks, CA: Sage.

Chan, C. S. (1989). Issues of identity formation among Asian-American lesbians and gay men. *Journal of Counseling Development, 68,* 16–20.

Chu, L. (1981, April). Asian-American women in educational research. Paper presented at annual conference of the American Educational Research Association, Los Angeles.

Chung, Y. B., & Katayama, M. (1999). Ethnic and sexual identity development of Asian American lesbian and gay adolescents. In K. S. Ng (Ed.), *Counseling Asian families from a systems perspective* (pp. 159–171). Alexandria, VA: American Counseling Association.

Chusmir, L. H. (1983). Characteristics and predictive dimensions of women who make nontraditional vocational choices. *Personnel and Guidance Journal, 62*(1), 43–48.

Clark-Stewart, A. (1993). *Daycare* (rev. ed.). Cambridge, MA: Harvard University Press.

Cochran, L. (1994). What is a career problem? *Career Development Quarterly, 42,* 204–215.

Cohn, D., & Fears, D. (2001, March 7). Hispanics draw even with Blacks in new census. *Washington Post,* A1.

Coleman, E., & Remafedi, G. (1989). Gay, lesbian, and bisexual adolescents: A critical challenge to counselors. *Journal of Counseling & Development, 68,* 36–40.

Colozzi, E. A. (2000). Toward the development of systematic guidance. In D. A. Luzzo (Ed.), *Career counseling of college students* (pp. 285–311). Washington, DC: American Psychological Association.

Coltrane, S. (2000). Research on household labor: Modeling and measuring the social embeddedness of routine family work. *Journal of Marriage and Family, 62,* 1208–1233.

Comas-Diaz, L. (1996). Cultural considerations in diagnosis. In F. W. Kaslow (Ed.), *Handbook on relational diagnosis and dysfunctional family patterns* (pp. 159–160). New York: Wiley.

Comas-Diaz, L., & Grenier, J. R. (1998). Migration and acculturation. In J. Sandoval, C. L. Frisby, K. F. Geisinger, J. D. Scheuneman, & J. R. Grenier, *Test interpretation and diversity* (pp. 213–241). Washington, DC: American Psychological Association.

Coon-Carty, H. M. (1995). *The relation of work-related abilities, vocational interests, and self-efficacy beliefs: A meta-analytic investigation.* Unpublished master's thesis, Loyola University, Chicago.

Coontz, S. (1997). *The way we really are.* New York: Basic Books.

Copeland, L., & Griggs, L. (1985). *Going international.* New York: Random House.

Corey, G. (1991). *Theory and practice of counseling and psychotherapy* (4th ed.). Pacific Grove, CA: Brooks/Cole.

Corey, G. (1986). *Theory and practice of counseling and psychotherapy* (3rd ed.). Pacific Grove, CA: Brooks/Cole.

Cormier, L. S., & Hackney, H. (1987). *The professional counselor: A process guide to help.* Englewood Cliffs, NJ: Prentice-Hall.

Cormier, W., & Cormier, L. S. (1991). *Interviewing strategies for helpers: Fundamental skills and cognitive behavioral interventions* (3rd ed.). Pacific Grove, CA: Brooks/Cole.

Cormier, S., & Nurius, P. S. (2003). *Interviewing and helping strategies for helpers* (5th ed.). Pacific Grove, CA: Brooks/Cole Thomson Learning.

Corrigan, P. W., River, L. P., Lundin, R. K., Wasowski, K. U., Campion, J., Mathisen, J., Goldstein, H., Bergman, M., Gagnon, C., & Kubiak, M. A. (2000). Stigmatizing attributions about mental illness. *Journal of Community Psychology, 28,* 91–102.

Cox, M. J., Owen, M. T., Henderson, V. K., & Margand, N. A. (1992). Prediction of infant–father and infant–mother attachment. *Developmental Psychology, 28,* 474–483.

Crace, R. K., & Brown, D. (1996). *Life values inventory.* Minneapolis: National Computer Systems.

Crites, J. O. (1973). *Theory and research handbook: Career maturity inventory.* Monterey, CA: CTB-MacMillan-McGraw-Hill.

Crites, J. O. (1981). *Career models: Models, methods, and materials.* New York: McGraw-Hill.

Crites, J. O., & Savickas, M. L. (1995). *The career maturity inventory—Revised form.* Clayton, NY: Careerware: ISM.

Crites, J. O., & Savickas, M. L. (1996). Revision of the career maturity inventory. *Journal of Career Assessment, 4*(2), 131–138.

Cronbach, L. J. (1990). *Essentials of psychological testing* (5th ed.). New York: Harper & Row.

Cropanzano, R., & Prehar, C. A. (2001). Progress in organizational justice: Tunneling through the maze. In C. L. Cooper & I. T. Robertson (Eds.), *International review in the workplace and organizational psychology* (Vol. 2). Mahwah, NJ: Erlbaum.

Cross, T. L., Bazron, B. J., Dennis, K. W., & Isaacs, M. R. (1989). *Toward a culturally competent system of care.* Washington, DC: Georgetown University Child Development Center.

D'Amico, M., Barrafato, A., Peterson, L., Snow, S., & Tanguay, D. (2001). Using theatre to examine children's attitudes toward individuals with disabilities. *Developmental Disabilities Bulletin, 29*(1), 231–238.

Dancer, L. S., & Gilbert, L. A. (1993). Spouses' family work participation and its relation to wives' occupational level. *Sex Roles, 28,* 127–145.

D'Augelli, A. R. (1991). Gay men in college: Identity processes and adaptations. *Journal of College Student Development, 32,* 140–146.

Davidson, S. L., & Gilbert, L. A. (1993). Career counseling is a personal matter. *Career Development Quarterly, 42,* 149–153.

Dawis, R. V. (1991). Vocational interests, values, and preferences. In M. D. Dunnette & L. M. Hough (Eds.), *Handbook of industrial and organizational psychology* (Vol. 2, 2nd ed., pp. 833–871). Palo Alto, CA: Consulting Psychologists Press.

Dawis, R. V. (1996). The theory of work adjustment and person-environment-correspondence counseling. In D. Brown, L. Brooks, & Associates (Eds.), *Career choice and development* (3rd ed.), pp. 75–115). San Francisco: Jossey-Bass.

Dawis, R. V. (2002). Person-environment-correspondence theory. In D. Brown & Associates (Ed.), *Career choice and development* (4th ed., pp. 427–465). San Francisco: Jossey-Bass.

Dawis, R. V., Dohm, T. E., Lofquist, L. H., Chartrand, J. M., & Due, A. M. (1987). *Minnesota occupational classification system III.* Minneapolis: Vocational Psychology Research, Department of Psychology, University of Minnesota.

Dawis, R. V., & Lofquist, L. H. (1984). *A psychological theory of work adjustment: An individual differences model and its application.* Minneapolis: University of Minnesota.

De Jong, P., & Berg, I. K. (2002). *Interviewing for solutions* (2nd ed.). Pacific Grove, CA: Brooks/Cole.

Denmark, F. (1994). Engendering psychology. *American Psychologist, 49,* 329–334.

Dent, H. S., Jr. (1998). *The roaring 2000's.* New York: Simon & Schuster.

DePoy, E., & Gilson, S. F. (2004). *Rethinking disability: Principles for professional and social change.* Belmont, CA: Brooks/Cole-Thomson Learning.

Diamond, E. E. (1975). Overview. In E. E. Diamond (Ed.), *Issues of sex bias and sex fairness in career interest movement.* Washington, DC: U.S. Government Printing Office.

Dickstein, L. J. (1996). Sexual harassment in medicine. In D. K. Shrier (Ed.), *Sexual harassment in the workplace and academia: Psychiatric issues* (pp. 223–243). Washington, DC: American Psychiatric Press.

Diller, J. V. (1999). *Cultural diversity: A primer for the human services.* Pacific Grove, CA: Wadsworth.

Diller, J. V. (2004). *Cultural diversity: A primer for the human services.* Belmont, CA: Brooks/Cole-Thomson Learning.

Dix, J. E., & Savickas, M. L. (1995). Establishing a career: Developmental tasks and coping responses. *Journal of Vocational Behavior, 47,* 93–107.

Doyle, R. E. (1992). *Essential skills and strategies in the helping process.* Pacific Grove, CA: Brooks/Cole.

Doyle, R. E. (1998). *Essential skills & strategies in the helping process* (3rd ed.). Pacific Grove, CA: Brooks/Cole.

Drucker, P. F. (1992). *Managing for the future.* New York: Truman Talley Books/Dutton.

Drucker, P. F. (2002). *Managing in the next society.* New York: Truman Talley Books.

Drummond, R. (1992). *Appraisal procedures for counselors and helping professionals* (2nd ed.). New York: Macmillan.

Drummond, R. J., & Ryan, C. W. (1995). *Career counseling: A developmental approach.* Columbus, OH: Merrill.

Dumenci, L. (1995). Construct validity of the *Self-Directed Search* using hierarchically nested structural models. *Journal of Vocational Behavior, 47,* 21–34.

Duran, E., & Duran, B. (1995). *Native American postcolonial psychology.* Albany: State University of New York Press.

Eagly, A. H., Karau, S. J., & Makhijani, M. G. (1995). Gender and the effectiveness of leaders. *Psychological Bulletin, 117,* 125–145.

Eccles, J. S. (1987). Gender roles and women's achievement-related decisions. *Psychology of Women Quarterly, 11,* 135–172.

Eccles, J. S. (1993). School and family effects on the ontogeny of children's interests, self-perceptions, and activity choices. In J. E. Jacobs (Eds.), *Nebraska Symposium on Motivation: 1992* (Vol. 40, pp. 145–208). Lincoln: University of Nebraska Press.

Eccles, J. S., Barber, B., & Jozefowicz, D. (1999). Linking gender to educational, occupational, and recreational choices: Applying the Eccles et al. model of achievement-related choices. In W. B. Swann, J. H. Langlois, & L. A. Gilbert (Eds.), *Sexism and stereotypes in modern society* (pp. 153–192). Washington, DC: American Psychological Association.

Educational Testing Service. (1996). SIGI PLUS. Princeton, NJ: Author.

Eldridge, N. S. (1987). Gender issues in counseling same-sex couples. *Professional Psychology: Research and Practice, 18*(6), 567–572.

Eldridge, N. S., & Barnett, D. C. (1991). Counseling gay and lesbian students. In N. J. Evans & V. A. Wall (Eds.), *Beyond tolerance: Gays, lesbians and bisexuals on campus* (pp. 147–178). Alexandria, VA: American College Personnel Association.

Elkind, D. (1968). Cognitive development in adolescence. In J. F. Adams (Ed.), *Understanding adolescence.* Boston: Allyn & Bacon.

Elliot, J. E. (1993). Career development with lesbian and gay clients. *Career Development Quarterly, 41*(3), 210–226.

Ellis, A. (1962). *Reason and emotion in psychotherapy.* Secaucus, NJ: Lyle Stuart.

Ellis, A. (1971). *Growth through reason.* Hollywood, CA: Wilshire.

Ellis, A. (1991). The philosophical basis of rational-emotive therapy (RET). *Psychotherapy in Private Practice, 8,* 97–106.

Ellis, A. (1994). *Reason and emotion in psychotherapy revisited.* New York: Carol Publishing.

Ellis, A., & Grieger, R. (1977). *Handbook of rational-emotive therapy.* New York: Springer.

Engels, D. W. (Ed.). (1994). *The professional practice of career counseling and consultation: A resource document* (2nd ed.). Alexandria, VA: American Counseling Association.

Epps, S. & Jackson, B. J. (2000). *Empowered families, successful children.* Washington DC: American Psychological Association.

Erikson, E. H. (1950). *Childhood and society.* New York: Norton.

Erikson, E. H. (1963). *Childhood and society* (2nd ed.). New York: Norton.

Espin, O. M. (1987). Issues of identity in psychology of Latina lesbians. In Boston Lesbian Psychologies Collective (Eds.), *Lesbian psychologies: Exploration and challenges* (pp. 35–55). Urbana: University of Illinois Press.

Etringer, B. D., Hillerbrand, E., & Hetherington, C. (1990). The influence of sexual orientation on career decision making: A research note. *Journal of Homosexuality, 19*(4), 103–111.

Ettinger, J. M. (Ed.). (1991). *Improved career decision making in a changing world.* Garrett Park, MD: Garrett Park.

Evanoski, P. O., & Tse, F. W. (1989). Career awareness program for Chinese and Korean American parents. *Journal of Counseling and Development, 67,* 472–474.

Eysenck, H. J. (1998). *Intelligence: A new book.* New Brunswick, NJ: Transaction Press.

Fagot, B. I., & Leinbach, M. D. (1989). The young child's gender schema: Environmental input, internal organization. *Child Development, 60,* 663–672.

Fassinger, R. E., & Schlossberg, N. K. (1992). Understanding the adult years: Perspectives and implications. In S. D. Brown & R. W. Lent (Eds.), *Handbook of counseling psychology* (2nd ed., pp. 217–249). New York: Wiley.

Feldman, D. C. (1988). *Managing careers in organizations.* Glenview, IL: Scott, Foresman.

Feldman, D. C. (Ed.). (2002). *Work careers: A developmental perspective.* San Francisco: Jossey-Bass.

Feller, R. (1994). *650 career videos: Ratings, reviews and descriptions.* Ft. Collins: Colorado State University.

Fernandez, J. P. (1999). *Race, gender, & rhetoric.* New York: McGraw-Hill.

Fernandez, M. S. (1988). Issues in counseling southeast Asian students. *Journal of Multicultural Counseling and Development, 16,* 157–166.

Fitzgerald, L. F., & Betz, N. E. (1994). Career development in cultural context: The role of gender, race, class and sexual orientation. In M. Savickas & R. Lent (Eds.), *Convergence in career development theories: Implications for science and practice* (pp. 103–115). Palo Alto, CA: Consulting Psychologists Press.

Fitzgerald, L. F., & Ormerod, A. J. (1991). Perceptions of sexual harassment: The influence of gender and academic context. *Psychology of Women Quarterly, 15,* 281–294.

Fong, R. (2003). Cultural competence with Asian Americans. In D. Lum (Ed.), *Culturally competent practice* (2nd ed., pp. 261–282). Pacific Grove; CA: Brooks/Cole-Thomson Learning.

Ford, D. H. (1987). *Humans as self-constructing living systems: A developmental perspective personality disorder.* Hillsdale, NJ: Erlbaum.

Ford, M. E., & Ford, D. H. (Eds.). (1987). *Humans as self-constructing living systems: Putting the framework to work.* Hillsdale, NJ: Erlbaum.

Fouad, N. A. (1995). Career behavior of Hispanics: Assessment and career intervention. In F. T. L. Leong (Ed.), *Career development and vocational behavior of racial and ethnic minorities* (pp. 165–187). Mahwah, NJ: Erlbaum.

Fouad, N. A. (1997). School-to-work transition: Voice from an implementer. *The Counseling Psychologist, 25,* 403–412.

Fouad, N. A., & Bingham, R. P. (1995). Career counseling with racial/ethnic minorities. In W. B. Walsh & S. H. Osipow (Eds.), *Handbook of vocational psychology* (2nd ed., pp. 331–366). Hillsdale, NJ: Erlbaum.

Fox, A. (1991). Development of a bisexual identity: Understanding the process. In L. Hutchins & L. Kaahumanu (Eds.), *Bi any other name: Bisexual people speak out* (pp. 29–36). Boston: Alyson.

Fox, S., & Spector, P. E. (2005). *Counterproductive work behavior: Investigations of actors and targets.* Washington, DC: American Psychological Association.

French, S. (1996). The attitudes of health professionals towards disabled people. In G. Hales (Ed.), *Beyond disability: Towards an enabling society* (pp. 151–162). London: Sage.

Friedman, M., & Rosenman, R. (1974). *Type A behavior and your heart.* Greenwich, CT: Fawcett.

Friskopp, A., & Silverstein, S. (1995). *Straight jobs, gay lives.* New York: Scribner.

Fullerton, H. N. (1999). Labor force projections to 2008: Steady growth and changing composition. *Monthly Labor Review, 122,* 19–32.

Furnham, A. (2001). Vocational preference and P-O fit: Reflections on Holland's theory of vocational choice. *Applied Psychology: An International Review Special Issue: P-O Fit, 50,* 5–29.

Galliano, G. (2003). *Gender: Crossing boundaries.* Belmont, CA: Wadsworth/Thomson Learning.

Garcia, E. E. (Ed.). (1995). *Meeting the challenge of linguistic and cultural diversity in early childhood education.* New York: Teachers College Press.

Garguilo, R. M., & Graves, J. B. (1991). Parental feelings. *Childhood Education, 67*(3), 176–178.

Gartrell, N. (1983). Gay patients in the medical setting. In C. C. Nadelson & D. B. Marcotte (Eds.), *Treatment and interventions in human sexuality*. New York: Plenium.

Geary, J. (1972). Forty newspapers forty. In J. E. Bottoms, R. N. Evans, K. B. Hoyt, & J. C. Willer (Eds.), *Career education resource guide.* Morristown, NJ: General Learning Corporation.

Geisinger, K. F. (1998). Psychometric issues in test interpretation. In J. Sandoval, C. L. Frisby, K. F. Geisinger, J. D. Scheuneman, & J. R. Grenier (Eds.), *Test interpretation and diversity* (pp. 17–31). Washington, DC: American Psychological Association.

Gelberg, S., & Chojnacki, J. T. (1996). *Career and life planning with gay, lesbian, & bisexual persons.* Alexandria, VA: American Counseling Association.

Gelso, C., & Fretz, B. (2001). *Counseling psychology.* Belmont, CA: Wadsworth.

Gilbert, L. A. (1993). *Two careers/one family.* Newbury Park, CA: Sage.

Gillies, P. (1989). A longitudinal study of the hopes and worries of adolescents. *Journal of Adolescence, 12,* 69–81.

Ginzberg, E. (1966). *Lifestyles of educated American women.* New York: Columbia University Press.

Ginzberg, E. (1972). Toward a theory of occupational choice: A restatement. *Vocational Guidance Quarterly, 20,* 169–176.

Ginzberg, E. (1984). Career development. In D. Brown & L. Brooks (Eds.), *Career choice and development.* San Francisco: Jossey-Bass.

Ginzberg, E., Ginsburg, S. W., Axelrad, S., & Herma, J. L. (1951). *Occupational choice: An approach to general theory.* New York: Columbia University Press.

Glasser, N. (Ed.). (1989). *Control theory in the practice of reality therapy: Case studies.* New York: Harper & Row.

Goldenberg, H., & Goldenberg, I. (2002). *Counseling families today.* Pacific Grove, CA: Brooks/Cole.

Golding, J. M. (1989). Role occupancy and role-specific stress and social support as predictors of depression. *Basic and Applied Social Psychology, 10,* 173–195.

Goldstein, I. L., & Ford, J. K. (2002). *Training in organizations* (4th ed.). Belmont, CA: Wadsworth.

Goodlad, J. I. (1984). *A place called school: Prospects for the future.* New York: McGraw-Hill.

Goodman, J. (1993, April 29). *Using nonstandardized appraisals, tools and techniques.* Presentation to Michigan Career Development Association Annual Conference, Kalamazoo.

Gordon, L. V. (1967). *Survey of personal values.* Chicago: Science Research Associates.

Gottfredson, G. D., & Holland, J. L. (1989). *Dictionary of Holland occupational codes.* Odessa, FL: Psychological Assessment Resources.

Gottfredson, G. D., & Holland, J. L. (1990). A longitudinal test of the influence of congruence: Job satisfaction, competency utilization, and counterproductive behavior. *Journal of Counseling Psychology, 37,* 389–398.

Gottfredson, G. D., & Holland, J. L. (1991). *The position classification inventory: Professional manual.* Odessa, FL: Psychological Assessment Resources.

Gottfredson, G. D., & Holland, J. L. (1994). *The career attitudes and strategies inventory.* Odessa, FL: Psychological Assessment Resources.

Gottfredson, G. D., Jones, E. M., & Holland, J. L. (1993). Personality and vocational interests: The relation of Holland's six interest dimensions to five robust dimensions of personality. *Journal of Counseling Psychology, 40,* 518–524.

Gottfredson, L. S. (1981). Circumscription and compromise: A developmental theory of occupational aspirations. *Journal of Counseling Psychology, 28*(6), 545–579.

Gottfredson, L. S. (1990). A longitudinal test of the influence of congruence: Job satisfaction competency utilization, and counterproductive behavior. *Journal of Counseling Psychology, 37,* 389–398.

Gottfredson, L. S. (1996). Gottfredson's theory of circumscription and compromise. In D. Brown, L. Brooks, & Associates (Eds.), *Career choice and development* (3rd ed.), (pp. 179–228). San Francisco: Jossey-Bass.

Gottfredson, L. S. (1997). Why g matters: The complexity of everyday life. *Intelligence, 24*(1), 79–132.

Gottfredson, L. S. (2002). Gottfredson's theory of circumscription, compromise, and self-creation. In D. Brown & Associates (Eds.), *Career choice and development* (4th ed., pp. 85–149). San Francisco: Jossey-Bass.

Green, L. B., & Parker, H. J. (1965). Parental influence upon adolescents' occupational choice: A test of an aspect of Roe's theory. *Journal of Counseling Psychology, 12,* 379–383.

Greene, B. (1997). Ethnic minority lesbians and gay men: Mental health and treatment issues. In B. Greene (Ed.), *Ethnic and cultural diversity among lesbians and gay men.* New York: Guilford Press.

Greenglass, E. R. (1991). Type A behavior, career aspirations, and role conflict in professional women. In M. J. Strube (Ed.), *Type A behavior* (pp. 277–292). Newbury Park, CA: Sage.

Grossman, G. M., & Drier, H. N. (1988). *Apprenticeship 2000: The status of and recommendations for improved counseling, guidance, and information processes.* Columbus: National Center for Research in Vocational Education, Ohio State University (ERIC Report No. ED 298 356).

Grubb, W. N., Davis, G., Lum, J., Plihal, J., & Mograine, C. (1991). *The cunning hand, the cultured mind: Models for integrating vocational and academic education.* Berkeley, CA: National Center for Research in Vocational Education (ERIC Report No. ED 334 421).

Guinn, B. (1999). Leisure behavior motivation and the life satisfaction of retired persons. *Activities, Adapting and Aging, 23,* 13–20.

Gunther-Mohr, C. (1997). Virtual reality training takes off. *Training and Development, 51,* 47–48.

Gysbers, N. C., & Henderson, P. (1988). *Developing and managing your school guidance program.* Alexandria, VA: American Association for Counseling and Development.

Gysbers, N. C., & Henderson, P. (2001). Comprehensive guidance and counseling programs: A rich history and bright future. *Professional School Counseling, 4,* 246–256.

Gysbers, N. C., & Moore, E. J. (1987). *Career counseling, skills and techniques for practitioners.* Englewood Cliffs, NJ: Prentice-Hall.

Hackett, G. (1993). Career counseling and psychotherapy: False dichotomies and recommended remedies. *Journal of Career Assessment, 1,* 105–117.

Hackett, G. (1995). Self-efficacy in career choice and development. In A. Bandura (Ed.), *Self-efficacy in changing societies* (pp. 232–258). Cambridge: Cambridge University Press.

Hackett, G., & Lent, R. W. (1992). Theoretical advances and current inquiry in career psychology. In S. D. Brown & R. W. Lent (Eds.), *Handbook of counseling psychology* (2nd ed., pp. 419–451). New York: Wiley.

Hackett, G., Lent, R. W., & Greenhaus, J. H. (1991). Advances in vocational theory and research: A 20-year retrospective. *Journal of Vocational Behavior, 38,* 3–38.

Hackett, R. D., & Betz, N. E. (1981). A self-efficacy approach to the career development of women. *Journal of Vocational Behavior, 18,* 326–329.

Hackney, H., & Cormier, L. S. (2001). *The professional counselor.* Boston: Allyn & Bacon.

Halaby, C. N., & Weakliem, D. L. (1989). Worker control and attachment to the firm. *American Journal of Sociology, 95,* 549–591.

Hall, D. T., & Associates (1996). *The career is dead: Long live the career.* San Francisco: Jossey-Bass.

Hall, D. T., & Mirvas, P. H. (1996). The new protean career: Psychological success and the path with a heart. In D. T. Hall & Associates (Eds.), *The career is dead: Long live the career: A relational approach to careers* (pp. 15–45). San Francisco: Jossey-Bass.

Hall, E. S., & Hall, D. T. (1979). *The two-career couple.* Reading, MA: Addison-Wesley.

Hall, D. T. (1971). *Beyond culture.* New York: Anchor/Doubleday.

Hall, E. T. (1982). *The hidden dimension.* New York: Anchor/Doubleday.

Hammer, M., & Champy, J. (1993). *Reengineering the corporation: A manifesto for business revolution.* New York: HarperCollins.

Hansen, J. C., Collins, R. C., Swanson, J. L., & Fouad, N. A. (1993). Gender differences in the structure of interests. *Journal of Vocational Behavior, 42,* 200–211.

Hansen, L. S. (1970). *Career guidance practices in school and community.* Washington, DC: National Vocational Guidance Association.

Hansen, L. S. (1978). *BORN FREE: Training packets to reduce stereotyping in career options.* Minneapolis: University of Minnesota Press.

Hansen, L. S. (1990, July). *Integrative life planning: Work, family and community.* Paper presented at International Round Table for the Advancement of Counseling, Helsinki, Finland.

Hansen, L. S. (1991). Integrative life planning: Work, family, community. [Special Issue from World Future Society Conference on "Creating the Future: Individual Responsibility," Minneapolis: July 25]. *Futurics, 14*(3 & 4), 80–86.

Hansen, L. S. (1996). ILP: Integrating our lives, shaping our society. In R. Feller & G. Walz (Eds.), *Career transitions in turbulent times* (pp. 21–30). Greensboro: ERIC Counseling and Student Services Clearinghouse, University of North Carolina.

Hansen, L. S. (2000). Integrative life planning: A new worldview for career professionals. In J. Kummerow (Ed.), *New directions in career planning and the workplace.* Palo Alto, CA: Consulting Psychologists Press.

Hansson, R. O., DeKoekkoek, P. D., Neece, W. M., & Patterson, D. W. (1997). Successful aging at work: Annual review, 1992–1996: The older worker and transitions to retirement. *Journal of Vocational Behavior, 51,* 202–233.

Harley, S. (1995). When your work is not who you are: The development of a working-class consciousness among Afro-American women. In D. Clark-Hine, W. King, & L. Reed (Eds.), *We specialize in the wholly impossible: A reader in Black women's history* (pp. 25–38). Brooklyn, NY: Carlson.

Harmon, L. W. (1996). A moving target: The widening gap between theory and practice. In M. L. Savickas & W. B. Walsh (Eds.), *Handbook of career counseling theory and practice* (pp. 37–45). Palo Alto, CA: Davies-Black.

Harmon, L., Hansen, J. C., Borgen, F., & Hammer, A. (1994). *Strong Interest Inventory Manual.* Palo Alto, CA: Consulting Psychologists Press.

Harmon, L. W., & Meara, N. M. (1994). Contemporary developments in women's career counseling: Themes of the past, puzzles for the future. In W. B. Walsh & S. H. Osipow (Eds.), *Career counseling for women: Contemporary topics in vocational psychology* (pp. 355–367). Hillsdale, NJ: Erlbaum.

Harrington, T. F., & O'Shea, A. J. (1992). *The Harrington/O'Shea system for career decision making manual.* Circle Pines, MN: American Guidance Service.

Harris-Bowlsbey, J., Dikel, M. R., & Sampson, J. P. (1998). *The Internet: A tool for career planning.* Columbus, OH: National Career Development Association.

Hartung, P. J. (1999). Interest assessment using card sorts. In M. L. Savickas & A. R. Spokane (Eds.), *Vocational interests: Meaning, measurement, and counseling use.* Palo Alto, CA: Davies-Black.

Hartung, P. J., & Niles, S. G. (2000). Established career theories. In D. A. Luzzo. (Ed.), *Career counseling of college students.* (pp. 3–23). Washington, DC: American Psychological Association.

Harway, M. (1980). Sex bias in educational-vocational counseling. *Psychology of Women Quarterly, 4,* 212–214.

Haverkamp, B. E., & Moore, D. (1993). The career-personal dichotomy: Perceptual reality, practical illusion, and workplace integration. *Career Development Quarterly, 42,* 154–160.

Havighurst, R. (1953). *Human development and education.* New York: Longman.

Havighurst, R. (1972). *Developmental tasks and education* (3rd ed.). New York: Longman.

Healy, C. C. (1982). *Career development: Counseling through life stages.* Boston: Allyn & Bacon.

Healy, C. C. (1990). Reforming career appraisals to meet the needs of clients in the 1990s. *Counseling Psychologist, 18,* 214–226.

Healy, C. C., & Quinn, O. H. (1977). *Project Cadre: A cadre approach to career education infusion.* Unpublished manuscript.

Helms, J. E. (1990b). An overview of Black racial identity theory. In J. E. Helms (Ed.), *Black and White racial identity: Theory, research and practice* (pp. 9–32). Westport, CT: Greenwood.

Helwig, A. A. (1992). Book review of career development and services. *Journal of Employment Counseling, 29,* 77–78.

Henderson, A. (1984). Homosexuality in the college years: Developmental differences between men and women. *Journal of American College Health, 32,* 216–219.

Hermans, H. J. M. (1992). Telling and retelling one's self-narrative: A contextual approach to life-span development. *Human Development, 35,* 361–375.

Herr, E. L. (1996). Toward convergence of career theory and practice: Mythology, issues, and possibilities. In M. L. Savickas & W. B. Walsh (Eds.), *Handbook of career counseling theory and practice* (pp. 70–85). Palo Alto, CA: Davies-Black.

Herr, E. L. (2001). Career development and its practice: A historical perspective. *Career Development Quarterly, 49*(3), 196–211.

Herr, E. L., & Cramer, S. H. (1996). *Career guidance and counseling through the life span: Systematic approaches* (5th ed.). New York: HarperCollins.

Herr, E. L., Cramer, S. H., & Niles, S. G. (2004). *Career guidance and counseling through the life span: Systematic approaches* (6th ed.). Boston: Pearson Education, Inc.

Herring, R. D. (1990). Attacking career myths among Native Americans: Implications for counseling. *School Counselor, 38,* 13–18.

Herring, R. D. (1998). *Career counseling in schools.* Alexandria, VA: American Counseling Association.

Heward, W. L. (1999). *Exceptional children: An introduction to special education* (6th ed.). Englewood Cliffs, NJ: Prentice-Hall.

Higginbotham, E. (1994). Black professional women: Job ceilings and employment sectors. In M. Zinn & B. Dill (Eds.), *Women of color in the U.S. society* (pp. 113–131). Philadelphia: Temple University Press.

Highwater, J. (1990). *Sex and myth.* Boston: Harper & Row.

Hochschild, A. R. (1997). *The time bind.* New York: Holt.

Hofstede, G. (1984). *Culture's consequences: International differences in work-related values.* Newbury Park, CA: Sage.

Hogan, R., & Blake, R. (1999). John Holland's vocational typology and personality theory. *Journal of Vocational Behavior, 55,* 41–56.

Holland, J. L. (1966). *The psychology of vocational choice.* Waltham, MA: Blaisdell.

Holland, J. L. (1985a). *Making vocational choices: A theory of careers* (2nd ed.). Englewood Cliffs, NJ: Prentice-Hall.

Holland, J. L. (1985b). *Manual for the vocational preference inventory.* Odessa, FL: Psychological Assessment Resources.

Holland, J. L. (1987a). Current status of Holland's theory of careers: Another perspective. *Career Development Quarterly, 36,* 31–34.

Holland, J. L. (1987b). *The self-directed search professional manual.* Odessa, FL: Psychological Assessment Resources.

Holland, J. L. (1987c). *The occupations finder.* Odessa, FL: Psychological Assessment Resources.

Holland, J. L. (1992). *Making vocational choices* (2nd ed.). Odessa, FL: Psychological Assessment Resources.

Holland, J. L. (1994a). *Self-directed search (SDS), Form R.* Odessa, FL: Psychological Assessment Resources.

Holland, J. L. (1994b). *You and your career booklet.* Odessa, FL: Psychological Assessment Resources.

Holland, J. L. (1996). Exploring careers with a typology: What we have learned and some new directions. *American Psychologist, 51,* 397–406.

Holland, J. L., Daiger, D., & Power, P. G. (1980). *My vocational situation.* Odessa, FL: Psychological Assessment Resources.

Holland, J. L., Fritzsche, B. A., & Powell, A. B. (1994). *The SDS technical manual.* Odessa, FL: Psychological Assessment Resources.

Holland, J. L., Johnston, J. H., & Asama, N. (1993). The vocational identity scale: A diagnostic and treatment tool. *Journal of Career Assessment, 1,* 1–12.

Holland, J. L., Powell, A. B., & Fritzsche, B. A. (1994). *The SDS: Professional user's guide.* Odessa, FL: Psychological Assessment Resources.

Holmberg, K., Rosen, D., & Holland, J. L. (1990). *Leisure activities finder.* Odessa, FL: Psychological Assessment Resources.

HOPE in Focus (2000, Spring). *CAT emerges as national technology research center.* Detroit, MI: Hope in Focus and Center for Advanced Technology.

Hopkinson, K., Cox, A., & Rutter, M. (1981). Psychiatric interviewing techniques III: Naturalistic study: Eliciting feelings. *British Journal of Psychiatry, 138,* 406–415.

Hotchkiss, L., & Borow, H. (1996). Sociological perspective on work and career development. In D. Brown, L. Brooks, & Associates (Eds.), *Career choice and development* (3rd ed., pp. 281–326). San Francisco: Jossey-Bass.

Houston, B. K., & Kelly, K. E. (1987). Type A behavior in housewives: Relation to work, marital adjustment, stress, tension, health, fear-of-failure and self-esteem. *Journal of Psychosomatic Research, 31,* 55–61.

Hsia, J. (1981, April). *Testing and Asian and Pacific Americans.* Paper presented at the National Association for Asian and Pacific American Education, Honolulu.

Hudson, J. S. (1992). *Vocational counseling with dual-career same-sex couples.* Unpublished manuscript, Southwest Texas State University.

Humes, C. W., Szymanski, E. M., & Hohenshil, T. H. (1989, Nov./Dec.). Roles of counseling in enabling persons with disabilities. *Journal of Counseling & Development, 68,* 145–149.

Hunter, J. E., & Hunter, R. F. (1984). Validity and utility of alternative predictors of job performance. *Psychological Bulletin, 96,* 72–98.

Icard, L. (1986). Black gay men and conflicting social identities: Sexual orientation versus racial identity. In J. Gripton & M. Valentich (Eds.), *Special issue of the Journal of Social Work & Human Sexuality, Social work practice in sexual problems, 4*(1/2), 83–93.

Issacson, L. E. (1985). *Basics of career counseling.* Boston: Allyn & Bacon.

Ivancevich, J. J., & Matteson, M. T. (1980). *Stress and work, a managerial perspective.* Dallas: Scott Foresman.

Ivey, A. E. (1986). *Development therapy.* San Francisco: Jossey-Bass.

Ivey, A. E., & Ivey, M. B. (1999). *Intentional interviewing & counseling* (4th ed.). Pacific Grove, CA: Brooks/Cole.

Ivey, A. E., & Ivey, M. B. (2003). *Intentional interviewing & counseling* (5th ed.). Pacific Grove, CA: Brooks/Cole-Thomson Learning.

Jackson, E. L. (1988). Leisure constraints: A survey of past research. *Leisure Sciences, 10,* 203–215.

Jacobson, E. (1938). *Progressive relaxation.* Chicago: University of Chicago Press.

Jahoda, M. (1981). Work, employment and unemployment: Values, theories, and approaches in social research. *American Psychologist, 36,* 184–191.

Jay, K., & Young, A. (Eds.). (1979). *The gay report: Lesbians and gay men speak out about their sexual experiences and lifestyles.* New York: Simon & Schuster.

Savickas & W. B. Walsh (Eds.). *Handbook of career counseling theory and practice* (pp. 135–155). Palo Alto, CA: Davies-Black.

Jiang, W., Babyak, M., Krantz, D. S., Waugh, R. A., Coleman, R. E., Hanson, M. M., Frid, D. J., McNulty, S., Morris, J. J., O'Connor, C. M., & Blumenthal, J. A. (1996). Mental stress-induced myocardial ischemia and cardiac events. *Journal of the American Medical Association, 275,* 1651–1656.

Johansson, C. B. (1975). *Self-description inventory.* Minneapolis: National Computer Systems.

Johnson, M. J., Swartz, J. L., & Martin, W. E., Jr. (1995). Applications of psychological theories for career development with Native Americans. In F. T. L. Leong (Ed.), *Career development and vocational behavior of racial and ethnic minorities* (pp. 103–129). Mahwah, NJ: Erlbaum.

Johnson, P. R., & Indvik, J. (1994). Workplace violence: An issue of the nineties. *Public Personnel Management, 23,* 515–523.

Johnston, R. (1995, June). *The effectiveness of instructional technology: A review of the research.* Proceedings of the Virtual Reality in Medicine and Developers' Exposition. Cambridge, MA: Virtual Reality Solutions, Inc.

Kail, R. V., & Cavanaugh, J. C. (1996). *Human development.* Pacific Grove, CA: Brooks/Cole.

Kail, R. V., & Cavanaugh, J. C. (2000). *Human development* (2nd ed.). Belmont, CA: Wadsworth.

Kail, R. V., & Cavanaugh, J. C. (2004). *Human development* (3rd ed.). Belmont, CA: Wadsworth.

Kando, T. M., & Summers, W. C. (1971). The impact of work on leisure: Toward a paradigm and research strategy. *Pacific Sociological Review, 14,* 310–327.

Kaneshige, E. (1979). Cultural factors in group counseling and interaction. In G. Henderson (Ed.), *Understanding and counseling ethnic minorities* (pp. 457–467). Springfield, IL: Charles C. Thomas.

Kanfer, G. H. (1980). Self-management methods. In F. H. Kanfer & A. P. Goldstein (Eds.), *Helping people change* (pp. 309–355). New York: Pergamon.

Kanter, M. (1989). *When giants learn to dance.* New York: Simon & Schuster.

Kapes, J. T., Borman, C. A., Garcia, G., Jr., & Compton, J. W. (1985, April). *Evaluation of microcomputer-based career guidance systems with college students: SIGI and DISCOVER.* Paper presented at the annual meeting of the American Educational Research Association, Chicago.

Karasek, R., & Theorell, T. (1990). *Healthy work: Stress, productivity, and the reconstruction of working life.* New York: Basic Books.

Kasl, S. V. (1978). Epidemiological contributions to the study of work stress. In C. L. Cooper & R. Payne (Eds.), *Stress at work* (pp. 119–128). New York: Wiley.

Katz, M. R. (1975). *SIGI: A computer-based system of interactive guidance and information.* Princeton, NJ: Educational Testing Service.

Katz, M. R. (1993). *Computer-assisted career decision-making: The guide in the machine.* Hillsdale, NJ: Erlbaum.

Keating, D. P. (1980). Thinking processes in adolescence. In J. Adelson (Ed.), *Handbook of adolescent psychology.* New York: Wiley.

Kelly, G. A. (1955). *The psychology of personal constructs.* New York: Norton

Kelly, J. R., (1996). Activities. In J. E. Birden (Ed.), *Encyclopedia of gerontology: Age, aging, and the aged* (Vol. 1, pp. 37–49). San Diego, CA: Academic Press.

Kinnier, R. T., & Krumboltz, J. D. (1984). Procedures for successful career counseling. In N. C. Gysbers (Ed.), *Designing careers: Counseling to enhance education, work, and leisure* (pp. 307–335). San Francisco: Jossey-Bass.

Kinsey, A. C., Pomeroy, W. B., & Martin, C. E. (1948). *Sexual behavior in the human male.* Philadelphia: Saunders.

Kivlighan, D. J., Jr., Johnston, J. A., Hogan, R. S., & Mauer, E. (1994). Who benefits from computerized career counseling? *Journal of Counseling and Development, 72,* 289–292.

Klinger, G. (1988). *Dual-role model.* Unpublished manuscript, Southwest Texas State University, San Marcos.

Kobylarz, L. (1996). *National career development guidelines: K-adult handbook.* Stillwater, OK: National Occupational Coordinating Committee Training and Support Center.

Kohlberg, L. (1973). Continuities in childhood and adult moral development revisited. In P. B. Baltes & K. W. Schase (Eds.), *Lifespan development psychology: Personality and socialization.* New York: Academic.

Kronenberger, G. K. (1991, June). Out of the closet. *Personnel Journal, 40–44.*

Krumboltz, J. D. (1983). *Private rules in career decision making.* Columbus, OH: National Center for Research in Vocational Education.

Krumboltz, J. D. (1988). *Career Beliefs Inventory.* Palo Alto, CA: Consulting Psychologists Press.

Krumboltz, J. D. (1991). *Career beliefs inventory.* Palo Alto, CA: Consulting Psychologists Press.

Krumboltz, J. D. (1992). Thinking about careers. *Contemporary Psychology, 37,* 113.

Krumboltz, J. D. (1993). Integrating career and personal counseling. *Career Development Quarterly, 42,* 143–148.

Krumboltz, J. D. (1996). A learning theory of career counseling. In M. L. Savickas & W. B. Walsh (Eds.), *Handbook of career counseling theory and practice* (pp. 55–81). Palo Alto, CA: Davies-Black.

Krumboltz, J., & Coon, D. W. (1995). Current professional issues in vocational psychology. In M. L. Savickas and W. B. Walsh (Eds.), *Handbook of career theory and practice* (pp. 55–80). Palo Alto, CA: Davies-Black.

Krumboltz, J. D., & Hamel, D. A. (1977). *Guide to career decision-making skills.* New York: Educational Testing Service.

Krumboltz, J. D., Mitchell, A., & Gelatt, H. G. (1975). Applications of social learning theory of career selection. *Focus on Guidance, 8,* 1–16.

Krumboltz, J., & Nichols, C. (1990). Integrating the social learning theory of career decision making. In W. B. Walsh & S. H. Osipow (Eds.), *Career counseling: Contemporary topics in vocational psychology* (pp. 159–192). Hillsdale, NJ: Erlbaum.

Krumboltz, J. D., & Sorenson, D. L. (1974). *Career decision making.* Madison, WI: Counseling Films.

Kuder, G. F. (1963). A rationale for evaluating interests. *Educational and Psychological Measurement, 23,* 3–10.

Kuder, G. F. (1964). *Kuder general interest survey: Manual.* Chicago: Science Research Associates.

Kuder, G. F. (1966). *Kuder occupational interest survey: General manual.* Chicago: Science Research Associates.

Kulik, L. (2001). Impact of length of unemployment and age on jobless men and women: A comparative analysis. *Journal of Employment Counseling, 38,* 15–27.

Kumata, R., & Murata, A. (1980, March). *Employment of Asian/Pacific American women in Chicago.* Report of conference sponsored by the Women's Bureau, U.S. Department of Labor, Chicago.

Kurpius, D., Burello, L., & Rozecki, T. (1990). Strategic planning in human service organizations. *Counseling and Human Development, 22*(9), 1–12.

LaFromboise, T. D., & Jackson, M. (1996). MCT theory and Native-American populations. In D. W. Sue, A. E. Ivey, & P. B. Pedersen, *A theory of multicultural counseling & therapy* (pp. 192–202). Pacific Grove, CA: Brooks/Cole.

LaFromboise, T. D., Trimble, J. E., & Mohatt, G. V. (1990). Counseling intervention and American Indian tradition: An integrative approach. *Counseling Psychologist, 18*(4), 628–654.

Lapan, R. T., & Jingeleski, J. (1992). Circumscribing vocational aspirations in junior high school. *Journal of Counseling Psychology, 39,* 81–90.

Lauer, R. H., & Lauer, J. C. (1986). Factors in long-term marriages. *Journal of Family Issues, 7,* 382–390.

Lazarus, A. A. (1989). *The practice of multimodal therapy.* Baltimore: Johns Hopkins University Press.

Lazarus, R. S. (2000). Toward better research on stress and coping. *American Psychologist, 55,* 655–673.

Leana, C. R. (2002). The changing organizational context of careers. In D. C. Feldman (Ed.), *Work careers: A developmental perspective* (pp. 274–294). San Francisco: Jossey-Bass.

Leana, C. R., & Feldman, D. C. (1991). Gender differences in responses to unemployment. *Journal of Vocational Behavior, 38,* 65–77.

Leana, C. R., & Feldman, D. C. (1992). *Coping with job loss: How individuals, institutions and communities deal with layoffs.* San Francisco: New Lexington Press.

Leclair, S. W. (1982). The dignity of leisure. *School Counselor, 29*(4), 289–296.

Lent, R. W., Brown, S. D., & Hackett, G. (1996). Career development from a social cognitive perspective. In D. Brown, L. Brooks, & Associates (Eds.), *Career choice and development* (3rd ed., pp. 373–416). San Francisco: Jossey-Bass.

Lent, R. W., Brown, S. D., & Hackett, G. (2002). Social cognitive career theory. In D. Brown & Associates (Eds.), *Career choice and development* (4th ed., pp. 255–312). San Francisco: Jossey-Bass.

Lenz, J. G. (2000). *Paraprofessionals in career services; The Florida State University model* (Tech. Rep. No. 27). Tallahassee: Florida State University, Center for the Study of Technology in Counseling and Career Development.

Leong, F. T. L. (1993). The career counseling process with racial/ethnic minorities: The case of Asian Americans. *Career Development Quarterly, 42,* 26–40.

Leong, F. T. L. (1996a). Challenges to career counseling: Boundaries, cultures, and complexity. In M. L. Savickas & W. B. Walsh, *Handbook of career counseling theory and practice* (pp. 333–347). Palo Alto, CA: Davies-Black.

Leong, F. T. L. (1996b). MCT theory and Asian-American populations. In D. W. Sue, A. E. Ivey, & P. B. Pedersen, *A theory of multicultural counseling and therapy* (pp. 204–214). Pacific Grove, CA: Brooks/Cole.

Leong, F. T. L., & Serafica, F. C. (1995). Career development of Asian Americans: A research area in need of a good theory. In F. T. L. Leong (Ed.), *Career development and vocational behavior of racial and ethnic minorities* (pp. 78–99). Mahwah, NJ: Erlbaum.

Leung, P., & Cheung, M. (2001). Competencies in practice evaluations with Asian American individuals and families. In R. Fong & S. B. C. L. Furuto (Eds.), *Culturally competent practice: Skills, interventions, and evaluations* (pp. 426–437). Boston: Allyn & Bacon.

Leung, S. A., Conoley, C. W., & Scheel, M. J. (1994). The career and educational aspirations of gifted high school students: A retrospective study. *Journal of Counseling & Development, 72,* 298–303.

Levi, L. (1984). *Preventing work stress.* Reading, MA: Addison-Wesley.

Levine, H., & Evans, N. J. (1991). The development of gay, lesbian, and bisexual identities. In N. J. Evans & V. A. Walls (Eds.), *Beyond tolerance: Gays, lesbians, and bisexuals on campus* (pp. 1–24). Alexandria, VA: American College Personnel Association.

Levinson, D. J. (1980). The mentor relationship. In M. A. Morgan (Ed.), *Managing career development* (pp. 22–37). New York: Van Nostrand.

Levinson, D. J. (1996). *The seasons of a woman's life.* New York: Knopf.

Levinson, D. J., Darrow, C. N., Klein, E. B., Levinson, M. H., & McKee, B. (1978). *The seasons of a man's life.* New York: Knopf.

Liptak, J. J. (2001). *Treatment planning in career counseling.* Belmont, CA: Wadsworth/Thomson Learning.

Livson, N., & Peskin, H. (1980). Perspectives on adolescence from longitudinal research. In J. Adelson (Ed.), *Handbook of adolescent psychology* (pp. 47–98). New York: Wiley.

Lofquist, L. H., & Dawis, R. V. (1984). Research on work adjustment and satisfaction: Implications for career counseling. In S. Brown & R. Lent (Eds.), *Handbook of counseling psychology* (pp. 216–237). New York: Wiley.

Lofquist, L. H., & Dawis, R. V. (1991). *Essentials of person-environment-correspondence counseling.* Minneapolis: University of Minnesota Press.

Loiacano, D. K. (1989). Gay identity issues among black Americans: Racism, homophobia, and the need for validation. *Journal of Counseling & Development, 68,* 21–25.

Loiacano, D. K. (1993). Gay identity issues among black Americans: Racism, homophobia, and the need for validation. In L. D. Garnets & D. C. Kimmel (Eds.), *Psychological perspectives on lesbian and gay male experiences* (pp. 364–376). New York: Columbia University Press.

London, M. (2002). Organizational assistance in career development. In D. C. Feldman (Ed.), *Work careers: A developmental perspective* (pp. 323–346). San Francisco: Jossey-Bass.

Lorde, A. (1984). *Sister outsider.* Trumansburg, NY: Crossing.

Lott, B. E. (1994). *Women's lives: Themes and variations in gender* (2nd ed.). Pacific Grove, CA: Brooks/Cole.

Lowman, R. L. (1993). *Counseling and psychotherapy of work dysfunctions.* Washington, DC: American Psychological Association.

Lucas, M. S. (1996). Building cohesiveness between practitioners and researchers: A practitioner-scientist model. In M. L. Savickas & W. B. Walsh (Eds.), *Handbook of career counseling theory and practice* (pp. 81–89). Palo Alto, CA: Davies-Black.

Lum, D. (Ed.) (2003). *Culturally competent practice* (2nd ed.). Pacific Grove, CA: Brooks/Cole-Thomson Learning.

Mackelprang, R., & Salsgiver, R. (1999). *Disability: A diversity model approach in human service practice.* Pacific Grove, CA: Brooks/Cole.

Magnuson, J. (1990). Stress management. *Journal of Property Management, 55,* 24–28.

Mankiller, W., & Wallis, M. (1993). *Mankiller.* New York: St. Martin's.

Manson, N. M. (Ed.). (1982). *Topics in American Indian mental health prevention.* Portland: Oregon Health Sciences University Press.

Mariani, M. (1995–96, Winter). Computers and career guidance: Ride the rising ride. *Occupational Outlook Quarterly, 39,* 16–27.

Mariani, M. (1998, Summer). Job shadowing for college students. *Occupational Outlook Quarterly, 40,* 46–49.

Martell, R. F., Parker, C., Emrich, C. G., & Crawford, M. S. (1998). Sex stereotyping in the executive suite: "Much ado about something." *Journal of Social Behavior and Personality, 13,* 127–138.

Martin, J. (1996). *Cybercorp: The new business revolution.* New York: AMACOM.

Martin, W. E., Jr. (1995). Career development assessment and intervention strategies with American Indians. In F. T. L. Leong (Ed.), *Career development and vocational behavior of racial and ethnic minorities* (pp. 227–246). Mahwah, NJ: Erlbaum.

Martin, C. L., & Ruble, D. N. (1997). A developmental perspective of self-construals and sex differences: Comment on Cross and Madson. *Psychological Bulletin, 122*(1), 45–50.

Matlin, M. W. (2000). *The psychology of women* (4th ed.) Belmont, CA: Wadsworth/Thomson Learning.

Matlin, M. W. (2004). *The psychology of women* (5th ed.) Belmont, CA: Wadsworth/Thomson Learning.

Matsumoto, David. (1996). *Culture and psychology.* Pacific Grove, CA: Brooks/Cole.

Matsumoto, David. (2000). *Culture and psychology* (2nd ed.). Belmont, CA: Wadsworth.

Matsumoto, D., & Juang, L. (2004). *Culture and psychology* (3rd ed.). Belmont, CA: Wadsworth/Thomson Learning.

Maze, M., & Cummings, R. (1982). Analysis of DISCOVER. In M. Maze & R. Cummings, *How to select a computer-assisted guidance system* (pp. 97–107). Madison: University of Wisconsin, Wisconsin Vocational Studies Center.

McBride, A. B. (1990). Mental health effects of women's multiple roles. *American Psychologist, 45,* 381–384.

McCarn, S. R., & Fassinger, R. E. (1996). Revisioning sexual minority identity formation: A new model of lesbian identity and its implications for counseling and research. *Counseling Psychologist, 24*(3), 508–534.

McCormac, M. E. (1988). Information sources and resources. *Journal of Career Development, 16,* 129–138.

McDaniels, C. (1990). *The changing workplace: Career counseling strategies for the 1990s and beyond.* San Francisco: Jossey-Bass.

McKinlay, B. (1990). *Developing a career information system.* Eugene, OR: Career Information System.

McLennan, N. A., & Arthur, N. (1999). Applying the cognitive information processing approach to career problem solving and decision making to women's career development. *Journal of Employment Counseling, 36,* 82–96.

McRoy, R. (2003). Cultural competence with African Americans. In D. Lum (Ed.), *Culturally competent practice* (2nd ed., pp. 217–238). Pacific Grove, CA: Brooks/Cole-Thomson Learning.

McWhirter, J. J., McWhirter, B. T., McWhirter, E. H., & McWhirter, R. J. (2004). *At-risk youth* (3rd ed.). Belmont, CA: Brooks/Cole Thomson Learning.

Meara, N. M. (1996). Prudence and career assessment: Making our implicit assumptions explicit. In M. L. Savickas & W. B. Walsh (Eds.), *Handbook of career counseling theory and practice* (pp. 315–331). Palo Alto, CA: Davies-Black.

Meichenbaum, D. (1977). *Cognitive behavior modification: An integrative approach.* New York: Plenum.

Meir, E. I., Esformes, Y., & Friedland, N. (1994). Congruence and differentiation as predictors of workers' occupational stability and job performance. *Journal of Career Assessment, 2,* 40–54.

Meister, J. C. (1994). *Corporate quality universities: Lessons in building a world-class workforce.* New York: Irwin.

Michael, R. T., Gagnon, J. H., Lauman, E. O., & Kolata, G. (1994). *Sex in America: A definitive survey.* Boston: Little, Brown.

Miller, J. M., & Springer, T. P. (1986). Perceived satisfaction of a computerized vocational counseling system as a function of monetary investment. *Journal of College Student Personnel, 27,* 142–146.

Miller, N. B. (1982). Social work services to urban Indians. In J. W. Green (Ed.), *Cultural awareness in the human services.* Englewood Cliffs, NJ: Prentice-Hall.

Miller-Tiedeman, A. (1988). *Lifecareer: The quantum leap into a process theory of career.* Vista, CA: LIFECAREER Foundation.

Miller-Tiedeman, A. L., & Tiedeman, D. V. (1990). Career decision making: An individualistic perspective. In D. Brown, L. Brooks, & Associates (Eds.), *Career choice and development: Applying contemporary theories to practice* (2nd ed., pp. 308–337). San Francisco: Jossey-Bass.

Mitchell, K. E., Levin, A. S., & Krumboltz, J. D. (1999). Planned happenstance: Constructing unexpected career opportunities. *Journal of Counseling and Development, 77,* 115–124.

Mitchell, L. K., & Krumboltz, J. D. (1987). Cognitive restructuring and decision-making training on career indecision. *Journal of Counseling and Development, 66,* 171–174.

Mitchell, L. K., & Krumboltz, J. D. (1990). Social learning approach to career decision making: Krumboltz's theory. In D. Brown & L. Brooks (Eds.), *Career choice and development: Applying contemporary theories to practice* (2nd ed., pp. 145–196). San Francisco: Jossey-Bass.

Mitchell, L. K., & Krumboltz, J. D. (1996). Krumboltz's learning theory of career choice and counseling. In D. Brown, L. Brooks, & Associates (Eds.), *Career choice and development* (3rd ed., pp. 233–276). San Francisco: Jossey-Bass.

Mondimore, F. M. (1996). *Homosexuality.* Baltimore: Johns Hopkins University Press.

Morales, E. S. (1992). Counseling Latino gays and Latina lesbians. In S. H. Dworkin and F. J. Gutierrea (Eds.), *Counseling gay men and lesbians: Journey to the end of the rainbow* (pp. 125–141). Alexandria, VA: American Counseling Association.

Morgan, R. B., & Hawkridge, D. G. (1999). Guest Editorial—Global distance learning. *Performance Improvement Quarterly, 12*(2), 6–8.

Morrison, W. W. (2002). The school-to-work transition. In D. C. Feldman (Ed.), *Work careers: A developmental response* (pp. 126–159). San Francisco: Jossey-Bass.

Muchinsky, P. M. (1997). *Psychology applied to work* (5th ed.). Pacific Grove, CA: Brooks/Cole.

Muchinsky, P. M. (2003). *Psychology applied to work* (6th ed.). Belmont, CA: Wadsworth/Thomson Learning.

Multon, K. D., Brown, S. D., & Lent, R. W. (1991). Relation of self-efficacy beliefs to academic outcomes: A meta-analytic investigation. *Journal of Counseling Psychology, 38,* 30–38.

Munk, N. (2000, March 5). The price of freedom. *New York Times Magazine,* pp. 50–54.

Munsterberg, H. (1913). *Psychology and industrial efficiency.* Boston: Houghton Mifflin.

Murphy, B. C., & Dillon. C. (2003). *Interviewing in action relationship, process, and change* (2nd ed.). Pacific Grove, CA: Brooks/Cole.

Myers, L. J., Speight, S. L., Highlen, P. S., Cox, C. I., Reynolds, A. L., Adams, E. M., & Hanley, C. P. (1991). Identity development and worldviews toward an optimal conceptualization. *Journal of Counseling and Development, 70,* 55–63.

National Board for Certified Counselors Inc. and Center for Credentialing and Education, Inc. (2001). *Standards of the ethical practice of Internet counseling.* Greensboro, NC: Author.

National Career Development Association. (1997). *Guidelines for the use of the Internet for provision of career information and planning services.* Alexandria, VA: Author.

National Career Development Association. (2003). National Career Development Association ethical standards. (On-line). Available: http://ncda.org/about/poles.html.

National Commission on Children. (1993). *Just the facts: A summary of recent information on America's children and their families.* Washington, DC: Author.

National Consortium of State Career Guidance Supervisors. (1996). *Planning for life: 1995 compendium of recognized career planning programs.* Columbus: Center on Education and Training for Employment, Ohio State University.

Neal, B. E. (2000). Native American women. In M. Julia (Ed.), *Constructing gender: Multicultural perspectives in working women* (pp. 157–174). Pacific Grove, CA: Brooks/Cole.

Neff, W. S. (1985). *Work and human behavior* (2nd ed.). Chicago: Aldine.

Neimeyer, G. J. (1989). Applications for repertory grid techniques to vocational assessment. *Journal of Counseling and Development, 67,* 585–589.

Neukrug, E. (1999). *The world of the counselor.* Pacific Grove, CA: Brooks/Cole.

Nevill, D. D., & Super, D. E. (1986). *The Salience Inventory manual: Theory, application, and research.* Palo Alto, CA: Consulting Psychologists Press.

Nevo, O. (1987). Irrational expectations in career counseling and their confronting arguments. *Career Development Quarterly, 35,* 239–250.

Newman, B. M., & Newman, P. R. (1995). *Development through life: A psychosocial approach.* Pacific Grove, CA: Brooks/Cole.

Newman, B. M., & Newman, P. R. (2003). *Development through life: A psychological approach* (8th ed.). Belmont, CA: Wadsworth.

Newman, B. S., & Muzzonigro, P. G. (1993). The effects of traditional family values on the coming out process of gay male adolescents. *Adolescence, 28,* 213–226.

NICHD Early Child Care Research Network. (2000). The relation of child care to cognitive and language development. *Child Development, 71,* 960–980.

Niles, S. G., & Hartung, P. J. (2000). Emerging career theories. In D. A. Luzzo (Ed.), *Career Counseling of College Students* (pp. 23–43). Washington, DC: American Psychological Association.

Noble, M. (1992). *Down is up for Aaron Eagle: A mother's spiritual journey with Down Syndrome.* San Francisco: Harper.

Ogbu, J. (1990). Cultural model, identity and literacy. In J. Stigler, R. Shweder, & G. Herdt (Eds.), *Cultural psychology* (pp. 520–541). New York: Cambridge University Press.

Okun, B. (2002). *Effective helping* (6th ed.). Pacific Grove, CA: Brooks/Cole.

Okun, B. F., Fried, J., & Okun, M. L. (1999). *Understanding diversity: A learning practice primer.* Pacific Grove, CA: Brooks/Cole.

O'Neil, J. M. (1982). Gender role conflict and strain in men's lives: Implications for psychiatrists, psychologists, and other human-services providers. In K. Solomon & N. B. Levy (Eds.), *Men in transition* (pp. 5–44). New York: Plenum.

O'Neil, J. M. (1990). Assessing men's gender role conflict. In D. Moore & F. Leafgren (Eds.), *Men in conflict* (pp. 23–38). Alexandria, VA: American Association of Counseling and Development.

O'Neil, J. M., Good, G. E., & Holmes, S. (1995). Fifteen years of theory and research on men's gender role conflict: New paradigms for empirical research. In R. Levant & W. Pollack (Eds.), *The new psychology of men* (pp. 164–206). New York: Basic Books.

Ortiz, V. (1996). Migration and marriage among Puerto Rican women. *International Migration Review, 30*(2), 460–484.

Osborn, D., & Zunker, V. (2006). *Using assessment results for career development.* Belmont, CA: Brooks/Cole-Thomson Learning.

Osipow, S. H. (1979). Occupational mental health: Another role for counseling psychologists. *The Counseling Psychologist, 8*(1), 65–70.

Osipow, S. H. (1983). *Theories of career development* (3rd ed.). New York: Appleton-Century-Crofts.

Osipow, S. H., & Fitzgerald, L. (1996). *Theories of career development* (4th ed.). Needham Heights, MA: Allyn & Bacon.

Ostroff, C., Shin, Y., & Feinberg, B. (2002). Skill acquisition and person-environment fit. In D. C. Feldman (Ed.), *Work Career: A developmental perspective* (pp. 63–93). San Francisco: Jossey-Bass.

Out! Resource Guide. (1994). Chicago: Lambda.

Paisley, P. O., & Hubbard, G. T. (1994). *Developmental school counseling programs: From theory to practice.* Alexandria, VA: American Counseling Association.

Palkovitz, R. (1984). Parental attitudes and fathers' interactions with their 5-month-old infants. *Developmental Psychology, 20,* 1054–1060.

Parcel, T. L., & Menaghan, E. G. (1994). Early parental work, family, social capital, and early childhood outcomes. *American Journal of Sociology, 9,* 972–1009.

Parham, T. (1996). MCT theory and African-American populations. In D. W. Sue, A. E. Ivey, & P. B. Pedersen (Eds.), *A theory of multicultural counseling & therapy* (pp. 177–190). Pacific Grove, CA: Brooks/Cole.

Parker, R. M., & Hansen, C. E. (1981). *Rehabilitation counseling.* Boston: Allyn & Bacon.

Parsons, F. (1909). *Choosing a vocation.* Boston: Houghton Mifflin.

Pascarella, E. T., & Terenzini, P. T. (1991). *How college affects students: Findings and insights from twenty years of research.* San Francisco: Jossey-Bass.

Patton, W., & McMahon, M. (1999). *Career development and systems theory.* Pacific Grove, CA: Brooks/Cole.

Peplau, L. A., Cochran, S. D., & Mays, V. M. (1997). A national survey of intimate relationships of African American lesbians and gay men: A look at commitment, satisfaction, sexual behavior, and HIV disease. In B. Greene (Ed.), *Ethnic and cultural diversity among lesbians and gay men* (pp. 11–39). Thousand Oaks, CA: Sage.

Pernanen, K. (1991). *Alcohol in human violence.* London: Guilford.

Peterson, G. W., Ryan-Jones, R. E., Sampson, J. P., Jr., Reardon, R. C., & Shahnasarian, M. (1987). *A comparison of the effectiveness of three computer-assisted career guidance systems on college students' career decision-making processes* (Technical Report No. 6). Tallahassee: Florida State University, Center for the Study of Technology in Counseling and Career Development.

Peterson, G. W., Sampson, J. P., & Reardon, R. C. (1991). *Career development and services: A cognitive approach.* Pacific Grove, CA: Brooks/Cole.

Peterson, G. W., Sampson, J. P., Jr., Reardon, R. C., & Lenz, J. G. (1996). A cognitive information processing approach to career problem solving and decision making. In D. Brown, L. Brooks, & Associates (Eds.), *Career choice and development* (3rd ed., pp. 423–467). San Francisco: Jossey-Bass.

Peterson, N., & Gonzalez, R. C. (2000). *The role of work in people's lives: Applied career counseling and vocational psychology.* Pacific Grove, CA: Brooks/Cole-Wadsworth.

Philips, S. D., & Imhoff, A. R. (1997). Women and career development: A decade of research. *Annual Review of Psychology, 48,* 31–59.

Piaget, J. (1929). *The child's conception of the world.* New York: Harcourt Brace.

Piaget, J., & Inhelder, B. (1969). *The psychology of the child.* New York: Basic.

Picchioni, A. P., & Bonk, E. C. (1983). *A comprehensive history of guidance in the United States.* Austin: Texas Personnel and Guidance Association.

Pietrofesa, J. J., & Splete, H. (1975). *Career development: Theory and research.* New York: Grune & Stratton.

Polkinghorne, D. E. (1990). Action theory approaches to career research. In R. A. Young & W. A. Borgen (Eds.), *Methodological approaches to the study of career* (pp. 87–105). New York: Praeger.

Ponterotto, J. G. (1987). Counseling Mexican Americans: A multimodal approach. *Journal of Counseling and Development, 65,* 308–311.

Pope, M. (2000). A brief history of career counseling in the United States. *Career Development Quarterly, 48,* 194–211.

Pope, M. S., Prince, J. P., & Mitchell, K. (2000). Responsible career counseling with lesbian and gay students. In D. A. Luzzo (Ed.), *Career counseling of college students* (pp. 267–285). Washington, DC: American Psychology Association.

Pope, R. L., & Reynolds, A. L. (1991). Including bisexuality: It's more than just a label. In N. J. Evans & V. A. Wall (Eds.), *Beyond tolerance: Gays, lesbians, and bisexuals on campus* (pp. 205–212). Alexandria, VA: American College Personnel Association.

Powell, D. H. (1957). Careers and family atmosphere: An empirical test of Roe's theory. *Journal of Counseling Psychology, 4,* 212–217.

Prediger, D. J. (1994). Multicultural assessment standards: A compilation for counselors. *Measurement and Evaluation in Counseling and Development, 27,* 68–73.

Prediger, D. J. (1995). *Assessment in career counseling.* Greensboro: ERIC Counseling and Student Services Clearinghouse, University of North Carolina.

Rabinowitz, F. E., & Cochran, S. V. (1994). *Man alive: A primer of men's issues.* Pacific Grove, CA: Brooks/Cole.

Ragheb, M. B., & Griffith, C. A. (1982). The contribution of leisure participation and leisure satisfaction to life satisfaction of older persons. *Journal of Leisure Research, 14,* 295–306.

Ragins, B. R., & Scandura, T. A. (1995). Antecedents and work-related correlates of reported sexual harassment: An empirical investigation of competing hypotheses. *Sex Roles, 32,* 429–455.

Rapoport, R., & Rapoport, R. (1978). The dual career family. In L. S. Hansen & R. S. Rapoza (Eds.), *Career development and the counseling of women.* Springfield, IL: Charles C. Thomas.

Rayman, J. (1996). Apples and oranges in the career center: Reaction to R. Reardon. *Journal of Counseling & Development, 74,* 286–287.

Reardon, R. C., & Lenz, J. G. (1998). *The self-directed search and related Holland materials: A practitioner's guide.* Odessa, FL: Psychological Assessment Resources.

Reardon, R. C., Lenz, J. G., Sampson, J. P., & Peterson, G. W. (2000). *Career development and planning: A comprehensive approach.* Pacific Grove, CA: Brooks/Cole.

Reardon, R. C., Petersen, G. W., Sampson, J. P., Ryan-Jones, R. E., & Shahnasarian, M. (1992). A comparative analysis of the impact of SIGI and SIGI PLUS. *Journal of Career Development, 18,* 315–322.

Reich, R. B. (1991). *The work of nations.* New York: Knopf.

Remafedi, G. (1999). Sexual orientation and suicide. *Journal of American Medical Association, 282*(13), 1291–1292.

Reskin, B. F. (1993). Sex segregation in the workplace. *Annual Review of Sociology, 19,* 241–270.

Reskin, B. F., & Pakavic, I. (1994). *Women and men at work.* London: Pine Forge.

Reynolds, A. L., & Hanjorgiris, W. F. (2000). Coming out: Lesbian, gay and bisexual identity development. In R. M. Perez, K. A. Debord, & K. J. Bieschke (Eds.), *Handbook of counseling and therapy with lesbians, gays, and bisexuals.* Washington, DC: American Psychology Association Press.

Reynolds, A. L., & Pope, R. (1991). The complexity of diversity: Exploring multiple oppressions. *Journal of Counseling and Development, 70,* 174–180.

Rice, P. L. (1999). *Stress and health* (3rd ed.). Pacific Grove, CA: Brooks/Cole.

Richards, M. H., & Larson, R. (1993). Pubertal development and the daily subjective states of young adolescents. *Journal of Research on Adolescence, 3,* 145–169.

Richardson, B. (1991). Utilizing the resources of the African American church: Strategies for counseling professionals. In C. Lee & B. Richardson (Eds.), *Multicultural issues in counseling: New approaches to diversity* (pp. 65–75). Alexandria, VA: American Association for Counseling and Development.

Richardson, M. S. (1993). Work in people's lives. *Journal of Counseling and Development, 40,* 425–433.

Richardson, M. S. (1996). From career counseling to counseling/psychotherapy and work, jobs, and career. In M. L. Savickas and W. B. Walsh (Eds.), *Handbook of career counseling theory and practice* (pp. 347–360). Palo Alto, CA: Davies-Black.

Rickel, J., & Johnston, W. L. (1999). Animated agents for procedural training in virtual reality: Perception, cognition, and motor control. *Applied Artificial Intelligence, 12,* 343–382.

Rider, E. A. (2000). *Our voices: Psychology of women.* Pacific Grove, CA: Wadsworth.

Rifkin, J. (1995). *The end of work: The decline of the global labor force and the dawn of the post-market era.* New York: Putnam's.

Rimer, S. (1996). The fraying of community. In *New York Times* (et al.), *The downsizing of America* (pp. 111–138). New York: Time Books.

Rodriguez, M., & Blocher, D. (1988). A comparison of two approaches to enhancing career maturity in Puerto Rican college women. *Journal of Counseling Psychology, 35,* 275–280.

Roe, A. (1956). *The psychology of occupations.* New York: Wiley.

Roe, A. (1972). Perspectives on vocational development. In J. M. Whiteley & A. Resnikoff (Eds.), *Perspectives on vocational development* (pp. 61–82). Washington, DC: American Personnel and Guidance Association.

Roe, A., & Lunneborg, P. W. (1990). Personality development and career choice. In D. Brown & L. Brooks (Eds.), *Career choice and development. Applying contemporary theories to practice* (pp. 68–101). San Francisco: Jossey-Bass.

Roessler, R., & Rubin, E. (1982). *Case management and rehabilitation counseling: Procedures and techniques.* Baltimore: University Park Press.

Rogers, C. R. (1942). *Counseling and psychotherapy.* Boston: Houghton Mifflin.

Rogler, L. H. (1994). International migrations: A framework for directing research. *American Psychologist, 49,* 701–708.

Roos, P. A., & Jones, K. W. (1993). Women's inroads into academic sociology. *Work and Occupations, 20,* 395–428.

Roselle, B., & Hummel, T. (1988). Intellectual development and interaction effectiveness with DISCOVER. *Career Development Journal, 35–36,* 241–251.

Rosen, D., Holmberg, K., & Holland, J. L. (1994a). *Dictionary of educational opportunities.* Odessa, FL: Psychology Assessment Resources.

Rosen, D., Holmberg, K., & Holland, J. L. (1994b). *Educational opportunities finder.* Odessa, FL: Psychological Assessment Resources.

Rotter, J. B. (1966). Generalized expectancies for internal versus external control of reinforcement. *Psychological Monographs, 80* (Whole No. 609).

Rounds, J. B. (1990). The comparative and combined utility of work value and interest data in career counseling with adults. *Journal of Vocational Behavior, 37,* 32–45.

Rounds, J. B., Henly, G. A., Dawis, R. V., Lofquist, L. H., & Weiss, D. J. (1981). *Manual for the Minnesota Importance Questionnaire.* Minneapolis: University of Minnesota, Psychology Department Work Adjustment Project.

Rounds, J. B., & Tinsley, H. E. A. (1984). Diagnosis and treatment of vocational problems. In S. D. Brown & R. W. Lent (Eds.), *Handbook of counseling psychology* (pp. 137–177). New York: Wiley.

Rounds, J. B., & Tracey, T. J. (1990). From trait-and-factor to person-environment-fit counseling: Theory and process. In W. B. Walsh & S. J. Osipow (Eds.), *Career counseling: Contemporary topics in vocational psychology* (pp. 1–44). Hillsdale, NJ: Erlbaum.

Rounds, J. B., & Tracy, T. J. (1993). Prediger's dimensional representation of Holland's RIASEC circumplex. *Journal of Applied Psychology, 78,* 875–890.

Rounds, J. B., & Tracey, T. J. (1996). Cross-cultural structural equivalence of RISEC models and measures. *Journal of Counseling Psychology, 43,* 310–329.

Rousseau, D. (1995). *Psychological contracts in organizations: Understanding written and unwritten agreements.* Thousands Oaks, CA: Sage.

Rowland, D. T. (1991). Family diversity and the life cycle. *Journal of Comparative Family Studies, 22,* 1–14.

Russo, N. F., Kelly, R. M., & Deacon, M. (1991). Gender and success-related attributions: Beyond individualistic conceptions of achievement. *Sex Roles, 25,* 331–350.

Rust, P. C. (1996). Managing multiple identities: Diversity among bisexual women and men. In B. A. Firestein (Ed.), *Bisexuality* (pp. 53–84). Thousand Oaks, CA: Sage.

Ryan, C., & Futterman, D. (1998). *Lesbian and gay youth: Care and counseling.* New York: Columbia University Press.

Ryan, E. S. (2000). Comparing 21st century job-skill acquisition with self-fulfillment for college students. *Education, 119,* 529–536.

Ryan, J. M., Tracey, T. J. & Rounds, J. (1996). Generalizability of Holland's structure of vocational interests across ethnicity, gender, and socioeconomic status. *Journal of Counseling Psychology, 43,* 330–337.

Ryan, L., & Ryan, R. (1982). *Mental health and the urban Indian.* Unpublished manuscript.

Rychlak, J. F. (1993). A suggested principle of complementarity for psychology. *American Psychologist, 48,* 933–942.

Rynes, S. L. & Gerhart, B. (2000). *Compensation in organizations.* San Francisco: Jossey-Bass.

Sadker, M., & Sadker, D. (1994). *Failing at fairness: How America's schools cheat girls.* New York: Scribners.

Sadri, G., & Robertson, L. T. (1993). Self-efficacy and work-related behavior: A review and meta-analysis. *Applied Psychology: An Internal Review, 42,* 139–152.

Saghir, M. T., & Robins, E. (1973). *Male and female homosexuality: A comprehensive investigation.* Baltimore: Williams and Wilkins.

Salomone, P. R. (1996, Spring). Tracing Super's theory of vocational development: A 40-year retrospective. *Journal of Career Development, 22*(3), 167–184.

Salsgiver, R. O. (1995 March 4). *Persons with disabilities and empowerment: Building a future of independent living.* Unpublished invitational speech to the Council on Social Work Education Annual Program Meeting, San Diego, CA.

Sampson, J. P. (1983). Computer-assisted testing and assessment: Current status and implications for the future. *Measurement and Evaluation in Guidance, 15*(3), 293–299.

Sampson, J. P. (1994). *Effective computer-assisted career guidance: Occasional paper number 2.* Center for the Study of Technology in Counseling and Career Development, Florida State University.

Sampson, J. P., Peterson, G. W., Lenz, J. G., & Reardon, R. C. (1992). A cognitive approach to career services: Translating concepts into practice. *Career Development Quarterly, 41,* 67–73.

Sampson, J. P., & Lumsden, J. A. (2000). Ethical issues in the design and use of Internet-based career assessment. *Journal of Career Assessment, 8,* 21–35.

Sampson, J. P., Jr., Peterson, G. W., Lenz, J. G., Reardon, R. C., & Saunders, D. E. (1996a). *Career thoughts inventory: Professional manual.* Odessa, FL: Psychological Assessment Resources.

Sampson, J. P., Jr., Peterson, G. W., Lenz, J. G., Reardon, R. C., & Saunders, D. E. (1996b). *Improving your career thoughts: A workbook for the Career Thoughts Inventory.* Odessa, FL: Psychological Assessment Resources.

Sampson, J. P., & Pyle, K. R. (1983). Ethical issues involved with the use of computer-assisted counseling, testing and guidance systems. *Personnel and Guidance Journal, 61*(3), 283–287.

Sampson, J. P., Reardon, R. C., Peterson, G. W., & Lenz, J. G. (2004). *Career counseling & services: A cognitive information processing approach.* Belmont, CA: Brooks/Cole-Thomson Learning.

Sandoval, J. (1998a). Testing in a changing world: An introduction. In J. Sandoval, C. L. Frisby, K. F. Geisinger, J. D. Scheuneman, & J. R. Grenier, *Test interpretation and diversity* (pp. 3–17). Washington, DC: American Psychological Association.

Sandoval, J. (1998b). Test interpretation in a diverse future. In J. Sandoval, C. L. Frisby, K. F. Geisinger, J. D. Scheuneman, & J. R. Grenier, *Test interpretation and diversity* (pp. 387–403). Washington, DC: American Psychological Association.

Sanguiliano, I. (1978). *In her time.* New York: Morrow.

Sastre, M. T. M., & Mullet, E. (1992). Occupational preferences of Spanish adolescents in relation to Gottfredson's theory. *Journal of Vocational Behavior, 40,* 306–317.

Saunders, L. (1995). Relative earnings of black and white men by region, industry. *Monthly Labor Review, 118*(4), 68–73.

Savickas, M. L. (1989). Career-style assessment and counseling. In T. Sweeney (Ed.), *Adelerian counseling: A practical approach for a new decade* (3rd ed., pp. 289–320). Muncie, IN: Accelerated Development Press.

Savickas, M. L. (1990). The use of career choice measures in counseling practice. In E. Watkins & V. Campbell (Eds.), *Testing in counseling practice* (pp. 373–417). Hillsdale, NJ: Erlbaum.

Savickas, M. L. (1993). Career counseling in the postmodern era. *Journal of Cognitive Psychotherapy: An International Quarterly, 7,* 205–215.

Savickas, M. L. (2002). Career construction: A developmental theory. In D. Brown & Associates (Eds.), *Career choice and development* (4th ed., pp. 149–206). San Francisco: Jossey-Bass.

Savickas, M. L., & Hartung, P. J. (1996). The career development inventory in review: Psychometric and research findings. *Journal of Career Assessment, 4,* 171–188.

Savickas, M. L., & Walsh, W. B. (Eds.). (1996). *Handbook of career counseling theory and practice.* Palo Alto, CA: Davies-Black.

Scandura, T. A. (2002). The establishment years: A dependence perspective. In D. C. Feldman (Ed.), *Work careers: A developmental perspective* (pp. 159–186). San Francisco: Jossey-Bass.

Scarr, S., Phillips, D., & McCartney, K. (1989). Working mothers and their families. *American Psychologist, 44,* 1402–1409.

Schafer, W. (2000). *Stress management for wellness.* Belmont, CA: Wadsworth/Thomson Learning.

Schien, E. H. (1990). *Career anchors: Discovering your real values.* San Diego, CA: University Associates.

Schultheiss, D. O. (2000). Emotional-social issues in the provision of career counseling. In D. S. Luzzo (Ed.), *Career counseling of college students* (pp. 43–63). Washington, DC: American Psychological Association.

Schunk, D. H. (1995). Self-efficacy and education and instruction. In J. E. Maddux (Ed.), *Self-efficacy, adaptation, and adjustment: Theory, research, and application* (pp. 281–303). New York: Plenum.

Schwartz, R. D., & Harstein, N. B. (1986). Group psychotherapy with gay men: Theoretical and clinical considerations. In T. Stein & C. J. Cohen (Eds.), *Perspectives on psychotherapy with lesbian and gay men* (pp. 157-177). New York: Plenum.

Sciarra, D. T. (2004). *School counseling: Foundations and contemporary issues.* Belmont, CA: Brooks/Cole-Thomson Learning.

Sexton, T. L., Whiston, S. C., Bleuer, J. C., & Walz, G. R. (1997). *Integrating outcome research into counseling practice and training.* Alexandria, VA: American Counseling Association.

Shaffer, D. R. (1999). *Developmental psychology: Childhood and adolescence* (5th ed.). Pacific Grove, CA: Brooks/Cole.

Shaffer, D. R. (2002). *Developmental psychology: Childhood & adolescence* (6th ed.). Belmont, CA: Wadsworth/Thomson Learning.

Sharf, R. S. (1992). *Applying career development theory to counseling.* Pacific Grove, CA: Brooks/Cole.

Sharf, R. S. (1996). *Theories of psychotherapy and counseling: Concepts and cases.* Pacific Grove, CA: Brooks/Cole.

Sharf, R. S. (2002). *Applying career development theory to counseling* (3rd ed.). Pacific Grove, CA: Brooks/Cole.

Shelton, B. A., & John, D. (1993). Ethnicity, race, and difference: A comparison of white, black, and Hispanic men's household labor time. In J. C. Hood (Ed.), *Men, work and family* (pp. 131–150). Newbury Park, CA: Sage.

Shostak, A. B. (1980). *Blue-collar stress.* Reading, MA: Addison-Wesley.

Shotter, J. (1993). *Conversational realities: Constructing life through language.* Newbury Park, CA: Sage.

Shulman, B. (2003). *The betrayal of work: How low-wage jobs fail 30 million Americans.* New York: New Press.

Shulman, L. (1999). *The skills of helping individuals, families, groups, and communities.* Itasca, IL: E. E. Peacock.

Sigelman, C. K., & Rider, E. A. (2003). *Life-span human development* (4th ed.). Belmont, CA: Wadsworth/Thomson Learning.

Sigelman, C. K., & Shaffer, D. R. (1995). *Life-span human development* (2nd ed.). Pacific Grove, CA: Brooks/Cole.

Signorile, M. (1993). *Queer in America: Sex, media, and the closets of power.* New York: Random House.

Silberstein, L. R. (1992). *Dual-career marriage: A system in transition.* Hillsdale, NJ: Erlbaum.

Simmons, R. G., & Blyth, D. A. (1987). *Moving into adolescence: The impact of pubertal change and school context.* New York: Aldine De Gruyter.

Simon, S. B., Howe, L. W., & Kirschenbaum, H. (1972). *Value clarification.* New York: Hart.

Skovholt, T. M. (1990). Career themes in counseling and psychotherapy with men. In D. Moore & F. Leafgren (Eds.), *Men in conflict* (pp. 39–56). Alexandria, VA: American Association for Counseling and Development.

Skovholt, T. M., Morgan, J. I., & Negron-Cunningam, H. (1989). Mental imagery in career counseling and life planning: A review of research and intervention methods. *Journal of Counseling and Development 67,* 287-292.

Slattery, J. M. (2004). *Counseling diverse clients: Bringing context into therapy.* Belmont, CA: Brooks/Cole-Thomson Learning.

Smith, A. (1997). Cultural diversity and the coming-out process: Implications for clinical practice. In B. Greene (Ed.), *Ethnic and cultural diversity among lesbians and gay men.* New York: Guilford Press.

Smith, P. L., & Fouad, N. A. (1999). Subject-matter specificity of self-efficacy, outcomes, expectations, interests, and goals: Implications for the social-cognitive model. *Journal of Counseling Psychology, 44,* 173–183.

Solomon, K. (1982). The masculine gender role: Description. In K. Solomon & N. B. Levy (Eds.), *Men in transition.* New York: Plenum.

Sophie, J. (1986). A critical examination of stage theories of lesbian identity development. *Journal of Homosexuality, 12*(2), 39–51.

Sorapuru, J., Theodore, R., & Young, W. (1972a). Financial facts of life. In J. E. Bottoms, R. N. Evans, K. B. Hoyt, & J. C. Willer (Eds.), *Career education resource guide* (pp. 218–220). Morristown, NJ: General Learning Corporation.

Sorapuru, J., Theodore, R., & Young, W. (1972b). Job hunting. In J. E. Bottoms, R. N. Evans, K. B. Hoyt, & J. C. Willer (Eds.), *Career education resource guide* (pp. 236–237). Morristown, NJ: General Learning Corporation.

Spearman, C. (1927). *The abilities of man.* New York: Macmillan.

Speight, S. L., Myers, L. J., Cox, C. I., & Highlen, P. S. (1991). A redefinition of multicultural counseling. *Journal of Counseling and Development, 70,* 29–35.

Spence, J. T. (1999). Thirty years of gender research: A personal chronicle. In W. B. Swann, J. H. Langlois, & L. A. Gilbert (Eds.), *Sexism and stereotypes in modern society* (pp. 255–290). Washington, DC: American Psychological Association.

Spencer, A. L. (1982). *Seasons.* New York: Paulist.

Splete, H., Elliott, B. J., & Borders, L. D. (1985). *Computer-assisted career guidance systems and career counseling services.* Unpublished manuscript, Oakland University, Adult Career Counseling Center, Rochester, MI.

Spokane, A. R. (1985). A review of research on person-environment congruence in Holland's theory of careers [Monograph]. *Journal of Vocational Behavior, 26,* 306–343.

Spokane, A. R. (1989). Are their psychological and mental health consequences of difficult career decisions? A reaction to Herr. *Journal of Career Counseling, 16,* 19–24.

Spokane, A. R. (1991). *Career intervention.* Englewood Cliffs, NJ: Prentice-Hall.

Spokane, A. R. (1996). Holland's theory. In D. Brown, L. Brooks, & Associates (Eds.), *Career choice and development* (3rd ed., pp. 33–69). San Francisco: Jossey-Bass.

Spokane, A. R., & Holland, J. L. (1995). The self-directed search: A family of self-guided career interventions. *Journal of Career Assessment, 3,* 373–390.

Spokane, A. R., Luchetta, E. J., & Richwine, M. H. (2002). Holland's theory of personalities. In D. Brown & Associates (Eds.), *Career choice and development* (4th ed., pp. 373–427). San Francisco: Jossey-Bass.

Stamps, D. (1999). Enterprise training: This changes everything. *Training, 36,* 40–48.

Steele-Johnson, D., & Hyde, B. G. (1997). Advanced technologies in training: Intelligent tutoring system and virtual reality. In J. K. Ford & Associates (Eds.), *Improving the effectiveness in work organizations.* Mahwah, NJ: LEA.

Steidl, R. (1972). Financial facts of life. In J. E. Bottoms, R. N. Evans, K. B. Hout, & J. C. Willer (Eds.), *Career education resource guide* (pp. 218–220). Morristown, NJ: General Learning Corporation.

Stephens, G. K., & Feldman, D. C. (1997). A motivational approach for understanding work versus personal life investments. *Research in Personnel and Human Resource Management, 15,* 333–378.

Stephenson, W. (1949). *Testing school children.* New York: Longmans, Green.

Sterns, H. L., & Subich, L. M. (2002). Career development in midcareer. In D. C. Feldman (Ed.), *Work career: A developmental perspective* (pp. 186–214). San Francisco: Jossey-Bass.

Stoltz-Loike, M. (1992). *Dual-career couples: New perspectives in counseling.* Alexandria, VA: American Association for Counseling and Development.

Strong, E. K. (1983). *Vocational interest blank for men.* Stanford, CA: Stanford University Press.

Strube, M. J. (Ed.). (1991). *Type A behavior.* Newbury Park, CA: Sage.

Sturdivant, S. (1980). *Therapy and women.* New York: Springer.

Subich, L. M. (1996). Addressing diversity in the process of career assessment. In M. L. Savickas & W. B. Walsh (Eds.), *Handbook of career counseling theory and practice* (pp. 277–291). Palo Alto, CA: Davies-Black.

Suchet, M., & Barling, J. (1985). Employed mothers: Interrole conflict, spouse support, and marital functioning. *Journal of Occupational Behavior, 7,* 167–178.

Sue, D. (1998). The interplay of sociocultural factors on the psychological development of Asians in America. In D. R. Atkinson, G. Morten, & D. W. Sue (Eds.), *Counseling American minorities* (5th ed., pp. 205–213). Boston: McGraw-Hill.

Sue, D. W. (1978). Counseling across cultures. *Personnel and Guidance Journal, 56,* 451.

Sue, D. W. (1981). *Counseling the culturally different.* New York: Wiley.

Sue, D. W. (1994). Asian American mental health and help-seeking behavior: Comment on Solberg et al. (1994), Tata & Leong (1994), and Lin (1994). *Journal of Counseling Psychology, 41,* 292–295.

Sue, D. W., Arredondo, A., & McDavis, R. J. (1992). Multicultural counseling competencies and standards: A call to the profession. *Journal of Counseling and Development, 70,* 477–486.

Sue, D. W., Ivey, A. E., & Pedersen, P. B. (1996). *A theory of multicultural counseling and therapy.* Pacific Grove, CA: Brooks/Cole.

Sue, D. W., & Sue, D. (1990). *Counseling the culturally different: Theory and practice* (2nd ed.). New York: Wiley.

Sue, D. W., & Sue, D. (2003). *Counseling the culturally diverse: Theory and practice* (4th ed.). New York: Wiley.

Sue, S., & Okazaki, S. (1990). Asian American educational achievements: A phenomenon in search of an explanation. *American Psychologist, 45*(8), 913–920.

Sulsky, L., & Smith, C. (2005). *Work stress.* Belmont, CA: Thomson Wadsworth.

Super, D. E. (1949). *Appraising vocational fitness.* New York: Harper & Brothers.

Super, D. E. (1957). *The psychology of careers.* New York: Harper & Row.

Super, D. E. (1970). *The work values inventory.* Boston: Houghton Mifflin.

Super, D. E. (1972). Vocational development theory: Persons, positions, and processes. In J. M. Whiteley & A. Resnikoff (Eds.), *Perspectives on vocational development* (pp. 17–31). Washington, DC: American Personnel and Guidance Association.

Super, D. E. (1974). *Measuring vocational maturity for counseling and evaluation.* Washington, DC: National Vocational Guidance Association.

Super, D. E. (1977). Vocational maturity in mid-career. *Vocational Guidance Quarterly, 25,* 297.

Super, D. E. (1980). A life-span, life-space approach to career development. *Journal of Vocational Behavior, 16,* 282–298.

Super, D. E. (1984). Career and life development. In D. Brown & L. Brooks (Eds.), *Career choice and development* (pp. 197–261). San Francisco: Jossey-Bass.

Super, D. E. (1990). A life-span, life-space approach to career development. In D. Brown, L. Brooks, & Associates (Eds.), *Career choice and development: Applying contemporary theories to practice* (2nd ed., pp. 197–261). San Francisco: Jossey-Bass.

Super, D. E. (1993). The two faces of counseling: Or is it three? *Career Development Quarterly, 42,* 132–136.

Super, D. E., & Overstreet, P. L. (1960). *The vocational maturity of ninth-grade boys.* New York: Teachers College, Columbia University.

Super, D. E., Savickas, M. L., & Super, C. M. (1996). The life-span, life-space approach to careers. In D. Brown, L. Brooks, & Associates (Eds.), *Career choice and development* (3rd ed., pp. 121–170). San Francisco: Jossey-Bass.

Super, D. E., Starishesky, R., Matlin, N., & Jordaan, J. P. (1963). *Career development: Self-concept theory.* New York: College Entrance Examination Board.

Super, D. E., Thompson, A. S., & Lindeman, R. H. (1988). *Adult career concerns inventory: Manual for research and exploratory use in counseling.* Palo Alto, CA: Consulting Psychologists Press.

Suro, R. (1998). *Strangers among us: How Latino immigration is transforming America.* New York: Knopf.

Swanson, J. L. (1992). Vocational behavior, 1989–1991: Life-span career development and reciprocal interaction of work and nonwork. *Journal of Vocational Behavior, 41,* 101–161.

Swanson, J. L. (1996). The theory is the practice: Trait-and-factor/person-environment. In M. L. Savickas & W. B. Walsh (Eds.), *Handbook of career counseling theory and practice* (pp. 93–109). Palo Alto, CA: Davies-Black.

Tafoya, T. (1997). Native gay and lesbian issues: The two-spirited. In B. Greene (Ed.), *Ethnic and cultural diversity among lesbians and gay men* (pp. 1–10). Thousand Oaks, CA: Sage.

Tang, M., Fouad, N. A., & Smith, P. L. (1999). Asian Americans' career choices: A path model to examine factors influencing their career choices. *Journal of Vocational Behavior, 54,* 142–157.

Telljohann, S. K., & Price, J. H. (1993). A qualitative examination of adolescents homosexuals' life experiences: Ramifications for secondary school personnel. *Journal of Homosexuality, 26*(1), 41–56.

Thomas, K. R., & Butler, A. J. (1981). Counseling for personal adjustment. In R. M. Parker & C. E. Hansen (Eds.), *Rehabilitation Counseling* (pp. 37–56). Boston: Allyn & Bacon.

Thomason, T. C. (1991). Counseling Native Americans: An introduction for non-Native American counselors. *Journal of Counseling & Development, 69,* 321–327.

Thomason, T. C. (2000). Issues in the treatment of Native Americans with alcohol problems. *Journal of Multicultural Counseling and Development, 28*(4), 243–252.

Thompson, A. S., Lindeman, R. H., Super, D. E., Jordaan, J. P., & Myers, R. A. (1984). *Career development inventory: Technical manual.* Palo Alto, CA: Consulting Psychologists Press.

Thompson, C. L., & Rudolph, L. B. (2000). *Counseling children* (5th ed.). Belmont, CA: Wadsworth.

Thompson, C. L., Rudolph, L. B., & Henderson, D. (2004). *Counseling children* (6th ed.). Belmont, CA: Brooks/Cole-Thomson Learning.

Thompson, E. H., Grisanti, C., & Pleck, J. H. (1987). Attitudes toward the male role and their correlates. *Sex Roles, 13,* 413–427.

Tiedeman, D. V., & O'Hara, R. P. (1963). *Career development: Choice and adjustment.* Princeton, NJ: College Entrance Examination Board.

Tinsley, H. E. A. (2000). The myth of congruence. *Journal of Vocational Behavior, 40,* 109–110.

Tomasko, R. T. (1987). *Downsizing.* New York: American Management Association.

Tower, K. D. (1994). Consumer-centered social work practice: Restoring client self-determination. *Social Work, 41*(1), 191–196.

Triandis, H. C. (1992, February). *Individualism and collectivism as a cultural syndrome.* Paper presented at the Annual Convention of the Society for Cross-Cultural Researchers, Santa Fe, NM.

Triandis, H. C. (1994). *Culture and social behavior.* New York: McGraw-Hill.

Trimble, J. E., & LaFromboise, T. (1985). American Indians and the counseling process: Culture, adaptation, and style. In P. Pedersen, *Handbook of cross-cultural counseling and therapy* (pp. 125–134). Westport, CT: Greenwood.

Trower, P., Casey, A., & Dryden, W. (1988). *Cognitive-behavioral counseling in action.* Newbury Park, CA: Sage.

Uchitelle, L., & Kleinfield, N. R. (1996). The price of jobs lost. In *New York Times* (et al.), *The downsizing of America* (pp. 3–36). New York: Time Books.

Unger, R. K. (Ed.). (2000). *Handbook of the psychology of women and gender.* San Francisco: Jossey-Bass.

Unger, R., & Crawford, M. (1992). *Women and gender: A feminist psychology.* Philadelphia: Temple University Press.

University of Minnesota. (1984). *Minnesota Importance Questionnaire.* Minneapolis: Author.

U.S. Bureau of the Census. (1993). *We the Americans: Pacific Islanders in the United States.* Washington, DC: U.S. Government Printing Office.

U.S. Bureau of Census. (1997). *Statistical abstract of the United States, 1997.* Washington, DC: U.S. Government Printing Office.

U.S. Bureau of the Census. (1999). *Current population survey, racial statistics branch, population division.* Washington, DC: U.S. Government Printing Office.

U.S. Bureau of the Census. (2000a). *Current population, racial statistics branch, population division.* Washington, DC: U.S. Government Printing Office.

U.S. Bureau of the Census. (2000b). *Poverty rate lowest in 20 years, household income at record high, Census Bureau reports.* Washington, DC: U.S. Government Printing Office.

U.S. Bureau of the Census, Bureau of Labor Statistics. (2002). *Occupational outlook handbook, 1997–1998 Edition.* Washington, DC: U.S. Government Printing Office.

U.S. Department of Commerce, Bureau of Census (1996). *Percentage of population by race: 1990, 2000, 2025, 2050.* Washington, DC: U.S. Government Printing Office.

U.S. Department of Education and U.S. Department of Labor. (1996). *School-to-work opportunities.* Washington, DC: National School-to-Work Office.

U.S. Department of Justice. (1991). *Americans with disabilities handbook.* Washington, DC: U.S. Government Printing Office.

U.S. Department of Labor. (1970a). *Career thresholds.* Washington, DC: U.S. Government Printing Office.

U.S. Department of Labor. (1970b). *Manual for the general aptitude test battery.* Washington, DC: U.S. Government Printing Office.

U.S. Department of Labor. (1992). *Learning for a living: A blueprint for high performance.* Washington, DC: U.S. Government Printing Office.

Uribe, V., & Harbeck, K. M. (1992). Addressing the needs of lesbian, gay, and bisexual youth: The origins of Project 10 and school-based intervention. *Journal of Homosexuality, 22*(3/4), 9–28.

Valach, L. (1990). A theory of goal-directed action in career analysis. In R. A. Young & W. A. Borgen (Eds.), *Methodological approaches to the study of career* (pp. 107–126). New York: Praeger.

Van Willigen, M. (2000). Differential benefits of volunteering across the life course. *Journal of Gerontology, 55,* 5308–5318.

Vargo, M. E. (1998). *Acts of disclosure: The coming-out process of contemporary gay men.* New York: Haworth.

Velasquez, J. S., & Lynch, M. M. (1981). Computerized information systems: A practice orientation. *Administration in Social Work, 5*(3/4), 113–127.

von Cranach, M., & Harre, R. (Eds.). (1982). *The analysis of action: Recent theoretical and empirical advances.* Cambridge, England: Cambridge University Press.

Vondracek, F. W., Lerner, R. M., & Schulenberg, J. E. (1986). *Career development: A life-span developmental approach.* Hillsdale, NJ: Erlbaum.

Vosler, N. R., & Page-Adams, D. (1996). Predictors of depression among workers at the time of a plant closing. *Journal of Sociology and Social Welfare, 23*(4), 25–42.

Wajcman, J. (1998). *Managing like a man: Women and men in corporate management.* University Park: Pennsylvania State University Press.

Walsh, W. B. (1990). A summary and integration of career counseling approaches. In W. B. Walsh & S. H. Osipow (Eds.), *Career counseling: Contemporary topics in vocational psychology* (pp. 263–283). Hillsdale, NJ: Erlbaum.

Walz, A. (1972). Required courses. In J. E. Bottoms, R. N. Evans, K. B. Hoyt, & J. C. Willer (Eds.), *Career education resource guide* (pp. 186–188). Morristown, NJ: General Learning Corporation.

Wanous, J. P. (1980). *Organizational entry.* Reading, MA: Addison-Wesley.

Ward, C. M., & Bingham, R. P. (1993). Career assessment of ethnic minority women. *Journal of Career Assessment, 1,* 246–257.

Ward, C. M., & Tate, G. (1990). *Career counseling checklist.* Atlanta: Georgia State University Counseling Center.

Warr, P. (1992). Age and occupational well-being. *Psychology and Aging, 7,* 37–45.

Warr, P. B. (1987). *Work, employment, and mental health.* Oxford: Clarendon.

Weaver, H. N. (2003). Cultural competence with First Nations Peoples. In D. Lum (Ed.), *Culturally competent practice* (2nd ed., pp. 197–216). Pacific Grove, CA: Brooks/Cole-Thomson Learning.

Wehrly, B. (1995). *Pathways to multicultural counseling competence.* Pacific Grove, CA: Brooks/Cole.

Weinrach, S. G., & Srebalus, D. J. (1990). Holland's theory of careers. In D. Brown & L. Brooks (Eds.), *Career choice and development: Applying contemporary theories to practice* (2nd ed., pp. 37–67). San Francisco: Jossey-Bass.

Welfel, E. R. (2002). *Ethics counseling psychotherapy* (2nd ed.). Pacific Grove, CA: Brooks/Cole.

Wentling, R. M. (1992, Jan./Feb.). Women in middle management: Their career development and aspirations. *Business Horizons,* 48–54.

Werbel, J. D., & Gilliland, S. W. (1999). Person-environment fit in the selection process. *Research in Personnel and Human Resource Management, 17,* 209–243.

Westermeyer, J. J. (1993). Cross-cultural psychiatric assessment. In A. Gaw (Ed.), *Culture, ethnicity, and mental illness* (pp. 125–144). Washington, DC: American Psychiatric Press.

Whiston, S. C. (2000). *Principles and applications of assessment in counseling.* Belmont, CA: Wadsworth/Thomson Learning.

Wiederhold, B. K., & Wiederhold, M. D. (2005). *Virtual reality therapy for anxiety disorders: Advances in treatment.* Washington, DC: American Psychological Association.

Wiinamaki, M. K. (1988). *My vocational experience.* Unpublished manuscript, Southwest Texas State University, San Marcos.

Wilcox-Matthew, L., & Minor, C. W. (1989). The dual career couple: Concerns, benefits, and counseling implications. *Journal of Counseling and Development, 68,* 194–198.

Williams, J. M., & Currie, C. (2000). Self-esteem and physical development in early adolescence: Pubertal timing and body image. *Journal of Early Adolescence, 20,* 129–149.

Williams, W. L. (1993). Persistence and change in the berdache tradition among contemporary Lakota Indians. In L. D. Garnets & D. C. Kimmel (Eds.), *Psychological perspectives on lesbian and gay male experiences* (pp. 339–348). New York: Columbia University Press.

Williamson, E. G. (1939). *How to counsel students: A manual of techniques for clinical counselors.* New York: McGraw-Hill.

Williamson, E. G. (1949). *Counseling adolescents.* New York: McGraw-Hill.

Williamson, E. G. (1965). *Vocational counseling: Some historical, philosophical, and theoretical perspectives.* New York: McGraw-Hill.

Winbush, G. B. (2000). African American women. In M. Julia (Ed.), *Constructing gender: Multicultural perspectives in working with women* (pp. 11–35). Pacific Grove, CA: Brooks/Cole.

Winfeld, L., & Spielman, S. (1995). *Straight talk about gays in workplace.* New York: AMACOM.

Wolpe, J. (1958). *Psychotherapy by reciprocal inhibition.* Palo Alto, CA: Stanford University Press.

Wood, J. T. (1994). *Gendered lives: Communication, gender, and culture.* Belmont, CA: Wadsworth.

Wooden, W. S., Kawasaki, H., & Mayeda, R. (1983). Lifestyles and identity maintenance among gay Japanese-American males. *Alternative Lifestyles, 5*(4), 236–243.

Woods, J. F., & Ollis, H. (1996). *Labor market & job information on the Internet.* Submitted for publication in the Winter (March 1996) issue of *Workforce Journal.*

Woody, B. (1992). *Black women in the workplace.* Westport, CT: Greenwood.

Worthington, R. L., & Juntunen, C. L. (1997). The vocational development of non-college bound youth: Counseling psychology and the school-to-work transition movement. *Counseling Psychologist, 25,* 323–363.

Wrenn, C. G. (1988). The person in career counseling. *Career Development Quarterly, 36*(4), 337–343.

Young, R. A., & Valach, L. (1996). Interpretation and action in career counseling. In M. L. Savickas & W. B. Walsh (Eds.), *Handbook of career counseling theory and practice* (pp. 361–376). Palo Alto, CA: Davies-Black.

Young, R. A., Valach, L., & Collin, A. (1996). A contextual explanation of career. In D. Brown, L. Brooks, & Associates (Eds.), *Career choice and development* (3rd ed., pp. 477–508). San Francisco: Jossey-Bass.

Young, R. A., Valach, L., & Collin, A. (2002). A contextual explanation of career. In D. Brown & Associates (Eds.), *Career choice and development* (4th ed., pp. 206–255). San Francisco: Jossey-Bass.

Zaccaria, J. (1970). *Theories of occupational choice and vocational development.* Boston: Houghton Mifflin.

Zaharlick, A. (2000). South Asian-American women. In M. Julia (Ed.), *Constructing gender: Multicultural perspectives in working with women* (pp. 177–205). Pacific Grove, CA: Brooks/Cole.

Zimmerman, B. J. (1995). Self-efficacy and educational development. In A. Bandura (Ed.), *Self-efficacy in changing societies (pp.* 72–85). Cambridge: Cambridge University Press.

Zmud, R. W., Sampson, J. P., Reardon, R. C., Lenz, J. G., & Byrd, T. A. (1994). Confounding effects of construct overlap. An example from IS user satisfaction theory. *Information Technology and People, 7,* 29–45.

Zuniga, M. E. (2003). Cultural competence with Latino Americans. In D. Lum (Ed.), *Culturally competent practice* (2nd ed., pp. 238–261). Pacific Grove, CA: Brooks/Cole-Thomson Learning.

Zunker, V. G. (1994). *Using assessment results for career development* (4th ed.). Pacific Grove, CA: Brooks/Cole.

Zunker, V. G. (1998). *Career counseling: Applied concepts of life planning* (5th ed.). Pacific Grove, CA: Brooks/Cole.

Zunker, V. G. (2002). *Career counseling: Applied concepts of life planning.* (6th ed.). Pacific Grove, CA: Brooks/Cole.

Zunker, V. G., & Brown, W. F. (1966). Comparative effectiveness of student and professional counselors. *Personnel and Guidance Journal, 44,* 733–743.

Zunker, V. G., & Norris, D. (1998). *Using assessment results for career development* (5th ed.) Pacific Grove, CA: Brooks/Cole.

Zunker, V. G., & Osborn, D. (2002). *Using assessment results for career development* (6th ed.). Pacific Grove, CA: Brooks/Cole.

Zytowski, D. G. (1969). Toward a theory of career development for women. *Personnel and Guidance Journal, 47,* 660–664.

Zytowski, D. G. (1994). Tests and counseling: We are still married, and living in discriminant analysis. *Measurement and Evaluation in Counseling and Development, 26,* 219–223.

Name Index

Subject Index

TO THE OWNER OF THIS BOOK:

I hope that you have found *Career Counseling: A Holistic Approach*, Seventh Edition useful. So that this book can be improved in a future edition, would you take the time to complete this sheet and return it? Thank you.

School and address:_____

Department:_____

Instructor's name:_____

1. What I like most about this book is:_____

_____

_____

2. What I like least about this book is:

_____

_____

3. My general reaction to this book is:

_____

_____

4. The name of the course in which I used this book is:

_____

5. Were all of the chapters of the book assigned for you to read?_____

   If not, which ones weren't?_____

6. In the space below, or on a separate sheet of paper, please write specific suggestions for improving this book and anything else you'd care to share about your experience in using this book.

_____

_____

_____

THOMSON

BROOKS/COLE ™

BUSINESS REPLY MAIL
FIRST-CLASS MAIL   PERMIT NO. 34   BELMONT CA

POSTAGE WILL BE PAID BY ADDRESSEE

Attn: Marquita Flemming, Counseling Editor

BrooksCole/Thomson Learning
10 Davis Drive
Belmont, CA   94002-9801

OPTIONAL:

Your name: _____ Date: _____

May we quote you, either in promotion for *Career Counseling: A Holistic Approach*, Seventh Edition, or in future publishing ventures?

Yes: _____ No: _____

Sincerely yours,

Vernon G. Zunker